| SAS Publishing

Multiple Comparisons and Multiple Tests

Using SAS®

Peter H. Westfall
Randall D. Tobias
Dror Rom
Russell D. Wolfinger
Yosef Hochberg

The Power to Know.

The correct bibliographic citation for this manual is as follows: Westfall, Peter H., Randall D. Tobias, Dror Rom, Russell D. Wolfinger, and Yosef Hochberg. 1999. *Multiple Comparisons and Multiple Tests Using SAS®*. Cary, NC: SAS Institute Inc.

Multiple Comparisons and Multiple Tests Using SAS®

SAS Institute Inc., SAS Campus Drive, Cary, North Carolina 27513.

1st printing, June 1999
2nd printing, February 2003

Note that text corrections may have been made at each printing.

SAS Publishing provides a complete selection of books and electronic products to help customers use SAS software to its fullest potential. For more information about our e-books, e-learning products, CDs, and hardcopy books, visit the SAS Publishing Web site at **support.sas.com/pubs** or call 1-800-727-3228.

Contents

Preface

This book is for users of statistics who need to make multiple inferences from a single study. Almost *all* users of statistical inference fall in this category, since almost nobody performs one and only one inference in a given study! The problem with analyses involving multiple inferences is that seemingly significant results occur more often than expected by chance alone. As a practical consequence, decision makers can easily make the wrong decisions.

There are numerous alternative solutions for multiple inference problems—some are very good, some perform reasonably well, and some are of questionable value. The wide variety of methods that are available can make the choice of technique difficult for the user. In this book we explain the various methods, their pitfalls and advantages, all in a self-contained format. We apply the methods to real data, giving examples from business, medicine, sociology, engineering, and other application areas.

One goal we had in writing this book was to unify the presentation of the diverse multiple comparisons methods, and to make the use of the software simple for the user. The proper choice of a multiple inference procedure depends upon your inference objectives and data structure. While many procedures for such inferences currently exist in the SAS System such as PROC GLM, PROC MIXED, and PROC MULTTEST, and in specialized macro packages such as MultComp, we realized through the course of writing the book that several types of problems fall through the cracks, and are not particularly well accommodated by any of the existing packages. To fill this gap, we developed a set of SAS macro language programs that implement more general and more recently developed multiple inference techniques than are available in the SAS/STAT procedures. In addition to handling the usual pairwise comparisons applications, these macros can be used for problems as diverse as

- confidence bands for regression functions (linear, logistic, survival analysis, etc.)
- simultaneous intervals for log-odds ratios in logistic regression
- closed testing for covariate-adjusted linear contrasts in multivariate analysis of covariance.

These macros, in conjunction with the existing software for multiple comparisons in the SAS System, allow you to carry out multiple inferences in most applications of practical interest.

Of course, no system is complete, and new methodologies are constantly being discovered. Thus, while we emphasize primarily methods found in the SAS System (through Version 7), along with the specialized macro set, we acknowledge that there are alternative analysis procedures not covered in this book, and offer references to those methods for the reader.

Most programs in this book are designed to run in Version 7 of the SAS System. We take liberal advantage of such features as long variable and data set names, and the Output Delivery System. Therefore, many of our programs will not run correctly in previous versions without suitable modifications. In particular, two of the more important macros, `%SimIntervals` and `%SimTests`, would require extensive modifications to run releases of the SAS System prior to Version 7.

Why is there a distinction between multiple comparisons and multiple tests shown in our title? Multiple comparisons usually refers to the comparison of mean values from an experiment on multiple treatments. For example, you might compare consumer perceptions of three different advertising displays: A, B, and C. Then, one uses the data to compare display A with display B, A with C, and B with C. This is the classic "multiple comparisons" application, and SAS has long offered a variety of methods for such analyses (for example, Tukey's method for comparing means in PROC GLM). Multiple testing, on the other hand, concerns a broader class of applications. For example, a clinical trial designed to assess efficacy of a pharmaceutical compound might be considered efficacious if it reduces fever, *or* if it speeds recovery time, *or* if it reduces headaches. Here, there are three tests—a comparison of active compound with placebo for each of the three outcomes. This is an example of multiple testing. The distinction between multiple comparisons and multiple tests is that, with multiple comparisons, you typically compare three or more mean values, in pairs or combinations, of the *same measurement*. With multiple testing, you can consider *multiple measurements*.

The following table summarizes some of the common characteristics of multiple comparisons and multiple tests. Note, however, that the distinctions are fairly loose, and there is plenty of overlap. You can almost use the terms interchangeably.

Multiple Comparisons	Multiple Tests
Comparisons of Means from ANOVA or ANCOVA data	More general inferences, especially involving multivariate data
Inference is based on confidence intervals	Inference is based on tests of hypotheses
Single-step methods	Stepwise methods

There has been relatively little software and methods for analyzing multiple test data, due to difficulties relating to the covariances among the variables. For example, Jason Hsu's excellent book on multiple comparisons, *Multiple Comparisons: Theory and Methods* (Chapman and Hall, 1996) does not treat this problem at all. One aim of this book is to address this issue. We will give numerous examples of multiple testing data, and we use the SAS System to solve the problems. We also give numerous examples from the multiple comparisons side, as well as examples that are a combination of both. One aim of our book is to balance the presentation of multiple comparisons with multiple testing, thereby filling a gap in previous expositions.

The area of multiple comparisons and multiple testing is large, and the details of the calculations can be tricky, which is why we have so many authors for this book. In our group we have an impressive collection of experts in the field, whose collective expertise include theory, practical application, and software development. Peter H. Westfall is the original developer of PROC MULTTEST, author (joint with S. S. Young) of the book *Resampling-Based Multiple Testing: Examples and Methods for P-Value Adjustment* (Wiley: New York, 1993), author of numerous papers on multiple comparisons and multiple testing in scientific journals, and teacher of numerous short courses on multiple tests and multiple comparisons. Randy Tobias, principal developer for PROC GLM, has implemented numerous multiple comparisons capabilities for both that procedure and PROC MIXED, following the framework of Jason Hsu's book (mentioned above). Dror Rom, the president of Prosoft Software Inc., has developed (joint with K. Chang) the multiple comparisons package MultComp (which runs as a macro facility from the SAS System), has published widely in the multiple comparisons and multiple testing field, has taught numerous short courses on multiple tests and multiple comparisons, and has years of experience consulting with pharmaceutical companies. Several of these macros are included with this book. Russ Wolfinger, principal developer of PROC MIXED, is also developer (along with Peter Westfall) of the recent versions of PROC MULTTEST, and has published in the area of multiple testing with discrete data. Finally, Yosef Hochberg is very prominent in the field, having authored (joint with A. Tamhane) the seminal book *Multiple Comparison Procedures* (Wiley, 1987), and having published dozens of articles in scientific journals on theory and applications of multiple comparisons methods.

The outline of this book is as follows.

Chapter 1	Discusses practical multiple testing examples, showing when to use such methods, and the real consequences of not using them.
Chapter 2	Lays the groundwork for understanding the methods, including the various error rate definitions and properties of the multiple comparisons and multiple testing methods. Examples of multiplicity adjustment that require only the *p*-values, which may come from any analysis, are included. We analyze such data using PROC MULTTEST and macros.
Chapter 3	Discusses the historically foundational "meat and potatoes" of the subject: multiple pairwise comparisons methods in the classical balanced analysis-of-variance (ANOVA) model, with analyses primarily done using PROC GLM.
Chapter 4	Extends Chapter 3 to unbalanced models, and introduces the simulation-based method of Edwards and Berry (1987).
Chapter 5	Extends to covariate models and introduces the %SimIntervals macro.
Chapter 6	Considers any collection of linear functions of parameters in the normal linear model, including infinite families and simultaneous confidence bands for regression functions.
Chapter 7	Computes power for a variety of multiple comparisons methods using new macros.
Chapter 8	Develops closure-based testing methods and explains the logic of the stepwise testing methods. Introduces the %SimTests macro.
Chapter 9	Discusses two-way and higher way ANOVAs.
Chapter 10	Shows how multiple comparisons can be obtained in repeated measures and general mixed linear models, and gives hands-on instructions for such implementations using PROC MIXED. Applications include heteroscedastic data, random blocks, repeated measures, multivariate tests, and multivariate analysis of covariance.
Chapter 11	Discusses tests for contrasts of means for the nonnormally distributed multivariate case, using PROC MULTTEST, with permutation and bootstrap sampling.
Chapter 12	Discusses the dramatic improvements that occur when the data are discrete. Examples using PROC MULTTEST and MultComp from Prosoft Inc. are used here.
Chapter 13	Discusses and provides macros for Bayesian simultaneous intervals and simultaneous tests.
Chapter 14	Discusses miscellaneous applications—multiple inferences following analyses using PROC LOGISTIC, PROC PHREG, etc., multiple comparisons with the best, multivariate infinite families, and interim analysis.

So, what's in this book for you? First of all, we hope to prompt you to consider the need to take multiple inference problems into account in your data analysis. Then we will present some of the best and most powerful multiple testing/multiple comparisons methods that are currently available. You will see, through our many examples, how to carry out such analyses and how to interpret the results. In some cases, you will find that the improvements obtained using more advanced methods over the usual multiple comparisons methods (like Bonferroni) are phenomenal, with no cost in terms of increased error rate. In other cases, you will see that there is little gain from using fancy multiplicity adjustment procedures. Overall, regardless of the situation, we will emphasize the magnitude of difference between multiplicity adjusted methods versus nonmultiplicity adjusted methods, and highlight the benefits of multiplicity adjusted analyses.

Acknowledgements

We want to acknowledge several individuals who helped in various ways. Stan Young and Keith Soper provided several examples that are used in our book. Chung-Kuei Chang developed (along with Dror Rom) several of the macros and methods we use. Reviewers who provided valuable feedback on statistical content include Jason Hsu, Mithat Gönen, Jack Berry, and Kathleen Kiernan. We are also greatly indebted to SAS Institute for logistical, editorial and technical support, including Jim Ashton, Kevin Scott, Gerardo Hurtado, and especially Julie Platt.

Introduction

1.1   The Multiplicity Problem

Practically every day, you find in the newspaper or other popular press, some claim of association between a stimulus and outcome, with consequences for health or general welfare of the population at large. Many of these associations are suspect at best, and often do not hold up under scrutiny. Examples taken from recent periodicals include the following claimed associations: cellular phones with brain tumors, power lines with leukemia (more recently overturned by the scientific community), vitamins with IQ, season of the year with mental performance (but only in men!), genetics with homosexuality (the "gay gene"), abortions with breast cancer (but not spontaneous abortions), remarriage with cancer, electric razors with cancer, and on and on. Many of these claims have shaky foundations *a priori*, and some have been found not to replicate in further studies. With so much conflicting information in the popular press, the general public has learned to mistrust the results of statistical studies, and to shy away from the use of statistics in general.

How do such incorrect conclusions become part of the scientific and popular landscape? While scientists typically fault such things as improper study design and poor data, there is another explanation that is the focus of this book. Data analysts can easily make such incorrect claims when they analyze data from large studies, reporting any test that is "statistically significant" (usually defined as "$p < 0.05$," where "p" denotes "p-value") as a "real" effect. On the surface, this practice seems innocuous. After all, isn't that the rule we learn in statistics classes—to report results where we find "$p < 0.05$" as "real"?

The problem, briefly stated, is that when multiple tests are performed, "$p < 0.05$" outcomes can often occur even when there are no real effects. Historically, the rule was devised for a single test, with the following logic: if the $p < 0.05$ outcome was observed, then the analyst has two options. He or she can believe that there is no real effect, and that the data are so anomalous that they are within the range of values that would be observed only 1 in 20 samples; or, he or she may choose to believe that the observed effect is real. Because the 1 in 20 chance is relatively small, the common decision is to "reject" the hypothesis of no real effect, and "accept" the conclusion that the effect is real.

This logic breaks down when you consider multiple tests or comparisons in a single study. If you consider 20 or more tests, then you *expect* at least one "1 in 20" significant outcome, even when none of the effects are real. Thus, there is little protection offered by the "1 in 20" rule, and incorrect claims can result. While problems of faulty study design, bad data, etc., can and do cause faulty conclusions, you should be aware that multiplicity is also a likely cause, especially in large studies where many tests or comparisons are made. Such studies are common, as the following examples indicate.

1.2   Examples of Multiplicity in Practice

Multiple comparisons and multiple tests occur in all areas of data analysis. The following sections contain descriptions of situations where the problem occurs, and discuss its practical consequences.

1.2.1   Multiple Comparisons in a Marketing Experiment

Suppose a market researcher shows five different advertisements (labeled, say, as A, B, C, D, and E) to focus groups of 20 males and 20 females. Advertisement E is the current one in circulation, and since there's a cost to pulling an old ad and starting up a new one, the market researcher would like to replace the current one with one that is assuredly better. Each person is shown all five ads via videotape, in random order, and each is allowed to return to previously viewed ads. At the end of the viewing each subject rates the ads on a standard set of attributes. Questions of interest include

- Is one of the new advertisements better than the old one?
- Are the males' ratings generally different than the females' ratings?

To answer these questions, researchers must perform many comparisons of advertisements, both within and between sexes. Without considering the multiple testing aspect, the analyst might be led to conclude, incorrectly, that advertisement "C" is better than "E," when in fact none of the new ads is really significantly better. In such a case, he or she might suggest a nationwide campaign for "C," potentially costing millions of dollars for no gain in revenue. With multiple comparisons methods, the conclusion of the data analysis is more likely to be that "E" and "C" are not significantly different.

On the other hand, if the conclusion that "C" is best is made after proper adjustment for multiple comparisons, then the analyst can proceed more confidently with the "C" recommendation.

An additional wrinkle to this problem is the analysis of the multiple questions on the questionnaire. The previous discussion presumes that there is a primary question of interest, such as "Overall, how much did you like this ad?" As such, the methodology is an example of multiple comparisons, although it is somewhat more complicated than usual with the different sources of variation (within and between subjects) and gender comparisons. However, in reality, there will be multiple questions pertaining to various aspects of "like" and "dislike." When all such questions are analyzed, the data analysis contains multiple tests as well as multiple comparisons.

Even in this simple example, there might be dozens or even hundreds of implicit multiple tests or comparisons. Thus, the opportunity for incorrect conclusions to arise by chance alone is great, unless the data are analyzed thoughtfully with this possibility in mind.

1.2.2   Subgroup Analysis in a Clinical Trial

As a part of the pharmaceutical development process, new therapies usually are evaluated using randomized clinical trials. In such studies, a cohort of patients is identified, and randomly assigned to either active or placebo therapy. After the conclusion of the study, the active and placebo groups are compared to see which is better, using a single predefined outcome of interest (e.g., whether the patient was cured). At this stage, there is no multiplicity problem, as there is only one test.

However, there are often good reasons to evaluate patient subgroups. The therapy might work better for men than for women, better for older patients, better for patients with mild conditions as opposed to severe, etc. While it is well and good to ask such questions, such data must be analyzed carefully, and with the multiplicity problem in mind. If the data are thus subdivided into many subgroups, it can easily happen that a patient subgroup shows "statistical significance" by chance alone, leading analysts to (incorrectly) recommend it for that subgroup, or worse yet, to recommend it for all groups based on the evidence from the single subgroup.

While such practice seems so obviously wrong, we recount two examples where it actually has happened. The first is reported in Fleming (1992), regarding a preoperative radiation therapy for colorectal cancer patients. The study was stopped early due to lack of significance; however, follow-up analysis revealed "significant" improvement in a particular subgroup. The trial's conclusions were then revised to recommend "universal use" of the therapy. A follow-up study involving the same therapy and a larger sample size revealed no statistical significance, so it seems likely that the original finding of a therapeutic effect was an incorrect claim, likely caused by the multiplicity effect.

Another case, reported in the *Wall Street Journal* (King, 1995) concerned the development of "Blue Goo," a salve meant to heal foot wounds of diabetic patients, by the Biotechnology firm ProCyte Corp. The firm decided to proceed with an expensive, large-scale clinical trial to assess efficacy of the salve, based on statistically significant efficacy results found in a subgroup of patients in a preliminary clinical trial. The larger study found no significant effect of the "Blue Goo" therapy, and as reported by King, "Within minutes [of the announcement of no therapeutic effect], ProCyte's stock fell 68% ..." As in the case of the preoperative radiation treatment, it seems likely that the statistically significant result was an incorrect conclusion caused by the multiplicity effect.

1.2.3   Analysis of a Sociological Survey

Blazer et al. (1985), report results of a survey of residents of North Carolina who were distributed nearly equally between urban and rural counties. Psychiatric interviews and questionnaires were given to a randomly selected set of about 3,900 people, one per household. Each person was classified dichotomously (yes/no) as agoraphobic, alcohol-dependent, antisocial, cognitive deficient, dysthymic, major depressive, obsessive-compulsive, and schizophrenic. These classifications result in eight-dimensional binary vectors, one for each subject. For example, the vector $(0, 0, 1, 0, 0, 0, 1, 0)$ denotes a person who was diagnosed as antisocial and obsessive-compulsive.

One goal of the study was to relate the diagnoses to the demographic variables age, sex, race (white and non-white), marital status (married with spouse, separated/divorced, widowed, nonmarried), education (non-high school, high school), mobility (moved in last year, did not move), and location (rural, urban). With eight diagnoses and seven demographic classifications, there are a total of $7 \times 8 = 56$ tests, all of which are interesting comparisons. Without considering the effect of multiplicity, it is clear that erroneously significant results might be claimed. Our point here is not to quibble with the claims of Blazer et al., but merely to point out (1) how easy it is for multiple tests to arise with survey data, and (2) that the multiplicity effect should be carefully considered in any such analysis.

1.2.4   An Epidemiology Example: Data Snooping

With the advent of the Information Revolution, researchers have access to ever larger databases. Methods have been developed to "mine" such databases for otherwise hidden information. However, it's all too easy for such "data mining" to become "data snooping"—turning up nuggets of fools' gold (to continue with the metaphor) which are artifacts of excessive data manipulation rather than indicators of real lodes of useful information.

How do researchers keep "data mining" from becoming "data snooping"? Recognition of the problems of multiple inference can be the key. Many data mining procedures have built-in safeguards against such problems. For example, in fitting complex statistical models, data mining procedures often use a "penalty function" to avoid sample-specific overfitting problems. Similarly, procedures for fitting tree-based classification models often use multiplicity-adjusted rules to choose the splitting points.

The following example illustrates the potential dangers of data snooping. Needleman et al. (1979), claimed that lead in drinking water adversely affected IQs of school children. While high levels of lead are indisputably toxic, the study aimed to prove that variations in levels of lead below the accepted "safe" level were in fact associated with mental performance. Ernhart et al. (1981), in a critical review of their finding, claimed that the statistically significant conclusions were "probably unwarranted in view of the number of nonsignificant tests." Ernhart, et al. essentially repeated the study and found no evidence for a decrease in IQ.

The analyses of Needleman et al. can be considered a classic case of "data snooping." In their analysis, various covariates and subgroup analyses were performed in an effort to find statistical significance. It was only after such analyses that significant lead and IQ associations were found. As reported in Palca (1991), "the printouts show[ed] that Needleman's first set of analyses failed to show a relationship between lead level and subsequent intelligence tests."

1.2.5   Industrial Experimentation and Engineering

In industry the first phase of experimentation often begins with a screening experiment, where many factors are studied using only a few experimental runs. Since many factors are tested, there is a multiplicity problem: factors that are truly inert can be easily called "significant."

As with any decision problem, errors of various types must be balanced against costs. In screening designs, there are costs of declaring an inactive factor to be active (Type I error), and costs of declaring an active effect to be inactive (Type II error). Type II errors are troublesome as addressed in Lin (1995). However, when there are enough runs in the experiment, linear regression and the usual t tests on the parameters provide sufficient protection against Type II errors; for saturated or nearly saturated designs, various other procedures have been devised (Box and Meyer, 1986; Lenth, 1989).

Type I errors also are troublesome, as they cause unnecessary experimental cost in the follow-up experiments, but are typically seen as having less importance than Type II errors in screening designs. Nevertheless, Type I errors are not necessarily free of cost. In particular, they can increase the cost of follow-up experimentation by including more factors than are really needed. Controlling Type I errors is a problem in multiple inference of the type considered in this book. While we consider Type II errors also to be important (see Chapter 7 in particular), the primary emphasis of most multiple comparisons and multiple testing procedures (including those in this book) is to find the most powerful method possible subject to global (familywise) Type I error control.

1.2.6   Identifying Clinical Practice Improvement Opportunities for Hospital Surgeries

As discussed by Pearce and Westfall (1997), health care has entered into the evidence-based decision making era. In no field is that more evident than cardiac surgery as evidenced by the publication of surgeon "report cards" of raw mortality data in New York and Pennsylvania newspapers (Green and Wintfeld, 1995). A principal reason for using such data is to identify continuous quality improvement (CQI) opportunities in clinical practice.

Hospital death, perioperative myocardial infarction, reoperation for bleeding, surgical wound infection, cerebrovascular accident, pulmonary complications, and renal failure are examined on a quarterly basis in these reports. Each of these adverse events is measured as a percentage of the total surgical procedures performed (individually and in total), and quarterly evaluations are made at the individual surgeon level. These examinations consist of testing the multiple hypotheses that each individual surgeon's outcomes for each adverse event do not differ significantly from the remainder of the group.

In order to drive out fear in the CQI process, the probability of declaring a false significance must be controlled. Without adjustment, the probability of declaring one surgeon worse than the others for at least one adverse outcome can approach 88 percent, even when the surgeons are identical in all respects except for patient assignment (assumed random). Such a high probability can cause fear and mistrust of the statistical methods. Pearce and Westfall (1997) used PROC MULTTEST to control this false significance probability at levels no higher than 5 percent, so that positive determinations could be viewed safely as a need for the improvement of a particular surgeon, and not as a spurious determination of differences between surgeons.

1.3   When Are Multiple Comparisons/Multiple Testing Methods (MCPs) Needed?

The previous examples show that multiple tests and multiple comparisons arise often in practice, and that improper conclusions can arise easily from such studies. In this book, we describe methods for overcoming the problem, and call such methods "MCPs," short for *Multiple Comparisons Procedures*, even though at times "MCP" will refer to a multiple testing method, or perhaps a simultaneous confidence interval method. Throughout this book, the term "MCP" will refer generically to *any* simultaneous inference procedure.

In general, then, when should you use an MCP? If *any* of the following apply to your multiple inferences, then you should be concerned about the multiple inference problem, and you should consider using an MCP. (Several of these are adapted from Westfall and Young 1993, p. 21.)

- It is plausible that many of the effects studied might truly be null.

- You want to ensure that any effects you claim are real, or reproducible, with the standard 95 percent level of confidence.

- You are prepared to perform much data manipulation to find a "significant" result. (For example, you perform many tests and play "pick the winner.")

- Your analysis is planned to be exploratory in nature, yet you still want to claim that any significant result is in fact real.

- Your experiment or survey is expensive and is unlikely to be repeated before serious actions are taken.

- There is a cost, real or implicit, that is associated with incorrectly declaring effects or differences to be "real."

1.4   Selecting an MCP Using This Book

Before deciding which test or procedure to use, you need to identify the three main components of your problem:

1. the assumptions of the statistical model that you are using
2. the comparison or testing objectives of your study
3. the collection of items that you want to test.

Once you have determined these three elements, you can identify an appropriate method of inference. What follows is a brief overview of the elements of each, with sections in the book where each item is discussed. Note that the chapters of this book are primarily arranged around 1, the assumptions of the model, with elements of 2 and 3 filling the subsections.

1.4.1   Statistical Modeling Assumptions

The choice of a statistical model is a completely separate issue from multiple tests and multiple comparisons, and is a choice that you must make before using any statistical procedure. Failure to identify an appropriate model invalidates MCPs, just as it invalidates any statistical procedure. Also, failure to use the structure of the data completely can result in inefficient methods. For example, methods that assume independence of comparisons or tests usually are valid, in the sense of controlling error probabilities, but are inefficient when compared to methods that fully utilize correlation information.

The following list contains major statistical model classes covered in this book:

Unstructured Models (or Models with Little Structure)
These are models where little is assumed about distributions, correlations, etc. Nonparametric procedures fall in this class. The models for the actual data in this case may be quite complicated, but the assumption is that the analysis has been distilled down to a collection of p-values. Multiple inference methods in this class consist essentially of adjusting these p-values for the purposes of making tests. Such methods work reasonably well for a variety of models, and if you have a model that is not contained in one of the major classes given below, then you can choose an MCP that assumes little structure. In particular, these methods are valid, though somewhat conservative, for all correlation structures, and can be termed "Generalized Bonferroni Methods." See Chapter 2.

Balanced One-way Analysis-of-Variance (ANOVA)
These are models for data from experiments where several groups are compared, and where the sample sizes are equal for all groups. Independence of data values is a crucial assumption for these models; and if they are not independent, then you might be able to use one of the alternatives listed below. Other assumptions strictly needed for these models are homogeneity of error variance and normality of the observations within each group, but these are not as important as the independence assumption (unless severely violated). See Chapter 3.

Unbalanced One-way ANOVA, or Analysis-of-Covariance (ANCOVA)
These data are similar to the balanced ANOVA except that sample sizes may be unbalanced, or the comparisons between means might be done while controlling one or more covariates (e.g., confounding variables, pre-experimental measurements). The distributional assumptions are identical to those of the ANOVA, with the exception that for ANCOVA, the normality assumption must be evaluated by using residuals and not actual data values. See Chapters 4 through 6.

Two-way and Higher-Way ANOVA

In these cases, you consider the effects of two or more factors, with possibly unbalanced sample sizes and/or covariates. The distributional assumptions are the same as for the unbalanced one-way ANOVA or ANCOVA (if there are covariates). See Chapter 9.

Repeated Measures ANOVA Data

When there are repeated measures on the same experimental unit, the crucial independence assumption that is used for the previous models no longer applies. For example, the data may contain repeated measures on blood pressure for an individual. In such cases, you can model the dependence of blood pressure measurements by using a variety of possible dependence structure models, and perform multiplicity-adjusted analyses within the context of such models. See Chapter 10.

Multivariate Responses with Normally Distributed Data

In these models, there are multiple measurements on the same individual. While repeated measures models usually assume that the measurements are taken on the same characteristic (like blood pressure), the multivariate response models allow completely different scales of measurement. For example, blood pressure and self-rated anxiety level form a multivariate response vector. Multiple inferences from such data are improved by incorporating the correlations among such measurements. In addition to the normality assumption, the multivariate observation vectors also are assumed independent, with constant covariance matrices. Our suggested method of analysis will allow covariates as well, so you can perform multiple comparisons with multivariate analysis of covariance (MANCOVA) data. See Chapter 10.

Nonnormally Distributed (but Continuous) Data

If the distributions are nonnormal, you still can make approximate inferences with multiplicity adjustment, using bootstrap and permutation methods. The general structure of the data is that the observation (vectors) are assumed independent, and the covariance matrices are assumed constant. However, the distributional form is not specified. The methods described herein also are valid if the distributions are normal. See Chapter 11.

Binary and Discrete Data

If your observations are binary (or more generally, if your distributions used for testing are discrete distributions), then there are fantastic gains in power that may be achieved for the multiple testing methods. An example was given previously in Section 1.2.3, where the observation vectors indicate presence or absence of a number of psychiatric conditions. In Chapter 14 we also give an application of large-sample multiple inferences from a logistic regression model for a binary outcome. See Chapters 12 and 14.

Heteroscedastic Responses

If the error variances are not constant, then the ordinary methods might be biased (in the sense of providing higher error rates than advertised) or inefficient (in the sense that the method lacks power to detect real differences). See Chapter 11.

Time-to-Event or Survival Data

If your data consist of time until an event (like death), with many censored observations, you can perform the multiple comparisons in a way that accounts for finite-sample discreteness of the observations (Chapter 12), or which uses large-sample approximations from a proportional-hazards model or a parametric survival analysis model. See Chapters 12 and 14.

1.4.2 Multiple Comparisons/Multiple Testing Objectives

Different MCPs may address different inferential objectives, so which procedure you should choose depends on which kinds of inferences you want to make. Perhaps the major distinction is whether you want to simply assess mean equality or whether you want to go further and construct confidence intervals for mean differences. A related decision is the choice of which error rate you want to control, though this is a decision to be approached cautiously. Or you might want to use an informal, graphically based method, rather than any formal error-rate-controlling method at all.

The following list contains major types of multiple inference methods, along with sections in the book where they are described. The types of inference are ordered from strongest to weakest, in a sense to be defined below, according to a classification first made by Hsu (1996).

Confidence Interval-Based Methods

These methods are useful for providing an explicit range of values for each parameter of interest. Such intervals are useful also for determining directional relationships and statistical significance. Confidence intervals are discussed throughout the book. Sections 2.3.1 and 2.3.2 define the concept, and Chapters 3 through 7 are devoted primarily to confidence interval applications. Further intervals-based applications are found later in the book, side-by-side with testing applications.

Confident Directions Methods

These methods allow you to assert inequalities involving parameters of interest—for example, that the mean for one group is less than the mean for another—without being able to give a likely range of values. Confident directions methods are introduced in Chapter 8, primarily in the context of one-sided stepwise testing methods.

Testing-Based Methods

You would use these methods if you just want to make yes/no decisions concerning hypotheses of interest. Many such methods are conveniently discussed within the context of "closed testing procedures," which we discuss in detail. Chapter 2 and Chapter 8 contain the fundamental ideas and applications of multiple testing. Further applications are given in Chapters 9 through 14.

Tests of Homogeneity

With these methods, all you can say is whether or not the hypotheses of interest are all true, without identifying which ones might be false. Such methods only control Type I errors in the "weak" sense, not in the more appropriate "strong" sense. Frankly, methods in this class are usually applied erroneously, with the mistaken idea that they provide the same type of inference as the stronger methods. Therefore, we will discuss these methods mainly in order to discourage their use.

Each item in this list provides weaker inference than the ones above it. For example, simultaneous confidence intervals for differences between means can be used to infer equality or inequality, but multiple tests for inequality cannot always be converted into confidence intervals. Conversely, methods that provide stronger inferences are often less powerful than those tailored specifically for less ambitious results. For example, if the goal of your study is just to make yes/no decisions concerning mean equality, then you can use a testing-based method with much greater power than interval-based procedures, while maintaining error rate control.

As far as error rates are concerned, the standard methods are those that control the "Familywise Error Rate" (or FWE) in the "Strong" sense (defined in Section 2.3.3). However, you might choose an alternative error rate to control, such as the "False Discovery Rate", discussed in Section 2.3.5. Also, sometimes tests of homogeneity are viewed as providing another, "weak" alternative to strong control of the FWE. **Note:** you should select a non-standard error rate *only after careful consideration of the consequences* of choosing an alternative to the strong control methods, which should be considered the "gold standard" of MCPs.

In some cases, the results of multiple inferences can be displayed nicely in graphs. For confidence interval applications of graphical display, see Section 3.3.2; for hypothesis testing applications see Section 2.6.

1.4.3   The Set (Family) of Elements to Be Tested

The type of MCP that is best for your data also depends on the set of elements which you want to compare. To control error rates, this set of items must be stated in advance, and strictly adhered to. Otherwise, the analysis is called "data snooping," as discussed in Section 1.2.4.

Here are some families of elements that you might want to test:

All Pairwise Comparisons in the ANOVA

Here, you decide to compare each mean value with every other mean value, which is useful to obtain a confident relative ranking of treatment means. This application is discussed primarily in Section 3.3, with additional applications in all remaining chapters.

All Pairwise Comparisons with the Control

If you decide, *a priori*, that your interest is in comparisons of individual groups against a standard (or control), and not against each other, then more power can be attained. This application is discussed primarily in Section 3.4, again with additional applications throughout the book.

Multiple Comparisons with the Best

If your interest only concerns comparing treatment means with the (unknown) "best" (highest or lowest, depending on the application) treatment mean, see Section 14.2.

General Contrasts

If your interest is in a general set of predefined contrasts, such as orthogonal contrasts, or cell means comparisons in a two-way ANOVA, see Section 3.5.2 and Chapter 6, with additional examples given throughout the book.

Dose-Response Contrasts

Sometimes the goal of multiple testing is to find the minimum effective dose. For this application, multiple dose-response comparisons are of interest; see Sections 6.2.2 and 8.5.

Comparisons of Multivariate Measures across Two or More Groups

The preceding applications generally presume multiple treatment groups and a univariate measure. If you have multivariate measures as well as multiple treatment groups, you might want to compare treatment groups for every one of the multivariate measures. This application is discussed in Chapters 10, 11, 12, and 13.

Infinitely many Comparisons

Although this category sounds like "data snooping," it is actually permissible when done properly. See Sections 6.3 and 14.3.

General Comparisons or Tests, Unstructured

General methods can be recommended for cases where the family is specified, but does not fit precisely into any of the categories above. These are given in Chapter 2.

Confidence Bounds for Regression Functions

These applications are discussed in Sections 6.3.2 through 6.3.5.

1.5   Controversial Aspects of MCPs

We would be wrong to suggest that all multiple testing inference issues are resolved by selecting an appropriate MCP, as suggested in the outline above, and proceeding. With MCPs, as with any statistical inference method, there is never one and only one method that is "the one and only correct method" for the analysis of any data. However, with MCPs, this issue is greatly compounded in that there can be enormous differences between the results obtained either with or without multiplicity adjustment; and there can be dramatic differences also depending upon the approach that you take to analyzing the data. This section discusses briefly some of the controversies.

1.5.1   Size of the Family

The size of the discrepancy between multiplicity-adjusted and nonmultiplicity-adjusted analysis is largely determined by the size of the "family" of tests considered: if you allow more inferences into your family, then your inferences are dramatically altered. Specifically, the larger the family, the less significant the results become.

Therefore, critics of MCPs point out that it seems easy to "cheat"; if your goal is to prove significance, then you can pare the family down to a suitably small size until statistical significance is obtained. Conversely, if your goal is to prove insignificance, then you can increase the family size until no significances remain.

There is a line of research that suggests *not* to multiplicity-adjust statistical tests, see Saville (1990), Rothman (1990), Cook and Farewell (1996), and Bailer (1991), among others. There are several issues brought up by these authors. First, the choice of the "family" is somewhat arbitrary, and inferences are *extremely* sensitive to the choice. Therefore, these authors argue that the most objective choice of a family is the test itself. Second, all MCPs lose power relative to the unadjusted methods. Thus, when Type II errors are considered as important or more important than Type I errors, the authors argue that some Type I error control should be sacrificed for the sake of controlling Type II errors. Third, these authors argue for unadjusted methods, but with complete disclosure of data analysis procedures, so that users can decide for themselves whether some of the claimed results are false significances.

Taken to its extreme, this practice of not considering multiplicity may cause scientists and experimenters to ignore completely the multiplicity problem. Appropriate use of multiple testing is a difficult and controversial subject; however, ignoring the problem will make it much worse, as shown in the examples of Section 1.2. Also, ignoring the problem makes it difficult for reviewers of scientific manuscripts to separate facts from Type I errors.

In response to these controversies, our view is that multiplicity effects are real, and that Type I errors can and do occur. You need to be aware of the various error rates to interpret your data properly. In answer to the issue concerning size of the family, our recommendation is to choose smaller, more focused families rather than broad ones, and that such a determination must be made *a priori* (preferably in writing!) to avoid the "cheating" aspect. Finally, assuming that you do decide to use a multiplicity adjustment method, you should use one that is as powerful as possible, subject to the appropriate error level constraint. In this book, you will find several examples of such methods.

1.5.2   Composite Inferences vs. Individual Inferences

Another controversial aspect of multiple testing is whether to analyze the data using a single composite inference (e.g., using meta-analytic procedures), or to require individual inferences. What is at issue is essentially the required strength of inference, as discussed in Section 1.4.2. You must make this choice on the basis of the subject matter under study, depending on what conclusions you want to be able to make. If your goal is to find whether there is a difference, overall, and you are not concerned with individual components that comprise the difference, then the composite inference is usually better (more powerful) than the individual, multiplicity-adjusted inferences. Here is an example to illustrate the difference:

EXAMPLE: Multiple Tests of ESP

While controversial, testing for extrasensory perception (ESP) has attracted interest in the scientific and government communities, particularly as it concerns possible application to international espionage (as discussed in Utts, 1995). While individual tests of significance of ESP might show marginal significance, such evidence usually disappears with appropriate definition of a family of tests and with analysis via an appropriate MCP. However, in this case it is perhaps more interesting to know whether ESP exists at all than whether ESP is found in a particular test, for a particular person. Utts (1991) discusses omnibus (meta-analytic) methods for such combined tests, finding convincingly significant evidence "for" the existence of ESP. (For discussions and rebuttals of the claims see the discussions following Utts' 1991 article.)

1.5.3 Bayesian Methods

(This section is written for Bayesians; if you are not a Bayesian, or if you don't know whether or not you are a Bayesian, then you may skip this section.)

We owe you (the Bayesian reader) an apology. Historically, the development of MCPs has been mostly along frequentist lines, and therefore, the methods that are commonly used are very non-Bayesian in flavor. In this book, our aim is to explain the commonly used tools for the analysis of multiple inferences, and since these methods are mostly frequentist, our discussions will largely follow the frequentist philosophy.

In simple inferences, there often are correspondences between frequentist and Bayesian methods that are comforting, and allow you to "compute as if a frequentist," but still to "act like a Bayesian." For example, the usual confidence intervals computed frequentist-style are Bayesian posterior intervals for suitable (usually flat) prior distributions. Similarly, p-values from one-sided tests of hypotheses that are calculated frequentist-style can be interpreted as Bayesian posterior probabilities, again with suitable priors (Casella and Berger, 1987). The correspondences break down somewhat in the case of two-sided tests as shown by Berger and Sellke (1987); nevertheless, there are broad correspondences that can be drawn even in that case.

Historically, there has been no such correspondence between frequentist and Bayesian methods in the case of multiple inferences that would allow you to take some comfort in the usual frequentist MCPs, should you be a Bayesian. It is, therefore, this issue of multiple comparisons that has, perhaps more than any other issue in statistics, polarized the Bayesian and frequentist communities, as recounted in Berry (1988) and Lindley (1990).

Recently, however, Westfall, Johnson and Utts (1997) demonstrated that some frequentist MCPs correspond roughly to Bayesian methods. The first list item in Section 1.3, which suggests that multiple inference methods are needed when it is suspected that many or all null hypotheses might be true, essentially refers to a Bayesian assessment of prior probabilities. If this condition holds, then, as noted by Westfall, Johnson, and Utts (1997), frequentist and Bayesian methods "need not be grossly disparate."

If you are in the Bayesian camp, we are sympathetic to your concerns. Please bear with us through the frequentist developments, keeping the idea in mind that frequentist and Bayesian conclusions need not be grossly disparate, when there is prior doubt about many of the hypotheses tested. We present methods that have Bayesian rationale in Chapter 13 of this book.

Chapter 2

Concepts and Basic Methods for Multiple Comparisons and Tests

2.1 Introduction

How do you protect yourself from making such erroneous claims as discussed in Chapter 1? The answer to the question and the methods that ensue are best understood by playing some probability games involving the "1 in 20" probabilities that are the foundation of standard statistical inferences. The following two SAS programs simulate statistical significance of comparisons of interest, in the case where there are in reality no true differences, using the fact that p-values are uniformly distributed under the null hypothesis. A "---" is generated if no significance is found, and a "SIG" is generated if significance is found. By construction, the long-term frequency of SIG's is only 5 percent, or 1 in 20.

Program 2.1 simulates significance from a single test.

PROGRAM 2.1   Simulated Significance from a Single Test

```
data test1;
   p_val  = ranuni(212121);
   if p_val < .05 then test="SIG"; else test="---";
proc print data=test1;
   var test;
run;
```

Program 2.2 simulates significances from 160 tests.

PROGRAM 2.2   Simulated Significances from 160 Tests

```
data test160;
   do i = 1 to 40;
      p_val1 =ranuni(212121);
      p_val2 =ranuni(0);
      p_val3 =ranuni(0);
      p_val4 =ranuni(0);
```

```
            if p_val1 < .05 then test1="SIG"; else test1="---";
            if p_val2 < .05 then test2="SIG"; else test2="---";
            if p_val3 < .05 then test3="SIG"; else test3="---";
            if p_val4 < .05 then test4="SIG"; else test4="---";
            output;
        end;
run;
proc print data=test160;
    var test1-test4;
run;
```

To be specific, imagine that the variables TEST1–TEST4 represent tests performed in the four subgroups: Young Male, Young Female, Older Male, Older Female, and that the 40 observations in the SAS data set `test160` refer to a characteristic of each subject that is compared for a treatment and control group. For example, observation 1 might be a statistical comparison of the frequency of headaches between treatment and control groups, observation 2 might denote comparison of nausea, ..., and observation 40 might denote comparison of flu-like symptoms.

What follows are outputs from these programs.

Output from Program 2.1

OBS	TEST
1	---

Output from Program 2.2

OBS	TEST1	TEST2	TEST3	TEST4
1	---	---	---	---
2	---	---	---	---
3	---	---	---	---
4	---	---	---	---
5	---	---	---	SIG
6	---	---	---	---
7	---	---	---	---
8	---	---	---	---
9	---	---	---	---
10	---	---	---	---
11	---	---	---	---
12	---	---	---	---
13	---	---	---	---
14	---	---	---	---
15	SIG	---	---	---
16	---	---	---	---
17	---	---	---	---
18	---	---	---	---
19	---	---	---	---
20	---	---	---	---
21	---	---	---	---
22	---	---	---	---
23	---	---	---	---
24	---	SIG	---	---
25	---	---	---	---
26	---	---	SIG	---
27	---	---	---	---
28	---	---	---	---

29	---	---	---	---
30	---	SIG	---	---
31	---	---	---	---
32	---	---	---	---
33	---	---	---	---
34	---	---	---	---
35	SIG	---	---	---
36	SIG	---	---	---
37	---	---	---	---
38	---	---	---	---
39	---	---	---	---
40	---	---	---	---

The first program produced "---" for the variable TEST. (It might have produced a "SIG," and if it did, you are reminded that significance tests at the 5 percent level are not infallible, even when only one test is performed.) The second program produced several SIG's, which are false significances in our simulation model. Further, if you look through the output, you might find some interesting patterns; for example, the fact that there are more SIG's in the first column than in the other columns might be taken to suggest that differences occur in the "Young Male subgroup." Finally, although it did not happen in this particular sample, you are likely to see two or more SIG's in a particular row suggesting "overall" treatment/control differences for a particular "affliction."

You are invited to run these programs yourself. If you do, you will get exactly the same result using the initial seed value 212121 in the `ranuni` function. Change the seed value to any other number and you will get different results. If you use "0" for the initial seed, then you will get different results every time you run the program, since the initial seed is taken from the computer clock in that case.

Thus, when multiple tests are performed, significances can arise easily by chance. With a 1 in 20 chance of a false significance for each individual test, you expect eight false significances in 160 tests. To correct the problem, a simple solution is to make the original 1 in 20 chance much smaller. In Program 2.3, we change the specifications (`ranuni(0) <.05`) to (`ranuni(0)<.0001`), which implies a 1 in 10,000 chance of error per test.

PROGRAM 2.3   Simulated Significances from 160 Tests where $\alpha = 0.0001$

```
data test160new;
   set test160;
   if p_val1 < .0001 then test1="SIG"; else test1="---";
   if p_val2 < .0001 then test2="SIG"; else test2="---";
   if p_val3 < .0001 then test3="SIG"; else test3="---";
   if p_val4 < .0001 then test4="SIG"; else test4="---";
run;
proc print data=test160new;
   var test1-test4;
run;
```

The output from Program 2.3 is not included. If you run this program, you will see no false significances; all values of the TEST variables are "---."

These simulation examples illustrate the general solution for the multiplicity problem: to protect yourself from false positives with multiple comparisons or tests, then you must use a significance level that is smaller than the usual 0.05 for the individual tests. In this chapter, we discuss specifically how to select such individual significance levels.

2.2   Families of Hypotheses or Inferences

The most important, and most controversial, aspect of multiple comparisons/multiple tests is the selection of a *family* of inferences. Statistical inferences can vary greatly depending upon how this family is selected, and specifically, upon how *many* tests or comparisons are included in the family.

A family of inferences is considered to be one in which the questions of interest meet these criteria:

- form a natural and coherent unit
- are considered simultaneously in the decision-making process.

For example, in the multiple comparison of treatment groups A, B, and C, one natural family of comparisons might be all pairs (A vs. B), (A vs. C), and (B vs. C), assuming the inference objective is to rank the treatments from worst to best. If instead this objective were to compare the treatments with one standard control (e.g. A), then this family may be safely reduced to just (A vs. B) and (A vs. C). The power of multiple testing methods can be improved by selecting the family to be as small as possible, while still addressing all questions of interest.

As we shall see, inferences can vary dramatically, depending upon the choice of the family of tests. Because of this problem, critics of multiple testing procedures have posed the farcical question, "why not let the family include all tests performed in your lifetime?" The principle that families should be as small as possible, in addition to the "natural and coherent unit" guideline, answers this question.

However, difficulties remain in the selection of a family. In large, complex studies, there are often multiple objectives, each of which contains a family of tests that can be considered a natural and coherent unit. For example, an animal carcinogenicity study might be performed using different species, and within each species, there are multiple tests for carcinogenic effects in multiple body organs. (The simulation examples of Section 2.1 are good models for this type of study: each variable represents a species, and each observation represents a body organ). In this case, we might have multiple families of tests, one for each species, or we might consider a single family including all organs in all species. We cannot give a firm recommendation for such examples, and suggest instead that you look to the specific subject matter for further guidance. If multiple families are adopted, then you need to be aware that erroneous conclusions can arise in one or more families, even if proper multiplicity adjustment is used within each family.

2.3   Error Rates

The fundamental idea of MCPs is that they control the probability of making a false claim, when the entire family of inferences is considered. This section contains an overview of the various error rates and simple methods for controlling them.

2.3.1   Comparisonwise Error Rate (CER)

Typical inferences are performed using the 95% confidence level or 5% significance level. In either case, the *comparisonwise error rate* (CER) is 5%. For confidence intervals, CER is defined as

$$CER = P(\text{Interval does not contain the parameter}).$$

A typical two-sided confidence interval has the form

(parameter estimate) $\pm$ (critical value) $\times$ (standard error of the estimate)

The CER is the probability that the actual parameter value lies outside the interval. The interval is called two-sided because the true parameter can be either below it or above it; that is, the interval can fail to contain the parameter either to the right or to the left. A one-sided interval, on the other hand, consists of all values beyond (i.e., below or above) a single endpoint, and endpoint is typically of the form

(parameter estimate) $+$ (critical value) $\times$ (standard error of the estimate)

or

(parameter estimate) $-$ (critical value) $\times$ (standard error of the estimate)

depending on which "side" is of interest. One-sided intervals have an obvious relation to one-sided tests, as discussed below.

For example, if the parameter of interest is a population mean, and the data are normally distributed, then the usual two-sided 95% confidence interval for the true mean is

$$\bar{y} \pm t_{.975, n-1} \times s_y/\sqrt{n}$$

where

- $\bar{y}$ is the estimate of the population mean
- s_y is the sample standard deviation
- n is the sample size
- $s_y/\sqrt{n}$ is the standard error of the estimate.

The critical value is $t_{.975, n-1}$, which is the $1 - 0.05/2$ quantile of the t distribution with $n - 1$ degrees of freedom. A one-sided upper confidence interval might be all values below

$$\bar{y} + t_{.95, n-1} \times s_y/\sqrt{n}.$$

For tests of hypotheses, CER is defined as

$$\text{CER} = P(\text{Reject } H_0 \mid H_0 \text{ is true}).$$

The statement "H_0" refers to a "null hypothesis" concerning a parameter or parameters of interest, which we shall always assume to be a strict equality, e.g., $H_0: \mu_1 = \mu_2$. The "$\mid$" symbol is read "given that," as in "given that H_0 is true." H_0 is "rejected" when a suitable test statistic (t, χ^2, F, etc.) exceeds the appropriate critical value. Rejecting H_0 means asserting some alternative hypothesis H_A, and it is the alternative which dictates the critical value for the test.

For example, in the one-sample problem discussed above, you might want to test whether the population mean is equal to a certain value μ_0. If the alternative is that the true mean is greater than μ_0, then a suitable test will reject the hypothesis of equality when the difference between the sample mean and μ_0 is large relative to its standard error—typically, if the difference is greater than $t_{.95, n-1} \times s_y/\sqrt{n}$. This is a one-sided test, and it corresponds to the one-sided confidence interval shown above in the sense that the null hypothesis that the true mean is equal to μ_0 will be rejected in favor of the alternative hypothesis that the true mean is greater than μ_0 if and only if μ_0 is not in the confidence interval. In this case the confidence interval is a *lower confidence* interval. The rejection rule

Conclude $H_A: \mu > \mu_0$ when $\bar{y} - \mu_0 > t_{.95, n-1} \times s_y/\sqrt{n}$

corresponds to the *lower* confidence bound for μ:

$$\bar{y} - t_{.95, n-1} \times s_y/\sqrt{n} < \mu < \infty.$$

On the other hand, if the alternative is just that the population mean is different from μ_0—either greater or less—then a suitable test will reject when the *absolute difference* $|\bar{y} - \mu_0|$ is large—say, greater than $t_{.975, n-1} \times s_y/\sqrt{n}$. This is a two-sided test, and as in the one-sided case, it will reject the null hypothesis precisely when the two sided interval does not contain μ_0.

The action, "Reject $H_0 \mid H_0$ is true" is called a "Type I error." The converse action, "Accept $H_0 \mid H_0$ is false" is a "Type II error." Occasionally, we may substitute the phrase "Retain H_0" or "Fail to reject H_0" for the phrase "Accept H_0." The "Accept H_0" action is a weak statement compared to the "Reject H_0" statement, as can be seen from the confidence interval correspondence. For example, when you "Accept" $H_0: \mu = \mu_0$, then you really are saying only that μ_0 is a *plausible value* for the population mean μ, since the corresponding confidence interval contains μ_0. However, you are not allowed to state that $\mu = \mu_0$, since the confidence interval also contains many values besides μ_0. On the other hand, the "Reject H_0" action is strong, since the confidence interval for μ does not contain the value μ_0, so we can state (with the prescribed confidence level) that $\mu \neq \mu_0$.

2.3.2   Familywise Error Rate (FWE)

Loosely stated, the *Familywise Error Rate* (FWE) is the probability of making a false claim when the entire family of inferences is considered. The specific definition of FWE depends on whether your inferences are interval-based or testing-based.

FWE for Simultaneous Confidence Intervals

Suppose that you have defined a family of inferences (tests or intervals) containing k elements. The FWE is the probability of at least one erroneous inference. This is defined for simultaneous confidence intervals as

$$\text{FWE} = P(\text{at least one interval is incorrect}) = 1 - P(\text{all intervals are correct}).$$

Here, there are multiple intervals, and the FWE is the probability that at least one of these intervals fails to contain the corresponding parameter; that is, the probability that the intervals do not all simultaneously contain their respective parameters. In the case where all intervals are independent and where the standard 95% confidence level is used for each interval (i.e., CER = 0.05), we have FWE $= 1 - (0.95)^k$. Thus, when $k = 5$, FWE $= 22.6\%$, and when $k = 20$, FWE rises to 64.2%. Another way to say this is that the *simultaneous* confidence for 20 independent 95% confidence intervals is only about 36%.

FWE for Multiple Tests of Hypotheses

In the case of multiple tests of hypotheses, some of the hypotheses H_{0j} could be true, and others could be false. Suppose the true state of nature is that the particular null hypotheses corresponding to $j_1, \ldots, j_m$ are true, and all other null hypotheses are false. In other words, $H_{0j_1}, H_{0j_2}, \ldots, H_{0j_m}$, are true, and the remaining $(k - m)$ hypotheses are false. The FWE is then defined as

$$\text{FWE} = P(\text{reject at least one of } H_{0j_1}, H_{0j_2}, \ldots, H_{0j_m} \mid H_{0j_1}, H_{0j_2}, \ldots, H_{0j_m} \text{ all are true})$$

For example, if there are $k = 20$ hypotheses tested each at the usual CER = 0.05 level, and $m = 8$ of these happen to be true nulls, then FWE $= 1 - (0.95)^8 = 33.7\%$ when the test statistics are independent. On the other hand, if all twenty nulls happen to be true, then FWE $= 64.2\%$, as shown above with the simultaneous confidence intervals.

Clearly, FWE depends on which nulls are true and which are false in the hypothesis testing application. To be unambiguous, therefore, we need to clarify that when we refer to "FWE" in multiple testing situations, we usually mean "maximum FWE." This maximum often occurs in the case where all nulls are true.

FWE depends not only on how many nulls are true, but also on the distributional characteristics of the data, including normality or lack thereof, and correlations among the test statistics. In the previous simple examples, we implicitly assumed that distributional assumptions were satisfied, which allowed us to state CER levels were 0.05; and we also assumed that the test statistics were independent. If these assumptions were always true, then this book would be much shorter than it is! The reason we need such a wide variety of multiple comparisons/multiple testing methods is to allow for varying dependence and distributional structures that arise in various problem settings.

2.3.3   Control of the FWE: Weak and Strong

To protect against incorrect decisions, you probably want your multiple comparisons/ multiple test procedure (MCP) to control the FWE at some low level, such as 0.05 or perhaps 0.10. Since you do not know in practice which nulls are true and which are false (If you did, why would you bother to test at all?), you must protect against the scenario where all nulls are true to fully control the FWE. Noting in the previous section that in the complete null scenario $FWE = 1 - (1 - CER)^k$, for k independent tests, you can control FWE to be no more than 0.05 by solving $1 - (1 - CER)^k = 0.05$, obtaining $CER = 1 - (1 - 0.05)^{1/k}$. Thus, to control the FWE at a level no more 0.05 with $k = 20$ independent inferences, you can use $CER = 0.002561$ for all individual inferences. Keep in mind that this is the simplest idea, though, and that it involves assumptions that usually are not true. Failure of these assumptions can hurt the performance of the MCP in one of two ways:

- the method might fail to actually control the FWE
- the method might control the FWE, but it might also be less powerful than an alternative method that also controls FWE.

An MCP is said to control the FWE *in the weak sense* if it protects the FWE under the complete null configuration, but not under all other configurations. Despite the fact that the terms "weak control" and "strong control" are used in conjunction with FWE, you should note that they really refer to different error rates. Weak control refers only to controlling the probability that the complete null hypothesis is rejected, and allows Type I errors in excess of the usual 5 percent value, for example, for the component hypotheses. On the other hand, a method that controls the FWE in the strong sense will result in a Type I error for *any component hypothesis* no more than 5% of the time.

Using $CER = 1 - (1 - 0.05)^{1/k}$ controls FWE in the *strong* sense, under independence. Usually, methods (such as the F-test) that test the composite null hypothesis control FWE only in the weak sense.

The following example is used to compare and contrast strong and weak control.

EXAMPLE: Flame-Retardant Pajamas

Flame-retardant pajamas were recently invented to protect babies from accidental fires. Later, concern was raised regarding the possibility that the flame-retarding chemical was carcinogenic, and a study was designed to test the basic chemical for carcinogenicity on 20 tissues. Testing was performed in two steps: first, a global test of whether the chemical affects carcinogenicity in *any* of the 20 tissues was performed, then follow-up tests were performed, all at the CER = 0.05 level, to see which *particular* tissues were affected.

In this example, the probability of incorrectly inferring that the chemical causes cancer in *some* tissue is controlled, since there is only a 5% chance that the initial hypothesis will be rejected. However, the probability of making an error in some of the individual follow-up tests is *not* controlled. To see why, suppose that the chemical causes cancer in tissue #20, but has absolutely no effect on the others. Further, assume that this effect is large, so that rejection of the initial hypothesis is virtually assured. Then, assuming independence as in the formulas above, the FWE for the remaining 19 tissues is $1 - (1 - 0.05)^{19} = 62.3\%$.

If the goal of the study is only to decide whether the chemical causes cancer at *any* of the tissues, with no concern as to *which particular* tissues are affected, then the method described previously, which controls the error rate for the global null hypothesis, is acceptable.

On the other hand, if you want to make specific inferences about the tissues, then the method described previously will be inadequate; you must control the FWE for the individual tests. Again, assuming independence, you can set the individual CER levels to $1 - (1 - 0.05)^{1/20} = 0.00256$ to do so. In this case, the FWE is less than 0.05 for all possible configurations of null and alternative hypotheses.

Some putative MCPs, such as "Fisher's Protected Least Significance" method, are really only appropriate for making inferences about the global null hypothesis, not for making multiple inferences about the individual hypotheses. Since these so-called "weak control" methods typically reject null hypotheses more often than MCPs that control FWE in the strong sense, they are fairly popular and have been widely used. However, please note the following:

- In cases where you want to make inferences about the individual hypotheses (e.g., the individual tumor tissues in the previous example), you should *not* use methods that really only test inferences about the global null hypothesis.

- When the global null hypothesis is the only concern, and there is no cost of (or concern about) making Type I errors about the individual null hypotheses, then you may use an MCP that only tests the over-all null hypothesis. Of course, in this case we would suggest that you *not* call the method an MCP, rather, it is more properly called a "test of the composite hypothesis."

Unless stated otherwise, all MCPs we discuss will control the error rate for testing individual hypotheses, not just the overall null.

2.3.4   Directional Decisions and (Type III) Error rates

A *directional error* (sometimes called a "Type III" error) is defined as the probability of misclassifying the *sign* of an effect. If you reject the hypothesis $H_0: \mu = 0$ in favor of the alternative $H_A: \mu \neq 0$ using a CER $= .05$ level test, can you then claim that the *sign* of the true mean μ is the same as the sign of the estimated mean $\bar{y}$? For the usual procedures, the answer is "yes" because of the strength-of-inference relations between confidence intervals, directional decisions, and hypothesis tests, as discussed in Section 1.4.2.

Specifically, suppose your test uses the t-statistic $t = \bar{y}/(s/\sqrt{30})$, with $n = 30$ observations, and you reject H_0 when $|t| > 2.045$ (taken from the t-distribution with 29 degrees of freedom). The associated confidence interval for μ is $\bar{y} \pm 2.045 s/\sqrt{30}$. In this case, a two-tailed rejection of H_0 at the CER $= 0.05$ significance level with a sample mean $\bar{y} > 0$ is equivalent to having the entire 95% confidence interval lie above the hypothesized value 0:

$$t > 2.045 \text{ implies } \bar{y} - 2.045 \, s/\sqrt{30} > 0$$

Conversely, two-tailed rejection of H_0 at the CER $= 0.05$ significance level with a sample mean $\bar{y} < 0$ is equivalent to having the entire 95% confidence interval lie below the hypothesized value 0:

$$t < -2.045 \text{ implies } \bar{y} + 2.045\,s/\sqrt{30} < 0$$

Thus, a rejection of H_0 in favor of the two-sided alternative at the CER level 0.05 allows one to claim that the *sign* of the parameter is the same as the sign of the estimated parameter. The CER level of the confidence interval is 0.05, so the Type III error rate of the testing method is also controlled at 0.05.

In the case where the true μ is zero, *any* classification of a significant direction is a Type III error. In this case, the Type III error is exactly 0.05. However, if $\mu > 0$, then the maximum Type III error rate is 0.025, since a Type III error can occur only when $\bar{y} < -2.045s/\sqrt{30}$. Similarly, when $\mu < 0$, then the maximum Type III error rate is 0.025. Thus, while the maximum Type III error rate is 0.05 over all possible μ (including $\mu = 0$), the Type III error rate is less than 0.025 for all $\mu \neq 0$.

For MCPs, the Type III FWE is the probability that the *sign* of *any* tested effect is misclassified. Again, we assume that if the true effect is 0, and if there is any significant determination (positive or negative), then a Type III error has occurred. When an MCP controls the Type III FWE, one may claim that the true signs of all significant effects are in the same directions as the estimated signs. As in the univariate testing situation, this property may be demonstrated when the simultaneous test procedure is equivalent to the simultaneous confidence interval procedure, since by the strength of inference relations discussed in Section 1.4.2 it will also then subsume a directional decision. Whenever you use simultaneous confidence intervals to test hypotheses, you also control the Type III FWE.

We provide the %SimPower macro to simulate Type III FWE, using this definition, in Chapter 7, Section 7.4.

2.3.5   False Discovery Rate

Benjamini and Hochberg (1995) referred to the expected proportion of erroneously rejected null hypotheses among the rejected ones as the *False Discovery Rate*, or FDR. Formally, for a given family of k null hypotheses and a given MCP, let R = number of hypotheses rejected, and let V = the (unknown) number of erroneously rejected ones. Define $V/R = 0$ in case $R = 0$ and $V = 0$ (since $V \leq R$). Then FDR is the expected value of V/R.

Under the overall null hypothesis, FDR and FWE are equal, since in this case $V/R = 1$ when there is at least one rejection, and $V/R = 0$ when there are no rejections. Thus, in the overall null hypothesis case, the expected value of V/R is just the probability of finding at least one significance, or FWE. However, under partial null configurations, the FDR is always smaller than the FWE. Thus, a method which assures that FWE $\leq \alpha$ also assures that FDR $\leq \alpha$, but it is possible—in fact, common—for FDR to be less than or equal to α while FWE $> \alpha$. Thus, FDR-controlling MCPs are usually more powerful than FWE-controlling counterparts, since a less stringent criterion is needed to achieve the same level of control.

To make a specific comparison of FWE and FDR, refer back to the pajama example in Section 2.3.3, and suppose that the 20 tissue types all are tested using (1) an MCP that has FWE = 0.10, (2) an MCP that has FDR = 0.10, and (3) an MCP that uses CER = 0.10 for all tests. Assume there is no preliminary composite test in any of these cases.

Suppose that in the FWE-controlling method (1) there are five rejections. In this case, we believe that the chemical in fact causes cancer in all five tissues, since the probability of finding one or more incorrect significances was only 0.10.

Now, suppose that in the FDR-controlling method (2) there are ten rejections. In this case, we expect that the chemical causes cancer in nine out the ten selected tissues, but we believe that one of the ten (unknown which one) may represent a false positive.

Finally, suppose that in the CER $= 0.10$ method (3) there are 15 rejections. In this case, we believe that two of the 15 (unknown which ones) may represent false positives, since the error rate per test is 10%. (CER makes no reference to how many hypotheses actually were rejected.)

As you can see, the strength of the conclusions decreases as you move from FWE to FDR to CER, however, you also see the power increase from FWE control to FDR control to CER control.

FDR-controlling and CER-controlling methods can be very useful to screen large numbers of tests, but the strength of evidence concerning particular hypotheses is weaker with such methods than it is with FWE-controlling methods.

2.4 Bonferroni and Šidák Methods

In the previous section, all calculations assumed independence. We found that if α is the desired FWE level then setting the CER levels to CER $= 1 - (1 - \alpha)^{1/k}$ controls the type I FWE level for simultaneous intervals and simultaneous tests. Further, these tests also control the simultaneous Type III error rate at or below FWE level α. This method is known as Šidák's method (Šidák, 1967). It is primarily useful in controlling the FWE when the comparisons are independent, although it also applies to certain dependent situations, to be discussed.

To guarantee strict control of the FWE when tests are not necessarily independent, the simplest and most common MCP is the Bonferroni method, which simply takes CER $= \alpha/k$.

The rationale for this method is the well-known *Bonferroni inequality*:

$$P(A_1 \text{ or } A_2 \text{ or } \ldots \text{ or } A_k) \le P(A_1) + P(A_2) + \cdots + P(A_k).$$

Figure 2.1 illustrates the inequality in the case where $k = 2$, where the probability of events is represented by the size of the corresponding set. The probability of the union of the event $\{A_1 \text{ or } A_2\}$ is clearly less than the sum of the probabilities individually, since when you sum the individual probabilities you count the intersection $\{A_1 \text{ and } A_2\}$ twice.

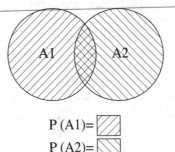

Figure 2.1
Illustration of Bonferroni's
Inequality

As an illustration of this method, suppose that you have constructed $k = 10$ simultaneous confidence intervals, all at the CER level $0.05/k = 0.05/10 = 0.005$. Then the FWE is calculated as

$$P(\{\text{Interval 1 incorrect}\} \text{ or } \{\text{Interval 2 incorrect}\} \text{ or } \ldots \{\text{Interval 10 incorrect}\})$$

$$\le \underbrace{0.005 + 0.005 + \cdots + 0.005}_{10 \text{ terms}} = 0.05.$$

2.4.1   Adjusted *p*-Values

To simplify the presentation of multiple tests, the *p*-values are often displayed as *adjusted p*-values. By definition, the adjusted *p*-value for any hypothesis equals the smallest FWE at which the hypothesis would be rejected. Therefore, adjusted *p*-values are readily interpretable as evidence against the corresponding null hypotheses, when all tests are considered as a family. To make a decision on any hypothesis H_{0j}, we can simply compare its corresponding adjusted *p*-value with the desired FWE level, α.

The Bonferroni procedure rejects any H_{0j} whose corresponding *p*-value, p_j, is less than or equal to α/k. This is equivalent to rejecting any H_{0j} for which kp_j is less than or equal to α. Thus, kp_j is the Bonferroni adjusted *p*-value for H_{0j}. We require any *p*-value to be less than 1.0, and therefore define it more specifically as follows, using the "$\tilde{p}$" symbol to denote "adjusted *p*-value":

Bonferroni Adjusted *p*-Value for Hypothesis H_{0j}:

$$\tilde{p}_j = \begin{cases} kp_j & \text{if} \quad kp_j \leq 1 \\ 1 & \text{if} \quad kp_j > 1. \end{cases}$$

For the Šidák method, recall that we can reject an individual hypothesis H_{0j} if $p_j \leq 1 - (1-\alpha)^{1/k}$; or equivalently, when $1 - (1-p_j)^k \leq \alpha$, where α is the desired FWE level. This gives us the Šidák adjusted *p*-values.

Šidák Adjusted *p*-Value for Hypothesis H_{0j}:

$$\tilde{p}_j = 1 - (1 - p_j)^k.$$

2.4.2   An Example with Multiple *p*-Values

Suppose you have calculated $k = 10$ ordinary (that is, nonmultiplicity adjusted) *p*-values using a standard testing method such as the two-sample *t*-test. These might be obtained, for example, from PROC TTEST using several variables or with BY variable processing. The *p*-values are $p_1 = 0.0911$, $p_2 = 0.8912$, $p_3 = 0.0001$, $p_4 = 0.5718$, $p_5 = 0.0132$, $p_6 = 0.9011$, $p_7 = 0.2012$, $p_8 = 0.0289$, $p_9 = 0.0498$, and $p_{10} = 0.0058$.

Program 2.4 calculates the Bonferroni and Šidák adjusted *p*-values "by hand".

PROGRAM 2.4   **Bonferroni and Šidák Adjusted *p*-Values Using the DATA Step**

```
data one;
   input test pval @@;
   bon_adjp = min(1,10*pval);
   sid_adjp = 1 - (1-pval)**10;
   datalines;
1 0.0911    2 0.8912
3 0.0001    4 0.5718
5 0.0132    6 0.9011
7 0.2012    8 0.0289
9 0.0498   10 0.0058
;
proc sort data=one out=one;
   by pval;
proc print data=one;
   run;
```

**Output from
Program 2.4**

OBS	TEST	PVAL	BON_ADJP	SID_ADJP
1	3	0.0001	0.001	0.00100
2	10	0.0058	0.058	0.05651
3	5	0.0132	0.132	0.12443
4	8	0.0289	0.289	0.25417
5	9	0.0498	0.498	0.40000
6	1	0.0911	0.911	0.61527
7	7	0.2012	1.000	0.89423
8	4	0.5718	1.000	0.99979
9	2	0.8912	1.000	1.00000
10	6	0.9011	1.000	1.00000

You can also perform these calculations using PROC MULTTEST as shown in Program 2.5.

PROGRAM 2.5   **Bonferroni and Šidák Adjusted *p*-Values Using PROC MULTTEST**

```
data one; set one;
   rename pval=raw_p;
   drop bon_adjp sid_adjp;
proc multtest pdata=one bon sid out=outp;
proc sort data=outp out=outp;
   by raw_p;
proc print data=outp;
run;
```

**Output from
Program 2.5**

OBS	TEST	RAW_P	BON_P	SID_P
1	3	0.0001	0.001	0.00100
2	10	0.0058	0.058	0.05651
3	5	0.0132	0.132	0.12443
4	8	0.0289	0.289	0.25417
5	9	0.0498	0.498	0.40000
6	1	0.0911	0.911	0.61527
7	7	0.2012	1.000	0.89423
8	4	0.5718	1.000	0.99979
9	2	0.8912	1.000	1.00000
10	6	0.9011	1.000	1.00000

Note that the use of PROC SORT allows for easy identification of the most significant tests. (PROC MULTTEST has many more advanced capabilities that will be discussed in Chapters 11 and 12.)

Comparing the Bonferroni and Šidák adjusted *p*-values, we see that there is little difference when the *p*-values are small. Also note that the Bonferroni *p*-values are always larger, so that you'll reject the null less often if you use Bonferroni-adjusted *p*-values. This is the price you pay to guarantee FWE control when the *p*-values are possibly not statistically independent.

2.4.3   Example: Multiple Comparisons from a Questionnaire

A data set reported by Johnson and Wichern (1998, p. 371) contains results of a survey in which each spouse of a married couple is asked (privately!)

1. What is the level of passionate love you feel for your partner?
2. What is the level of passionate love your partner feels for you?
3. What is the level of companionate love you feel for your partner?
4. What is the level of companionate love your partner feels for you?

All responses are given on a 1–5 Likert scale.

There are several questions of interest in this study. First, do the husbands and wives differ, overall, in their responses? Second, what husband/wife differences do the data support concerning

- each of the four questions, individually
- the average of all four questions
- the average of the "companionate" questions
- the average of the "passionate" questions
- the average of the "feel for partner" questions
- the average of the "partner feels for you" questions?

This example illustrates issues involved in the choice of a "family" of tests: you should decide, *a priori*, which contrasts or hypotheses best answer the questions of your study. Then, you need to select a multiplicity adjustment method that works best, given your particular set of contrasts or tests of interest. In this example, we use simultaneous, Bonferroni-adjusted confidence intervals. This gives reasonable results, but the resulting intervals are somewhat conservative (i.e. a little wider than they should be) because the Bonferroni method ignores the correlation structure.

Some statistics texts use the preliminary test (the overall difference) to decide whether to do the follow-up tests, but we do not recommend this approach. We especially discourage using this approach with unadjusted follow-up tests, as described above in Section 2.3.3. Even if the initial test finds insufficient evidence to reject the hypothesis of an overall difference between husbands and wives, there remains interest in the estimated directions of the differences, and in their associated confidence limits, to understand the level of precision of the current study and to suggest directions for additional research.

(As a parenthetical note, the overall test *is* important in the "Closure" method, described in Chapter 8. This method does allow inferences about individual hypotheses with strong FWE control, but its application is much more complex than simply following the global test with simple tests.)

While the use of multivariate analysis testing procedures is somewhat outside the scope of this book, Program 2.6 performs these tests using multivariate methods. Note that the data are one-sample data, not two-sample data, since the observational units are married couples, not individual spouses.

The program also computes simultaneous Bonferroni intervals, the simultaneous Šidák intervals, and the ordinary unadjusted confidence intervals, all at the usual 95% level of confidence. We treat the problem as pure multivariate and make no special assumptions (e.g., sphericity) about the covariance matrix.

PROGRAM 2.6   Conservative Simultaneous Confidence Intervals with Multivariate Data

```
data _null_;
   call symput('bonalpha',0.05/9             );
   call symput('sidalpha',1-(1-0.05)**(1/9));
data HusbWive;
   input HusbQ1-HusbQ4 WifeQ1-WifeQ4 @@;
   DiffQ1 = HusbQ1-WifeQ1;
   DiffQ2 = HusbQ2-WifeQ2;
```

```
      DiffQ3 = HusbQ3-WifeQ3;
      DiffQ4 = HusbQ4-WifeQ4;
      DiffQAvg = sum(of HusbQ1-HusbQ4)/4 - sum(of WifeQ1-WifeQ4)/4;
      DiffComp = sum(of HusbQ1-HusbQ2)/2 - sum(of WifeQ1-WifeQ2)/2;
      DiffPass = sum(of HusbQ3-HusbQ4)/2 - sum(of WifeQ3-WifeQ4)/2;
      DiffFFP  = sum(of HusbQ1 HusbQ3)/2 - sum(of WifeQ1 WifeQ3)/2;
      DiffFFY  = sum(of HusbQ2 HusbQ4)/2 - sum(of WifeQ2 WifeQ4)/2;
   datalines;
2 3 5 5   4 4 5 5     5 5 4 4   4 5 5 5     4 5 5 5   4 4 5 5
4 3 4 4   4 5 5 5     3 3 5 5   4 4 5 5     3 3 4 5   3 3 4 4
3 4 4 4   4 3 5 4     4 4 5 5   3 4 5 5     4 5 5 5   4 4 5 4
4 4 3 3   3 4 4 4     4 4 5 5   4 5 5 5     5 5 4 4   5 5 5 5
4 4 4 4   4 4 5 5     4 3 5 5   4 4 4 4     4 4 5 5   4 4 5 5
3 3 4 5   3 4 4 4     4 5 4 4   5 5 5 5     5 5 5 5   4 5 4 4
5 5 4 4   3 4 4 4     4 4 4 4   5 3 4 4     4 4 4 4   5 3 4 4
4 4 4 4   4 5 4 4     3 4 5 5   2 5 5 5     5 3 5 5   3 4 5 5
5 5 3 3   4 3 5 5     3 3 4 4   4 4 4 4     4 4 4 4   4 4 5 5
3 3 5 5   3 4 4 4     4 4 3 3   4 4 5 4     4 4 5 5   4 4 5 5
;

proc glm;
   model HusbQ1-HusbQ4 WifeQ1-WifeQ4 = / nouni;
   repeated Spouse 2, Question 4 identity;
   run;

proc means alpha=0.05 n mean lclm uclm;
   title "Unadjusted Confidence Intervals";
   var DiffQ1-DiffQ4 DiffQAvg DiffComp DiffPass DiffFFP DiffFFY;
proc means alpha=&sidalpha n mean lclm uclm;
   title "Simultaneous Sidak Intervals";
   var DiffQ1-DiffQ4 DiffQAvg DiffComp DiffPass DiffFFP DiffFFY;
proc means alpha=&bonalpha n mean lclm uclm;
   title "Simultaneous Bonferroni Intervals";
   var DiffQ1-DiffQ4 DiffQAvg DiffComp DiffPass DiffFFP DiffFFY;
   run;
```

Output from Program 2.6

```
                    General Linear Models Procedure
                   Repeated Measures Analysis of Variance


                 Manova Test Criteria and Exact F Statistics for
                    the Hypothesis of no SPOUSE*QUESTION Effect
       H = Type III SS&CP Matrix for SPOUSE*QUESTION   E = Error SS&CP Matrix


                         S=1    M=1    N=12

Statistic                     Value         F     Num DF   Den DF  Pr > F

Wilks' Lambda              0.68838089    2.9424       4       26   0.0394
Pillai's Trace             0.31161911    2.9424       4       26   0.0394
Hotelling-Lawley Trace     0.45268415    2.9424       4       26   0.0394
Roy's Greatest Root        0.45268415    2.9424       4       26   0.0394
```

Unadjusted Confidence Intervals

Variable	N	Mean	Lower 95.0% CLM	Upper 95.0% CLM
DIFFQ1	30	0.0666667	-0.2720826	0.4054159
DIFFQ2	30	-0.1333333	-0.4692319	0.2025652
DIFFQ3	30	-0.3000000	-0.5799473	-0.0200527
DIFFQ4	30	-0.1333333	-0.4231261	0.1564594
DIFFQAVG	30	-0.1250000	-0.2889963	0.0389963
DIFFCOMP	30	-0.0333333	-0.2830207	0.2163541
DIFFPASS	30	-0.2166667	-0.4926500	0.0593167
DIFFFFP	30	-0.1166667	-0.3341955	0.1008621
DIFFFFY	30	-0.1333333	-0.3290468	0.0623802

Simultaneous Sidak Intervals

Variable	N	Mean	Lower 99.4% CLM	Upper 99.4% CLM
DIFFQ1	30	0.0666667	-0.4280355	0.5613688
DIFFQ2	30	-0.1333333	-0.6238724	0.3572057
DIFFQ3	30	-0.3000000	-0.7088290	0.1088290
DIFFQ4	30	-0.1333333	-0.5565404	0.2898737
DIFFQAVG	30	-0.1250000	-0.3644966	0.1144966
DIFFCOMP	30	-0.0333333	-0.3979715	0.3313048
DIFFPASS	30	-0.2166667	-0.6197068	0.1863735
DIFFFFP	30	-0.1166667	-0.4343411	0.2010077
DIFFFFY	30	-0.1333333	-0.4191491	0.1524825

Simultaneous Bonferroni Intervals

Variable	N	Mean	Lower 99.4% CLM	Upper 99.4% CLM
DIFFQ1	30	0.0666667	-0.4295431	0.5628765
DIFFQ2	30	-0.1333333	-0.6253674	0.3587007
DIFFQ3	30	-0.3000000	-0.7100750	0.1100750
DIFFQ4	30	-0.1333333	-0.5578302	0.2911635
DIFFQAVG	30	-0.1250000	-0.3652265	0.1152265
DIFFCOMP	30	-0.0333333	-0.3990827	0.3324161
DIFFPASS	30	-0.2166667	-0.6209352	0.1876018
DIFFFFP	30	-0.1166667	-0.4353092	0.2019759
DIFFFFY	30	-0.1333333	-0.4200202	0.1533535

Note that the composite multivariate test rejects the hypothesis of overall equal treatment means for the husbands and wives ($F(4, 26) = 2.9424$, $p = 0.0394$). The follow-up tests attempt to discover which component, or linear combination of the component means, have significant differences for the husbands and wives.

Most of the estimated differences are negative, indicating that the husbands' sample averages are lower than the wives' averages, except for the first question, "What is the level of passionate love you feel for your partner?" Using the unadjusted confidence intervals, you would claim that the husbands' average is significantly lower than the wives' for the third question, "What is the level of companionate love you feel for your partner?" However, since the unadjusted simultaneous intervals admit an FWE of $1 - (1 - .05)^9 = 40.0\%$, the conclusion that there is difference for this variable is questionable.

The Šidák and Bonferroni intervals show no significant differences, since all the intervals include 0. In general, the safest of the two is the Bonferroni method, which guarantees FWE control for all correlation structures. However, the Šidák method also controls the FWE conservatively in the case of two-sided intervals or tests, and usually controls the FWE conservatively in the case of one-sided intervals or tests. In any event the difference between the two is very small, with the Bonferroni intervals only slightly wider (and therefore more conservative).

We will return to this example in Chapter 14. Because the composite F test is found significant, we know that there is at least one linear combination of the means that also can be declared legitimately significant. In this example, it turns out that the most significant linear combination is $-0.04\text{DIFFQ1} + 0.10\text{DIFFQ2} + .41\text{DIFFQ3} - 0.27\text{DIFFQ4}$, which is essentially a comparison of the difference between the third and fourth questions. This measure can be interpreted as a measure of "perceived reciprocation of companionate love." A significant difference between husbands and wives can be claimed legitimately along this dimension, even though it was not suspected *a priori*.

If you prefer to analyze the data using tests of hypotheses rather than confidence intervals, then you may use Program 2.7.

PROGRAM 2.7   Multiple Tests with Multivariate Data

```
proc means data=HusbWive n mean std prt;
   title "Tests of Hypotheses With Husband/Wife Data";
   var DiffQ1-DiffQ4 DiffQAvg DiffComp DiffPass DiffFFP DiffFFY;
run;
```

Output from Program 2.7

Tests of Hypotheses With Husband/Wife Data

Variable	N	Mean	Std Dev	Prob>|T|
DIFFQ1	30	0.0666667	0.9071871	0.6903
DIFFQ2	30	-0.1333333	0.8995529	0.4235
DIFFQ3	30	-0.3000000	0.7497126	0.0366
DIFFQ4	30	-0.1333333	0.7760792	0.3545
DIFFQAVG	30	-0.1250000	0.4391901	0.1299
DIFFCOMP	30	-0.0333333	0.6686751	0.7868
DIFFPASS	30	-0.2166667	0.7390970	0.1192
DIFFFFP	30	-0.1166667	0.5825528	0.2817
DIFFFFY	30	-0.1333333	0.5241304	0.1741

Note that these are *unadjusted* p-values; therefore, they correspond to the unadjusted confidence intervals in the Output from Program 2.6. The p-value that is less than 0.05 corresponds to the unadjusted 95% confidence interval that excludes 0 (for the difference in Question 3).

However, none of the p-values shown above are less than either the Bonferroni CER value of 0.00556 or the Šidák CER value of 0.005683. This observation corresponds to the observation that none of the Bonferroni or Šidák confidence intervals exclude 0. Had any of the Bonferroni p-values been less than 0.00556, then the corresponding Bonferroni interval would have excluded 0. Thus, if you only perform the comparisons using two-sided t-tests, either with the appropriate Bonferroni or Šidák CER level, you still may conclude directional inequalities with confidence whenever you find a statistically significant result.

2.5   Sequentially Rejective Methods

In the previous section we defined Bonferroni and Šidák methods for testing hypotheses and forming confidence intervals, and we noted that the FWE is controlled when you use these methods (guaranteed with Bonferroni, usually true with Šidák). Because there is a direct correspondence between simultaneous confidence intervals and simultaneous hypothesis tests using these methods, directional decisions are allowed whenever a rejection of a hypothesis is found.

These methods are called "single-step" methods because only one "step" is needed to find the appropriate critical value for all tests or intervals. With single-step methods, each individual interval or test is calculated without reference to the significance or insignificance of the remaining inferences.

Sequentially rejective methods, also called "stepwise" methods differ in that the result of a given test depends upon the results of the other tests. When comparing means, sequentially rejective methods are purely for testing mean equality; they cannot be used to infer a confidence interval for mean differences. If you are interested only in tests of hypotheses, with no confidence intervals, then the power can be improved dramatically while retaining FWE control by using sequentially rejective methods.

Whether and when stepwise methods allow directional decisions with Type III error control depends on the particulars of the method. For example, stepwise one-sided tests generally allow directional decisions, but stepwise two-sided tests may not. Defining situations for which stepwise two-sided tests in fact control the Type III FWE is largely an open research area. You can estimate the Type III FWE using the %SimPower macro, discussed in Chapter 7.

2.5.1   Bonferroni-Holm Method

Assume that there are k hypotheses of interest, $H_{01}, \ldots, H_{0k}$ with corresponding p-values $p_1, \ldots, p_k$. The simple (single-step) Bonferroni procedure rejects any H_{0j} if the corresponding p-value is $\leq \alpha/k$, where α is the desired FWE level. Holm (1979) offered the following modification of the simple Bonferroni procedure: order the p-values, $p_{(1)} \leq \cdots \leq p_{(k)}$ and the corresponding hypotheses $H_{(1)}, \ldots, H_{(k)}$. Now, if $p_{(1)} > \alpha/k$ then all hypotheses are retained, otherwise, $H_{(1)}$ (the hypothesis corresponding to $p_{(1)}$) is rejected and one goes on to compare $p_{(2)}$ with $\alpha/(k-1)$. If $p_{(2)} > \alpha/(k-1)$, then all the remaining hypotheses are retained, otherwise, $H_{(2)}$ is rejected and one goes on to compare $p_{(3)}$ with $\alpha/(k-2)$, etc. Clearly, Holm's procedure is more powerful than the simple Bonferroni procedure because the critical points are no smaller and are in fact larger for all steps after the first.

For example, suppose two hypotheses have been tested with corresponding p-values of $p_{(1)} = 0.02$ and $p_{(2)} = 0.03$. The Bonferroni procedure rejects only $H_{(1)}$ (at $\alpha = 0.05$) since only $p_{(1)} < 0.05/2$. Both hypotheses are rejected by Holm's procedure; however, $H_{(1)}$ is rejected since $p_{(1)} < 0.05/2$, and $H_{(2)}$ is rejected since $p_{(2)} < 0.05/1$ (and the fact that $H_{(1)}$ is rejected).

Adjusted p-values simplify the presentation of the Holm procedure. Recall that the adjusted p-value is the smallest nominal FWE level α leading to a rejection of the given hypothesis. In the previous example $p_{(1)} = 0.02$ will be significant for α as low as 0.04; hence, $\tilde{p}_{(1)} = 0.04$. Note further that $H_{(2)}$ is also rejected for α as low as 0.04, but for α less than 0.04, $H_{(2)}$ is retained because $H_{(1)}$ is. Thus $\tilde{p}_{(2)} = 0.04$ as well.

As another example, suppose the p-values were $p_{(1)} = 0.02$ and $p_{(2)} = .045$. In this case, the adjusted p's would be $\tilde{p}_{(1)} = 2 \times 0.02 = 0.040$ and $\tilde{p}_{(2)} = 1 \times 0.045 = 0.045$. The essential idea for the Holm step-down adjusted p-values is that the smallest p-value is multiplied by k, the second smallest by $k-1$, the third smallest by $k-2$, etc., but with a correction as shown above in the $p_{(1)} = 0.02$, $p_{(2)} = 0.03$ case, to ensure that the ordering of the adjusted p-values is the same as the ordering of the unadjusted p-values.

In general, the adjusted p-values for the Holm method can be defined sequentially as follows:

Adjusted *p*-Values for Holm's Method

$$\tilde{p}_{(1)} = kp_{(1)}$$
$$\tilde{p}_{(2)} = \max(\tilde{p}_{(1)}, \; (k-1)p_{(2)})$$
$$\vdots$$
$$\tilde{p}_{(j)} = \max(\tilde{p}_{(j-1)}, \; (k-j+1)p_{(j)})$$
$$\vdots$$
$$\tilde{p}_{(k)} = \max(\tilde{p}_{(k-1)}, \; p_{(k)})$$

As usual, any Bonferroni adjusted p-value greater than 1.0 is truncated to 1.0.

You can use PROC MULTTEST to perform these calculations. Using the example from Program 2.5, Program 2.8 computes the Holm step-down adjusted p-values.

PROGRAM 2.8   HOLM Adjusted *p*-Values Using PROC MULTTEST

```
data one;
   set one;
   rename pval=raw_p;
   drop bon_adjp sid_adjp;
proc multtest pdata=one bon stepbon out=outp;
proc sort data=outp out=outp;
   by raw_p;
proc print data=outp;
run;
```

Output from Program 2.8

OBS	TEST	RAW_P	BON_P	STPBON_P
1	3	0.0001	0.001	0.0010
2	10	0.0058	0.058	0.0522
3	5	0.0132	0.132	0.1056
4	8	0.0289	0.289	0.2023
5	9	0.0498	0.498	0.2988
6	1	0.0911	0.911	0.4555
7	7	0.2012	1.000	0.8048
8	4	0.5718	1.000	1.0000
9	2	0.8912	1.000	1.0000
10	6	0.9011	1.000	1.0000

The column "STPBON_P" contains the Holm adjusted p-values. This output also could be obtained using PROC MULTTEST with the "HOLM" option in place of the "STEPBON" option. To use this method, simply note whether the STEP_BON p-value is less than your desired FWE level, such as 0.05. In this example, only Test 3 is significant at the FWE = 0.05 level, and Tests 3 and 10 are significant at the FWE = 0.10 level.

The gain in power that is possible by using Holm instead of Bonferroni is apparent because the adjusted p-values are smaller, leading one to reject hypotheses more often. In the preceding example, however, both methods rejected exactly the same hypotheses at the FWE = 0.050 and FWE = 0.10 levels.

2.5.2   Šidák-Holm Method

As an alternative to Holm's step-down Bonferroni method, you can perform the multiplicity adjustments in step-down fashion by using the Šidák-Holm method. Adjusted *p*-values are calculated sequentially as follows:

Adjusted *p*-Values (Step-Down) Using Šidák's Method

$$\tilde{p}_{(1)} = 1 - (1 - p_{(1)})^k$$
$$\tilde{p}_{(2)} = \max(\tilde{p}_{(1)}, \ 1 - (1 - p_{(2)})^{k-1})$$
$$\vdots$$
$$\tilde{p}_{(j)} = \max(\tilde{p}_{(j-1)}, \ 1 - (1 - p_{(j)})^{k-j+1})$$
$$\vdots$$
$$\tilde{p}_{(k)} = \max(\tilde{p}_{(k-1)}, \ p_{(k)})$$

Program 2.9 shows how to use `PROC MULTTEST`.

PROGRAM 2.9   **Šidák-Holm Adjusted *p*-Values Using `PROC MULTTEST`**

```
data one; set one;
   rename pval=raw_p;
   drop bon_adjp sid_adjp;
proc multtest pdata=one sid stepsid out=outp;
proc sort data=outp out=outp;
   by raw_p;
proc print data=outp;
run;
```

Output from Program 2.9

OBS	TEST	RAW_P	SID_P	STPSID_P
1	3	0.0001	0.00100	0.00100
2	10	0.0058	0.05651	0.05101
3	5	0.0132	0.12443	0.10085
4	8	0.0289	0.25417	0.18558
5	9	0.0498	0.40000	0.26398
6	1	0.0911	0.61527	0.37973
7	7	0.2012	0.89423	0.59285
8	4	0.5718	0.99979	0.92149
9	2	0.8912	1.00000	0.98816
10	6	0.9011	1.00000	0.98816

Note that the Šidák-Holm adjustments (single-step or step-down) are slightly smaller than the corresponding Bonferroni adjustments that are shown in the output from Program 2.8. FWE control is guaranteed only under independence, but Šidák's method also provides FWE control for most types of dependence structures that occur in practice as well, as discussed in Holland and Copenhaver (1987). In fact, the adjusted *p*-values are usually made even smaller by incorporating specific dependence structures, as we show throughout this book.

2.5.3 Simes' Modified Bonferroni Procedure

Simes (1986) offered another test for the global H_0 which is based on the individual p-values: reject H_0 if $p_{(j)} \le j\alpha/k$, for at least one j. For two hypotheses, for example, you would reject H_0 if $p_{(1)} \le \alpha/2$ or $p_{(2)} \le \alpha$. This is obviously an improvement over the Bonferroni procedure that rejects H_0 if $p_{(1)} \le \alpha/2$. Simes proved that his procedure controls the global Type I error rate only under independence, and performed some simulations indicating that his procedure also controls the FWE weakly under a variety of situations. Recent research in this area indicates that the Simes test does provide satisfactory control of the FWE, but can sometimes exceed α (Hochberg and Rom, 1995; Sarkar and Chang, 1998). Simes' procedure cannot be used to make inferences on individual hypotheses, since it tests only the global null hypothesis. Thus, while the Simes method provides a useful foundation for other multiple testing procedures, we do not recommend its use.

2.5.4 Hommel's Procedure

Hommel (1988), employed the "Closure Principle," (see Chapter 8), and devised a sequential procedure based on Simes' test to allow inferences on individual hypotheses.

Compute $j = \max_{i \in \{1,\dots,k\}} p_{k-i+i'} > i'\alpha/i$, $i' = 1,\dots,i$. If the maximum does not exist, reject all H_i, $i = 1,\dots,k$; otherwise, reject H_i with $p_i \le \alpha/j$.

Hommel's procedure is *coherent* but not *consonant*. This means that it is possible to reject the global null hypothesis without a rejection of any of the individual hypotheses; see Hochberg and Tamhane (1987) and Chapter 8 of this book for further discussion of these concepts.

2.5.5 Hochberg's Method—A Step-Up Test

Bonferroni and Šidák tests of the preceding sections are performed in "step-down" fashion; that is, you adjust the smallest p-value, then the second-smallest, and so on to the largest. The term "step-down" refers to the fact that you start with the "most significant" test and "step down" to the "least significant" test.

"Step-up" procedures work in the reverse direction: you start by adjusting the p-value for the least significant test and "step up" to the most significant.

Hochberg (1988) derived such a step-up procedure, based on Simes's test, and extended Simes' test of the global H_0 to testing the component H_{0j}'s. The critical points are identical to those of the step-down Bonferroni (or Holm) method, but the testing is performed in step-up fashion rather than step-down. If the least significant p-value $p_{(k)} \le \alpha$ then all hypotheses are rejected, otherwise, $H_{(k)}$ is retained and one goes on to compare $p_{(k-1)}$ with $\alpha/2$. If $p_{(k-1)} \le \alpha/2$, all the remaining hypotheses are rejected; otherwise $H_{(k-1)}$ is retained and one goes on to compare $p_{(k-2)}$ with $\alpha/3$ etc. At the last step (should one get this far) $p_{(1)}$ is compared with α/k, as in the Holm procedure.

Any hypothesis rejected by the Holm procedure also will be rejected by the Hochberg procedure, but the Hochberg procedure can find *more* significances than the Holm procedure, and therefore has more power. However, unlike the Holm procedure, FWE control is not guaranteed for all types of dependence among p-values. Nevertheless, simulation studies have shown that the Hochberg method is typically conservative, particularly for large positive dependence structures, and therefore can be recommended in such cases.

Adjusted *p*-Values for Hochberg's Method

$$\tilde{p}_{(k)} = p_{(k)}$$

$$\tilde{p}_{(k-1)} = \min(\tilde{p}_{(k)},\ 2p_{(k-1)})$$

$$\vdots$$

$$\tilde{p}_{(k-j)} = \min(\tilde{p}_{(k-j+1)},\ (j+1)p_{(k-j+1)})$$

$$\vdots$$

$$\tilde{p}_{(1)} = \min(\tilde{p}_{(2)},\ kp_{(k)})$$

The Hochberg adjusted *p*-values are less than or equal to the Holm adjusted *p*-values. Program 2.10 compares the two methods, using the data from Program 2.5.

PROGRAM 2.10   **Hochberg's Adjusted *p*-Values Using PROC MULTTEST**

```
data one; set one;
   rename pval=raw_p;
   drop bon_adjp sid_adjp;
proc multtest pdata=one holm hoc out=outp;
proc sort data=outp out=outp;
   by raw_p;
proc print data=outp;
run;
```

Output from Program 2.10

OBS	TEST	RAW_P	STPBON_P	HOC_P
1	3	0.0001	0.0010	0.0010
2	10	0.0058	0.0522	0.0522
3	5	0.0132	0.1056	0.1056
4	8	0.0289	0.2023	0.2023
5	9	0.0498	0.2988	0.2988
6	1	0.0911	0.4555	0.4555
7	7	0.2012	0.8048	0.8048
8	4	0.5718	1.0000	0.9011
9	2	0.8912	1.0000	0.9011
10	6	0.9011	1.0000	0.9011

We see that the Hochberg adjustments, "HOC_P" are similar to the Holm adjustments "STPBON_P" in this example, except that they are in some cases smaller.

2.5.6   Rom's Method

While Hochberg's procedure does not control FWE for all correlation structures, it does control FWE at a level slightly lower than α when the *p*-values are independent. Rom (1990) devised another step-up procedure similar to Hochberg's procedure, but with slightly more power because it has FWE $= \alpha$ exactly under independence of *p*-values. Rather than use the cutpoints α, $\alpha/2$, etc., Rom calculated cutpoints $C_1, \ldots, C_k$: if $p_{(k)} \le C_k$ then all hypotheses are rejected; otherwise, $H_{(k)}$ is retained and one goes on to compare $p_{(k-1)}$ with C_{k-1}. If $p_{(k-1)} \le C_{k-1}$, all the remaining hypotheses are rejected, otherwise $H_{(k-1)}$ is retained and one goes on to compare $p_{(k-2)}$ with C_{k-2}, etc. The critical values in this procedure are calculated using a recursive formula given in Rom (1990).

While the Rom method is not available in any SAS/STAT procedure, macros for such calculations are given in the appendix. Using the DATA=ONE example from Program 2.10, and invoking the %ROM macro, we get the following output:

Output from %ROM macro

```
                        ROM STEP-UP PROCEDURE

   I   CRITICAL VALUE    P-VALUE        ADJUSTED P      DECISION
  ---------------------------------------------------------------
   1    .050000          0.9011         .901100         retain
   2    .025000          0.8912         .901100         retain
   3    .016875          0.5718         .901100         retain
   4    .012713          0.2012         .634677         retain
   5    .010193          0.0911         .385432         retain
   6    .008505          0.0498         .265304         retain
   7    .007296          0.0289         .186008         retain
   8    .006388          0.0132         .100940         retain
   9    .005681          0.0058         .051023         retain
  10    .005115          0.0001         .001000         reject
  ---------------------------------------------------------------
  ALPHA=  0.05
```

Comparing the adjusted p-values from Rom's method with Hochberg's method shown in the output from Program 2.9 (the "HOC_P" adjustments) (and noting that the output from Program 2.9 is from most to least significant, while the output from the %ROM macro is the reverse), you can see that the Rom method produces smaller adjusted p-values, and is therefore more powerful.

2.5.7   Benjamini and Hochberg's FDR-Controlling Method

Benjamini and Hochberg (1995) proposed a new approach for handling multiple comparison problems that controls the False Discovery Rate (FDR), discussed in Section 2.3.5, instead of the FWE. Like Hochberg's method discussed in Section 2.5.5, this method adjusts the p-values in step-up fashion. However, instead of using cutpoints $\alpha, \alpha/2, \ldots, \alpha/(k-1), \alpha/k$, Benjamini and Hochberg suggest using cutpoints $\alpha, [(k-1)/k]\alpha, \ldots, [2/k]\alpha, [1/k]\alpha$. Adjusted p-values are as follows:

Adjusted p-Values for Benjamini and Hochberg's Method

$$\tilde{p}_{(k)} = p_{(k)}$$
$$\tilde{p}_{(k-1)} = \min(\tilde{p}_{(k)}, \ [k/(k-1)]p_{(k-1)})$$
$$\vdots$$
$$\tilde{p}_{(k-j)} = \min(\tilde{p}_{(k-j+1)}, \ [k/(k-j)]p_{(k-j)})$$
$$\vdots$$
$$\tilde{p}_{(1)} = \min(\tilde{p}_{(2)}, \ kp_{(1)})$$

The Benjamini and Hochberg method has adjusted p-values that can be much smaller than the previous methods. Consider Program 2.11 that uses PROC MULTTEST.

PROGRAM 2.11   **FDR-controlling *p*-Values Using PROC MULTTEST**

```
data one; set one;
   rename pval=raw_p;
   drop bon_adjp sid_adjp;
proc multtest pdata=one hoc fdr out=outp;
proc sort data=outp out=outp;
   by raw_p;
proc print data=outp;
run;
```

Output from Program 2.11

OBS	TEST	RAW_P	HOC_P	FDR_P
1	3	0.0001	0.0010	0.00100
2	10	0.0058	0.0522	0.02900
3	5	0.0132	0.1056	0.04400
4	8	0.0289	0.2023	0.07225
5	9	0.0498	0.2988	0.09960
6	1	0.0911	0.4555	0.15183
7	7	0.2012	0.8048	0.28743
8	4	0.5718	0.9011	0.71475
9	2	0.8912	0.9011	0.90110
10	6	0.9011	0.9011	0.90110

Note that in using Benjamini and Hochberg's method (corresponding to the "FDR" column), there are three significances at the $\alpha = 0.05$ level, and five at the $\alpha = 0.10$ level. However, be very careful to note that this method *only* controls the FDR, the proportion of erroneous significances, and *not* the FWE, which is the probability of *any* erroneous significances. As such, Benjamini and Hochberg's method should be used *only if you feel comfortable controlling FDR and not FWE.*

2.5.8   Sequential Testing with Fixed Sequences

Suppose your hypotheses follow a logical sequence, in the sense that H_{01} precedes (in implication or importance) H_{02}, H_{02} precedes H_{03}, and so on. Then it is reasonable to test them in order: first test H_{01}, and if rejected, then test H_{02}, and if rejected, then test H_{03}, etc. In contrast to the examples of the previous sections, the order of the hypotheses in this application is determined *a priori* by the researcher, rather than determined *a posteriori* by the ordering of the *p*-values.

EXAMPLE: **Testing for Dose-Response Relationships**

Suppose you have a control group and treatment groups that represent increasing levels of a compound that is administered to the experimental units. Suppose there are four treatment levels: low, medium, high, and extreme. You may decide to test the treatment vs. control hypotheses in the sequence (extreme vs. control), then (high vs. control), then (medium vs. control), then (low vs. control). If any test is insignificant, then no more testing is performed. The treatments are all expected to affect the response in the same direction, so one-tailed tests are appropriate.

Suppose that the *p*-values (one-tailed) for the comparisons are

- For the (extreme, control) comparison, $p_1 = 0.021$.
- For the (high, control) comparison, $p_2 = 0.043$.

- For the (medium, control) comparison, $p_3 = 0.402$.
- For the (low, control) comparison, $p_4 = 0.004$.

You may then declare tests 1 and 2 significant, but not test 3 and hence not 4, using the fixed sequence method with FWE $= 0.05$.

The logic of this testing method is that, in the previous example, you might feel that if a significant difference cannot be found for the control vs. extreme comparison, then there is no point examining the remaining comparisons. On the other hand, if the dose-response relationship is nonlinear, then the method might fail to detect real differences between lower doses and control, following an insignificant (extreme vs. control) comparison.

If you are comfortable with the possibility of missing some important information in the tests later in the sequence (e.g., in the example, if you are comfortable assuming linearity or at least monotonicity), then you may perform tests sequentially in the given order, without adjusting the significance levels of the individual comparisons. The resulting method controls the FWE at level α.

To see how the method can miss important tests later in the sequence when the treatment effect is nonlinear, it is instructive to recast the inferences in terms of adjusted p-values. Suppose $p_1, p_2, \ldots, p_k$ are your ordinary (unadjusted) p-values for the tests, in the intended sequence.

Adjusted *p*-Values for Fixed Sequence Testing

$$\tilde{p}_1 = p_1$$
$$\tilde{p}_2 = \max(\tilde{p}_1, \ p_2)$$
$$\vdots$$
$$\tilde{p}_j = \max(\tilde{p}_{j-1}, \ p_j)$$
$$\vdots$$
$$\tilde{p}_k = \max(\tilde{p}_{k-1}, \ p_k)$$

In the example above, the p-values are adjusted to $\tilde{p}_1 = 0.021$, $\tilde{p}_2 = \max(0.021, 0.043) = 0.043$, $\tilde{p}_3 = \max(0.043, 0.402) = 0.402$, and $\tilde{p}_4 = \max(0.402, 0.004) = 0.402$. As these adjusted p-values show, you must be willing to ignore the extreme significance of p-values at later steps, should you choose to use this procedure.

Consider again the example from Program 2.5, with the following program to calculate the fixed-sequence adjusted p-values. Also, assume the sequence is in order of the test number.

PROGRAM 2.12   Adjusted *p*-Values from Fixed-sequence Tests

```
data a;
   input p @@;
   if (_N_ = 1) then pseq = 0;
   pseq = max(pseq,p);
   retain pseq;
   cards;
0.021
0.043
0.402
0.004
;
proc print data=a;
run;
```

Output from Program 2.12

Obs	p	pseq
1	0.021	0.021
2	0.043	0.043
3	0.402	0.402
4	0.004	0.402

To use the fixed sequential method for multiple testing, you must compare the adjusted p-values ("pseq" in the output above) to the desired FWE level, e.g., $\alpha = 0.05$.

For more information about dose-response testing, see Chapter 8, Section 8.5.

2.6   Graphical Presentation of Multiple Testing Results

It is useful to supplement the results of multiple tests with graphical presentation, particularly when there are very many tests, for which the display of large tables can be tedious. In this section we describe a graphical method due to Schweder and Spjøtvoll (1982) for visualizing such data, and formal testing methods based on this graph.

2.6.1   The Schweder-Spjøtvoll *p*-Value Plot

A very useful plot for assessing multiplicity, this plot depicts the relationship between values $q = 1 - p$ and their rank order. Specifically, if $q_{(1)} \leq \cdots \leq q_{(k)}$ are the ordered values of the q's, then $q_{(1)} = 1 - p_{(k)}$, $q_{(2)} = 1 - p_{(k-1)}$, etc. The method is to plot j vs. $q_{(j)}$. If the hypotheses all are truly null, then the p-values will behave like a sample from the uniform distribution, and the graph should lie approximately on a straight line. Deviations from linearity, particularly points below the line in the upper-right corner of the graph, suggest hypotheses that are false, since their p-values are too small to be consistent with the uniform distribution.

To construct the p-Value plot using the data from Program 2.5, you can use the following program.

PROGRAM 2.13   **Schweder-Spjøtvoll *p*-Value Plot**

```
data one; set one;
proc sort out=pplot;
   by descending pval;
run;
data pplot;  set pplot;
   q = 1-pval;
   order = _n_;
run;
goptions ftext=simplex hsize=5 in vsize=3.33 in;
axis1 style=1 width=2 major=(number=5) minor=none label=('q = 1-p');
axis2 style=1 width=2 major=(number=6)
   order=(0 2 4 6 8 10) minor=none label=('Order');
proc gplot data=pplot;
   title "SCHWEDER-SPJOTVOLL PLOT";
   plot order*q / vaxis=axis2 haxis=axis1 frame;
run;
```

Output from
Program 2.13

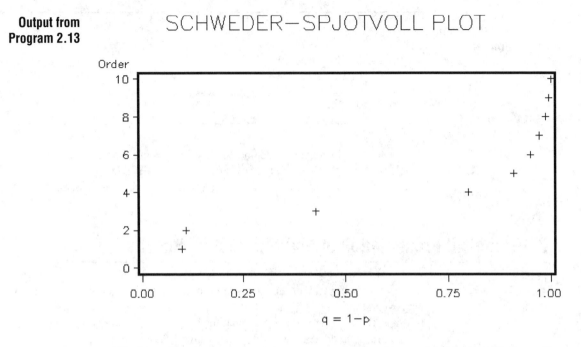

The data points in the upper-right corner are not consistent with the trend for the earlier points, suggesting that some of these points correspond to false nulls.

2.6.2   A Testing Procedure for Nominal FWE Protection

In Section 2.3.2, we noted that the FWE of an MCP depends upon the number of true null hypotheses, m. In order to protect the FWE in all possible circumstances, we had to protect it for the complete null hypothesis where all nulls are true, i.e., where $m = k$.

Thus, in the Bonferroni method we used k as a divisor for the critical value (and as a multiplier for the adjusted p-value).

If you know m, the number of true nulls, then you may use m as a divisor (or multiplier for adjusted p-values), instead of k, and still control the FWE. From the examination of the Schweder-Spjøtvoll plot, you can estimate the total number of true null hypotheses, say $\hat{m}$, and modify the critical value of the Bonferroni procedure by rejecting any hypothesis H_{0j} for which $p_j \leq \alpha/\hat{m}$.

The number of true null hypotheses is estimated as follows. Recalling that truly null hypotheses yield p-values that are uniformly distributed, the $q_{(j)}$'s corresponding to true hypotheses should appear in the left-hand side of the plot as an approximately straight line with slope $\beta = 1/(m + 1)$. The rest of the $q_{(j)}$'s, which correspond to false hypotheses, should concentrate in the right-hand side of the plot, with decreasing slope. From the left-hand side of the graph, one can estimate the number of true hypotheses using $\hat{\beta} = 1/(\hat{m} + 1)$, or $\hat{m} = (1/\hat{\beta}) - 1$ (rounding $\hat{m}$ to get an integer estimate). Hochberg and Benjamini (1990) start by fitting straight lines from the rightmost (highest) point in the plot to the origin, and working down as long as the slopes of successive lines increase. They stop when for the first time the next slope decreases, and use the last slope to estimate $\hat{m} = (1/\hat{\beta}) - 1$. The estimate $\hat{m}$ can then be used to correct the Bonferroni critical value α/k to $\alpha/\hat{m}$.

A more powerful approach is to use Holm's step-down procedure, replacing $\alpha/(k - j + 1)$ in the jth step by $\max(\alpha/(k - j + 1), \alpha/\hat{m})$. (Yet more powerful procedures can be devised by using $\hat{m}$ adaptively in either Hochberg's or Rom's procedures; however, they are more complicated to implement). The Hochberg and Benjamini procedure can be more powerful than all other modified Bonferroni procedures, but does not always control the FWE. There is yet substantial research to be conducted in order for a clear recommendation regarding this procedure to be made.

For the graphical procedure of Hochberg and Benjamini, the adjusted p-values are calculated similarly to Holm's adjusted p-values, but with k replaced by $\min(k + j - 1, \hat{m})$.

This graphical procedure is implemented in the %HOCHBEN macro, provided in the appendix. This macro is invoked with the p-value data set (DATA=ONE) used in this chapter, shown in Program 2.14.

PROGRAM 2.14   Hochberg and Benjamini Graphical Analysis of Multiple p-Values

```
%hochben(dataset=one, pv=pval);
```

Output from Program 2.14

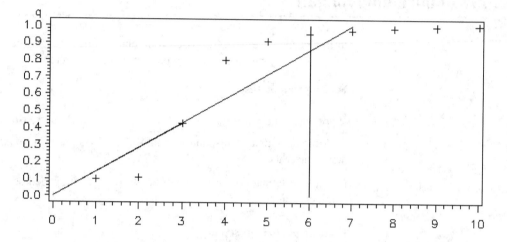

HOCHBERG & BENJAMINI GRAPHICAL ANALYSIS OF MULTIPLE P-VALUES
PLOT of 1-PVALUES VS. THEIR ORDER

For these data, the slopes get successively larger (going from right to left) up to $i = 4$, at which point the next slope gets smaller. We now use $i = 3$ to fit the final slope. From the point where the line intersects the horizontal $q = 1$ line, we subtract 1 to get an estimate of the number of true hypotheses, in this case 6.

Note that the Hochberg-Benjamini graph has axes that are reversed from the Schweder-Spjøtvoll graph, but otherwise, the graphs are identical.

The following output displays the results of inferences on individual hypotheses.

Output from Program 2.14

HOCHBERG & BENJAMINI GRAPHICAL ANALYSIS OF MULTIPLE P-VALUES

CRITICAL VALUES ADJUSTED BY ESTIMATED NUMBER OF TRUE HYPOTHESES

I	CRITICAL VALUE	P-VALUE	ADJUSTED P	DECISION
1	.008333	0.0001	.000600	reject
2	.008333	0.0058	.034800	reject
3	.008333	0.0132	.079200	retain
4	.008333	0.0289	.173400	retain
5	.008333	0.0498	.298800	retain
6	.010000	0.0911	.455500	retain
7	.012500	0.2012	.804800	retain
8	.016667	0.5718	1.00000	retain
9	.025000	0.8912	1.00000	retain
10	.050000	0.9011	1.00000	retain

ALPHA= 0.05
ESTIMATED NUMBER OF TRUE HYPOTHESES: 6

The first column shows the critical points adjusted by the estimated number of true hypotheses (last row in the table) which is 6. Note how this procedure capitalizes on the fact that only six of ten hypotheses are estimated to be true. Instead of the $0.05/10 = 0.005$ critical value for comparing with the minimum p-value used by the Bonferroni procedure, we use $0.05/6 = 0.00833$ as the starting point for the step-down procedure. Now two hypotheses are rejected compared with only one by all other Bonferroni procedures. Note also that while six hypotheses are estimated to be true, eight actually remain unrejected. You should not be tempted to reject the four hypotheses with the smallest p-values as this may result in a FWE in excess of 0.05.

2.7 Concluding Remarks

In this chapter we have discussed a number of methods for the analysis of multiple p-values. Our recommendations can be summarized as follows:

For Dependent Tests:

If you want these inferences . . .	**. . . then use this method.**
Multiple tests that correspond to confidence intervals	Single-step Bonferroni
Multiple tests that do not correspond to confidence intervals	Holm's method

For Independent Tests:

If you want these inferences . . .	**. . . then use this method.**
Multiple tests that correspond to confidence intervals	Single-step Šidák
Multiple tests that do not correspond to confidence intervals	Hochberg (easy to do by hand) or Rom (use %ROM macro)

To elaborate, single-step methods (Bonferroni and Šidák) are easy to implement and they correspond naturally to confidence intervals; Šidák's method provides slightly more power, but occasionally does not control the FWE. However, when confidence intervals are not required, stepwise procedures are more powerful than the single-step methods. Among the stepwise procedures, Holm's procedure is the simplest and is the only one that is guaranteed to control the FWE in all circumstances. Hochberg's and Rom's step-up methods control the Type I error under independence; however, substantial evidence supports the use of these procedures in most cases. Among these procedures, Hochberg's can be implemented easily; Rom's procedure is more powerful than Hochberg's procedure but requires a specialized program (provided in the %ROM macro given in the appendix).

The graphical procedure of Hochberg and Benjamini can be used in an exploratory analysis. More research is needed to support the use of this procedure under general settings. And finally, you can use FDR-controlling methods if you are comfortable with a less stringent criterion than strong FWE control.

Chapter 3

Multiple Comparisons among Treatment Means in the One-Way Balanced ANOVA

3.1 Introduction

In Chapter 2 we discussed various multiplicity adjustment methods that are formulated mostly without reference to the underlying distribution of the data. In this chapter, and in most of the succeeding chapters, we incorporate information on the distribution of the data, along with correlations among the intervals or tests, to produce more powerful procedures. To do this, we must make certain assumptions about the form of the underlying statistical model. In this chapter, we begin with the simplest of such models: the balanced one-way analysis of variance (ANOVA) model with additive, independent, homoscedastic, and normally distributed observations.

Historically, multiple testing and multiple comparisons procedures got their start in the ANOVA model. The one-way ANOVA model is commonly used to compare mean values in different groups. The model can be used whether the data are obtained *observationally* or *experimentally*. An example of observational data is the comparison of average salaries for different ethnic groups; an example of experimental data is the comparison of average cholesterol reduction in response to different medical treatments. In the experimental example the subjects are assigned (usually at random) to the treatment groups; in the observational example, demographic or other personal characteristics of the subjects themselves define the groups.

Conclusions regarding causal effects of treatment differences are more easily obtained in the experimental ANOVA setting. In observational studies, the treatment effects may be (and frequently are) *confounded* with uncontrolled variables. For example, in the ethnic-group-by-salary study mentioned above, socio-economic background factors may be confounded with a measured relationship between ethnicity and current salary. If confounding factors can be measured, then it may be possible to correct for their effects by "partialing them out"—that is, using the confounding variables as covariates in an analysis of covariance (ANCOVA) model. ANCOVA methods can strengthen arguments in studies involving observational data. They can also be useful in experimental studies where they are employed to reduce the level of underlying noise, thus making tests more powerful and confidence intervals more accurate (or shorter). Multiplicity adjustments in ANCOVA are discussed in detail in Chapter 5.

In this chapter we confine our attention to the simplest of ANOVA cases, that is, the one-way ANOVA with equal sample sizes per group. While it may be fairly rare that your data fits this classification, it is the easiest setting for introducing important general ideas. Most of the methods for analysis of balanced data carry over easily to cases with unbalanced data and/or covariates.

To fix ideas, consider the following example.

EXAMPLE: **Comparing Weight Loss for Five Different Regimens**

Ott (1988) reports an experiment undertaken to evaluate the effectiveness of five weight-reducing agents. There are 10 male subjects in each group who have been randomly assigned to one of the regimens A,B,C,D or E. This is a classic example of the balanced one-way ANOVA setup.

After a fixed length of time, the weight loss of each of the 50 subjects is measured. The goal of the study is to rank the treatments, to the extent possible, using the observed weight loss data for the 50 subjects.

TABLE 3.1   **Means and Standard Deviations of Weight Loss Data**

	A	B	C	D	E
Mean	12.05	11.02	10.27	9.27	12.17
Std. Dev.	0.829	1.121	1.026	1.159	0.792

Reprinted with permission of Brooks/Cole Publishing Company, a division of International Thompson Publishing Inc.; fax 800-930-2215. From *An Introduction to Statistical Methods and Data Analysis, 3rd Ed.* by Ott (1988).

3.2   Overview of Methods

To develop the basic methods of MCPs that incorporate dependence structures, you must specify the model. We present the model in Section 3.2.1 and the general structure of simultaneous intervals in Section 3.2.2.

3.2.1   The Model and Estimates

The model for the data throughout this chapter is assumed to be

$$y_{ij} = \mu_i + \epsilon_{ij},$$

where the y_{ij} are the observed data, with $i = 1, \ldots, g$ indicating which group contains each observation ($i = 1, \ldots, 5$ in the weight-loss example), and $j = 1, \ldots, n$ indexing the measurements observed within a group ($j = 1, \ldots, 10$ in the weight-loss example). The μ_i are assumed to be fixed, unknown population mean values, and the errors ϵ_{ij} are assumed to be random variables that

- are independent
- are normally distributed
- have constant variance σ^2.

Discussion of the Assumptions

You can check the assumption of normality by checking the data within each group, e.g., via a normal quantile-quantile (q-q) plot, or by examining the residuals as a whole via a q-q plot. Note, however, that it is usually not critical that this assumption be precisely true, if the other two are. The Central Limit Theorem states that group means are approximately normally distributed even if the observations have nonnormal distributions. (However, if the sample sizes are small and the distributions are asymmetrical, then the Central Limit Theorem may not apply.)

The assumption of constant variance can be examined informally by looking at the standard deviations; in the previous example, they seem reasonably similar.

There are statistical tests for normality and constant variance (also called homoscedasticity) that might be used in conjunction with the informal descriptive and graphical assessments of these assumptions. To test for normality, you can analyze the residuals with PROC UNIVARIATE using the NORMAL option to obtain the test for normality. To test for equal within-group variances, you can use the HOVTEST option in the MEANS statement in PROC GLM. However, these tests should not be used exclusively in deciding whether the model is useful. Even when one or the other of these assumptions are violated, the inferences still are approximately valid, provided the assumptions are not violated too badly.

With regard to the homogeneity of variances assumption, here are some prototype situations where the assumption might be so badly violated that an alternative method is needed.

- The within-group sample sizes are small (say less than ten per group), yet the homogeneity of variance test is highly significant.
- The sample sizes are very unbalanced, such as in the 20, 20, 20, 100 configuration, and the within-group standard deviation for the (100) group differs from the pooled within-group standard deviation of the 20 groups by a factor of 1.5 or more.
- The sample sizes are large in all groups, and the largest within-group standard deviation differs from the smallest within-group standard deviation by a factor of two.

Note that these items do not comprise a complete test.

We do not recommend assessing the assumption of homogeneity of variances based on the HOVTEST results with large sample sizes, since minor (and unimportant) deviations from homogeneity will be flagged as "significant" in this case. Also, the test procedure does not consider degree of balance. As it turns out, heterogeneity is more damaging when designs are unbalanced than when they are balanced.

Regarding the normality assumption, we recommend basing decisions about how to analyze the data on a testing procedure even less. Here are some prototype situations where you need to use an alternative method:

- There are one or two extreme outliers in the data set, and removal of the outlier(s) substantially changes the inferences.
- The data are binary or categorical with few categories.
- The data are censored, such as with survival data.

The assumption of independence is more crucial than the normality and homoscedasticity assumptions. Usually, the specific aspects of the design will tell you if this assumption is satisfied. Here are prototype situations where you need to use an alternative method:

- There are repeated measurements on the subjects (since measurements on the same subject are usually correlated).
- Subjects are "paired" in some fashion, such as the husband/wife example in Chapter 2.
- The data involve time series.
- Some data points are closer geographically to each other, which makes them correlated ("spatial data").

In Chapters 10, 11, 12 and 14 we provide alternative methods for cases where one or more of these assumptions is violated. The benefits of using such alternative methods are that they have better power and are more robust.

The Parameter Estimates

The estimated population means are the individual sample means for each group,

$$\hat{\mu}_i = \bar{y}_i = \frac{\sum_{j=1}^{n} y_{ij}}{n},$$

and the estimated common variance of the errors is the pooled mean squared error (MSE),

$$\hat{\sigma}^2 = \text{MSE} = \frac{\sum_{i=1}^{g} \sum_{j=1}^{n} (y_{ij} - \bar{y}_i)^2}{g(n-1)}.$$

In the weight loss example, the $\bar{y}_i$ values are given directly in the equation above. When all sample sizes are equal, the value of $\hat{\sigma}^2$ is just the average of the individual variances:

$$\hat{\sigma}^2 = \frac{0.829^2 + 1.121^2 + 1.026^2 + 1.159^2 + 0.792^2}{5}$$

$$= 0.9934,$$

and the root mean squared error (RMSE) is $\hat{\sigma} = \sqrt{0.9934} = 0.9967$.

3.2.2 Simultaneous Confidence Intervals

Confidence intervals for the difference of means $\mu_i - \mu_{i'}$ have the form

$$\bar{y}_i - \bar{y}_{i'} \pm c_\alpha \hat{\sigma} \sqrt{2/n},$$

that is, all the values between $\bar{y}_i - \bar{y}_{i'} - c_\alpha \hat{\sigma} \sqrt{2/n}$ and $\bar{y}_i - \bar{y}_{i'} + c_\alpha \hat{\sigma} \sqrt{2/n}$, where c_α is a critical value that is selected to make the FWE $= \alpha$ (or as close as possible to α, for some methods). The term $\hat{\sigma} \sqrt{2/n}$ is the square root of the estimated variance of the difference, also called the standard error of the estimated difference.

In the case of nonmultiplicity adjusted confidence intervals, you set c_α to the $1 - \alpha/2$ quantile of the t distribution, $t_{1-\alpha/2, g(n-1)}$. Each confidence interval thus constructed will contain the true difference with confidence $100 \times (1 - \alpha)\%$, but all k intervals will contain their respective true differences *simultaneously* with much lower confidence. The Bonferroni inequality gives a pessimistic estimate of the simultaneous confidence of k intervals thus constructed as $100 \times (1 - k\alpha)\%$. This implies that you can construct Bonferroni-adjusted confidence intervals by setting $c_\alpha = t_{1-\alpha'/2, g(n-1)}$, where $\alpha' = \alpha/k$. However, the Bonferroni method is *conservative*; the value of c_α is larger than it needs to be, in the sense that the actual simultaneous confidence level will be somewhat larger than the nominal $100 \times (1 - \alpha)\%$. We can improve upon this value by taking into account the distribution of the differences. Among other factors, this distribution depends upon the set of differences of interest, that is, all pairs, comparisons with a control (one- or two-sided), or other comparisons.

To understand the general methods of multiple comparisons, we need to refer to some fundamental technical details. These details are very important, particularly for understanding how the methods work in more complex situations.

3.3 All Pairwise Comparisons

If you want to order the treatment means from smallest to largest, identifying significant differences where possible, then you probably want to examine all pairwise comparisons. In this case, you need a c_α for which the confidence intervals for all pairwise differences capture simultaneously their respective true differences with the specified level of confidence. Mathematically, c_α must satisfy

$$P(\bar{y}_i - \bar{y}_{i'} - c_\alpha \hat{\sigma}\sqrt{2/n} \leq \mu_i - \mu_{i'} \leq \bar{y}_i - \bar{y}_{i'} + c_\alpha \hat{\sigma}\sqrt{2/n}, \text{ for all } i, i') = 1 - \alpha,$$

or equivalently

$$P\left(\max_{i,i'} \frac{|(\bar{y}_i - \mu_i) - (\bar{y}_{i'} - \mu_{i'})|}{\hat{\sigma}\sqrt{2/n}} \leq c_\alpha\right) = 1 - \alpha.$$

This last formula makes it clear that c_α is related to the *studentized range distribution*.

DEFINITION: The Studentized Range Distribution

If $Z_1, \ldots, Z_g$ are independent standard normal random variables, and V is a random variable distributed as Chi-Square with df degrees of freedom, independent of the Z's, then

$$Q_{g,\text{df}}^R = \max_{i,i'} \frac{|Z_i - Z_{i'}|}{\sqrt{V/\text{df}}}$$

has the studentized range distribution with parameters g and df.

With the definition above and some algebraic manipulation, along with well-known results concerning distributions involving normally distributed variables, you can see that c_α satisfies

$$P(Q_{g,g(n-1)}^R / \sqrt{2} \leq c_\alpha) = 1 - \alpha,$$

or that $c_\alpha = q_{1-\alpha,g,g(n-1)}^R / \sqrt{2}$, where $q_{1-\alpha,\cdot,\cdot}^R$ is the $1 - \alpha$ quantile of the studentized range distribution.

Tukey's Method   Confidence intervals for all pairwise comparisons in the balanced ANOVA that use the critical value $q_{1-\alpha,g,g(n-1)}^R / \sqrt{2}$ from the studentized range distribution are commonly said to be constructed by "Tukey's Method," after Tukey (1953).

The quantiles of the studentized range distribution can be calculated using the PROBMC function in SAS, which evaluates the cumulative probability distribution function of the random variable $Q_{g,\nu}^R$. This distribution is given as

$$P(Q_{g,\nu}^R \leq q) = g \int_0^\infty \left[\int_{-\infty}^\infty \{\Phi(y) - \Phi(y - qx)\}^{g-1} d\Phi(y)\right] dF_\nu(x),$$

where

$$\frac{d\Phi(z)}{dz} = \frac{1}{\sqrt{2\pi}} e^{-\frac{z^2}{2}}$$

is the standard normal density function and

$$\frac{dF_\nu(u)}{du} = \frac{\nu^{\frac{\nu}{2}}}{\Gamma(\frac{\nu}{2}) 2^{\frac{\nu}{2}-1}} u^{\nu-1} e^{-\frac{\nu u^2}{2}}$$

is the density of $\sqrt{\chi_\nu^2 / \nu}$, or the density of the square root of a Chi-squared random variable with ν degrees of freedom, divided by its degrees of freedom (see, e.g., Hochberg and Tamhane, 1987, p. 376). The double integral is evaluated numerically with excellent precision (numerical error on the order of 10^{-8}) by the PROBMC function.

The PROBMC function takes as its arguments a distribution label, either a quantile or a probability, and various parameters. Either the quantile or the probability should be missing in input, in which case the function returns that value given all the other parameters. For the weight-loss example, the critical value for the 95 percent simultaneous confidence intervals is $c_{.05} = q^R_{.95,5,45}/\sqrt{2}$, calculated in Program 3.1.

PROGRAM 3.1   **Studentized Range Critical Value**

```
data;
   qval = probmc("RANGE",.,.95,45,5);
   c_alpha = qval/sqrt(2);
run;
proc print; run;
```

Output from Program 3.1

```
         OBS     QVAL     C_ALPHA

          1     4.01842   2.84145
```

Thus, the confidence intervals (via Tukey's method) for the pairwise comparisons in the weight loss example are given by

$$\bar{y}_i - \bar{y}_{i'} \pm 2.84145 \times .9967 \times \sqrt{2/10}$$

or

$$\bar{y}_i - \bar{y}_{i'} \pm 1.2665.$$

By comparison, we note that the unadjusted confidence intervals would use the critical value $t_{.975,45} = 2.0141$, rather than $q^R_{.95,5,45}/\sqrt{2} = 2.84145$, yielding intervals with radius 0.8978. The unadjusted intervals are much narrower, but the unadjusted method does not control the FWE.

Let's also compare Tukey's adjustment with Bonferroni's. Since there are $5 \times 4/2 = 10$ pairwise comparisons among the five groups, the Bonferroni critical value uses $0.05/10 = 0.005$, and the critical value is $t_{.9975,45} = 2.9521$. The reason for the difference between the Bonferroni critical value and the Tukey critical value, 2.9521 vs. 2.84145, is that the Tukey critical value is based on the precise distribution of the 10 pairwise statistics $(\bar{y}_i - \bar{y}_{i'})/(\hat{\sigma}\sqrt{2/n})$. There are correlations among the estimates because there are lots of comparisons with common elements. For example, the statistics $(\bar{y}_1 - \bar{y}_2)/(\hat{\sigma}\sqrt{2/n})$ and $(\bar{y}_1 - \bar{y}_3)/(\hat{\sigma}\sqrt{2/n})$ are correlated because both contain the common elements $\bar{y}_1$ and $\hat{\sigma}$.

In summary, Tukey's intervals control the FWE precisely (under the assumptions of the model given in Section 3.2.1) while the Bonferroni intervals *over*-control and the unadjusted intervals *under*-control. That is, FWE is *greater than 5 percent* for the unadjusted intervals, *less than 5 percent* for the Bonferroni intervals, and *exactly equal to 5 percent* for the Tukey intervals.

3.3.1   Example of Pairwise Comparisons with Simultaneous Confidence Intervals

Program 3.2 analyzes the weight loss data using the unadjusted, Bonferroni, and Tukey intervals. The Tukey method is the recommended one; the Bonferroni and unadjusted intervals are included for comparison purposes only.

PROGRAM 3.2   Simultaneous Intervals for Mean Differences

```
data wloss;
   do diet = 'A','B','C','D','E';
      do i = 1 to 10;
         input wloss @@;
         output;
         end;
      end;
datalines;
12.4 10.7 11.9 11.0 12.4 12.3 13.0 12.5 11.2 13.1
 9.1 11.5 11.3  9.7 13.2 10.7 10.6 11.3 11.1 11.7
 8.5 11.6 10.2 10.9  9.0  9.6  9.9 11.3 10.5 11.2
 8.7  9.3  8.2  8.3  9.0  9.4  9.2 12.2  8.5  9.9
12.7 13.2 11.8 11.9 12.2 11.2 13.7 11.8 11.5 11.7
;
proc glm data=wloss;
   class diet;
   model wloss=diet;
   means diet/cldiff t bon tukey;
run;
```

The CLASS and MODEL statements specify a one-way model with the groups that are defined by the variable `diet`, and the MEANS statement requests group means for `diet`. The MEANS statement options request confidence limits for the mean differences with three different types of adjustment. The output contains four main sections: the overall ANOVA test and the confidence intervals for the differences (because we used the CLDIFF option) for each of the three methods. We show each of the confidence interval summaries in turn.

Output from Program 3.2: Unadjusted Intervals

The GLM Procedure

t Tests (LSD) for wloss

NOTE: This test controls the type I comparisonwise error rate not the experimentwise error rate.

Alpha	0.05
Error Degrees of Freedom	45
Error Mean Square	0.993422
Critical Value of t	2.01410
Least Significant Difference	0.8978

Comparisons significant at the 0.05 level are indicated by ***.

diet Comparison		Difference Between Means	95% Confidence Interval		
E	- A	0.1200	-0.7778	1.0178	
E	- B	1.1500	0.2522	2.0478	***
E	- C	1.9000	1.0022	2.7978	***
E	- D	2.9000	2.0022	3.7978	***
A	- E	-0.1200	-1.0178	0.7778	
A	- B	1.0300	0.1322	1.9278	***

A	– C	1.7800	0.8822	2.6778	***
A	– D	2.7800	1.8822	3.6778	***
B	– E	-1.1500	-2.0478	-0.2522	***
B	– A	-1.0300	-1.9278	-0.1322	***
B	– C	0.7500	-0.1478	1.6478	
B	– D	1.7500	0.8522	2.6478	***
C	– E	-1.9000	-2.7978	-1.0022	***
C	– A	-1.7800	-2.6778	-0.8822	***
C	– B	-0.7500	-1.6478	0.1478	
C	– D	1.0000	0.1022	1.8978	***
D	– E	-2.9000	-3.7978	-2.0022	***
D	– A	-2.7800	-3.6778	-1.8822	***
D	– B	-1.7500	-2.6478	-0.8522	***
D	– C	-1.0000	-1.8978	-0.1022	***

Intervals that exclude zero are shown with "***" to indicate statistical significance of the comparison. The critical value $t_{.975,45} = 2.01410$ for the unadjusted intervals is reported in the top summary, as is $\hat{\sigma}^2 = \text{MSE} = 0.993422$, and the least significant difference, $2.01410 \times \sqrt{0.993422} \times \sqrt{2/10} = 0.8978$, is the smallest the difference $\bar{y}_i - \bar{y}_{i'}$ can be and still be a statistically significant difference, that is, as small as the difference can be and still have the confidence interval exclude zero.

Note also that a warning is printed.

```
NOTE: This test controls the type I comparisonwise error rate, not the
      experimentwise error rate.
```

Note that "type I comparisonwise error rate" refers to CER; and "experimentwise error rate" refers to "familywise error rate," which is abbreviated FWE.

Output from Program 3.2: Bonferroni Intervals

```
                        The GLM Procedure

                Bonferroni (Dunn) t Tests for wloss
```

```
NOTE: This test controls the type I experimentwise error rate but generally
      has a higher type II error rate than Tukey's for all pairwise comparisons.
```

Alpha	0.05
Error Degrees of Freedom	45
Error Mean Square	0.993422
Critical Value of t	2.95208
Minimum Significant Difference	1.3159

Comparisons significant at the 0.05 level are indicated by ***.

diet Comparison		Difference Between Means	Simultaneous 95% Confidence Interval		
E	– A	0.1200	-1.1959	1.4359	
E	– B	1.1500	-0.1659	2.4659	
E	– C	1.9000	0.5841	3.2159	***
E	– D	2.9000	1.5841	4.2159	***
A	– E	-0.1200	-1.4359	1.1959	

A	- B	1.0300	-0.2859	2.3459	
A	- C	1.7800	0.4641	3.0959	***
A	- D	2.7800	1.4641	4.0959	***
B	- E	-1.1500	-2.4659	0.1659	
B	- A	-1.0300	-2.3459	0.2859	
B	- C	0.7500	-0.5659	2.0659	
B	- D	1.7500	0.4341	3.0659	***
C	- E	-1.9000	-3.2159	-0.5841	***
C	- A	-1.7800	-3.0959	-0.4641	***
C	- B	-0.7500	-2.0659	0.5659	
C	- D	1.0000	-0.3159	2.3159	
D	- E	-2.9000	-4.2159	-1.5841	***
D	- A	-2.7800	-4.0959	-1.4641	***
D	- B	-1.7500	-3.0659	-0.4341	***
D	- C	-1.0000	-2.3159	0.3159	

The only difference between the analysis for the Bonferroni intervals and the analysis for the unadjusted intervals is that the critical value is computed with CER = 0.05/10 rather than CER = 0.05. Therefore, the least significant difference is larger, and there are fewer significant differences. A warning message is printed:

```
NOTE: This test controls the type I experimentwise error rate but
      generally has a higher type II error rate than Tukey's for all
      pairwise comparisons.
```

This warning means that the tests can be made more powerful when you incorporate correlations among the comparisons, thereby reducing the critical value.

Output from Program 3.2: Tukey Intervals

```
                         The GLM Procedure

               Tukey's Studentized Range (HSD) Test for wloss

      NOTE: This test controls the type I experimentwise error rate.
```

Alpha	0.05
Error Degrees of Freedom	45
Error Mean Square	0.993422
Critical Value of Studentized Range	4.01842
Minimum Significant Difference	1.2665

Comparisons significant at the 0.05 level are indicated by ***.

diet Comparison		Difference Between Means	Simultaneous 95% Confidence Interval		
E	- A	0.1200	-1.1465	1.3865	
E	- B	1.1500	-0.1165	2.4165	
E	- C	1.9000	0.6335	3.1665	***
E	- D	2.9000	1.6335	4.1665	***
A	- E	-0.1200	-1.3865	1.1465	
A	- B	1.0300	-0.2365	2.2965	
A	- C	1.7800	0.5135	3.0465	***
A	- D	2.7800	1.5135	4.0465	***

B	– E	-1.1500	-2.4165	0.1165	
B	– A	-1.0300	-2.2965	0.2365	
B	– C	0.7500	-0.5165	2.0165	
B	– D	1.7500	0.4835	3.0165	***
C	– E	-1.9000	-3.1665	-0.6335	***
C	– A	-1.7800	-3.0465	-0.5135	***
C	– B	-0.7500	-2.0165	0.5165	
C	– D	1.0000	-0.2665	2.2665	
D	– E	-2.9000	-4.1665	-1.6335	***
D	– A	-2.7800	-4.0465	-1.5135	***
D	– B	-1.7500	-3.0165	-0.4835	***
D	– C	-1.0000	-2.2665	0.2665	

The output for Tukey's intervals contain no warning messages, as this is the preferred method. Note that while the intervals and statistics all are calculated correctly, the reported critical value 4.018 is not comparable to the Bonferroni and unadjusted critical values. To make them comparable, you must divide by $\sqrt{2}$, $(4.018/\sqrt{2} = 2.841)$ as shown in the output from Program 3.1.

You can directly compare (without having to divide anything by $\sqrt{2}$) the values of Minimum Significant Difference (MSD) to see the gain (or loss) in efficiency. For example, the Tukey intervals have MSD = 1.3159, whereas the Bonferroni intervals have MSD = 1.2665. Therefore, the Tukey intervals are 3.75% shorter.

The conclusions from the study are that the mean for diet E is significantly larger than the means of C or D, that the mean for A is significantly larger than the means of C or D, and that the mean for B is significantly larger than the mean for D. The remaining five comparisons are statistically insignificant. (Note that while there are 20 comparisons with 10 significances that are shown in the output, actually there are 10 comparisons and five significances because, E-A and A-E are equivalent.)

3.3.2   Displaying Pairwise Comparisons Graphically

As an alternative to the somewhat cumbersome listing of which comparisons are and are not statistically significant, you can use a graph to display the results simply and effectively.

Program 3.3 uses the LINES option which provides a listing of the means in descending order and a text graph that displays the results of the tests. Nonsignificant subsets are shown using line segments (shown as text lines with the letter A, B, etc.) beside the corresponding means.

PROGRAM 3.3   Graphical Presentation for Comparing Means: LINES Option

```
proc glm data=wloss;
    class diet;
    model wloss=diet;
    means diet/lines tukey;
run;
```

**Output from
Program 3.3**

```
                    Tukey's Studentized Range (HSD) Test for wloss

NOTE: This test controls the type I experimentwise error rate but generally
            has a higher type II error rate than REGWQ.


              Alpha                                    0.05
              Error Degrees of Freedom                   45
              Error Mean Square                     0.993422
              Critical Value of Studentized Range   4.01842
              Minimum Significant Difference          1.2665


        Means with the same letter are not significantly different.


              Tukey Grouping          Mean       N    diet

                             A      12.1700      10    E
                             A
                             A      12.0500      10    A
                             A
                      B      A      11.0200      10    B
                      B
                      B      C      10.2700      10    C
                             C
                             C       9.2700      10    D
```

Because there is no line (or vertical grouping along the left side) that connects "E" or "A" with "C" or "D," we can conclude that the means for E and A are significantly different from those of "C" and "D." Further, because there is no line connecting "B" with "D," we conclude that those are significantly different. All means that share a grouping are not significantly different.

Recall that differences are determined to be significant when the corresponding confidence interval excludes zero. In addition to merely claiming inequality, when the interval excludes zero you may in fact make a more ambitious directional inference. Specifically, in this case you may claim that the means for "E" and "A" are larger than the means for "C" and "D," and that the mean for "B" is larger than the mean for "D," while maintaining directional error control.

Note that there is a warning message.

```
NOTE: This test controls the type I experimentwise error rate, but
        generally has a higher type II error rate than REGWQ.
```

The REGWQ method referred to is an example of a *closed testing procedure* and is discussed in Chapter 8. If you are interested in testing whether there is a difference only, and not in making directional decisions, then you can obtain more powerful tests for pairwise comparisons than the Tukey method. The Tukey method provides a confidence interval for the difference, which is a more ambitious inference than either inequality or direction.

3.3.3   Simultaneous Tests of Hypotheses

While the simultaneous confidence intervals allow you to infer the possible size of the differences between the pairs of means, the practical aspect of the intervals that is usually of interest is whether they contain zero. The hypothesis $H_{0i,i'}: \mu_i - \mu_{i'} = 0$ can be tested simply by noting whether the value zero lies inside the associated confidence interval. While more powerful methods are available, this method controls the FWE for simple null hypotheses as well as for directional determinations.

To find the exact significance level of a test using Tukey's method for simultaneous intervals, you need the value of $c_\alpha = \frac{1}{\sqrt{2}} q_{1-\alpha,g,g(n-1)}^R$ for which $\bar{y}_i - \bar{y}_{i'} + c_\alpha \hat{\sigma} \sqrt{2/n} = 0$ (if $\bar{y}_i - \bar{y}_{i'} < 0$) or $\bar{y}_i - \bar{y}_{i'} - c_\alpha \hat{\sigma} \sqrt{2/n} = 0$ (if $\bar{y}_i - \bar{y}_{i'} < 0$). Solving for c_α, you can see that $c_\alpha = |t_{i,i'}|$, where $t_{i,i'}$ is the usual statistic used to test $H_{0i,i'}: \mu_i - \mu_{i'} = 0$,

$$t_{i,i'} = \frac{\bar{y}_i - \bar{y}_{i'}}{\hat{\sigma} \sqrt{2/n}}.$$

Thus, the adjusted p-value for the test is

$$\tilde{p}_{i,i'} = P(Q_{g,g(n-1)}^R \geq \sqrt{2}|t_{i,i'}|).$$

By comparison, the ordinary (unadjusted) p-value is given by

$$p_{i,i'} = 2 \cdot P(T_{g(n-1)} \geq |t_{i,i'}|),$$

where T_ν denotes a Student's t-distributed random variable with ν degrees of freedom.

Program 3.4 shows how to calculate the adjusted and unadjusted p-values corresponding to the "A versus B" comparison in the weight loss data.

PROGRAM 3.4   **"Hand" Calculation of Adjusted p-values**

```
data;
    n=10; g=5; df=g*(n-1);
    MeanA=12.05; MeanB=11.02; mse=0.993422;
    tab = (MeanA-MeanB)/(sqrt(mse)*sqrt(2/n));
    p = 2*(1-probt(abs(tab),df));
    adjp = 1-probmc('RANGE',sqrt(2)*abs(tab),.,df,g);
run;
proc print; var tab p adjp;
run;
```

Output from Program 3.4

OBS	TAB	P	ADJP
1	2.31076	0.025485	0.16038

Thus, as shown in the output from Program 3.4, the unadjusted "A versus B" comparison is statistically significant—the unadjusted $p = 0.025485 < 0.05$ corresponds to the fact that the unadjusted 95 percent confidence interval excludes zero. Also, the multiplicity-adjusted "A versus B" comparison is statistically insignificant—the adjusted p-value $\tilde{p} = 0.16038 > 0.05$ corresponds to the fact that the Tukey 95 percent confidence interval includes zero.

To calculate all adjusted p-values automatically, use Program 3.5.

PROGRAM 3.5   **PROC GLM Calculation of Adjusted p-values**

```
proc glm data=wloss;
   class diet;
   model wloss=diet;
   lsmeans diet/pdiff adjust=tukey;
run;
```

Least squares means are discussed more fully in Chapter 5, but note for now that in the case of one-way designs (balanced or unbalanced) they are precisely the same as the simple group means. Program 3.5 produces all pairwise adjusted p-values in tabular format.

**Output from
Program 3.5**

```
                    Least Squares Means for effect diet
                      Pr > |t| for HO: LSMean(i)=LSMean(j)

                         Dependent Variable: wloss

      i/j          1          2          3          4          5

       1                   0.1604     0.0021     <.0001     0.9988
       2        0.1604                0.4547     0.0026     0.0914
       3        0.0021     0.4547                0.1828     0.0009
       4        <.0001     0.0026     0.1828                <.0001
       5        0.9988     0.0914     0.0009     <.0001
```

Output 3.5 shows the FWE levels that are needed to achieve statistical significance using Tukey's method. For example, the "B versus E" comparison (or 2/5 comparison), with adjusted *p*-value 0.0914, is statistically significant at the FWE = 0.10 level but not at the FWE = 0.05 level.

3.4 Pairwise Comparisons with a Control

If you are interested *only* in whether (or by how much) your treatment averages differ from a control or baseline average, then you can make your tests more powerful by restricting the family to include only comparisons with the control, rather than all pairs. The gain in power can be substantial; for example, if you have seven groups, one with a control, your family has only $k = 6$ elements if you consider comparisons with a control, but it has $k = 7 \times 6/2 = 21$ elements if you include all pairwise comparisons. Using the Bonferroni critical value, you would use CER = 0.05/6 = 0.0083 as the CER in the comparisons with control case, and CER = 0.05/21 = 0.0024 in the all pairwise comparisons case.

However, we refer to Bonferroni CERs for comparison only. The Bonferroni critical levels are too conservative because they are not based on the precise distribution of the statistics. As is the case with all pairwise comparisons, the statistics that are used for making all comparisons against the control also are correlated, because they all involve the data of the control group.

EXAMPLE: Comparing Growth of Mice against a Control

Suppose you are performing a toxicology study in which six different chemical solutions are applied to young mice, and weight change is measured after a fixed time interval. Your study is designed to screen out the solutions that are obviously harmful, retaining solutions that are not demonstrably different from the control group. Suppose you want to consider only the comparisons of the six solutions with the control, and are not interested in comparisons among the six solutions.

TABLE 3.2   Means and Standard Deviations of Mouse Growth Data

	Control	1	2	3	4	5	6
Mean	105.38	95.90	80.48	72.14	91.88	84.68	74.24
Std. Dev.	13.44	23.89	12.68	8.41	9.44	18.35	7.81
n	4	4	4	4	4	4	4

Principles and Procedures of Statistics: A Biometrical Approach, 2nd Ed, Steele, R. et al. (1980). McGraw-Hill. Reprinted with permission.

The pooled variance is $\hat{\sigma}^2 = 210.0048$.

3.4.1 Two-Sided Comparisons with a Control

If you want to make a claim about whether the treated groups' means are *either larger or smaller* than the control group mean, then you should use two-sided intervals. In the previous toxicology example, for example, you might want to exclude solutions that cause either too much or too little weight gain.

Following the development of Section 3.3, and letting $\bar{y}_0$ denote the mean of the control group, you need a c_α for which

$$P(\bar{y}_i - \bar{y}_0 - c_\alpha \hat{\sigma}\sqrt{2/n} \leq \mu_i - \mu_0 \leq \bar{y}_i - \bar{y}_0 + c_\alpha \hat{\sigma}\sqrt{2/n}, \text{ for all } i) = 1 - \alpha.$$

Algebraically rearranging terms, we see that c_α must satisfy

$$P\left(\max_i \frac{|(\bar{y}_i - \mu_i) - (\bar{y}_0 - \mu_0)|}{\hat{\sigma}\sqrt{2/n}} \leq c_\alpha\right) = 1 - \alpha.$$

The value c_α is then seen to be related to *Dunnett's two-sided range distribution*.

DEFINITION: **Dunnett's Two-Sided Range Distribution**

If $Z_0, Z_1, \ldots, Z_g$ are independent standard normal random variables, and V is a random variable distributed as Chi-Square with df degrees of freedom, independent of the Z's, then

$$Q_{g,\text{df}}^{D2} = \frac{\max_i |Z_i - Z_0|}{\sqrt{2V/\text{df}}}$$

has Dunnett's two-sided range distribution with parameters g and df.

You can see that c_α satisfies

$$P(Q_{g,(g+1)(n-1)}^{D2} \leq c_\alpha) = 1 - \alpha,$$

or equivalently $c_\alpha = q_{1-\alpha,g,(g+1)(n-1)}^{D2}$, where $q_{1-\alpha,\cdot,\cdot}^{D2}$ is the $1 - \alpha$ quantile of Dunnett's two-sided range distribution.

In contrast to the definition of the critical value using Tukey's method, the $1/\sqrt{2}$ factor is incorporated directly into the definition of the critical value for Dunnett's method, and no division by $\sqrt{2}$ is needed.

Dunnett's Method (two-sided)   Confidence intervals for comparisons with a control in the balanced ANOVA that use the critical value $q_{1-\alpha,g,(g+1)(n-1)}^{D2}$ from Dunnett's two-sided range distribution are called *Dunnett's two-sided confidence intervals* after Dunnett (1955).

As with Tukey's range distribution, the quantiles of this distribution can be calculated using the PROBMC function in SAS, which evaluates the cumulative probability distribution function of the random variable $Q_{g,v}^{D2}$. This distribution is given as (see, e.g., Hochberg and Tamhane, 1987, p. 141)

$$P(Q_{g,v}^{D2} \leq q) = \int_0^\infty \left[\int_{-\infty}^\infty \{\Phi(y + q\sqrt{2}x) - \Phi(y - q\sqrt{2}x)\}^g \, d\Phi(y) \right] dF_v(x),$$

where $d\Phi(z)/dz$ and $dF_v(u)/du$ are, as defined above for the range distribution, the standard normal and the $\sqrt{\chi_v^2/v}$ density functions, respectively. The double integral is evaluated numerically by the PROBMC function.

For the toxicology example, the critical value for the 95 percent simultaneous confidence intervals is $c_{.05} = q_{.95,6,21}$, as calculated in Program 3.6.

PROGRAM 3.6   Dunnett's Critical Value (two-sided)

```
data;
   c_alpha = probmc("DUNNETT2",.,.95,21,6);
run;
proc print; run;
```

Output from Program 3.6

```
          OBS     C_ALPHA

           1      2.78972
```

The two-sided Dunnett confidence intervals for the pairwise comparisons against the control in the toxicology example are then given by

$$\bar{y}_i - \bar{y}_0 \pm 2.78972 \times \sqrt{210.0048} \times \sqrt{2/4}$$

or

$$\bar{y}_i - \bar{y}_0 \pm 28.586.$$

Table 3.3 shows the effects of using the precise distribution of the comparisons using Dunnett's method as the critical value of the interval.

TABLE 3.3   Comparison of Critical Values for $k = 6$ Comparisons with Control

Unadjusted	Dunnett	Bonferroni
2.07961	2.78972	2.91209

The difference between the Dunnett critical point and Bonferroni's shows the specific effect of calculating the probability directly rather than bounding it with the Bonferroni approximation. Since the Dunnett critical value is smaller while still providing FWE control, you can see that the Dunnett method is more powerful, providing intervals that are about 4 percent tighter than Bonferroni's.

The effect of reducing the family size is even more dramatic. Table 3.4 compares the Dunnett critical point (family size is $k = 6$) with the corresponding critical point from the Tukey all-pairwise intervals ($k = 21$).

TABLE 3.4   Comparison of Critical Values for $k = 6$ Comparisons with Control vs. $k = 21$ Pairwise Comparisons

Unadjusted ($k = 1$)	Dunnett ($k = 6$)	Tukey ($k = 21$)
2.07961	2.78972	3.25078

Comparing the Dunnett 2.78972 multiplier with the Tukey 3.25078 critical value, we see that reducing the family size greatly increases the power of the inference, providing intervals that are about 14 percent tighter than Tukey's.

Program 3.7 analyzes the toxicology data using two-sided Dunnett intervals.

PROGRAM 3.7   Simultaneous Two-sided Comparisons with a Control

```
data tox;
   input g @;
   do j = 1 to 4;
      input gain @; output;
   end;
datalines;
0 97.76 102.56 96.08 125.12
1 91.28 129.20 90.80  72.32
2 67.28  85.76 95.60  73.28
3 80.24  64.88 64.88  78.56
4 96.08  98.24 77.84  95.36
5 57.68  89.84 98.48  92.72
6 68.72  85.28 68.72  74.24
;
proc glm data=tox;
   class g;
   model gain=g;
   means g/dunnett;
run;
```

Output from Program 3.7

```
                         The GLM Procedure

                      Dunnett's t Tests for gain

NOTE: This test controls the type I experimentwise error for comparisons of
                  all treatments against a control.


           Alpha                               0.05
           Error Degrees of Freedom              21
           Error Mean Square                210.0048
           Critical Value of Dunnett's t    2.78972
           Minimum Significant Difference    28.586
```

```
Comparisons significant at the 0.05 level are indicated by ***.


                            Difference      Simultaneous
                   g        Between         95% Confidence
              Comparison     Means            Interval

              1   - 0         -9.48      -38.07    19.11
              4   - 0        -13.50      -42.09    15.09
              5   - 0        -20.70      -49.29     7.89
              2   - 0        -24.90      -53.49     3.69
              6   - 0        -31.14      -59.73    -2.55   ***
              3   - 0        -33.24      -61.83    -4.65   ***
```

The conclusion is that the animals in the solutions 6 and 3 groups have significantly lower mean weight gain than do the animals in the control group.

The statistics Critical Value of Dunnett's t (2.78972) and Minimum Significant Difference (28.586) are explained by Program 3.6. There are no warning methods listed because the method is exact in the sense that the FWE for the confidence intervals is exactly 0.05. However, if you are only interested in tests of hypotheses, then you can have more power by analyzing the data by using stepwise methods, as described in Chapter 8.

3.4.2   One-Sided Comparisons with a Control

If you want to reject the null hypothesis *only* when the treated groups' means are on one side of (e.g., lower than) the control group mean, *and if you are willing to ignore any difference in the opposite direction*, then you can get more power by using one-sided tests or one-sided confidence intervals. In the toxicology example above, for example, if you want to exclude only solutions that result in significantly less weight gain than control, retaining solutions for which weight gain is equal to *or larger* than the control, then you should use one-sided tests or intervals.

Confidence bounds for lower-tailed inferences have the form

$$\mu_i - \mu_0 \le \bar{y}_i - \bar{y}_0 + c_\alpha \hat{\sigma} \sqrt{2/n},$$

so that a significant difference can be claimed when $\bar{y}_i - \bar{y}_0 + c_\alpha \hat{\sigma} \sqrt{2/n} < 0$; that is, when $\bar{y}_i - \bar{y}_0$ is significantly less than 0. The corresponding test of hypothesis rejects the null hypothesis in favor of the alternative $H_{Ai}: \mu_i - \mu_0 < 0$, when the *t*-statistic based on the difference between sample means,

$$t_i = \frac{\bar{y}_i - \bar{y}_0}{\hat{\sigma} \sqrt{2/n}}$$

is less than the critical value, c_α.

Thus, to obtain the critical points for lower-tailed bounds and tests, you need a c_α for which

$$P(\mu_i - \mu_0 \le \bar{y}_i - \bar{y}_0 + c_\alpha \hat{\sigma} \sqrt{2/n}, \text{ for all } i) = 1 - \alpha.$$

Similarly, for upper-tailed bounds and tests, you need a c_α for which

$$P(\mu_i - \mu_0 \ge \bar{y}_i - \bar{y}_0 - c_\alpha \hat{\sigma} \sqrt{2/n}, \text{ for all } i) = 1 - \alpha.$$

Rearranging terms algebraically and using the symmetry of the normal distribution, we see that in both cases c_α must satisfy

$$P\left(\max_i \frac{(\bar{y}_i - \mu_i) - (\bar{y}_0 - \mu_0)}{\hat{\sigma} \sqrt{2/n}} \le c_\alpha \right) = 1 - \alpha.$$

The value c_α thus defined is related to *Dunnett's one-sided range distribution*.

DEFINITION: Dunnett's One-Sided Range Distribution

If $Z_0, Z_1, \ldots, Z_g$ are independent standard normal random variables, and V is a random variable distributed as Chi-Square with df degrees of freedom, independent of the Z's, then

$$Q_{g,\text{df}}^{D1} = \frac{\max_i (Z_i - Z_0)}{\sqrt{2V/\text{df}}}$$

has Dunnett's one-sided range distribution with parameters g and df.

The constant c_α you need for forming one-sided bounds and tests is related to the one-sided range distribution as follows:

$$P(Q^{D1}_{g,(g+1)(n-1)} \leq c_\alpha) = 1 - \alpha,$$

or $c_\alpha = q^{D1}_{1-\alpha,g,(g+1)(n-1)}$, where $q^{D1}_{1-\alpha,\cdot,\cdot}$ is the $1-\alpha$ quantile of Dunnett's one-sided range distribution.

Dunnett's Method (one-sided)   The values

$$\bar{y}_i - \bar{y}_0 + q^{D1}_{1-\alpha,g,(g+1)(n-1)}\hat{\sigma}\sqrt{2/n}, \ i = 1, \ldots, g$$

are simultaneous upper-confidence bounds for the comparisons $\mu_i - \mu_0$, with FWE $= \alpha$. The corresponding (lower-tailed) test rejects the null hypothesis in favor of the alternative $H_{Ai}: \mu_i < \mu_0$ when

$$(\bar{y}_i - \bar{y}_0)/[\hat{\sigma}\sqrt{2/n}] < -q^{D1}_{1-\alpha,g,(g+1)(n-1)}.$$

The values

$$\bar{y}_i - \bar{y}_0 - q^{D1}_{1-\alpha,g,(g+1)(n-1)}\hat{\sigma}\sqrt{2/n}, \ i = 1, \ldots, g$$

are simultaneous lower-confidence bounds for the comparisons $\mu_i - \mu_0$, with FWE $= \alpha$. The corresponding (upper-tailed) test rejects the null hypothesis in favor of the alternative $H_{Ai}: \mu_i > \mu_0$ when

$$(\bar{y}_i - \bar{y}_0)/[\hat{\sigma}\sqrt{2/n}] > q^{D1}_{1-\alpha,g,(g+1)(n-1)}.$$

The testing methods allow directional claims when rejection is made because they correspond to the confidence intervals. However, more powerful one-sided procedures using step-down testing methods are available that also allow directional claims. See Chapter 8.

The quantiles of this distribution can be calculated using the PROBMC function, which evaluates the cumulative probability distribution function of the random variable $Q^{D1}_{g,\nu}$. This distribution is given as

$$P(Q^{D1}_{g,\nu} \leq q) = \int_0^\infty \left[\int_{-\infty}^\infty \{\Phi(y + q\sqrt{2}x)\}^g \, d\Phi(y) \right] dF_\nu(x),$$

where $\frac{d\Phi(z)}{dz}$ and $\frac{dF_\nu(u)}{du}$ are, as defined above for the range distribution, the standard normal and the $\sqrt{\chi^2_\nu/\nu}$ density functions, respectively. (See, e.g., Hochberg and Tamhane, 1987, p. 141.) The double integral is evaluated numerically by the PROBMC function.

For the toxicology example, the critical value for the 95 percent simultaneous upper-confidence is $q^{D1}_{.95,6,21}$, calculated in Program 3.8.

PROGRAM 3.8   **Dunnett's Critical Value (one-sided)**

```
data;
    c_alpha = probmc("DUNNETT1",.,.,95,21,6);
run;
proc print; run;
```

Output from Program 3.8

```
              OBS    C_ALPHA

               1     2.44786
```

Dunnett's one-sided, upper-confidence bounds for the pairwise comparisons against the control in the toxicology example are then given by

$$\bar{y}_i - \bar{y}_0 + 2.44786 \times \sqrt{210.0048} \times \sqrt{2/4}$$

or

$$\bar{y}_i - \bar{y}_0 + 25.083.$$

Looking back at Section 3.4.1 you can clearly see the power advantage of the one-sided method over the two-sided method, because in the two-sided method the treatment mean had to be 28.586 units less than the control mean to declare a significant difference. With one-sided tests the upper bound is about 12 percent tighter, so that the treatment mean only has to be 25.083 units less than the control mean to declare a significant difference. However, note that if you choose the one-sided method, you must not claim significant differences for any treatment mean that is higher than the control mean (no matter how much higher).

Program 3.9 analyzes the toxicology data using two-sided Dunnett intervals. The data set `data=tox` is defined in Program 3.7.

PROGRAM 3.9   **Simultaneous One-sided Comparisons with a Control**

```
proc glm data=tox;
   class g;
   model gain=g;
   means g/dunnettl;
run;
```

Output from Program 3.9

```
                    The GLM Procedure

            Dunnett's One-tailed t Tests for gain

NOTE: This test controls the type I experimentwise error for comparisons of
              all treatments against a control.


                Alpha                            0.05
                Error Degrees of Freedom           21
                Error Mean Square            210.0048
                Critical Value of Dunnett's t 2.44786
                Minimum Significant Difference  25.083


     Comparisons significant at the 0.05 level are indicated by ***.


                        Difference    Simultaneous
                 g      Between       95% Confidence
            Comparison    Means          Interval


            1   - 0       -9.48    -Infinity   15.60
            4   - 0      -13.50    -Infinity   11.58
            5   - 0      -20.70    -Infinity    4.38
            2   - 0      -24.90    -Infinity    0.18
            6   - 0      -31.14    -Infinity   -6.06  ***
            3   - 0      -33.24    -Infinity   -8.16  ***
```

The conclusion is that animals receiving solutions 6 and 3 have significantly lower mean weight gain than do animals receiving the control solution, as in the case of the two-sided intervals that are shown in the Output from Program 3.7. However, the critical difference is shorter.

Important Note: In releases of SAS/STAT software prior to Version 7, the GLM procedure displayed finite lower limits as well as upper limits for the DUNNETTL confidence bounds. These lower limits were not valid, since there are no lower limits for the Dunnett lower-tailed confidence bounds (the DUNNETTL option). Similarly, the finite upper limits displayed in previous releases for DUNNETTU confidence bounds should be ignored.

3.5   Multiple Inferences for Independent Estimates

In this section we consider another type of studentized range distribution. Whereas the distributions used in Tukey's and Dunnett's tests concern estimates that are dependent, the studentized maximum modulus distribution concerns estimates that are independent. The most common applications of this distribution are confidence intervals for means and for orthogonal comparisons, which are covered in the following sections.

3.5.1   Simultaneous Intervals for the Treatment Means

Suppose that you want simultaneous confidence intervals for the group means themselves, rather than for their differences. Then following the development of Section 3.3, you need a c_α for which

$$P(\bar{y}_i - c_\alpha \hat{\sigma}/\sqrt{n} \leq \mu_i \leq \bar{y}_i + c_\alpha \hat{\sigma}/\sqrt{n}, \text{ for all } i) = 1 - \alpha.$$

Rearranging terms algebraically, we see that c_α must satisfy

$$P\left(\max_i \frac{|(\bar{y}_i - \mu_i)|}{\hat{\sigma}\sqrt{1/n}} \leq c_\alpha\right) = 1 - \alpha.$$

Since the $\bar{y}_i$ are independent, the $t = \bar{y}_i/(\hat{\sigma}/\sqrt{n})$ values are *nearly* independent, too. (They're not quite so because they share a common pooled variance estimate.) Thus, we could use Šidák's method to approximate c_α as the t-distribution quantile of CER $= 1 - (1-\alpha)^{1/g}$. However, an exact value for c_α can be calculated using Tukey's (1953) *maximum modulus distribution*.

DEFINITION: The Maximum Modulus Distribution

If $Z_1, \ldots, Z_g$ are independent standard normal random variables, and V is a random variable distributed as Chi-Square with df degrees of freedom, independent of the Z's, then

$$Q_{g,\text{df}}^{MM} = \frac{\max_i |Z_i|}{\sqrt{V/\text{df}}}$$

has the maximum modulus distribution with parameters g and df.

You can see that the c_α satisfies

$$P(Q_{g,g(n-1)}^{MM} \leq c_\alpha) = 1 - \alpha,$$

or that $c_\alpha = q_{1-\alpha,g,g(n-1)}^{MM}$, where $q_{1-\alpha,\cdot,\cdot}^{MM}$ is the $1 - \alpha$ quantile of the maximum modulus distribution.

The quantiles of the maximum modulus distribution can also be calculated using the PROBMC function in SAS, which evaluates the cumulative probability distribution function of the random variable $Q_{g,v}^{MM}$. This distribution is given as

$$P(Q_{g,v}^{MM} \le q) = \int_0^\infty \{2\Phi(qx) - 1\}^g \, dF_v(x),$$

where $d\Phi(z)/dz$ and $dF_v(u)/du$ are, as defined above, the standard normal and the $\sqrt{\chi_v^2/v}$ density functions, respectively. The integral is evaluated numerically by the PROBMC function.

Program 3.10 calculates simultaneous confidence intervals for the weight loss data of Program 3.2.

PROGRAM 3.10   Simultaneous Confidence Intervals for Means

```
proc glm data=wloss;
   class diet;
   model wloss=diet;
   means diet / clm smm sidak;
run;
```

Output from Program 3.10

The GLM Procedure

Studentized Maximum Modulus Confidence Intervals for wloss

Alpha	0.05
Error Degrees of Freedom	45
Error Mean Square	0.993422
Critical Value of Studentized Maximum Modulus	2.67592
Half Width of Confidence Interval	0.843414

diet	N	Mean	Simultaneous 95% Confidence Interval	
E	10	12.1700	11.3266	13.0134
A	10	12.0500	11.2066	12.8934
B	10	11.0200	10.1766	11.8634
C	10	10.2700	9.4266	11.1134
D	10	9.2700	8.4266	10.1134

Sidak t Confidence Intervals for wloss

Alpha	0.05
Error Degrees of Freedom	45
Error Mean Square	0.993422
Critical Value of t	2.68165
Half Width of Confidence Interval	0.845218

diet	N	Mean	Simultaneous 95% Confidence Interval	
E	10	12.1700	11.3248	13.0152
A	10	12.0500	11.2048	12.8952
B	10	11.0200	10.1748	11.8652
C	10	10.2700	9.4248	11.1152
D	10	9.2700	8.4248	10.1152

Note the following about the output from Program 3.10:

- Since the intervals are *almost* independent, Šidák's adjustment provides a very close approximation to the maximum modulus method, as discussed earlier. Using the maximum modulus distribution yields very slightly (about 0.2%) tighter intervals.

- It is valid to judge whether means are significantly different by noting whether the maximum modulus confidence intervals overlap, in the sense that the FWE for all pairwise comparisons will be less than or equal to α. In this example, we can conclude that significant differences exist for exactly the same pairs of means that are different using Tukey's method shown in the output from Program 3.2. However, Tukey's method is generally more powerful than this method. If your goal is to compare means, then you should use Tukey's method, not the method of "overlapping simultaneous intervals."

3.5.2 Orthogonal Comparisons

There is a misconception among some users of MCPs that MCPs are necessary only when the tests are correlated. This is false; in fact, the largest FWE rates will occur when the tests are independent or nearly so. Thus, MCPs are needed *most* in this case.

Orthogonal comparisons provide one such example where tests are nearly independent. As in the case of independent group means discussed in the previous section, the estimates that correspond to orthogonal comparisons are independent, but the intervals themselves are slightly dependent because they all use the same pooled variance estimate.

Orthogonal comparisons are often used in dose-response analysis to identify effects that are linear, quadratic, cubic, and so on. They have the attractive property that the sums of squares attributable to each component add up to the sum of squares for the overall F-test. Thus, you can use orthogonal contrasts to decompose the overall F-test into components that show relative importance of linear, quadratic, and higher-order effects.

EXAMPLE: **Purchase Amounts with Discount Coupons**

A mail-order agency offered discounts of 0 percent (no discount), 10 percent, 15 percent, and 20 percent as an insert in their catalog. For each purchase, they recorded the net price (after discount) of goods purchased. Program 3.11 analyzes data from this example, with orthogonal contrasts to investigate the relationship between net purchase and discount rate.

PROGRAM 3.11 **Orthogonal Comparisons***

```
data coupon;
   input discount purchase @@;
datalines;
0 32.39   10 98.47   15 71.62   20 60.85
0 38.32   10 74.80   15 59.92   20 46.45
```

***Business Cases in Statistical Decision Making*, Peters, Lawrence H., and Gray, J. Brian. (1994). Prentice Hall. Reprinted with permission. Currently out of print. Contact Professor Brian Gray (bgray@cba.us.edu) at the University of Alabama for more information

```
0 35.66   10 52.97   15 75.37   20 68.49
0 74.24   10 46.72   15 77.04   20 63.83
0 63.05   10 76.81   15 72.84   20 75.38
0 66.53   10 69.01   15 52.53   20 70.60
0 46.36   10 53.77   15 80.47   20 52.23
0 41.90   10 54.21   15 72.55   20 57.14
0 44.94   10 83.14   15 78.94   20 60.17
0 41.09   10 49.00   15 64.00   20 60.46
;
run;
proc glm data=coupon;
   class discount;
   model purchase = discount;
   estimate "linear" discount   -3 -1  1  3;
   estimate "quad"   discount   -2  2  2 -2;
   estimate "cubic"  discount   -1  3 -3  1;
run;
data alevel;
   input FWE @@;
   qMM = probmc('maxmod',.,1-FWE,36,3);
   CER = 2*(1-probt(qMM,36));
   output;
datalines;
0.05 0.10
;
proc print data=alevel noobs;
   title1 "CER is the ALPHA level for orthogonal contrasts";
   title2 "that yields the corresponding FWE";
run;
title1; title2;
```

Output from Program 3.11

Source	DF	Type III SS	Mean Square	F Value	Pr > F
discount	3	2710.898190	903.632730	5.51	0.0032

Contrast	DF	Contrast SS	Mean Square	F Value	Pr > F
linear	1	966.856338	966.856338	5.90	0.0203
quad	1	1743.720250	1743.720250	10.63	0.0024
cubic	1	0.321602	0.321602	0.00	0.9649

CER is the ALPHA level for orthogonal contrasts
that yields the corresponding FWE

FWE	qMM	CER
0.05	2.49910	0.017151
0.10	2.19084	0.035020

Note the following about Program 3.11 and its output:

- You need to specify the degrees of freedom and the number of estimates for the PROBMC function. In this example, there are four groups, but only three tests; hence, "3" is used as the last PROBMC parameter rather than "4."

- The contrast sums of squares add up to the Type III sum of squares for `discount`, so it is clear that the quadratic effect is most responsible for the rejection of the overall hypothesis that the means are equal.

- Use the CER critical values shown in the output to interpret the orthogonal contrasts simultaneously. Thus, the `quad` contrast is highly significant at either the FWE = 5 percent or FWE = 10 percent levels, but the `linear` contrast is significant only at the FWE = 10 percent level. Again, the dominant effect in this data is the quadratic effect.

- Strictly speaking, the contrasts are not linear, quadratic, etc., since the discount levels are not equally spaced. So technically, we should say that the contrasts are linear, quadratic, etc., in the *ordinal*, rather than *actual* discount levels.

- A simple plot of the group means by discount rate also shows that the dominant effect is quadratic.

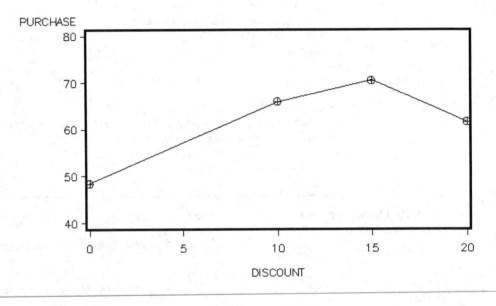

In this chapter we have developed the standard MCPs for the balanced one-way ANOVA layout. The methods described are Tukey's method, Dunnett's one- and two-sided methods, and the method for independent estimates that uses the maximum modulus distribution. These methods are the best methods available for simultaneous confidence intervals with balanced data. However, if you don't need a confidence interval for each difference and only want to make decisions regarding the hypotheses tested, then more powerful procedures are available. The simple step-down Bonferroni method (or Holm method) described in Chapter 2 can, in some cases, be more powerful than the methods in this chapter. Step-down procedures that use the specific dependence structures of the tests are even more powerful than the Bonferroni step-down procedure. These are described in the ANOVA context and in more general models starting with Chapter 8.

3.6 Concluding Remarks

Chapter 4

Multiple Comparisons among Treatment Means in the One-Way Unbalanced ANOVA

4.1   Introduction

In Chapter 3 we discussed various multiple comparisons methods in the balanced one-way ANOVA. This is the simplest structure, and it allows for exact calculation of critical values and adjusted p-values using simple distributions (and their integrals).

In many cases, however, sample sizes are unbalanced. In planned experiments, you frequently lose a few observations at random, resulting in unbalanced data. Sometimes, you want to estimate data in a control group very precisely, and therefore, *plan* to have unbalanced data, with more observations in the control group. In observational studies, the number of observations falling in each group is usually a random variable, and the studies are generally unbalanced.

There is nothing wrong with having unbalanced sample sizes. However, when this occurs, the simple distributions such as Tukey's Studentized range and Dunnett's range distributions become more complicated. Before the advent of advanced computing power that we now enjoy, this simple change from balanced to unbalanced caused numerous problems. Various researchers devised alternative solutions to circumvent these problems, and this is one reason there are so many alternative MCPs available today.

In this chapter we show what modifications are needed for the unbalanced case, and we identify the appropriate procedures to use for simultaneous intervals and their associated tests. The following applications are covered in this chapter:

- all pairwise comparisons
- all comparisons with a control (two-sided)
- all comparisons with a control (one-sided).

These are the same topics covered in Chapter 3, except that we do not discuss the topic of independent estimates (Section 3.5) further. If you have independent estimates, you can use Šidák's method. As discussed in Chapter 3 (following the output from Program 3.10), Šidák's method provides an extremely close approximation in the case of independent estimates.

If you want exact methods for general linear functions of the parameters, instead of just the pairwise comparisons, or pairwise comparisons with a control, see Chapter 6 and Chapter 8.

To fix ideas, consider the following example.

EXAMPLE: Comparing Temperature Recovery Times

Have you ever had a surgical procedure? If you remember how you felt when the anesthetic wore off, you were probably very cold. A company developed specialized heating blankets designed to help the body heat following a surgical procedure. They performed an experiment, trying four types of blankets on surgical patients. They then wanted to compare the recovery times of the patients who used different types of blankets. One of the blankets they considered was a standard blanket that had been in use already in various hospitals. The sample sizes differ greatly because of difficulties in carrying out the study, both with patients and hospital administrators.

PROGRAM 4.1   Recovery Time Data Set

```
data recover;
    input blanket$ minutes @@;
datalines;
b0 15 b0 13 b0 12 b0 16 b0 16 b0 17 b0 13 b0 13 b0 16 b0 17
b0 17 b0 19 b0 17 b0 15 b0 13 b0 12 b0 16 b0 10 b0 17 b0 12
b1 13 b1 16 b1  9
b2  5 b2  8 b2  9
b3 14 b3 16 b3 16 b3 12 b3  7 b3 12 b3 13 b3 13 b3  9 b3 16
b3 13 b3 18 b3 13 b3 12 b3 13
;
```

The blanket called "b0" is the standard blanket, and the types "b1-b3" are the new types. Note that the sample sizes are very unbalanced, in particular with few observations for the "b1" and "b2" type.

The Model and Estimates

The model we consider in this chapter is identical to that of Chapter 3,

$$y_{ij} = \mu_i + \epsilon_{ij},$$

with independent, homoscedastic, and normally distributed ϵ_{ij}. In the balanced case, the within-group samples all have the same size n; in this case we allow them to differ, denoting the size of the ith sample by n_i, for $i = 1, \ldots, g$. The estimated parameters are $\hat{\mu}_i = \bar{y}_i = (1/n_i)\Sigma_{j=1}^{n_i} y_{ij}$, and $\hat{\sigma}^2 = \Sigma_{i=1}^{g}\{(n_i - 1)s_i^2\}/\Sigma_{i=1}^{g}(n_i - 1)$, where s_i^2 is the ordinary sample variance estimate for group i, $s_i^2 = \Sigma_{j=1}^{n_i}(y_{ij} - \bar{y}_i)^2/(n_i - 1)$. The degrees of freedom for the estimate of σ^2 is $df = \Sigma_{i=1}^{g}(n_i - 1) = N - g$, where N is the total of all within-group sample sizes.

4.2 All Pairwise Comparisons

The confidence intervals for the difference of means $\mu_i - \mu_{i'}$ have the form

$$\bar{y}_i - \bar{y}_{i'} \pm c_\alpha \hat{\sigma} \sqrt{1/n_i + 1/n_{i'}}.$$

In the case of nonmultiplicity adjusted confidence intervals, you set c_α to the $1 - \alpha/2$ quantile of the t distribution, $t_{1-\alpha/2,df}$, with $df = N - g$. As always, you can construct Bonferroni-adjusted confidence intervals by setting $c_\alpha = t_{1-\alpha'/2,g(n-1)}$, where $\alpha' = \alpha/k$, and where k is the number of inferences (e.g., pairwise comparisons) in the family. And, as always, you can improve upon the Bonferroni value by taking into account the distribution of the differences.

Mathematically, c_α must satisfy

$$P(\bar{y}_i - \bar{y}_{i'} - c_\alpha \hat{\sigma} \sqrt{1/n_i + 1/n_{i'}} \leq \mu_i - \mu_{i'}$$

$$\leq \bar{y}_i - \bar{y}_{i'} + c_\alpha \hat{\sigma} \sqrt{1/n_i + 1/n_{i'}}, \text{ for all } i, i') = 1 - \alpha,$$

or equivalently

$$P(\max_{i,i'} \frac{|(\bar{y}_i - \mu_i) - (\bar{y}_{i'} - \mu_{i'})|}{\hat{\sigma} \sqrt{1/n_i + 1/n_{i'}}} \leq c_\alpha) = 1 - \alpha.$$

Unlike the balanced case, the denominator of the previous expression is not constant for all i, i' pairs. Thus, the statistic does not have the studentized range distribution and actually has a quite complicated form.

4.2.1   The Tukey-Kramer Method

Tukey (1953) and Kramer (1956) independently proposed a method to approximate the critical value c_α in unbalanced designs. Recall that when the sample sizes are all equal $n_1 = \ldots = n_g = n$, the statistic

$$\max_{i,i'} |T_{i,i'}| = \max_{i,i'} \frac{|(\bar{y}_i - \mu_i) - (\bar{y}_{i'} - \mu_{i'})|}{(1/\sqrt{2})\hat{\sigma} \sqrt{1/n + 1/n}}$$

is distributed as $Q^R_{g,g(n-1)}$, which has the studentized range distribution. In the Tukey-Kramer procedure, you use the distribution of $Q^R_{g,df}$ to approximate the distribution of

$$\max_{i,i'} \frac{|(\bar{y}_i - \mu_i) - (\bar{y}_{i'} - \mu_{i'})|}{(1/\sqrt{2})\hat{\sigma} \sqrt{1/n_i + 1/n_{i'}}},$$

which gives us the Tukey-Kramer simultaneous confidence intervals:

$$\bar{y}_i - \bar{y}_{i'} \pm (q^R_{1-\alpha,g,df}/\sqrt{2})\hat{\sigma} \sqrt{1/n_i + 1/n_{i'}}.$$

Note that, as in the balanced case, the critical value c_α is the upper $1 - \alpha$ quantile of the range distribution divided by $\sqrt{2}$. Thus, there are no real differences in the form of the Tukey-Kramer intervals and the Tukey intervals. If you apply the above formula in the case where all n_i are equal (to n), you get exactly the Tukey intervals for all pairwise comparisons.

However, the Tukey-Kramer intervals are not exact in the sense of providing exact simultaneous $1 - \alpha$ coverage rate and exact FWE= α when the sample sizes are unequal. Hayter (1984) proved that the method is in fact conservative; that is, that the true FWE is less than or equal to α for all possible sample size configurations, but with equality (exactness) when the sample sizes are equal.

Program 4.2 uses PROC GLM to compare the recovery times for the different types of blankets using the Tukey-Kramer method.

PROGRAM 4.2   Tukey-Kramer Simultaneous Intervals with Unbalanced ANOVA

```
proc glm data=recover;
   class blanket;
   model minutes=blanket;
   means blanket/tukey;
run;
```

When you specify TUKEY as an option for the MEANS statement, the Tukey-Kramer method is used automatically when the sample sizes are unequal. This code produces the following output.

Output from Program 4.2

```
                            The GLM Procedure

                 Tukey's Studentized Range (HSD) Test for minutes

        NOTE: This test controls the type I experimentwise error rate.


             Alpha                                   0.05
             Error Degrees of Freedom                  37
             Error Mean Square                      6.70991
             Critical Value of Studentized Range    3.80389


        Comparisons significant at the 0.05 level are indicated by ***.
```

blanket Comparison		Difference Between Means	Simultaneous 95% Confidence Interval		
b0	– b3	1.6667	-0.7132	4.0465	
b0	– b1	2.1333	-2.1805	6.4471	
b0	– b2	7.4667	3.1529	11.7805	***
b3	– b0	-1.6667	-4.0465	0.7132	
b3	– b1	0.4667	-3.9399	4.8732	
b3	– b2	5.8000	1.3934	10.2066	***
b1	– b0	-2.1333	-6.4471	2.1805	
b1	– b3	-0.4667	-4.8732	3.9399	
b1	– b2	5.3333	-0.3555	11.0222	
b2	– b0	-7.4667	-11.7805	-3.1529	***
b2	– b3	-5.8000	-10.2066	-1.3934	***
b2	– b1	-5.3333	-11.0222	0.3555	

We see that the control blanket and the blanket "b3" have significantly longer average recovery times than the blanket "b2." However, even though the difference between "b1" and "b2" is not much less than the difference between "b3" and "b2", "b1 - b2" is not significant because of the smaller sample sizes involved in this comparison. This is one consequence of an unbalanced experimental design.

There are no warning messages because the method does protect the FWE (as proven by Hayter, 1984); however, it is conservative. We will provide an alternative, less conservative method in Section 4.2.3.

Although the output does not indicate "Tukey-Kramer," that is in fact the method that is used.

Let's calculate the first interval

```
        b0    – b3         1.6667    -0.7132   4.0465
```

to understand the Tukey-Kramer method. Noting that there are $g = 4$ groups and $df = 37$, the Studentized range and associated c_α values can be calculated as follows:

```
data;
   qval = probmc("RANGE",.,.95,37,4);
   c_alpha = qval/sqrt(2);
run;
proc print; run;
```

which provides values $q^R_{.95,4,37} = 3.80389$ and $c_\alpha = 3.80389/\sqrt{2} = 2.68976$. The difference between sample means for blankets "b0" and "b3" is 1.6667, and the sample sizes for those groups are $n_0 = 20$ and $n_3 = 15$, respectively. The estimate $\hat{\sigma}^2 = 6.70991$ is shown in the output as `Error Mean Square`. Thus, the Tukey-Kramer confidence interval is given by

$$1.6667 \pm 2.68976\sqrt{6.70991}\sqrt{1/20 + 1/15},$$

which provides the indicated lower and upper confidence limits -0.7132 and 4.0465 for the "b0 - b3" mean difference.

4.2.2   Graphical Comparisons - LINES Option

A very important difference between the balanced and unbalanced cases is that the graphical output provided by the LINES option in the MEANS statement can be incorrect. The problem is that the ordering of the sample means, e.g., $\bar{y}_0 > \bar{y}_3 > \bar{y}_1 > \bar{y}_2$, does not necessarily imply the same ordering to the significance of the differences. For example, the "1" versus "2" comparison might be significant (the confidence interval for the difference excludes zero), while the "3" versus "2" comparison is insignificant. This anomaly can happen when the sample size in group 3 is smaller than the sample size in group 1, leading to a less precise estimate for the "3" versus "2" difference (wider confidence interval) than for the "1" versus "2" difference. With equal sample sizes, this cannot happen, as the widths of all confidence intervals are equal.

When this case occurs, you cannot draw a line connecting "3", "1", and "2", since this would imply no significant difference for the "1" vs. "2" comparison. However, you would like to connect "3" and "2" with a line, indicating no significant difference.

There is no easy solution for presenting the results graphically using LINES with unequal sample sizes. Here is what happens when you specify LINES in PROC GLM, using the following:

PROGRAM 4.3   **LINES Option with Unequal Sample Sizes**

```
proc glm data=recover;
   class blanket;
   model minutes=blanket;
   means blanket/tukey lines;
run;
```

Output from Program 4.3

```
                        The GLM Procedure

            Tukey's Studentized Range (HSD) Test for minutes

NOTE: This test controls the type I experimentwise error rate but generally
                has a higher type II error rate than REGWQ.
```

```
                    Alpha                                   0.05
                    Error Degrees of Freedom                  37
                    Error Mean Square                     6.70991
                    Critical Value of Studentized Range   3.80389
                    Minimum Significant Difference         4.3604
                    Harmonic Mean of Cell Sizes          5.106383

                         NOTE: Cell sizes are not equal.


            Means with the same letter are not significantly different.


            Tukey Grouping          Mean      N    blanket

                        A          14.800     20    b0
                        A
                        A          13.133     15    b3
                        A
                        A          12.667      3    b1

                        B           7.333      3    b2
```

Unlike the previous analysis without the LINES option (Program 4.2), this analysis suggests that the difference between blankets 1 and 2 is statistically significant. The note explains what is going on. In order to have constant-width confidence intervals, the procedure uses the Tukey method, but replaces all n_i with the harmonic mean $\tilde{n} = 5.106383$, a method suggested by Winer (1971). Using this approach, the confidence interval for the "b1" versus "b2" difference is

$$5.33333 \pm 2.68976\sqrt{6.70991}\sqrt{1/5.1064 + 1/5.1064},$$

with limits 0.973 to 9.694, showing a significant difference.

Our purpose in showing this analysis is to **discourage** you from using it. In particular, we recommend **not** using the LINES option with unequal sample sizes because it does not control the FWE and can lead to incorrect inferences. At the very least, you should verify that the inferences shown from the LINES option are valid using a more appropriate method when you have unbalanced sample sizes.

An Alternative Graphical Comparison

In cases where the sample sizes differ, there are alternative graphical methods that represent the confidence interval inferences correctly; see Hsu (1996, pp. 146–153). One of these is implemented in JMP software. For further discussions of graphical methods, see Hochberg et al. (1982).

4.2.3   Simulation-based Methods

The Tukey-Kramer method is conservative because the critical value $q^R_{1-\alpha,g,N-g}$ is really larger than the true c_α, which is the $1 - \alpha$ quantile of the distribution of $\max_{i,i'} |T_{i,i'}|$. To calculate this critical value analytically requires a complex multidimensional integration using the *multivariate t distribution* (described in Chapter 5), and is often not feasible. However, you can approximate this critical value very easily by simulation, as follows:

1. Generate a random sample y_{ij}^* from the standard normal distribution.
2. Analyze the data exactly as you would if it were an actual data set, getting sample means $\bar{y}_i^*$ and a pooled variance estimate $(\hat{\sigma}^*)^2$. Compute the test statistics for all pairwise comparisons, $T_{i,i'}^* = (\bar{y}_i^* - \bar{y}_{i'}^*)/(\hat{\sigma}^* \sqrt{1/n_i + 1/n_{i'}})$.
3. Calculate the value $\max_{i,i'} |T_{i,i'}^*|$ and store it.
4. Repeat steps 1 through 3 NSAMP times, and estimate c_α using the $1 - \alpha$ quantile of the resulting maxima. Call the resulting value $\hat{c}_\alpha$.

The resulting value $\hat{c}_\alpha$ is a *simulation-consistent* estimate; that is, as the number of simulations (NSAMP) tends to infinity, the value $\hat{c}_\alpha$ gets closer to the value c_α. Thus, with sufficient computing resources, you can obtain the true value of c_α with adequate precision, and there is no need to resort to approximations such as Tukey-Kramer.

Program 4.4 illustrates this approach. Note that there are more efficient methods for simulating critical values than this (some discussed in Chapter 5), but this program gives the general idea.

PROGRAM 4.4   Simulation of Correct Tukey-Kramer Critical Value

```
data sim;
   array nsize{4} (20,3,3,15);
   do rep = 1 to 500;
      do i=1 to dim(nsize);
         do j=1 to nsize{i};
            y = rannor(121211);
            output;
         end;
      end;
   end;
run;

ods listing close;
proc glm data=sim;
   by rep;
   class i;
   model y=i;
   lsmeans i/ tdiff;
   ods output Diff=GDiffs;
quit;
   ods listing;

proc transpose data=GDiffs out=t(where=(_label_ > RowName));
   by rep  RowName;
   var _1 _2 _3 _4;
data t;
   set t;
   abst = abs(COL1);
   keep rep abst;
proc means noprint data=t;
   var abst;
   by rep;
   output out=maxt max=maxt;
run;
```

```
      ods select Quantiles;
proc univariate;
      var maxt;
run;
```

The results from PROC UNIVARIATE are shown in the output from Program 4.4.

**Output from
Program 4.4**

Quantiles (Definition 5)

Quantile	Estimate
100% Max	3.783023
99%	3.372945
95%	2.676082
90%	2.206895
75% Q3	1.838108
50% Med	1.385222
25% Q1	0.977111
10%	0.693883
5%	0.538896
1%	0.354717
0% Min	0.231491

Thus, the correct 95th percentile is estimated to be 2.676082, based on 500 simulations. The Tukey-Kramer approximation resulted in a slightly higher number, 2.68976, which suggests a slight level of conservatism of the Tukey-Kramer method. Note, however, that the error of the simulation method can be larger than the minor difference that is shown between these two critical values.

Edwards and Berry (1987) show how to simulate to obtain estimates $\hat{c}_\alpha$ with prescribed accuracy for the true FWE $P(\max_{i,i'} |T_{i,i'}| \geq \hat{c}_\alpha)$. Their method sets the size of the simulation to ensure that this probability is within γ of $1 - \alpha$ with confidence $100(1 - \epsilon)\%$. You can adjust γ and ϵ to set the level of accuracy.

The Edwards and Berry method is implemented in the ADJUST=SIMULATE option for the LSMEANS statement in both PROC GLM and PROC MIXED. In general, the LSMEANS statement computes and compares "least squares means," which are a generalization of simple group means. Least squares means are discussed more fully in Chapters 5 and on, but note for now that in the case of one-way designs (balanced or unbalanced) they are precisely the same as the simple group means. The default values for γ and ϵ are 0.005 and 0.01, respectively, so the resulting estimated critical value for FWE= 0.05 will ensure that the true FWE is between 0.045 and 0.055, with 99 percent confidence. If this is deemed to be too imprecise, you can improve the accuracy by lowering the value of γ or lowering the value of ϵ, or simply setting the number of samples in the simulation directly. However, note that the default accuracy provides fast answers on most hardware. Be advised that cutting γ in half quadruples the sample size and the execution time. If you want to adjust γ, you should try a couple of moderate values first, then choose γ as small as possible, subject to time limitations.

If you specify the ADJUST=SIMULATE option then PROC GLM uses the simulation-estimated quantile in forming multiplicity-adjusted confidence intervals for the differences. Although PROC GLM doesn't display the actual value of the quantile by default, you can use the previously undocumented REPORT option for the simulation to print the quantile and other information to the log window, as demonstrated in Program 4.5.

PROGRAM 4.5   **Simulation-based Critical Value and Intervals**

```
proc glm data=recover;
   class blanket;
   model minutes=blanket;
   lsmeans blanket/cl adjust=simulate(seed=121211 report);
run;
```

Log Output from Program 4.5

```
NOTE: Comparison type: All
NOTE: Simulation seed = 121211, sample size = 12604.
Test=MCA, Simulated p =    0.95 +-   0.005 (  99 %)
Means are uncorrelated but unbalanced.
                            Simulated
                      Q         P
      Simulated     2.6344 ( 0.9500)
      Tukey-Kramer  2.6898 ( 0.9568)
      Bonferroni    2.7876 ( 0.9662)
      Sidak         2.7792 ( 0.9654)
      GT-2          2.7708 ( 0.9650)
      Scheffe       2.9285 ( 0.9763)
      T             2.0262 ( 0.8130)
```

The critical value 2.6344 has the property that the true FWE of the simulated method using $\hat{c}_\alpha = 2.6344$ is between 0.045 and 0.055 with 99 percent confidence. The phrase "99 percent confidence" here refers to the fact that 99 percent of the critical values obtained through this program (with random SEED values generated from the computer clock for example), will give true FWE between 0.045 and 0.055.

The critical value $\hat{c}_\alpha = 2.6344$ is more accurate than the simulated value 2.676082 from Program 4.4 because Program 4.4 used a smaller simulation size (500 instead of 12,604). Note also that the Tukey-Kramer critical value 2.6898 is too large, corroborating our previous statement that the method is conservative.

4.2.4   Tests of Hypotheses—Adjusted *p*-Values

Suppose you don't require confidence intervals for the mean differences, but you only want to know which ones are significant. As in the balanced case, confidence intervals for the differences can be used to test the hypotheses $H_{0i,i'}: \mu_i = \mu_{i'}$ by noting whether zero lies within the interval. As discussed in Chapter 2, more powerful methods for making "Accept and Reject" decisions can be devised using the "closure principle," discussed further in Chapter 8. However, if you are interested in the confidence intervals, then you probably are also interested in the implied significance levels of test procedures that use such intervals.

The adjusted *p*-value using this method is the smallest FWE level at which $H_{0i,i'}$ is still rejected. To define these quantities we must distinguish between random values of test statistics and the fixed, observed values. Let $\{T_{i,i'}\}$ denote the random value of the test statistic (considered under the null hypothesis) and let $t_{i,i'}$ denote the fixed, observed value of the test statistic from the actual study.

We can calculate the adjusted *p*-value using the distribution of $\max_{i,i'} |T_{i,i'}|$ as follows:

Adjusted *p*-Values for All Pairwise Comparisons

$$\tilde{p}_{i,i'} = P(\max_{j,j'} |T_{j,j'}| \geq |t_{i,i'}|).$$

For example, the test statistic for comparing blanket 1 with blanket 2 is

$$t_{2,3} = \frac{5.33333333}{\sqrt{6.70991}\sqrt{1/3 + 1/3}} = \frac{5.3333333}{2.11501} = 2.52166.$$

The adjusted p-value for this test is then

$$\tilde{p}_{2,3} = P(\max_{j,j'} |T_{j,j'}| \geq 2.52166).$$

Note that we get adjusted p-values for all six pairwise comparisons, defined identically except for the different values of the pairwise test statistics.

As with the Tukey-Kramer method of constructing confidence intervals discussed in Section 4.2.1, the distribution of $\max_{j,j'} |T_{j,j'}|$ can be approximated by the studentized range distribution. The Tukey-Kramer method for calculating the adjusted p-values used the studentized range distribution approximation to the distribution of $\max_{i,i'} |T_{i,i'}|$, approximating adjusted p-values as $\tilde{p}_{i,i'} = P(Q^R_{g,N-g} \geq \sqrt{2}|t_{i,i'}|)$.

Using the test statistic 2.52166, the adjusted p-value using the Tukey-Kramer method can be obtained as follows:

```
data;
   adjp= 1-probmc('RANGE',sqrt(2)*2.52166,.,37,4); run;
proc print; run;
```

which produces ADJP = 0.072940. Of course, you don't need to calculate all of the adjusted p-values yourself, as shown above. All of the adjusted p-values are calculated automatically by the GLM procedure and are displayed in a convenient matrix, as shown in Program 4.6:

PROGRAM 4.6   Tukey-Kramer Adjusted p-Values in an Unbalanced ANOVA

```
proc glm data=recover;
   class blanket;
   model minutes=blanket;
   lsmeans blanket/ pdiff cl adjust=tukey;
run;
```

The adjusted p-values from Program 4.6 are displayed here.

Output from Program 4.6

```
                      Least Squares Means
        Adjustment for Multiple Comparisons: Tukey-Kramer

                          minutes      LSMEAN
        blanket           LSMEAN       Number

        b0            14.8000000          1
        b1            12.6666667          2
        b2             7.3333333          3
        b3            13.1333333          4
```

```
              Least Squares Means for effect blanket
                 Pr > |t| for H0: LSMean(i)=LSMean(j)

                   Dependent Variable: minutes

     i/j            1            2            3            4

      1                        0.5501       0.0002       0.2524
      2          0.5501                     0.0729       0.9918
      3          0.0002       0.0729                     0.0058
      4          0.2524       0.9918       0.0058
```

The adjusted p-value from the "b1 versus b2" comparison is shown above as 0.0729, in the (2,3) and (3,2) elements of the comparison matrix.

Simulation-based Adjusted p-Values for Pairwise Comparisons

Instead of using the Tukey-Kramer approximation, you can use the ADJUST=SIMULATE option to estimate the precise values of the adjusted p-values $\tilde{p}_{i,i'} = P(\max_{j,j'} |T_{j,j'}| \geq |t_{i,i'}|)$. For example, using the PROC UNIVARIATE output from Program 4.4, we would estimate the adjusted p-value for $t_{2,3} = 2.52166$ from 500 simulations to be some number between 0.05 and 0.10, since 2.52166 lies between the estimated 90th and 95th percentiles (2.206895 and 2.676082, respectively) of the distribution of $\max_{j,j'} |T_{j,j'}|$.

The simulation-based estimate of the adjusted p-value can be obtained in essentially the same manner as the critical values.

1. Generate a random sample y_{ij}^* from the standard normal distribution.
2. Analyze the data exactly as you would if it were an actual data set, getting sample means $\bar{y}_i^*$ and a pooled variance estimate $(\hat{\sigma}^*)^2$. Compute the test statistics for all pairwise comparisons, $T_{i,i'}^* = (\bar{y}_i^* - \bar{y}_{i'}^*)/(\hat{\sigma}^* \sqrt{1/n_i + 1/n_{i'}})$.
3. Calculate the value $M = \max_{j,j'} |T_{j,j'}^*|$ and compare it to each of the observed $|t_{i,i'}|$. Create counters $c_{i,i'}$, with $c_{i,i'} = 1$ if $M \geq |t_{i,i'}|$, and $c_{i,i'} = 0$ otherwise.
4. Repeat steps 1 through 3 NSAMP times and estimate the adjusted p-value $\tilde{p}_{i,i'}$ as the proportion of samples for which $c_{i,i'} = 1$. Call the resulting estimate $\hat{\tilde{p}}_{i,i'}$.

You can set the accuracy of the adjusted p-values easily by using the NSAMP= option. The standard error of the estimate $\hat{\tilde{p}}_{i,i'}$ is

$$s.e.(\hat{\tilde{p}}_{i,i'}) = \sqrt{\frac{\hat{\tilde{p}}_{i,i'}(1 - \hat{\tilde{p}}_{i,i'})}{NSAMP}}.$$

Thus, if you set NSAMP $= 10000$, the standard error of an estimated adjusted p-value $\hat{\tilde{p}}_{i,i'} = 0.06$ is $\sqrt{0.06(1 - 0.06)/10000} = 0.0024$. This means that the true adjusted p-value $\tilde{p}_{i,i'} = P(\max_{j,j'} |T_{j,j'}| > |t_{i,i'}|)$ would be within $\pm 2.576(0.0024)$ of 0.06, or between 0.054 and 0.066, with 99 percent confidence. Again, the idea of "confidence" in the simulation setting refers to the fact that 99 percent of the simulations (using random seeds as generated, for example, by the computer clock) will yield a similarly constructed interval estimate that contains the true adjusted p-value $\tilde{p}_{i,i'}$.

The default value of NSAMP ensures that a p-value around 0.05 will be estimated between 0.045 and 0.055 with 99 percent confidence. If you want more accuracy then you can choose a value of NSAMP as large as your time and computing resources allow. Computing time is approximately linear in the value of NSAMP, so you can determine approximately the time for a large NSAMP by extrapolating from the times of two runs with smaller, distinct NSAMP values. Be advised that the largest values of NSAMP also require more RAM, so it might not be feasible to evaluate estimates with extremely large NSAMP values due to memory constraints.

Program 4.7 is used to calculate the adjusted *p*-values for the recovery data using NSAMP=4000000. It takes less than 2 minutes on a Pentium 300 MhZ personal computer with 64 Megabytes of RAM.

PROGRAM 4.7   **Getting Greater Simulation Accuracy Using the NSAMP= Option**

```
proc glm data=recover;
   class blanket;
   model minutes=blanket;
   lsmeans blanket/ pdiff cl adjust=simulate (NSAMP=4000000 seed=121211);
run;
```

Output from Program 4.7

```
            Least Squares Means for effect blanket
              Pr > |t| for H0: LSMean(i)=LSMean(j)

                  Dependent Variable: minutes

       i/j          1           2           3           4

        1                     0.5329      0.0002      0.2382
        2        0.5329                   0.0673      0.9912
        3        0.0002      0.0673                   0.0053
        4        0.2382      0.9912      0.0053
```

The true value of $\tilde{p}_{2,3}$ is between $0.0673 \pm 2.576\sqrt{0.0673(1 - 0.0673)/4000000}$, or between 0.06727 and 0.06733, with 99 percent confidence. Note that the Tukey-Kramer approximation shown in the output from Program 4.6 is 0.0729, clearly conservative. In fact, all of the Tukey-Kramer adjusted *p*-values shown in the output from Program 4.6 are larger than the simulation-based adjusted *p*-values shown in the output from Program 4.7.

4.3 Pairwise Comparisons with Control

In the recovery example that we are using in this chapter, you might only be interested in whether the new blanket types differ from the existing standard blanket. If you are willing to ignore any comparisons between the new blanket types, then your confidence intervals will be narrower and your tests more powerful if you compare the new types with the standard only. This is Dunnett's method, described in Chapter 3, Section 3.4.

Unlike the case of all pairwise comparisons, the critical value c_α and the adjusted *p*-values can be calculated analytically for Dunnett's method in the case of all pairwise comparisons with a control. In other words, there is no need to use approximations (like Tukey-Kramer) or simulations to obtain these values.

4.3.1 Distributions

Following Chapter 3, suppose the means are $\bar{y}_0, \bar{y}_1, \ldots, \bar{y}_g$, where $\bar{y}_0$ denotes the sample mean for the control group.

To get the critical values and adjusted p-values for two-sided intervals and tests, you need the distribution of

$$M_2 = \max_i \frac{|\bar{y}_i - \bar{y}_0|}{\hat{\sigma}\sqrt{1/n_i + 1/n_0}}.$$

The critical value c_α for the two-sided confidence intervals for $\mu_i - \mu_0$ is the $1 - \alpha$ quantile of the distribution of this M_2, and adjusted p-values for two-sided tests are given as $\tilde{p}_i = P(M_2 \geq |t_i|)$, where t_i is the test statistic for $H_{0i}: \mu_i - \mu_0 = 0$, $t_i = (\bar{y}_i - \bar{y}_0)/(\hat{\sigma}\sqrt{1/n_i + 1/n_0})$.

Similarly, to get the critical values and adjusted p-values for one-sided intervals and tests, you need the distribution of

$$M_1 = \max_i \frac{\bar{y}_i - \bar{y}_0}{\hat{\sigma}\sqrt{1/n_i + 1/n_0}}.$$

The critical value c_α for the one-sided confidence bounds is the $1 - \alpha$ quantile of the distribution of this M_1. Adjusted p-values for one-sided, upper-tail tests are given as $\tilde{p}_i = P(M_1 \geq t_i)$, and adjusted p-values for one-sided, lower-tail tests are given as $\tilde{p}_i = P(M_1 \geq -t_i)$.

The distributions of M_1 and M_2 are reasonably simple two-dimensional integrals that can be evaluated numerically with excellent precision. As given by Hochberg and Tamhane (1987, p. 141),

$$P(M_1 \leq m) = \int_0^\infty \int_{-\infty}^\infty \prod_{i=1}^g \Phi\left[\frac{\lambda_i z + mu}{(1 - \lambda_i^2)^{1/2}}\right] d\Phi(z)\, dF_{df}(u)$$

and

$$P(M_2 \leq m) = \int_0^\infty \int_{-\infty}^\infty \prod_{i=1}^g \left\{\Phi\left[\frac{\lambda_i z + mu}{(1 - \lambda_i^2)^{1/2}}\right] - \Phi\left[\frac{\lambda_i z - mu}{(1 - \lambda_i^2)^{1/2}}\right]\right\} d\Phi(z)\, dF_{df}(u),$$

where

$$\frac{d\Phi(z)}{dz} = \frac{1}{\sqrt{2\pi}} e^{-\frac{z^2}{2}}$$

is the standard normal density function and

$$\frac{dF_\nu(u)}{du} = \frac{\nu^{\frac{\nu}{2}}}{\Gamma(\frac{\nu}{2})2^{\frac{\nu}{2}-1}} u^{\nu-1} e^{-\frac{\nu u^2}{2}}$$

is the density of $\sqrt{V/\nu}$, where V is a Chi-squared random variable with ν degrees of freedom.

The parameters λ_i are given as

$$\lambda_i = \left(\frac{n_i}{n_0 + n_i}\right)^{1/2}.$$

These distributions are calculated using the PROBMC function. In Program 4.8, we calculate the critical value that is used for the two-sided confidence intervals comparing new blankets with the standard blanket, and we calculate the adjusted p-value for the test of blanket "b3" against the standard "b0".

PROGRAM 4.8   **Dunnett's Exact Two-sided Critical Value for Unbalanced ANOVA**

```
data;
   n0=20; n1=3; n2=3; n3=15;
   lambda1 = sqrt(n1/(n0+n1));
   lambda2 = sqrt(n2/(n0+n2));
   lambda3 = sqrt(n3/(n0+n3));
   c_alpha = probmc('DUNNETT2',.,.,.95,37,3,lambda1,lambda2,lambda3);
   t3 = -1.66666667/0.88477275;
   adjp_3 = 1-probmc('DUNNETT2',abs(t3),.,37,3,lambda1,lambda2,lambda3);
run;
proc print; var c_alpha adjp_3; run;
```

Output from Program 4.8

```
      OBS    C_ALPHA    ADJP_3

       1     2.48867    0.18198
```

The critical value 2.48867 is smaller than the simulation-based value from the all pairwise comparisons analysis, 2.65379. This demonstrates how you get more power by restricting your attention only to pairwise comparisons with the control. Note that the adjusted p-value for the comparison of "b3" with "b0" is 0.18198 in this analysis, which is less than the simulation-based adjusted p-value 0.2382 for all pairwise comparisons, again indicating more power.

The big difference between comparisons with a control and all-pairwise comparisons is that the critical value and adjusted p-values can be calculated exactly, rather than merely approximated (e.g., using simulation or Tukey-Kramer).

4.3.2   Two-Sided Comparisons

You don't need to compute Dunnett's quantiles and p-values by hand; the GLM procedure will do it for you. For example, all two-sided intervals and tests for comparing the new blankets to the standard blankets are computed using Program 4.9.

PROGRAM 4.9   **Dunnett's Two-Sided Comparisons with Unbalanced Data**

```
proc glm data=recover;
   class blanket;
   model minutes = blanket;
   lsmeans blanket/pdiff cl adjust=dunnett;
run;
```

Output from Program 4.9: Simultaneous Confidence Intervals

		Least Squares Means for Effect blanket		
i	j	Difference Between Means	Simultaneous 95% Confidence Interval for LSMean(i)-LSMean(j)	
2	1	-2.133333	-6.124626	1.857959
3	1	-7.466667	-11.457959	-3.475374
4	1	-1.666667	-3.868572	0.535239

The intervals show that the mean for the control group "b0" is significantly larger than the mean for blanket "b2", but as in the case of all pairwise comparisons, no other comparisons are significant. The specific significance levels are given by the adjusted p-values.

Output from Program 4.9: Adjusted p-Values

```
                  General Linear Models Procedure
                       Least Squares Means
              Adjustment for multiple comparisons: Dunnett


            BLANKET        MINUTES        Pr > |T| H0:
                           LSMEAN       LSMEAN=CONTROL


              b0         14.8000000
              b1         12.6666667        0.4559
              b2          7.3333333        0.0001
              b3         13.1333333        0.1820
```

An application of these adjusted p-values would be that the comparison "b3" versus "b0" is significant when using confidence intervals with FWE > 0.1820. Since this error rate is usually considered too large, we would not claim that "b3" differs from "b0".

Note that the value 0.1820 is calculated directly in Program 4.7.

4.3.3 One-Sided Comparisons

If you feel comfortable in restricting your inferences further, so that you make a claim only when a new blanket has significantly lower recovery time than the existing blanket, then you can improve the power of your tests by restricting to one-sided inferences. In the case of the blankets, you can calculate simultaneous upper confidence bounds for the differences $\mu_i - \mu_0$ and find significant differences when the upper bound is less than zero. Using tests, you can calculate the adjusted p-values for the hypotheses $H_{0i} : \mu_i - \mu_0 = 0$ versus $H_{Ai} : \mu_i - \mu_0 < 0$. The critical value c_α for the upper confidence bounds and the adjusted p-value for the test of "b3" versus "b0" in the blanket data are found using Program 4.10.

PROGRAM 4.10   **Dunnett's Exact One-sided Critical Value for Unbalanced ANOVA**

```
data;
   n0=20; n1=3; n2=3; n3=15;
   lambda1 = sqrt(n1/(n0+n1));
   lambda2 = sqrt(n2/(n0+n2));
   lambda3 = sqrt(n3/(n0+n3));
   c_alpha = probmc('DUNNETT1',.,.,.90,37,3,lambda1,lambda2,lambda3);
   t3 = -1.66666667/0.88477275;
   adjp_3 = 1-probmc('DUNNETT1',-t3,.,.,37,3,lambda1,lambda2,lambda3);
run;
proc print; var c_alpha adjp_3; run;
```

Output from Program 4.10

```
            OBS     C_ALPHA      ADJP_3

             1      1.84307     0.092439
```

The critical value $c_\alpha = 1.84307$ is incorporated automatically in the analysis using Program 4.11.

PROGRAM 4.11   **Dunnett's One-Sided Comparisons with Unbalanced Data**

```
proc glm data=recover;
   class blanket;
   model minutes = blanket;
   lsmeans blanket/pdiff=controll cl alpha=0.10;
run;
```

Output from Program 4.11

```
                        The GLM Procedure
                      Least Squares Means
              Adjustment for Multiple Comparisons: Dunnett
```

		H0:LSMean=
	minutes	Control
blanket	LSMEAN	Pr < t
b0	14.8000000	
b1	12.6666667	0.2412
b2	7.3333333	<.0001
b3	13.1333333	0.0924

	minutes		
blanket	LSMEAN	90% Confidence Interval	
b0	14.800000	13.822802	15.777198
b1	12.666667	10.143553	15.189781
b2	7.333333	4.810219	9.856447
b3	13.133333	12.004962	14.261704

```
             Least Squares Means for Effect blanket
```

		Difference Between	Simultaneous 90% Confidence Interval for	
i	j	Means	LSMean(i)-LSMean(j)	
2	1	-2.133333	-Infinity	0.822564
3	1	-7.466667	-Infinity	-4.510770
4	1	-1.666667	-Infinity	-0.035965

The upper confidence bound 0.822564 for the "b1-b0" mean comparison is $-2.1333 + 1.84307(1.60378681)$. Note that with the more powerful, one-sided comparisons, and with the more liberal ALPHA=0.10 significance level, the "b3-b0" comparison is now significant.

4.4   Concluding Remarks

In this chapter we have presented analyses for simultaneous intervals and tests in the unbalanced one-way ANOVA. Where possible, exact methods should be used. Thus, for pairwise comparisons with a control (one- or two-sided), you should use Dunnett's method (either the one-sided or the two-sided version, depending on the goals of the study), and definitely not the more conservative methods, like Bonferroni.

For all pairwise comparisons, the choice is less clearcut because there is no software for calculating the critical values exactly. Thus, we recommend either using the Tukey-Kramer or the simulation-based methods.

Regarding the choice between these, we recommend the following:

- If the slight variation in the simulation-based approach will not affect your decisions appreciably, or if you have sufficient time and computing resources to ensure that this is so, then you should use the LSMEANS statement and the ADJUST=SIMULATE option.

- If you are uncomfortable using confidence intervals and adjusted p-values that will differ slightly with each re-analysis of the same data (with different random number seeds for the simulation) then use the MEANS statement and the TUKEY method.

A final note: if the sample sizes differ only slightly, then the Tukey-Kramer approach will be quite accurate and only slightly conservative. The less balanced the data, the more you should prefer using the simulation-based method.

Chapter 5

Multiple Comparisons among Treatment Means in the General Linear Model

5.1 Introduction

In Chapter 3 we discussed various multiple comparisons methods in the balanced one-way ANOVA. This model is fairly restrictive, and we discussed the necessary modifications for the unbalanced case in Chapter 4. However, the unbalanced one-way ANOVA model is still restrictive in that it does not allow covariates.

Fortunately, many of the methods developed in Chapters 3 and 4 have simple counterparts for more general linear models. As in Chapters 3 and 4, the methods discussed in this chapter will account for specific distributional characteristics of the estimates, implying that these methods are more powerful than the methods of Chapter 2 based on Bonferroni's and other probability bounds. In this chapter we develop simultaneous confidence intervals and tests for comparing mean values in the general linear model; however, we still assume independent, normally distributed, and homoscedastic errors. We give the form of the general linear model and discuss the associated comparisons. The balanced ANOVA, unbalanced ANOVA, and the analysis of covariance (ANCOVA) can be viewed as special cases of the general framework.

Because the material in this chapter is so general, we will frequently refer back to it in later chapters.

The following example is a five-group unbalanced ANCOVA, with two covariates.

EXAMPLE: Comparing Housing Prices in Different Sectors

Location, location, location! As real estate agents will tell you, the price of a house depends on its location within a city. It also depends on the size of the house, its age and other characteristics. If homes in a given neighborhood tend to be older and smaller than homes in another neighborhood, then the prices will be lower, even if the neighborhoods are equally attractive in other ways (low crime rates, short distance from schools, etc.) Thus, to compare locations fairly, you need to adjust for such factors.

We will use the data set defined in the following SAS program repeatedly in this section to compare average prices of homes in different locations. The data set has the classic ANCOVA structure, with one classification variable (`location`), two covariates (`age` and `sqfeet`), and unbalanced sample sizes (unequal numbers of houses at each location). The response variable is the price (in $1,000's) of the home.

PROGRAM 5.1   Selling Prices of Homes

```
data house;
    input location$ price sqfeet age @@;
datalines;
A 113.5 2374 4    A 119.9 2271 8    A 127.9 2088 5
A  92.5 1645 8    A 103.0 1814 6    A 142.1 2553 7
A 120.5 1921 9    A 105.5 1854 2    A 101.2 1536 9
A  94.7 1677 3    A 129.0 2342 5    A 108.7 1862 4
A  99.7 1894 7    A 112.0 1774 9    A 104.8 1476 8
A  86.1 1466 7    A 103.5 1800 8    A  93.0 1491 5
A  99.5 1749 8    A  98.1 1690 7    A 144.8 2741 5
A  96.3 1460 5    A  95.1 1614 6    A 125.8 2244 6
A 126.9 2165 6    A 104.7 1828 4    B  74.2 1503 6
B  69.9 1689 6    B  77.0 1638 2    B  67.0 1276 6
B  98.9 2101 9    B  81.2 1668 5    B  85.7 2123 4
B  99.8 2208 5    B  55.7 1273 8    B 120.1 2519 4
B 109.1 2303 6    B  82.4 1800 3    B 102.7 2336 8
B  92.0 2100 6    B  84.1 1697 4    C  90.8 1674 4
C  98.2 2307 7    C  94.6 2152 5    C  87.9 1948 9
D 102.5 2258 2    D  81.3 1965 6    D  86.1 1772 3
D  94.7 2385 1    D  64.7 1345 4    D  93.5 2220 8
D  80.1 1883 8    D  92.3 2012 6    D  80.6 1898 5
E 105.3 2362 7    E 106.3 2362 7    E  84.3 1963 9
E  76.6 1941 7    E  82.4 1975 5    E  98.8 2529 6
E  86.8 2079 5    E  88.5 2190 4    E  77.5 1897 5
E  86.9 1946 4
;
```

The goal of the study is to compare all locations, controlling for size and age, using simultaneous confidence intervals. Program 5.2 contains our recommended method of analysis. It produces the resulting confidence intervals for differences of locations, adjusted for size and age as shown in the output. Notice that, as in Chapter 4, we consider the ADJUST=SIMULATE method to be the generally preferred analysis. Also, notice that we use the new *Output Delivery System* (ODS), available starting with Version 7, to customize the reported output. You will see the ODS feature more and more as we progress through this book.

PROGRAM 5.2   Simultaneous Confidence Intervals for Mean Differences in ANCOVA

```
ods select LSMeanDiffCL;
proc glm data=house;
    class location;
    model price = location sqfeet age;
    lsmeans location / pdiff cl adjust=simulate(seed=12345 cvadjust);
run;
```

**Output from
Program 5.2**

The GLM Procedure
Least Squares Means

Adjustment for Multiple Comparisons: Simulated

Least Squares Means for Effect location

i	j	Difference Between Means	Simultaneous 95% Confidence Interval for LSMean(i)-LSMean(j)	
1	2	22.203200	16.585689	27.820711
1	3	21.528513	12.289095	30.767932
1	4	26.015221	19.189281	32.841160
1	5	29.089325	22.533429	35.645222
2	3	-0.674687	-10.406621	9.057247
2	4	3.812020	-3.473484	11.097524
2	5	6.886125	-0.317347	14.089597
3	4	4.486707	-5.951959	14.925373
3	5	7.560812	-2.605157	17.726781
4	5	3.074105	-4.976947	11.125157

Note that level 1 corresponds to location A, 2 to B, and so on. See the ORDER= option of PROC GLM for details. (In PROC MIXED, discussed in Chapter 10 of this book, the levels of the class variables are displayed directly in the output.)

The `Difference Between Means` column shows the difference in average price, adjusted to average levels of the covariates SIZE and AGE. Since the model assumes no interaction, the differences in mean price for the different location pairs are assumed constant for all SIZE and AGE values.

As usual, significant differences between groups (locations in this case) are determined by noting whether the confidence interval excludes zero. In this case, location 1 (coded A in the input data set) has a significantly higher adjusted mean than all other locations, but no significant differences are found between any of the remaining locations B–E.

Note also that we have recommended the ADJUST=SIMULATE option rather than any of the more familiar methods such as Tukey's, Bonferroni's, etc. The reason for this is that these other methods incorporate the correlation structures only in an approximate sense. The ADJUST=SIMULATE method, on the other hand, incorporates the exact correlation structure, and the critical values can be estimated adequately with a sufficient number of simulations. Our general recommendation is to use the ADJUST=SIMULATE method, although as we shall see, in many cases the approximations such as Tukey-Kramer that are provided by default are reasonably adequate. However, it is somewhat difficult to characterize how well the various approximations work in all applications, while the ADJUST=SIMULATE method always works well.

In the remainder of this chapter, we develop the methodology for this and related analyses of ANCOVA data. To do so, we will develop a more general notation that applies beyond the ANCOVA case.

5.2   The Model and Estimates

To develop the basic methods of MCPs that incorporate dependence structures, you must specify the model and the parameters of interest. In this section we present the general linear model, the estimates obtained from it, and the multivariate t distribution, which is fundamentally important for simultaneous inferences in these more general settings.

5.2.1   The Model

The model for the data throughout this chapter is assumed to be

$$\mathbf{Y} = \mathbf{X}\boldsymbol{\beta} + \boldsymbol{\epsilon},$$

where $\mathbf{Y}$ is the $n \times 1$ observation vector, $\mathbf{X}$ is the fixed and known $n \times p$ design matrix, $\boldsymbol{\beta}$ is the fixed and unknown $p \times 1$ parameter vector, and $\boldsymbol{\epsilon}$ is the random, unobservable $n \times 1$ error vector. The model implies that each observation y_i follows the linear model

$$y_i = x_{i1}\beta_1 + \cdots + x_{ip}\beta_p + \epsilon_i.$$

Using the data from the housing price example, a standard parameterization of the model might be

$$\mathbf{Y} = \begin{pmatrix} 113.5 \\ 119.9 \\ \vdots \\ 104.7 \\ 74.2 \\ 69.9 \\ \vdots \\ 84.1 \\ \vdots \\ \vdots \\ 105.3 \\ 106.3 \\ \vdots \\ 86.9 \end{pmatrix}, \quad \mathbf{X} = \begin{pmatrix} 1 & 1 & 0 & 0 & 0 & 0 & 2374 & 4 \\ 1 & 1 & 0 & 0 & 0 & 0 & 2271 & 8 \\ \vdots & \vdots & \vdots & \vdots & \vdots & \vdots & \vdots & \vdots \\ 1 & 1 & 0 & 0 & 0 & 0 & 1828 & 4 \\ 1 & 0 & 1 & 0 & 0 & 0 & 1503 & 6 \\ 1 & 0 & 1 & 0 & 0 & 0 & 1689 & 6 \\ \vdots & \vdots & \vdots & \vdots & \vdots & \vdots & \vdots & \vdots \\ 1 & 0 & 1 & 0 & 0 & 0 & 1697 & 4 \\ \vdots & \vdots & \vdots & \vdots & \vdots & \vdots & \vdots & \vdots \\ \vdots & \vdots & \vdots & \vdots & \vdots & \vdots & \vdots & \vdots \\ 1 & 0 & 0 & 0 & 0 & 1 & 2362 & 7 \\ 1 & 0 & 0 & 0 & 0 & 1 & 2362 & 7 \\ \vdots & \vdots & \vdots & \vdots & \vdots & \vdots & \vdots & \vdots \\ 1 & 0 & 0 & 0 & 0 & 1 & 1946 & 4 \end{pmatrix},$$

$$\boldsymbol{\beta} = \begin{pmatrix} \gamma \\ \mu_1 \\ \mu_2 \\ \mu_3 \\ \mu_4 \\ \mu_5 \\ \beta_1 \\ \beta_2 \end{pmatrix}, \quad \text{and } \boldsymbol{\epsilon} = \begin{pmatrix} \epsilon_1 \\ \epsilon_2 \\ \vdots \\ \vdots \\ \epsilon_{64} \end{pmatrix}.$$

For this parameterization,

- the first column of $\mathbf{X}$ containing all 1's corresponds to the intercept parameter γ
- the next five columns correspond to the five different location groups, with parameters $\mu_1, \ldots, \mu_5$
- the last two columns correspond to the two covariates, with parameters β_1 and β_2.

This is the typical model that is used for analysis of covariance in PROC GLM. Note that it is *over-determined*. Because of linear dependencies in the $\mathbf{X}$ matrix, you can't estimate all of the parameters unbiasedly. In particular, since the intercept column is the sum of the columns that are associated with the location groups, the parameters $\gamma, \mu_1, \ldots, \mu_5$ are not estimable. However, with this parameterization, quantities of interest such as the location means adjusted for the covariates *can be* represented as certain (estimable) linear combinations of the parameters, despite the fact that the individual parameters themselves are not estimable. For more information on how and why PROC GLM and PROC MIXED use this parameterization, see the PROC GLM chapter in the *SAS/STAT User's Guide, Version 7-1*.

The assumptions of the model can be stated in terms of $\boldsymbol{\epsilon} = (\epsilon_1, \epsilon_2, \ldots, \epsilon_n)$:

1. $\epsilon_1, \epsilon_2, \ldots, \epsilon_n$ all have mean zero.
2. $\epsilon_1, \epsilon_2, \ldots, \epsilon_n$ all have common variance, σ^2.
3. $\epsilon_1, \epsilon_2, \ldots, \epsilon_n$ all are independent random variables.
4. $\epsilon_1, \epsilon_2, \ldots, \epsilon_n$ all are normally distributed.

Except for the first assumption, these are the same assumptions that we discussed in Section 3.2 of Chapter 3.

Assumption 1 is equivalently stated as $E(\mathbf{Y}) = \mathbf{X}\boldsymbol{\beta}$, which means that the means of the distributions of $\mathbf{Y}$ are specified by $\mathbf{X}\boldsymbol{\beta}$. This assumption is violated when, for example, the covariates affect the response in nonlinear fashion, but are modelled with a simple linear effect. Scatterplots are useful diagnostics tools for assessing this assumption, as are residual plots. These are discussed further in regression analysis textbooks.

Assumption 2 can also be checked using residual plots; see regression analysis textbooks.

Assumption 3 is crucial, as discussed in Chapter 3, and can be assessed using subject matter considerations. Repeated observations on an individual usually leads to a violation of this assumption. The assumption also is violated often with time-series data, and in such cases you can examine the autocorrelation of the residuals to assess violation of this assumption. Methods for dealing with correlated residuals are discussed in Chapter 10.

Assumption 4 can be assessed using the residual q-q plot.

5.2.2   The Estimates

In the model, $\mathbf{X}'\mathbf{X}$ may be noninvertible, hence we use a generalized inverse $(\mathbf{X}'\mathbf{X})^-$ rather than the ordinary inverse $(\mathbf{X}'\mathbf{X})^{-1}$ in computing the parameter estimates. This implies that some functions of the parameters in $\boldsymbol{\beta}$ are nonestimable. For discussion of generalized inverses and estimability conditions in overparameterized models, see Searle (1971). The covariate-adjusted differences $\mu_i - \mu_j$ are estimable, and our focus is on multiple comparisons of such estimable parameters. Such estimable functions are expressed in terms of

$$\hat{\boldsymbol{\beta}} = (\mathbf{X}'\mathbf{X})^-\mathbf{X}'\mathbf{Y}.$$

The estimate of variance is the mean square for error

$$\hat{\sigma}^2 = (\mathbf{Y} - \mathbf{X}\hat{\boldsymbol{\beta}})'(\mathbf{Y} - \mathbf{X}\hat{\boldsymbol{\beta}})/df,$$

where $df = (n - \text{rank}\mathbf{X})$. The degrees of freedom parameter (df) is the sample size, minus the number of linearly independent columns in $\mathbf{X}$. In the housing example, there is a perfect dependency among the columns of $\mathbf{X}$, the first column is the sum of columns 2 through 6. Removing one of columns 2 through 6 (the standard "dummy variable" parameterization used in regression analysis) results in an $\mathbf{X}$ matrix with full column rank. Thus, the degrees of freedom for error in the housing example are $df = 64 - 7 = 57$.

A general form of estimable linear function is $\mathbf{c}'\boldsymbol{\beta}$ (see Scheffé, 1959, p. 13 for characterization of estimable functions), which is a linear combination of the parameters in $\boldsymbol{\beta}$. In the housing example above, for example, $\mu_1 - \mu_2 = \mathbf{c}'\boldsymbol{\beta}$, where $\mathbf{c}' = (0\ 1\ -1\ 0\ 0\ 0\ 0)$. The estimated difference is then $\hat{\mu}_1 - \hat{\mu}_2 = \mathbf{c}'\hat{\boldsymbol{\beta}}$.

To obtain simultaneous inferences, we need the standard errors of the estimates. For a general estimable function $\mathbf{c}'\boldsymbol{\beta}$, the variance of the estimate is

$$Var(\mathbf{c}'\hat{\boldsymbol{\beta}}) = \sigma^2 \mathbf{c}'(\mathbf{X}'\mathbf{X})^{-}\mathbf{c}.$$

The standard error is the estimated standard deviation of the estimate, or

$$s.e.(\mathbf{c}'\hat{\boldsymbol{\beta}}) = \hat{\sigma}\sqrt{\mathbf{c}'(\mathbf{X}'\mathbf{X})^{-}\mathbf{c}}.$$

A family of inferences can be characterized by a collection of linear combination vectors $\mathbf{c}_i$. For example, in the case of all pairwise comparisons of covariate-adjusted means, the vectors are

$$
\begin{array}{rcrrrrrrrr}
\mathbf{c}_1' = & (0 & 1 & -1 & 0 & 0 & 0 & 0 & 0) \\
\mathbf{c}_2' = & (0 & 1 & 0 & -1 & 0 & 0 & 0 & 0) \\
 & \vdots & \vdots & \vdots & \vdots & \vdots & \vdots & \vdots & \vdots \\
\mathbf{c}_{10}' = & (0 & 0 & 0 & 0 & 1 & -1 & 0 & 0)
\end{array}
$$

$$\text{corresponding to} \quad \gamma \quad \mu_1 \quad \mu_2 \quad \mu_3 \quad \mu_4 \quad \mu_5 \quad \beta_1 \quad \beta_2.$$

5.2.3 The Multivariate *t* Distribution

To get accurate simultaneous intervals for a given family of estimable parameters $\{\mathbf{c}_1'\boldsymbol{\beta}, \mathbf{c}_2'\boldsymbol{\beta}, \ldots, \mathbf{c}_k'\boldsymbol{\beta}\}$ you need to know the dependence structure of their estimates. As usual, the simultaneous inferences use the joint distribution of the pivotal quantities

$$T_i = \frac{\mathbf{c}_i'\hat{\boldsymbol{\beta}} - \mathbf{c}_i'\boldsymbol{\beta}}{\hat{\sigma}\sqrt{\mathbf{c}_i'(\mathbf{X}'\mathbf{X})^{-}\mathbf{c}_i}}.$$

The joint distribution of $\{T_1, \ldots, T_k\}$ is called the multivariate t distribution, defined formally as follows.

DEFINITION: **The Multivariate *t* Distribution**

If $Z_1, \ldots, Z_k$ are distributed as standard normal variables, with zero means and unit variances, and with known correlation matrix $\mathbf{R}$, and if V is a random variable distributed as Chi-Square with df degrees of freedom, independent of $\mathbf{Z} = (Z_1, \ldots, Z_k)$, then $\mathbf{t} = \mathbf{Z}/\sqrt{V/df}$ has the multivariate t distribution with dispersion matrix $\mathbf{R}$ and degrees of freedom df.

The mathematical form of the multivariate t density function can be found in Hochberg and Tamhane (1987, p. 375).

The multivariate t distribution arises if you want to calculate the critical value c_α for simultaneous intervals for an arbitrary family of estimable linear combinations in the general model.

5.2.4 Simultaneous Inferences for Estimable Functions

Confidence intervals for the estimable functions $\mathbf{c}_i'\boldsymbol{\beta}$ have the form

$$\mathbf{c}_i'\hat{\boldsymbol{\beta}} \pm c_\alpha s.e.(\mathbf{c}_i'\hat{\boldsymbol{\beta}}),$$

where c_α is a critical value that is selected to make the FWE $= \alpha$ for the collection of inferences concerning your parameters $\mathbf{c}_1'\boldsymbol{\beta}, \mathbf{c}_2'\boldsymbol{\beta}, \ldots, \mathbf{c}_k'\boldsymbol{\beta}$.

In the case of nonmultiplicity adjusted confidence intervals, you set $c_\alpha = t_{1-\alpha/2, df}$. Conservative Bonferroni-based inferences are obtained simply by using $\alpha' = \alpha/k$ in place of α in the critical value. However, as discussed in Chapter 3, the Bonferroni method is conservative in that the value of c_α is larger than it needs to be. In other words, the Bonferroni intervals will be wide enough to simultaneously contain the true $\mathbf{c}_i'\boldsymbol{\beta}$ values *more than* $(1 - \alpha) \cdot 100\%$ of the time. We can improve upon this value by using the Multivariate t distribution, which depends upon the correlations among the estimates $\mathbf{c}_i\hat{\boldsymbol{\beta}}$. These correlations in turn depend on specific design characteristics given by the design matrix $\mathbf{X}$, and on the specific set of linear functions that you have specified.

The desired value of c_α satisfies

$$P(\mathbf{c}_i'\hat{\boldsymbol{\beta}} - c_\alpha s.e.(\mathbf{c}_i'\hat{\boldsymbol{\beta}}) < \mathbf{c}_i'\boldsymbol{\beta} < \mathbf{c}_i'\hat{\boldsymbol{\beta}} + c_\alpha s.e.(\mathbf{c}_i'\hat{\boldsymbol{\beta}}), \text{ for all } i) = 1 - \alpha,$$

or, re-arranging terms,

$$P\left(\left|\frac{\mathbf{c}_i'\hat{\boldsymbol{\beta}} - \mathbf{c}_i'\boldsymbol{\beta}}{\hat{\sigma}\sqrt{\mathbf{c}_i'(\mathbf{X}'\mathbf{X})^-\mathbf{c}_i}}\right| \leq c_\alpha, \text{ for all } i\right) = 1 - \alpha.$$

Now the joint distribution of the quantities

$$T_i = \frac{\mathbf{c}_i'\hat{\boldsymbol{\beta}} - \mathbf{c}_i'\boldsymbol{\beta}}{\hat{\sigma}\sqrt{\mathbf{c}_i'(\mathbf{X}'\mathbf{X})^-\mathbf{c}_i}}$$

is multivariate t, with degrees of freedom $df = (n - \text{rank}\mathbf{X})$ and dispersion matrix $\mathbf{R} = \mathbf{D}^{-1/2}\mathbf{C}'(\mathbf{X}'\mathbf{X})^-\mathbf{C}\mathbf{D}^{-1/2}$, where $\mathbf{C} = (\mathbf{c}_1, \ldots, \mathbf{c}_k)$, and where $\mathbf{D}$ is a diagonal matrix having ith element equal to $\mathbf{c}_i'(\mathbf{X}'\mathbf{X})^-\mathbf{c}_i$. The value of c_α is thus the $1 - \alpha$ quantile of the distribution of $\max_i |T_i|$, where the vector $\mathbf{T}' = (T_1, \ldots, T_k)$ has the indicated multivariate t distribution.

An important feature of the multivariate t distribution is that it is *pivotal*, or free of unknown parameters. Therefore, exact inferences are possible, at least in principle, when using quantiles derived from this distribution. In practice, the critical values and significance levels might have to be calculated via simulation, as analytic calculations are unavailable using current technology. But, with large simulation sizes, the correct critical values can be obtained with sufficient precision. Simulation-based methods are described in detail in the next section.

The assumptions of the general linear model we consider in this chapter are particularly important for the pivotality of the $\max |T_i|$ statistic. In later chapters, (Chapters 10 and on), where the models are more complex, such pivotal distributions are unavailable, meaning that the distributions of statistics like $\max |T_i|$ depend on unknown parameters. In such cases, it is impossible to obtain the correct critical values, no matter how large the simulation size, since they depend on the particular values of the unknown parameters. However, as we will show, in many cases it is reasonable to substitute the appropriate estimated parameters to obtain the distribution of $\max |T_i|$. The resulting inferences are only approximately correct, but usually are adequate, particularly with moderately large sample sizes.

5.3 All Pairwise Comparisons in ANCOVA Models

In Chapter 3 we used Tukey's range, Dunnett's range, and maximum modulus distributions to account for dependencies among the estimates. As we saw in Chapter 4, the Range distribution becomes inexact in the case of unbalanced data, while the Dunnett one- and two-sided distributions remain exact (with suitable modifications). When we include covariates, none of these distributions is exact in general; however, the quantiles can be simulated with relative ease and adequate accuracy from the appropriate multivariate t distribution. This is the approach taken in Program 5.2 with the housing data and the ADJUST=SIMULATE option.

5.3.1 Confidence Intervals

To obtain simultaneous confidence intervals, the general form of c_α described above will be calculated using the contrasts $c_1, \ldots, c_{10}$ shown earlier in Section 5.2.2.

You can display the estimated critical value c_α along with other useful information by specifying the REPORT suboption with the ADJUST=SIMULATE option. Note again the use of the ODS feature.

PROGRAM 5.3   **Viewing Simulation Details when Using `adjust=simulate`**

```
ods select SimDetails
           SimResults
           LSMeanDiffCL;
proc glm data=house;
   class location;
   model price = location sqfeet age;
   lsmeans location / pdiff cl adjust=simulate(seed=12345 report cvadjust);
run;
```

Output from Program 5.3

The GLM Procedure
Least Squares Means

Details for Quantile Simulation

Random number seed	12345
Comparison type	All
Sample size	12604
Target alpha	0.05
Accuracy radius (target)	0.005
Accuracy radius (actual)	0.003
Accuracy confidence	99%

Simulation Results

Method	95% Quantile	Estimated Alpha	99% Confidence Interval	
Simulated	2.795352	0.0500	0.0470	0.0529
Tukey-Kramer	2.817012	0.0474	0.0445	0.0503
Bonferroni	2.920420	0.0374	0.0342	0.0406
Sidak	2.912166	0.0382	0.0350	0.0413
GT-2	2.905590	0.0390	0.0359	0.0421
Scheffe	3.183447	0.0174	0.0133	0.0215
T	2.002465	0.2702	0.2607	0.2798

```
                        The GLM Procedure
                       Least Squares Means
              Adjustment for Multiple Comparisons: Simulated

                   Least Squares Means for Effect location
```

		Difference Between Means	Simultaneous 95% Confidence Interval for LSMean(i)-LSMean(j)	
i	j			
1	2	22.203200	16.585689	27.820711
1	3	21.528513	12.289095	30.767932
1	4	26.015221	19.189281	32.841160
1	5	29.089325	22.533429	35.645222
2	3	-0.674687	-10.406621	9.057247
2	4	3.812020	-3.473484	11.097524
2	5	6.886125	-0.317347	14.089597
3	4	4.486707	-5.951959	14.925373
3	5	7.560812	-2.605157	17.726781
4	5	3.074105	-4.976947	11.125157

The estimated value of c_α is the first number in the "95% Quantile" column, 2.795352, and is obtained by using the simulation-based approximation algorithm.

The Simulation-based Approximation Algorithm

In Chapter 4 we described how the critical value c_α can be simulated in cases where it is difficult to calculate analytically. This method can also be used in more general cases as follows:

1. Generate a vector $\mathbf{Z}^*$ that is multivariate normal with mean vector $\mathbf{0}$ and covariance matrix $\mathbf{R} = \mathbf{D}^{-1/2}\mathbf{C}'(\mathbf{X}'\mathbf{X})^-\mathbf{C}\mathbf{D}^{-1/2}$, defined in Section 5.2.4.

2. Generate V^*, a chi-squared random variable with $df = (n-\text{rank}\mathbf{X})$ degrees of freedom, independent of $\mathbf{Z}^*$, and compute $\mathbf{T}^* = \mathbf{Z}^*/\sqrt{V^*/df}$.

3. Compute and store $M^* = \max |t_j^*|$ or $M^* = \max t_j$, depending upon whether you want to perform two-sided or one-sided inferences.

4. Repeat steps 1 through 3 NSAMP times. The estimated value $\hat{c}_\alpha$ is the $1 - \alpha$ quantile of the M^* values.

These are the calculations performed using the ADJUST=SIMULATE option of the LSMEANS statement in PROC GLM and PROC MIXED. The default value of NSAMP is the sample size that makes the tail area beyond $\hat{c}_\alpha$ within 0.005 of α with 99 percent probability (i.e., the tail area for the simulated value is within 0.005 of the of $1 - \alpha$ in 99 percent of simulations). These defaults can be changed using the ACC= and EPS= options. For example, using ACC=0.002 and EPS=0.05, the tail probability of $\hat{c}_\alpha$ will be within 0.002 of $1 - \alpha$ with 95 percent probability.

A drawback of this method is that the endpoints of the confidence intervals are simulation-dependent. For example, if SEED=12345 is changed to SEED=54321, then the estimated value of c_α becomes 2.7945 instead of 2.7954. It is often important that these discrepancies be made as small as possible; if this is the case, you can allow the computer to run as long as possible to obtain more accurate estimates. To predict how long a run will take, you can use the NSAMP= option, rather than the ACC= and EPS= options. If the program takes 25 seconds with NSAMP=1000000, then it should take approximately 2500 seconds, or about 41 minutes with NSAMP=100000000. These figures are actual times obtained using the above program on the housing data, run on a Pentium 300MhZ computer with 64 M of RAM.

The results of the REPORT suboption of the ADJUST=SIMULATE option exhibit the degree of conservativeness of the various alternatives directly. For the example analyzed in the output from Program 5.3, the true FWE levels are estimated to be lower than 0.05 for all "usual" methods, Tukey-Kramer (0.0474), Bonferroni (0.0374), Šidák (0.0382), GT-2 (0.0390), and Scheffé (to be discussed in more detail in Chapter 6, 0.0174). Of course, the ordinary unadjusted t method is liberal, with FWE estimated to be 0.2702.

5.3.2 The `%SimIntervals` Macro

We now introduce a very flexible and powerful macro that can be used in a variety of multiple comparisons problems. The macro is called `%SimIntervals`, which can be shorthand for either Simultaneous Intervals, or Simulation-Based Simultaneous Intervals. We will use this macro and a closely related macro `%SimTests` in later chapters. Both are included in the appendix. For now, all we want to do is show how to use `%SimIntervals`, and show how it corresponds to the perhaps more familiar ADJUST=SIMULATE option of PROC GLM.

The simulation algorithm of the preceding section is implemented in the `%SimIntervals` macro. You can use this macro to obtain the critical value, adjusted p-values, and confidence limits for any collection of multiple contrasts in any general linear model. You may invoke the macro as follows:

```
%SimIntervals(nsamp= <number> ,
              seed = <number> ,
              conf = <number> ,
              side = <value>  );
```

where

`nsamp` is the simulation size, with 20000 as the default

`seed` is the random number seed, with 0 (the computer clock time) as the default

`conf` is the desired confidence level, with 0.95 as the default

`side` determines whether upper-tailed (`side=U`), lower-tailed (`side=L`) or two-tailed (`side=B`) are needed. The default is `side=B`.

So, how does the macro know what data to analyze? Well, the `%SimIntervals` macro uses two macros internally, `%Contrasts` and `%Estimates` that contain, respectively, the contrasts of interest and the data to which the contrasts are applied. You can specify these macros in one of three ways:

- If you have the summary statistics, you can specify the two macros directly, writing SAS/IML code to identify the needed quantities.
- Use the `%MakeGLMStats` macro, also provided in the appendix, to create the summary statistics macro (`%Estimates`) automatically. Then you specify the `%Contrasts` macro directly to identify your contrasts of interest.
- Use the `%MakeGLMStats` macro to create both the summary statistics macro (`%Estimates`) and the contrasts macro (`%Contrasts`) automatically.

(A quick note: while the word "Contrasts" is used to define the macro, and while we have suggested that you supply linear combinations that are contrasts, you do not have to specify contrasts. You can define any linear combinations using the `%Contrasts` macro, whether or not they are contrasts.)

The easiest way to learn how to use this very flexible collection of macros is by examples. The following three examples show each of the three methods for specifying the inputs using the weight loss data from Program 3.2 in Section 3.3.1. In the first of the three programs, the sample means, estimated covariance matrix, and degrees of freedom are used. (Table 3.1 in Section 3.1 shows the sample means.) In the second and third programs, the summary statistics are computed using the PROC GLM.

PROGRAM 5.4   **Invocation of %SimIntervals Using Direct Specification of %Estimates and %Contrasts**

```
%macro Estimates;
   EstPar = { 12.05 , 11.02 , 10.27 , 9.27 , 12.17 };
   Mse    = 0.9934;
   Cov    = Mse * I(5)/10 ;   /* sample size is 10 per group */
   df     = 45;
%mend;


%macro Contrasts;
   C = { 1 -1  0  0  0 ,
         1  0 -1  0  0 ,
         1  0  0 -1  0 ,
         1  0  0  0 -1 ,
         0  1 -1  0  0 ,
         0  1  0 -1  0 ,
         0  1  0  0 -1 ,
         0  0  1 -1  0 ,
         0  0  1  0 -1 ,
         0  0  0  1 -1 };
   C = C' ;                     /* transposed to coincide with notation in 5.2.2 */

   Clab = {"1-2", "1-3", "1-4", "1-5",
                  "2-3", "2-4", "2-5",
                         "3-4", "3-5",
                                "4-5" };  /* Contrast labels */
%mend;


%SimIntervals(nsamp=50000, seed=121211, conf=0.95, side=B);
```

Output from Program 5.4

Estimated 95% Quantile = 2.834955

Contrast	Estimate	Standard Error	t Value	Pr > |t| Raw	Pr > |t| Adjusted	95% Confidence Interval	
1-2	1.0300	0.4457	2.31	0.0255	0.1625	-0.2336	2.2936
1-3	1.7800	0.4457	3.99	0.0002	0.0020	0.5164	3.0436
1-4	2.7800	0.4457	6.24	<.0001	<.0001	1.5164	4.0436
1-5	-0.1200	0.4457	-0.27	0.7890	0.9987	-1.3836	1.1436
2-3	0.7500	0.4457	1.68	0.0994	0.4614	-0.5136	2.0136
2-4	1.7500	0.4457	3.93	0.0003	0.0024	0.4864	3.0136
2-5	-1.1500	0.4457	-2.58	0.0132	0.0923	-2.4136	0.1136
3-4	1.0000	0.4457	2.24	0.0298	0.1859	-0.2636	2.2636
3-5	-1.9000	0.4457	-4.26	0.0001	0.0008	-3.1636	-0.6364
4-5	-2.9000	0.4457	-6.51	<.0001	<.0001	-4.1636	-1.6364

Note that the output is the same as that given by the Tukey Intervals output from Program 3.2 shown in Section 3.3.1, with slight differences due to Monte Carlo error. In particular, the 1-2 difference shown above corresponds to the A-B difference shown in the output from Program 3.2. Above the interval is -0.2336 2.2936, and in the Tukey method the interval is -0.2365 2.2965. The Monte Carlo estimated value of c_α shown above is 2.834955, and the exact critical value (shown under the Tukey output from Program 3.2) is $c_\alpha = 2.841$.

In this situation, the exact Tukey method is recommended, rather than the approximate method of %SimIntervals. The points of doing this exercise are (1) to illustrate that the methods do in fact correspond, and (2) to demonstrate the use of %SimIntervals, which we will find to be very useful in more complex applications.

As shown in Program 5.4, the variables EstPar, Cov and df must be specified using SAS/IML code within the %Estimates macro, as these are the specific variables that eventually are used by %SimIntervals. The variables C and Clab must be created using SAS/IML code in the %Contrasts macro.

If your data come from a simple linear model, you can avoid having to specify the %Estimates macro by using the %MakeGLMStats macro that is provided in the appendix. It is invoked as follows:

```
%MakeGLMStats(dataset   = <dataset name>           ,
              classvar  = <class variable(s)>      ,
              yvar      = <response variable>       ,
              model     = <variables in model>      ,
              contrasts = <value(class variable)> );
```

where

dataset   is the SAS data set, a required input. There is no default value.

classvar is the listing of CLASS variables, separated by spaces if there is more than one. If blank, no CLASS variables are assumed for the GLM syntax.

yvar   is the response variable. There is no default; this is a required input.

model   is the GLM model specification. Again, this is a required input, with no default.

contrasts define the type of contrasts to be created, and the classification variable to which the contrasts are applied. The possible values are CONTROL(classvariable), ALL(classvariable), and USER. CONTROL(classvariable) creates pairwise contrasts with the control level (the "first" encountered level of classvariable), and ALL(classvariable) creates all pairwise contrasts of the levels of classvariable. If you specify either CONTROL(classvariable) or ALL(classvariable), then the %Contrasts macro is created automatically. If you specify contrasts=USER (the default), then you must create the %Contrasts macro yourself.

Program 5.5 shows how to use the %MakeGLMStats macro with the default value contrasts=USER.

PROGRAM 5.5   Invocation of %SimIntervals Using %MakeGLMStats

```
%MakeGLMStats(dataset=wloss, classvar=diet, yvar=wloss, model=diet);
```

```
%macro Contrasts;
   C = { 0    1 -1  0  0  0 ,
         0    1  0 -1  0  0 ,
         0    1  0  0 -1  0 ,
         0    1  0  0  0 -1 ,
         0    0  1 -1  0  0 ,
         0    0  1  0 -1  0 ,
         0    0  1  0  0 -1 ,
         0    0  0  1 -1  0 ,
         0    0  0  1  0 -1 ,
         0    0  0  0  1 -1 };
   C = C' ;                      /* transposed to coincide with notation in 5.2.2 */

   Clab = {"1-2", "1-3", "1-4", "1-5",
                  "2-3", "2-4", "2-5",
                         "3-4", "3-5",
                                "4-5" };  /* Contrast labels */
%mend;

%SimIntervals(nsamp=50000, seed=121211);
```

The output from Program 5.5 is identical to that from Program 5.4, with very slight deviations due to roundoff error in the specification of the estimates in the %Estimates macro of Program 5.4.

Note also the following comparisons of Program 5.5 and Program 5.4:

- The C matrix of the %Contrasts macro in Program 5.5 has an extra column of 0's. This accounts for the intercept in the PROC GLM model.

- The call to %SimIntervals in Program 5.5 is really identical to that of Program 5.4, since the defaults are conf=0.95 and side=B.

Finally, Program 5.6 shows how to use the %MakeGLMStats macro to create the %Contrasts macro as well as the %Estimates macro.

PROGRAM 5.6   **Invocation of %SimIntervals Using %MakeGLMStats to Create %Contrasts and %Estimates**

```
%MakeGLMStats(dataset=wloss, classvar=diet, yvar=wloss, model=diet,
              contrasts=all(diet));

%SimIntervals(nsamp=50000, seed=121211);
```

This is the simplest of the three programs, and it can be used if you want to perform all pairwise comparisons with data from a general linear model. In more complex cases, including examples with alternative linear combinations or nonnormal models, such as logistic regression of survival analysis, the more general forms shown in Programs 5.5 and 5.6 are needed.

Of course, Programs 5.4, 5.5, and 5.6 really shouldn't be used at all in this case, since the Tukey method provided in PROC GLM is exact. However, in more complex cases involving covariates or unbalanced data, either the ADJUST=SIMULATE option of PROC GLM or the %SimIntervals macro can be used; both use the same simulation-based method. The benefit of using %SimIntervals is that it applies to many more possible families of inference and in many more modelling situations than does PROC GLM.

An example where either %SimIntervals or PROC GLM could be used is in the multiple comparison of covariate-adjusted location means in housing example of Program 5.3. The %SimIntervals analysis of that data is performed in Program 5.7; note that the model= parameter now includes the covariates.

PROGRAM 5.7   %SimIntervals Analysis for Comparing Covariate-Adjusted Means

```
%MakeGLMStats(dataset=house, classvar=location, yvar=price,
              model=location sqfeet age, contrasts=all(location));

%SimIntervals(seed=121211);
```

Output from Program 5.7

```
              Estimated 95% Quantile = 2.799929

                    Standard          --- Pr > |t| --    95% Confidence
Contrast  Estimate  Error  t Value   Raw   Adjusted        Interval

  1-2     22.2032   2.0096  11.05   <.0001  <.0001     16.5765   27.8299
  1-3     21.5285   3.3053   6.51   <.0001  <.0001     12.2740   30.7831
  1-4     26.0152   2.4419  10.65   <.0001  <.0001     19.1781   32.8523
  1-5     29.0893   2.3453  12.40   <.0001  <.0001     22.5227   35.6560
  2-3     -0.6747   3.4815  -0.19    0.8470  0.9995    -10.4226    9.0732
  2-4      3.8120   2.6063   1.46    0.1491  0.5825     -3.4854   11.1095
  2-5      6.8861   2.5769   2.67    0.0098  0.0672     -0.3291   14.1014
  3-4      4.4867   3.7343   1.20    0.2345  0.7419     -5.9691   14.9425
  3-5      7.5608   3.6367   2.08    0.0421  0.2353     -2.6218   17.7434
  4-5      3.0741   2.8802   1.07    0.2903  0.8162     -4.9901   11.1383
```

The confidence interval outputs from Program 5.3 and Program 5.7 are identical except for Monte Carlo error, shown by the difference of the respective estimated critical values 2.795352 and 2.799929.

5.3.3   Tests of Hypotheses and Adjusted *p*-values

In the output from Programs 5.4 and 5.7, you see that there is an adjusted *p*-value column. Adjusted *p*-values are defined in this section.

For testing hypotheses of the form $H_{0i} : \mathbf{c}'\boldsymbol{\beta} = f_i$ (f_i is a fixed value, usually 0), the test statistic is

$$t_i = \frac{\mathbf{c}_i'\hat{\boldsymbol{\beta}} - f_i}{\hat{\sigma}\sqrt{\mathbf{c}_i'(\mathbf{X}'\mathbf{X})^-\mathbf{c}_i}},$$

which is distributed as Student's t with $df = n - \text{rank}(\mathbf{X})$ when H_{0i} is true.

You can use the simultaneous confidence intervals to test these hypotheses simply by noting whether the value f_i lies inside the given interval. Algebraically, this method results in the following procedures:

- For two-sided alternatives $H_{Ai} : \mathbf{c}'\boldsymbol{\beta} \neq f_i$: reject H_{0i} and conclude H_{Ai} when $|t_i| > c_\alpha$, where c_α is as defined above for the two-sided intervals.

- For one-sided alternatives $H_{Ai} : \mathbf{c}'\boldsymbol{\beta} < f_i$: reject H_{0i} and conclude H_{Ai} when $t_i < -c_\alpha$, where c_α is as defined above for the one-sided intervals.

- For one-sided alternatives $H_{Ai} : \mathbf{c}'\boldsymbol{\beta} > f_i$: reject H_{0i} and conclude H_{Ai} when $t_i > c_\alpha$, where c_α is as defined above for the one-sided intervals.

These tests control the FWE in the strong sense because they are directly related to the confidence intervals. However, more powerful procedures that also control the FWE are available, provided you are interested only in "accept/reject" decisions or directional determinations, rather than interval estimates or bounds. Such methods are described in Chapter 8.

The adjusted p-value for H_{0i}: $\mathbf{c}'\boldsymbol{\beta} = f_i$ is the smallest FWE level at which H_{0i} is still rejected. To define these quantities we must distinguish between random values of test statistics and the fixed, observed values. Let $\mathbf{T} = (T_1, \ldots, T_k)$ represent a random multivariate Student's t vector with dispersion R and df as given above, and let $\mathbf{t} = (t_1, \ldots, t_k)$ denote a vector of fixed, observed values.

Then the adjusted p-values are expressed as

- For two-sided alternatives H_{Ai}: $\mathbf{c}'\boldsymbol{\beta} \neq f_i$: the adjusted p-value for testing H_{0i} is $\tilde{p}_i = P(\max |T_j| > |t_i|)$.

- For one-sided alternatives H_{Ai}: $\mathbf{c}'\boldsymbol{\beta} < f_i$: the adjusted p-value for testing H_{0i} is $\tilde{p}_i = P(\min T_j < t_i)$.

- For one-sided alternatives H_{Ai}: $\mathbf{c}'\boldsymbol{\beta} > f_i$: the adjusted p-value for testing H_{0i} is $\tilde{p}_i = P(\max T_j > t_i)$.

Note that the distribution of $\min T_j$ is the same as that of $-\max T_j$. Thus, in all cases, whether adjusted p-values or simultaneous confidence intervals, the inference requires the distribution of $\max |T_j|$ or $\max T_j$. In principle, exact critical values and p-values can be calculated from these distributions, since they are pivotal, that is, free of unknown parameters. However, as in the case with confidence intervals, it can be difficult to calculate these quantities exactly except in balanced situations, such as those described in Chapter 3.

As described in Westfall and Young (1993, p. 108, 130), the adjusted p-values can be be approximated via simulation as follows.

Calculating the Adjusted *p*-values via Simulation

1. Generate a vector $\mathbf{Z}^*$ that is multivariate normal with mean vector $\mathbf{0}$ and covariance matrix $\mathbf{R}$.

2. Generate V^*, a chi-squared random variable with $df = (n - \mathrm{rank}\mathbf{X})$ degrees of freedom, independent of $\mathbf{Z}^*$, and compute $\mathbf{T}^* = \mathbf{Z}^*/\sqrt{V/df}$.

3. Compute $M_2^* = \max_{j=1}^{k} |t_j^*|$, $M_U^* = \max_{j=1}^{k} t_j^*$, or $M_L^* = \min_{j=1}^{k} t_j^*$, depending upon whether you want to perform two-sided, upper-tailed, or lower-tailed inferences.

4. For each of the observed test statistics t_i from the analysis of the original data, note whether $M_2^* \geq |t_i|$, or $M_U^* \geq t_i$, or $M_L^* \leq t_i$, for two-sided, upper-tailed, or lower-tailed tests, respectively.

5. Repeat steps 1 through 3 nsamp times. The estimated adjusted p-value for each test is $\hat{\tilde{p}}_i$, the proportion of samples for which the M^* value is as extreme as the observed t_i.

Program 5.8 and output 5.8 show these adjusted p-values that result from the PROC GLM analysis of the housing price data given by Program 5.2 and uses the ods feature to select them specifically.

PROGRAM 5.8   **Adjusted *p*-values from PROC GLM**

```
ods select DiffMat;
proc glm data=house;
   class location;
   model price = location sqfeet age;
   lsmeans location / pdiff cl adjust=simulate(seed=12345 nsamp=100000);
run;
```

Output from Program 5.8

```
                        The GLM Procedure
                       Least Squares Means
              Adjustment for Multiple Comparisons: Simulated

                  Least Squares Means for effect location
                    Pr > |t| for H0: LSMean(i)=LSMean(j)

                       Dependent Variable: price

      i/j         1          2          3          4          5

       1                   <.0001     <.0001     <.0001     <.0001
       2      <.0001                  0.9996     0.5781     0.0696
       3      <.0001     0.9996                  0.7414     0.2345
       4      <.0001     0.5781     0.7414                  0.8153
       5      <.0001     0.0696     0.2345     0.8153
```

These adjusted p-values correspond directly to the simultaneous confidence interval analysis. If the interval excludes zero, then the adjusted p-value is less than 0.05, and conversely. In this case, we see the same conclusions as provided by the intervals. The advantage of the intervals is that you see the actual range of plausible differences. The advantage of the p-values is that you get a direct quantification of "significance", e.g., we can see directly from the adjusted p-values that the comparison of location 2 versus 5 (B versus E) is statistically significant at the FWE = 0.10 level.

Note also that the adjusted p-values shown above are identical to those in the output from Program 5.7, except for Monte Carlo error.

You can set the accuracy of the adjusted p-values easily by using the NSAMP= option. The standard error of the estimate $\hat{\tilde{p}}_i$ is

$$s.e.(\hat{\tilde{p}}_i) = \sqrt{\frac{\hat{\tilde{p}}_i(1 - \hat{\tilde{p}}_i)}{nsamp}}.$$

Thus, if you set `nsamp` = 100000000, the standard error of an estimated adjusted p-value $\hat{\tilde{p}}_i = 0.06$ is only $\sqrt{0.06(1 - 0.06)/100000000} = 0.000024$. This means that the true adjusted p-value obtained from the multivariate t distribution would be within $\pm 1.96(0.000024)$ of 0.06, or between 0.05995 and 0.06005, with 95 percent confidence.

5.4 Comparisons with a Control

The general methods described previously for inferences with all pairwise comparisons carry over equally well to the case of comparisons with a control. In some cases, as described in Chapter 3, Section 3.4.2, you might want to perform one-sided inferences, and in that case, you need to consider the distribution of max T_i instead of max $|T_i|$. As before, our general recommendation is to use the simulation-based approach for intervals and tests, as these are correct (or at least, simulation-consistent) for all correlation structures.

EXAMPLE: **Growth Curve Data**

Box (1950) analyzes data on rat growth with three treatment groups (control, Thyroxin and Thiouracil). The questions of interest are whether Thyroxin weights or Thiouracil weights differ from control. Initial body weights, W_0, and four weekly weights, W_1–W_4, are given in Program 5.9.

PROGRAM 5.9   Rat Growth Data

```
data ratgrwth;
   length trt $ 10;
   input trt$ W0-W4 @@;
datalines;
Control     46 70 102 131 153    Control     49 67  90 112 140
Control     49 67 100 129 164    Control     51 71  94 110 141
Control     52 77 111 144 185    Control     56 81 104 121 151
Control     57 82 110 139 169    Control     57 86 114 139 172
Control     60 93 123 146 177    Control     63 91 112 130 154
Thyroxin    52 70 105 138 171    Thyroxin    52 73  97 116 140
Thyroxin    54 71  90 110 138    Thyroxin    56 75 108 151 189
Thyroxin    57 72  97 120 144    Thyroxin    59 85 116 148 177
Thyroxin    59 85 121 156 191    Thiouracil 46 61  78  90 107
Thiouracil 51 75  92 100 119    Thiouracil 51 75 101 123 140
Thiouracil 53 79 100 106 133    Thiouracil 53 72  89 104 122
Thiouracil 56 78  95 103 108    Thiouracil 58 69  93 114 138
Thiouracil 59 80 101 111 122    Thiouracil 59 88 100 111 122
Thiouracil 61 86 109 120 129
;
```

A simple plot of the data (see the graphic below) shows that Thiouracil seems to adversely affect the weights, and this can be verified easily with virtually any statistical analysis. Another question of interest, however, is whether the Thiouracil effect *persists* at the fourth week. That is, controlling for rat size at weeks 0 through 3, does Thiouracil *still* appear to adversely impact weight comparisons, or has the effect of Thiouracil been completely incorporated in the early weeks? In addition, since initial looks at the data are not sufficient to restrict attention to Thiouracil only, the analysis should consider the comparison of Thyroxin against control as well, and multiplicity-adjust over the resulting family of two tests.

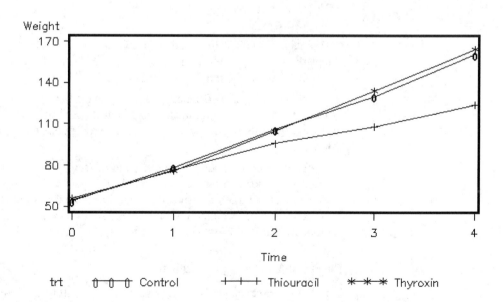

To answer the question posed in the example, we use a one-way ANCOVA model with the week four weight as the response variable and week 0 through 3 weights as covariates. The tests are lower-tailed comparisons with control and are given in Program 5.10.

PROGRAM 5.10   Covariate-Adjusted One-Sided Comparisons with a Control

```
ods select LSMeans LSMeanDiffCL;
proc glm data=ratgrwth;
   class trt;
   model w4 = trt w0-w3;
   lsmeans trt /  pdiff=controll cl adjust=dunnett;
run;
```

Output from Program 5.10

```
                            The GLM Procedure
                          Least Squares Means
               Adjustment for Multiple Comparisons: Dunnett-Hsu


                                            HO:LSMean=
                                              Control
                    trt          W4 LSMEAN     Pr < t

                    Control      152.050831
                    Thiouracil   142.592571     0.0098
                    Thyroxin     149.937997     0.4218



                    Least Squares Means for Effect trt

                         Difference        Simultaneous 95%
                           Between      Confidence Interval for
               i    j       Means          LSMean(i)-LSMean(j)


               2    1     -9.458260     -Infinity      -2.603613
               3    1     -2.112834     -Infinity       4.469897
```

Note the following about Output 5.10:

- The comparison of Thiouracil with control remains statistically significant (adjusted lower-tail $p = 0.0098$), even after controlling for weight up to week 3. This suggests that the effect of Thiouracil persists into week 4.

- The default analysis is Dunnett-Hsu, after the method given by Hsu (1992, 1996). This method involves an approximate (but extremely accurate) factor-analytic representation of the correlation matrix and uses exact integral calculations (further details given below).

- The simultaneous upper-confidence bounds, which also use the Dunnett-Hsu critical value, correspond to the adjusted p-values in that the upper bound is less than zero whenever the adjusted p-value is less than 0.05. In this example, we can state further that the adjusted mean weight in week 4 for the control group exceeds that of the Thiouracil group by at least 2.6036.

The Factor-Analytic Approximation

Both Tukey's and Dunnett's tests are based on the multivariate t distribution given in Section 5.2.3. In general, as we have discussed, evaluating the critical values and adjusted p-values for the distribution of max $|T_i|$ and max T_i is usually intractable, but the problem reduces to a feasible 2-fold integral when $\mathbf{R}$ has a certain symmetry in the case of Tukey's test, and a *factor analytic structure* (cf. Hsu 1992) in the case of Dunnett's test.

The **R** matrix has the required symmetry for exact computation of Tukey's test if the t_is are studentized differences between

- $k(k-1)/2$ pairs of k uncorrelated means with equal variances, that is, equal sample sizes
- $k(k-1)/2$ pairs of k LS-means from a *variance-balanced* design (for example, a balanced incomplete block design).

Refer to Hsu (1992, 1996) for more information. The **R** matrix has the factor analytic structure for exact computation of Dunnett's test if the t_is are studentized differences between

- $k-1$ means and a control mean, all uncorrelated. (Dunnett's one-sided methods depend on a similar probability calculation, without the absolute values.) Note that it is not required that the variances of the means (that is, the sample sizes) be equal.
- $k-1$ LS-means and a control LS-mean from either a *variance-balanced* design, or a design in which the other factors are *orthogonal* to the treatment factor (for example, a randomized block design with proportional cell frequencies).

However, other important situations that do **not** result in a correlation matrix **R** that has the structure for exact computation include

- all pairwise differences with unequal sample sizes
- differences between LS-means in many unbalanced designs.

In these situations, exact calculation of critical values and adjusted p-values is intractable in general. For comparisons with a control when the correlation **R** does not have a factor analytic structure, Hsu (1992) suggests approximating **R** with a matrix $\mathbf{R}^F$ that does have such a structure and, correspondingly, approximating the multivariate t critical values and p-values by assuming that the true correlation matrix is $\mathbf{R}^F$. The resulting critical values and adjusted p-values are calculated exactly for the correlation $\mathbf{R}^F$, but are approximate for the true correlation **R**.

When you request Dunnett's test for LS-means (the PDIFF=CONTROL and ADJUST=DUNNETT options), the GLM procedure automatically uses Hsu's approximation when appropriate.

Simulation-based Approximation

While Hsu's factor-analytic approximation is the default for the ADJUST=DUNNETT option, it is prudent to check the results using the simulation-based approach, which incorporates the correct covariance information exactly. Hsu (1992) developed an algorithm, which uses the factor-analytic method as a "control variate," for simulating critical values. This method produces more accurate estimates than the ordinary simulation approach, with the same number of simulations. Using the rat growth data, the control-variate, simulation-based method is implemented in Program 5.11.

PROGRAM 5.11   **Using Hsu's Control-Variate Simulation Method for Reducing Monte Carlo Error**

```
ods select LSMeans LSMeanDiffCL;
proc glm data=ratgrwth;
   class trt;
   model w4 = trt w0-w3;
   lsmeans trt /  pdiff=controll cl adjust=simulate
      (cvadjust nsamp=100000 report seed=121211);
run;
```

Output from Program 5.11

```
                          The GLM Procedure
                        Least Squares Means
           Adjustment for Multiple Comparisons: Simulated

                                             H0:LSMean=
                                              Control
              trt              W4 LSMEAN       Pr < t

              Control         152.050831
              Thiouracil      142.592571       0.0103
              Thyroxin        149.937997       0.4232


                  Least Squares Means for Effect trt

                        Difference        Simultaneous 95%
                         Between        Confidence Interval for
          i     j          Means          LSMean(i)-LSMean(j)

          2     1        -9.458260      -Infinity      -2.605177
          3     1        -2.112834      -Infinity       4.468395
```

The results of the simulation-based analysis virtually match the default Dunnett-Hsu method, implying that the factor-analytic approximation method is reasonable.

5.5   Multiple Comparisons when There Are CLASSvar × Covariate Interactions

Often, there are important interactions between the CLASS variable and one or more covariates. When this occurs, the difference between the means depends on the value of the covariates, and you must specify covariate settings of interest prior to performing your multiple comparisons. Different settings of the covariate values can have dramatically different effects upon estimated differences, and the associated simultaneous inferences are likewise affected.

EXAMPLE: Comparing Therapies for Alzheimer's Patients

Five therapies are tested for improving memory in Alzheimer's patients. Some of these therapies are chemical (pharmaceutical products) and some are holistic (e.g., special exercise and diet regimens). The study includes as covariates the age (in years) of the patient and the length of time (in months) since the patient was first diagnosed with Alzheimer's disease. Patients are given a memory test after a regimen of therapy, and the response variable is the score on that test, on a scale of 1 to 100. There is some concern that differences between therapies may depend upon the advancement of the disease.

Program 5.12 shows how to specify comparisons at a particular value of the covariate. There are two analyses, one with a comparison of mean values when the time since first diagnosis is 10 months (months=10), and the other with a similar comparison when months=20. The adjusted confidence intervals for the comparison at since=10 and since=20 are shown in output from Program 5.12.

PROGRAM 5.12   **Multiple Comparisons at Fixed Covariate Levels**

```
data alz;
   input therapy age since score @@;
cards;
1 69   22 66   1 68 14   60   1 66 14 55   1 68 31 70   1 71   27 50
1 55   28 56   1 71 24   62   1 68 28 67   1 71 25 72   1 71   16 48
1 88 123 59   1 67 27   58   1 71 25 70   2 72 54 47   2 90 121 44
2 72   44 64   2 75 19   65   2 69 28 56   2 65 27 71   2 76   22 68
2 68   29 53   2 61 18   60   2 65 20 65   2 71 20 60   2 72   21 64
3 70   27 54   3 70 23   45   3 64 11 60   3 66 45 30   3 67   19 46
3 68   24 45   3 69 16   49   3 79 23 49   3 68 31 34   3 72   15 40
4 67   28 89   4 65 17  100   4 66 32 81   4 75 23 76   4 83   60 64
4 70   12 58   4 63 16   85   4 68 17 86   4 65 18 89   4 68   27 76
4 63   18 95   4 67 37   85   4 75 18 96   4 66 27 90   4 71   23 83
4 70   36 75   5 66 18   68   5 69 25 77   5 76 13 87   5 70    9 95
5 70   11 95   5 71 13   82
;
proc glm data=alz outstat=stat;
   ods select LSMeanDiffCL;
   class therapy;
   model score = therapy since age therapy*since;
   lsmeans therapy / pdiff cl adjust=simulate at since  = 10;
run;
proc glm data=alz outstat=stat;
   ods select LSMeanDiffCL;
   class therapy;
   model score = therapy since age therapy*since;
   lsmeans therapy / pdiff cl adjust=simulate at since  = 20;
run;
```

Output from Program 5.12

```
                        The GLM Procedure
            Least Squares Means at since=10, age=69.77193
            Adjustment for Multiple Comparisons: Simulated


                 Least Squares Means for Effect therapy


                       Difference        Simultaneous 95%
                        Between       Confidence Interval for
              i    j      Means          LSMean(i)-LSMean(j)


              1    2   -4.065032     -16.499233     8.369169
              1    3    6.293719      -9.714140    22.301578
              1    4  -27.757653     -40.788530   -14.726776
              1    5  -30.429616     -46.567575   -14.291657
              2    3   10.358751      -6.027908    26.745409
              2    4  -23.692621     -37.346797   -10.038444
              2    5  -26.364584     -42.834936    -9.894232
              3    4  -34.051371     -51.108976   -16.993767
              3    5  -36.723335     -55.405654   -18.041015
              4    5   -2.671963     -19.890790    14.546863
```

```
                              The GLM Procedure
                 Least Squares Means at since=20, age=69.77193
                 Adjustment for Multiple Comparisons: Simulated

                      Least Squares Means for Effect therapy

                            Difference        Simultaneous 95%
                             Between        Confidence Interval for
          i      j            Means           LSMean(i)-LSMean(j)

          1      2          -2.014865        -12.500231      8.470500
          1      3          13.253509          2.534580     23.972437
          1      4         -24.096237        -33.711052    -14.481422
          1      5         -16.228190        -31.432688     -1.023693
          2      3          15.268374          4.154117     26.382631
          2      4         -22.081372        -32.233116    -11.929628
          2      5         -14.213325        -29.704671      1.278021
          3      4         -37.349746        -47.743102    -26.956389
          3      5         -29.481699        -45.056538    -13.906860
          4      5           7.868047         -7.108649     22.844742
```

Note the following about Output 5.12:

- The (1,3) and (2,3) comparisons are insignificant at SINCE=10 but significant at SINCE=20. The differences between the inferences can be seen in the following graph, which shows how the estimated differences depend on the covariate when there is interaction.

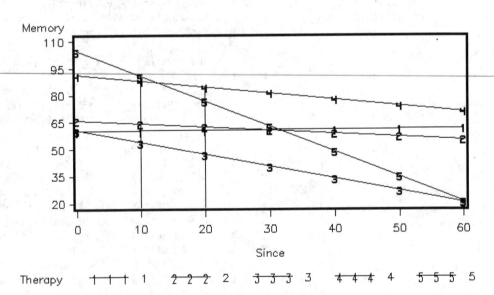

- All comparisons are done at a common level of the AGE variable. Since the variable AGE was not included in the AT option of the LSMEANS statement, the average age (69.77193) was selected as default. Since the model included no interaction of AGE and THERAPY, the resulting differences shown above will be identical, no matter what value of AGE is used.

- The FWE for each of the two confidence interval outputs individually is 0.05. If the set of inferences at both SINCE=10 and SINCE=20 is considered as a family with $k = 10 + 10 = 20$ elements, then the FWE will be more than 0.05, but less than the Bonferroni upper bound of 0.10. If you want to include the SINCE=10 and SINCE=20 inferences in the same family, and perform multiplicity adjustment over this family while taking advantage of the large correlations between elements in this expanded family, you can easily do so by using the %SimIntervals or %SimTests macros. See Chapter 6 and later chapters for further examples using the %Sim* macros.

5.6   Concluding Remarks

Our recommendation in this chapter is to use the ADJUST=SIMULATE method for ANCOVA applications. The reason for this recommendation is that the more common methods, such as Bonferroni, Šidák, Tukey-Kramer, etc., tend to be conservative, in that they do not fully exploit the correlation structure.

Hsu's factor-analytic method (the default of LSMEANS for comparisons with a control) appears to provide excellent approximations to the critical and adjusted p-values; however, it is prudent to validate the analysis using the simulation adjustment.

Finally, we recommend Hsu's control-variate simulation method (obtained using CVADJUST) generally, since it provides more accurate simulated critical values with the same number of simulations.

Chapter 6

Inferences for General Linear Functions of Means

6.1 Introduction

In the previous chapters, we have mainly considered the cases of all pairwise comparisons among means, and comparisons with a control (perhaps covariate-adjusted). However, you may have other comparisons in mind.

- If two of the treatments are different dose levels of a new drug, and a third treatment is a placebo, you might be interested in whether the average response for the two doses of the drug differs from the placebo.

- Recall the HOUSE data from Chapter 5, studying home prices in different locations. Suppose you want to compare the average price of homes in the north side of town with those in the south side. If the north side is comprised of locations A, B, and C, and the south side of D and E, then you are interested in comparing the average of the first three with the average of the last two.

- Suppose you want to construct a simultaneous confidence band for a regression line. In this case your inferences are not contrasts, but predicted values of the response, which are linear combinations of the intercept and slope parameters β_0 and β_1 of the form $\beta_0 + \beta_1 x_0$, where x_0 ranges over an entire interval of interest. This example illustrates two of the important points of this chapter: inferences need not be restricted to contrasts, and the family of inferences can be infinite.

While these types of linear functions do not fit into the "all pairwise comparisons" or "comparisons with control" mode, the general methods described in Chapter 5 apply. Further, you can perform these analyses easily using the %SimIntervals macro or the %SimTests macro discussed in Chapter 8.

In this chapter we assume the same general linear model as in Chapter 5; namely,

$$\mathbf{Y} = \mathbf{X}\boldsymbol{\beta} + \boldsymbol{\epsilon},$$

where the elements of $\boldsymbol{\epsilon}$ are independent, homoscedastic, and normally distributed error terms with zero means.

In Section 6.2 we show how to analyze a finite set of linear functions of $\boldsymbol{\beta}$ from this model. In Section 6.3 we consider infinite sets of linear functions, with 6.3.1 concerning contrasts in the ANOVA and ANCOVA, and with Section 6.3.2 and 6.3.3 concerning simultaneous confidence bands for regression functions.

6.2   Inferences for Any Finite Set of Linear Functions

As introduced in Chapter 5, the general elements of simultaneous inferences for a set of linear functions (assumed estimable) are as follows.

Elements of Simultaneous Inference for General Linear Functions

- You need to identify the family of functions. As discussed in Chapter 5, these can be written as $\mathbf{c}_1'\boldsymbol{\beta}, \mathbf{c}_2'\boldsymbol{\beta}, \ldots, \mathbf{c}_k'\boldsymbol{\beta}$. The estimates of these parameters are $\mathbf{c}_1'\hat{\boldsymbol{\beta}}, \mathbf{c}_2'\hat{\boldsymbol{\beta}}, \ldots, \mathbf{c}_k'\hat{\boldsymbol{\beta}}$.

- The t-statistics for these functions are $T_i = (\mathbf{c}_i'\hat{\boldsymbol{\beta}} - \mathbf{c}_i'\boldsymbol{\beta})/\{\hat{\sigma}\sqrt{\mathbf{c}_i'(\mathbf{X}'\mathbf{X})^{-}\mathbf{c}_i}\}$. The joint distribution of these t-statistics is multivariate t, and is free of any unknown parameters. Critical values for confidence intervals and adjusted p-values for tests are derived from the distribution of $\max |T_i|$ or $\max T_i$, depending on whether you're interested in two-sided or one-sided inferences, respectively.

- Where possible, you should use the exact distribution of $\max |T_i|$ or $\max T_i$. Otherwise, you can simulate this distribution.

- For simultaneous confidence intervals, the critical value for the confidence intervals, c_α, is the $1 - \alpha$ quantile of the distribution of these simulated values $\max |t_i^*|$ or $\max t_i^*$.

- For simultaneous (single-step) tests, the hypothesis $H_{0i} : \mathbf{c}_i'\boldsymbol{\beta} = f_i$ can be tested using the adjusted p-value, which is the proportion of simulations for which $\max |t_j^*| \geq |t_i|$ for two-sided tests. For upper-tailed tests, the adjusted p-value is the proportion of simulations for which $\max t_j^* \geq t_i$, and for lower-tailed tests, the adjusted p-value is the proportion of simulations for which $\min t_j^* \leq t_i$, which can be simulated as the proportion for which $\max t_j^* \geq -t_i$.

6.2.1   Comparisons with Control, Including Dose-response Contrasts

When the treatments are varying levels of doses, you often want to detect a dose-response trend. These trends can have various functional forms, for example, linear, exponential, logarithmic, quadratic, etc. Tests for trend that are most sensitive to a particular form of dose-response function use contrast coefficients that mimic the assumed functional form. (We saw this in the example from Chapter 3 concerning coupon redemption; the orthogonal contrasts were defined so as to mimic linear, quadratic, and cubic functional forms.)

In practice, the assumed form is unknown, thus you might want to try a few different contrasts to get an idea about which is most significant. If you adopt this method, you should correct the tests for multiplicity; otherwise, your chance of declaring a significant trend where none exists will exceed the nominal (usually 0.05) Type I error level.

There are two special features about this type of analysis that you should note.

- The contrasts are not necessarily orthogonal, so the maximum modulus method described in Section 3.5.2 may no longer apply. Even when the tests *are* orthogonal, the maximum modulus method only applies for the balanced ANOVA. You should use the methods of this chapter for orthogonal contrasts in all cases but balanced ANOVA, since the contrasts are no longer independent with unbalanced designs or covariates or both.

- The correlations between multiple trend contrasts can be very high. This means that Bonferroni-type methods can be highly conservative in these applications.

6.2.2 Example: Evaluating Dose Response of Litter Weights in Rats

In the 1950s, the drug Thalidomide was introduced in some countries to combat nausea and insomnia in pregnant women. When taken in the first trimester of pregnancy, Thalidomide prevented the proper growth of the fetus resulting in horrific birth defects in thousands of children around the world. Since this event, government agencies that regulate the sale of new pharmaceutical products have taken particular care to evaluate whether drugs cause birth defects.

One part of this evaluation process involves testing of the drug on pregnant mice. The pregnant females are typically divided into control, low, medium, and high dose groups, and the compound is administered throughout their pregnancy. Their litters are then evaluated for defects and birth weights.

The data set in Program 6.1 is taken from Westfall and Young (1993, p. 100–101). The response variable is the average post-birth weights in the entire litter (WEIGHT). Covariates are gestation time (GESTTIME) and number of animals in the litter (NUMBER). DOSE is the treatment indicator.

PROGRAM 6.1   **Litter weight data**

```
data litter;
   input dose weight gesttime number @@;
datalines;
  0 28.05 22.5 15     0 33.33 22.5 14     0 36.37 22.0 14
  0 35.52 22.0 13     0 36.77 21.5 15     0 29.60 23.0  5
  0 27.72 21.5 16     0 33.67 22.5 15     0 32.55 22.5 14
  0 32.78 21.5 15     0 31.05 22.0 12     0 33.40 22.5 15
  0 30.20 22.0 16     0 28.63 21.5  7     0 33.38 22.0 15
  0 33.43 22.0 13     0 29.63 21.5 14     0 33.08 22.0 15
  0 31.53 22.5 16     0 35.48 22.0  9     5 34.83 22.5 15
  5 26.33 22.5  7     5 24.28 22.5 15     5 38.63 23.0  9
  5 27.92 22.0 13     5 33.85 22.5 13     5 24.95 22.5 17
  5 33.20 22.5 15     5 36.03 22.5 12     5 26.80 22.0 13
  5 31.67 22.0 14     5 30.33 21.5 12     5 26.83 22.5 14
  5 32.18 22.0 13     5 33.77 22.5 16     5 21.30 21.5  9
  5 25.78 21.5 14     5 19.90 21.5 12     5 28.28 22.5 16
 50 31.28 22.0 16    50 35.80 21.5 16    50 27.97 21.5 14
 50 33.13 22.5 15    50 30.60 22.5 15    50 30.17 21.5 15
 50 27.07 21.5 14    50 32.02 22.0 17    50 36.72 22.5 13
 50 28.50 21.5 14    50 21.58 21.5 16    50 30.82 22.5 17
 50 30.55 22.0 14    50 27.63 22.0 14    50 22.97 22.0 12
 50 29.55 21.5 12    50 31.93 22.0 14    50 29.30 21.5 16
500 24.55 22.0  7   500 33.78 22.5 13   500 32.98 22.0 10
500 25.38 21.5 11   500 30.32 22.0 15   500 19.22 22.5 11
500 26.37 21.5 14   500 28.60 22.5  9   500 19.70 22.0 11
500 32.88 22.5 15   500 26.12 22.5 13   500 33.20 22.0 12
500 32.97 22.5 14   500 38.75 23.0 16   500 33.15 22.5 12
500 30.70 21.5 13   500 35.32 22.0 17
;
```

Suppose you are interested in comparisons of average weight with the control, as well as in dose-response contrasts, all adjusted for the covariates GESTTIME and NUMBER. Letting $\mu' = (\mu_1\ \mu_2\ \mu_3\ \mu_4)$ denote the covariate-adjusted means for the control, low, mid, and high dose groups, these contrasts can be expressed as $c_i'\mu$. For the comparisons with control, the coefficients are

$$\begin{aligned}
\mathbf{c}_1' &= (1 \quad -1 \quad 0 \quad 0) \\
\mathbf{c}_2' &= (1 \quad 0 \quad -1 \quad 0) \\
\mathbf{c}_3' &= (1 \quad 0 \quad 0 \quad -1),
\end{aligned}$$

and it is anticipated that the contrasts will be positive, with higher weight in the control group.

For the dose-response contrasts, we may assume that the effect is linear in dose order, linear in actual dose, or linear in the log-ordinal dose. These functions can be represented as $(0,1,2,3)$, $(0,5,50,500)$, and $(\ln(1), \ln(2), \ln(3), \text{and } \ln(4))$, respectively. The linear contrasts that capture these effects are obtained by centering these linear combinations to have a mean of zero. We also scale them so that the sum of all absolute values of the contrasts is equal to 2, for comparability with the comparisons with control. Thus, the linear, arithmetic, and log-ordinal dose-response contrasts are given by, respectively,

$$\begin{aligned}
\mathbf{c}_4' &= (0.750 \quad 0.250 \quad -0.250 \quad -0.750) \\
\mathbf{c}_5' &= (0.384 \quad 0.370 \quad 0.246 \quad -1.000) \\
\mathbf{c}_6' &= (0.887 \quad 0.113 \quad -0.339 \quad -0.661).
\end{aligned}$$

You can estimate these contrasts and obtain comparisons that ignore correlation structure using methods from Chapter 2, such as the Bonferroni method. Program 6.2 shows how to obtain the contrasts of interest for unadjusted comparisons by using the ESTIMATE statement.

PROGRAM 6.2   Estimation of Contrasts Using PROC GLM

```
proc glm data=litter;
   class dose;
   model weight = dose gesttime number;
   estimate 'cont-low ' dose 1    -1     0     0    ;
   estimate 'cont-mid ' dose 1     0    -1     0    ;
   estimate 'cont-high' dose 1     0     0    -1    ;
   estimate 'ordinal  ' dose 0.750 0.250 -0.250 -0.750;
   estimate 'arith    ' dose 0.384 0.370  0.246 -1.000;
   estimate 'log ord  ' dose 0.887 0.113 -0.339 -0.661;
run;
```

Output from Program 6.2

Parameter	Estimate	Standard Error	t Value	Pr > |t|
cont-low	3.35239986	1.29075327	2.60	0.0115
cont-mid	2.29087893	1.33838960	1.71	0.0915
cont-high	2.67524263	1.33431207	2.00	0.0490
ordinal	1.74105174	1.04333741	1.67	0.0998
arith	0.87129846	1.13215373	0.77	0.4442
log ord	2.16612215	1.07353210	2.02	0.0476

Note the following about the output:

- The *p*-values shown are two-sided. To obtain the appropriate one-sided *p*-values, you divide the two-sided *p*-value by two *when the sign is in the anticipated direction*. If the sign is in the unanticipated direction, you divide the two-tailed *p*-value by two and subtract the result from 1.0. In this example, all signs are in the anticipated direction, so you can divide all *p*-values by two to obtain the one-sided *p*-values.

- Suppose you want to perform one-sided inferences. Then the multiplicity-adjusted *p*-values, using Bonferroni, would be obtained by multiplying the appropriate one-sided *p*-values by $k = 6$ (that is, multiplying the listed *p*-values by $6/2 = 3$), giving 0.0345, 0.2745, 0.1470, 0.2994, 1.0000 (this value truncated to 1.0), and 0.1428. Thus, by using Bonferroni there is only one significant result at either the FWE $= 0.05$ or FWE $= 0.10$ levels.

- For simultaneous one-sided Bonferroni confidence intervals, use the critical value $t_{1-0.05/6,68} = 2.455$. Thus, the lower confidence bound on the control-low comparison is $3.3524 - 2.455 \times 1.2908 = 0.1839$. That is, the covariate-adjusted difference between the control and the low dose means is at least 0.1839 with 95 percent confidence; this is greater than zero, corresponding to the statistical significance of the Bonferroni *p*-value. All other lower 95 percent Bonferroni bounds, calculated similarly, are less than zero, which corresponds to the fact that all other Bonferroni adjusted *p*-values are greater than 0.05.

The preceding analysis ignores correlation structure, and is therefore conservative. To obtain the critical values and adjusted *p*-values that incorporate correlations, you can use the %SimIntervals macro described in Chapter 5 and given in the appendix, as shown in Program 6.3.

PROGRAM 6.3   **Simultaneous Intervals for General Contrasts in an ANCOVA Model**

```
%MakeGLMStats(dataset  = litter,
              classvar = dose  ,
              yvar     = weight,
              model    = dose gesttime number);

%macro Contrasts;
   C = {0   1     -1     0      0     0 0,
        0   1      0    -1      0     0 0,
        0   1      0     0     -1     0 0,
        0   0.750  0.250 -0.250 -0.750 0 0,
        0   0.384  0.370  0.246 -1.000 0 0,
        0   0.887  0.113 -0.339 -0.661 0 0};
   C = C';
   Clab = { "Control-Low" , "Control-Med"  , "Control-High",
            "Ordinal"    , "Arithmetic", "Log-Ordinal"};
%mend;

%SimIntervals(nsamp=100000,seed=121221,side=U);
```

Output from Program 6.3

Estimated 95% Quantile = 2.219251

Contrast	Estimate	Standard Error	t Value	---- Pr > t --- Raw	Adjusted	95% Confidence Interval	
Control-Low	3.3524	1.2908	2.60	0.0058	0.0210	0.4879	Infty
Control-Med	2.2909	1.3384	1.71	0.0458	0.1365	-0.6793	Infty
Control-High	2.6752	1.3343	2.00	0.0245	0.0779	-0.2859	Infty
Ordinal	1.7411	1.0433	1.67	0.0499	0.1477	-0.5744	Infty
Arithmetic	0.8713	1.1322	0.77	0.2221	0.5006	-1.6412	Infty
Log-Ordinal	2.1661	1.0735	2.02	0.0238	0.0760	-0.2163	Infty

Note the following about the output:

- The conclusion of the study is that the weights are significantly smaller in the low dose group than in the control, using FWE = 0.05. If we are willing to relax the FWE level to 0.10, we may also claim a significant difference between the high dose group and the control, and a significant log-ordinal trend.

- Interestingly, the parameter estimates show that the largest difference occurs in the control versus low dose comparison. Thus, the estimated trend shows a decrease from control to low dose, then either a leveling-off, or perhaps even an increase. (See the graph below.) The log-ordinal contrast best mimics this trend, which explains why this contrast was the most significant among the three.

- Because the estimated critical value, 2.219251, incorporates dependencies among the contrasts, it is smaller (9.6 percent) than the corresponding Bonferroni critical value $t_{1-0.05/6,68} = 2.455$.

- The Bonferroni adjusted *p*-values would be obtained by multiplying the "raw" *p*-values from the %SimIntervals output by $k = 6$, yielding values 0.0348, 0.2748, 0.1470, 0.2994, 1.0000, and 0.1428. (The value 1.000 has been truncated.) In this case we would have only one statistically significant test at the 0.05 and 0.10 levels. By accounting for correlations, we found one significance at the 0.05 level and two others at the 0.10 level.

- The simulation standard errors for the adjusted *p*-values are given by $\sqrt{\tilde{p}(1-\tilde{p})/100000}$ in this example, since there are 100000 simulations. Multiplying these by 2.576 to obtain the 99 percent margins of error, we get 0.0210 ± 0.0012, 0.1365 ± 0.0028, 0.0779 ± 0.0022, 0.1477 ± 0.0029, 0.5006 ± 0.0041, and 0.0760 ± 0.0022, respectively for the six adjusted *p*-values. Clearly, these values are very small, and the inferences are not affected adversely by Monte Carlo error.

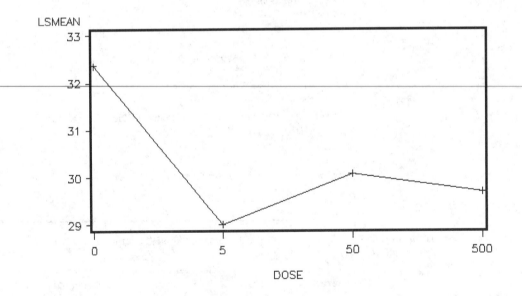

6.3 Inferences for Infinite Sets of Linear Functions

You might think that a section called "Inferences for Infinite Sets of Linear Functions" is too esoteric to be of practical use. On the contrary! In many cases of practical interest, it is very difficult to pin down a finite family of inferences, *a priori*. Rather, you might allow yourself to explore a large, unspecified set of comparisons, but still you want to claim that any significances are in fact real, and unlikely to be Type I errors. In this case, you should use an infinite family of comparisons.

It may seem that definitive inferences are impossible with infinite families. After all, the Bonferroni method requires that you divide α by k, the number of elements in the family. If k is infinity (symbolically, if $k = \infty$), then you must use α/∞, which can only be defined as zero, for all your inferences. Since p-values are always greater than zero, your tests will never be significant. Similarly, critical values using $\alpha = 0$ can only be defined as infinitely large; hence, confidence intervals would be infinitely wide in this case.

Evidently, the Bonferroni approach is not appropriate for infinite contrasts. As we have seen, the greater the degree of dependence among the tests or intervals, the less appropriate the Bonferroni correction. What often happens with infinite collections of tests is that, as more and more tests are considered, the dependencies among the tests increase. After a certain point, the dependencies become so great that essentially no more correction is needed. So, in fact, infinite families *are* allowed, and MCPs that use them are reasonably powerful for detecting effects.

Perhaps the most important criteria for deciding whether to use an infinite family is whether your comparisons of interest are determined *after looking at the data*. For example, after having observed that $\bar{y}_1$ and $\bar{y}_2$ are smallest, and $\bar{y}_3$ and $\bar{y}_4$ are largest among the four means in an ANOVA, you might decide to test $H_0: (\mu_1 + \mu_2)/2 = (\mu_3 + \mu_4)/2$. Such a test can *only* be considered within the context of an infinite family of tests, since there are infinitely many possible tests that you could have picked using this method.

(As a technical point, you might be interested only in the family of contrasts that involve comparisons of equally weighted means, which is a very large but finite family. This special family can be reasonably considered infinite in that the difference between critical values for this family and the infinite family will be small.)

It is not valid to include the comparisons suggested by the data (like $H_0: (\mu_1 + \mu_2)/2 = (\mu_3 + \mu_4)/2$) with other comparisons that are preplanned such as all pairwise comparisons, and then perform multiplicity adjustment as shown in Section 6.1. While it might seem that the additional comparison simply increases the number of inferences by one, in reality the size of the family is infinite (or virtually so), since you have implicitly considered infinitely many comparisons before arriving at the maximal one. Using a family other than the infinite one will not protect the FWE in this case.

6.3.1 ANOVA tests

To motivate the problem, we consider a common occurrence. It can happen that the overall F-test in the ANOVA is significant, but none of the pairwise comparisons tests are significant. This seems contradictory because if the hypothesis tested by the overall F-test, $H_0: \mu_1 = \mu_2 = \cdots = \mu_g$, is truly false (not just "significantly" false), then it is a mathematical fact that at least one of the $\mu_i - \mu_{i'}$ pairs must be different from 0. However, when the overall F is statistically significant, then it is possible that none of the pairwise differences are significant, even if you use unadjusted pairwise comparisons.

Program 6.4 shows a revised data set like the "Weight loss data" (data=wloss) from Chapter 3 that illustrates the problem. We have added random error to weight loss values to make the results less significant. Please do not try this at home!!! We are only adding random error to the data to create a data set that illustrates the point.

PROGRAM 6.4   **Overall *F*-test Significant but Pairwise Comparisons Insignificant**

```
data wlossnew;
   set wloss;
   wloss=wloss + 6*rannor(121211);   /* Random error added */
proc glm;
```

```
      class diet;
      model wloss=diet;
      means diet/cldiff tukey;
run;
```

Output from Program 6.4

The GLM Procedure

Dependent Variable: wloss

Source	DF	Sum of Squares	Mean Square	F Value	Pr > F
Model	4	252.693538	63.173385	2.65	0.0456
Error	45	1074.610625	23.880236		
Corrected Total	49	1327.304163			

R-Square	Coeff Var	Root MSE	wloss Mean
0.190381	40.93625	4.886741	11.93744

Source	DF	Type I SS	Mean Square	F Value	Pr > F
diet	4	252.6935382	63.1733846	2.65	0.0456

Source	DF	Type III SS	Mean Square	F Value	Pr > F
diet	4	252.6935382	63.1733846	2.65	0.0456

The GLM Procedure

Tukey's Studentized Range (HSD) Test for wloss

NOTE: This test controls the type I experimentwise error rate.

Alpha	0.05
Error Degrees of Freedom	45
Error Mean Square	23.88024
Critical Value of Studentized Range	4.01842
Minimum Significant Difference	6.2098

Comparisons significant at the 0.05 level are indicated by ***.

diet Comparison	Difference Between Means	Simultaneous 95% Confidence Interval	
A - E	1.572	-4.638	7.781
A - C	2.927	-3.283	9.136

A	– B	5.025	–1.185	11.235
A	– D	6.198	–0.012	12.408
E	– A	–1.572	–7.781	4.638
E	– C	1.355	–4.855	7.565
E	– B	3.454	–2.756	9.663
E	– D	4.626	–1.583	10.836
C	– A	–2.927	–9.136	3.283
C	– E	–1.355	–7.565	4.855
C	– B	2.098	–4.111	8.308
C	– D	3.271	–2.939	9.481
B	– A	–5.025	–11.235	1.185
B	– E	–3.454	–9.663	2.756
B	– C	–2.098	–8.308	4.111
B	– D	1.173	–5.037	7.382
D	– A	–6.198	–12.408	0.012
D	– E	–4.626	–10.836	1.583
D	– C	–3.271	–9.481	2.939
D	– B	–1.173	–7.382	5.037

With these data the overall F test is significant with $F(4, 45) = 2.65$, $p = 0.0456$, yet all Tukey intervals contain 0. Fortunately, it is possible to make a specific claim about at least one contrast involving the means, when the overall F-test is significant. The solution involves expanding the family to an infinite size and locating the most extreme statistics within that set. This family is the set of all contrasts $c'_i \mu = c_1 \mu_1 + c_2 \mu_2 + \cdots + c_g \mu_g$, where the sum of the elements is zero ($\sum c_i = 0$). Examples of such contrast vectors are the usual pairwise comparisons like $c' = (0\ -1\ 0\ 1\ 0)$, contrasts that compare one set of means with another, like $c' = (-0.5\ -0.5\ 0.333\ 0.333\ 0.333)$, and also the weighted contrasts for trend shown in the dose-response analysis of Section 6.2, such as $c' = (0.887\ 0.113\ -0.339\ -0.661\ 0)$.

The general method for infinite families is essentially the same as that for finite families. In either case, you need to know the distribution of max $|T_i|$ to obtain critical values for the simultaneous confidence intervals and multiplicity-adjusted p-values. The only difference is that, in the infinite case, the maximum is taken over an infinite collection of test statistics T_i rather than a finite collection.

Scheffé's Method

Scheffé's (1953) method involves finding the distribution of $\max_c T_c^2$, where T_c is the t statistic for the contrast $c'\mu$,

$$T_c = \frac{c'\hat{\mu} - c'\mu}{s.e.(c'\hat{\mu})}.$$

In the case of the one-way ANOVA without covariates (balanced or unbalanced), the standard error of $c'\hat{\mu}$ is given as

$$s.e.(c'\hat{\mu}) = \hat{\sigma}\sqrt{\sum \frac{c_i^2}{n_i}}.$$

The method can be used in models with covariates as well, in which case the standard error is as given in Chapter 5.

Scheffé showed that the distribution of $\max_c T_c^2$ over all contrasts is $(g-1)F_{g-1,df}$, which is the distribution of $g-1$ times an F-distributed random variable with $g-1$ numerator and df denominator degrees of freedom. The term df is just the usual error degrees of freedom.

Thus, the $1-\alpha$ quantile of the distribution of $\max_{\mathbf{c}} |T_{\mathbf{c}}|$ is just $c_\alpha = \sqrt{(g-1)F_{1-\alpha,g-1,df}}$, and the simultaneous Scheffé intervals are

$$\mathbf{c}'\hat{\boldsymbol{\mu}} \pm \sqrt{(g-1)F_{1-\alpha,g-1,df}}\,s.e.(\mathbf{c}'\hat{\boldsymbol{\mu}}).$$

The Scheffé method for all pairwise comparisons can be computed using PROC GLM as shown in Program 6.5.

PROGRAM 6.5   Scheffé Intervals

```
proc glm data=wlossnew;
   class diet;
   model wloss=diet;
   means diet/cldiff scheffe;
run;
```

Output from Program 6.5

Scheffe's Test for wloss

NOTE: This test controls the type I experimentwise error rate but generally has a higher type II error rate than Tukey's for all pairwise comparisons.

Alpha	0.05
Error Degrees of Freedom	45
Error Mean Square	23.88024
Critical Value of F	2.57874
Minimum Significant Difference	7.0189

Comparisons significant at the 0.05 level are indicated by ***.

diet Comparison			Difference Between Means	Simultaneous 95% Confidence Interval	
A	-	E	1.572	-5.447	8.590
A	-	C	2.927	-4.092	9.946
A	-	B	5.025	-1.994	12.044
A	-	D	6.198	-0.821	13.217
E	-	A	-1.572	-8.590	5.447
E	-	C	1.355	-5.664	8.374
E	-	B	3.454	-3.565	10.472
E	-	D	4.626	-2.393	11.645
C	-	A	-2.927	-9.946	4.092
C	-	E	-1.355	-8.374	5.664
C	-	B	2.098	-4.920	9.117
C	-	D	3.271	-3.748	10.290
B	-	A	-5.025	-12.044	1.994
B	-	E	-3.454	-10.472	3.565
B	-	C	-2.098	-9.117	4.920
B	-	D	1.173	-5.846	8.192
D	-	A	-6.198	-13.217	0.821
D	-	E	-4.626	-11.645	2.393
D	-	C	-3.271	-10.290	3.748
D	-	B	-1.173	-8.192	5.846

Comparing this output with the output from Program 6.4, you see that the Scheffé intervals are clearly wider (13 percent wider) than the Tukey intervals. There is a warning message

```
NOTE: This test controls the type I experimentwise error rate but generally
 has a higher type II error rate than Tukey's for all pairwise comparisons.
```

that also tells you of this problem. You should *not* use the Scheffé method if you want only to analyze pairwise comparisons. Use Tukey's method instead.

Note, however, that Scheffé's method does have a characteristic that Tukey's does not; it is partially consistent with the ANOVA F-test in the sense that if the F-test is insignificant, then Scheffé's method will never judge any mean difference to be significant.

Before discussing further uses of the Scheffé method, let us review some items from the output. First, the reported `Critical Value of F= 2.57874` is obtained as $F_{0.95,5-1,45}$, and the associated critical value c_α is $\sqrt{(5-1)F_{0.95,5-1,45}} = 3.212$. These can also be obtained using the following program:

```
data;
   fwe = 0.05;
   g   = 5;
   df  = 45;
   fcrit   = finv(1-fwe,g-1,df);
   c_alpha = sqrt((g-1)*fcrit);
proc print; run;
```

The value of the minimum significant difference is just the radius of the confidence interval, obtained as $3.212 \times \sqrt{23.88024} \times \sqrt{2/10} = 7.0189$.

The only reason for using Scheffé's method is for use with the infinite family of contrasts . You can use the critical value $c_\alpha = 3.212$ for *all possible* contrasts involving the means, even those that are *suggested by the data*, and still have FWE control at the 0.05 level.

An interesting application of this statement is that *any* contrast t-statistic that is in excess of 3.212 (in absolute value) is statistically significant, even if the contrast is suggested by the data. Thus, the p-value must be less than $P(|T_{45}| > 3.212) = 2 \times (1 - P(T_{45} \leq 3.212)) = 0.002436$. This corresponds to an "effective Bonferroni divisor" of $k^* = 0.05/0.002436 = 20.5$. Referring back to our discussion at the beginning of this section about $k = \infty$ and the seeming impossibility of detecting significant effects using infinite families, you can see that you never need to consider a Bonferroni correction factor of more than $k^* = 20.5$ when considering contrasts between 5 means (data-dependent or preselected). This occurs because of the very large correlations among the set of infinite contrasts.

To summarize the Bonferroni and Scheffé discussion in this example:

- If you have a family of 20 or fewer preselected contrasts, the Bonferroni critical value will be *smaller than* the Scheffé critical value, and thus, Bonferroni's is the better of the two closed-form methods. However, the simulation-based method described in Section 6.2 using the `%SimIntervals` macro would be preferable to either Bonferroni or Scheffé.

- If you have a family of more than 20 preselected contrasts, the Bonferroni critical value will be *larger than* the Scheffé critical value, and thus, Scheffé's is the better of the two closed-form methods. However, again the simulation-based method from Section 6.2 using the `%SimIntervals` macro would be preferable to either Bonferroni or Scheffé.

- If you want to test a contrast that has been *suggested by the data*, then your family size is implicitly infinite (or, at least very large, certainly larger than 20), and you should use the Scheffé critical value. The simulation-based method is not appropriate because the family is not prespecified.

Note that the cutoff of about 20 contrasts (for whether Bonferroni's or Scheffé's method is better) is specific to comparisons among 5 groups. In general, Scheffé's is better than Bonferroni's if the number of preselected contrasts of interest is greater than $k^* = 0.05/P(|T_{df}| > c_\alpha)$ where c_α is the Scheffé critical value.

You can test hypotheses using ordinary p-values, comparing them to the Scheffé critical adjusted α level (0.002436 in this example), or you can use Scheffé adjusted p-values and compare them to 0.05. The adjusted p-values for the Scheffé procedure are given by

$$\tilde{p} = P\left(\sqrt{(g-1)F_{g-1,df}} \geq |t_c|\right) = 1 - P\left(F_{g-1,df} < t_c^2/(g-1)\right).$$

Program 6.6 calculates tests for linear contrasts of interest, some obviously suggested by the data. The output contains unadjusted p-values from the ESTIMATE statements, and we must use the Scheffé critical point 0.002436 to determine significance for them. The output also contains the pairwise difference adjusted p-values using the Scheffé method. Since we are considering various contrasts among the means, including some suggested by the data, in addition to the pairwise comparisons, we must also use the Scheffé method for the pairwise comparisons. Seemingly, there are a total of $k = 16$ tests in the following analysis (10 pairwise comparisons plus 6 specified contrasts), and since $k^* = 20.5 > 16$, the Bonferroni method would provide smaller critical values and adjusted p-values than the Scheffé method. However, some of the comparisons are selected *post hoc* (after looking at the data) as discussed below; hence, the seeming family size of $k = 16$ is not valid. Had the specified contrasts been preselected, then Bonferroni would be more appropriate than Scheffé, but the simulation-based method would be more appropriate than either method.

PROGRAM 6.6   Multiple Contrasts, Where Some Are Suggested by the Data

```
data;
   fwe = 0.05;
   g   = 5;
   df  = 45;
   fcrit   = finv(1-fwe,g-1,df);
   c_alpha = sqrt((g-1)*fcrit);
   p_crit  = 2*(1 - probt(c_alpha, df));
   call symput ('scheffep',p_crit);
run;
proc glm data=wlossnew;
   title "Use &Scheffep to determine significance of contrasts";
   class diet;
   model wloss=diet;
   lsmeans diet/pdiff adjust=scheffe;
   estimate "c1" diet  1   1 -1 -1   0 /divisor=2;
   estimate "c2" diet -1  -1  1  0   1 /divisor=2;
   estimate "c3" diet  4  -1 -1 -1  -1 /divisor=4;
   estimate "c4" diet  2  -3  2 -3   2 /divisor=6;
   estimate "c5" diet  1  -1  0 -1   1 /divisor=2;
   estimate "c6" diet  2  -1  0 -2   1 /divisor=3;
run;
```

Output from Program 6.6

The GLM Procedure
Least Squares Means
Adjustment for Multiple Comparisons: Scheffe

Least Squares Means for effect diet
Pr > |t| for H0: LSMean(i)=LSMean(j)

Dependent Variable: wloss

i/j	1	2	3	4	5
1		0.2764	0.7730	0.1091	0.9710
2	0.2764		0.9198	0.9902	0.6476
3	0.7730	0.9198		0.6928	0.9832
4	0.1091	0.9902	0.6928		0.3588
5	0.9710	0.6476	0.9832	0.3588	

Use 0.0024383322 to determine significance of contrasts

The GLM Procedure

Dependent Variable: wloss

Parameter	Estimate	Standard Error	t Value	Pr > |t|
c1	2.04973510	1.54532314	1.33	0.1914
c2	0.26341885	1.54532314	0.17	0.8654
c3	3.93033236	1.72772380	2.27	0.0277
c4	4.11207646	1.41068057	2.91	0.0055
c5	4.82572576	1.54532314	3.12	0.0031
c6	5.28311048	1.62891362	3.24	0.0022

None of the pairwise comparisons can be called statistically significant, since all adjusted p-values are greater than 0.05. Comparing the unadjusted p-values for the additional contrasts c1–c6 with 0.0024383322, we see that the contrast $c_6'\mu = \frac{2}{3}\mu_1 - \frac{1}{3}\mu_2 - \frac{2}{3}\mu_4 + \frac{1}{3}\mu_5$ is significantly different from zero.

Thus, there does indeed exist a significant contrast that is associated with the significant F-test. This always occurs, since $\max_c t_c^2 = (g-1)F$, where F is the usual F-statistic for the ANOVA hypothesis. The F test is significant when $F > F_{0.95,g-1,df}$; hence, when this occurs, we then have $\max_c |t_c| > \sqrt{(g-1)F_{0.95,g-1,df}}$ for the contrast c that maximizes $|t_c|$.

What is the c that maximizes the significance? In the simple ANOVA (balanced or unbalanced), c is anything proportional to the vector $\left(n_1(\bar{y}_1 - \bar{\bar{y}}), \ldots, n_g(\bar{y}_g - \bar{\bar{y}})\right)$, where $\bar{\bar{y}} = \sum n_i \bar{y}_i / \sum n_i$ is the grand mean of all observations. Thus, in the new weight loss data, the maximal c is proportional to $\left(10(15.08 - 11.94), \ldots, 10(13.51 - 11.94)\right) = (31.44, -18.81, 2.18, -30.54, 15.73)$. Rescaling to make the comparison reflect a difference of weighted averages, we may take $c = (0.64, -0.38, 0.04, -0.62, 0.32)$, which is essentially the c6 contrast shown in Program 6.6.

Often, the maximal contrasts themselves are not easily interpretable. However, they might suggest simple forms that are of interest. For example, you might choose to test the hypothesis $H : (\mu_1 + \mu_5)/2 = (\mu_2 + \mu_4)/2$ after seeing that the maximal contrast has coefficients of reasonable size for all but μ_3.

Finding the Maximal Contrast for General ANCOVA Applications

The maximal contrast **c** also can be found to correspond with the general ANCOVA hypothesis, but its form is more complicated. In fact, it is the eigenvector that is associated with the maximal eigenvalue of a certain matrix that appears in multivariate analysis methods. You can use the code from Program 6.7 to find the maximal vector **c** in the general ANCOVA. We use the data set data=house from Chapter 5 to illustrate the calculations.

Program 6.7 begins by creating an output data set from the LSMEANS analysis that includes both the estimates and their covariance (compare the COV specification in the LSMEANS statement). This data set is then used in PROC IML to compute the most significant contrast.

PROGRAM 6.7   Finding the Most Significant Contrast in ANCOVA

```
%let classvar = location;
proc glm data=house;
   class location;
   model price = location sqfeet age;
   lsmeans location / out=stats cov;
proc iml;
   use stats;
   read all into alldata;
   read all var {&classvar} into classvar;
   read all var {LSMEAN} into ests;
   classvar = char(classvar);
   classvar = classvar';
   ncall    = ncol(alldata);
   nclass   = nrow(ests);
   ncstart  = ncall-nclass+1;
   covs     = alldata[,ncstart:ncall];
   cont1    = j(nclass-1,1,1);
   cont2    = -i(nclass-1);
   cont     = cont1||cont2;
   nummat   = (cont*ests)*(ests'*cont');
   denmat   = cont*covs*cont';
   h        = half(denmat);
   evec     = eigvec(inv(h')*nummat*inv(h));
   e1       = inv(h)*evec[,1];
   contrast = e1'*cont;
   contrast = contrast/sum((contrast>0)#contrast);
   print "Most Significant Contrast",
   contrast [label="&classvar" colname=classvar];
quit;
```

Output from Program 6.7

```
                           Most Significant Contrast

        location        A          B          C          D          E

               1 -0.307122 -0.074921 -0.249097  -0.36886
```

The coefficients corresponding to locations B, D, and E are all similar and add up to approximately the negative of the coefficient for location A, while the coefficient for C is nearly zero. Thus, the most significant comparison involves houses in location A with the average of houses in locations B, D, and E. Should you choose to use comparisons like this that are suggested by the data, you must use the Scheffé critical value $c_\alpha = \sqrt{(5-1)F_{0.95,5-1,57}} = 3.183$.

6.3.2   Confidence Bands for Regression Functions

Infinite families need not be concerned contrasts. Suppose you have a simple linear regression model

$$y_i = \beta_0 + \beta_1 x_i + \epsilon_i,$$

with fixed x_i values, and the usual assumptions of independence, constant variance, and normality of the mean-zero error terms ϵ_i. The estimated regression function is $\hat{y} = \hat{\beta}_0 + \hat{\beta}_1 x$, where $(\hat{\beta}_0, \hat{\beta}_1) = \hat{\boldsymbol{\beta}} = (\mathbf{X}'\mathbf{X})^{-1}\mathbf{X}'\mathbf{Y}$. You might want to obtain simultaneous confidence intervals for the regression function in a meaningful range of values, say as x ranges from a lower bound a to an upper bound b (one or both of these bounds could be infinite). In other words, you want simultaneous confidence intervals for $\beta_0 + \beta_1 x$ for all $a \leq x \leq b$. The intervals we consider are the usual intervals of the form

$$\hat{\beta}_0 + \hat{\beta}_1 x \pm c_\alpha s.e.(\hat{\beta}_0 + \hat{\beta}_1 x),$$

where

$$s.e.(\hat{\beta}_0 + \hat{\beta}_1 x) = \hat{\sigma}\sqrt{\mathbf{x}'(\mathbf{X}'\mathbf{X})^{-1}\mathbf{x}},$$

$\hat{\sigma} = $ RMSE, and $\mathbf{x}' = (1\ x)$. The difficult question is, how do you choose c_α?

Even if the bounds a and b are both finite, the set of inferences still is infinite because there are infinitely many points in the interval from a to b. Thus, the solution to the problem requires something similar to the Scheffé method. The Working-Hotelling method (described in, for example, Neter et al., 1996, p. 156) uses the same essential technique as the Scheffé method. It is based on the fact that the intervals

$$\ell_0\hat{\beta}_0 + \ell_1\hat{\beta}_1 \pm \sqrt{2F_{1-\alpha,2,n-2}}\,\hat{\sigma}\sqrt{\boldsymbol{\ell}'(\mathbf{X}'\mathbf{X})^{-1}\boldsymbol{\ell}}$$

are *exact* simultaneous $1 - \alpha$ confidence intervals for the parameters $\boldsymbol{\ell}'\boldsymbol{\beta} = \ell_0\beta_0 + \ell_1\beta_1$, over the infinite set of *all* linear combinations $\boldsymbol{\ell} = (\ell_0, \ell_1)'$. (These intervals are based on the same premise as the Scheffé intervals, but use "2" instead of "2-1" because we are considering all linear combinations, not just contrasts. You get to lose a degree of freedom with Scheffé's method because you are restricting your attention to contrasts.)

The problem with the Working-Hotelling intervals is that they are too conservative. The infinite family contains all points in the range $-\infty < x < +\infty$, which is too big, since you are only interested in a finite interval $a \leq x \leq b$.

Rather than use the Working-Hotelling approach, we prefer to use the exact distribution of $\max_{a \leq x \leq b}|T_x|$, where T_x is the usual pivotal statistic

$$T_x = \frac{\hat{\beta}_0 + \hat{\beta}_1 x - (\beta_0 + \beta_1 x)}{s.e.(\hat{\beta}_0 + \hat{\beta}_1 x)}.$$

Letting c_α be the $1 - \alpha$ quantile of the distribution of $\max_{a \leq x \leq b}|T_x|$, the simultaneous confidence intervals are $\hat{\beta}_0 + \hat{\beta}_1 x \pm c_\alpha s.e.(\hat{\beta}_0 + \hat{\beta}_1 x)$. These intervals will be exact in the sense that they will contain the true regression line with approximately $(1 - \alpha) \times 100$ percent confidence, and they will be narrower than the Working-Hotelling intervals.

The distribution of $\max_{a \leq x \leq b}|T_x|$ is practically uncomputable, but can be approximated easily. As a first approximation, we suggest approximating the distribution of $\max_{a \leq x \leq b}|T_x|$ using the distribution of $\max_{x_i}|T_{x_i}|$, where the values x_i are equally spaced values with $a = x_1 < x_2 < \cdots < x_k = b$. The critical value c_α from this distribution is slightly smaller than the correct critical value, but should be very close when k is large.

You can use the %SimIntervals macro for this "discrete approximation" method. For our example, we will compute simultaneous confidence bounds for the mean price of a house as a function of its size, using the data set `data=house` from Chapter 5 and restricting our attention only to houses in location A.

To create a data set with houses only in region A we specify

```
data house_a;
    set house;
    if location = 'A';
run;
```

The program that produces simultaneous confidence bounds over the region from 1,000 to 3,000 square feet (using increments of 200) is shown in Program 6.8.

PROGRAM 6.8   Simultaneous Confidence Bounds for Regression Function

```
%MakeGLMStats(dataset=house_a,
                  yvar=price,
                  model=sqfeet);

%macro Contrasts;
    free c clab;
    do x = 1000 to 3000 by 200;
        c = c // (1 || x);
        clab = clab // x;
        end;
        c = c';
%mend;

%SimIntervals(nsamp=50000,seed=121211);

data xvalues;
    do x = 1000 to 3000 by 200;
    output;
    end;
run;

data confplot;
    merge xvalues SimIntOut;
run;

goptions ftext=swissb hsize=4 in vsize=4 in;
axis1 style=1 width=2 major=(number=5) minor=none
    label=('Square Feet');
axis2 style=1 width=2 major=(number=5) minor=none
    label=('Price');

symbol1 w=1 c=black i=spline v=none;
symbol2 w=1 c=black i=spline v=none l=2;

proc gplot data=confplot;
        title;
        plot Estimate*x=1 (LowerCL UpperCL)*x=2/
            haxis=axis1 vaxis=axis2 frame overlay;
run;
```

Note that the %SimIntervals macro creates an output data set, SimIntOut, which we have used for the graphics.

The ordinary output from the %SimIntervals macro is as follows.

**Output from
Program 6.8: Statistics**

```
                 Estimated 95% Quantile = 2.582993

                    Standard        --- Pr > |t| --   95% Confidence
   Contrast Estimate  Error t Value  Raw Adjusted        Interval

      1000  73.4435  3.6973  19.86  <.0001  <.0001  63.8934  82.9936
      1200  81.4959  2.9917  27.24  <.0001  <.0001  73.7684  89.2234
      1400  89.5483  2.3269  38.48  <.0001  <.0001  83.5379  95.5586
      1600  97.6006  1.7500  55.77  <.0001  <.0001  93.0804  102.1
      1800   105.7   1.3765  76.76  <.0001  <.0001   102.1   109.2
      2000   113.7   1.3823  82.26  <.0001  <.0001   110.1   117.3
      2200   121.8   1.7638  69.03  <.0001  <.0001   117.2   126.3
      2400   129.8   2.3442  55.38  <.0001  <.0001   123.8   135.9
      2600   137.9   3.0105  45.79  <.0001  <.0001   130.1   145.6
      2800   145.9   3.7169  39.26  <.0001  <.0001   136.3   155.5
      3000   154.0   4.4443  34.64  <.0001  <.0001   142.5   165.4
```

The estimated quantile 2.582993 is only slightly smaller than the Working-Hotelling critical value $\sqrt{2F_{.95,2,26-2}} = 2.6088$, so that there is only slight savings in using the discrete simulation-based method. Moreover, recall that the discrete simulation-based method results in a slightly liberal critical value relative to the 95th percentile of the true distribution of $\max_{a \leq x \leq b} |T_x|$; therefore, the correct critical value should be even closer to the Working-Hotelling critical value. These observations suggest that, for this example, the Working-Hotelling critical value will suffice, and there is no need to simulate.

The reason the Working-Hotelling method works so well in this instance is that the range $1000 \leq x \leq 3000$ covers the entire range of the x data, and is, therefore, "almost like" considering an infinite collection. With a narrower range of x values of interest, the savings when using the simulation-based method can be more substantial. For example, suppose the range of interest only involves houses between 2,000 and 2,500 square feet. If you change the code in Program 6.8 from do x = 1000 to 3000 by 200; to do x = 2000 to 2500 by 25; then the simulation-based critical value is 2.323194, substantially smaller than the Working-Hotelling critical value 2.609.

The graph of the confidence bounds from Program 6.8 is shown here:

**Output from
Program 6.8:
Confidence Bounds for
Mean Price of a House**

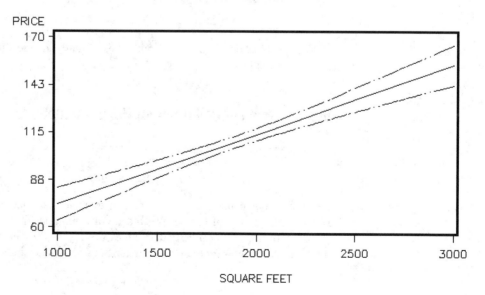

Confidence Bounds for Mean Price

Because the simulation-based critical value and the Working-Hotelling critical value are virtually identical, you can essentially reproduce the confidence bounds using the Working-Hotelling method, as given in Program 6.9.

PROGRAM 6.9   Working-Hotelling Confidence Bounds for Regression Function

```
%let conf=.95;
data housplt;
   set house_a end=eof;
   output;
   if eof then do;
      call symput('n',left(_n_));
      price=.;
      do sqfeet=1000 to 3000 by 200;
         output;
         end;
      end;
run;
proc reg data=housplt;
   model price = sqfeet;
   output out=ests p=pred stdp=se;
run;
data plot;
   set ests;
   if _n_ > &n;
   c_a = sqrt(2*finv(&conf,2,&n-2));
   lower = pred - c_a*se;
   upper = pred + c_a*se;
run;
goptions ftext=swissb hsize=4 in vsize=4 in;
axis1 style=1 width=2 major=(number=5) minor=none
   label=('Square Feet');
axis2 style=1 width=2 major=(number=5) minor=none
   label=('Price');
Symbol1 W=1 C=Black I=Spline V=None;
Symbol2 W=1 C=Black I=Spline V=None L=2;
proc gplot data=plot;
   title;
      plot pred*sqfeet=1 (lower upper)*sqfeet=2/
         haxis=axis1 vaxis=axis2 frame overlay;
run;
```

The graphical output from Program 6.9 is virtually identical to that of Program 6.8, and is not repeated here.

6.3.3   Confidence Bands for Partial Functions

Suppose you have a multiple regression model

$$y = \beta_0 + \beta_1 x_1 + \beta_2 x_2 + \cdots + \beta_r x_r + \epsilon,$$

and you want to depict the relationship of y to a particular one of the r regressor variables, say x_1, without loss of generality. To show this relationship in a two-dimensional graph, you must fix $x_2, \ldots, x_r$ at particular values $x_{02}, \ldots, x_{0r}$ (for example, the variable means). In this case you want to obtain simultaneous confidence intervals for all values

$$\beta_0 + \beta_1 x_1 + \beta_2 x_{02} + \cdots + \beta_r x_{0r}$$

where x_1 ranges from a to b. These intervals will be constructed as

$$\hat{\beta}_0 + \hat{\beta}_1 x_1 + \hat{\beta}_2 x_{02} + \cdots + \hat{\beta}_r x_{0r} \pm c_\alpha \hat{\sigma} \sqrt{\mathbf{x}_1'(\mathbf{X}'\mathbf{X})^{-1}\mathbf{x}_1},$$

where $\mathbf{x}_1' = (1 \; x_1 \; x_{02} \; \dots \; x_{0r})$.

Using the Working-Hotelling method, you would select $c_\alpha = \sqrt{(r+1)F_{1-\alpha,r+1,n-r-1}}$, since there are $r+1$ parameter estimates whose variability must be accounted for. However, this critical value is much too large because it considers inferences over the family of all linear combinations of β. The simulation-based approach provides substantial savings in this case, since it only concerns the linear combinations where x_1 varies and all other coefficients are fixed.

The following example illustrates the point concerning conservativeness of Working-Hotelling in the case of partial functions.

EXAMPLE: Patient Satisfaction as a Function of Severity of Illness

Do you live in a city with more than one medical center? If you do, then you are probably often subjected to a barrage of advertising by the various medical centers, each promising the best care, or the most competence, or special services. Hospitals are increasingly concerned with patient satisfaction, since satisfied patients typically tell others of their experiences, and this translates into more patients in the long term. Moreover, market research suggests that the multiplier effect of *loss* from a *dissatisfied* customer is even greater than the multiplier effect of *gain* from a *satisfied* customer. For these reasons, it is very important for businesses, and hospitals in particular, to understand customer satisfaction.

Neter et al. (1996, p. 254–255) report an example where patient satisfaction, age, severity of illness, and anxiety level are measured for a sample of $n = 23$ patients. The data are given in Program 6.10.

PROGRAM 6.10   Patient Satisfaction Data

```
data pat_sat;
   input age severe anxiety satisf @@;
   cards;
50 51 2.3 48   36 46 2.3 57   40 48 2.2 66   41 44 1.8 70
28 43 1.8 89   49 54 2.9 36   42 50 2.2 46   45 48 2.4 54
52 62 2.9 26   29 50 2.1 77   29 48 2.4 89   43 53 2.4 67
38 55 2.2 47   34 51 2.3 51   53 54 2.2 57   36 49 2.0 66
33 56 2.5 79   29 46 1.9 88   33 49 2.1 60   55 51 2.4 49
29 52 2.3 77   44 58 2.9 52   43 50 2.3 60
;
```

We will investigate the effect of severity of illness on patient satisfaction. Simple analysis shows a significant correlation between these variables ($r = -0.58$, $p = 0.0032$), but this analysis does not include the variables age and anxiety. It is possible that older or more anxiety-prone patients also have more severe illnesses, and thus, that this pairwise correlation is driven more by age or anxiety than by severity.

You can use a partial effect plot to remove the effect of age and `anxiety`, thus revealing a clearer picture of the satisfaction-satisfaction relationship. Average values of age and `anxiety` are 39.6 and 2.30, respectively. Program 6.11 estimates the satisfaction-severity relationship, along with its simultaneous 95 percent confidence bounds, when age and `anxiety` are held fixed at their respective averages.

PROGRAM 6.11   Confidence Bounds for a Partial Function

```
%MakeGLMStats(dataset   = pat_sat,
                 yvar     = satisf,
                 model    = age severe anxiety);

%macro Contrasts;
    free c clab;
    do x = 45 to 60 by 1;
        c = c // (1 || 39.6 || x || 2.30);
        clab = clab // x;
        end;
        c = c';
%mend;

%SimIntervals(nsamp=100000,seed=121221);

data xvalues;
    do x = 45 to 60 by 1;
    output;
    end; run;
data confplot;
    merge xvalues SimIntOut; run;

goptions ftext=swissb hsize=4 in vsize=4 in;
axis1 style=1 width=2 major=(number=6) minor=none
    label=('Illness Severity');
axis2 style=1 width=2 major=(number=6) minor=none
    label=('Satisfaction');
Symbol1 W=1 C=Black I=Spline V=None;
Symbol2 W=1 C=Black I=Spline V=None L=2;

proc gplot data=confplot;
      title;
      plot estimate*x=1 (lowercl uppercl)*x=2/
        haxis=axis1 vaxis=axis2 frame overlay;
run;
```

The output from the %SimIntervals macro looks very much like the output from Program 6.8, and is not shown here. However, the estimated critical value provided by %SimIntervals is 2.627, substantially smaller than the corresponding Working-Hotelling critical value of $\sqrt{4F_{.95,4,23-4}} = 3.403$. Thus, in the case of partial regression plots, the Working-Hotelling method is very wasteful.

The partial regression function plot, with associated confidence limits, is given in the output from Program 6.11.

**Output from
Program 6.11**

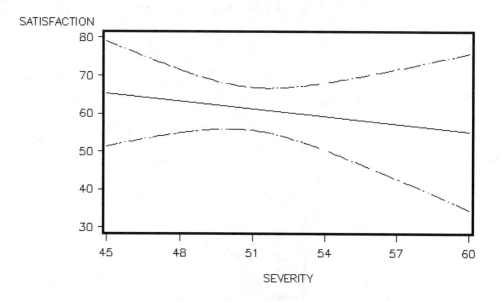

Confidence Bounds For Satisfaction

As you can see, it is unclear whether severity increases or decreases satisfaction, when age and anxiety are held constant. While logic suggests that the effect should not be an increase, the confidence bounds show that no effect at all (a flat line) is plausible. More data are needed to characterize the precise relationship between satisfaction and severity of illness.

6.3.4   Confidence Band for Difference of Regression Functions; Interaction with Classification Variable and Covariate

When you have interaction between a two-level classification variable and a covariate, then the estimated difference between response means depends on the value of the covariate. For some values of the covariate the estimated differences could be significantly positive; for other values the direction of the difference could be statistically indeterminable, or perhaps even significantly negative.

EXAMPLE: Comparing Two Product Formulations when there is a Significant Covariate

In an example data set from Neter et al. (1996, p. 493), engineers want to compare operating costs per mile of two brands of truck tires. They measure wear on the tires at various operating speeds (measured in miles per hour, or MPH). The data set is given in Program 6.12.

PROGRAM 6.12   Tire Wear Data

```
data tire;
   input make$ mph cost @@;
datalines;
A 10  9.8  A 20 12.5  A 20 14.2  A 30 14.9  A 40 19.0
A 40 16.5  A 50 20.9  A 60 22.4  A 60 24.1  A 70 25.8
B 10 15.0  B 20 14.5  B 20 16.1  B 30 16.5  B 40 16.4
B 40 19.1  B 50 20.9  B 60 22.3  B 60 19.8  B 70 21.4
;
run;
```

A graph of the resulting data is given as follows. Note that the tire type "A" seems to have a lower cost at low MPH, while tire type "B" seems to have a lower cost at high MPH. The question is, for which values of MPH can we confidently conclude a cost difference?

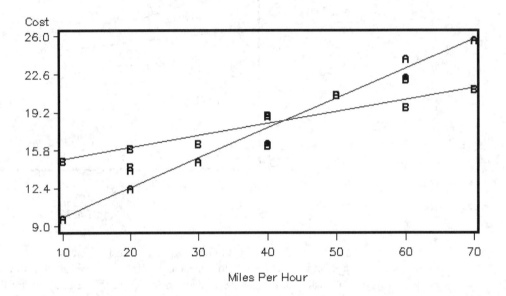

The plot of the data and fitted regression lines shows a dramatic interaction—for some MPH the tire "A" seems preferred, and for others "B" seems preferred. For which MPH can we make statistically significant directional determinations? For this we consider a confidence band for the difference of regression lines.

The model is

$$\text{cost}_{ij} = \beta_{0i} + \beta_{1i}\text{mph}_{ij} + \epsilon_{ij},$$

where $i = 1, 2$ denotes group and j denotes an observation within the group. The difference function is

$$\delta(x) = (\beta_{01} - \beta_{02}) + (\beta_{11} - \beta_{12})x,$$

and we consider only those x values that lie in a relevant range. Program 6.13 uses the %SimIntervals macro to find the appropriate critical value for the confidence band.

PROGRAM 6.13   Simultaneous Confidence Bounds for Difference of Regression Functions

```
%MakeGLMStats(dataset  = tire ,
              classvar = make ,
              yvar     = cost ,
              model    = make mph make*mph);

%macro Contrasts;
   free c clab;
   do x = 10 to 70 by 5;
      c = c // (0 || 1 || -1 || 0 || x || -x);
      clab = clab // x ;
   end;
   c = c`;
%mend;
```

```
%SimIntervals(nsamp=100000, seed=121211);

data xvalues;
   do x = 10 to 70 by 5;
   output;
   end;
run;

data confplot;
   merge xvalues SimIntOut;
run;

goptions ftext=swissb hsize=5 in vsize=4 in;
axis1 style=1 width=2 major=(number=7) minor=none
   label=('Miles Per Hour');
axis2 style=1 width=2 major=(number=5) minor=none
   label=('CostA-CostB');
symbol1 w=1 c=black i=spline v=none;
symbol2 w=1 c=black i=spline v=none l=2;
proc gplot data=confplot;
   title;
   plot estimate*x=1 (lowercl uppercl)*x=2/
      haxis=axis1 vaxis=axis2 frame overlay vref=0;
run;
```

The output from the %SimIntervals macro is as follows:

Output from %SimIntervals Macro from Program 6.13

Estimated 95% Quantile = 2.638264

Contrast	Estimate	Standard Error	t Value	Pr > |t| Raw	Adjusted	95% Confidence Interval	
10	-4.1067	0.9143	-4.49	0.0004	0.0013	-6.5189	-1.6945
15	-3.4539	0.8084	-4.27	0.0006	0.0019	-5.5867	-1.3211
20	-2.8011	0.7101	-3.94	0.0012	0.0037	-4.6745	-0.9277
25	-2.1483	0.6230	-3.45	0.0033	0.0105	-3.7920	-0.5047
30	-1.4956	0.5524	-2.71	0.0155	0.0444	-2.9531	-0.0381
35	-0.8428	0.5054	-1.67	0.1149	0.2660	-2.1762	0.4906
40	-0.1900	0.4887	-0.39	0.7026	0.9235	-1.4794	1.0994
45	0.4628	0.5054	0.92	0.3734	0.6531	-0.8706	1.7962
50	1.1156	0.5524	2.02	0.0605	0.1531	-0.3419	2.5731
55	1.7683	0.6230	2.84	0.0119	0.0346	0.1247	3.4120
60	2.4211	0.7101	3.41	0.0036	0.0114	0.5477	4.2945
65	3.0739	0.8084	3.80	0.0016	0.0050	0.9411	5.2067
70	3.7267	0.9143	4.08	0.0009	0.0029	1.3145	6.1389

Note that, in this case, the differences between the tire types is significant for MPH from 10 to 30, and for MPH from 55 to 70. These differences are clearly seen in the graphical output that follows:

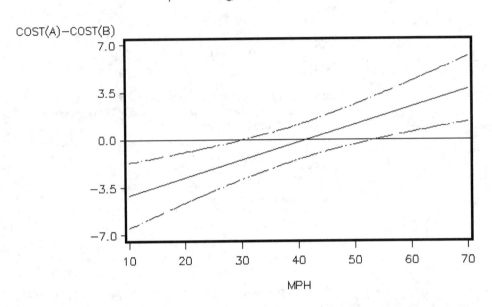

When both confidence limits are completely on one side of the horizontal reference line (at difference $= 0$), the difference between the tire types is statistically significant. Furthermore, you may make a directional determination with confidence in this situtation.

As is the case with the simple regression line, the difference between simulation-based and Working-Hotelling critical values is small in this case. Here, the Working-Hotelling critical value is $c_{0.05} = \sqrt{2F_{0.95,2,20-4}} = 2.696$, only slightly larger than the simulation-based critical value 2.638264 shown in the output from Program 6.13. The Working-Hotelling critical value is identical to the case with the confidence band for the simple regression line, except for using $df = n - 4$ instead of $df = n - 2$.

Since there is so little difference between the simulation-based and Working-Hotelling methods for this case, you could just as well employ the Working-Hotelling method by suitably modifying Program 6.9. However, the Working-Hotelling method can sometimes be needlessly conservative when

- the range of interest is appreciably less than the range of the data
- there are many more parameters estimated whose x-multipliers are not varied (as is the case with the partial plots).

In each of these cases, the set of inferences of interest is more restricted than the set considered in the Working-Hotelling procedure.

Thus, even though the Working-Hotelling procedure is perfectly adequate, and only barely wasteful in many cases, it is prudent to use the simulation-based method always to avoid unnecessary conservativeness.

6.3.5 Comparing the Discrete Method with the Continuous Method

In the examples from the preceding sections, we recommend using the %SimIntervals macro to estimate the critical values that are needed for simultaneous confidence bands.

This macro requires that you make the interval discrete by choosing intermediate points x_i with $a \leq x_1 < x_2 < \cdots < x_k = b$. Clearly, the $1 - \alpha$ quantile of the discrete maximum $\max |T_{x_i}|$ will *underestimate* the $1 - \alpha$ quantile of the continuous $\max_{a \leq x \leq b} |T_x|$. Thus, your inferences might be incorrect in that the true simultaneous confidence level of the regression band is less than the desired $100(1 - \alpha)\%$. However, as the number of points k increases, the discrete quantile should approach the continuous quantile. Thus, there should be no problem when k is large.

It is possible to simulate the distribution of $\max_{a \leq x \leq b} |t_x|$ using a constrained optimization technique to calculate the value of $\max_{a \leq x \leq b} |T_x^*|$ for each simulated data set. Program 6.14 uses the nlp* subroutines from SAS/IML software to perform this optimization in a simulation for the comparison of the tire types.

PROGRAM 6.14 **Finding the Critical Value for Comparing Two Regression Lines Using the Continuous Method (Constrained Optimization)**

```
options nonotes;
%let nsamp     = 100000;    /* Number of simulations */
%let seed      = 121021;
%let dataset   = tire;
%let yvar      = cost;
%let classvar  = make;      /* Must be a two-level variable */
%let xvar      = mph;
%let lowerX    = 10;
%let upperX    = 70;
%let conf      = 0.95;
%let npoints   = 100;       /* Number of points to plot on the graph */

proc iml;
    use &dataset;
    read all var {&yvar} into Y;
    read all var {&xvar} into X1;
    read all var {&classvar} into X2;
    D = design(X2)[,1];
    DX = D#X1;
    n = nrow(X1);
    one = j(n,1,1);
    X = one||X1||D||DX;
    XPXI   = INV(X'*X);
    XPXIXP = XPXI*X';
    b = XPXIXP*Y;
    df = n-ncol(X);
    mse = (Y'-b'*X')*(Y-X*b)/df;
    lowerX = &lowerX;  upperX = &upperX;
    xbar = x1[+,]/n;
    optn={1 0};
    bc = lowerX//UpperX;
    maxt=j(&nsamp,1,0);
    inc = (UpperX-LowerX)/&npoints;

start tstat(x0) global(n,XPXI,bstar,msestar );
    c0 = {0}||{0}||{1}||x0;
    est = c0*bstar;
    t = est/sqrt(msestar*c0*XPXI*c0');
    t = abs(t);
    return(t);
finish;
```

```
do isim = 1 to &nsamp;
  Ystar = rannor(j(n,1,&seed));
  bstar = xpxixp*Ystar;
  msestar = (Ystar'-bstar'*X')*(Ystar-X*bstar)/df;
  call nlpqn(rc,xmax,"tstat",xbar,optn,bc,,,,,);
  mx = tstat(xmax);
  maxt[isim] = mx;
end;

temp = maxt;
maxt[rank(maxt),] = temp;
critindx = round(&nsamp*&conf,1);
sim_crit = maxt[critindx];
wh_crit  = sqrt(2*finv(&conf,2,df));
t_crit   = tinv(1-(1-&conf)/2,df);
print "The simulation-based, Working-Hotelling, and t critical values are";
print  sim_crit wh_crit t_crit;
```

Output from Program 6.14

```
The simulation-based, Working-Hotelling, and t critical values are


       SIM_CRIT       WH_CRIT       T_CRIT

     2.6440823111   2.6958202713   2.1199052992
```

To see the effect of discreteness (the %SimIntervals method) versus using the continuous method from Program 6.14, you can compare the output with the output from %SimIntervals for various numbers of points k in the interval. Table 6.1 compares the results. In all cases, the number of simulations is nsamp=100000.

TABLE 6.1   Comparison of Discrete and Continuous Critical Values

x values	k	95% Quantile
10,70	2	2.430
10,40,70	3	2.575
10,20,30,40,50,60,70	7	2.632
10,15,20,25,...,70	15	2.638
$10 \leq x \leq 70$	∞	2.644
Working-Hotelling	–	2.696

The correct critical value is 2.644, corresponding to the $10 \leq x \leq 70$ entry. (This is not exactly correct because of Monte Carlo error, but is reasonably close.) The %SimIntervals method produces the first four lines of Table 6.1. You can see that the more discrete points you include in the interval, the more accurate are the %SimIntervals results.

6.4   Concluding Remarks

- If you want to perform inferences for a general set of linear functions (contrasts or otherwise) in the linear model, you can adjust for the specific correlation structure using simulation-based methods. The %SimIntervals macro is provided for that purpose.

- If you want to search through your data to identify the most significant contrasts, then you should use the Sheffé critical value, since your family is virtually infinite.

- If you want to calculate simultaneous confidence bands for regression functions or for differences of regression functions, you can safely use the Working-Hotelling critical value in many cases. However, since the Working-Hotelling critical value can be needlessly conservative, we recommend using the %SimIntervals macro for this purpose as well, using the discrete approximation method.

Chapter 7

Power and Sample Size in Simultaneous Inference

7.1   Introduction

As we have shown, a major drawback of multiple comparisons and multiple testing procedures is their reduced power. Adjusted *p*-values are larger and simultaneous confidence intervals are wider, making it more difficult to reach firm conclusions. You can avoid these difficulties if you *design* your study with multiple inferences in mind. If you do this, you can guarantee that meaningful differences will be flagged as "statistically significant" with high probability, even when you use an MCP.

Before you perform any study, you should consider beforehand which inferences you want to make and which statistical procedures you will use to make them, and you should be careful to design the study so that those procedures will provide those inferences with an acceptable level of confidence. The same goes for multiple comparisons and multiple testing: you should design your group-comparison studies with multiple inferences in mind.

In this chapter we show how to calculate power for various MCPs, and how to determine sample sizes to achieve high power. As we shall see, power is not so easily defined in multiple testing situations as it is in single testing situations. Further, there are difficulties in evaluating power for many methods.

A potential complexity of power calculations in the context of multiple inference is that in principle they require you to compute with the joint noncentral distribution of all test statistics. This is a daunting task even when it's possible to write down a formula for this distribution, and it isn't even always possible. However, a recurring theme of this book is that, in cases where analytic evaluations are difficult, it is often easy to obtain reasonable results through simulation. This solution is perhaps the best approach, in general, for power calculations involving MCPs. In this chapter we provide programs to calculate power analytically in simple situations, and to simulate it in more complex ones.

EXAMPLE: Comparisons of Assays

A laboratory wants to compare five alternative formulations of a compound. They can feasibly handle no more than 400 assays in all, but because of cost constraints they'd like to do many fewer than that. From historical information, the scientists know that mean differences of 5.0 units are "meaningful," and they also know that the background standard deviation of the measurement is roughly 6.0 units. What sample sizes should be used for each assay group?

The most important items, the number of groups, the size of the meaningful difference, and the size of the background standard deviation are already given in the example. However, you need to answer more questions before determining sample sizes.

1. Do you want to use the same sample size in every group? Usually, the answer is "yes"; however, in some cases, you might require more precision for a particular group (e.g., the control group), and allocate more units there.

2. You obviously would like to detect meaningful differences, but how high a probability do you require to detect such differences? Noting that 100 percent probability is impossible, and that extremely high probabilities like 99.9 percent are needlessly stringent, analysts typically choose a "reasonably high" value in the 80 percent to 95 percent range.

3. Do you want to perform all pairwise comparisons or only comparisons with a control? If the goal is only to screen solutions that are significantly worse than control, then you should use comparisons with control. If you want to compare all treatments with the goal of ranking them, then you should use all pairwise comparisons.

4. Most tricky of all, which power definition will you use? In simple testing, there is only one definition, but the situation is more complex in multiple testing because there are so many more parameters.

Program 7.1 simulates how the analysis might turn out after a single run. We are simulating data here, using "true mean" values $\mu_1 = 10$, $\mu_2 = 5$, $\mu_3 = 5$, $\mu_4 = 0$, and $\mu_5 = 0$, and a "true standard deviation" of $\sigma = 6.0$. We analyze all pairwise differences using Tukey's method with a balanced design and $n_i = 10$ assays per treatment group.

PROGRAM 7.1   Simulation of ANOVA Data

```
data a;
    array mu{5} (10,5,5,0,0);
    do a = 1 to dim(mu);
        do i = 1 to 10;
            y = mu{a} + 6*rannor(12345);
            output;
            end;
        end;
    run;

proc glm data=a;
    class a;
    model y = a;
    means a / tukey cldiff;
    ods select CLDiffs;
    run;
```

**Output from
Program 7.1**

```
                              The GLM Procedure

                  Tukey's Studentized Range (HSD) Test for y

          Comparisons significant at the 0.05 level are indicated by ***.


                             Difference      Simultaneous
                    a        Between         95% Confidence
              Comparison      Means            Interval


                1  - 2        2.863        -4.364    10.089
                1  - 3        5.949        -1.277    13.176
                1  - 5       10.096         2.870    17.323     ***
                1  - 4       12.319         5.092    19.545     ***
                2  - 1       -2.863       -10.089     4.364
                2  - 3        3.087        -4.140    10.313
                2  - 5        7.234         0.008    14.460     ***
                2  - 4        9.456         2.230    16.682     ***
                3  - 1       -5.949       -13.176     1.277
                3  - 2       -3.087       -10.313     4.140
                3  - 5        4.147        -3.079    11.373
                3  - 4        6.369        -0.857    13.596
                5  - 1      -10.096       -17.323    -2.870     ***
                5  - 2       -7.234       -14.460    -0.008     ***
                5  - 3       -4.147       -11.373     3.079
                5  - 4        2.222        -5.004     9.449
                4  - 1      -12.319       -19.545    -5.092     ***
                4  - 2       -9.456       -16.682    -2.230     ***
                4  - 3       -6.369       -13.596     0.857
                4  - 5       -2.222        -9.449     5.004
```

In this simulation, Tukey's method detects the difference between the means where the true difference is 10.0 units (the 1 - 4 and 1 - 5 comparisons). It also detects two of the comparisons where the true difference is 5.0 units (the 2 - 4 and 2 - 5 comparisons), but misses four other comparisons where the true difference is 5.0 units (1 - 2, 1 - 3, 3 - 4, and 3 - 5). The remaining comparisons (2 - 3 and 4 - 5) are correctly determined as "statistically insignificant."

So, what would you like to have happened in this simulation? Presumably, you would like all of the differences except (2 - 3 and 4 - 5) to be "statistically significant," since these are the only true nulls, and all other differences are real differences. However, it is statistically ambitious (and unlikely) that all nonnull effects will be detected. You can try to design a study with this objective in mind, but the sample size requirements might be too large. In the next section, we offer alternative objectives that might serve your purposes as well, without requiring large sample sizes.

7.2   Definitions of Power

In single testing situations, power is defined as

$$\text{Power} = P(\text{reject } H_0 \mid H_0 \text{ is false}).$$

To perform this calculation, you must specify the condition "H_0 is false" precisely. For example, when testing $H_0: \mu_1 = \mu_2$, the condition "H_0 is false" must be specified by giving a particular nonnull value for $\mu_1 - \mu_2$, such as $\mu_1 - \mu_2 = 5$ or $\mu_1 - \mu_2 = 10$. The power is, therefore, a function of the size of the difference, and the usual approach to designing studies is to ensure that a "meaningful" difference will be detected with sufficiently high probability. For example, if $\mu_1 - \mu_2 = 5$ is considered a "meaningful" difference, then you can choose to design the study so that the power is, say, 80 percent when $\mu_1 - \mu_2 = 5$.

In multiple testing and multiple comparisons applications, power is more complex since there are multiple parameters with multiple null hypotheses H_{0i}. Definitions include

- Complete Power $= P$(reject *all* H_{0i} that are false)
- Minimal Power $= P$(reject *at least one* H_{0i} that is false)
- Individual Power $= P$(reject *a particular* H_{0i} that is false)
- Proportional Power = average *proportion* of false H_{0i} that are rejected.

7.2.1   Complete Power

As suggested in the assay example, *complete power* appears the most attractive, since you obviously would like to reject all false hypotheses. However, it is usually very difficult to obtain rejections for all false hypotheses, since reasonable designs often have low power by this definition. For example, with 10 independent tests, all with individual power of 0.8, the complete power is $(0.8)^{10} = 0.107$. Computing the complete power requires that you specify all the alternatives precisely; exact computations are infeasible, but simulation yields results that are accurate enough for design purposes.

As a parenthetical comment, we note that in the International Conference for Harmonisation Guidelines on Statistical Principle for Clinical Trials (ICH, 1998), there is a reference to what we refer to as complete power.

> "If the purpose of the trial is to demonstrate effects on all of the designated primary variables, then there is no need for adjustment of the type I error, but the impact on type II error and sample size should be carefully considered."

It is a fact that such a method controls the type I error, but it is rather stringent in that insignificance for just one test implies a failure to reject the null. Thus, power implications must be considered carefully. This method is known as the "Intersection-Union" method; see, e.g., Hochberg and Westfall (1999).

7.2.2   Minimal Power

Minimal power tells you the probability that you will find at least one significant result in your study, among hypotheses that are truly false. If your study only requires that at least one effect be demonstrated then you should use minimal power.

Minimal power is useful because it corresponds to the FWE rate: when the alternative differences all tend toward zero, the minimal power tends toward FWE.

As with the complete power, computing the minimal power requires that you specify all the alternatives precisely; and again, while exact computations are infeasible, simulation yields results that are accurate enough for design purposes.

7.2.3   Individual Power

Individual power is most closely related to the ordinary definition of power. It differs only in that it presumes that your tests use critical points from MCPs. The disadvantage of individual power is that, from the multiple inference standpoint, it presumes a particular interest in just one of the multiple hypotheses. This is a disadvantage because if you are really just interested in one hypothesis, then you can test that one without any multiplicity adjustment. Also, if you use this method, you need to interpret the results carefully; an individual power of 0.8 refers only to a specific, predetermined hypothesis. You cannot interpret this probability as "the power of detecting all false nulls is 0.8," or "the probability of detecting at least one false null is 0.8." You can only interpret this power figure as "the probability of detecting a false null for (say) test # 3 is 0.8," where "test # 3" is a particular test among the collection that has been predetermined.

7.2.4 Proportional Power

Proportional power tells you what proportion of false nulls you may expect to detect. For example, in the assay simulation in Section 7.1, there were eight false nulls, and four were detected. Thus, the proportion of false nulls detected is $4/8 = 50$ percent for this simulation. Another simulation (with a different seed) might produce $6/8 = 75$ percent as the proportion of false nulls that are detected. Suppose you simulate 10,000 times, and compute the average of all such proportions; this would be an estimate of proportional power. In more precise mathematical terms, the proportional power is the average of all possible proportions weighted by their respective probabilities (or the *expected value* of the proportion).

Note that all four definitions of power reduce to the usual univariate definition of power when there is only one test (i.e., when $k = 1$).

7.3 Examples Using Individual Power

Among the various methods, individual power is the easiest to calculate, since it is just like "ordinary" power, except with multiplicity-adjusted critical values. Also, it can be calculated exactly, without resorting to simulations. In this section we provide examples and code to calculate individual power in the cases of all pairwise comparisons, comparisons with a control, and simultaneous confidence intervals for means.

7.3.1 All Pairwise Comparisons

Suppose that you plan to use Tukey's method in a balanced one-way ANOVA layout, and you want to detect a significant difference for a particular $\mu_i - \mu_{i'}$ comparison when $\mu_i - \mu_{i'} = \delta$. The value δ is a specified number that is a "meaningful" difference in the particular problem context.

To detect a significant difference between μ_i and $\mu_{i'}$, you must have either

$$t_{i,i'} = \frac{\bar{y}_i - \bar{y}_{i'}}{\hat{\sigma}\sqrt{2/n}} > c_\alpha$$

or

$$t_{i,i'} = \frac{\bar{y}_i - \bar{y}_{i'}}{\hat{\sigma}\sqrt{2/n}} < -c_\alpha,$$

where $c_\alpha = q^R_{1-\alpha,g,g(n-1)}/\sqrt{2}$ is the critical value used for Tukey's method. The sum of the probabilities of these two events is the power of the test using the individual power definition. To calculate these probabilities, use the fact that $t_{i,i'}$ has a noncentral Student's t distribution with $g(n-1)$ degrees of freedom and a noncentrality parameter $(\delta/\sigma)\sqrt{n/2}$. Thus, the probabilities can be computed using the PROBT function.

In order to compute the individual power, you need to specify the following:

d is the "meaningful difference"

σ is an estimate (or guess) of the within-group standard deviation of the response

g is the number of groups

n is the within-group sample size

α is the desired FWE level of the Tukey intervals.

The %IndividualPower macro, defined in the appendix, computes the individual power given d, σ, g, and α for a range of group sizes n, plotting the power as a function n and identifying the value of n closest to a target power. In Program 7.2, the input parameters are specified as $\delta = 4$, $\sigma = 3$, $g = 5$, and FWE=.05, and the target power is the default 0.80.

PROGRAM 7.2   **Using the %IndividualPower Macro to Calculate Power Analytically for All Pairwise Comparisons**

```
%IndividualPower(
    MCP = RANGE,  /* RANGE, DUNNETT2, DUNNETT1, OR MAXMOD          */
    g   = 5,      /* number of groups (exclude control for DUNNETT) */
    d   = 4,      /* meaningful mean difference                     */
    s   = 3       /* estimate (guess) of standard deviation         */
    );
```

**Output from
Program 7.2**

Power for detecting an individual difference of 4
Using the RANGE method with FWE=0.05
With 5 groups and standard deviation = 3

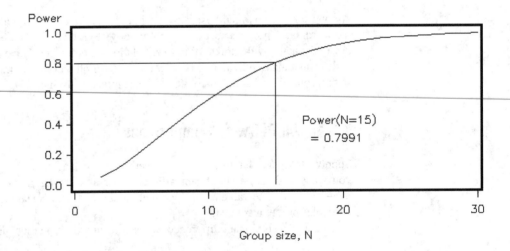

Power(N=15)
= 0.7991

Note that you would need about $n = 15$ observations per cell to achieve an individual power of 0.80 for the given difference $\delta = 5$ when $\sigma = 4$. The power refers to a particular, prespecified pairwise comparison using Tukey's method with FWE $= 0.05$ in a balanced ANOVA with $g = 5$ groups.

7.3.2   Comparisons with a control

Suppose that you plan to use Dunnett's method in a balanced one-way ANOVA, and you want to detect a significant difference for a particular $\mu_i - \mu_0$ comparison when $\mu_i - \mu_0 = \delta$. Again, the value δ is a specified number that is a "meaningful" difference in the particular problem context. Then you need to have either

$$t_{i0} = \frac{\bar{y}_i - \bar{y}_0}{\hat{\sigma}\sqrt{2/n}} > q_{1-\alpha,g,(g+1)(n-1)}^{D2}$$

or

$$t_{i0} = \frac{\bar{y}_i - \bar{y}_j}{\hat{\sigma}\sqrt{2/n}} < -q_{1-\alpha,g,(g+1)(n-1)}^{D2}.$$

The sum of the probabilities of these two events is the power of the test, using definition 3. To calculate these probabilities, use the fact that the distribution of t_{i0} is non-central Student's t with $(g+1)(n-1)$ degrees of freedom and noncentrality parameter ncp $= \sqrt{n/2}(\delta/\sigma)$.

For example, suppose that you have $g = 6$ groups (excluding control), and you want to detect a difference of $\mu_i - \mu_0 = 5$ for a particular comparison, and guess that the standard deviation of the measurement is $\sigma = 3.5$. The appropriate %IndividualPower invocation is shown in Program 7.3.

PROGRAM 7.3   **Using the %IndividualPower Macro to Calculate Power Analytically for Dunnett's Two-sided Comparisons with a Control**

```
%IndividualPower(MCP=DUNNETT2,g=6,d=5,s=3.5);
```

Output from Program 7.3

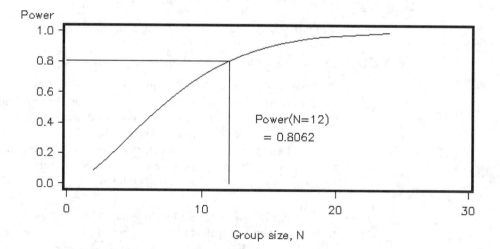

Power for detecting an individual difference of 5
Using the DUNNETT2 method with FWE=0.05
With 6 groups and standard deviation = 3.5

Power analysis for one-sided tests can be performed in the same way, changing DUNNETT2 to DUNNETT1. If you make the change you will see that there is higher power for the one-sided method; consequently, smaller sample sizes are needed to achieve the same power. Using the two-sided method, you need $n = 12$ observations per cell to detect a particular difference $\mu_i - \mu_0 = 5$ when $\sigma = 3.5$ with probability 0.80 (see output from

Program 7.3), but with one-sided tests you only need $n = 10$ observations per cell to achieve the same power (see the following graph).

Power for detecting an individual difference of 5
Using the DUNNETT1 method with FWE=0.05
With 6 groups and standard deviation = 3.5

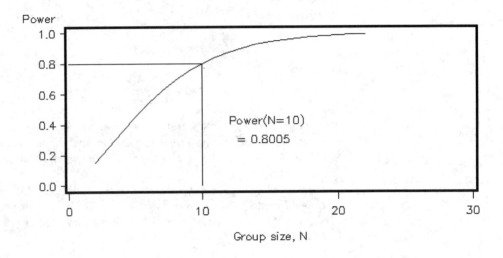

Group size, N

7.3.3   Simultaneous Confidence Intervals for Means

You can use the simultaneous confidence intervals for the means to test whether a particular mean differs significantly from a given standard. The hypotheses are stated as $H_0: \mu_i = \mu_{i0}$, and can be tested by noting whether the value μ_{i0} lies inside the confidence interval. If it lies outside the interval, then you reject the hypothesis, otherwise, you fail to reject it.

Power calculations for these tests require that you specify the "meaningful difference" $\delta = \mu_i - \mu_{i0}$. You can then use Program 7.2 easily as with the previous applications, but specifying the MAXMOD value for the mcp variable.

EXAMPLE: Changes from Baseline Measurements

An alternative design for the lab assay example from Section 7.1 is to use baseline measurements as controls, and evaluate assays for significant changes from baseline measurement. Suppose there are 10 formulations being assayed, with measurements taken before and after administration of the treatment. The variable of interest is the difference from baseline, and the question of interest is whether the mean difference is significantly different from zero. How large a sample size per group is needed to assure that the power for detecting a particular mean difference of 5 units is 0.80, while maintaining FWE = 0.05?

The pairwise differences in the 10 groups form a balanced one-way ANOVA, and we are testing the means against a known standard (0 in this case), so we can use Program 7.2 with the MAXMOD option. We need to know (or guess) the standard deviation σ of the difference measures; assume $\sigma = 5$. Supplying these inputs leads us to the following power curve:

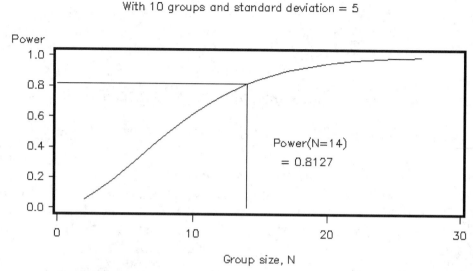

Power for detecting an individual difference of 5
Using the MAXMOD method with FWE=0.05
With 10 groups and standard deviation = 5

7.4   Examples Using Combined Power Definitions

While *individual* power refers to a particular hypothesis, *complete*, *minimal*, and *proportional* power involve several hypotheses simultaneously. As such, their calculations are complicated by the fact that they depend on the specific alternative settings for *all* nonnull hypotheses, not just the alternative setting for a particular test of interest. Calculations are further complicated for complete and proportional power because they require the joint noncentral distribution of the test statistics.

While calculating the power analytically is often infeasible for the combined power definitions, simulation can yield useful, if slightly imprecise, results. The %SimPower macro, defined in the appendix, computes the complete, minimal, and proportional power for specified input parameters. It is invoked as follows:

```
%SimPower(method    = <value>                      ,
          nrep      = <number>                      ,
          n         = <number> or <(n1,n2,...)>     ,
          s         = <number>                      ,
          FWE       = <number>                      ,
          TrueMeans = <(m1,m2,...)>                 ,
          seed      = <value>                       );
```

where

method   is the multiple comparisons method, whether all pairwise comparisons (method = TUKEY), two-sided comparisons with control (method = DUNNETT), one-sided comparisons with a control (either method = DUNNETTL or method = DUNNETTU) or REGWQ (defined in Chapter 8). The default is TUKEY.

nrep   is the number of simulations, with 1000 as the default.

n   is the within-group sample size (if equal) or list of within-group sample sizes (if unequal). You must specify n; there is no default.

s   is the underlying population standard deviation; there is no default.

FWE   is the desired FWE, with 0.05 as the default.

TrueMeans   is a listing of the true group means. You must specify this list; there is no default. An example: TrueMeans = (10,5,5,0,0).

seed   is the seed value, with 0 (computer clock time) as the default.

7.4.1   All Pairwise Comparisons

Program 7.4 simulates the same situation as in Program 7.1 and computes the three measures of composite power. The parameters method, FWE, and nrep are not given, and thus, are left at their defaults of TUKEY, 0.05, and 1000, respectively.

PROGRAM 7.4   Simulating Combined Power Measures for all Pairwise Comparisons

```
%SimPower(TrueMeans=(10, 5, 5, 0, 0),s=5,n=10,seed=12345);
```

Output from Program 7.4

```
Method=TUKEY, Nominal FWE=0.05, nrep=1000, Seed=12345
      True means = (10, 5, 5, 0, 0), n=10, s=5


Quantity                 Estimate      ---95% CI----

Complete Power            0.00700      (0.002,0.012)
Minimal Power            0.97500      (0.965,0.985)
Proportional Power       0.44263      (0.431,0.454)
True FWE                 0.01200      (0.005,0.019)
Directional FWE          0.01200      (0.005,0.019)
```

If you change the sample size from 10 to 20 in Program 7.4, and tabulate the results as shown above, you get

Power estimates with $n = 20$ per group, all pairwise comparisons

```
Method=TUKEY, Nominal FWE=0.05, nrep=1000, Seed=12345
      True means = (10, 5, 5, 0, 0), n=20, s=5


Quantity                 Estimate      ---95% CI----

Complete Power            0.13400      (0.113,0.155)
Minimal Power            1.00000      (1.000,1.000)
Proportional Power       0.73063      (0.720,0.741)
True FWE                 0.01500      (0.007,0.023)
Directional FWE          0.01500      (0.007,0.023)
```

We note the following:

- Power increases with larger sample sizes, for all power types.
- Complete power is very low, while minimal power is very high, both for $n = 10$ and $n = 20$.

7.4.2   True FWE and Directional FWE

Take a look at the output from Program 7.4. We snuck two new measures in on you—"True FWE" and "Directional FWE." While these topics are perhaps out of place here (perhaps belonging more to Chapter 1 or Chapter 2), they are computed essentially as a by-product of the power calculations done by %SimPower, and we would like to revisit these concepts at this time.

In Section 2.3.2 we discuss FWE for confidence intervals and hypothesis tests. Under the usual assumptions, FWE is exactly α for simultaneous confidence intervals, assuming you have selected an MCP with nominal α level control. However, the nominal α FWE level for multiple hypothesis tests is actually an upper bound for the true FWE level, which depends upon the number of true nulls. %SimPower simulates this true FWE level for you. In the output from Program 7.4, the true FWE is estimated at 0.012, meaning that at least one of the hypotheses $H: \mu_2 = \mu_3$ or $H: \mu_4 = \mu_5$ was rejected in only 1.2 percent of the 1000 simulated samples.

In Section 2.3.4, we define the *Directional* error rate as the probability of at least one incorrect sign determination. If the true sign is zero, then any determination of significant effect is a Type III error by this definition. If the true sign is negative, then a Type III error occurs when the claimed sign is positive and vice versa. Thus, the Type III FWE rate is *greater than* the true Type I FWE, by an amount equal to the proportion of samples yielding an incorrect directional determination, when the true difference is nonnull. In the output from Program 7.4 (both for n=10 and n=20), there were no such occurrences in the 1000 samples, thus the Type III FWE and the true Type I FWE coincide.

The Type III FWE is more interesting in cases where none of the effects are truly null. (Some statisticians take this point of view strictly, that no effects are truly null, and for them the Type III FWE is much more relevant than Type I FWE.) In Program 7.5 we evaluate power and FWE measures for such a case, where the size of all effects are "virtually null," but where no effects are truly null.

PROGRAM 7.5   **Evaluating Directional FWE When There Are No Null Effects**

```
%SimPower(TrueMeans = (-.1, -.2, .1, .05),
          s          = 500            ,
          n          = 2              ,
          nrep       = 4000           ,
          seed       = 12345          );
```

Output From Program 7.5

```
          Method=TUKEY, Nominal FWE=0.05, nrep=4000, Seed=12345
               True means = (-.1, -.2, .1, .05), n=2, s=500


               Quantity          Estimate      ---95% CI----

          Complete Power          0.00000      (0.000,0.000)
          Minimal Power           0.04525      (0.039,0.052)
          Proportional Power      0.01425      (0.012,0.017)
          Directional FWE         0.02775      (0.023,0.033)
```

Note the following about the output:

- Since there are no true null differences, there is no "True FWE" reported.

- The Type III directional FWE is between 0.023 and 0.033. Because of the confidence interval correspondence of Tukey's method, the Type III FWE is guaranteed to be less than 0.05.

- In applications from Chapter 8, where control of Type III directional FWE is not known theoretically, you can use the %SimPower macro to estimate the Type III FWE for various parameter configurations.

7.4.3   Comparisons with a Control

Continuing with the example from the previous section, suppose you are concerned only with comparisons with the control. Your power for this more focused set of comparisons will be uniformly higher than the power for comparing all pairs (when using identical sample sizes). Here is the appropriate program:

PROGRAM 7.6   **Simulating Combined Power of Two-sided Comparisons with a Control**

```
%SimPower(TrueMeans=(10, 5, 5, 0, 0),s=5,n=10,seed=12345,method=DUNNETT);
```

Output from Program 7.6: Power (two-sided DUNNETT) with $n = 10$

```
          Method=DUNNETT, Nominal FWE=0.05, nrep=1000, Seed=12345
                 True means = (10, 5, 5, 0, 0), n=10, s=5

          Quantity            Estimate      ---95% CI----

          Complete Power        0.2380     (0.212,0.264)
          Minimal Power         0.9900     (0.984,0.996)
          Proportional Power    0.6785     (0.664,0.693)
          Directional FWE       0.0000     (0.000,0.000)
```

If you increase to $n = 20$, using the same two-sided comparisons with combined power estimates, then you get

Power (two-sided DUNNETT) with $n = 20$

```
          Method=DUNNETT, Nominal FWE=0.05, nrep=1000, Seed=12345
                 True means = (10, 5, 5, 0, 0), n=20, s=5

          Quantity            Estimate      ---95% CI----

          Complete Power       0.59400     (0.564,0.624)
          Minimal Power        1.00000     (1.000,1.000)
          Proportional Power   0.86575     (0.855,0.877)
          Directional FWE      0.00000     (0.000,0.000)
```

Again, the powers increase with larger sample sizes. Note that, for the given parameter configuration, there can be no Type I errors since none of the "treatment" means (5,5,0,0) are equal to the "control" mean (10). Also, there were no instances in either simulation where a treatment mean was declared larger than the control mean, hence the directional FWE is reported as 0.00000.

Power is even larger if you specify one-sided tests instead of two-sided. Program 7.7 uses one-sided (lower-tailed) comparisons with control using $n = 10$ observations per group.

PROGRAM 7.7   **Simulating Combined Power of One-sided Comparisons with a Control**

```
%SimPower(TrueMeans=(10, 5, 5, 0, 0),s=5,n=10,seed=12345,method=DUNNETTL);
```

Output from Program 7.7

```
Method=DUNNETTL, Nominal FWE=0.05, nrep=1000, Seed=12345
          True means = (10, 5, 5, 0, 0), n=10, s=5


       Quantity        Estimate    ---95% CI----

   Complete Power       0.34800    (0.318,0.378)
   Minimal Power        0.99700    (0.994,1.000)
   Proportional Power   0.74575    (0.732,0.760)
   Directional FWE      0.00000    (0.000,0.000)
```

If you increase to $n = 20$, using the same one-sided comparisons with combined power estimates, then you get

Power (one-sided DUNNETT) with $n = 20$

```
Method=DUNNETTL, Nominal FWE=0.05, nrep=1000, Seed=12345
          True means = (10, 5, 5, 0, 0), n=20, s=5


       Quantity        Estimate    ---95% CI----

   Complete Power        0.706     (0.678,0.734)
   Minimal Power         1.000     (1.000,1.000)
   Proportional Power    0.907     (0.897,0.917)
   Directional FWE       0.000     (0.000,0.000)
```

So with $n = 20$, using one-sided comparisons with control, even complete power becomes reasonably high for this parameter configuration.

7.4.4   A Macro to Simulate and Graph Combined Power

If you don't mind letting your computer run for a while, you can run the %SimPower macro repeatedly, for different sample sizes, then tabulate and graph the results. We provide a macro, %PlotSimPower (given in the appendix), for this purpose. You invoke %PlotSimPower as

```
%PlotSimPower(method    = <value>              ,
             nrep       = <number>             ,
             s          = <number>             ,
             FWE        = <number>             ,
             TrueMeans  = <(m1,m2,...)>         ,
             seed       = <value>              ,
             stop       = <value>/<number>    ,
             target     = <value>             );
```

where

method   is the multiple comparisons method, whether all pairwise comparisons (method = TUKEY), two-sided comparisons with control (method = DUNNETT), one-sided comparisons with a control (either method = DUNNETTL or method = DUNNETTU), or REGWQ (defined in Chapter 8). The default is TUKEY.

nrep   is the number of simulations to be performed at each sample size, with 100 as the default.

s   is the value of σ (there is no default value).

FWE is the FWE, (0.05 is the default).

TrueMeans are the true mean values; identical to the %SimPower macro.

seed is the random number seed (the default is 0, which specifies computer clock time).

stop specifies type of power and stopping criterion. The syntax is type/max, where type is either Complete, Minimal, or Porportional, and where max is a maximum power to stop the simulation. The default is Complete/0.9, meaning that the simulation stops at the *n* for which the complete power is greater than or equal to 0.9 (with 95 percent confidence).

target is the desired power level. The default is 0.8.

An example of the %PlotSimPower macro is shown in Program 7.8.

PROGRAM 7.8   Plotting Simulated Complete Power of Two-sided Comparisons with a Control

```
%PlotSimPower(TrueMeans=(10,5,5,0,0),s=5,seed=12345,method=Dunnett);
```

Output from Program 7.8

Complete power using the Dunnett method with FWE=0.05

With true means (10,5,5,0,0) and standard deviation = 5

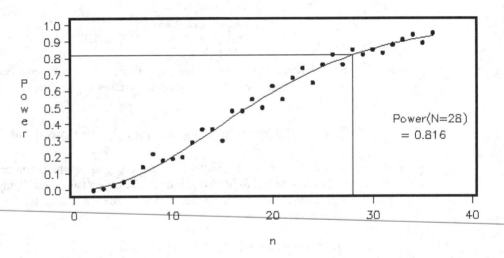

7.5 Concluding Remarks

In this chapter we have given programs to perform power calculations with multiple comparisons. With simple balanced designs, and using individual power, you can calculate power exactly and design your studies accordingly. We have provided the %IndividualPower macro for that purpose.

We have also noted that there are other definitions of power that combine information from all tests. For such definitions, it is simplest to simulate the power for the purposes of study design. We have provided the %SimPower macro and the %PlotSimPower macro for this purpose.

Chapter 8

Stepwise and Closed Testing Procedures

8.1 Introduction

In this chapter we discuss improvements to testing-based MCPs that were introduced in Chapter 2, with special application to testing in linear models as discussed in Chapters 3 through 7. In Chapters 3 through 7, the idea was primarily to perform treatment comparisons via confidence intervals. This approach is called *single-step* analysis. If your primary goal in conducting an experiment is to qualitatively assess treatment differences, rather than to estimate their mean differences, then you might want to consider stepwise MCPs that do not necessarily provide you with confidence intervals. These procedures are often more powerful for these less ambitious inferences, with the same familywise error rate. To start, we will consider the balanced one-way design with the same model assumptions as presented in Section 3.2.1, but we will later allow the generality and scope of applications discussed in Chapters 5 and 6.

The closure method discussed in this chapter can be applied to any collection of hypotheses. We consider testing all pairwise hypotheses, testing treatments against a common control, dose-response comparisons, the Fisher combination test, and more general sets of contrasts.

8.2 The Closure Principle

Although stepwise MCPs have been around for many years, it is in the past two decades that a unified approach to this area has been developed. We will use principles that were primarily introduced in Marcus, Peritz and Gabriel (1976), with the notation of Hochberg and

Tamhane (1987). In much of the recent development of stepwise MCPs, the fundamental idea is the *Closure Principle*. MCPs based on this principle are called *closed testing methods* because they address families of hypotheses that are *closed* under intersection. A *closed* family, by definition, is one for which any subset intersection hypothesis involving members of the family of tests is also a member of the family.

To illustrate the closure concept, suppose that you want to test the pairwise equality of four means. There are six such pairwise comparisons to be made. To form a closed family, we take all possible intersections among the pairwise hypotheses. Remember that a hypothesis that is formed by an intersection of two or more hypotheses is true if and only if all the components are true. For example, if we intersect $H_{1,2}: \mu_1 = \mu_2$ with $H_{2,3}: \mu_2 = \mu_3$, we get $H_{1,2,3}: \mu_1 = \mu_2 = \mu_3$ because if $\mu_1 = \mu_2$, and $\mu_2 = \mu_3$, then necessarily $\mu_1 = \mu_2 = \mu_3$. If we continue to take all possible intersections in this family, we will get the following augmented closed family:

- Original pairwise homogeneity hypotheses: $H_{1,2}: \mu_1 = \mu_2$, $H_{1,3}: \mu_1 = \mu_3$, $H_{1,4}: \mu_1 = \mu_4$, $H_{2,3}: \mu_2 = \mu_3$, $H_{2,4}: \mu_2 = \mu_4$, $H_{3,4}: \mu_3 = \mu_4$.
- Three means homogeneity hypotheses: $H_{1,2,3}: \mu_1 = \mu_2 = \mu_3$, $H_{1,2,4}: \mu_1 = \mu_2 = \mu_4$, $H_{1,3,4}: \mu_1 = \mu_3 = \mu_4$, $H_{2,3,4}: \mu_2 = \mu_3 = \mu_4$.
- Four means homogeneity hypothesis: $H_{1,2,3,4}: \mu_1 = \mu_2 = \mu_3 = \mu_4$.
- Subset intersection (disjoint) hypotheses: $H_{(1,2)\cap(3,4)}: \mu_1 = \mu_2$ and $\mu_3 = \mu_4$, $H_{(1,3)\cap(2,4)}: \mu_1 = \mu_3$ and $\mu_2 = \mu_4$, $H_{(1,4)\cap(2,3)}: \mu_1 = \mu_4$ and $\mu_2 = \mu_3$.

In all, there are fourteen hypotheses in this closed family. In some cases, the subset intersection hypotheses are as interesting as the individual component hypotheses. For example, suppose the four groups correspond to four different treatments for headaches, two different dosages each of an aspirin-based (1,2) and an ibuprofen-based (3,4) drug. The result of our testing procedure might be the important conclusion that the dosage makes a difference for at least one of the two types of drug, which is implied by rejecting the subset intersection hypothesis $H_{(1,2)\cap(3,4)}: \mu_1 = \mu_2$ and $\mu_3 = \mu_4$.

Another point to note in closed families is the hierarchical structure: if $H_{(1,2)\cap(3,4)}: \mu_1 = \mu_2$ and $\mu_3 = \mu_4$ is true, then necessarily $H_{1,2}: \mu_1 = \mu_2$ and $H_{3,4}: \mu_3 = \mu_4$ are both true. We have an implication relationship among the hypotheses; we say that $H_{(1,2)\cap(3,4)}: \mu_1 = \mu_2$ and $\mu_3 = \mu_4$ *implies* both $H_{1,2}: \mu_1 = \mu_2$ and $H_{3,4}: \mu_3 = \mu_4$. The implication relations lead to a property of MCPs, termed *coherence*. If H' implies H'', then whenever H' is retained, so must be H''. Coherence is related to another property of MCPs, called *consonance*. Whenever H' is rejected, at least one of its components is rejected too. Coherence is a required property of closed testing procedures; consonance is desirable but not an absolute requirement. This is due to the lack of symmetry in the hypothesis testing paradigm. When H is rejected, we conclude (albeit, with some uncertainty), that it is false. On the other hand, when H is retained (not rejected by our test procedure), we do not conclude that it is true; rather, we say that there is no sufficient evidence to reject it. It turns out that MCPs that satisfy the Closure Principle (defined on the following page) are always coherent but not necessarily consonant.

Here is a graphical display of the family.

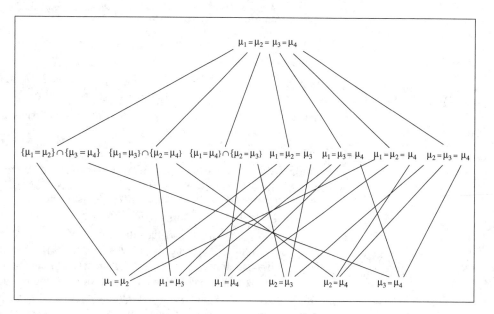

Figure 8.1
Peritz's Closed Family of
All Subset Homogeneity
Hypotheses

The reason to address a closed family is based on Peritz's (1970) Closure Principle, which was more fully developed in Marcus, Peritz, and Gabriel (1976). This principle asserts that you can ensure strong control of the FWE, and coherence at the same time, by conducting the following procedure:

1. Test every member of the closed family by a (suitable) α level test. (Here, α refers to comparison-wise error rate, not family-wise error rate).

2. A hypothesis can be rejected provided (1) its corresponding test was significant at α, and (2) every other hypothesis in the family that implies it has also been rejected by its corresponding α level test.

While the Closure Principle outlines the general method for obtaining stepwise procedures that are powerful and control the FWE, it is still up to you to come up with appropriate α level tests for the subset and component hypotheses. Moreover, all tests are not created equal. Different tests can be computationally easier to implement or more statistically powerful; unfortunately, these two characteristics are typically at variance. We will see later how to choose appropriate tests for given situations.

8.3 Step-down Procedures for Testing All Subset Homogeneity Hypotheses

8.3.1 Tukey-Welsch

Although closed testing procedures were developed in the late 70's, the principles were known early on, but lack of high-speed computing forced researchers to look for simplified procedures. Like procedures based on the Closure Principle, the Tukey-Welsch procedure is a step-down approach that has more power for detecting treatment differences than single-step procedures. However, the stepwise tests of the Tukey-Welsch procedure are generally performed at α levels lower than those implied by the Closure Principle, so Tukey-Welsch is not as powerful as a full-blown closure-based approach.

Assuming there are g means, the method is as follows:

Tukey-Welsch Step-down Procedure

- Test every subset hypothesis $H: \mu_{i_1} = \mu_{i_2} = \cdots = \mu_{i_k}$ at level $\alpha_k = (k/g)\alpha$ for $k = 2, \ldots, m - 2$, and at level $\alpha_k = \alpha$ for $k = g - 1, g$.

- Start by testing $H: \mu_1 = \mu_2 = \cdots = \mu_g$ (i.e., the homogeneity of all g means) and then step down, testing subsets of $g - 1$ means, $g - 2$ means, etc.

- Whenever any homogeneity hypothesis is retained, all subset hypotheses implied by it are retained without testing.

Using a Šidák-type method, the Tukey-Welsch procedure can be improved slightly under some mild assumptions by replacing the "additive" critical values $\alpha_k = (k/g)\alpha$ with "multiplicative" critical values $\alpha_k = 1 - (1 - \alpha)^{k/g}$ for $k = 2, \ldots, g - 2$.

The Tukey-Welsch procedure controls the FWE strongly at level α with balanced designs. It be implemented using either an ANOVA F test or a Range test for each homogeneity hypothesis. If you use an F-test, then when you reject a homogeneity hypothesis, you must proceed to test all of its subsets. On the other hand, if you use a Range test and reject the homogeneity of a certain set of means, it is valid to test just two subsets: the one containing the smallest mean up to the next to the largest mean, and the other containing the next to the smallest mean up to the largest. For example, suppose you test the homogeneity of the four means ordered as $\bar{y}_1 < \bar{y}_2 < \bar{y}_3 < \bar{y}_4$.

- If the F test rejects the homogeneity of all four means, you must proceed to test the four hypotheses: $H: \mu_1 = \mu_2 = \mu_3$, $H: \mu_1 = \mu_3 = \mu_4$, $H: \mu_1 = \mu_2 = \mu_4$, and $H: \mu_2 = \mu_3 = \mu_4$.

- If the range test rejects the homogeneity of all four means, you only need to test the homogeneity of the two contiguous subsets: $H: \mu_1 = \mu_2 = \mu_3$, and $H: \mu_2 = \mu_3 = \mu_4$.

Clearly, using the Range test requires testing fewer hypotheses. In fact, in the computationally worst case that all g means are unequal, using the F-test will require on the order of 2^g tests, whereas using the Range test will only require about $g^2/2$ tests. In addition, the Range test has the advantage that when you reject a subset homogeneity hypothesis, you can immediately reject the equality of the smallest and largest means in the set.

You can compute the Tukey-Welsch procedure using the Range test with the REGWQ option on the MEANS statement in PROC GLM. The option is named after Ryan, Einot, Gabriel, and Welsch, who at various times proposed this approach. (For some reason, Tukey has been omitted.)

8.3.2 Example: Comparing Cholesterol Reduction Using Five Treatments

A pharmaceutical company has conducted a clinical study to assess the effect of three formulations of the same drug on reducing cholesterol. The formulations were 20 mg once a day (A), 10 mg twice a day (B), and 5 mg four times a day (C). In addition, two competing drugs were used as control groups. One drug was in the same class as the test drug (D), the other was in a different class (E). The purpose of the study was to find which of the formulations, if any, is efficacious and how these formulations compare with the existing drugs.

You can use REGWQ to answer the research questions as shown in Program 8.1.

PROGRAM 8.1   Tukey-Welch (REGWQ) Comparisons for Balanced ANOVA

```
data Cholesterol;
do trt = 'A','B','C','D','E';
   do i = 1 to 10;
      input response @@;
      output;
   end;
end;
datalines;
 3.8612 10.3868  5.9059  3.0609  7.7204  2.7139  4.9243  2.3039  7.5301  9.4123
10.3993  8.6027 13.6320  3.5054  7.7703  8.6266  9.2274  6.3159 15.8258  8.3443
13.9621 13.9606 13.9176  8.0534 11.0432 12.3692 10.3921  9.0286 12.8416 18.1794
16.9819 15.4576 19.9793 14.7389 13.5850 10.8648 17.5897  8.8194 17.9635 17.6316
21.5119 27.2445 20.5199 15.7707 22.8850 23.9527 21.5925 18.3058 20.3851 17.3071
;
proc glm data=Cholesterol;
   class trt;
   model response=trt;
   means trt/regwq;
run;
```

Output from Program 8.1

```
                    The GLM Procedure

        Ryan-Einot-Gabriel-Welsch Multiple Range Test for response

        NOTE: This test controls the type I experimentwise error rate.


                    Alpha                         0.05
                    Error Degrees of Freedom        45
                    Error Mean Square          10.41668


Number of Means          2          3          4          5
Critical Range   3.4724829  3.8036748  3.8504947  4.1012849


        Means with the same letter are not significantly different.


            REGWQ Grouping          Mean      N    trt

                          A        20.948     10    E

                          B        15.361     10    D
                          B
                    C     B        12.375     10    C
                    C
                    C     D         9.225     10    B
                          D
                          D         5.782     10    A
```

We can see from the output generated from REGWQ that treatment E is significantly different from all other treatments. The other treatment groups have some complicated relationships. For example, D is significantly different from B, but C is not significantly different from either D or B. Similar relationships hold among A, B, and C.

8.3.3   More about REGWQ

REGWQ strongly controls the FWE, although it provides direct tests only for the subset homogeneity hypotheses. However, it does provide implied (indirect) tests for subset intersection hypotheses based on the following argument: consider $H: \mu_1 = \mu_2$ and $\mu_3 = \mu_4$, which is not tested directly by REGWQ. According to the Closure Principle, this hypothesis must be tested and rejected at level α before testing $H: \mu_1 = \mu_2$ and $H: \mu_3 = \mu_4$. However, $\mu_1 = \mu_2$ and $\mu_3 = \mu_4$ are both tested at level $2\alpha/5$ by REGWQ, and if either is rejected, you can reject $\{\mu_1 = \mu_2$ and $\mu_3 = \mu_4\}$ at level less than $2\alpha/5 + 2\alpha/5 = 4\alpha/5$ (using the Bonferroni inequality). By using REGWQ, strong control is conservatively ensured by testing *directly* all subset homogeneity hypotheses, and *indirectly* all subset intersection hypotheses.

Note that other stepwise MCP options in the MEANS statement, such as DUNCAN and SNK, do not control the FWE strongly. Consider the SNK option which uses $\alpha_k = \alpha$ at all levels of the procedure, i.e., all subset hypotheses are tested at the same level. Clearly, subset intersection hypotheses like $\{\mu_1 = \mu_2$ and $\mu_3 = \mu_4\}$ are not protected at level α. Similarly, the DUNCAN option which is even more liberal with the critical values does not strongly control the FWE. In fact, DUNCAN does not even weakly control the FWE.

Thus, since we usually require strong control of the FWE, neither SNK nor DUNCAN should be used.

Note that in releases of the SAS System prior to 6.10, the MEANS statement also included a REGWF option intended to implement the Tukey-Welsch procedure using the ANOVA F test for each homogeneity hypothesis. However, the procedure was erroneously implemented; the implementation assumed that only contiguous subsets of the groups ordered by sample means needed to be tested for equality, as is the case with REGWQ. When the error was discovered, it was decided that a proper implementation of REGWF would be impractical, since it potentially involves a number of tests exponential in the number of groups. Thus, the REGWF option was disabled beginning with release 6.11.

8.3.4   Power of the REGWQ Method

In Chapter 7 we introduced two macros, %SimPower and %PlotSimPower for various MCPs. Although not described at that time because we had not yet covered closed methods, these macros can also compute power functions for the REGWQ method.

In Program 7.3, we used %SimPower to calculate the various power measures for Tukey's method in a one-way ANOVA. Program 8.2 uses the same inputs, but with the REGWQ method.

PROGRAM 8.2   Power Calculation for the REGWQ Method

```
%SimPower(TrueMeans=(10, 5, 5, 0, 0),s=5,n=10,seed=12345,
          method=REGWQ);
```

Output from Program 8.2

```
Method=REGWQ, Nominal FWE=0.05, nrep=1000, Seed=12345

        True means = (10, 5, 5, 0, 0), n=10, s=5

    Quantity              Estimate      ---95% CI----

    Complete Power        0.02200       (0.013,0.031)
    Minimal Power         0.97500       (0.965,0.985)
    Proportional Power    0.50663       (0.494,0.519)
    True FWE              0.03100       (0.020,0.042)
    Directional FWE       0.03100       (0.020,0.042)
```

For ease of comparison, the corresponding calculations using Tukey's method are shown here.

Output from Program 7.3: Power Calculations for Tukey's Method

```
Method=TUKEY, Nominal FWE=0.05, nrep=1000, Seed=12345
        True means = (10, 5, 5, 0, 0), n=10, s=5

    Quantity              Estimate      ---95% CI----

    Complete Power        0.00700       (0.002,0.012)
    Minimal Power         0.97500       (0.965,0.985)
    Proportional Power    0.44263       (0.431,0.454)
    True FWE              0.01200       (0.005,0.019)
    Directional FWE       0.01200       (0.005,0.019)
```

As expected, all power estimates are as high or higher using REGWQ. Note that REGWQ is less wasteful in that the true FWE is closer to the nominal 0.05 value.

8.3.5   Begun and Gabriel

Recall that the Closure Principle allows you to test every hypothesis at level α, provided that you preserve the implication hierarchy when testing hypotheses. Consider testing $\mu_1 = \mu_2$. If you tested and rejected at level α all hypotheses implying it, then you can test $\mu_1 = \mu_2$ at level α, not at level $2\alpha/5$ as in REGWQ. Begun and Gabriel (1981) propose improving REGWQ as follows:

- Reject a subset homogeneity hypothesis H_K if it is rejected by REGWQ's (conservative) critical level of α_k.

- Retain H_K if it is not rejected at level α (required by the Closure Principle).

- Otherwise, if all subset homogeneity hypotheses containing H_K are rejected, and all subset homogeneity concerning means outside of K are rejected at REGWQ's critical points, then you can proceed to test H_K at level α.

This procedure is obviously more complicated than REGWQ, however, it can provide additional power. The %BEGGAB macro given in the appendix performs this procedure, and Program 8.3 can be used to analyze the data used in Program 8.1.

(Note: The macro uses exact calculations in the balanced case, but uses the conservative Tukey-Kramer approximation in unbalanced cases.)

PROGRAM 8.3   The Begun and Gabriel Method

```
%beggab(dataset=Cholesterol,groups=trt,response=response);
```

Output from Program 8.3

OBS	TRT	MEAN	SD	N
1	A	5.7820	2.87811	10
2	B	9.2250	3.48305	10
3	C	12.3748	2.92312	10
4	D	15.3612	3.45464	10
5	E	20.9475	3.34500	10

Begun-Gabriel Closed Testing Procedure
Based on the Range Statistic, FWE=0.05

t_i	-	t_j	P-VALUE	DECISION
A	-	B	0.0213	Retain
A	-	C	0.0001	Reject
A	-	D	<.0001	Reject
A	-	E	<.0001	Reject
B	-	C	0.0344	Reject
B	-	D	0.0003	Reject
B	-	E	<.0001	Reject
C	-	D	0.0443	Retain
C	-	E	<.0001	Reject
D	-	E	0.0003	Reject

Based on the Range Statistic, FWE=0.05
Schematic Plot of Significant Differences

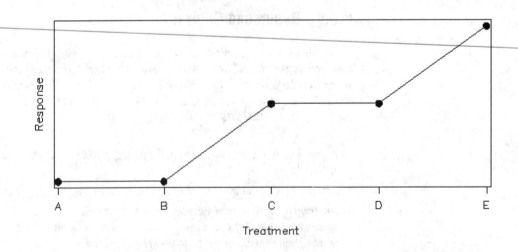

The output from the %beggab macro gives both decisions on subset homogeneity hypotheses, and a graphical display of the results. The output table shows all subset homogeneity hypotheses tested, and their corresponding α level range test p-value. The hypothesis 1-5 represents the global null hypothesis $\mu_1 = \mu_2 = \mu_3 = \mu_4 = \mu_5$ whose corresponding range test p-value is < 0.0001. The decisions on individual hypotheses are made using the Begun and Gabriel algorithm which can be displayed schematically. Note the following points:

1. The response to treatment 5 is significantly different from any other response.

2. The responses to treatment 3 and 4 are significantly different from the responses to treatment 1 and 2.

3. There are no significant differences in the responses to treatments 1 and 2, and the responses to treatments 3 and 4. These are indicated by the two corresponding horizontal lines connecting the responses.

Note that the Begun and Gabriel procedure rejects all hypotheses that are rejected by REGWQ, and additionally rejects the equality of μ_2 and μ_3. With REGWQ, this hypothesis is tested using a critical value of $\alpha_2 = 2\alpha/5$. Since the corresponding p-value is 0.0344, greater than 0.02, this hypothesis is retained by REGWQ. With the Begun and Gabriel procedure, this hypothesis can be rejected if its corresponding p-value is less than α, provided that:

1. Every homogeneity hypothesis containing it is rejected; this is easily seen in the tabular output, for example $\mu_1 = \mu_2 = \mu_3$.

2. All hypotheses concerning means outside of $\{\mu_2, \mu_3\}$ are rejected by the REGWQ critical levels; these hypotheses are $\mu_1 = \mu_4$, $\mu_1 = \mu_5$, $\mu_4 = \mu_5$, and $\mu_1 = \mu_4 = \mu_5$. All of the corresponding p-values are less than the REGWQ critical levels; therefore, $\mu_2 = \mu_3$ is ultimately rejected.

Note that the Begun and Gabriel procedure is still conservative, and can be improved further as shown in Rom and Holland (1995), however, their improvement has not been implemented yet.

8.3.6   On Shortcut Closure Procedures

Suppose there are k hypotheses H_1 to H_k which have the *free combination* property (see Holm, 1979; Westfall and Young, 1993, pp. 62–72), defined as follows.

DEFINITION: Free Combinations

If, for every subcollection of j hypotheses $\{H_{i_1}, \ldots, H_{i_j}\}$, the simultaneous *truth* of $\{H_{i_1}, \ldots, H_{i_j}\}$ and *falsehood* of the remaining hypotheses is a plausible event, then the hypotheses satisfy the *free combinations* condition. In other words, each of the 2^k outcomes of the k-hypothesis problem is possible.

We form the closure of the family by taking all intersections among these hypotheses. Thus, we create a closed family consisting of the original hypotheses and the following intersection hypotheses:

- All k hypotheses intersection: $H_1 \cap H_2 \cap \ldots \cap H_k$ (the global null hypothesis) …
- Three hypotheses intersection: $H_1 \cap H_2 \cap H_3, \ldots, H_{k-2} \cap H_{k-1} \cap H_k$
- Two hypotheses intersection $H_1 \cap H_2, \ldots, H_{k-1} \cap H_k$

Now suppose that we want to devise a closed testing procedure for this family using the Bonferroni test for each member of the closed family. Each member will then be tested by comparing the minimum p-value corresponding to the hypotheses in the set under consideration with $\alpha/$(number of hypotheses in the set). We can start by testing the global null hypothesis $H_1 \cap H_2 \cap \ldots \cap H_k$, and then test sequentially all other intersection hypotheses. Suppose (without loss of generality) that H_2 has the minimum p-value, $p_{(1)}$. If $p_{(1)} > \alpha/k$ then we must stop and retain all null hypotheses. Otherwise, the global null can be rejected, and we can proceed to test intersections of $k - 1, k - 2, \ldots$, hypotheses. Note that when testing any $k - 1, (k - 2, \ldots)$ intersection hypothesis containing H_2 as a component, we compare $p_{(1)}$ with $\alpha/(k-1), (\alpha/(k-2), \ldots)$. But since we already found $p_{(1)} \leq \alpha/k$ in the first step (otherwise we would not have been able to proceed) any such $k - 1, (k - 2, \ldots)$ intersection hypothesis would be rejected too since $p_{(1)} \leq \alpha/k \rightarrow p_{(1)} \leq \alpha/(k - 1)$, $(p_{(1)} \leq \alpha/(k - 2), \ldots)$. This means that:

1. If $p_{(1)} \leq \alpha/k$ we can automatically reject the hypothesis corresponding to $p_{(1)}$ (in our example, H_2), since every intersection hypothesis consisting of H_2 is rejected too at level α.

2. In the second step, we can test only the one intersection of $k - 1$ hypotheses that does not consist of H_2. This hypothesis would be tested by comparing the minimum p-value corresponding to the remaining $k - 1$ hypotheses with $\alpha/(k - 1)$.

You can now see the emerging pattern. Whenever we reject an intersection hypothesis, we can automatically reject the hypothesis corresponding to the minimum p-value in the set of the remaining hypotheses. This leads to the following procedure:

1. Start by comparing $p_{(1)}$ with α/k. If larger, stop and retain all hypotheses; otherwise, reject the hypothesis corresponding to $p_{(1)}$ and proceed.

2. Compare $p_{(2)}$ with $\alpha/(k - 2)$. If larger, stop and retain the remaining hypotheses; otherwise, reject the hypothesis corresponding to $p_{(2)}$ and proceed.

3. Continue in this fashion until a stop or until all hypotheses are rejected.

This is in fact Holm's step-down Bonferroni procedure. What we have observed in this example is what is called "The Shortcut Version of the Closed Testing Procedure" which is possible due to the property of the Bonferroni test that $p_{(1)} \leq \alpha/k \rightarrow p_{(1)} \leq \alpha/(k - 1), p_{(1)} \leq \alpha/(k - 2) \ldots$, sometimes referred to as "monotonicity of the critical values." Other tests possess similar properties, for example, the range test when applied to equal sample sizes. Using the range test in conjunction with testing all pairwise comparisons among treatment means yields the (step-down) Tukey-Welsch procedure as implemented by REGWQ. Dunnett's test is another example where monotonicity of critical values affords a simple step-down procedure. The Bonferroni, range, and Dunnett tests belong to the class of "Union Intersection Tests" for which the shortcut version often yields simple step-down procedures. Shortcut versions can also be used with other types of tests, for example, Hochberg, Rom, and Dunnett and Tamhane, yielding step-up procedures, using a similar argument as for Holm's test. Hommel's procedure is another simplification of a closed procedure based on Simes' test. As can be seen from the foregoing discussion, the closure method can sometimes be applied without having to go through testing the entire family.

For further reading on monotonicity of critical values, and shortcut procedures, see Finner and Roters (1998) and Grechanovsky and Hochberg (1999).

8.3.7   A Closed Procedure for Combination Tests

You can test for the global null hypothesis H_0 using a Fisher's combination statistic $\chi^2 = -2\Sigma ln(p_j)$. Under H_0, *and independence* of the p-values, the statistic χ^2 is distributed as a chi-squared statistic with $2k$ degrees of freedom, so an α level test for H_0 rejects it if $\chi^2 \geq \chi^2_{2k, 1-\alpha}$.

Program 8.4 illustrates the closure method with Fisher's combination statistic.

PROGRAM 8.4   Closed Testing Using Fisher's Combination Test

```
data fishcomb;
input p1 p2 p3;
   t123= -2*(log(p1) + log(p2) + log(p3));
   p123= 1-probchi(t123,6);
   t12 = -2*(log(p1) + log(p2));
   p12=  1-probchi(t12,4);
   t13 = -2*(log(p1) + log(p3));
   p13= 1-probchi(t13,4);
   t23 = -2*(log(p2) + log(p3));
   p23= 1-probchi(t23,4);
datalines;
0.076 0.081 0.0201
;
run;
proc print;
   var p123 p12 p13 p23 p1 p2 p3;
run;
```

Output from Program 8.4

OBS	P123	P12	P13	P23	P1	P2	P3
1	.0062454	0.037492	0.011433	0.012081	0.076	0.081	0.0201

The overall chi-squared statistic has a p-value of 0.0062, leading to the rejection of H_0 at 0.05 level, despite the fact that the smallest p-value is 0.0201, not small enough to reject the corresponding hypothesis by any of the Bonferroni procedures. To make assessments on an individual hypothesis, you should test every subset of the p-values containing the p-value in question, as dictated by the Closure Principle. For example, to test the hypothesis H_3 corresponding to the smallest p-value, 0.0201, you must consider the p-values p_{13}, p_{23}, and p_3. In this example, all combinations of tests containing the smallest p-value reject the corresponding hypotheses, leading to the rejection of the hypothesis corresponding to the smallest p-value. For this example, we not only conclude the rejection of the global null hypothesis, but also manage to reject an individual hypothesis, corresponding to the smallest p-value.

Note that the adjusted p-value for H_3 is the *maximum* of the p-values for the containing tests (H_{123}, H_{13}, H_{23}, and H_3); in this case, $\tilde{p}_3 = 0.0201$, identical to the unadjusted p-value.

We could test the remaining two hypotheses H_1 and H_2 in similar fashion. It is readily obvious that these hypotheses cannot be rejected due to the fact that neither of the corresponding p-values is smaller than 0.05 (which is required under this scheme). However, adjusted p-values are obtained using the maxima over containing tests (including the marginal test itself) as described above for p_3, and we have $\tilde{p}_1 = 0.076$ and $\tilde{p}_2 = 0.081$. Thus, for this example, no multiplicity adjustment at all is required!

We conclude this section noting that Fisher's combination procedure is often used to test related or similar hypotheses in order to support or refute a common research question. It is also important to emphasize that this procedure controls the FWE only under independence and may reach very high error rates when the statistics are correlated.

8.3.8   Caveats Concerning Closed Testing Methods

There are two caveats concerning closed testing that you need to know. The first has to do with your ability to claim directional inferences, and the second has to do with possible inconsistency of rank ordering of raw and adjusted p-values.

The extent to which directional inferences are allowed with Begun and Gabriel's method, as with all stepwise methods, is a subject of ongoing research. For one-sided tests, it can be shown in most cases that the directional error is controlled with closed testing; however, with two-sided testing we still are not sure. At this point, we simply recommend making the safe but less ambitious claim that a difference exists, when you reject a null in a closed testing scheme.

Another concern with closed testing is that it sometimes leads to situations where test H_2 (say) has a smaller unadjusted p-value than test H_5 (say), yet test H_5 is rejected and H_2 is retained. This was shown in the output from Program 8.3. The A – B comparison, with unadjusted p-value 0.0213, was not rejected; whereas the B – C comparison, with unadjusted p-value 0.0344, was rejected. While this type of situation is somewhat unpleasant, it does allow more power in some instances. On the other hand, some closed-based methods do not have this problem; see Section 8.6 and our %SimTests macro for a closed procedure that guarantees the same ordering of raw and adjusted p-values.

8.4   Step-down Procedures for Testing against a Common Control

In Chapter 3 we discussed Dunnett's procedure for comparing several means with a common control mean. The procedure was presented in its single-step form. Simply put, the test was based on the calculation of a common critical point that exploits the correlation structure among the statistics, the familiar pairwise t-tests of all group means with the control mean. The single-step Dunnett procedure allows you to convert it into simultaneous confidence intervals, as is shown in Chapter 3. In this section, we discuss a step-down procedure that uses Dunnett's test within a closed testing scheme. To do that, we first need to form a closed family.

Consider testing the equality of three treatment means with a control mean. Denote the control group mean by μ_0, and the other three group means by μ_1, μ_2, and μ_3. The three pairwise hypotheses of interest are $\mu_0 = \mu_1$, $\mu_0 = \mu_2$, and $\mu_0 = \mu_3$. To form a closed family, we take all intersections among these pairwise hypotheses, and we get the following augmented family:

- Original two means homogeneity hypotheses: $\mu_1 = \mu_0$, $\mu_2 = \mu_0$, and $\mu_3 = \mu_0$.
- Three means homogeneity hypotheses: $\mu_0 = \mu_1 = \mu_2$, $\mu_0 = \mu_1 = \mu_3$, and $\mu_0 = \mu_2 = \mu_3$.
- Four means homogeneity hypothesis: $\mu_0 = \mu_1 = \mu_2 = \mu_3$.

We will illustrate the step-down procedure with one-sided hypothesis tests. Let c_g denote Dunnett's critical value for comparing g noncontrol means to a control mean for given values of FWE (α) and degrees of freedom (df). As discussed in Chapter 3, the single-step Dunnett's test ensures strong control of the FWE by testing all differences from the control using the distribution of $\max_j(\bar{y}_j - \bar{y}_0)/(\hat{\sigma}\sqrt{2/n})$, where $\hat{\sigma}$ is the regular square root of the MSE, and comparing it with Dunnett's critical value c_3. This is in fact the start of the following step-down procedure:

1. Order the means by the t-values of their differences from the control so that $t_{(1)} < t_{(2)} < t_{(3)}$, where $t_{(i)} = (\bar{y}_0 - \bar{y}_{(i)})/(\hat{\sigma}\sqrt{2/n})$.
2. Compare $t_{(3)}$ to c_3. If it is smaller, then stop and retain all equalities. Otherwise, reject $\mu_0 = \mu_{(3)}$ and proceed to step 3.

3. Compare $t_{(2)}$ to c_2. If it is smaller, then stop and retain $\mu_0 = \mu_{(2)}$ and $\mu_0 = \mu_{(1)}$. Otherwise, reject $\mu_0 = \mu_{(2)}$ and proceed to step 4.

4. Compare $t_{(1)}$ to c_1. If it is smaller, then retain $\mu_0 = \mu_{(1)}$. Otherwise, reject $\mu_0 = \mu_{(1)}$.

We will now illustrate this procedure with the toxicology example from Chapter 3. For the purpose of illustration, we will use a one-sided testing approach. Since drugs are generally considered potentially toxic, it is reasonable to assume that mice who are administered the solutions may exhibit a lower weight gain. Therefore, we will test the null hypotheses of no mean difference in weight gain versus the one-sided alternative hypotheses of a reduced weight gain. Under the alternative hypotheses, $\mu_j - \mu_0 < 0$. With the toxicology data, MSE $= \hat{\sigma}^2 = 210.0048$, $n = 4$, and there are 21 error degrees of freedom. The mean differences from the control are shown in the Output from Program 3.5 of Chapter 3; these values also are reproduced in Table 8.1.

TABLE 8.1   Mean Differences from Control in Toxicology Data

Means Being Compared	Difference
1 - 0	-9.48
4 - 0	-13.50
5 - 0	-20.70
2 - 0	-24.90
6 - 0	-31.14
3 - 0	-33.24

Program 8.5 gives the critical points for the step-down Dunnett procedure.

PROGRAM 8.5   Step-down Dunnett Critical Points

```
data;
   do i=1 to 6;
      c_i =-probmc("DUNNETT1",.,.95,21,i);
      diff_i=c_i*(210.0048*2/4)**0.5;
      output;
   end;
proc print; run;
```

Output from Program 8.5

```
          OBS    I      C_I        DIFF_I

           1     1    -1.72076    -17.6327
           2     2    -2.02178    -20.7174
           3     3    -2.18578    -22.3978
           4     4    -2.29722    -23.5398
           5     5    -2.38102    -24.3985
           6     6    -2.44786    -25.0834
```

The output shows the critical values c_k which can be used with the t-statistics, and DIFF_I's which can be used to compare the mean differences. Using the step-down procedure, we start at the bottom and

1. reject $\mu_3 = \mu_0$ since $-33.24 < -25.0834$

2. reject $\mu_6 = \mu_0$ since $-31.14 < -24.3985$

3. reject $\mu_2 = \mu_0$ since $-24.90 < -23.5398$

4. retain $\mu_5 = \mu_0$ since $-20.70 > -22.3978$, and therefore retain all remaining hypotheses.

Comparing with the Output from Program 3.7 in Chapter 3, you can see that the stepwise procedure allows you to reject one more hypothesis ($\mu_2 = \mu_0$). The step-down procedure enabled us to enhance power by modifying the critical points from one step to the next. With this procedure, however, you give up the correspondence with the usual confidence intervals.

8.5   Step-down and Closed Testing Procedures for Dose-Response Analysis

Dose-response studies explore the relationship between different dosages of a drug and some response to that drug. Often, dose-response studies are undertaken in order to find optimal differences from the control or zero dose. For example,

- In efficacy studies the goal is to find the lowest efficacious dose, that is, the lowest dose whose response is different from the control.

- Conversely, in safety studies the response is a negative one, such as the likelihood of side effects, and the goal is to identify the *highest* dose whose response is *not* different from the control.

While responses to drugs vary, there are two major types of response curves encountered in these studies. The most common is an 'S' shaped curve, in which there is little or no response up to a certain dose level, then there is a steep rise in the curve and then a plateauing of the response. The second type has the same 'S' shape initially, but with a decline in the response beyond a certain dose level. This second phenomenon, while rare, can be encountered, for example, in vaccine studies.

For various reasons, not the least of which is cost, dose response studies are relatively small, and the amount of information that is available from them is limited. Thus, it is important to use efficient methods. The underlying constraints on these studies are (1) small number of doses, typically two or three in addition to the control group, and (2) small number of observations per dose group.

One of the most important considerations in these studies is the choice of the doses. A wrong choice may result in having all doses on the flat curve of no response, leading to the (wrong) conclusion that there is no dose response. These considerations obviously should be addressed at the design stage. In this section we will focus on the analysis of such studies, assuming the study has been properly designed, with doses whose expected responses reflect the overall behavior (from initial rise through plateau) of the underlying dose-response curve.

The common statistical hypothesis testing setup for these studies is as follows. Test the null hypothesis, $H_{0,g} : \mu_1 = \cdots = \mu_g$ against an ordered alternative $H_{A,g} : \mu_1 \leq \cdots \leq \mu_g$ with at least one strict inequality. The highest dose for which the equality holds is called the (true) *No Effect* dose. The problem of a dose response is formulated here as an upward trend, with obvious changes necessary when the response is downward. Note that

- The procedures discussed in this section generally require the monotonicity assumption to hold (see Bauer 1997). When monotonicity is not guaranteed, these procedures should be used with a great degree of caution, as they may lead to erroneous conclusions.

- Hypothesis testing does not in general identify the No Effect dose. Rather, the maximal dose that is not *significantly* different from control, also known as the *No Statistical Significance of Trend* (NOSTASOT) dose. This is frequently higher than the true No Effect dose, due to lack of power.

8.5.1   Tukey's Trend Test

Tukey, Ciminera, and Heyse (1985) have proposed a simple step-down test for identifying the "No Statistical Significance Of Trend" (NOSTASOT) Dose. Their procedure can be summarized as follows:

1. Test the null hypothesis, $H_{0,g}: \mu_1 = \cdots = \mu_g$ at level α using an appropriate test (to be discussed later). If not rejected, then stop and conclude that the doses are homogeneous (or at least not sufficiently different). Otherwise, conclude that the high dose is significantly different from the zero dose, and proceed to step 2.

2. Test $H_{0,g-1}: \mu_1 = \cdots = \mu_{g-1}$. If not rejected, then stop and conclude that the next to the highest dose is the NOSTASOT dose, otherwise, conclude that the next to the highest dose is significantly different from the zero dose, and proceed to step 3.

3. Continue in this manner until you retain a homogeneity hypothesis, or there are no more tests to perform.

The are a few issues important to note with this scheme.

- If we define the family of interest in this setting as the hypotheses of homogeneity of means from the zero dose to successively higher doses, then this procedure has strong control of the FWE. As discussed in Section 2.5.8 ("Sequential Testing with Fixed Sequences") in Chapter 2, you can test hypotheses in a predetermined sequence without adjusting significance levels for each test.

- You can choose one or two-sided tests. If one-sided tests are used throughout, then directional decisions can be made whenever you reject a hypothesis. It is not clear whether you can make directional decisions with two-sided tests.

- Tukey et al. offer several tests for this family. Basically, they propose using contrasts that are powerful for detecting deviations from the null hypothesis of increasing severity response, corresponding to the assumption that increasing doses yield increasing responses. Since it is rarely known in advance what the shape of the dose response is, they propose using three types of contrasts simultaneously, each powerful for detecting a specific dose-response shape: an ordinal contrast, a linear contrast, and a log-arithmic contrast. Tukey et al. acknowledge that using multiple contrast types leads to a slight increase in the Type I error but they note that this would result in a conservative approach in safety studies, when the purpose is to identify safe doses.

- This method will fail badly when the dose-response function is "U"-shaped, in which case the first test will suggest to retain all nulls, where the reality is that the nulls should be rejected for mid-dose versus control comparisons.

This procedure is simple but is quite competitive when compared with other procedures. To simplify things, and to control the Type I error exactly, we will illustrate this procedure with just the ordinal contrast. This contrast is derived by assigning equally spaced integer scores to the ordered doses, centered around zero. For example, with two groups, assign 1 and 2 to the control and low dose respectively, then center around zero by subtracting the mean of the scores (1.5) yielding $-0.5, 0.5$. To get rid of the fractions we multiply by 2 to get $-1, 1$. The ordinal contrast for three groups is $-1, 0, 1$; for four groups $-3, -1, 1, 3$; and for five groups $-2, -1, 0, 1, 2$.

EXAMPLE: Dose Response Study of an Angina Drug

A study was conducted to assess the effect of increasing doses of a new angina drug on the ability to walk free of pain, relative to pretreatment ability. Change from pretreatment as measured in minutes of pain-free walking was collected on 50 patients. Five treatment groups were studied including a control (dose = 0), and four doses of a drug (treatments 1, 2, 3, and 4, respectively). Program 8.6 is used to perform Tukey's trend test.

PROGRAM 8.6   Dose-Response Contrasts for the Analysis of Angina Drug Data

```
data angina;
do dose = 0 to 4;
   do i = 1 to 10;
      input response @@;
      output;
   end;
end;
datalines;
12.03 19.06 14.24 11.17 16.19 10.80 13.18 10.35 15.99 18.01
17.54 15.48 21.26  9.63 14.53 15.51 16.20 12.86 23.78 15.18
18.97 18.96 18.92 13.51 16.27 17.49 15.67 14.41 17.93 22.86
20.60 19.19 23.38 18.52 17.45 14.93 21.16 13.03 21.51 21.20
25.29 32.32 24.08 18.25 26.98 28.29 25.39 21.36 23.91 20.14
;
proc glm data=angina;
   class dose;
   model response=dose;
   contrast 'all doses       ' dose -2 -1 0 1 2;
   contrast 'next to highest' dose -3 -1 1 3 0;
   contrast 'middle dose     ' dose -1  0 1 0 0;
   contrast 'low dose        ' dose -1  1 0 0 0;
run;
```

Output from Program 8.6

General Linear Models Procedure

Contrast	DF	Contrast SS	F Value	Pr > F
all doses	1	571.11440400	47.61	0.0001
next to highest	1	132.63318450	11.06	0.0018
middle dose	1	57.69804500	4.81	0.0335
low dose	1	21.94512500	1.83	0.1830

With this data, you reject the homogeneity of all means and conclude that

- the three highest doses are significantly different than the placebo
- the low dose is the NOSTASOT dose.

Note that with this test, we cannot say anything about the relative effectiveness of the three doses that were found to be different from the zero dose, since they are not compared directly. In this example, the use of the F test gives us a two-sided test. If a one-sided test is required, then you'll need to use an ESTIMATE statement. For example, the one-sided p-value for the test of control through the middle dose is 0.0168; thus, if we use a one-sided test with this procedure, we could say that the mid-dose group has a greater pain free walking distance improvement than the control group. The decision of whether to use a one or a two-sided test should be done at the design stage, and should be based on clinical judgments.

8.5.2   A Closed Testing Procedure for Dose Response

Marcus, Peritz, and Gabriel (1976) have formed a closed family of hypotheses for the problem of testing ordered responses, and they used the Closure Principle to devise a closed testing procedure based on Bartholomew's (1959) isotonic regression test. This closed testing scheme is the most powerful procedure known for this problem. However, Bartholomew's test is analytically intractable when the sample sizes are not equal for more than four treatments. Rom, Costello and Connell (1994) used the same principle to devise a closed testing procedure based on Tukey's trend test, and the Begun and Gabriel (1981) algorithm.

Consider the family of subset homogeneity hypotheses $H_{i,j}: \mu_i = \mu_{i+1} = \cdots = \mu_j$. These are homogeneity hypotheses on successive means. Form the closure of this family by taking all possible intersections. The closed family resembles the one we formed for testing all pairwise hypotheses, but is much smaller; it consists of hypotheses of homogeneity of successive means and their intersections. For example, with four means, the closed family consists of

- Pairwise homogeneity hypotheses: $\mu_1 = \mu_2$, $\mu_2 = \mu_3$, $\mu_3 = \mu_4$
- Three means homogeneity hypotheses: $\mu_1 = \mu_2 = \mu_3$, $\mu_2 = \mu_3 = \mu_4$
- The four means homogeneity hypothesis: $\mu_1 = \mu_2 = \mu_3 = \mu_4$
- The subset intersection (disjoint) hypothesis: $\{\mu_1 = \mu_2 \text{ and } \mu_3 = \mu_4\}$.

This family has half the hypotheses as the one for testing all pairs of means, described in Section 8.2. We test the family in a step-down manner as we did with the Begun and Gabriel procedure.

- We reject a subset homogeneity hypothesis H_K if it is rejected at level of $(k/g)\alpha$.
- We retain H_K if it is not rejected at level α.
- Otherwise, if all subset homogeneity hypotheses containing H_K are rejected, and every subset homogeneity, R, concerning means outside of K are rejected at $(r/g)\alpha$, then we can proceed to test H_K at level α.

To satisfy coherence, whenever any homogeneity hypothesis is retained, all hypotheses implied by it are retained without formal testing. The resulting inferences from this procedure enable you to assess homogeneity of successive means. When $H_{i,j}$ is rejected, we conclude that the response increases from the ith to the jth dose. You should be aware of the following point. Whenever a homogeneity hypothesis is rejected, there is still the question of which of the subsets implied by it are false. It may happen that the procedure terminates without identifying such subsets, due to lack of consonance. Most studies are designed to have sufficient power to detect a global dose response but may not have sufficient power for some of the intermediate comparisons. As an example of this point, suppose the means i, j, and, k have been found different. We conclude that there is an increase in the response from i to k. If, however, the homogeneity of i and j and that of j and k were not rejected, we cannot be sure whether there is a monotonic response from i to k, an increase from i to j and then a leveling off of the response, or a flat response between i and j and then an increase from j to k.

The %rcc macro, given in the appendix, implements the Rom-Costello-Connell procedure discussed earlier. Note that Program 8.7 demonstrates its use on the Angina data from Section 8.5.2; both tabular and graphical outputs are generated.

PROGRAM 8.7   Rom-Costello-Connell Closed Dose-Response Testing

```
%rcc(DataSet  = angina   ,
     Groups   = dose      ,
     Response = Response ,
     FWE      = 0.05      );
```

Output from Program 8.7

```
ROM-COSTELLO-CONNELL CLOSED TESTING PROCEDURE
FOR UPPER-TAILED DOSE RESPONSE ANALYSIS

d_i  -  d_j   P-VALUE   DECISION
---------------------------------------
0    -   1    0.0915    Retain
0    -   2    0.0168    Reject
0    -   3    0.0009    Reject
0    -   4    0.0000    Reject
1    -   2    0.2025    Retain
1    -   3    0.0338    Reject
1    -   4    0.0000    Reject
2    -   3    0.1539    Retain
2    -   4    0.0000    Reject
3    -   4    0.0005    Reject
---------------------------------------
ALPHA=  0.05
```

ROM—COSTELLO—CONNELL CLOSED TESTING PROCEDURE

SCHEMATIC PLOT OF THE DOSE RESPONSE

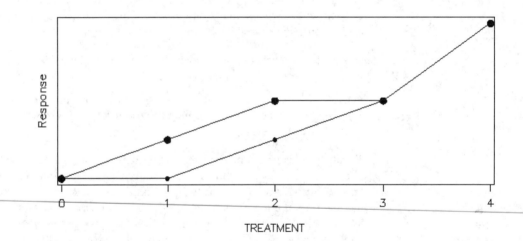

TREATMENT

The output from the %rcc macro gives both decisions on subset homogeneity hypotheses, and a graphical display of the results. The output table shows all subset homogeneity hypotheses tested, and their corresponding one-sided *p*-values. Notice that these *p*-values are exactly half of the *p*-values seen in the output from Tukey's trend test, since we chose to do one-sided tests. The indices $d_i - d_j$ refer to the hypotheses of equality of successive means. Hypotheses 0-1, 0-2, 0-3, 0-4 correspond to Tukey's trend test ordinal contrasts, from which we conclude that the NOSTASOT dose is the low dose. The remaining hypotheses give you additional information. For example, hypothesis 2-4 is rejected, leading to the conclusion that there is an increase in the response from dose 2 to dose 4. Hypothesis 3-4 is rejected, leading to the conclusion that there is also an increase in the response from dose 3 to dose 4. Thus, dose 4 has a significantly higher response than all the rest in this example. This information is not available from Tukey's trend test. The schematic display of the results shows these findings as well. Two responses that can be connected with a horizontal line correspond to a retained hypothesis of all intermediate means. Note that the response to dose 4 is not connected horizontally to any other response. On the other hand, dose 1 and dose 2 responses can be connected, dose 2 and dose 3 responses can be connected, but dose 1 and dose 3 responses cannot be connected. Therefore, we can conclude that dose 3 has a higher response than dose 1, but there is some uncertainty about dose 2, since we are not able to reject the equality of its response to either dose 3 or dose 1. This is due to lack of consonance. A similar situation exists for dose 1 between doses 0 and 2.

8.5.3 Williams' Test

Williams (1971, 1972) has proposed a test for identifying the Minimal Effective Dose (MED), which is a dose just above the No Effect Dose. It requires equal sample sizes of the dose groups, but not necessarily equal to the control group sample size. With this test, the maximum likelihood estimate of the population means, under the order restriction, is calculated using the *Pool Adjacent Violators* algorithm. Then pairwise t-type statistics are calculated using the low (zero) dose as a reference $\bar{t}_i = (\hat{\mu}_i - \bar{y}_0)/\{s\sqrt{1/n_0 + 1/n}\}$, where n_0 and n are the sample sizes of the control and the dose groups respectively, $\bar{y}_i$ is the sample mean of the ith group, and $\hat{\mu}_i$ is the maximum likelihood estimate of ith group mean. The hypotheses of homogeneity are tested in a step-down manner, starting with the highest dose mean (assume g dose groups plus a control).

1. Test the null hypothesis $H_{0,g}: \mu_1 = \cdots = \mu_g$ at level α using $\bar{t}_g$ and compare with $c_g = \bar{t}_{g,\alpha}$. If smaller, then stop and conclude that the doses are homogeneous (or at least not sufficiently different). Otherwise, conclude that the high dose is significantly different from the control, and proceed to step 2.
2. Test $H_{0,g-1}: \mu_1 = \cdots = \mu_{g-1}$ by comparing $\bar{t}_{g-1}$ with $c_{g-1} = \bar{t}_{g-1,\alpha}$. If smaller, then stop and conclude that the highest dose is the MED, otherwise conclude that the next to the highest dose is significantly different from the control, and proceed to step 3.
3. Continue in this manner until you retain a homogeneity hypothesis, or there are no more tests to perform.

The critical values c_k are calculated using the algorithm of Williams (1971, 1972). These can be computed using the PROBMC function in SAS, but the calculation is computationally intense and may take a while.

The calculation of the maximum likelihood estimates $\hat{\mu}_i$ is done as follows. First, order the group means. Compare the control mean with the first dose mean. If ordered in the right way (control mean $\leq$ dose mean), use $\bar{y}_0$ and $\bar{y}_1$ as the respective estimates, otherwise use $(\bar{y}_0+\bar{y}_1)/2$ as $\hat{\mu}_0$ and $\hat{\mu}_1$. Compare these estimates to the next group mean. If ordered in the right way, use $\bar{y}_2$ as the estimate for the second group mean, otherwise use $(\bar{y}_0 + \bar{y}_1 + \bar{y}_3)/3$ as the estimate of the control, first dose, and second dose group means. Continue in this manner until all means are included.

EXAMPLE: **Effect of Drug Dose on Heart Rate**

A study was conducted to assess the effect of increasing doses of a new drug on heart rate. Change from pretreatment as measured in heart beats per minute was collected on 60 patients. Five treatment groups were studied, including a control (trt=1), and four doses of a drug (treatments 2, 3, 4, and 5, respectively). Program 8.8, which uses the %Williams macro from the appendix, performs Williams' test to identify the MED.

PROGRAM 8.8 **Williams' Test on Heart Rate Data**

```
data hr;
do trt = 1 to 5;
     do j = 1 to 12;
        input response @@;
        output;
        end;
     end;
```

```
cards;
    5 7 10  3 -6 10 11 13 -2 -4 5  8
   -3 -5 7 6 -8 -5 7 2 -4 -5 -1 3
   -1 6 -2 -3 5 6 -1 -5 5 7 0 -2
   12 8 0 -3 7 9 2 -2 5 2 -1 10
    5 11 9 9 7 0 10 11 14 9 8  10
;

%Williams(dataset=hr,trt=trt,response=response);
```

**Output from
Program 8.8**

```
              WILLIAMS STEP-DOWN TEST

     i   Mean_1  Mean_i   T_i    P-VALUE
    ---------------------------------------
     2   1.917   1.917   0.000   .5000
     3   1.917   1.917   0.000   .5833
     4   1.917   4.083   1.074   .1830
     5   1.917   8.583   3.305   .0009
    ---------------------------------------
```

The output shows the estimates of the treatment means under the order restriction using the Pool Adjacent Violators algorithm, the t-type statistics, and the corresponding p-values from Williams' procedure. Note that the control and two lowest dose groups have the same estimate of the mean, resulting in t-type statistics that are equal to zero for the first and second doses. The procedure starts by comparing the p-value associated with treatment 5 (p5) to α. Since it is smaller, we conclude that the high dose increases heart rate more than the control. Since the p-value for treatment 4 (p4) is not significant, we stop and declare the highest dose as the MED. We conclude that doses 1,2, and 3 are not significantly different from the control. Note that the number of groups included for the calculation of the p-values equals the number of dose groups for the comparison, i.e., when we compare all doses, we include four dose groups. If we conclude that the high dose is different from the control, we include only three doses, etc.

8.6 Closed Tests for General Contrasts

As shown in previous sections, you can gain power by using closed testing procedures. In this section, we provide a macro for general testing which

- is a closed testing procedure that incorporates logical dependencies among hypotheses
- allows *any collection* of linear combinations, not just pairwise contrasts
- incorporates correlations correctly, thus allowing imbalance, covariates, and more general models.

Following Shaffer (1986), Westfall (1997) developed a procedure to test multiple contrasts in the general homoscedastic normal linear model. The procedure works as follows:

1. Order the t-statistics from most to least significant: $t_1 \geq \cdots \geq t_k$. (With lower-tail tests, reverse the sign; with two-tailed tests use absolute values.) The hypotheses corresponding to these ordered test statistics are $H_1, \ldots, H_k$.

2. Reject H_1 if $t_1 \geq c_{\alpha,1}$, where $c_{\alpha,1}$ is the $1 - \alpha$ quantile of the distribution of max T_i. (This first step is identical to the single-step method of Chapter 5, Section 5.3.2.) If H_1 is rejected, proceed to the next step; otherwise, do not reject any of $H_1, \ldots, H_k$ and stop.

3. Reject H_2 if $t_2 \geq c_{\alpha,2}$, where $c_{\alpha,2}$ is the *maximum* of all $1 - \alpha$ quantiles of $\max_{S_2} T_i$. The maximum is taken over all sets of null hypotheses S_2 that (1) contain H_2 and (2) whose joint truth does not contradict falseness of H_1. If H_2 is rejected, proceed to the next step; otherwise, do not reject any of $H_2, \ldots, H_k$ and stop.

4. Reject H_3 if $t_2 \geq c_{\alpha,3}$, where $c_{\alpha,3}$ is the *maximum* of all $1 - \alpha$ quantiles of $\max_{S_3} T_i$. The maximum is taken over all sets of null hypotheses S_3 that (1) contain H_3 and (2) whose joint truth does not contradict falseness of either H_1 or H_2. If H_3 is rejected, proceed to the next step; otherwise, do not reject any of $H_3, \ldots, H_k$ and stop.

5. Continue in this fashion until a stop, or until all nulls have been rejected.

This method is due to Shaffer (1986), and Conforti and Hochberg (1987) showed that this is in fact a closed testing method. Westfall (1997) re-expressed the above algorithm using adjusted p-values so that the decisions to retain or reject particular nulls can be made simply by noting whether the adjusted p-value is less than α. The method uses the actual distribution of the joint test statistics, simulated using a hybrid of Bonferroni control variate and simple simulation that gives more accurate estimates than either method individually. (Westfall, 1997, called this method the generalized least squares, or GLS method.)

The %SimTests macro provided in the appendix performs these adjustments. You invoke this macro in exactly the same way that you invoke the %SimIntervals macro, described in Chapters 5 and 6. You need to supply the linear contrasts and their labels using the %Contrasts macro, as discussed previously in Chapter 5. You also need to supply the estimated parameters, their estimated covariance matrix, and the degrees of freedom using SAS/IML code embedded in the %Estimates macro. In some cases you can use the %MakeGLMStats macro, described in Chapter 5, to avoid having to specify the %Contrasts and %Estimates macros. Examples of using the %SimTests macro are given below.

The macro is invoked as

```
%SimTests(nsamp=  <value>   ,
          seed=   <value>  ,
          side=   <value>  ,
          type=   <value>  );
```

where

nsim   is the number of simulations. The default is 20000. Using nsim=0 suppresses simulation and calculates all adjustments using the Bonferroni multiplier. The Bonferroni adjustments are properly attributed to Shaffer (1986) when the type argument defined below is set to type=LOGICAL or to Holm (1979) when the type argument defined below is set to type=FREE.

seed   is the seed value for the random number generator; 0 is the default, meaning it uses the computer clock time.

side   is either side=L, side=U, or side=B, for lower-, upper-, or two-tailed tests, respectively. The default is side=B.

type   determines whether the logical constraint method of Shaffer (1986) and Westfall (1997) will be used (type=LOGICAL), or whether the free (unconstrained) step-down method of Holm will be used (type=FREE). The default is type=FREE because the more statistically powerful LOGICAL method can be computationally prohibitive when the number of contrasts is twenty or more. Note, however, that even though `type=FREE` is less powerful than `type=LOGICAL`, it still uses step-down testing and correlations, and is thus much more powerful than the single-step testing. (`type=FREE` essentially applies Holm's method, but uses correlations to improve the power.)

As with the `%SimIntervals` macro, you must run the `%Contrasts` macro first to define the contrasts of interest and their labels, and the `%Estimates` macro to define the estimates, the estimated covariance matrix, and the degrees of freedom. Setting degrees of freedom as `df=0` corresponds to using the asymptotic standard normal distribution for the *p*-values, and to simulating from the appropriate multivariate normal distribution, rather than multivariate *t*. Thus, with the `%Estimates` macro, you can

- input summary statistics directly.
- use output from PROC GLM to define the estimates and to obtain exact (modulo Monte Carlo error) simultaneous inferences.
- use output from a variety of SAS procedures, such as PROC LOGISTIC, PROC PHREG, PROC LIFEREG, etc., to define the estimates, specifying `df=0` to obtain the asymptotic multiple comparisons using the multivariate normal distribution.

8.6.1   All Pairwise Comparisons—Cholesterol Reduction Data Revisited

Consider the cholesterol reduction example and Program 8.1. There are $g = 5$ groups with $n = 10$ observations per group. The code for the `%Contrasts` macro defines all 10 pairwise comparisons contrasts. The code for the `%Estimates` macro uses the estimates shown in the output from Program 8.1, which includes the estimated means, MSE, and df. `%SimTests` processes this information to perform the multiple tests.

PROGRAM 8.9   Logically Constrained Tests on Cholesterol Reduction Data

```
%macro Contrasts;
   C =   {-1 1 0 0 0, -1 0 1 0 0, -1 0 0 1 0, -1 0 0 0 1 ,
                      0 -1 1 0 0,  0 -1 0 1 0,  0 -1 0 0 1 ,
                                   0  0 -1 1 0,  0  0 -1 0 1 ,
                                                 0  0  0 -1 1 };
   C=C';
   clab =     {"2-1", "3-1", "4-1", "5-1",
                      "3-2", "4-2", "5-2",
                             "4-3", "5-3",
                                    "5-4"};
%mend;

%macro Estimates;
   mse = 10.41668;
   df = 45;
   EstPar = {5.782 , 9.225 , 12.375 , 15.361 , 20.948  };
   cov = mse*(1/10)*I(5);
%mend;

%SimTests(seed=121211, type=LOGICAL);
```

Output from Program 8.9

```
Logically Constrained (Restricted Combinations) Step-Down Tests

                      Standard   ----- Pr > |t| -----
       Contrast  Estimate  Error     Raw    Bon    Adj    SE(AdjP)

         2-1      3.4430   1.4434  0.0213 0.0427 0.0422  0.000155
         3-1      6.5930   1.4434  <.0001 0.0002 0.0002  0
         4-1      9.5790   1.4434  <.0001 <.0001 <.0001  0
         5-1     15.1660   1.4434  <.0001 <.0001 <.0001  0
         3-2      3.1500   1.4434  0.0343 0.0427 0.0422  0.000155
         4-2      6.1360   1.4434  0.0001 0.0003 0.0003  0
         5-2     11.7230   1.4434  <.0001 <.0001 <.0001  0
         4-3      2.9860   1.4434  0.0443 0.0443 0.0443  0
         5-3      8.5730   1.4434  <.0001 <.0001 <.0001  0
         5-4      5.5870   1.4434  0.0003 0.0007 0.0007  0
```

Note that, in contrast to the Begun and Gabriel method shown in the output from Program 8.3, this procedure finds all comparisons significant, whether using the Bonferroni adjusted *p*-values in the Bon column, or the more powerful adjustments that utilize correlations in the Adj column. In this example, correlations do not affect the results much; however, in cases where the *p*-values are larger, correlations have a larger affect.

This gain in power is not a general rule; in some cases this method is more powerful, in other cases the Begun and Gabriel approach is more powerful. However, using this method, you will never reject a hypothesis whose unadjusted *p*-value is larger than that of a hypothesis that has been retained. Such an anomaly is possible with the Begun and Gabriel and other closed methods.

The %Contrasts macro can be simplified in the case of pairwise comparisons. Instead of typing the contrasts and their labels in manually, you can use Program 8.10.

PROGRAM 8.10   Simplifying the %Contrasts Macro for Pairwise Comparisons

```
%macro Contrasts;
   g = 5;
   free c clab;
   do i = 1 to g-1;
      do j = i+1 to g;
         c    = c    // ((1:g)=i) - ((1:g)=j);
         clab = clab // (     trim(left(char(i,5)))
                           +'-'+trim(left(char(j,5))));
      end;
   end;
   c=c`;
%mend;
```

Using this macro produces the same result as the %Contrasts macro shown in Program 8.9; however, this one is more general. All you have to do is change g=5 to the number of groups you have.

8.6.2   Using the %SimTests Macro with General Contrasts

The methods of the %SimTests macro are quite powerful for all pairwise comparisons, and are competitive with the best available closed methods. However, perhaps the greatest utility of the methodology is that you can analyze data using any set of contrasts of interest, not just pairwise comparisons or comparisons with control. For example, in the cholesterol reduction example, the formulations were 20 mg once a day (A), 10 mg twice a day (B), and 5 mg four times a day (C), a drug in the same class as the test drug (D), and a drug in a different class (E).

Instead of all pairwise comparisons, you might only be interested in the comparisons among the treatment combinations involving the test drug, as well as overall comparisons involving the test drug and the two competitors. In this case you can use Program 8.11.

PROGRAM 8.11   **Analysis of More General Contrasts Using %SimTests**

```
%macro Contrasts;
   C =  {-1  1  0 0 0, -1  0 1 0 0,  0 -1  1 0 0,
         -1 -1 -1 3 0,
         -1 -1 -1 0 3 };

   C=C';
   clab =   {"2-1"    , "3-1", "3-2",
             "D-test"  ,
             "E-test"  };
%mend;


%macro Estimates;
   mse = 10.41668;
   df = 45;
   EstPar = {5.782 , 9.225 , 12.375 , 15.361 , 20.948  };
   cov = mse*(1/10)*I(5);
%mend;

%SimTests(seed=121211, type=LOGICAL, nsamp=50000);
```

Output from Program 8.11

Logically Constrained (Restricted Combinations) Step-Down Tests

Contrast	Estimate	Standard Error	----- Pr > |t| ----- Raw	Bon	Adj	SE(AdjP)
2-1	3.4430	1.4434	0.0213	0.0213	0.0213	0
3-1	6.5930	1.4434	<.0001	0.0001	0.0001	0
3-2	3.1500	1.4434	0.0343	0.0343	0.0343	0
D-test	18.7010	3.5355	<.0001	<.0001	<.0001	0
E-test	35.4620	3.5355	<.0001	<.0001	<.0001	0

8.6.3 Using the %SimTests Macro with General Contrasts and Covariates

As shown above, you can use the %Estimates macro manually by inputting the data yourself. In our examples, the design was balanced, leading to the following which was coded in the %Estimates macro as cov = mse*(1/10)*I(5);.

Estimated Covariance Matrix of the Sample Mean Vector for Balanced One-Way ANOVA

$$\text{COV} = \hat{\sigma}^2 \begin{pmatrix} \frac{1}{n} & 0 & \cdots & 0 \\ 0 & \frac{1}{n} & \cdots & 0 \\ \vdots & \vdots & \ddots & \vdots \\ 0 & 0 & \cdots & \frac{1}{n} \end{pmatrix},$$

When the design is unbalanced, the covariance matrix is only slightly more complex:

Estimated Covariance Matrix of the Sample Mean Vector for Unbalanced One-Way ANOVA

$$\text{COV} = \hat{\sigma}^2 \begin{pmatrix} \frac{1}{n_1} & 0 & \cdots & 0 \\ 0 & \frac{1}{n_2} & \cdots & 0 \\ \vdots & \vdots & \ddots & \vdots \\ 0 & 0 & \cdots & \frac{1}{n_g} \end{pmatrix},$$

This can be coded as, for example, n = 10,3,4,21,23; cov = mse*inv(diag(n)); assuming sample sizes $n_1 = 10, \ldots, n_5 = 23$.

In general, covariance matrices of the means or adjusted means (LS-means) do not have such simple forms. Fortunately, many SAS procedures put estimates and their covariance matrices to output files, and you can import such values from these data sets into the %Estimates macro.

8.6.4 Example: Evaluating Dose Response of Litter Weights in Rats—Revisited

In Chapter 6, Section 6.2.2, we analyzed the LS-means comparing doses with control, evaluating trend contrasts for rat weights, and controlling litter size and gestation time. We considered $k = 6$ contrasts in total, three pairwise comparisons with control, three alternative dose-response contrasts, and upper-tailed tests. Noting that there are large correlations between the estimated contrasts, we used the %SimIntervals macro to analyze the data, incorporating these correlations. The analysis used in %SimIntervals is a single-step analysis that has the handy confidence interval correspondence. If you are willing to forgo this correspondence in order to use more powerful tests, then you can use the %SimTests macro instead, as shown in Program 8.12.

PROGRAM 8.12 **Multiple Tests with General Contrasts and Correlations**

```
proc glm data=litter outstat=stat;
   class dose;
   model weight = dose gesttime number;
   lsmeans dose/out=ests cov;
run;

%macro Estimates;
   use ests;
   read all var {lsmean} into EstPar;
   read all var {cov1 cov2 cov3 cov4} into Cov;
   use stat(where=(_TYPE_='ERROR'));
   read all var {df} into df;
%mend;
```

```
%macro Contrasts;
   c = { 1     -1     0     0    ,
         1      0    -1     0    ,
         1      0     0    -1    ,
       0.750  0.250 -0.250 -0.750 ,
       0.384  0.370  0.246 -1.000 ,
       0.887  0.113 -0.339 -0.661 };
   c=c';
   clab = { "cont-low " ,
            "cont-mid " ,
            "cont-high" ,
            "ordinal  " ,
            "arith    " ,
            "log ord  " };
%mend;

%SimTests(nsamp=50000,seed=121211,type=LOGICAL,side=U);
```

**Output from
Program 8.12**

Logically Constrained (Restricted Combinations) Step-Down Tests

		Standard	------ Pr > t ------			
Contrast	Estimate	Error	Raw	Bon	Adj	SE(AdjP)
cont-low	3.3524	1.2908	0.0058	0.0345	0.0209	0.000329
cont-mid	2.2909	1.3384	0.0458	0.0915	0.0894	0.000194
cont-high	2.6752	1.3343	0.0245	0.0490	0.0457	0.000219
ordinal	1.7411	1.0433	0.0499	0.0998	0.0894	0.000194
arith	0.8713	1.1322	0.2221	0.2221	0.2221	0
log ord	2.1661	1.0735	0.0238	0.0476	0.0402	0.000274

Comparing this analysis with the analysis shown in the output from Program 6.3 in Section 6.2.2, you can see that there are three significances at the FWE $= 0.05$ here, but only one significance shown in the output from Program 6.3.

8.7 Concluding Remarks

In this chapter we have shown how you can have much more powerful tests using the closure method, provided you are willing to give up confidence intervals. The REGWQ option of PROC GLM provides an example of such a method; others are provided in the %BegGab, %RCC, and %SimTests macros.

To summarize:

- If you have a balanced ANOVA and want to perform closed tests on all pairwise comparisons, then you can use the REGWQ option in PROC GLM, or either of the %BegGab or the %SimTests macros. %BegGab and %SimTests are both more powerful than REGWQ, but neither is uniformly more powerful than the other. If you have many treatment groups (more than seven), then %SimTests will probably be too time-consuming and you should use %BegGab. With fewer groups you can use either, but %SimTests has the advantage that the ordering of the adjusted *p*-values is always the same as the ordering of the unadjusted *p*-values.

- If you have an unbalanced ANOVA and want to perform closed tests on all pairwise comparisons, REGWQ is not recommended. You may use the %BegGab macro or the %SimTests macro, with the same caveats noted above. However, in this case, an additional element favoring %SimTests is that the %BegGab macro uses the conservative Tukey-Kramer approximation, whereas %SimTests estimates the precise critical values.

- If you want to perform closed tests for all comparisons with a control, you can use the step-down Dunnett method described in Section 8.4. Note that %SimTests also does this analysis, with identical results (identical up to Monte Carlo error). See "Sequential Testing and Fixed Sequences" in Chapter 2, Section 2.5.8 for an alternative method.

- If you want to perform dose-response analysis with closed tests in the ANOVA, you can use one of the several methods described in Section 8.5. There is ongoing research concerning which of these dose-response methods is most appropriate.

- If you want to perform dose-response analysis in the general linear model with covariates using closed tests, you can use contrasts described in Section 8.5 and the %SimTests macro.

- The %SimTests macro is quite generally applicable, allowing inference on any collection of linear combinations in the general linear model. However, if the family size is large (say, 20 or more), the more powerful type=LOGICAL method becomes infeasible, and you should use the default type=FREE, which still incorporates correlations in a step-down method, but not logical constraints.

Chapter 9

Simultaneous Inference in Two-Way and Higher-Way ANOVA and ANCOVA

9.1 Introduction

Two-way and higher-way ANOVA and ANCOVA models use multiple classification variables and often contain interactions among them. In such models, there is interest in comparisons among the main effects and in comparisons involving the interactions. In this chapter, we show how to use PROC GLM for common standard simultaneous inferences, and how to use the specialized macros %SimIntervals and %SimTests for less standard situations.

To start with a simple illustration, we consider a balanced two-way ANOVA.

EXAMPLE: **Industrial Waste Experiment**

To remain competitive, businesses have adopted a philosophy of continuous improvement of their manufacturing and service processes. An important element of this philosophy is experimentation, to better understand systems and to optimize performance. The data in the following study are from an experiment designed to study the effect of temperature (at low, medium, and high levels) and environment (five different environments) on waste output in a manufacturing plant. Two replicate measurements are taken at each temperature/environment combination.

The data are given in Program 9.1.

PROGRAM 9.1 **Industrial Waste Output**

```
data waste;
   do temp = 1 to 3;
      do envir = 1 to 5;
         do rep=1 to 2;
         input waste @@;
         output;
         end;
      end;
   end;
datalines;
```

```
7.09 5.90   7.94 9.15 9.23 9.85   5.43   7.73   9.43 6.90
7.01 5.82   6.18 7.19 7.86 6.33   8.49   8.67   9.62 9.07
7.78 7.73 10.39 8.78 9.27 8.90 12.17 10.95 13.07 9.76
;
run;
```

Among the questions of interest are

- Overall, are there significant differences among the temperature levels?
- Overall, are there significant differences among the environment levels?
- Do the differences between temperature levels depend on the environment (or vice versa)?

Each of these three families defines a family of hypotheses, within which the FWE can be controlled using various MCPs. It is also possible to control the FWE over the entire collection of tests.

9.2   Two-Way ANOVA

9.2.1   Balanced with Replication

With equal sample sizes, interpretations are simplest. The usual model for the data is

$$y_{ijk} = \mu + \alpha_i + \beta_j + (\alpha\beta)_{ij} + \epsilon_{ijk},$$

where the indexes are $1 \le i \le I$, $1 \le j \le J$, $1 \le k \le K$, and where the error terms ϵ_{ijk} satisfy the usual conditions. This parameterization is consistent with the PROC GLM syntax, for example,

```
proc glm;
   class a b;
   model y = a b a*b;
run;
```

Note that the product operator "*" in the a*b model term does *not* refer to multiplication of the main effects; it simply denotes a general effect that depends on the levels of both A and B.

9.2.2   The Cell Means Model

The model is easiest to understand in the cell means framework. Here, we view the data just like a one-way ANOVA, but with the mean value μ_{ij} indexed by the cell location (i, j); hence μ_{ij} is called a "cell mean". The cell means model is

$$y_{ijk} = \mu_{ij} + \epsilon_{ijk}.$$

In the context of this model, the main effect comparisons are simply comparisons of cell mean averages: $\bar{\mu}_{i\cdot} - \bar{\mu}_{i'\cdot}$ and $\bar{\mu}_{\cdot j} - \bar{\mu}_{\cdot j'}$. The "·" notation means to average over the subscript, for example,

$$\bar{\mu}_{i\cdot} = \frac{1}{J} \sum_{j=1}^{J} \mu_{ij}.$$

Returning to the example of industrial waste output, you can use Program 9.2.

PROGRAM 9.2   **Multiple Comparisons of Main Effects in Balanced ANOVA**

```
proc glm data=waste;
   class envir temp;
   model waste = envir temp envir*temp;
   lsmeans temp envir/pdiff cl adjust=tukey;
run;
```

Note that for this balanced data (that is, all cells are of the same size) the MCP options on both the MEANS and the LSMEANS statements give the same results. We prefer to demonstrate how you use the LSMEANS statement, however, since it applies more generally. The confidence limit results from the above statements are shown in the output from Program 9.2.

Output from Program 9.2

Least Squares Means for Effect temp

i	j	Difference Between Means	Simultaneous 95% Confidence Interval for LSMean(i)-LSMean(j)	
1	2	0.241000	-1.018054	1.500054
1	3	-2.015000	-3.274054	-0.755946
2	3	-2.256000	-3.515054	-0.996946

Least Squares Means for Effect envir

i	j	Difference Between Means	Simultaneous 95% Confidence Interval for LSMean(i)-LSMean(j)	
1	2	-1.383333	-3.315680	0.549013
1	3	-1.685000	-3.617346	0.247346
1	4	-2.018333	-3.950680	-0.085987
1	5	-2.753333	-4.685680	-0.820987
2	3	-0.301667	-2.234013	1.630680
2	4	-0.635000	-2.567346	1.297346
2	5	-1.370000	-3.302346	0.562346
3	4	-0.333333	-2.265680	1.599013
3	5	-1.068333	-3.000680	0.864013
4	5	-0.735000	-2.667346	1.197346

These results allow you to make the following inferences:

- When averaged over temperatures, Environment 1 has significantly less waste than Environments 4 or 5.

- When averaged over environments, Temperature 3 has significantly more waste than either Temperature 1 or 2.

These inferences about Environment and Temperature differences hold with FWE = 0.05 *within* each set of comparisons. The FWE level over both sets together is larger than 0.05, but less than 0.10 (using the Bonferroni inequality).

Alternatively, you can control the FWE over both sets of main effects contrasts at the simultaneous FWE level by choosing 0.025 as the FWE level for each subfamily. For another method of controlling the FWE over both sets of contrasts, see Section 9.2.3.

Note that more powerful inferences are available, as discussed in Chapter 8, if you are willing to accept the less ambitious inference of deciding only whether the averages differ, rather than trying to place limits on the size of the differences.

9.2.3   Simultaneous Inference for Both Sets of Main Effects

If you want to control the FWE for both sets of main effect contrasts *simultaneously* at the 0.05 FWE level, you can use FWE of 0.025 (using the ALPHA=0.025 option of LSMEANS, for example). This method controls the FWE for the joint family conservatively at less than the 0.05 level. However, using the cell means approach and the %Sim* macros defined in previous chapters, you can include both sets of main effects contrasts in the family of tests so that the FWE is closer to the 0.05 level (and therefore the tests are less conservative). We demonstrate this approach in this section.

Assuming you are willing to accept the less ambitious inference of simply deciding which contrasts are non-null, you can test the entire family simultaneously using the %SimTests macro defined in Chapter 8. Here is the program:

PROGRAM 9.3   **Simultaneous Tests of Both Sets of Main Effects Contrasts**

```
%MakeGLMStats(dataset  = waste      ,
              classvar = envir temp ,
              yvar     = waste      ,
              model    = envir*temp );

%macro Contrasts;
   C = {0  1  1  1 -1 -1 -1  0  0  0  0  0  0  0  0  0 ,
        0  1  1  1  0  0  0 -1 -1 -1  0  0  0  0  0  0 ,
        0  1  1  1  0  0  0  0  0  0 -1 -1 -1  0  0  0 ,
        0  1  1  1  0  0  0  0  0  0  0  0  0 -1 -1 -1 ,
        0  0  0  0  1  1  1 -1 -1 -1  0  0  0  0  0  0 ,
        0  0  0  0  1  1  1  0  0  0 -1 -1 -1  0  0  0 ,
        0  0  0  0  1  1  1  0  0  0  0  0  0 -1 -1 -1 ,
        0  0  0  0  0  0  0  1  1  1 -1 -1 -1  0  0  0 ,
        0  0  0  0  0  0  0  1  1  1  0  0  0 -1 -1 -1 ,
        0  0  0  0  0  0  0  0  0  0  1  1  1 -1 -1 -1 };
   C=C/3;
   C1 = {0  1 -1  0  1 -1  0  1 -1  0  1 -1  0  1 -1  0 ,
         0  1  0 -1  1  0 -1  1  0 -1  1  0 -1  1  0 -1 ,
         0  0  1 -1  0  1 -1  0  1 -1  0  1 -1  0  1 -1 };
   C1 = C1/5;
   C = C//C1;
   C=C`;
   Clab = {"e1-e2","e1-e3","e1-e4","e1-e5",
                   "e2-e3","e2-e4","e2-e5",
                          "e3-e4","e3-e5",
                                  "e4-e5",
           "t1-t2","t1-t3",
                   "t2-t3"};
%mend;

%SimTests(seed=121211, type=LOGICAL);
```

Output from Program 9.3

```
        Logically Constrained (Restricted Combinations) Step-Down Tests


                          Standard    ----- Pr > |t| -----
          Contrast  Estimate   Error    Raw    Bon    Adj    SE(AdjP)

          e1-e2     -1.3833   0.6258   0.0430 0.2151 0.1671   0.00109
          e1-e3     -1.6850   0.6258   0.0167 0.0835 0.0704   0.000640
          e1-e4     -2.0183   0.6258   0.0057 0.0396 0.0309   0.000519
          e1-e5     -2.7533   0.6258   0.0005 0.0057 0.0046   0.000176
          e2-e3     -0.3017   0.6258   0.6367 1.0000 0.8557   0.00166
          e2-e4     -0.6350   0.6258   0.3263 1.0000 0.7088   0.00200
          e2-e5     -1.3700   0.6258   0.0448 0.3136 0.1975   0.00139
          e3-e4     -0.3333   0.6258   0.6021 1.0000 0.8356   0.00170
          e3-e5     -1.0683   0.6258   0.1084 0.4336 0.3067   0.00147
          e4-e5     -0.7350   0.6258   0.2585 0.7755 0.5719   0.00186
          t1-t2      0.2410   0.4847   0.6263 1.0000 0.8557   0.00166
          t1-t3     -2.0150   0.4847   0.0008 0.0059 0.0050   0.000169
          t2-t3     -2.2560   0.4847   0.0003 0.0041 0.0034   0.000124
```

The following notes provide more details concerning Program 9.3 and its output.

- Since we have specified just the interaction term `envir*temp` as the model, contrasts correspond to the cell means μ_{ij} of the study. The first row in the C matrix is the contrast $(\mu_{11} + \mu_{12} + \mu_{13})/3 - (\mu_{21} + \mu_{22} + \mu_{23})/3$, which is the comparison of Environment 1 with Environment 2 averages. The "0" in the first position is for the intercept term.

- The order of the indexes (i, j) is determined by the order of the variables in the `classvar = envir temp` input.

- The first 10 contrasts in the "C" matrix are main effect contrasts for the `envir` factor; the last three are main effect contrasts for the `temp` factor.

- Conclusions from the outputs of Program 9.2 and Program 9.3 are the same with regard to significances: the same four differences (two Environment and two Temperature differences) are flagged as "statistically significant." However, the differences flagged on the output of Program 9.2 are collectively significant at an FWE of 0.10, whereas the output of Program 9.3 allows us to claim the same differences at a lower overall significance level of FWE=0.05.

- If the ALPHA=0.025 option is used in Program 9.2 for the LSMEANS statement, then the overall FWE level for the `temp` and `envir` pairwise comparisons is at most 0.05. However, in this case the comparison of Environments 1 and 4 becomes insignificant. The output of Program 9.3 shows this comparison (row 4) to be significant because

  - It incorporates logical constraints. (The Bonferroni multiplier is only 7 at this step, implying a Bonferroni adjusted *p*-value of 0.03964.)

  - It incorporates correlations. (The adjusted *p*-value is 0.03087, which is smaller still than the Bonferroni adjusted *p*-value.)

9.2.4 Interaction Contrasts

There is interaction when the effect of one factor depends on the level of the other factor. You can measure effect by changes in mean level; for example, the pairwise comparisons shown in the preceding section are measures of effects (overall effects). When there are interactions, the overall effects might miss important information. It is therefore useful to compare the pairwise differences for one factor at different levels of the other factor. These statistics are called *tetrad differences*, and have the form

$$(\mu_{ij} - \mu_{ij'}) - (\mu_{i'j} - \mu_{i'j'}).$$

If there are I levels of one factor and J levels of the other, then there are $\{I(I-1)/2\} \times \{J(J-1)/2\}$ such interaction contrasts.

You might think you could analyze interaction contrasts using the following GLM syntax:

```
lsmeans envir*temp / pdiff cl adjust=tukey;
```

However, this code performs pairwise comparisons among all 15 combinations of the mean levels, and therefore does not address the interactions at all. Instead, you can use either of the %Sim* macros, defining the interaction contrasts yourself.

Program 9.4 performs the analysis using the %SimIntervals macro to obtain confidence intervals for the interaction contrasts.

PROGRAM 9.4   Simultaneous Confidence Intervals for Interaction Contrasts

```
%MakeGLMStats(dataset  = waste      ,
              classvar = envir temp ,
              yvar     = waste      ,
              model    = envir*temp );

%let a=5;   /* Levels of first CLASS variable */
%let b=3;   /* Levels or second CLASS variable */

%macro Contrasts;
   start tlc(n); return(trim(left(char(n,20)))); finish;

   idi=(1:&a);
   idj=(1:&b);
   free C clab;
   do i1=1 to &a-1; do i2=i1+1 to &a;
     do j1=1 to &b-1; do j2=j1+1 to &b;
       C     = C    // (0 || ( ((idi=i1) - (idi=i2))
                            @((idj=j1) - (idj=j2))));
       clab = clab //   "("+tlc(i1)+tlc(j1)+"-"+tlc(i1)+tlc(j2)+")"
                      +"-("+tlc(i2)+tlc(j1)+"-"+tlc(i2)+tlc(j2)+")";
     end; end;
   end; end;
   C=C`;
%mend;

%SimIntervals(nsamp=100000,seed=12345);
```

Output from Program 9.4

Estimated 95% Quantile = 3.559044

Contrast	Estimate	Standard Error	t Value	--- Pr > |t| --- Raw	Adjusted	95% Confidence Interval	
(11-12)-(21-22)	-1.7800	1.5328	-1.16	0.2637	0.9514	-7.2354	3.6754
(11-13)-(21-23)	-0.2200	1.5328	-0.14	0.8878	1.0000	-5.6754	5.2354
(12-13)-(22-23)	1.5600	1.5328	1.02	0.3249	0.9772	-3.8954	7.0154
(11-12)-(31-32)	-2.3650	1.5328	-1.54	0.1437	0.8122	-7.8204	3.0904
(11-13)-(31-33)	-1.7150	1.5328	-1.12	0.2808	0.9605	-7.1704	3.7404
(12-13)-(32-33)	0.6500	1.5328	0.42	0.6775	1.0000	-4.8054	6.1054

(11-12)-(41-42)	2.0800	1.5328	1.36	0.1949	0.8918	-3.3754	7.5354
(11-13)-(41-43)	3.7200	1.5328	2.43	0.0283	0.3260	-1.7354	9.1754
(12-13)-(42-43)	1.6400	1.5328	1.07	0.3016	0.9695	-3.8154	7.0954
(11-12)-(51-52)	1.2600	1.5328	0.82	0.4239	0.9937	-4.1954	6.7154
(11-13)-(51-53)	1.9900	1.5328	1.30	0.2138	0.9118	-3.4654	7.4454
(12-13)-(52-53)	0.7300	1.5328	0.48	0.6408	0.9999	-4.7254	6.1854
(21-22)-(31-32)	-0.5850	1.5328	-0.38	0.7081	1.0000	-6.0404	4.8704
(21-23)-(31-33)	-1.4950	1.5328	-0.98	0.3449	0.9823	-6.9504	3.9604
(22-23)-(32-33)	-0.9100	1.5328	-0.59	0.5616	0.9994	-6.3654	4.5454
(21-22)-(41-42)	3.8600	1.5328	2.52	0.0236	0.2861	-1.5954	9.3154
(21-23)-(41-43)	3.9400	1.5328	2.57	0.0213	0.2649	-1.5154	9.3954
(22-23)-(42-43)	0.0800	1.5328	0.05	0.9591	1.0000	-5.3754	5.5354
(21-22)-(51-52)	3.0400	1.5328	1.98	0.0660	0.5635	-2.4154	8.4954
(21-23)-(51-53)	2.2100	1.5328	1.44	0.1699	0.8583	-3.2454	7.6654
(22-23)-(52-53)	-0.8300	1.5328	-0.54	0.5961	0.9997	-6.2854	4.6254
(31-32)-(41-42)	4.4450	1.5328	2.90	0.0110	0.1580	-1.0104	9.9004
(31-33)-(41-43)	5.4350	1.5328	3.55	0.0029	0.0514	-0.0204	10.8904
(32-33)-(42-43)	0.9900	1.5328	0.65	0.5281	0.9989	-4.4654	6.4454
(31-32)-(51-52)	3.6250	1.5328	2.36	0.0319	0.3557	-1.8304	9.0804
(31-33)-(51-53)	3.7050	1.5328	2.42	0.0288	0.3305	-1.7504	9.1604
(32-33)-(52-53)	0.0800	1.5328	0.05	0.9591	1.0000	-5.3754	5.5354
(41-42)-(51-52)	-0.8200	1.5328	-0.53	0.6005	0.9997	-6.2754	4.6354
(41-43)-(51-53)	-1.7300	1.5328	-1.13	0.2768	0.9585	-7.1854	3.7254
(42-43)-(52-53)	-0.9100	1.5328	-0.59	0.5616	0.9994	-6.3654	4.5454

Note the following about the output:

- The most significant interaction contrast is for the comparison (31-33)-(41-43), eighth from the bottom. The difference in waste output for temperature 1 versus temperature 3 is 5.435 units higher in environment 3 than it is in environment 4.

- The most significant interaction is significant at the FWE = 0.10 level, but its significance cannot be determined at the FWE = 0.05 from this simulation because the Monte Carlo estimate 0.0514 is within simulation error of 0.05. (The simulation standard error here is $\sqrt{.0514(1-.0514)/100000} = 0.0007$.) You need a larger simulation size to make the comparison with 0.05 precise.

- The interaction F-test in this analysis (not shown above, but found using PROC GLM) yields $F(8, 15) = 2.44$, $p = 0.0651$. This result is significant at 0.10, but not at 0.05. However, in this case the test using the %SimIntervals macro appears more sensitive, since the p-value 0.0514 is smaller than 0.0651 (and not within simulation error). In general, this is not expected. The F-test usually, but not always, has higher power than tests using the max T statistic.

Note that if testing were the only objective and confidence intervals for the differences were not required, more powerful tests could be obtained from the %SimTests macro. Because there are $\{5(5-1)/2\} \times \{3(3-1)/2\} = 30$ interaction contrasts, the logical constraint method (type=LOGICAL) of the %SimTests macro would be too time-consuming. The less powerful "FREE" method (type=FREE) of the %SimTests macro can easily be used, however.

9.2.5   Balanced ANOVA without Replication

If there is only one observation per cell in a two-way design, you cannot estimate both the interaction effect and the underlying level of noise. However, if you assume that there is no interaction, you can still compare the overall averages for the factors using the interaction sum of squares as the error sum of squares. The assumption here is that the interaction is truly null; if this is not the case, then the inferences tend to be conservative, since the estimate of the variance of the errors tends to be too large.

Program 9.5 performs the REGWQ comparisons of main effects using the WASTE data, using only the first observation of each replication.

PROGRAM 9.5   **Multiple Comparisons with One Observation Per Cell**

```
data waste1;
   set waste;
   if rep=1; run;
proc glm;
   class envir temp;
   model waste = envir temp;
   means envir temp/regwq lines;
   ods select MCLinesInfo MCLines;
run;
```

Output from Program 9.5

The GLM Procedure

Ryan-Einot-Gabriel-Welsch Multiple Range Test for waste

Alpha	0.05
Error Degrees of Freedom	8
Error Mean Square	2.164787

Means with the same letter are not significantly different.

REGWQ Grouping		Mean	N	envir
A		10.707	3	5
A				
A		8.787	3	3
A				
A		8.697	3	4
A				
A		8.170	3	2
A				
A		7.293	3	1

Ryan-Einot-Gabriel-Welsch Multiple Range Test for waste

Alpha	0.05
Error Degrees of Freedom	8
Error Mean Square	2.164787

Means with the same letter are not significantly different.

REGWQ Grouping	Mean	N	temp
A	10.5360	5	3
B	7.8320	5	2
B			
B	7.8240	5	1

Note the following about the output:

- There are fewer significances in this case than in the previous analysis of Program 9.2 with the complete data set (despite using the more powerful REGWQ method in Program 9.5) for two reasons:

  1. The sample sizes are smaller, implying larger variances of estimated parameters.
  2. The estimate of the error variance in Program 9.5 uses the interaction sum of squares, which tends to be inflated.

  In this case, the analysis of Program 9.5 uses an MSE of 2.16, nearly twice as large as the MSE of Program 9.2.

- The FWE for each set of comparisons individually is 0.05. Taking both sets together, you would have to claim FWE of 0.10. If you specify ALPHA=0.025 in the MEANS options, you can claim FWE = 0.05 over the entire set of comparisons, but you will see that no comparisons are significant.

- The significances shown are reasonably consistent with the F-test for the main effects, which shows the ENVIR effect to be insignificant ($F(4, 8) = 2.18$, $p = 0.1619$) and the TEMP effect to be significant ($F(2, 8) = 5.65$, $p = 0.0296$).

- The following note is printed in the LOG:

```
NOTE: Means from the MEANS statement are not adjusted for
      other terms in the model.  For adjusted means, use
      the LSMEANS statement.
```

Because the design is balanced, the LSMEANS comparisons are identical to the ordinary MEANS comparisons. Note, however, that REGWQ is not an option for multiplicity adjustment using LSMEANS.

If you want to include both sets of main effects comparisons in a single family, you can use the %SimTests macro as shown in Program 9.6.

PROGRAM 9.6   Comparisons with One Observation Per Cell: Global Family

```
%MakeGLMStats(dataset  = waste1    ,
              classvar = envir temp ,
              yvar     = waste     ,
              model    = envir temp );
```

```
%macro Contrasts;
   C = {0   1 -1  0  0  0     0  0  0 ,
        0   1  0 -1  0  0     0  0  0 ,
        0   1  0  0 -1  0     0  0  0 ,
        0   1  0  0  0 -1     0  0  0 ,
        0   0  1 -1  0  0     0  0  0 ,
        0   0  1  0 -1  0     0  0  0 ,
        0   0  1  0  0 -1     0  0  0 ,
        0   0  0  1 -1  0     0  0  0 ,
        0   0  0  1  0 -1     0  0  0 ,
        0   0  0  0  1 -1     0  0  0 ,
        0   0  0  0  0  0     1 -1  0 ,
        0   0  0  0  0  0     1  0 -1 ,
        0   0  0  0  0  0     0  1 -1 };
   C=C`;
   Clab = {"e1-e2","e1-e3","e1-e4","e1-e5",
                   "e2-e3","e2-e4","e2-e5",
                           "e3-e4","e3-e5",
                                   "e4-e5",
           "t1-t2","t1-t3",
                   "t2-t3"};
%mend;


%SimTests(seed=121211, type=LOGICAL);
```

Output from Program 9.6

Logically Constrained (Restricted Combinations) Step-Down Tests

		Standard	----- Pr > |t| -----			
Contrast	Estimate	Error	Raw	Bon	Adj	SE(AdjP)
e1-e2	-0.8767	1.2013	0.4864	1.0000	0.8472	0.00186
e1-e3	-1.4933	1.2013	0.2490	1.0000	0.6962	0.00224
e1-e4	-1.4033	1.2013	0.2764	1.0000	0.6962	0.00224
e1-e5	-3.4133	1.2013	0.0218	0.2529	0.1358	0.00144
e2-e3	-0.6167	1.2013	0.6216	1.0000	0.9429	0.00135
e2-e4	-0.5267	1.2013	0.6727	1.0000	0.9429	0.00135
e2-e5	-2.5367	1.2013	0.0677	0.4740	0.2674	0.00169
e3-e4	0.0900	1.2013	0.9421	1.0000	0.9954	0.000453
e3-e5	-1.9200	1.2013	0.1487	0.7433	0.4565	0.00195
e4-e5	-2.0100	1.2013	0.1328	0.6642	0.4181	0.00188
t1-t2	-0.00800	0.9305	0.9934	1.0000	0.9954	0.000453
t1-t3	-2.7120	0.9305	0.0195	0.2529	0.1358	0.00144
t2-t3	-2.7040	0.9305	0.0197	0.2529	0.1358	0.00144

Here, note that nothing is significant, whereas in the two separate runs of the REGWQ shown in the output of Program 9.5, the t1-t3 and t2-t3 comparisons were in fact significant. This discrepancy is reconciled as follows:

- In the analysis of Program 9.5, each family of comparisons is at the FWE = 0.05 level. Thus the overall level of the two families is FWE = 0.10. However, the discrepancy remains, since the t1-t3 and t2-t3 comparisons are significant at the FWE = 0.10 level, whereas in the output from Program 9.6, nothing is significant at the FWE = 0.10 since all adjusted *p*-values are greater than 0.10.

- The method of the %SimTests macro is to weigh each hypothesis equally with all other hypotheses. In a simple Bonferroni sense, you would use 0.10/13 to judge significance of an unadjusted *p*-value using this method.

- The separate families approach of the Program 9.5 analysis, on the other hand, weighs hypotheses equally *within a family*. Thus, in a simple Bonferroni sense, you would use $0.05/3$ to compare the unadjusted p-values for each of the Temperature comparisons, but you would use $0.05/10$ to compare the unadjusted p-values for each of the Environment comparisons. In this case, the Temperature comparisons are given higher weight.

- The separate families approach implicitly weighs hypotheses by the number of elements within a family. When there are more elements within a family, there is less weight (less likelihood of being found significant).

- It is possible to incorporate differential weights of hypotheses directly into the multiplicity adjustments, without resorting to the Bonferroni inequality as we have done here. See Westfall and Young (1993, pp. 184–188).

9.2.6   Unbalanced Designs

With unbalanced designs, LS-means typically are more relevant than arithmetic means for quantifying general population characteristics, since the LS-means estimate the marginal means over a balanced population, whether or not the design itself is balanced; the arithmetic means only estimate the balanced population margins when the design itself is balanced. We illustrate multiple comparisons of LS-means for unbalanced designs with an example from drug development.

EXAMPLE: **Outcomes of Alternative Drugs on Different Diseases**

Developing pharmaceutical drugs is a long and laborious process, often taking 10 years from discovery to marketing. During the process the drug must be tested, first on animals, and later on humans, for evidence of safety and efficacy. Human testing alone requires four phases of clinical trials (labeled Phase I though Phase IV). Development can be stopped at any point in the process should the candidate drug be determined unsafe and/or ineffective. Multiplicity adjustment is important because it is costly for the drug company to pursue false leads. However, the tests should be as powerful as possible to avoid halting development of a promising drug.

Phase I trials tend to be small and exploratory. The following data, taken from *SAS/STAT User's Guide, Version 6, Fourth Edition, Volumes 1 and 2* on the GLM procedure (SAS Institute, Inc., 1989, p. 972) shows how patients with different diseases respond to alternative drug formulations. While there were plans for six patients at each drug/disease combination, in many cases there were fewer than that number.

The main questions here are

- Are there differences in effect between drugs?
- To what extent do the differences in effect between drugs depend on type of disease?

The data are given in Program 9.7, with an analysis to answer question 1.

PROGRAM 9.7   **Drug Study Data: Comparisons of LS-Means with Unbalanced Data**

```
data drug;
   input drug disease @;
   do i=1 to 6;
      input response @;
      output;
      end;
cards;
```

```
1 1 42 44 36 13 19 22
1 2 33  . 26  . 33 21
1 3 31 -3  . 25 25 24
2 1 28  . 23 34 42 13
2 2  . 34 33 31  . 36
2 3  3 26 28 32  4 16
3 1  .  .  1 29  . 19
3 2  . 11  9  7  1 -6
3 3 21  1  .  9  3  .
4 1 24  .  9 22 -2 15
4 2 27 12 12 -5 16 15
4 3 22  7 25  5 12  .
;
proc glm;
   class drug disease;
   model response = drug disease drug*disease/ss3;
   lsmeans drug/ pdiff cl adjust=simulate(seed=121211 acc=.001);
   ods select  OverallANOVA ModelANOVA LSMeanDiffCL;
run;
```

Output from Program 9.7

The GLM Procedure

Dependent Variable: response

Source	DF	Sum of Squares	Mean Square	F Value	Pr > F
Model	11	4259.338506	387.212591	3.51	0.0013
Error	46	5080.816667	110.452536		
Corrected Total	57	9340.155172			

Source	DF	Type III SS	Mean Square	F Value	Pr > F
drug	3	2997.471860	999.157287	9.05	<.0001
disease	2	415.873046	207.936523	1.88	0.1637
drug*disease	6	707.266259	117.877710	1.07	0.3958

The GLM Procedure
Least Squares Means
Adjustment for Multiple Comparisons: Simulated

Least Squares Means for Effect drug

i	j	Difference Between Means	Simultaneous 95% Confidence Interval for LSMean(i)-LSMean(j)	
1	2	-0.561111	-10.918737	9.796515
1	3	16.250000	5.214704	27.285296
1	4	12.450000	2.304498	22.595502
2	3	16.811111	5.775815	27.846408
2	4	13.011111	2.865609	23.156613
3	4	-3.800000	-14.636446	7.036446

We can say that the LS-Means for drugs 1 and 2 are higher than those of drugs 3 and 4, but we cannot determine whether 1 differs from 2, nor whether 3 differs from 4. These conclusions reflect "overall" comparisons, somewhat like averaging over different disease levels. For a precise interpretation of the LS-Means in this situation, see Searle, Speed, and Milliken (1980) and the material on LS-means in "The GLM Procedure" in the *SAS/STAT User's Guide, Fourth Edition* (1989).

To answer the question of whether drug effect depends on disease type, you can use the method shown in Program 9.4. However, since the interaction F-test is nowhere near significance ($F(4, 46) = 1.07$, $p = 0.3958$), it is unlikely that the multiple interaction comparisons will show significant differences.

9.2.7   Incomplete Two-way Designs

An incomplete two-way design is a design for two factors in which, as the name implies, not all combinations of the factor levels are observed. As with unbalanced designs, the LS-means are more appropriate for measuring population characteristics than the arithmetic means. Also, since these designs are usually unreplicated, the interaction sum of squares must be used to estimate the error variance.

In this section we will demonstrate how you can compare LS-means for an incomplete two-way design using either simultaneous confidence intervals for their differences computed by the GLM procedure, or simultaneously valid adjusted *p*-values computed by the %SimTests macro.

EXAMPLE: **Durability of Detergents**

Industrial experiments typically have the following features: (1) there are many controllable inputs to the process, and (2) it is too costly and/or time-consuming to run all possible input combinations. Fractional designs provide a simple solution whereby you run only a fraction of the possible combinations, choosing the levels in a balanced fashion. In the following example, from Sheffé (1959, p. 189) plates are washed with five detergent varieties, in 10 blocks. A complete design would have $5 \times 10 = 50$ combinations; however, you can reduce the number of runs to 30 by using a balanced incomplete block design, running only three detergent varieties in each block.

Program 9.8 shows the structure of the design. Note that there are six observations taken at each detergent level, distributed in a balanced way among the 10 blocks.

PROGRAM 9.8   **BIBD Data for Detergents**

```
data detergent;
   do detergent=1 to 5;
      do block =1 to 10;
      input plates @@;
      output;
      end;
   end;
datalines;
27 28 30 31 29 30  .  .  .  .
26 26 29  .  .  . 30 21 26  .
30  .  . 34 32  . 34 31  . 33
 . 29  . 33  . 34 31  . 33 31
 .  . 26  . 24 25  . 23 24 26
;
```

You can analyze the data by constructing simultaneous confidence intervals for the detergent differences shown in Program 9.9.

PROGRAM 9.9   Simultaneous Confidence Intervals for Treatment Differences

```
proc glm data=detergent;
   class block detergent;
   model plates = block detergent;
   lsmeans detergent/pdiff cl adjust=simulate
       (acc=.001 report seed=121211);
run;
```

Output from Program 9.9

The GLM Procedure
Least Squares Means
Adjustment for Multiple Comparisons: Simulated

detergent	plates LSMEAN	LSMEAN Number
1	29.0000000	1
2	26.8666667	2
3	32.6000000	3
4	31.2000000	4
5	24.6666667	5

Least Squares Means for effect detergent
Pr > |t| for H0: LSMean(i)=LSMean(j)

Dependent Variable: plates

i/j	1	2	3	4	5
1		0.1499	0.0059	0.1314	0.0010
2	0.1499		<.0001	0.0010	0.1314
3	0.0059	<.0001		0.5095	<.0001
4	0.1314	0.0010	0.5095		<.0001
5	0.0010	0.1314	<.0001	<.0001	

Least Squares Means for Effect detergent

i	j	Difference Between Means	Simultaneous 95% Confidence Interval for LSMean(i)-LSMean(j)	
1	2	2.133333	-0.521827	4.788494
1	3	-3.600000	-6.255160	-0.944840
1	4	-2.200000	-4.855160	0.455160
1	5	4.333333	1.678173	6.988494
2	3	-5.733333	-8.388494	-3.078173
2	4	-4.333333	-6.988494	-1.678173
2	5	2.200000	-0.455160	4.855160
3	4	1.400000	-1.255160	4.055160
3	5	7.933333	5.278173	10.588494
4	5	6.533333	3.878173	9.188494

Conclusions, in order of most durable to least durable detergent, are as follows:

- Detergent 3 lasts significantly longer than 1,2, and 5, but is not significantly different from detergent 4.
- Detergent 4 lasts longer than 2 and 5, but is not significantly different from detergent 1.
- Detergent 1 lasts significantly longer than detergent 5 but is not significantly different from detergent 2.
- Detergent 2 is not significantly different from detergent 5.

The `report` option displays the following results:

```
                    Details for Quantile Simulation

              Random number seed           121211
              Comparison type                 All
              Sample size                  315156
              Target alpha                   0.05
              Accuracy radius               0.001
              Accuracy confidence             99%



                          Simulation Results

                                        Estimated    99% Confidence
            Method         95% Quantile     Alpha        Interval

            Simulated        3.059124      0.0500    0.0490   0.0510
            Tukey-Kramer     3.063673      0.0495    0.0485   0.0505
            Bonferroni       3.251993      0.0344    0.0336   0.0353
            Sidak            3.241074      0.0351    0.0343   0.0360
            GT-2             3.198542      0.0381    0.0372   0.0390
            Scheffe          3.468093      0.0223    0.0217   0.0230
            T                2.119905      0.2582    0.2562   0.2602
```

This shows that the Tukey-Kramer method is essentially correct in this case, and that the remaining methods are clearly conservative (with the exception of the unadjusted t intervals, for which FWE = 0.2582).

If you only want to perform closed tests of equality of detergent types, and forego the confidence intervals, you can use the `%SimTests` macro as shown in Program 9.10:

PROGRAM 9.10   Step-down Comparisons of BIBD Means

```
%MakeGLMStats(dataset   = detergent        ,
              classvar  = block detergent ,
              yvar      = plates          ,
              model     = block detergent ,
              contrasts = all(detergent)  );

%SimTests(nsamp=100000,seed=121211,type=LOGICAL);
```

**Output from
Program 9.10**

```
Logically Constrained (Restricted Combinations) Step-Down Tests

                       Standard    ----- Pr > |t| -----
      Contrast  Estimate    Error     Raw    Bon    Adj    SE(AdjP)

        1-2      2.1333    0.8679   0.0258 0.0515 0.0499   0.000118
        1-3     -3.6000    0.8679   0.0008 0.0030 0.0028   0.000042
        1-4     -2.2000    0.8679   0.0221 0.0441 0.0430   0.000102
        1-5      4.3333    0.8679   0.0001 0.0005 0.0005   0.000013
        2-3     -5.7333    0.8679   <.0001 <.0001 <.0001          0
        2-4     -4.3333    0.8679   0.0001 0.0005 0.0005   0.000013
        2-5      2.2000    0.8679   0.0221 0.0441 0.0430   0.000102
        3-4      1.4000    0.8679   0.1263 0.1263 0.1263          0
        3-5      7.9333    0.8679   <.0001 <.0001 <.0001          0
        4-5      6.5333    0.8679   <.0001 <.0001 <.0001          0
```

Using the %SimTests macro, we are able to claim two more significant differences: the
(2–5) and (1–4) comparisons are now statistically significant. In addition, the (1–2) comparison is quite near significance. You can compare the adjusted *p*-values to see exactly
how much has been gained using the step-down procedure versus the single step procedure.
For the single-step analysis shown in the output from Program 9.9, the adjusted *p*-values
for the (1–2), (1–4) and (2–5) comparisons are, respectively, 0.1499, 0.1314, and 0.1314.
For the step-down analysis shown in the output from Program 9.10, the adjusted *p*-values
are, respectively, 0.0499, 0.0430, and 0.0430.

9.2.8   More Complex ANOVAS

Of course, ANOVAs can be more complex, with three or more factors, covariates, and interactions among the factors, among the covariates, and between the factors and covariates.
There are essentially no new differences involved in these cases. With pairwise comparisons between LS-means and comparisons with a control, you can use the ADJUST= option on the LSMEANS statement in PROC GLM to compute appropriately adjusted confidence
intervals and confidence-interval-based *p*-values. In cases involving more complex comparisons, such as interaction contrasts and interactions between the classification variables
and the covariates, you can use the %SimIntervals and %SimTests macros. You can even
include the parameter of the covariate itself (the regression coefficient) as a parameter to
test within the family of inferences.

   However, as the designs become more complex, the number of possible parameters to
test also gets larger. Thus, more caution is needed in defining the family of relevant inferences. If your family is too large, then it will be difficult to find any significant differences.
If your family is too small, you might miss some important effects.

9.3   Examples

The following two examples illustrate the power of the %Sim* macros for handling complex
experiments.

9.3.1   Example: Effect of Protein in Diet on Weight Gain in Pigs: Three Way ANOVA with a Covariate

Scheffé (1959, p. 217) reports data on weight gain (measured as rate of growth) of pigs for different diets. The three factors are Feed, Sex and Pen, and the covariate is initial weight. The Feed factor has levels 1, 2, and 3, associated with increasing amounts of protein in the diet. There are five pens, labeled 1 to 5; sex is labeled as M for males and F for females.

The data are given in Program 9.11.

PROGRAM 9.11   **Weight Gain in Pigs**

```
data pigs;
   do pen = 1 to 5;
      do feed = 1 to 3;
         do sex = 'M','F';
            input gain initial @@;
            output;
         end;
      end;
   end;
datalines;
 9.52 38  9.94 48   8.51 39 10.00 48   9.11 48  9.75 48
 8.21 35  9.48 32   9.95 38  9.24 32   8.50 37  8.66 28
 9.32 41  9.32 35   8.43 46  9.34 41   8.90 42  7.63 33
10.56 48 10.90 46   8.86 40  9.68 46   9.51 42 10.37 50
10.42 43  8.82 32   9.20 40  9.67 37   8.76 40  8.57 30
;
```

The following questions are of interest:

- Are there differences in weight gain between the different feeds?
- Are there differences in weight gain between the sexes?
- Does initial weight have an effect on weight gain?

You can express these questions in terms of linear combinations involving the model parameters. Scheffé suggested using the model

$$y_{ijk} = \mu + \alpha_i + \beta_j + \gamma_k + (\beta\gamma)_{jk} + \delta x_{ijk} + \epsilon_{ijk},$$

where α_i denotes pen, β_j denotes feed, γ_k denotes sex, $(\beta\gamma)_{jk}$ denotes feed×sex interaction, δ denotes effect of initial weight, and the ϵ_{ijk} denote random error terms with the usual assumptions.

Since there is an interaction term in the model, the differences involving feed and sex must be determined carefully. For a particular pen i and initial weight x, the average gain for diet 1 is $\mu + \alpha_i + \beta_1 + (1/2)(\gamma_M + \gamma_F) + (1/2)\{(\beta\gamma)_{1M} + (\beta\gamma)_{1F}\} + \delta x$, when averaged for both sexes. Similarly, the average gain for diet 2 is $\mu + \alpha_i + \beta_2 + (1/2)(\gamma_M + \gamma_F) + (1/2)\{(\beta\gamma)_{2M} + (\beta\gamma)_{2F}\} + \delta x$, when averaged for both sexes. Thus, the difference between average of diet 1 and average of diet 2, for any pen and initial weight, is $\beta_1 - \beta_2 + (1/2)\{(\beta\gamma)_{1M} + (\beta\gamma)_{1F} - (\beta\gamma)_{2M} - (\beta\gamma)_{2F}\}$, when averaged for both sexes. It is this latter linear combination that you must specify to calculate the contrasts. Note also that this difference is the parameter tested when using `lsmeans feed/pdiff` in PROC GLM.

Program 9.12 provides an answer to these questions.

PROGRAM 9.12   Simultaneous Intervals in a Three-Factor ANCOVA with Interaction

```
%MakeGLMStats(dataset  = pigs,
              classvar = pen feed sex,
              yvar     = gain,
              model    = pen feed sex feed*sex initial);

%macro Contrasts;
Cfeed = {0   0 0 0 0 0   2 -2  0   0  0   1  1 -1 -1  0  0   0 ,
         0   0 0 0 0 0   2  0 -2   0  0   1  1  0  0 -1 -1   0 ,
         0   0 0 0 0 0   0  2 -2   0  0   0  0  1  1 -1 -1   0 };
Cfeed = Cfeed/2;
Csex  = {0   0 0 0 0 0   0  0  0   3 -3   1 -1  1 -1  1 -1   0 };
Csex  = Csex/3;
Cinit = {0   0 0 0 0 0   0  0  0   0  0   0  0  0  0  0  0   1 };
C = Cfeed//Csex//Cinit;
C=C';
Clab = {"Feed1-Feed2","Feed1-Feed3","Feed2-Feed3","F-M","Init"};
%mend;

%SimIntervals(nsamp=50000,seed=121211);
```

Output from Program 9.12

```
                   Estimated 95% Quantile = 2.800029

                     Standard           --- Pr > |t| --   95% Confidence
Contrast   Estimate  Error  t Value    Raw  Adjusted        Interval

Feed1-Feed2  0.4410  0.2262   1.95    0.0661  0.2506    -0.1923  1.0743
Feed1-Feed3  0.6730  0.2251   2.99    0.0075  0.0336     0.0426  1.3034
Feed2-Feed3  0.2320  0.2262   1.03    0.3179  0.7812    -0.4013  0.8653
F-M          0.4243  0.1904   2.23    0.0381  0.1532    -0.1068  0.9555
Init         0.0889  0.0239   3.72    0.0015  0.0064     0.0219  0.1559
```

As you can see, the weight gain average is less for the feed with the highest protein than it is for the feed with the least protein. Also, initial weight has a positive effect on weight gain. Other comparisons are insignificant, although the signs of the coefficients suggest a consistent ordering of less weight gain with higher protein; they also suggest that females experience greater weight gain, but this is not statistically confirmed because the adjusted *p*-value for the F–M comparison is 0.1532.

As an alternative, you can run the %SimTests macro to assess significance levels without out regard for intervals and directional determinations. Just use the same %Contrasts and %MakeGLMStats setting shown in Program 9.12. If you have already run the code from Program 9.12, then all you have to do to run %SimTests is to submit the code in Program 9.13.

PROGRAM 9.13   Simultaneous Tests in a Three-Factor ANCOVA with Interaction

```
%SimTests(nsamp=50000, seed=121211, type=LOGICAL);
```

Output from Program 9.13

```
          Logically Constrained (Restricted Combinations) Step-Down Tests

                         Standard    ----- Pr > |t| -----
          Contrast   Estimate   Error    Raw    Bon    Adj    SE(AdjP)

          Feed1-Feed2   0.4410   0.2262  0.0661 0.0761 0.0736  0.000210
          Feed1-Feed3   0.6730   0.2251  0.0075 0.0302 0.0267  0.000213
          Feed2-Feed3   0.2320   0.2262  0.3179 0.3179 0.3179         0
          F-M           0.4243   0.1904  0.0381 0.0761 0.0736  0.000207
          Init          0.0889   0.0239  0.0015 0.0073 0.0067  0.000094
```

Comparing the outputs from Program 9.12 and Program 9.13, please note the following:

- Using the strictly testing method of Program 9.13, the same two tests are significant as in the interval-based method of Program 9.12 at the FWE = 0.05 level; however, there are an additional two significances at the FWE = 0.10 level using the testing method. The additional power results from the "less ambitious inference" of simply deciding whether the effect is not zero, rather than quantifying its precise magnitude.

- The use of the logical constraints allows the Bonferroni multiplier of 2 for the F-M comparison, rather than 3, as it would be for the Holm procedure (obtained using type=FREE in the %SimTests macro). This multiplier is 2 because only two of the hypotheses associated with the comparisons F-M, Food1-Food2, and Food2-Food3 can be null, and still not contradict falseness of the Food1-Food2 null. However, if all three were null, then the Food1-Food2 null also would be implied.

- Since the Init effect is the most significant of the five tested effects, the adjusted p-values for this effect, 0.0064 and 0.0067, both estimate the same quantity. This difference seems large in light of the reported standard error 0.000094 shown in the output from Program 9.13. However, the %SimTests macro uses a more efficient method for estimating the adjusted p-values than does %SimIntervals. For %SimIntervals, the Monte Carlo standard error is $\sqrt{.0064(1 - .0064)/50000} = .000357$, and the difference between the two estimates of 0.0064 and 0.0067 are thus easily within Monte Carlo error of one another.

9.3.2   Example: Sub-group and Whole-group Analysis of a Respiratory Therapy Drug: Three-Way ANOVA with Weighted Contrasts

As discussed in Chapter 1, Section 1.2.2, subgroup analysis refers to separating the data into various groups (such as younger and older, male and female, US-born and non-US-born) and testing the main effects in every subgroup. This method can easily lead to spurious, and in some cases costly, Type I errors. Koch et al. (1990) report data from a clinical trial to evaluate the effectiveness of an active respiratory treatment versus a placebo treatment. The data contain physicians' ratings of a patient's respiratory health prior to treatment, and at four post-treatment evaluations. The ratings are scored from 0 to 4, where 0 represents poor health and 4 represents good health.

Since greater therapeutic gains are possible with longer exposure to the drug, we use a time-weighted score comprised of the four post-treatment evaluations as the primary endpoint:

$$\text{Score} = (R_1 + 2R_2 + 3R_3 + 4R_4)/10.$$

In addition to the active versus placebo classification, the data can be stratified by Age ("Older" patients being those older than 30 years) and by Initial Health ($R_0 \le 2$ denoting "poor" and $R_0 > 2$ denoting "good" Initial Health). In all cases, the Active versus Placebo test is of primary interest, but there is also interest in the Active versus Placebo test in the various subgroups defined by Age and Initial Health. The data are shown in Program 9.14, with a frequency tabulation showing subgroup membership.

PROGRAM 9.14   Frequency Tabulation of Respiratory Health Data

```
data respiratory;
   input  T$ Age R0-R4 @@;
   Score = (R1 + 2*R2 + 3*R3 + 4*R4)/10;
   if (T = 'A')  then Treatment  = 'Active ';
   else                Treatment  = 'Placebo'; drop T;
   if (Age > 30) then AgeGroup   = 'Older  ';
   else                AgeGroup   = 'Younger';
   if (R0 > 2)   then InitHealth = 'Good';
   else                InitHealth = 'Poor';
datalines;
A 32 1 2 2 4 2  A 47 2 2 3 4 4  A 11 4 4 4 4 2  A 14 2 3 3 3 2
A 15 0 2 3 3 3  A 20 3 3 2 3 1  A 22 1 2 2 2 3  A 22 2 1 3 4 4
A 23 3 3 4 4 3  A 23 2 3 4 4 4  A 25 2 3 3 2 3  A 26 1 2 2 3 2
A 26 2 2 2 2 2  A 26 2 4 1 4 2  A 28 1 2 2 1 2  A 28 0 0 1 2 1
A 30 3 3 4 4 2  A 30 3 4 4 4 3  A 31 1 2 3 1 1  A 31 3 3 4 4 4
A 31 0 2 3 2 1  A 32 3 4 4 3 3  A 34 1 1 2 1 1  A 46 4 3 4 3 4
A 48 2 3 2 0 2  A 50 2 2 2 2 2  A 57 3 3 4 3 4  P 13 4 4 4 4 4
P 31 2 1 0 2 2  P 35 1 0 0 0 0  P 36 2 3 3 2 2  P 45 2 2 2 2 1
P 13 3 4 4 4 4  P 14 2 2 1 2 3  P 15 2 2 3 3 2  P 19 2 3 3 0 0
P 20 4 4 4 4 4  P 23 3 3 1 1 1  P 23 4 4 2 4 4  P 24 3 4 4 4 3
P 25 1 1 2 2 2  P 26 2 4 2 4 3  P 26 1 2 1 2 2  P 27 1 2 2 1 2
P 27 3 3 4 3 3  P 23 2 1 1 1 1  P 28 2 0 0 0 0  P 30 1 0 0 0 0
P 37 1 0 0 0 0  P 37 3 2 3 3 2  P 43 2 3 2 4 4  P 43 1 1 1 3 2
P 44 3 4 3 4 2  P 46 2 2 2 2 2  P 49 2 2 2 2 2  P 63 2 2 2 2 2
A 37 1 3 4 4 4  A 39 2 3 4 4 4  A 60 4 4 3 3 4  A 63 4 4 4 4 4
A 13 4 4 4 4 4  A 14 1 4 4 4 4  A 19 3 3 2 3 3  A 20 2 4 4 4 3
A 20 2 1 1 0 0  A 21 3 3 4 4 4  A 24 4 4 4 4 4  A 25 3 4 3 3 1
A 25 3 4 4 3 3  A 25 2 2 4 4 4  A 26 2 3 4 4 4  A 28 2 3 2 2 1
A 31 4 4 4 4 4  A 34 2 4 4 2 4  A 35 4 4 4 4 4  A 37 4 3 2 2 4
A 41 3 4 4 3 4  A 43 3 3 4 4 2  A 52 1 2 1 2 2  A 55 4 4 4 4 4
A 55 2 2 3 3 1  A 58 4 4 4 4 4  A 68 2 3 3 3 4  P 31 3 4 4 4 4
P 32 3 2 2 3 4  P 36 3 3 2 1 3  P 38 1 2 0 0 0  P 39 1 2 1 1 2
P 39 3 2 3 0 0  P 44 3 4 4 4 4  P 47 2 3 3 2 3  P 48 2 2 1 0 0
P 48 2 2 2 2 2  P 51 3 4 2 4 4  P 58 1 4 2 2 0  P 11 3 4 4 4 4
P 14 2 1 2 3 2  P 15 3 2 2 3 3  P 15 4 3 3 3 4  P 19 4 2 2 3 3
P 20 3 2 4 4 4  P 20 1 4 4 4 4  P 33 3 3 3 2 3  P 36 2 4 3 3 4
P 38 4 3 0 0 0  P 42 3 2 2 2 2  P 43 2 1 0 0 0  P 45 3 4 2 1 2
P 48 4 4 0 0 0  P 52 2 3 4 3 4  P 66 3 3 3 4 4
;
proc freq;
   tables Treatment*AgeGroup*InitHealth / nocum list;
run;
```

Output from Program 9.14

Treatment	AgeGroup	InitHealth	Frequency	Percent
Active	Older	Good	13	11.71
Active	Older	Poor	13	11.71
Active	Younger	Good	11	9.91
Active	Younger	Poor	17	15.32
Placebo	Older	Good	14	12.61
Placebo	Older	Poor	19	17.12
Placebo	Younger	Good	12	10.81
Placebo	Younger	Poor	12	10.81

Questions of interest concern whether respiratory health is better for Active than Placebo subjects in the following groups:

- overall
- the older subgroup
- the younger subgroup
- the subgroup with initial good health
- the subgroup with initial poor health
- the subgroup of older patients with initial good health
- the subgroup of older patients with initial poor health
- the subgroup of younger patients with initial good health
- the subgroup of younger patients with initial poor health.

You can formulate each of these hypotheses as upper-tail tests in terms of contrasts involving the subgroup means. For these estimated differences to be identical to the estimated differences when simple averages are used, you must weigh the subgroup averages appropriately using the frequencies shown in the output from Program 9.14. Here is the program for testing these nine hypotheses, using logical constraints and upper-tailed tests.

PROGRAM 9.15   Multiple Tests for Treatment Efficacy in Subgroups

```
%MakeGLMStats(dataset  = respiratory             ,
              classvar = Treatment AgeGroup InitHealth ,
              yvar     = Score                    ,
              model    = Treatment*AgeGroup*InitHealth );

%macro Contrasts;
   CA  = { 0 13 13 11 17  0  0  0  0 }; CA = CA/sum(CA);
   CP  = { 0  0  0  0  0 14 19 12 12 }; CP = CP/sum(CP);
   C1  = CA - CP;

   CAO = { 0 13 13  0  0  0  0  0  0 }; CAO = CAO/sum(CAO);
   CPO = { 0  0  0  0  0 14 19  0  0 }; CPO = CPO/sum(CPO);
   C2  = CAO - CPO;

   CAY = { 0  0  0 11 17  0  0  0  0 }; CAY = CAY/sum(CAY);
   CPY = { 0  0  0  0  0  0  0 12 12 }; CPY = CPY/sum(CPY);
   C3  = CAY - CPY;

   CAG = { 0 13  0 11  0  0  0  0  0 }; CAG = CAG/sum(CAG);
   CPG = { 0  0  0  0  0 14  0 12  0 }; CPG = CPG/sum(CPG);
   C4  = CAG - CPG;
```

```
CAP = { 0  0 13  0 17  0  0  0  0 }; CAP = CAP/sum(CAP);
CPP = { 0  0  0  0  0  0 19  0 12 }; CPP = CPP/sum(CPP);
C5 =  CAP - CPP;

C6 = { 0  1  0  0  0 -1  0  0  0 };
C7 = { 0  0  1  0  0  0 -1  0  0 };
C8 = { 0  0  0  1  0  0  0 -1  0 };
C9 = { 0  0  0  0  1  0  0  0 -1 };

C = C1//C2//C3//C4//C5//C6//C7//C8//C9;
C = C';

Clab = {"Overall","Older","Younger","Good","Poor",
        "OldGood","OldPoor","YoungGood","YoungPoor"};
%mend;

%SimTests(nsamp=50000, seed=121211, type=LOGICAL, side=U);
```

Output from Program 9.15

Logically Constrained (Restricted Combinations) Step-Down Tests

Contrast	Estimate	Standard Error	Raw	Bon	Adj	SE(AdjP)
Overall	0.7360	0.1908	0.0001	0.0006	0.0005	0.000024
Older	1.0733	0.2635	<.0001	0.0004	0.0003	0.000034
Younger	0.3190	0.2795	0.1281	0.2563	0.1962	0.000644
Good	0.6093	0.2844	0.0173	0.0593	0.0482	0.000349
Poor	0.8611	0.2573	0.0006	0.0034	0.0029	0.000070
OldGood	1.2187	0.3870	0.0011	0.0064	0.0057	0.000094
OldPoor	0.8154	0.3616	0.0131	0.0593	0.0482	0.000349
YoungGood	-0.1045	0.4194	0.5982	0.5982	0.5982	0
YoungPoor	0.8696	0.3788	0.0119	0.0593	0.0482	0.000349

You can see that the increases are significant for all subgroups except for the combined younger group, and for the younger group with initial good health. Since these are one-sided tests, directional determinations are allowed, as discussed in Westfall and Young (1993, p. 74–75).

9.4   Multiple *F*-Tests

With higher-way ANOVAs and ANCOVAs, you often are faced with a number of tests for the various interactions and main effects terms. Here, multiplicity comes into play as well. For example, in a four-factor model with covariates, should the significance of a particular three-factor interaction (say, with $p = 0.0087$) be considered important enough to investigate it further?

To illustrate the question, consider the following output, taken from a real experiment used to predict number of bottles of wine purchased as a function of several factors. The variables CustomerType, light and music are classification variables; the variables handle and examine are covariates. This data set is used with permission of Dr. James Wilcox of the Marketing Department at Texas Tech University.

PROGRAM 9.16   Multiple *F*-tests in a Multifactorial ANOVA

```
data wine;
  input Purchase CustomerType light music handle examine @@;
  datalines;
0 4 0 0 0  0  0 4 0 0 0  0  0 3 0 0 0  0  0 3 0 0 0 16
0 3 0 0 1  1  0 4 0 0 0  1  1 3 0 0 3 11  0 4 0 0 0  0
0 3 0 0 0  0  0 3 0 0 2  8  0 4 0 0 0  0  0 3 0 0 0  2
0 3 0 0 0  2  0 3 0 0 0  0  0 3 0 0 0  0  0 . 0 1 0  3
0 3 0 1 0  0  0 3 0 1 5  8  0 3 0 1 0  1  0 4 0 1 0  2
0 3 0 1 0  0  0 . 0 1 0  0  0 4 0 1 0  0  0 4 0 1 1  3
0 4 0 1 0  1  1 3 0 1 2  2  0 3 0 1 1  2  0 3 0 1 0  2
0 1 0 1 0  0  0 4 0 1 2  2  0 3 1 1 1  2  0 4 1 1 0  0
3 1 1 1 9 11  0 3 1 1 0  0  0 3 1 1 0  3  1 4 1 1 0  0
0 3 1 1 5  8  0 . 1 1 1  1  0 4 1 1 3  7  0 3 1 1 0  0
0 3 1 1 0  0  0 2 1 0 0  2  0 3 1 0 0  0  0 1 1 0 0  4
0 4 1 0 0  0  0 4 1 0 12 21  0 3 1 0 1  1  0 3 0 0 0  1
0 3 0 0 1  0  0 3 0 0 1  1  0 3 0 0 3  8  0 3 0 0 0  8
0 1 0 0 1  1  0 4 0 0 0  0  0 3 0 0 0  4  1 4 0 0 1  2
0 3 0 0 1  4  1 3 0 0 1  6  0 4 0 1 0  0  0 2 0 1 0  0
0 4 0 1 0  2  0 3 0 1 0  0  0 4 0 1 0  2  0 3 0 1 2  4
0 3 0 1 0  0  0 3 0 1 0  0  0 4 0 1 0  2  0 3 0 1 0  0
1 1 0 1 1  2  0 3 0 1 0  2  0 3 0 1 0  0  0 3 0 1 1  1
0 4 0 1 0  8  0 4 0 1 0  0  0 4 1 0 0  7  0 3 1 0 0  2
0 4 1 0 1  4  0 4 1 0 2  5  0 4 1 0 0  2  0 3 1 0 1  2
0 4 1 0 0  2  0 3 1 0 2  6  0 4 1 0 1  2  0 3 1 0 0  0
0 3 0 1 0  4  0 4 0 1 0  3  0 4 0 1 1  7  0 3 0 1 0  1
0 2 0 1 4  7  0 3 0 1 2  2  0 . 0 1 0  0  0 3 0 1 1  7
0 4 0 1 1 11  0 4 0 1 3 13  0 1 1 0 0  2  0 3 1 0 1  6
0 3 1 0 3  4  0 3 1 0 5  3  0 3 1 0 2 10  0 4 1 0 6  7
0 3 1 0 4  3  0 3 0 0 3 12  0 4 0 0 0  1  1 3 0 0 0  2
0 3 0 0 3  5  0 4 0 0 3  3  2 3 0 0 1  3  0 3 0 0 4  6
0 3 0 0 0  1  0 1 0 0 1  4  1 3 0 0 0  5  0 3 0 0 3  8
0 3 1 1 0  0  0 3 1 1 0  3  0 3 1 1 1  7  0 3 1 1 0 14
0 3 1 1 0 14  0 . 1 1 0  6  6 3 1 1 6  6  0 4 1 1 3  3
0 4 1 1 1  3  0 3 1 1 0  3  0 3 1 1 0  2  1 4 0 0 0  1
0 3 0 0 0  0  0 3 0 0 0 11  0 4 0 0 0  1  0 4 0 0 0  4
0 4 1 1 1  4  0 1 1 1 0  4  0 3 1 1 0  0  1 3 1 1 0  0
1 3 1 1 1 15  0 3 1 1 0  7  0 4 1 1 1  3  0 4 1 1 0  5
0 3 1 1 0  4  0 4 1 1 0  2  0 4 1 1 5 12  0 4 1 1 2  8
0 4 1 1 1  1  0 3 0 1 0  3  0 3 0 1 0  1  1 1 0 1 3  5
0 1 0 1 1 10  0 4 0 1 0  3  0 4 0 1 0  3  0 3 0 1 0  0
0 4 0 1 0  6  0 3 0 1 0  5  0 3 0 1 0  0  0 4 1 0 0  3
0 3 1 0 1  5  0 3 1 0 1  1  2 3 1 0 13 6  0 3 1 0 0  2
0 3 1 0 0  2  0 3 1 0 0  4  0 3 1 0 0  4  1 3 1 0 0  2
0 3 1 0 4  8  0 4 1 0 2  6  0 4 1 1 0  5  0 4 1 1 0  1
0 3 1 1 1 11  0 4 1 1 13 9  0 3 1 1 0  2  0 4 1 1 0  3
0 4 1 1 0  2
;
proc glm data=wine;
   class CustomerType light music;
   model purchase = CustomerType light music
      CustomerType*light CustomerType*music light*music
      CustomerType*light*music handle examine/SS3;
run;
```

Output from Program 9.16

The GLM Procedure

Dependent Variable: Purchase

Source	DF	Sum of Squares	Mean Square	F Value	Pr > F
Model	15	13.80991628	0.92066109	2.83	0.0006
Error	148	48.06813250	0.32478468		
Corrected Total	163	61.87804878			

R-Square	Coeff Var	Root MSE	Purchase Mean
0.223180	359.4746	0.569899	0.158537

Source	DF	Type III SS	Mean Square	F Value	Pr > F
CustomerType	3	1.66728446	0.55576149	1.71	0.1672
light	1	0.17427064	0.17427064	0.54	0.4650
music	1	1.36822668	1.36822668	4.21	0.0419
CustomerType*light	2	1.08320919	0.54160459	1.67	0.1922
CustomerType*music	2	1.27567629	0.63783814	1.96	0.1440
light*music	1	0.81190218	0.81190218	2.50	0.1160
Customer*light*music	2	0.29094607	0.14547304	0.45	0.6398
handle	1	6.92219763	6.92219763	21.31	<.0001
examine	1	0.71227908	0.71227908	2.19	0.1408

As you can see, the main factor contributing to purchases is the variable `handle`, the number of bottles of wine handled by the customer. Using the Type III SS, you might also be inclined to consider the `music` factor also to be significant. However, with $k = 9$ tests of effects, it is not very unusual to see a *p*-value of 0.0419 or lower even when there is no real effect.

You can use the *p*-value-based methods of Chapter 2 to test the multiple effects. If you want to obtain more powerful tests by using correlations among the tests, as is done, for example, in the %SimTests macro, then you will need to write your own program. If you do this, you need to base the inference on the distribution of min p_i rather than max F_i, because the *F*-distributions with different degrees of freedom are not comparable. See Westfall and Young (1993, pp. 50–51, 66–67) for further details.

Multifactorial experiments are often analyzed sequentially, using a forward-selection type of approach (start only with main effects, then add higher-order interactions sequentially, by significance), or backward-deletion (start with all interactions, then delete interactions sequentially, by significance). Once a "final model" has been determined, multiple comparisons involving the remaining terms are performed. While this approach has merit and a logical basis, we cannot give it our unqualified recommendation in cases where Type I errors are costly, because it does not control the FWE. In particular, the significance of the terms in the final model is typically overstated for two reasons:

- The selected effects have resulted from testing many hypotheses, and their *p*-values are essentially the min *p*'s resulting from these tests. As estimates of the true statistical significance of the corresponding effects, these *p*-values are biased downwards.

- The residual MSE tends to be understated in such selected models. This will result in confidence intervals that are narrower than they should be, and in tests with excessive Type I errors.

So, what should you do? This is a difficult question, but we have the following general recommendations:

- When in doubt, start with a simpler model. Very often, models involving main effects only are used. Use higher order interactions when theory suggests that they are needed.

- If variable selection is needed to identify higher-order interactions, use it sparingly. Automatic variable selection procedures are notorious for distorting significance levels. Require a somewhat more stringent level of significance when you use this method, and be sure to divulge the variable selection method in the discussion of the data analysis.

- Use an appropriate multiple comparisons method on the final model (for example, `%SimTests`). If the model has been pre-specified, then the FWE is controlled. If the model has been determined using a variable selection process, then the FWE is not controlled, but it should be reasonably low, with limited variable selection.

9.5   Concluding Remarks

In this chapter we have shown how to analyze data from complex ANOVAs and ANCOVAs. If you want to perform interval-based inference on the main effect parameters, with separate families for each main effect, you can use LSMEANS in PROC GLM. In other cases, you need to use one of the `%Sim*` macros.

Cases where you need to use the `%Sim*` macros include

- combined families of inferences for main effect terms
- inferences for interaction contrasts
- inferences where a covariate term is included in the family
- inferences involving non-standard (for example, weighted) contrasts
- stepwise testing-based inferences.

Chapter 10

Multiple Comparisons in Heteroscedastic, Mixed, and Multivariate Models Using PROC MIXED

10.1 Introduction

In previous chapters, we have given a fairly complete treatment of classical multiple inference methods in the simple linear model. By *simple linear model*, we mean the model with the usual assumptions of linearity, normality, constant variance, and uncorrelated errors. PROC MIXED allows you to relax the last two assumptions, fitting models that have correlated error structures and nonconstant variances. Applications where PROC MIXED is used abound in recent statistical practice.

When the assumptions of homoscedasticity and uncorrelated errors are violated, then even the simple, non-multiplicity-adjusted inferences can be grossly inaccurate if the analysis ignores the true error structure. As you would expect, this inaccuracy carries over to multiplicity-adjusted inferences. To overcome this problem, you can fit an appropriate model using PROC MIXED, as it allows you to fit models with various types of dependence among residuals or models with nonconstant variance. You can then carry out your inferences assuming the error structure of the fitted model.

While this approach can improve greatly upon analyses such as those shown in previous chapters that don't take the complex error structure into account at all, you should be aware that this is not a free lunch. Typically, MCPs using PROC MIXED fitted models are *inexact*, as opposed to the methods described in previous chapters, which often were exact (at least to within Monte Carlo error). Reasons for the inexactness include the following:

- PROC MIXED treats estimated variances (and other parameters) as if they were fixed and known, instead of as random quantities, in the multiplicity adjustment methods.

- The degrees of freedom used by PROC MIXED are, in many cases, only an approximation to what the true degrees of freedom should be. (And in many cases, a true degrees of freedom does not even exist!)

- In some mixed models, the degrees of freedom differ from contrast to contrast. In such cases, use of the max T_i distribution for multiplicity adjustment can implicitly weight some tests more heavily than others. This can, in extreme cases, lead to adjusted *p*-values that are actually *smaller* than raw *p*-values.

Despite these difficulties, we are reasonably comfortable in recommending that you use MCPs based on PROC MIXED in these more complex models because the problems with using analyses based on PROC GLM can be much worse. But we must state some caveats clearly. PROC MIXED is a fairly new procedure, and further study is needed to identify the specific properties (power and FWE control) of MCPs using PROC MIXED. We still do not completely know

- when and where such applications succeed or fail
- when MCPs based on PROC GLM are likely to offer improvement over MCPs based on PROC MIXED (despite failed assumptions for the analysis based on PROC GLM)
- what alternative methods are available in situations where both approaches fail.

We do not intend this chapter to be a general tutorial on the use of PROC MIXED, or on mixed models in general. For such information, please consult Littell *et al.* (1996).

10.2 Multiple Comparisons in the Heteroscedastic ANOVA

In Chapter 3, we discussed the balanced one-way ANOVA, and various methods for multiple comparisons in that case. The main recommendation was that, for the more ambitious interval-based inferences, Tukey's method is best. Later, in Chapter 8, we revised that recommendation to include the Begun and Gabriel method (as implemented in the %BegGab macro), or the logical constraint method using the %SimTests macro for less ambitious inferences which can decide inequality only.

In models with nonconstant variance, we revise these recommendations further to include the use of

- the ADJUST=SIMULATE option of the LSMEANS statement in PROC MIXED for the more ambitious interval-based inference
- the %SimTests macro using PROC MIXED output for the less ambitious testing-based inference.

These recommendations are more tenuous than before because the methods are not exact. However, despite these problems, among the currently available methods that are easily implemented, we feel that these are the best.

10.2.1 Simultaneous Intervals

Consider again the weight loss data of Chapter 3, which consists of the weight lost by subjects under five different dietary treatments. As discussed in Section 3.1, the standard one-way analysis requires the assumption that all treatment groups have the same variance. To relax this assumption, you might consider fitting the following model

$$y_{ij} = \mu_i + \epsilon_{ij}, \quad Var(\epsilon_{ij}) = \sigma_i^2$$

to the data, allowing a separate variance for each diet type. Program 10.1 demonstrates how to use PROC MIXED to fit such a model and to compare treatment means, using a Satterthwaite approximation to the error degrees of freedom.

PROGRAM 10.1   Multiple Comparisons with Nonconstant Variance

```
data wloss;
   do diet = 'A','B','C','D','E';
      do i = 1 to 10;
         input wloss @@;
         output;
         end;
      end;
cards;
12.4 10.7 11.9 11.0 12.4 12.3 13.0 12.5 11.2 13.1
 9.1 11.5 11.3  9.7 13.2 10.7 10.6 11.3 11.1 11.7
 8.5 11.6 10.2 10.9  9.0  9.6  9.9 11.3 10.5 11.2
 8.7  9.3  8.2  8.3  9.0  9.4  9.2 12.2  8.5  9.9
12.7 13.2 11.8 11.9 12.2 11.2 13.7 11.8 11.5 11.7
;

proc mixed data=wloss;
   class diet;
   model wloss=diet/ddfm=satterth;
   repeated /group=diet;
   lsmeans diet/ adjust=simulate(seed=121211) cl;
   ods select tests3;
   ods output diffs=diffs;
run;

proc print data=diffs noobs;
   title "Multiple Heteroscedastic Comparisons";
   var  diet _diet Estimate StdErr DF tValue Probt Adjp AdjLow AdjUpp;
run;
```

Output from Program 10.1

Type 3 Tests of Fixed Effects

Effect	Num DF	Den DF	F Value	Pr > F
diet	4	18.5	15.39	<.0001

Multiple Heteroscedastic Comparisons

diet	_diet	Estimate	StdErr	DF	tValue	Probt	Adjp	AdjLow	AdjUpp
A	B	1.0300	0.4410	16.6	2.34	0.0324	0.1768	-0.2932	2.3532
A	C	1.7800	0.4172	17.2	4.27	0.0005	0.0025	0.5281	3.0319
A	D	2.7800	0.4505	16.3	6.17	<.0001	<.0001	1.4282	4.1318
A	E	-0.1200	0.3625	18	-0.33	0.7444	0.9971	-1.2077	0.9677
B	C	0.7500	0.4807	17.9	1.56	0.1363	0.5317	-0.6924	2.1924
B	D	1.7500	0.5099	18	3.43	0.0030	0.0198	0.2201	3.2799
B	E	-1.1500	0.4341	16.2	-2.65	0.0174	0.1024	-2.4525	0.1525
C	D	1.0000	0.4895	17.7	2.04	0.0562	0.2825	-0.4687	2.4687
C	E	-1.9000	0.4099	16.9	-4.64	0.0002	0.0013	-3.1300	-0.6700
D	E	-2.9000	0.4437	15.9	-6.54	<.0001	<.0001	-4.2315	-1.5685

Note the following about the output:

- Examining this output in conjunction with the comparable homoscedastic analysis shown in the Tukey Interval from Program 3.2 in Section 3.3.1, the heteroscedastic intervals generally are wider, reflecting greater uncertainty in the variance estimates. On average, the heteroscedastic intervals have width 2.664, 5.2% wider than the Tukey intervals.

- For the individual unadjusted comparisons, the `adjust=satterth` option provides a different df for every contrast. The Satterthwaite formula is data dependent and involves the within-group variance estimates for the groups that are compared: for comparing μ_i with $\mu_{i'}$,

$$df_{i,i'} = \frac{(\hat{\sigma}_i^2/n_i + \hat{\sigma}_{i'}^2/n_{i'})^2}{(\hat{\sigma}_i^2/n_i)^2/(n_i - 1) + (\hat{\sigma}_{i'}^2/n_{i'})^2/(n_{i'} - 1)}.$$

- The adjusted confidence limits and p-values are calculated from a multivariate t distribution, as described in Chapter 5, Section 5.3.

- The correlation matrix of the multivariate t distribution is based on the estimated covariance matrix of the differences, $\mathbf{C}'(\mathbf{X}'\hat{\mathbf{V}}\mathbf{X})^-\mathbf{C}$, where $\mathbf{C} = (\mathbf{c}_1, \ldots, \mathbf{c}_k)$ is the contrast matrix for all pairwise differences. Here, $\mathbf{V} = Cov(\boldsymbol{\epsilon})$ and $\hat{\mathbf{V}}$ denotes the estimate of it using the PROC MIXED estimates of variance components.

- The degrees of freedom used for the multivariate t distribution is the Satterthwaite approximation to the denominator degrees of freedom for the corresponding F-test of $\mathbf{C}\boldsymbol{\beta} = \mathbf{0}$, where $\mathbf{C}$ is the contrast matrix for all pairwise differences. Calculation of this particular df is considerably more complex than for the individual pairwise comparisons; refer to SAS Institute Inc. (1999). As shown in the output, this value is $df = 18.5$.

There are two major elements that make this analysis inexact: (i) the approximation of the degrees of freedom using the Satterthwaite method, and (ii) the treatment of $\hat{\mathbf{V}}$ as if it were in fact equal to $\mathbf{V}$ in the estimated correlation matrix. These problems should be negligible with larger sample sizes; however, the likely result of using this approximation in smaller samples is that the method is probably too liberal (that is, the FWE is really greater than 0.05); see Westfall and Young (1993, pp. 88–91) for further analysis and discussion. You can also perform the above analysis using the `%SimIntervals` and `%SimTests` macros introduced in earlier chapters by plugging in the appropriate estimates and degrees of freedom from the PROC MIXED output. In the next section, we will show how to do this with the `%SimTests` macro. Of course, if your interest lies more in intervals (the more ambitious inference) than in tests, you can always substitute `%SimIntervals` for `%SimTests` because the inputs are identical.

10.2.2   Simultaneous Tests

Program 10.2 shows how to perform logically constrained step-down tests for all pairwise comparisons in the weight loss example, assuming the heteroscedastic model of PROC MIXED.

PROGRAM 10.2   Logically Constrained Step-Down Tests in Heteroscedastic ANOVA

```
%MakeGLMStats(dataset  = wloss,
              classvar = diet ,
              yvar     = wloss,
              model    = diet ,
              contrasts = all(diet));
```

```
ods output Tests3   =Tests3
            SolutionF=SolutionF
            CovB     =CovB    ;
proc mixed data=wloss;
   class diet;
   model wloss = diet/ddfm=satterth solution covb;
   repeated/group=diet;
run;

%macro Estimates;
   use Tests3;    read all var {DenDf}          into df;
   use CovB;      read all var ("Col1":"Col6") into cov;
   use SolutionF; read all var {Estimate}       into EstPar;
%mend;

%SimTests(seed=121211, type=LOGICAL);
```

Output from Program 10.2

Logically Constrained (Restricted Combinations) Step-Down Tests

| | | Standard | ----- Pr > \|t\| ----- | | | |
Contrast	Estimate	Error	Raw	Bon	Adj	SE(AdjP)
1-2	1.0300	0.4410	0.0310	0.0643	0.0603	0.000268
1-3	1.7800	0.4172	0.0004	0.0013	0.0013	0.000047
1-4	2.7800	0.4505	<.0001	<.0001	<.0001	0
1-5	-0.1200	0.3625	0.7443	0.7443	0.7443	0
2-3	0.7500	0.4807	0.1357	0.2714	0.2484	0.000885
2-4	1.7500	0.5099	0.0029	0.0115	0.0106	0.000202
2-5	-1.1500	0.4341	0.0161	0.0643	0.0547	0.000536
3-4	1.0000	0.4895	0.0556	0.1112	0.1067	0.000439
3-5	-1.9000	0.4099	0.0002	0.0012	0.0011	0.000090
4-5	-2.9000	0.4437	<.0001	<.0001	<.0001	0

Note that the unadjusted *p*-values from this analysis differ from those of the output in
PROC MIXED because, in this analysis, they all use a common error degrees of freedom
(the Satterthwaite value from the Type III *F*-test). This is one of the compromises that you
must settle for when doing this type of analysis.

By comparison, consider Program 10.3, which analyzes the same data, using logically
constrained step-down tests in the homoscedastic model.

PROGRAM 10.3   Logically Constrained Step-Down Tests in Homoscedastic ANOVA

```
%MakeGLMStats(dataset   = wloss,
              classvar  = diet,
              yvar      = wloss,
              model     = diet,
              contrasts = all(diet));

%SimTests(seed=121211, type=LOGICAL);
```

Output from Program 10.3

Logically Constrained (Restricted Combinations) Step-Down Tests

Contrast	Estimate	Standard Error	Pr > |t| Raw	Bon	Adj	SE(AdjP)
1-2	1.0300	0.4457	0.0255	0.0529	0.0499	0.000225
1-3	1.7800	0.4457	0.0002	0.0007	0.0007	0
1-4	2.7800	0.4457	<.0001	<.0001	<.0001	0
1-5	-0.1200	0.4457	0.7890	0.7890	0.7890	0
2-3	0.7500	0.4457	0.0994	0.1988	0.1871	0.000672
2-4	1.7500	0.4457	0.0003	0.0012	0.0012	0
2-5	-1.1500	0.4457	0.0132	0.0529	0.0469	0.000454
3-4	1.0000	0.4457	0.0298	0.0597	0.0585	0.000226
3-5	-1.9000	0.4457	0.0001	0.0006	0.0006	0
4-5	-2.9000	0.4457	<.0001	<.0001	<.0001	0

Note that the adjusted *p*-values are generally smaller using the homoscedastic model than they are using the heteroscedastic model.

General Recommendation Regarding Homoscedastic versus Heteroscedastic Models

If the true error variances differ greatly, it is best to use heteroscedastic methods like PROC MIXED; otherwise, it is best to use homoscedastic methods such as PROC GLM. For the difficult and much more likely situation that the true error structure is unknown, our recommendations are necessarily more vague. Even if the error variances differ somewhat, in small sample sizes the homoscedastic model might be preferred for parsimony and statistical precision (despite some bias). Westfall and Young (1993, pp. 88–89) discuss this issue in more detail.

With large data sets, the PROC MIXED analysis always has approximately the correct size (that is, the nominal FWE is accurately protected), although it will have less power than PROC GLM if the errors are truly homoscedastic. On the other hand, if the true variances differ substantially but you use the homoscedastic method, then the FWE may no longer be protected, and the true standard errors of some contrast estimates will be larger or smaller than their displayed values.

Thus, you should explore the character of the heteroscedasticity using data and subject matter considerations. If the variances differ, in a way that affects the inferences substantively, then we recommend that you use the heteroscedastic model. More precise answers could be given through simulation studies.

Note: We do *not* recommend that the choice be governed solely by test of significance for equality of variances (for example, using the HOVTEST option of PROC GLM) because the hypothesis test for variances does not address the issue of quality of inference on the mean values.

10.3   Multiple Comparisons Among Treatments When Blocks Are Random

In Chapter 9 we considered two-way ANOVAs. In such models, you often have a main treatment variable of interest and a block variable that defines collections of similar experimental units. Often the effects of the block variable can be considered as a random sample from a larger population. For example, in a quality control setting, blocks of production material can be selected randomly from all produced items in order to perform a statistical experiment. In this case, with respect to inferences that refer to the population of all block effects, the blocks can affect the individual responses by causing values in the same block to be correlated, violating the assumption that the experimental observations are independent. Other examples of intra-block correlation include cluster effects due to familial relationships or proximity in space or time. In these cases, you should use an analysis method that correctly incorporates the true random structure of the data because such a method will provide more accurate estimates of uncertainty about the parameters of interest.

10.3.1   RCBD with One Observation per Cell

The waste data of Chapter 9 provides an example of a randomized block design. The temperature levels are considered to be fixed effects, and the environment levels are considered to be random effects. Using the data with one observation per cell defined in Program 9.5, Section 9.2.5 (the WASTE1 data set), the random block model is

$$y_{ij} = \mu + \alpha_i + \beta_j + \epsilon_{ij},$$

where i denotes temperature level and j environment level, and we assume that

- μ and the temperature effects α_i are fixed constants
- the environmental effects β_j and the random residuals ϵ_{ij} are random terms
- $E(\beta_j) = 0$, $E(\epsilon_{ij}) = 0$
- $Var(\beta_j) = \sigma_\beta^2$ and $Var(\epsilon_{ij}) = \sigma_\epsilon^2$ (σ_β^2 and σ_ϵ^2 are called the variance components)
- the β_j are independent of the ϵ_{ij}
- the β_j and the ϵ_{ij} are normally distributed.

You can perform multiple comparisons of environment effects using this model with Program 10.4.

PROGRAM 10.4   **Multiple Comparisons in the Random Block RCBD**

```
data waste;
    do temp = 1 to 3;
        do envir = 1 to 5;
            do rep=1 to 2;
            input waste @@;
            output;
            end;
        end;
    end;
datalines;
7.09 5.90   7.94 9.15 9.23 9.85   5.43   7.73   9.43 6.90
7.01 5.82   6.18 7.19 7.86 6.33   8.49   8.67   9.62 9.07
7.78 7.73 10.39 8.78 9.27 8.90 12.17 10.95 13.07 9.76
;
data waste1;
   set waste;
   if rep=1;
run;

proc mixed data=waste1;
   class envir temp;
   model waste = temp/ddfm=satterth;
   random envir;
   lsmeans temp/cl adjust=tukey;
   ods output diffs=diffs;
run;
```

```
proc print data=diffs noobs;
   title "Multiple Comparisons in Random Block Model";
   var temp _temp Estimate StdErr df AdjLow AdjUpp;
run;
```

Output from Program 10.4

		Multiple Comparisons in Random Block Model				
temp	_temp	Estimate	StdErr	DF	AdjLow	AdjUpp
1	2	-0.00800	0.9305	8	-2.6670	2.6510
1	3	-2.7120	0.9305	8	-5.3710	-0.05304
2	3	-2.7040	0.9305	8	-5.3630	-0.04504

Note the following concerning Program 10.4 and its output:

- The conclusion seems identical to that obtained using a fixed block model, shown in Chapter 9, in the Output from Program 9.5. Namely, level 3 of the `temp` variable differs from the other two. This correspondence between GLM and MIXED is no accident! In fact, they coincide exactly in this case, but you should not count on it in general.

- The Satterthwaite approximation for the degrees of freedom is exact in this case; $df = 8$ is identical to the fixed-effects denominator $df = (I-1)(J-1) = (5-1)(3-1)$ because the design is balanced (see also the output from Program 9.5).

- While we generally recommend the `adjust=simulate` option, in this particular case of balanced data and simple model structure, the `adjust=tukey` option is exact (without Monte Carlo error), and therefore appropriate.

- If you analyze the data using the GLM code

```
proc glm data=waste1;
   class envir temp;
   model waste = envir temp;
   lsmeans temp/pdiff cl adjust=tukey;
run;
```

you then get simultaneous intervals identical to those provided by PROC MIXED.

It turns out that the balanced nature of the design and the specific structure of the model allow you to use either PROC GLM or PROC MIXED in this case. However, to be on the safe side, we generally recommend using PROC MIXED because it provides more flexible modeling options.

10.3.2 Incomplete Blocks

One example where there are differences between the fixed effect and random effect analyses is in the case of incomplete block designs. In this case, the standard errors of the estimated LS-Means treatment differences differ for the two models, and the LS-Means themselves differ. Thus, it becomes extremely important that you identify the blocks as either fixed or random before proceeding with the inferences.

Consider the detergent data of Program 9.8 in Section 9.2.7. The blocks most likely represent batches of plates grouped together for experimental convenience, and thus do not represent unique experimental situations of interest, but rather are representative of a larger collection of possible experimental situations. Thus, the random effects model

$$y_{ij} = \mu + \alpha_i + \beta_j + \epsilon_{ij}$$

with i denoting detergent and j denoting the block, seems reasonable. This model corresponds to that shown above for the waste data with the difference that it is incomplete—that is, not all levels of detergent are present in each block. Otherwise, the models are identical. However, the fact that the design is incomplete means that the GLM and MIXED analyses differ.

You can use Program 10.5 to analyze the data assuming random block effects.

PROGRAM 10.5   Multiple Comparisons with Random Block Levels: Incomplete Blocks

```
data detergent;
   do detergent=1 to 5;
      do block =1 to 10;
      input plates @@;
      output;
      end;
   end;
datalines;
27 28 30 31 29 30  .  .  .  .
26 26 29  .  .  . 30 21 26  .
30  .  . 34 32  . 34 31  . 33
 . 29  . 33  . 34 31  . 33 31
 .  . 26  . 24 25  . 23 24 26
;

proc mixed data=detergent;
   class block detergent;
   model plates = detergent/ddfm=satterth;
   random block;
   lsmeans detergent/cl adjust=simulate(seed=121211);
   ods output diffs=diffs;
run;

proc print data=diffs noobs;
   title "Multiple Comparisons in Random Block Model - Incomplete Blocks";
   var detergent _detergent Estimate StdErr df AdjLow AdjUpp;
run;
```

Output from Program 10.5

Multiple Comparisons in Random Block Model - Incomplete Blocks

detergent	_detergent	Estimate	StdErr	DF	AdjLow	AdjUpp
1	2	2.3240	0.8473	17.6	-0.2289	4.8768
1	3	-3.4820	0.8473	17.6	-6.0348	-0.9291
1	4	-2.3271	0.8473	17.6	-4.8799	0.2257
1	5	4.3787	0.8473	17.6	1.8259	6.9316
2	3	-5.8060	0.8473	17.6	-8.3588	-3.2531
2	4	-4.6511	0.8473	17.6	-7.2039	-2.0983
2	5	2.0547	0.8473	17.6	-0.4981	4.6076
3	4	1.1549	0.8473	17.6	-1.3980	3.7077
3	5	7.8607	0.8473	17.6	5.3079	10.4135
4	5	6.7058	0.8473	17.6	4.1530	9.2587

Comparing this output with the corresponding fixed-block-effect output from Program 9.9 in Section 9.2.7, we see the same general conclusions regarding significant differences. However, note that the parameter estimates differ, as do the confidence limits. Interestingly, the limits are *narrower* for the random block model. The average width is 5.1057 for the random block model, and 5.3103 for the fixed block output of Program 9.9. While the usual effect of making factors random is to increase the width of the intervals for LS-Mean differences because of modeling additional sources of variability, in some incomplete block designs the reverse holds. This phenomenon has traditionally been called *recovery of interblock information*; refer to Patterson and Thompson (1971) and Giesbrecht (1986).

Note also that the df given by the Satterthwaite approximation is, in this case, fractional, and therefore approximate. Using the default df calculation in PROC MIXED (the containment method described in SAS Institute Inc, 1999), you get $df = 16$, identical to the fixed-effects residual error $df = 30 - (5 + 10 - 1)$. Because the default df value is smaller and thus more conservative, it is perhaps more prudent to use it. In general, you may want to try both methods to see if they qualitatively affect conclusions. If they do, you may have to conduct your own custom simulation study to investigate the differences. The SAS macros we have provided in this book provide good templates for constructing such simulation code.

10.3.3   Comparing Means When Random Factors Interact

Returning to the waste example, consider the full data set with two replications at each environment×temperature combination. Here, you can model interaction between environment and temperature, but if you assume environment is random, then you also should assume the environment×temperature interaction is random. A model is

$$y_{ijk} = \mu + \alpha_i + \beta_j + (\alpha\beta)_{ij} + \epsilon_{ijk},$$

which is identical to the previous model for the data, with the additional assumption that the interaction effects $(\alpha\beta)_{ij}$ also are random, independent of the other random effects, with mean zero and variance $\sigma^2_{(\alpha\beta)}$.

To perform multiple comparisons on the temperature means in this model, use Program 10.6.

PROGRAM 10.6   Multiple Comparisons in Random Block Model with Interaction

```
proc mixed data=waste;
   class envir temp;
   model waste = temp/ddfm=satterth;
   random envir envir*temp;
   lsmeans temp/cl adjust=tukey;
   ods output diffs=diffs;
run;

proc print data=diffs noobs;
   title "Multiple Comparisons in Random Block Model with Interaction";
   var temp _temp Estimate StdErr df AdjLow AdjUpp;
run;
```

Output from Program 10.6

Multiple Comparisons in Random Block Model with Interaction						
temp	_temp	Estimate	StdErr	DF	AdjLow	AdjUpp
1	2	0.2410	0.7568	8	-1.9216	2.4036
1	3	-2.0150	0.7568	8	-4.1776	0.1476
2	3	-2.2560	0.7568	8	-4.4186	-0.09342

Comparing this output with that of Program 9.2, the corresponding fixed block analysis, we see that the intervals are much wider in the case where the environmental main effect and the environment×temperature interaction are considered random. The reason is that the fixed effects analysis considers differences between temperature levels, averaged over the *specific* environment conditions in the given experiment. By contrast, in the random effects model, the inference concerns effects of differences in temperature levels, averaged over *all* environment conditions in the population. The latter inference must account for variability in environment conditions, and therefore gives wider intervals. No interblock information is available here to offset this effect because the design is balanced.

Note also that we again used adjust=tukey in this example, which is appropriate given the balanced nature of the design. If you are uncertain about whether Tukey's method is appropriate, we suggest that you simply use adjust=simulate because you will get the right answer (modulo a small amount of Monte Carlo error) even when the design has the appropriate balanced structure.

10.4   Repeated Measures Analysis

Another application of the mixed model involves analyzing data consisting of repeated measurements on the same experimental unit. These repeated measures are likely to be correlated, but instead of modeling these correlations with random effects as in the previous sections, we specify the variance-covariance structure directly. In PROC MIXED, this involves switching from the RANDOM statement to the REPEATED statement. You use the TYPE= option in the REPEATED statement to specify an appropriate covariance structure.

10.4.1   Repeated Measures Experimental Design

In a repeated measures design, different treatments are applied repeatedly to each experimental unit. The advantage of doing so is that you can get a given number of observations with far fewer experimental units, while possibly also reducing the underlying level of noise. For example, if you have five treatments, you can get 10 observations per treatment with only 10 units (perhaps human subjects), while with a completely randomized design you would need 50 units.

However, the savings in number of units comes with costs:

- you must account for the correlation among the responses in the analysis of the data, making the analysis more complicated

- you must try to avoid carry-over effects, where the effect of the first applied treatment biases the outcome from subsequently applied treatments.

Randomizing the order of treatment application, or allowing sufficient time between applications, often can alleviate carry-over biases. Because correlation structures can now be dealt with fairly easily with proper statistical analysis, the carry-over effects are the major difficulty with these designs. Whether the design is appropriate often depends more on subject-specific considerations than on statistical ones. Despite these difficulties, repeated measures designs are a staple for the analysis of clinical trials in pharmaceutical development, in which patients typically are evaluated for responses to multiple therapeutic agents via a cross-over design.

For our repeated measures example, we consider an experiment in which $n = 19$ dogs are each subjected to four distinct treatments. Here, dog is the experimental unit, and the four repeated measurements represent a (2×2) factorial application of Halothane (Present or Absent), in combination with CO_2 pressure (Low or High). The response data are milliseconds between heartbeats.

Here is a model for the data:

$$\mathbf{y}_i = \boldsymbol{\mu} + \boldsymbol{\epsilon}_i,$$

where

- $\mathbf{y}_i = (y_{i1} \ y_{i2} \ y_{i3} \ y_{i4})$, the response profile for the ith dog.
- $\boldsymbol{\mu} = (\mu_1 \ \mu_2 \ \mu_3 \ \mu_4)$, the population mean profile, where

  - μ_1 denotes mean response for high CO_2 with Halothane absent
  - μ_2 denotes mean response for low CO_2 with Halothane absent
  - μ_3 denotes mean response for high CO_2 with Halothane present
  - μ_4 denotes mean response for low CO_2 with Halothane present.

- $\boldsymbol{\epsilon}_i$ denotes the random error vector for the ith dog. Assume the $\boldsymbol{\epsilon}_i$ are independent, with $E(\boldsymbol{\epsilon}_i) = \mathbf{0}$, $Cov(\boldsymbol{\epsilon}_i) = \Sigma$, and that the $\boldsymbol{\epsilon}_i$ are distributed as multivariate normal.

For this example, we assume that Σ has the most general form possible, a 4×4 unstructured covariance matrix with 10 unknown parameters. You can also model the covariance structure more parsimoniously using a variety of possible structures from PROC MIXED, comparing the fits using likelihood-based measures. By using a more structured covariance matrix, you get more error degrees of freedom and more powerful tests. However, note that in the process of fitting a covariance structure to the data, you can introduce biases from over-fitting. That is, your inferences might be overly optimistic (resulting in inflated FWE) because you have tailored the model to fit the data at hand, much in the same way the regression tests are biased when based on a linear model selected for how well it fits the data.

In Program 10.7 you will find the data, as well as the analysis of all pairwise comparisons of the components of the mean vector.

PROGRAM 10.7   **Comparison of Repeated Measures Means**

```
data Halothane;
   do Dog =1 to 19;
      do Treatment = 'HA','LA','HP','LP';
         input Rate @@;
         output;
         end;
      end;
```

```
datalines;
426 609 556 600    253 236 392 395    359 433 349 357
432 431 522 600    405 426 513 513    324 438 507 539
310 312 410 456    326 326 350 504    375 447 547 548
286 286 403 422    349 382 473 497    429 410 488 547
348 377 447 514    412 473 472 446    347 326 455 468
434 458 637 524    364 367 432 469    420 395 508 531
397 556 645 625
;
proc mixed data=Halothane;
   class Dog Treatment;
   model Rate = Treatment / ddfm=satterth;
   repeated / type=un subject=Dog;
   lsmeans Treatment / adjust=simulate(nsamp=200000 seed=121211) cl pdiff;
   ods output Diffs=Diffs;
run;

proc print data=Diffs noobs;
   title "Multiple Comparisons in Repeated Measures Model";
   var Treatment _Treatment Estimate StdErr df AdjLow AdjUpp;
run;
```

Output from Program 10.7

Multiple Comparisons in Repeated Measures Model

Treatment	_Treatment	Estimate	StdErr	DF	AdjLow	AdjUpp
HA	HP	-111.05	14.1116	18	-150.86	-71.2453
HA	LA	-36.4211	13.8518	18	-75.4956	2.6535
HA	LP	-134.68	12.7889	18	-170.76	-98.6081
HP	LA	74.6316	14.8793	18	32.6587	116.60
HP	LP	-23.6316	11.9891	18	-57.4515	10.1883
LA	LP	-98.2632	15.7467	18	-142.68	-53.8435

Note the following about the output:

- Using this analysis, all differences are significant except for the HA-LA and HP-LP differences. These insignificant differences refer to differences between high and low CO_2 when, respectively, Halothane is absent or Halothane is present,

- The reported degrees of freedom obtained using the Satterthwaite approximation algorithm, $df = 18$, is correct for the unadjusted pairwise comparisons. You can verify this easily by noting that the appropriate multivariate test reduces to a paired sample t-test in this case, with degrees of freedom $n - 1$, where n is the number of experimental units (in this case, $n = 19$ dogs). The standard errors reported above using PROC MIXED also are identical to the paired sample t-test standard errors.

- The adjusted confidence limits are obtained by sampling from a multivariate t distribution, as described in Chapter 5, using an estimated correlation matrix and 18 degrees of freedom. There are two approximations coming into play here, each of which can contribute to error.

  The first level of approximation is the one previously noted that applies to almost all PROC MIXED modeling, namely the assumption that the estimated variances (or, in the case of our Halothane example, the variances and covariances) are in fact the true values. The second level of approximation is the related fact that the usual multivariate t distribution is not the correct joint distribution of the paired sample t statistics because there are many variances to estimate, not just one. The correct distribution is a separately standardized type of multivariate t, discussed by, e.g., Siddiqui (1967). Nevertheless, the correct multivariate t distribution and the one used by PROC MIXED to obtain the simultaneous inferences agree in (1) their marginal distributions and in (2) their correlation structure. These two facts suggest that the PROC MIXED approximation should be reasonable in this example.

Treatments in the Halothane experiment have a two-way factorial structure. In addition to (or instead of) the usual pairwise comparisons, you might want to test the usual main effects and interaction contrasts. In Program 10.8, you will see how to extend the family of all pairwise comparisons to include these contrasts. Because the resulting set of contrasts have many logical interrelationships, we use step-down testing with the type=LOGICAL setting in the %SimTests macro to exploit this feature.

PROGRAM 10.8   Logically Constrained Step-Down Tests with Repeated Measures Data

```
proc mixed data=Halothane;
    class Dog Treatment;
    model Rate = Treatment / ddfm=satterth;
    repeated / type=un subject=Dog;
    lsmeans Treatment / cov;
    ods output LSmeans = LSmeans;
    ods output Tests3  = Tests3;
run;

%macro Contrasts;
    C = {  1  -1   0   0 ,
           1   0  -1   0 ,
           1   0   0  -1 ,
           0   1  -1   0 ,
           0   1   0  -1 ,
           0   0   1  -1 ,
         -.5 -.5  .5  .5 ,
          .5 -.5  .5 -.5 ,
           1  -1  -1   1 };
    C = C` ;

    Clab = {"HA-HP","HA-LA","HA-LP",
                   "HP-LA","HP-LP",
                          "LA-LP",
            "Halo"                 ,
            "CO2"                  ,
            "Interaction"          };  /* Contrast labels */
%mend;

%macro Estimates;
    use tests3;
    read all var {DenDf} into df;
    use lsmeans;
    read all var {Cov1 Cov2 Cov3 Cov4} into cov;
    read all var {Estimate} into EstPar;
%mend;

%SimTests(nsamp=40000, seed=121211, type=LOGICAL);
```

Output from Program 10.8

Logically Constrained (Restricted Combinations) Step-Down Tests

Contrast	Estimate	Standard Error	Raw	Bon	Adj	SE(AdjP)
			----- Pr > |t| -----			
HA-HP	-111.1	14.1116	<.0001	<.0001	<.0001	0
HA-LA	-36.4211	13.8518	0.0170	0.0170	0.0170	0
HA-LP	-134.7	12.7889	<.0001	<.0001	<.0001	0
HP-LA	74.6316	14.8793	<.0001	0.0002	0.0002	0
HP-LP	-23.6316	11.9891	0.0643	0.0643	0.0643	0
LA-LP	-98.2632	15.7467	<.0001	<.0001	<.0001	0
Halo	30.0263	8.2684	0.0019	0.0076	0.0058	0.000130
CO2	-104.7	11.1404	<.0001	<.0001	<.0001	0
Interaction	-12.7895	19.9439	0.5294	0.5294	0.5294	0

In this analysis, you see that all comparisons are significant except for HP-LP and Interaction. Interestingly, the HA-LA comparison now is significant, despite the larger family size in this example ($k = 9$ is more than $k = 6$ pairwise comparisons). This occurs in this example because the logical constraint method allows you to test the HA-LA contrast without multiplicity adjustment, as you can see by comparing the Raw and Bon p-values. Of course, the inferences in the latter analysis are less ambitious, as we have noted in previous chapters.

10.5   Multivariate Analysis

In addition to repeated measures models, you can also analyze general multivariate models using PROC MIXED and obtain approximate multiple comparisons for the parameters as shown in the preceding sections. PROC MIXED mimics the usual multivariate analysis procedures via the unstructured covariance matrix estimates (the type=un option). One very useful benefit of this approach is that missing values are incorporated directly into the estimation. If you are interested in one-dimensional differences between groups, then you can fit multivariate ANOVA (MANOVA) models and multivariate ANCOVA (MANCOVA) models using PROC MIXED, then perform multiplicity adjustments, as we show in this section. However, if you are interested in differences between groups that are composite (multidimensional) hypotheses (for example, multiple F-tests or multiple likelihood ratio tests), then you need more general methods than provided in this book, some of which are discussed by Westfall and Young (1993).

10.5.1   Testing Mean Differences in the MANOVA Model—Multiple Outcomes

A repeated measures experiment has the characteristic that the different treatments are applied to the same experimental unit. By contrast, a MANOVA model assumes the treatments are applied to different experimental units, as in the case of ANOVA, but with multiple response variables. A similarity is that the data are multivariate in either case: in a repeated measures ANOVA, you measure the same item under different experimental conditions for a particular unit; and in a MANOVA, you measure distinct items for a particular unit, all under the same experimental condition.

EXAMPLE: Multiple Endpoints in a Randomized Clinical Trial

Clinical trials are used to evaluate the efficacy of a pharmaceutical product. Often, it can be difficult to identify a single, measurable quantity that represents efficacy of the drug better than all other quantities. For example, the patient's self-rated perception of health is important, as is the physician's assessment, as are various measurements, for example, blood analysis. If a drug company wants to declare "The drug is efficacious" when it positively affects *at least one* of a collection of endpoints, *and* the company wants to make *specific* claims about which endpoints are affected, then they must analyze their data using multiplicity-adjusted methods.

Program 10.9 concerns data from an actual Phase II clinical trial conducted at a large pharmaceutical company. There are four endpoints. The first 54 records represent patients under a placebo control, and the last 57 records represent patients who have taken the experimental drug. There are 111 patients in total. The data and analysis using PROC MIXED and the %SimTests macro are as follows.

PROGRAM 10.9   Multiple Comparisons of Multiple Outcomes in the MANOVA Framework

```
data MultipleEndpoints;
    Treatment = 'Placebo';
    do Subject = 1 to 54;
        do Endpoint = 1 to 4; input y @@; output;
        end;
    end;
    Treatment = 'Drug';
    do Subject = 54+1 to 54+57;
        do Endpoint = 1 to 4; input y @@; output;
        end;
    end;
datalines;
4 3 3 5   5 0 1 7   1 0 1 9   4 0 3 5   3 0 2 9   4 1 2 6   2 0 4 6
2 2 5 5   3 0 1 7   2 0 1 9   4 6 5 5   2 0 2 8   2 7 1 7   1 2 2 9
4 0 3 7   3 0 1 6   3 0 1 6   4 1 4 6   6 0 4 7   3 0 1 8   3 0 1 9
2 1 2 7   6 2 3 5   3 0 4 7   3 0 1 9   2 0 1 9   6 9 6 3   4 9 2 6
2 0 1 7   1 0 1 9   4 0 4 7   3 1 4 6   3 0 3 7   1 0 1 8   6 7 5 4
4 6 2 5   6 19 7 5   6 3 6 6   3 0 5 6   2 4 2 8   1 0 1 8   4 21 5 5
2 0 2 9   4 7 3 5   3 1 2 8   3 3 3 8   4 3 4 6   1 0 1 10  1 0 2 9
3 0 4 5   3 1 1 6   3 4 4 6   5 8 5 5   5 1 5 4   1 0 4 8   1 0 1 10
1 0 1 9   2 1 2 7   4 1 2 5   5 0 5 6   1 4 5 6   5 6 4 6   2 0 2 9
2 2 2 5   1 0 1 10  3 2 3 6   5 4 6 6   2 1 2 8   2 1 2 6   2 1 1 8
3 0 3 9   3 1 2 6   1 0 2 9   1 0 1 9   3 0 3 9   1 0 1 10  1 0 1 9
1 0 1 10  2 0 4 7   5 1 2 6   4 0 5 7   4 0 4 6   2 1 3 6   2 1 1 6
4 0 4 6   1 0 1 8   1 0 2 9   4 1 3 6   4 3 4 5   4 2 5 5   1 0 1 10
3 0 2 8   4 2 2 8   3 0 2 9   1 0 1 10  1 0 1 9   2 0 2 9   2 1 2 8
3 0 3 8   2 4 2 6   2 1 1 9   2 2 2 9   4 0 1 4   3 3 1 8   4 4 3 6
2 0 1 10  4 2 3 6   1 0 1 8   2 0 2 8   5 1 5 5   4 0 4 6
;
proc mixed data=MultipleEndpoints;
    title "Two-Sample Multivariate Mean Comparisons";
    class Endpoint Treatment Subject;
    model y = Treatment*Endpoint / ddfm=satterth;
    repeated / type=un subject=Subject;
    lsmeans Treatment*Endpoint / cov;
    contrast 'F test' Treatment*Endpoint 1 -1  0  0  0  0  0  0 ,
                      Treatment*Endpoint 0  0  1 -1  0  0  0  0 ,
                      Treatment*Endpoint 0  0  0  0  1 -1  0  0 ,
                      Treatment*Endpoint 0  0  0  0  0  0  1 -1 ;
```

```
        ods output LSmeans    = LSmeans;
        ods output Contrasts = Contrasts;
run;

%macro Contrasts;
    C = { 1 -1  0  0  0  0  0  0 ,
          0  0  1 -1  0  0  0  0 ,
          0  0  0  0  1 -1  0  0 ,
          0  0  0  0  0  0  1 -1 };
    C = C' ;

    Clab = {"Endpoint 1", "Endpoint 2", "Endpoint 3", "Endpoint 4"};
%mend;

%macro Estimates;
    use Contrasts; read all var {DenDf} into df;
    use LSmeans;
    read all var {Cov1 Cov2 Cov3 Cov4 Cov5 Cov6 Cov7 Cov8} into cov;
    read all var {Estimate} into EstPar;
%mend;

%SimTests(seed=121211, nsamp=100000);
```

Output from Program 10.9

Two-Sample Multivariate Mean Comparisons

Logically Constrained (Restricted Combinations) Step-Down Tests

Contrast	Estimate	Standard Error	----- Pr > |t| -----			SE(AdjP)
			Raw	Bon	Adj	
Endpoint 1	-0.6784	0.2658	0.0121	0.0483	0.0393	0.000245
Endpoint 2	-1.5146	0.6079	0.0142	0.0483	0.0393	0.000245
Endpoint 3	-0.3743	0.2893	0.1986	0.1986	0.1986	0
Endpoint 4	0.7505	0.3154	0.0191	0.0483	0.0393	0.000245

We see that all treatment-control comparisons are significant after multiplicity adjustment, except for variable 3. The effect of incorporating the correlation among the endpoints is to reduce the significant Bonferroni adjusted p-values from 0.0483 to 0.0393. Also, the effect of using a stepwise procedure rather than a single-step procedure is that more variables are significant: using the single-step Bonferroni adjustments of ($4 \times$ {raw p-value}), only the first variable would be called significant. In the next chapter we show how to analyze these data using PROC MULTTEST. The syntax is considerably simpler, and the method incorporates non-normal characteristics (as shown in the raw data) via bootstrap resampling.

Here are some other comments concerning the program and its output:

- The logical choice for the df parameter seems to be the Satterthwaite approximation for the F-test of the composite null. That is why we had to use the special `contrast` test in the PROC MIXED code. The df parameter was given as $df = 109$ for this test.

- The $df = 109$ value is exactly the same value as for the usual two-sample t-test ($54 + 57 - 2$). Coupled with the fact that the estimated variance parameters are identical to the two-sample pooled variances for each variable, the unadjusted p-values shown above correspond exactly with the two-sample (pooled variance) t-test p-values.

- Similarly, the 4×4 covariance matrix estimated by the PROC MIXED model is identical to the two-sample pooled covariance matrix of the four endpoints.

- One place where the correspondence of PROC MIXED and the usual types of analyses fails is in the reported value of the F-test for the equality of group means. The program above reports $F(4, 109) = 2.67$, whereas the proper two-sample multivariate test (either Hotelling's T^2 or Wilks' Lambda) has a converted F of $F(4, 106) = 2.60$. Thus, the error df are slightly off using the PROC MIXED contrast formulation, as is the value of the F statistic itself. You can obtain the Hotelling-Lawley trace statistics for within-subject effects by adding the HLM and HLPS options to the REPEATED statement.

10.5.2   Multiple Comparisons in MANCOVA using `PROC MIXED`

Suppose you have multivariate multiple-group response data, as in the preceding section, but want to adjust your comparisons for covariates—that is, you want to perform a multi-variate analysis of covariance, or MANCOVA. No problem! As long as you can accept the various approximations used by PROC MIXED, there are essentially no new difficulties.

A MANCOVA example discussed by Morrison (1990, pp. 234–236), has response variables are Y_1=amount of the pigment creatinine and Y_2=amount of chloride in urine samples; these are to be compared for four different obesity groups (lighter underweight, heavier underweight, lighter obese, heavier obese) of subjects, adjusting for a single covariate X=Volume (mL). There are six pairwise comparisons of the amount of creatinine and six pairwise comparisons of the amount of chloride. For our family of inferences, we will form all 12 confidence intervals for the differences in means, all covariate-adjusted.

The data and program are given as follows.

PROGRAM 10.10   **Multiple Comparisons of Means in MANCOVA**

```
data Obesity;
    input Group $ Creatinine Chloride Volume @@;
    Subject = _n_;
    datalines;
LU 17.6  5.15 205  LU 13.4  5.75 160  LU 20.3  4.35 480
LU 22.3  7.55 230  LU 20.5  8.50 235  LU 18.5 10.25 215
LU 12.1  5.95 215  LU 12.0  6.30 190  LU 10.1  5.45 190
LU 14.7  3.75 175  LU 14.8  5.10 145  LU 14.4  4.05 155
HU 18.1  9.00 220  HU 19.7  5.30 300  HU 16.9  9.85 305
HU 23.7  3.60 275  HU 19.2  4.05 405  HU 18.0  4.40 210
HU 14.8  7.15 170  HU 15.6  7.25 235  HU 16.2  5.30 185
HU 14.1  3.10 255  HU 17.5  2.40 265  HU 14.1  4.25 305
HU 19.1  5.80 440  HU 22.5  1.55 430  LO 17.0  4.55 350
LO 12.5  2.65 475  LO 21.5  6.50 195  LO 22.2  4.85 375
LO 13.0  8.75 160  LO 13.0  5.20 240  LO 10.9  4.75 205
LO 12.0  5.85 270  LO 22.8  2.85 475  LO 16.5  6.55 430
LO 18.4  6.60 490  HO 12.5  2.90 105  HO  8.7  3.00 115
HO  9.4  3.40  97  HO 15.0  5.40 325  HO 12.9  4.45 310
HO 12.1  4.30 245  HO 13.2  5.00 170  HO 11.5  3.40 220
;

data ObesityU;   /* Change multivariate data format to MIXED data format */
    set Obesity;
    Compound = 'Creatinine'; Amount = Creatinine; output;
    Compound = 'Chloride'  ; Amount = Chloride;   output;
    keep Subject Group Compound Amount Volume;
run;
```

```
proc mixed data=ObesityU order=data;
   class Group Compound Subject;
   model Amount = Group*Compound Volume*Compound / ddfm=satterth s;
   repeated / type=un subject = Subject;
   lsmeans Group*Compound / cov;
   contrast 'F test' Group*Compound 1  0 -1  0  0  0  0  0 ,
                     Group*Compound 1  0  0  0 -1  0  0  0 ,
                     Group*Compound 1  0  0  0  0  0 -1  0 ,
                     Group*Compound 0  1  0 -1  0  0  0  0 ,
                     Group*Compound 0  1  0  0  0 -1  0  0 ,
                     Group*Compound 0  1  0  0  0  0  0 -1 ;
   ods output LSmeans   = LSmeans;
   ods output Contrasts = Contrasts;
run;

%macro Contrasts;
      C = { 1  0 -1  0  0  0  0  0 ,
            1  0  0  0 -1  0  0  0 ,
            1  0  0  0  0  0 -1  0 ,
            0  0  1  0 -1  0  0  0 ,
            0  0  1  0  0  0 -1  0 ,
            0  0  0  0  1  0 -1  0 ,
            0  1  0 -1  0  0  0  0 ,
            0  1  0  0  0 -1  0  0 ,
            0  1  0  0  0  0  0 -1 ,
            0  0  0  1  0 -1  0  0 ,
            0  0  0  1  0  0  0 -1 ,
            0  0  0  0  0  1  0 -1 };

      C = C' ;

      Clab = {"Creatine,LU-HU","Creatine,LU-LO","Creatine,LU-HO",
                        "Creatine,HU-LO","Creatine,HU-HO",
                                      "Creatine,LO-HO",
              "Chloride,LU-HU","Chloride,LU-LO","Chloride,LU-HO",
                        "Chloride,HU-LO","Chloride,HU-HO",
                                      "Chloride,LO-HO"};
%mend;

%macro Estimates;
   use Contrasts; read all var {DenDf} into df;
   use LSmeans;
   read all var {Cov1 Cov2 Cov3 Cov4 Cov5 Cov6 Cov7 Cov8} into cov;
   read all var {Estimate} into EstPar;
%mend;

%SimIntervals(seed=121211, nsamp=50000);
```

Output from Program 10.10

```
              Two-Sample Multivariate Mean Comparisons

                    Estimated 95% Quantile = 2.941194

                         Standard       --- Pr > |t| --   95% Confidence
Contrast         Estimate  Error t Value  Raw  Adjusted      Interval

Creatine,LU-HU   -0.7685  1.2700  -0.61  0.5485  0.9944  -4.5037  2.9667
Creatine,LU-LO    1.5011  1.4203   1.06  0.2969  0.9121  -2.6763  5.6785
Creatine,LU-HO    3.6803  1.4213   2.59  0.0133  0.1136  -0.5000  7.8606
Creatine,HU-LO    2.2695  1.2740   1.78  0.0824  0.4889  -1.4776  6.0166
Creatine,HU-HO    4.4488  1.4435   3.08  0.0037  0.0354   0.2031  8.6945
Creatine,LO-HO    2.1792  1.5905   1.37  0.1783  0.7600  -2.4988  6.8573
Chloride,LU-HU    0.5073  0.7805   0.65  0.5194  0.9918  -1.7882  2.8029
Chloride,LU-LO    0.1501  0.8729   0.17  0.8643  1.0000  -2.4172  2.7174
Chloride,LU-HO    2.1061  0.8735   2.41  0.0206  0.1678  -0.4630  4.6752
Chloride,HU-LO   -0.3572  0.7830  -0.46  0.6507  0.9989  -2.6601  1.9456
Chloride,HU-HO    1.5988  0.8872   1.80  0.0791  0.4752  -1.0105  4.2081
Chloride,LO-HO    1.9560  0.9775   2.00  0.0522  0.3535  -0.9190  4.8310
```

Thus, the covariate-adjusted Creatinine level is significantly larger for the heavier underweight group than for the heavier overweight group, with no other comparisons statistically significant.

This analysis agrees with that performed by Westfall and Young (1993, p. 130), who analyzed these data using the same model. They implicitly resampled data from the proper (separately standardized) multivariate t distribution, rather than sample from the multivariate t distribution that uses a common standardization. The correspondence between these two analyses suggests that the multivariate t approximation (common standardization) used by PROC MIXED is reasonable.

10.5.3   Multiple Comparisons of Simple Effects in Repeated Measures

Simple effects analyze an interaction by comparing cell means for different levels of one or more factors while holding the other factors fixed. You can perform global F-tests of simple effects using the SLICE= option in the LSMEANS statement of either PROC GLM or PROC MIXED. However, neither of these procedures currently allows slice-wise multiple comparisons of the cell means.

The example is taken from Milliken and Johnson (1992, pp. 326–332). There are 24 subjects, randomly divided into three groups of eight each. Two groups are active drugs, ax23 and bww9, the third group is a placebo control. Heart rate following administration of the drug or placebo is measured at four time points, labeled t1, t2, t3, and t4.

The data and program are given as follows.

PROGRAM 10.11   Global Tests of 'Sliced' Effects

```
data heart;
   do drug = 'ax23', 'bww9', 'ctrl';
      do person = 1 to 8;
         do time = 't1', 't2', 't3', 't4';
            input hr @@;
            output;
            end;
```

```
            end;
        end;
    datalines;
    72 86 81 77  78 83 88 81  71 82 81 75  72 83 83 69
    66 79 77 66  74 83 84 77  62 73 78 70  69 75 76 70
    85 86 83 80  82 86 80 84  71 78 70 75  83 88 79 81
    86 85 76 76  85 82 83 80  79 83 80 81  83 84 78 81
    69 73 72 74  66 62 67 73  84 90 88 87  80 81 77 72
    72 72 69 70  65 62 65 61  75 69 69 68  71 70 65 63
    ;
    proc mixed data=heart;
        class time drug person;
        model hr = time*drug / ddfm=satterth;
        repeated time / type=un subject=person(drug);
        lsmeans time*drug / slice=time;

    run;
    ;
```

Output from Program 10.11

The Mixed Procedure

Tests of Effect Slices

Effect	time	Num DF	Den DF	F Value	Pr > F
time*drug	t1	2	21	9.29	0.0013
time*drug	t2	2	21	7.25	0.0040
time*drug	t3	2	21	6.26	0.0074
time*drug	t4	2	21	5.10	0.0157

Thus, you can say that the drugs differ significantly, overall, at each time point (ignoring the multiplicity problem of several time points for the moment). However, you probably would like to make statements about the particular three drugs, rather than an overall assessment. Program 10.12 shows how you can perform such comparisons using the %SimTests macro.

PROGRAM 10.12   Multiple Comparisons of Sliced Effects

```
proc mixed data=heart;
    class time drug person;
    model hr = time*drug / ddfm=satterth;
    repeated / type=un subject = person(drug);
    lsmeans time*drug / cov;
    contrast 'F test' time*drug 1 -1  0   0  0  0   0  0  0   0  0  0 ,
                      time*drug 1  0 -1   0  0  0   0  0  0   0  0  0 ,
                      time*drug 0  0  0   1 -1  0   0  0  0   0  0  0 ,
                      time*drug 0  0  0   1  0 -1   0  0  0   0  0  0 ,
                      time*drug 0  0  0   0  0  0   1 -1  0   0  0  0 ,
                      time*drug 0  0  0   0  0  0   1  0 -1   0  0  0 ,
                      time*drug 0  0  0   0  0  0   0  0  0   1 -1  0 ,
                      time*drug 0  0  0   0  0  0   0  0  0   1  0 -1 ;
    ods output LSmeans   = LSmeans;
    ods output Contrasts = Contrasts;
run;
```

```
%macro Contrasts;
    C = { 1 -1  0   0  0  0    0  0  0   0  0  0 ,
          1  0 -1   0  0  0    0  0  0   0  0  0 ,
          0  1 -1   0  0  0    0  0  0   0  0  0 ,
          0  0  0   1 -1  0    0  0  0   0  0  0 ,
          0  0  0   1  0 -1    0  0  0   0  0  0 ,
          0  0  0   0  1 -1    0  0  0   0  0  0 ,
          0  0  0   0  0  0    1 -1  0   0  0  0 ,
          0  0  0   0  0  0    1  0 -1   0  0  0 ,
          0  0  0   0  0  0    0  1 -1   0  0  0 ,
          0  0  0   0  0  0    0  0  0   1 -1  0 ,
          0  0  0   0  0  0    0  0  0   1  0 -1 ,
          0  0  0   0  0  0    0  0  0   0  1 -1 };
    C = C' ;
    Clab = {"Time1, a-b","Time1, a-c","Time1, b-c",
            "Time2, a-b","Time2, a-c","Time2, b-c",
            "Time3, a-b","Time3, a-c","Time3, b-c",
            "Time4, a-b","Time4, a-c","Time4, b-c"};
%mend;

%macro Estimates;
    use Contrasts; read all var {DenDf} into df;
    use LSmeans;
    read all var {Cov1 Cov2 Cov3 Cov4 Cov5 Cov6 Cov7 Cov8 Cov9
                    Cov10 Cov11 Cov12} into cov;
    read all var {Estimate} into EstPar;
%mend;

%SimTests(seed=121211, nsamp=50000, type=LOGICAL);
```

Output from Program 10.12

```
        Logically Constrained (Restricted Combinations) Step-Down Tests
```

		Standard	----- Pr > |t| -----			
Contrast	Estimate	Error	Raw	Bon	Adj	SE(AdjP)
Time1, a-b	-11.2500	2.7624	0.0005	0.0066	0.0043	0.000143
Time1, a-c	-2.2500	2.7624	0.4245	1.0000	0.7286	0.00128
Time1, b-c	9.0000	2.7624	0.0038	0.0226	0.0177	0.000239
Time2, a-b	-3.5000	3.1318	0.2764	1.0000	0.6072	0.00137
Time2, a-c	8.1250	3.1318	0.0169	0.0677	0.0538	0.000386
Time2, b-c	11.6250	3.1318	0.0013	0.0129	0.0084	0.000200
Time3, a-b	2.3750	2.7943	0.4049	1.0000	0.7286	0.00128
Time3, a-c	9.5000	2.7943	0.0027	0.0216	0.0148	0.000248
Time3, b-c	7.1250	2.7943	0.0186	0.0746	0.0613	0.000397
Time4, a-b	-6.6250	2.8585	0.0306	0.1226	0.0849	0.000591
Time4, a-c	2.1250	2.8585	0.4655	1.0000	0.7286	0.00128
Time4, b-c	8.7500	2.8585	0.0059	0.0356	0.0268	0.000306

Note the following about the output:

- The conclusions are determined by *p*-values in the Adj column, with all such *p*-values less than 0.05 determining significant differences at the familywise 0.05 level.

- The family consists of 12 tests in this instance, with three pairwise sliced effects within each time point.

- You can fit simpler covariance structures and gain more power. In this example, the type=ar(1) covariance structure fits well, and allows more degrees of freedom, thereby improving power.

- Consider the results for Time2, a-c. The Bonferroni adjusted p-value of 0.0667 tells you that there are only $0.0667/0.0169 = 4$ hypotheses that can possibly be true at this stage in the hierarchy, given that all hypotheses corresponding to smaller p-values are false. Thus, the logical constraint method offers substantial improvement over the simple Bonferroni method, which uses 12 as a multiplier instead of 4. It also improves upon the Bonferroni-Holm method, which would use six as a multiplier for this test because there are six tests with p-values as large as 0.0169.

- Consider again the results for Time2, a-c. Comparing the adjusted p-value 0.0538 with the Bonferroni p-value 0.0667 shows the specific effect of incorporating the dependencies among the test statistics for the particular four tests that can be true at this point in the hierarchy. The p-value 0.0538 is computed using 50000 simulations, and the standard error is 0.000386; thus the simulation-based estimate shows that the true value is clearly more than 0.05 ($z = (0.0538 - 0.05)/0.000386 = 9.84$.)

10.6   Concluding Remarks

In this chapter, we have introduced a broad collection of models for which PROC MIXED provides reasonable approximations to the multiplicity adjustment problem. You can perform multiplicity adjustment for many possible choices of a family of tests using PROC MIXED output data and the %SimIntervals and %SimTests macros; further, you can get very powerful tests that incorporate correlations and logical constraints using the %SimTests macro.

You should realize, however, that in most cases these analyses are approximate, unlike the exact methods from previous chapters. While our experience shows that these approximations are reasonably accurate in many situations, problems can and do occur in PROC MIXED applications, not only for multiple comparisons, but for general analyses. You should verify that the degrees of freedom used in the approximations appear reasonable for your problem. If they don't, you may consider specifying your own degrees of freedom with the DDF= option in the MODEL statement. A more ambitious alternative is to conduct your own simulation study by iteratively calling the methods in this chapter over replications of a suitable data structure.

Chapter 11

Multiple Comparisons of Means in Univariate and Multivariate Models, Allowing Nonnormality, Using PROC MULTTEST

11.1 Introduction

In this chapter and in the following chapter we drop the normality assumption. PROC MULTTEST was designed specifically to allow for nonnormality using bootstrap and permutation resampling methods. In many cases we find that the analyses using PROC MULTTEST and the corresponding parametric analyses (for example, LSMEANS in PROC GLM) are very similar, and in such cases either method is acceptable. However, PROC MULTTEST was written specifically for the purpose of doing multiple inferences, and therefore, the syntax can be much simpler than that of PROC GLM and PROC MIXED, particularly for applications where the %Contrasts, %Estimates, and %SimTests macros are required.

While there is considerable overlap between the analyses of preceding chapters and those of PROC MULTTEST, there are also major differences. Besides the differences in syntax, PROC MULTTEST has the following additional capabilities:

- It allows the normality assumption to be relaxed using either bootstrap or permutation resampling. In fact, some researchers prefer permutation tests to the usual t and F tests regardless of the distribution of the data (Ludbrook and Dudley, 1998). While our position is not as extreme on this issue, we do recognize that such methods are important tools for practical statisticians.

- It has extensive capabilities for handling binary data, including multiple tests using Fisher exact tests, Cochran-Armitage linear trend tests, and Freeman-Tukey transformed tests. With sparse binary data, you can greatly improve the power of the tests by properly incorporating the discreteness of the distributions (more on this in Chapter 12).

A little history concerning PROC MULTTEST will help to explain how it came into being, and why its syntax looks as it does. Its development began in 1988 when a consortium of pharmaceutical companies funded the effort through a grant between the Pharmaceutical Manufacturer's Association (PMA) and Texas Tech University (TTU). From this project came PROC MBIN, a precursor to PROC MULTTEST, whose initial focus was to analyze binary data with particular emphasis on the analysis of animal carcinogenicity experiments. In 1989 the grant was extended to allow continuous responses following the same structure used by PROC MBIN, and the resulting procedure was dubbed PROC MTEST. In 1990 the software was unveiled at the 1990 SAS User Group International Conference in Nashville, Tennessee, and its capabilities were reported in the conference *Proceedings* (Westfall, Lin, and Young, 1990). An important and useful feature of PROC MTEST, as reported in those *Proceedings*, was its display of multiplicity-adjusted tests (including step-down and resampling-based) using adjusted *p*-values.

As stipulated in the contract between TTU and PMA, PROC MTEST was given to SAS Institute in 1990. Since SAS products already had a number of options called MTEST, they decided to change the name to PROC MULTTEST. After extensive testing, debugging, and fine-tuning, PROC MULTTEST became a SAS supported procedure in 1992, as of Release 6.07. In 1995, Russ Wolfinger and Peter Westfall made several enhancements to the procedure, notably to improve binary data handling, to add newer and more powerful testing methods (like hoch and fdr), to improve the input and output capabilities, and to make the animal carcinogenicity tests essentially conform with the industry standard method. See Westfall and Wolfinger (1997) for more on these enhancements, especially the binary data handling. These latest improvements have been in place since 1996, as of Release 6.11.

Although originally designed to address a narrow problem of the pharmaceutical industry, the techniques currently available in PROC MULTTEST address a broad range of practical problems.

The resampling methodologies of PROC MULTTEST are described in great detail by Westfall and Young (1993).

11.2   Univariate Means Tests Using PROC MULTTEST

In this section we show how PROC MULTTEST works in the simplest of applications; namely, the one-way ANOVA model (with or without balanced sample sizes). These applications are essentially the same as we discussed in Chapters 3 and 4, except now we allow nonnormal error distributions.

11.2.1   Bootstrap Resampling

PROC MULTTEST offers two options for bootstrap analysis, bootstrap for single-step tests and stepboot for step-down tests. When you use one of these options to compare univariate means, you are implicitly assuming the standard additive model:

$$y_{ij} = \mu_i + \epsilon_{ij}.$$

However, instead of assuming that the ϵ_{ij} come from a normal distribution, you now assume that they come from some unspecified distribution, say G.

Recognizing that proper multiplicity adjustment should account for the character of G, the bootstrap procedure works by *estimating* G as $\hat{G}$ then calculating the multiplicity adjustments using $\hat{G}$ as if it were the true G. This process is similar to replacing the true error variance $\mathbf{V}$ with $\hat{\mathbf{V}}$ in PROC MIXED. Of course, this approach is inexact in either PROC MIXED or PROC MULTTEST, but you can expect the errors to diminish as sample sizes increase in either case.

We have seen that adjusted p-values can be calculated as $\tilde{p}_j = P(\max_i |T_i| \geq |t_j|)$. In many cases, this is equivalent to $\tilde{p}_j = P(\min_i P_i \leq p_j)$. For example, the adjusted p-values for Tukey's pairwise comparisons can be calculated using either method, since the p-value is a monotonic function of the absolute value of the test statistic. PROC MULTTEST uses the $\min P_i$ formulation because in cases where there are differing degrees of freedom for the tests, the two approaches are not equivalent. The $\min P_i$ approach provides a more balanced multiplicity adjustment in this case (Westfall and Young, p. 50–51). In addition, the $\min P_i$ approach is more natural for the binary data applications in Chapter 12.

How do you estimate G? A simple approach is to compute the sample residuals $\hat{\epsilon}_{ij} = y_{ij} - \hat{\mu}_i = y_{ij} - \bar{y}_{i.}$, and let $\hat{G}$ be the empirical distribution function of the pooled sample residuals. Bootstrap sampling refers to generating data from such a $\hat{G}$. In this example, a simple way to generate data from $\hat{G}$ is to sample the pooled collection of residuals *with replacement*. Such a sample is thus called a *bootstrap sample*.

PROC MULTTEST estimates the adjusted p-values $\tilde{p}_j = P(\min_i P_i \leq p_j \,|\, \hat{G})$ as follows:

- Generate bootstrap data y_{ij}^* by resampling *with replacement* from the pooled sample residuals. (Note that a sample residual from group i can easily wind up in a different group in the bootstrap sample.)

- Compute the p-values $p_1^*, \ldots, p_k^*$ from the bootstrap sample. (This might be all pairwise p-values, or p-values from more general contrasts.)

- Repeat this process `nsamp` times. The single-step adjusted p-value for test i is the proportion of samples for which $\min p_j^* \leq p_i$.

- If step-down tests are requested, then PROC MULTTEST uses minima over appropriately restricted subsets.

It can be shown that this method is identical to the ADJUST=SIMULATE option in the LSMEANS statement, except that for LSMEANS the data y_{ij}^* are sampled from a normal distribution rather than from $\hat{G}$, the empirical distribution of the residuals. For more detailed algorithms, consult Westfall and Young (1993).

In Program 11.1, we compare the PROC MULTTEST bootstrap analysis to the PROC GLM analysis of the weight loss data discussed in Chapter 3.

PROGRAM 11.1   Bootstrap Multiple Comparisons of Means in the ANOVA

```
proc multtest data=wloss bootstrap seed=121211 n=50000;
   class diet;
   test mean(wloss);
   contrast "A-B"  1 -1  0  0  0 ;
   contrast "A-C"  1  0 -1  0  0 ;
   contrast "A-D"  1  0  0 -1  0 ;
   contrast "A-E"  1  0  0  0 -1 ;
   contrast "B-C"  0  1 -1  0  0 ;
   contrast "B-D"  0  1  0 -1  0 ;
   contrast "B-E"  0  1  0  0 -1 ;
   contrast "C-D"  0  0  1 -1  0 ;
   contrast "C-E"  0  0  1  0 -1 ;
   contrast "D-E"  0  0  0  1 -1 ;
   ods select continuous pValues;
run;
```

Output for Program 11.1

```
                    Continuous Variable Tabulations


                                                      Standard
     Variable     diet    NumObs          Mean       Deviation

     wloss        A         10          12.0500       0.8290
     wloss        B         10          11.0200       1.1213
     wloss        C         10          10.2700       1.0264
     wloss        D         10           9.2700       1.1586
     wloss        E         10          12.1700       0.7917



                            p-Values


         Variable     Contrast        Raw      Bootstrap

         wloss        A-B           0.0255      0.1598
         wloss        A-C           0.0002      0.0019
         wloss        A-D          <.0001      <.0001
         wloss        A-E           0.7890      0.9989
         wloss        B-C           0.0994      0.4565
         wloss        B-D           0.0003      0.0024
         wloss        B-E           0.0132      0.0909
         wloss        C-D           0.0298      0.1834
         wloss        C-E           0.0001      0.0009
         wloss        D-E          <.0001      <.0001
```

The `raw` p-values are the ordinary p-values obtained from the t-distribution, which in this case has $df = 5(10 - 1) = 45$. Under the `Bootstrap` column are the multiplicity-adjusted p-values obtained from the bootstrap resampling of the residuals. Note that these adjusted p-values agree very well with those obtained using the normality assumption, as shown in the output from Program 3.5 in Section 3.3.3. We conclude that possible non-normality affects the simultaneous inferences little, if any.

You can get more powerful tests using PROC MULTTEST by using step-down tests. Just specify `stepboot` instead of `bootstrap` in the PROC MULTTEST statement and you get the following:

Output Using Stepdown Bootstrap Tests (the STEPBOOT Option)

```
                            p-Values


                                              Stepdown
         Variable     Contrast        Raw     Bootstrap

         wloss        A-B           0.0255      0.0882
         wloss        A-C           0.0002      0.0015
         wloss        A-D          <.0001      <.0001
         wloss        A-E           0.7890      0.7901
         wloss        B-C           0.0994      0.1897
         wloss        B-D           0.0003      0.0016
         wloss        B-E           0.0132      0.0554
         wloss        C-D           0.0298      0.0882
         wloss        C-E           0.0001      0.0007
         wloss        D-E          <.0001      <.0001
```

Note that these are uniformly smaller, and therefore, more desirable than the simple bootstrap *p*-values. These adjusted *p*-values are equivalent to the `type=FREE` default *p*-values of the `%SimTests` macro, except they use bootstrap sampling rather than sampling from the normal distribution. There is no option to incorporate logical constraints in PROC MULTTEST, as in the `type=LOGICAL` specification of `%SimTests`.

Marginal Bootstrap Tests

You can get PROC MULTTEST to perform bootstrap tests of hypotheses, without multiplicity adjustment, simply by specifying a single test. In Program 11.2 we do this for the B–E comparison in the weight loss data set.

PROGRAM 11.2   **Bootstrap Two-Sample *t*-Test Using PROC MULTTEST**

```
data wlossBE;
   set wloss;
   if diet="B" or diet="E"; run;

proc multtest data=wlossBE bootstrap n=100000;
   class diet;
   test(mean);
   contrast "B-E" 1 -1;
run;
```

Output from Program 11.2

		p-Values	
Variable	Contrast	Raw	Bootstrap
wloss	B-E	0.0163	0.0146

The `Raw` *p*-value here, 0.0163, differs from that in the Output from Program 11.1 since

- the denominator variance is pooled over only two groups, not all five
- the degrees of freedom are only 18 instead of 45.

The `Bootstrap` *p*-value (0.0146) is from the bootstrap test. Since it is so close to the normality-assuming *p*-value (0.0163), we again conclude that nonnormality is not a concern when using tests with these data.

11.2.2   Permutation Resampling

When treatments are assigned to experimental units at random, and when the units themselves are not randomly selected from a larger population, some would argue that the only probability mechanism that you can appeal to is the random assignment of the treatments to the units. In this case, permutation methods are the only legitimate form of inference (Ludbrook and Dudley, 1998). They seek to answer inferential questions by calculating what would have occurred in other randomizations, and by comparing the data that was actually observed to what would have occurred. This idea traces back to Fisher (1936).

In the two-sample comparison with a single hypothesis test, it works like this: you assign n_1 units at random to group 1 and n_2 units to group 2, perform the experiment, and observe data $y_{11}, \ldots, y_{1n_1}, y_{21}, \ldots, y_{2n_2}$. Since you are interested in comparing the groups, you wonder whether the statistic $\bar{y}_1 - \bar{y}_2$ is extreme, in some sense. If there really were no difference between groups 1 and 2, then the observed value of $\bar{y}_1 - \bar{y}_2$ should be typical when considered against the values of $\bar{y}_1^* - \bar{y}_2^*$ that are obtained by randomly assigning the observed data to the two groups, that is, randomly permuting (or "shuffling") the $n_1 + n_2$ data values, then computing $\bar{y}_1^*$ from the first n_1 permuted values and $\bar{y}_2^*$ from the last n_2 permuted values. A permutational p-value then can be computed as $p = P(\bar{Y}_1^* - \bar{Y}_2^* \geq \bar{y}_1 - \bar{y}_2)$ (assuming the uppertail is of interest, and with appropriate modifications for lower and two-tailed tests).

Of course, you can use other statistics as well. Instead of comparing $\bar{y}_1$ with $\bar{y}_2$, you might compare the average group ranks, $\bar{r}_1$ and $\bar{r}_2$. The permutational p-value can be computed permuting the ranks rather than the raw data. This method gives the p-value for Wilcoxon-Mann-Whitney Rank Sum test, $p = P(\bar{R}_1^* - \bar{R}_2^* \geq \bar{r}_1 - \bar{r}_2)$.

Program 11.3 shows how to use PROC MULTTEST to compute permutation tests, again using the B–E comparison in the weight loss data.

PROGRAM 11.3   Two-Sample Permutation Test and Rank Test Using PROC MULTTEST

```
proc multtest data=wlossBE permutation;
   title "Permutation Test using Raw Data";
   class diet;
   test mean(wloss);
   contrast "B-E" 1 -1;
   ods select continuous pValues;
run;

proc rank data=wlossBE;
   var wloss;
   ranks wlossranks;
run;

proc multtest data=wlossBE permutation;
   title "Permutation Test using Ranks";
   class diet;
   test mean(wlossranks);
   contrast "B-E" 1 -1;
   ods select continuous pValues;
run;
```

Output from Program 11.3

```
                         Permutation Test using Raw Data

                         Continuous Variable Tabulations

                                                           Standard
            Variable    diet    NumObs        Mean         Deviation

            wloss        B        10        11.0200         1.1213
            wloss        E        10        12.1700         0.7917


                                    p-Values

            Variable    Contrast           Raw      Permutation

            wloss        B-E             0.0163        0.0167
```

Permutation Test using Ranks

Continuous Variable Tabulations

Variable	diet	NumObs	Mean	Standard Deviation
wlossranks	B	10	6.9500	5.2623
wlossranks	E	10	14.0500	4.2325

p-Values

Variable	Contrast	Raw	Permutation
wlossranks	B-E	0.0038	0.0053

Note that the permutational p-value on the raw data, 0.0167, is quite similar to the bootstrap p-value 0.0146. This occurs because the permutation and bootstrap methods are quite similar, with the only these differences:

- Permutation tests use resampling *without replacement*, whereas bootstrap tests use resampling *with replacement*.
- With permutation tests, the underlying theory suggests that you should resample the raw data values. With bootstrap tests, the theory suggests that you should resample the centered data values (that is, the residuals). These are in fact the defaults of PROC MULTTEST, but you can override them using the CENTER and NOCENTER options.

On the other hand, the rank test gives different results since it is a fundamentally different approach. While the bootstrap and permutation tests on the raw data are testing equality of means, the rank test is essentially testing equality of average ranks, which relate more to medians than means. Note that the Raw p-value 0.0038 from the rank analysis is the approximate p-value for the rank test using the t-distribution approximation to the standardized difference of rank averages (the RANK TRANSFORM method of Conover and Iman, 1981), whereas the Permutation value 0.0053 is an estimate of the true permutational p-value obtained by sampling 100000 random permutations.

The permutational method can be extended to simultaneous inferences as well. If you have multiple groups, you can permute the data as described above, but into the multiple groups instead of just two, then recompute the test statistics. Adjusted p-values are calculated as $\tilde{p}_j = P(\min P_i^* \le p_j)$, where the P_i^* are computed from the rerandomized data. Program 11.4 shows how to do this using PROC MULTTEST.

PROGRAM 11.4   Pairwise Comparisons Using the Global Permutation Distribution

```
proc multtest data=wloss permutation seed=121211 n=50000;
   class diet;
   test mean(wloss);
   contrast "A-B"  1 -1  0  0  0 ;
   contrast "A-C"  1  0 -1  0  0 ;
   contrast "A-D"  1  0  0 -1  0 ;
   contrast "A-E"  1  0  0  0 -1 ;
   contrast "B-C"  0  1 -1  0  0 ;
   contrast "B-D"  0  1  0 -1  0 ;
   contrast "B-E"  0  1  0  0 -1 ;
```

```
    contrast "C-D"  0  0  1 -1  0 ;
    contrast "C-E"  0  0  1  0 -1 ;
    contrast "D-E"  0  0  0  1 -1 ;
    ods select pValues;
run;
```

**Output from
Program 11.4**

p-Values

Variable	Contrast	Raw	Permutation
wloss	A-B	0.0255	0.1597
wloss	A-C	0.0002	0.0023
wloss	A-D	<.0001	<.0001
wloss	A-E	0.7890	0.9987
wloss	B-C	0.0994	0.4518
wloss	B-D	0.0003	0.0029
wloss	B-E	0.0132	0.0925
wloss	C-D	0.0298	0.1829
wloss	C-E	0.0001	0.0011
wloss	D-E	<.0001	<.0001

Note that the multiplicity-adjusted *p*-values obtained using the permutation method are virtually identical to those obtained using bootstrapping, as shown in the output from Program 11.1. Again, the differences between the calculations are minor (with replacement versus without replacement and centering versus not centering); the major difference concerns inferential philosophy rather than actual results.

11.2.3   A Caveat: The Subset Pivotality Condition, Heteroscedasticity and Excess Type I Errors

As noted by Petrondas and Gabriel (1983), the permutational method shown in Program 11.4 is, strictly speaking, not valid for simultaneous inference. The problem occurs because you are using the global permutation distribution to make inferences concerning individual pairs. In some cases, the global permutation distribution can be inappropriate for judging individual pairs, leading to "excess Type I errors," or uncontrolled FWE.

Experience shows that this issue is most likely to arise in cases of extreme heteroscedasticity and unbalanced sample sizes. Westfall and Young (1993) show that the method of re-sampling the global null distribution is valid when the statistics satisfy the subset pivotality condition; and examples of cases where the condition either is satisfied or is not satisfied are given throughout their book. The analysis of pairwise comparisons by rerandomization is a case where the condition does not hold.

Westfall and Young (1993, p. 42) give the following definition of subset pivotality:

The distribution of the vector of *p*-values **P** has the *subset pivotality* property if the joint distribution of the subvector $\{P_i; \ i \in K\}$ is identical under the restrictions $\cap_{i \in K} H_{0i}$ and the global null H_0, for all subsets $K = \{i_1, \ldots, i_j\}$ of true null hypotheses.

In the bootstrap testing case, the subset pivotality condition holds for location shift data, which implies homoscedasticity. If you perform multiplicity adjustments using simple bootstrap sampling in cases of extreme heteroscedasticity, you will get incorrect results, just as if you perform multiplicity adjustments using permutation resampling. To correct for the heteroscedasticity problem using bootstrap resampling; see Westfall and Young, p. 88–91.

Of course, ordinary (not resampling-based) multiplicity adjustments also fail in cases of extreme heteroscedasticity. If you are comfortable with the normality assumption and the other approximations of PROC MIXED, then you can always perform multiplicity adjustments for the heteroscedastic case as shown in Chapter 10.

These issues can become even more problematic when testing binary data, as we will see in Chapter 12.

11.2.4   Incorporating Covariates with PROC MULTTEST

Because PROC MULTTEST was originally designed to handle tests for animal carcinogenicity, it is somewhat limited in the scope of models that it allows you to fit. Only one CLASS variable is allowed, and covariates are not allowed directly. However, you can introduce covariate information with the STRATA variable. The resulting analyses are combined over levels of the STRATA variable, and multiplicity adjustments are performed by resampling independently within STRATA levels. Further information concerning stratification is given in SAS Institute Inc. (1989), and we will discuss the STRATA statement in more detail in Chapter 12 when we discuss tests using binary data.

11.3   Testing Means from Multivariate Data Using PROC MULTTEST

PROC MULTTEST was designed specifically for the analysis of multivariate data, and the syntax for performing multivariate tests is very straightforward. The resampling methods used in the case of multivariate continuous data are identical to those used for univariate continuous data, except that the data *vectors* are resampled, rather than the individual values. By doing so, you incorporate the correlations between the multivariate observations automatically.

11.3.1   Bootstrap and Permutation Resampling

Return to the "multiple endpoints" example in Chapter 10, Program 10.9, Section 10.5.1. You can perform the given analysis somewhat more easily than shown in Program 10.9 using PROC MULTTEST, as shown below in Program 11.5. Note that the PROC MULTTEST requires the multivariate input data format, as opposed to the single Y column format used by PROC MIXED.

PROGRAM 11.5   Testing Multiple Endpoints in Clinical Trials Using PROC MULTTEST

```
proc multtest data=multiple_endp_mv stepboot n=100000 seed=121211;
   class tx;
   test mean(y1-y4);
   contrast "t vs c" -1 1;
run;
```

Output from Program 11.5

```
                    Continuous Variable Tabulations

                                                   Standard
        Variable    tx    NumObs         Mean      Deviation

        y1          0       54         3.2222       1.4623
        y1          1       57         2.5439       1.3372
        y2          0       54         2.4444       4.3683
        y2          1       57         0.9298       1.3740
        y3          0       54         2.7778       1.6673
        y3          1       57         2.4035       1.3740
        y4          0       54         6.7407       1.6390
        y4          1       57         7.4912       1.6810


                              p-Values

                                                  Stepdown
        Variable    Contrast          Raw         Bootstrap

        y1          t vs c          0.0121         0.0379
        y2          t vs c          0.0142         0.0379
        y3          t vs c          0.1986         0.1991
        y4          t vs c          0.0191         0.0379
```

Note that the unadjusted *p*-values are identical to those shown in the output from Program 10.9. Despite the rather serious nonnormality of these data, the conclusions regarding the multiple endpoints do not seem to change much from the normality-assuming Program 10.9 to the nonnormality-allowing bootstrap method. However, the code for the analysis using PROC MULTTEST is substantially simpler.

Another interesting point concerns the least significant y3 variable. In the output from Program 10.9, the step-down multiplicity adjusted *p*-value is identical to the unadjusted *p*-value, since at this point in the step-down procedure, we consider only that test (and not the minimum *p* over two or more tests). However, in the output from Program 11.5 the raw and adjusted *p*-values differ, since PROC MULTTEST calculates $P(P_3^* \leq 0.1986)$ at this step using the bootstrap resampled data. Thus, the value 0.1991 is in fact the *bootstrap* unadjusted *p*-value for the third variable.

If you prefer the permutation resampling framework, then you can replace `stepboot` in the PROC MULTTEST step in Program 11.5 with `stepperm`, obtaining the following:

Permutational Step-Down Tests for Multiple Endpoints

```
                              p-Values

                                                  Stepdown
        Variable    Contrast          Raw         Permutation

        y1          t vs c          0.0121         0.0363
        y2          t vs c          0.0142         0.0363
        y3          t vs c          0.1986         0.2166
        y4          t vs c          0.0191         0.0363
```

Again, the bootstrap and permutation resampling approaches are virtually identical, and the choice of method depends largely on personal philosophy. More discussion of bootstrap versus permutation sampling is given by Westfall and Young, pp. 169–177.

11.3.2   Multiple Endpoints and the Subset Pivotality Condition

The issue concerning possibly invalid inferences occurs when you have multiple comparisons among the treatment means, but not when you have multiple tests involving the variables, one per variable (Westfall and Young, p. 115). Examples of such applications include treatment versus control comparisons, one per variable, and trend tests involving ordered dose groups, again assuming one per variable. In these cases the subset pivotality assumption is valid, and inferences using PROC MULTTEST with permutation tests can be considered valid (at least asymptotically). Thus, PROC MULTTEST is ideally suited for analyzing clinical trials data with multiple endpoints.

In addition, as we have indicated previously, the bootstrap inferences under location shift models also are asymptotically valid, even with multiple comparisons per variable. Closeness of the permutation-based multiplicity adjustments and the bootstrap-based multiplicity adjustments suggests that the permutation approach also is reasonably valid (though not strictly so) in this case. The problems occur with both approaches when you have multiple comparisons per variable and extreme heteroscedasticity between treatment groups for a given variable.

11.3.3   Missing Value Handling

Like PROC MIXED, PROC MULTTEST allows missing data for its multivariate analyses. Both procedures use all data and do not delete multivariate observations where a single variable has a missing value. With PROC MULTTEST, the degrees of freedom for individual tests are adjusted to account for the missing values so that different tests can have different degrees of freedom. Also, the missing values remain in the vectors when they are resampled, so the resampled data sets also will contain missing values, and the degrees of freedom for the individual tests in the resampled data sets become random variables, as they will vary from simulation to simulation.

11.4   Inferences for Multiple Contrasts and Multiple Variables Simultaneously

In this final section, we give a more complex example to show more of the scope and capability of PROC MULTTEST. We return to the respiratory drug example from Chapter 9, Section 9.3.2 and define an additional endpoint that contrasts the weighted average response variable used previously with the initial health variable. Further, we

- test for treatment effect separately in "younger" and "older" patients, in addition to performing an overall test
- use upper-tail tests for all
- perform step-down multiplicity adjustments using bootstrap resampling with 100000 samples.

Program 11.6 shows how to do all of this.

PROGRAM 11.6   Inferences over Multiple Variables and Subgroup Contrasts

```
data respiratory1;
   set respiratory;
   treat_x_age=compress(Treatment||'_'||AgeGroup,' ');
   score_control = score-r0;
run;
proc sort data=respiratory1 out=respiratory2;
   by treat_x_age; run;
proc multtest data=respiratory2 stepboot n=100000 seed=121211;
   class treat_x_age;
   test mean(score score_control/upper);
   contrast "Active-Placebo"        1  1 -1 -1 ;
   contrast "Active-Placebo, Old"   1  0 -1  0 ;
   contrast "Active-Placebo, Young" 0  1  0 -1 ;
run;
```

Note that you can get PROC MULTTEST to analyze two factors, but you have to create a single factor that contains all combination levels of the multiple factors, as shown with the treat_x_age variable.

Output from Program 11.6

		p-Values	
			Stepdown
Variable	Contrast	Raw	Bootstrap
Score	Active-Placebo	0.0008	0.0029
Score	Active-Placebo, Old	0.0002	0.0012
Score	Active-Placebo, Young	0.1539	0.1549
score_control	Active-Placebo	0.0006	0.0026
score_control	Active-Placebo, Old	0.0027	0.0081
score_control	Active-Placebo, Young	0.0282	0.0509

Output from 11.6 shows all significant improvements for all placebo versus control comparisons, except in the case of younger patients. Assuming normality, you can get the same analysis using PROC MIXED in conjunction with the %Estimates, %Contrasts, and %SimTests macros, but the code would be considerably more complicated.

11.5   Concluding Remarks

PROC MULTTEST allows you to perform multiple inferences for means in much the same way as we have seen in previous chapters. The advantages of PROC MULTTEST over previously discussed analyses are as follows:

- It allows you to incorporate possibly nonnormal distributions into the inferences, either by bootstrap or permutation resampling.
- The syntax can be much simpler than other methods for one-way designs, particularly when you have multivariate observations and multiple comparisons among them.
- It has very good capabilities for multiple tests with multivariate binary data (see Chapter 12).

On the other hand, the procedures developed in previous sections have great flexibility that is not available in PROC MULTTEST. Here are some types of multiple comparisons analysis that you can perform with PROC GLM, PROC MIXED, and the %Sim* macros that are *not* available in PROC MULTTEST:

- continuous covariate adjustment
- logical restrictions
- LS-Means
- single-sample multivariate comparisons (for example, the "dog" example in Chapter 10)
- normality-assuming multiplicity adjustments
- simultaneous confidence intervals.

Despite these limitations, we think PROC MULTTEST is an important component of the multiplicity adjustment software arsenal. It is very simple to use for a wide variety of problems of interest, including multiple endpoints in clinical trials, provides randomization tests, and provides a simple way to assess the effects of nonnormality on your multiple inferences. But perhaps the best feature of PROC MULTTEST is its handling of binary data, which we describe in Chapter 12.

Multiple Comparisons with Binary Data Using PROC MULTTEST

12.1 Introduction

If you have been following the examples of the preceding chapters carefully, you probably have noticed that proper multiplicity adjustments that account for correlations are not much different from simple Bonferroni adjustments. To be sure, the adjusted *p*-values *are* somewhat smaller when you incorporate correlations, and you should *definitely* incorporate correlation structures whenever possible in your multiple tests; but in most cases, the improvement is not dramatically better than Bonferroni.

With discrete distributions, however, incorporating correlations *does* lead to dramatic differences from the Bonferroni method. When you use the right multiplicity adjustment, the adjusted *p*-values might be *one-tenth* the size of the Bonferroni-adjusted *p*-values!

How can you get such improvements? The method for calculating adjusted *p*-values in the binary case is identical to that for the continuous case, namely adjusted *p*-values are $\tilde{p}_j = P(\min_i P_i^* \le p_j)$. But with binary data (and more generally, with discrete data in general), you often have many *p*-values P_i whose distributions do not even allow a small p_j. In such a case, that variable is effectively (and automatically) dropped from the calculation of $\tilde{p}_j$, thereby reducing the multiplier.

Another way that discreteness comes into play in the calculation of the $\tilde{p}_j$ is in the fact that the value p_j often is not attained in the distribution of P_i. In such a case, test H_i has less effect on the multiplicity adjustment of p_j than is assumed by the usual Bonferroni method. When such effects are accumulated over all tests, the savings can be enormous.

More technical details concerning multiple testing with binary data are found in Westfall and Young (1993, pp. 146–183) and Westfall and Wolfinger (1997).

12.2 Multivariate Two-Sample Binary Outcomes

We start with the analysis of two samples with binary outcomes because, as described in Chapter 11, it is a case where the subset pivotality condition holds, and where the global resampling method is most appropriate. As an example, we consider a common application in clinical trials, namely, determining adverse events associated with a new compound. The following discussion follows Hochberg and Westfall (1999).

EXAMPLE: Adverse Events in Clinical Trials

New drugs must be tested on human subjects for evidence of safety and efficacy. The data arising from safety studies typically have a multivariate binary form, that is, a 0/1 indicator for each of several adverse events, also called side effects. There are typically very many adverse events that might occur, and if all such events are tested without adjusting for multiplicity, false positive determinations are likely. This is just to say that while drugs often do have side effects, statistical determinations based on the simple $p \leq .05$ rule can incorrectly flag side effects too often.

As with any screening procedure, there are errors and costs. A Type I error in the analysis of adverse events implies making a claim that a drug causes some problem, say, headache for example, when the drug has no such effect in reality. The costs of such Type I errors include delayed approval of a drug, and possibly even cancelation of development of a good drug in the case of a serious adverse event, with costs both to the drug company and the consumer. A Type I error can also be very costly if a competitor makes an essentially equivalent drug, and finds (correctly) that there is no adverse event of the given type. In this case, doctors are more likely to prescribe the "clean" drug, resulting in lost revenue for the first company to market the drug.

On the other hand, Type II errors are also very serious, as they may cause undue suffering for the public and possibly lawsuits for the drug company. Because of the concern for Type II errors, some have advocated de-emphasizing the multiplicity problem, even analyzing all sites individually at the unadjusted $\alpha = 0.10$ level (Edwards et al., 1990, p. 144).

Our view is that, because Type I errors can and do occur, the data analysis should acknowledge this fact in some direct fashion. The discrete multiplicity adjustment method of PROC MULTTEST provides a simple, valid, and powerful method for handling the multiplicity problem. It is certainly reasonable to provide multiplicity-adjusted p-values, side-by-side with unadjusted p-values, to assess the extent of the multiplicity problem for any adverse events study.

12.2.1   Resampling-based Multiplicity Adjustment

The following adverse events data are from a real clinical trial, and Program 12.1 shows the recommended PROC MULTTEST analysis.

PROGRAM 12.1   Multiple Two-Sample Binary Data Tests

```
data Adverse; keep Group AE1-AE28;
   array AE{28};
   length Group $ 9;

   input Group nTotal nNone;
   do i = 1 to dim(AE); AE{i} = 0; end;
   do iobs = 1 to nNone; output; end;
   do iobs = 1 to nTotal-nNone;
      input nAE @@;
      do i = 1 to dim(AE); AE{i} = 0; end;
      do i = 1 to nAE; input iAE @@; AE{iAE} = 1; end;
      output;
      end;
   datalines;
```

```
Control   80 46
4 2 3 17 28    2 18 28      2 2 28       3 4 22 28
3 1 3 28       2 1 28       4 2 3 11 28  2 2 28
3 12 27 28     2 1 28       3 2 19 28    3 1 9 28
2 14 28        2 7 28       2 4 28       2 4 28
2 2 28         2 3 28       4 1 4 9 28   3 1 26 28
2 1 28         3 5 12 28    2 2 28       2 4 28
3 5 13 28      2 16 28      2 9 28       3 1 2 28
2 24 28        2 2 28       2 7 28       2 7 28
2 25 28        5 3 14 19 21 28
Treatment 80 44
2 23 28        2 1 28       3 1 4 28     2 2 28
2 1 28         4 1 3 6 28   4 1 5 8 28   3 1 21 28
3 1 10 28      3 3 8 28     5 1 2 3 10 28 3 2 15 28
2 1 28         3 2 6 28     4 1 5 9 28   3 1 5 28
3 1 15 28      2 7 28       2 7 28       3 1 8 28
3 1 6 28       3 1 3 28     3 1 6 28     3 2 8 28
3 1 4 28       3 1 2 28     3 1 20 28    3 1 4 28
3 1 2 28       2 1 28       4 1 5 16 28  3 2 8 28
2 1 28         4 1 4 5 28   2 3 28       2 3 28
;

proc multtest data=Adverse stepperm seed=121211;
   class Group;
   test fisher(AE1-AE28/upper);
   contrast ''Treatment-Control'' -1 1;
   ods output Discrete=Discrete;
   ods output pValues=pValues;
run;

proc sort data=Discrete out=Discrete; by Variable;
proc sort data=pValues  out=pValues ; by Variable;
data both; merge Discrete pValues;    by Variable;
   run;

proc sort data=both out=both;
   by Raw;
data best5; set both; if _n_<=10;
   run;

proc print noobs data=best5;
   title ''Counts and Percentages for the Most Significant AEs'';
   var Variable Group count NumObs Percent;
run;

proc print noobs
   data=best5(where =(Group            ='Control')
              rename=(Raw               =RawPValue
                     StepdownPermutation=AdjustedPValue));
   title ''Fisher Exact (Raw) and Multivariate Permutation-Adjusted p-Values'';
   var Variable RawPValue AdjustedPValue;
run;
```

Output from Program 12.1

```
                 Counts and Percentages for the Most Significant AEs

        Variable      Group       Count    NumObs    Percent

          AE1        Control         8        80      10.00
          AE1        Treatment      25        80      31.25
          AE8        Control         0        80       0.00
          AE8        Treatment       5        80       6.25
          AE6        Control         0        80       0.00
          AE6        Treatment       4        80       5.00
          AE5        Control         2        80       2.50
          AE5        Treatment       5        80       6.25
          AE10       Control         0        80       0.00
          AE10       Treatment       2        80       2.50


      Fisher Exact (Raw) and Multivariate Permutation-Adjusted p-Values

                                  Raw        Adjusted
                    Variable     PValue       PValue

                      AE1        0.0008       0.0018
                      AE8        0.0293       0.1317
                      AE6        0.0601       0.2560
                      AE5        0.2213       0.6253
                      AE10       0.2484       0.9279
```

Note that we have printed only the results from the five most significant tests. There are actually a total of $k = 28$ tests, not five.

Conclusions from the study are that the adverse outcome AE1 has a higher treatment incidence than control, and no other effects are statistically significant when the family of $k = 28$ tests is considered.

The adjusted p-values are obtained by resampling (permuting) the 160 binary data vectors, taking the first 80 for the resampled "control" data, and the last 80 for the resampled "treatment" data. Then the 28 p-values are recomputed from the resampled data set, the process is repeated 20000 times (the default), and the step-down adjusted p-values are computed using the min P^* statistics.

By resampling vectors, the correlation among binary outcomes is incorporated. Noting that AE28 is in fact a binary indicator of whether the patient suffered *any* side effect (in SAS code, AE28 = (sum(of AE1-AE27) >0)), there is certainly some correlation between this adverse event and the others.

As an aside, note that the combined AE28 variable appears nowhere in the list of significant results, adjusted or unadjusted. This observation contradicts the common assumption that omnibus-type tests are more sensitive than multiplicity-adjusted component tests. In fact, unadjusted omnibus tests will be less powerful than multiplicity-adjusted component tests when there is a dominant signal for one component, with all other components effectively "noise," as appears to be the case here. In such a case, the dominant signal can be swamped by the noise of the other components, when the omnibus test is used. Multiplicity-adjusted component tests, on the other hand, allow the signal to be seen clearly.

While the resampling method of PROC MULTTEST does incorporate correlations, the fantastic gains over the Bonferroni method come from incorporating discreteness, not from incorporating correlations. The major point concerning discrete tests is illustrated well in the above output. For the most significant test AE1, the adjusted p-value is only $.0018/.0008 = 2.25$ times the unadjusted p-value. Contrasting this figure with the Bonferroni multiplier of $k = 28$ for this most significant test, which yields an adjusted p-value of $28 \times .0008 = .0224$, you see how great the improvement can be. You see also that the degree of improvement depends on the size of the raw p-value. For the remaining four tests, the implied Bonferroni multipliers are 4.5, 4.3, 2.8, and 3.7, respectively; contrasting these values with the corresponding step-down Bonferroni multipliers 27, 26, 25, and 24, you see again the enormous improvement.

The FISHER option produces the Fisher exact test for comparing binary data in two samples. This test is a permutation test, as described in the previous chapter. Because the data have the simple 0/1 structure, the raw p-values are computed exactly from the hypergeometric distribution, and do not require simulation.

The Cochran-Armitage linear trend test (hereafter abbreviated ca, its PROC MULTTEST representation) is a generalization of the Fisher exact test. It uses a statistic $T = \sum_{i=1}^{g} c_i X_i$, where the X_i are the observed counts in the treatment groups, and where the c_i are constants that you specify. PROC MULTTEST computes exact (raw) permutation p-values for ca tests, as well as for Fisher exact tests.

When you have only two groups, the ca test and the Fisher test coincide, so you can use either one in PROC MULTTEST. However, you can output the permutation distributions using ca tests, but not with the Fisher test. Program 12.2 shows how to use the ca tests, and outputs the permutation distribution of the test for AE6.

PROGRAM 12.2   **Multiple Cochran-Armitage Permutation Tests with Permutation Distribution Output**

```
proc multtest data=Adverse outperm=permdists;
   class Group;
   test ca(AE1-AE28/upper permutation=100);
   contrast ''Treatment-Control'' -1 1;
   ods output pValues=pValues;
run;

proc sort data=pValues out=pValues;
   by Raw;
proc print noobs data=pValues(obs=5 rename=(Raw = ExactCAPValue));
   title ''Exact Permutation pValues for CA Tests'';
run;

proc print noobs data=permdists;
   where (_var_=''AE6'');
   title ''Permutation Distribution of CA test for AE6'';
run;
```

Output from Program 12.2

Exact Permutation pValues for CA Tests

Variable	Contrast	Exact CAPValue
AE1	Treatment-Control	0.0008
AE8	Treatment-Control	0.0293
AE6	Treatment-Control	0.0601
AE5	Treatment-Control	0.2213
AE10	Treatment-Control	0.2484

```
          Permutation Distribution of CA test for AE6

          _contrast_        _var_    _value_     upper_p

        Treatment-Control     AE6        -4       1.00000
        Treatment-Control     AE6        -2       0.93985
        Treatment-Control     AE6         0       0.68988
        Treatment-Control     AE6         2       0.31012
        Treatment-Control     AE6         4       0.06015
```

Note that the `ca` *p*-values are identical to the Fisher exact *p*-values. You must specify `permutation=` to make this correspondence, otherwise PROC MULTTEST computes the asymptotic *z*-score approximation to the distribution. The value of `permutation=` must be as large as the largest total number of within-variable outcomes to have all *p*-values be computed exactly. If the `permutation=` value is smaller than a particular within-variable total, then PROC MULTTEST uses the asymptotic *z*-score approximation for that variable.

You can see from the permutation distribution that an upper-tailed *p*-value of .0008 is impossible for the AE6 test; therefore, this variable does not at all contribute to the multiplicity adjustment for AE1. PROC MULTTEST automatically makes this adjustment for you; you do not need to think about dropping variables manually because of low total occurrences.

12.2.2 Multiplicity Adjustments Ignoring Correlations

You can also use PROC MULTTEST to perform multiplicity adjustments without resampling, improving the execution time. The discrete characteristics still are incorporated, and since this is the major component of the discrete variable multiplicity adjustments, you do not lose much by doing so.

Westfall and Wolfinger (1997, equation 4) describe Bonferroni-based multiplicity adjustments that incorporate discrete characteristics of the data. Their method is an improvement of methods published by Tarone (1990) and Hommel and Krummenaur (1998). Use Program 12.3 to perform the Westfall and Wolfinger discrete multiplicity adjustments using the adverse events data.

PROGRAM 12.3   **Discrete Bonferroni-based Multiple Tests Using Binary Data**

```
proc multtest data=Adverse stepbon;
   class Group;
   test ca(AE1-AE28/upper permutation=100);
   contrast ''Treatment-Control'' -1 1;
   ods output pValues=pValues;
run;

proc sort data=pValues out=pValues;
   by Raw;
proc print data=pValues(obs=5 rename=(Raw=ExactCAPValue));
   title ''Exact Raw pValues and Discrete Bonferroni Adjustments'';
   var variable ExactCAPValue StepdownBonferroni;
run;
```

Output from Program 12.3

```
          Exact Raw pValues and Discrete Bonferroni Adjustments

                          Exact       Stepdown
              Variable    CAPValue    Bonferroni

                AE1       0.0008       0.0021
                AE8       0.0293       0.1483
                AE6       0.0601       0.3115
                AE5       0.2213       1.0000
                AE10      0.2484       1.0000
```

Comparing this output with the correlation-incorporating resampling method shown in the output from Program 12.1, we see little difference, demonstrating that the main contributor to the reduction in the effective Bonferroni mutliplier is indeed the use of the discreteness, rather than the incorporation of the correlations. To be sure, the *p*-values are generally larger in the previous output than in the output from Program 12.1, so you would rather incorporate the correlations if you have the time. However, you might prefer to use the discrete Bonferroni method if you find that the resampling-based method takes too long (as it might when your data set is very large).

Finally, you can get a slightly better approximation by using the independence approximation of Šidák, although, for one-sided tests, the independence assumption can be anticonservative, as shown by Westfall and Wolfinger (1997). Simply substitute `stepsid` (short for "step-down Šidák") for `stepbon`, "StepdownSidak" for "StepdownBonferroni," and change the title appropriately in Program 12.3, and you get the following:

Discrete Independence-Based Multiple Tests Using Binary Data

```
            Exact Raw pValues and Discrete Sidak Adjustments

                          Exact       Stepdown
              Variable    CAPValue    Sidak

                AE1       0.0008       0.0021
                AE8       0.0293       0.1394
                AE6       0.0601       0.2732
                AE5       0.2213       0.6730
                AE10      0.2484       0.9533
```

While the resampling-based values shown in the output from Program 12.1 are generally smaller than the step-down Šidák values, you see that the independence approximation provides an even closer fit than the Bonferroni approximation for this example.

12.3   Multiple Pairwise Comparisons with Binary Data

As described in Chapter 11, failure of the subset pivotality condition can invalidate multiple comparisons when using the global permutation distribution. The worst-case scenario appears to be situations where there are extremely unbalanced sample sizes and heteroscedasticity.

The heteroscedasticity problem is more dramatic with binary data than with continuous data, since, when you have binary data, difference in proportions implies difference in variances. You can get very odd, and essentially invalid, results using PROC MULTTEST in some situations because of this problem.

12.3.1   The Good and the Bad of Multiple Pairwise Comparisons: Two Examples

First, we consider a well-behaved example, using data taken from Mantel (1963). In this example, rabbits are given a lethal injection of the streptococci bacillus and are then inoculated with five doses of penicillin. We then compare the death rates for all 10 pairs of penicillin dose comparisons.

PROGRAM 12.4   **All Binary Pairwise Comparisons Using the Global Permutation Distribution: Example 1**

```
data rabbits;
   input died freq Penicillin$ @@;
datalines;
0  0 1/8   1 11 1/8
0  3 1/4   1  9 1/4
0  8 1/2   1  4 1/2
0 11 1     1  1 1
0  7 4     1  0 4
;
proc multtest order=data stepperm;
   class Penicillin;
   freq freq;
   test fisher(died);
   contrast ''1/8 vs 1/4'' -1  1  0  0  0 ;
   contrast ''1/8 vs 1/2'' -1  0  1  0  0 ;
   contrast ''1/8 vs 1''   -1  0  0  1  0 ;
   contrast ''1/8 vs 4''   -1  0  0  0  1 ;
   contrast ''1/4 vs 1/2''  0 -1  1  0  0 ;
   contrast ''1/4 vs 1''    0 -1  0  1  0 ;
   contrast ''1/4 vs 4''    0 -1  0  0  1 ;
   contrast ''1/2 vs 1''    0  0 -1  1  0 ;
   contrast ''1/2 vs 4''    0  0 -1  0  1 ;
   contrast ''1 vs 4''      0  0  0 -1  1 ;
   ods select Discrete pValues;
run;
```

Output from Program 12.4

Discrete Variable Tabulations

Variable	Penicillin	Count	NumObs	Percent
died	1/8	11	11	100.00
died	1/4	9	12	75.00
died	1/2	4	12	33.33
died	1	1	12	8.33
died	4	0	7	0.00

p-Values

Variable	Contrast	Raw	Stepdown Permutation
died	1/8 vs 1/4	0.2174	0.4307
died	1/8 vs 1/2	0.0013	0.0036
died	1/8 vs 1	<.0001	<.0001
died	1/8 vs 4	<.0001	<.0001
died	1/4 vs 1/2	0.0995	0.2574

died	1/4 vs 1	0.0028	0.0068
died	1/4 vs 4	0.0031	0.0090
died	1/2 vs 1	0.3168	0.4307
died	1/2 vs 4	0.2451	0.4307
died	1 vs 4	1.0000	1.0000

These results appear entirely sensible, with adjusted p-values larger than unadjusted and with results substantially better than Bonferroni, as you would expect given our discussion of the effects of discreteness.

Consider now a made-up example, where the identical method runs amok.

PROGRAM 12.5 **All Binary Pairwise Comparisons Using the Global Permutation Distribution: Example 2**

```
data trouble;
   input b f g;
datalines;
0   2000 1
0    1 2
1    3 2
0    3 3
1    1 3
;
proc multtest data=trouble stepperm n=1000;
   class g;
   freq f;
   test fisher(b);
   contrast ''1 vs 2''  1 -1  0 ;
   contrast ''1 vs 3''  1  0 -1 ;
   contrast ''2 vs 3''  0  1 -1 ;
run;
```

Output from Program 12.5

Discrete Variable Tabulations

Variable	g	Count	NumObs	Percent
b	1	0	2000	0.00
b	2	3	4	75.00
b	3	1	4	25.00

p-Values

Variable	Contrast	Raw	Stepdown Permutation
b	1 vs 2	<.0001	<.0001
b	1 vs 3	0.0020	<.0001
b	2 vs 3	0.4857	<.0001

Here, there is an obvious problem. The adjusted p-value for the 2 vs 3 comparison is a highly significant <.0001, while the raw p-value is clearly insignificant at $p = 0.4857$. The problem here is the use of the global null hypothesis to generate a p-value for the 2 vs 3 test. In the global randomization test, the four occurrences are randomly assigned to groups 1, 2, and 3. Since there are 2000 observations in group 1 and only 8 in groups 2 and 3 combined, it is most likely (98.4 percent likely, it turns out) that all four occurrences will end up in group 1. For these situations, the p-value for the 2 vs 3 comparison will be 1.0 (certainly not less than 0.4857). Thus, the adjusted p-value is much *less than* the raw p-value, contrary to common sense and to the closure principle, which dictate that the adjusted p-value for a given test must be at least as large as its unadjusted p-value.

Even if there are no real differences between group 2 and group 3 proportions, it is clear that this method will produce statistically significant differences much more often than 5 percent. This is an example of the problem of "excess Type I errors" associated with testing individual hypotheses using the global randomization distribution, noted by Petrondas and Gabriel (1983).

When you have a situation such as this, you cannot use the adjusted p-values to make individual claims about null hypotheses. The only claim that can be made is that the smallest adjusted p-value is valid for testing the global null hypothesis; in this case, the global null of equality of the three proportions is rejected since the adjusted p-value for the 1 vs 2 comparison is less than .0001.

12.3.2   Using the Discrete Bonferroni Method to Avoid the Subset Pivotality Pitfall

You can avoid the problem shown in the preceding section by using a simple trick. You need to create a multivariate data set, with one variable per test, and lots of missing values, to perform the discrete Bonferroni (DB) method. Program 12.6 shows how to do it with the anomalous data of Program 12.5.

PROGRAM 12.6   **A Workaround for the Subset Pivotality Problem: Discrete Bonferroni Method for Pairwise Binary Comparisons**

```
data Test1vs2; set trouble(where=(g in (1,2)));
   Test1vs2 = b; DummyGroup = (g=2);
data Test1vs3; set trouble(where=(g in (1,3)));
   Test1vs3 = b; DummyGroup = (g=3);
data Test2vs3; set trouble(where=(g in (2,3)));
   Test2vs3 = b; DummyGroup = (g=3);
data TroubleNoMore; set Test1vs2 Test1vs3 Test2vs3;
run;

proc multtest data=TroubleNoMore stepbon;
   class DummyGroup;
   freq f;
   test ca(Test1vs2 Test1vs3 Test2vs3/permutation=10);
   contrast ''Pairwise Test'' -1 1;
run;
```

As you can see, the trick here is to create a separate variable for every test, and to use missing values for all other variables so that PROC MULTTEST calculates all of the marginal permutation distributions correctly. Further, the discrete Šidák and Bonferroni methods do not require correlation information, and the missing value handling capabilities of PROC MULTTEST allows it to calculate these discrete multiplicity adjustments without requiring the multivariate binary records.

Since each variable uses data only pertaining to that particular test, we avoid the use of the global permutation distribution, and therefore, avoid the problem of failure of subset pivotality.

Output from Program 12.6

```
                            Discrete Variable Tabulations

                    Dummy
          Variable  Group      Count     NumObs     Percent

          Test1vs2    0          0        2000        0.00
          Test1vs2    1          3           4       75.00
          Test1vs3    0          0        2000        0.00
          Test1vs3    1          1           4       25.00
          Test2vs3    0          3           4       75.00
          Test2vs3    1          1           4       25.00



                               p-Values


                                                        Stepdown
          Variable   Contrast              Raw        Bonferroni

          Test1vs2   Pairwise Test       <.0001        <.0001
          Test1vs3   Pairwise Test       0.0020        0.0020
          Test2vs3   Pairwise Test       0.4857        0.4857
```

Here, we have the outcome where proper multiplicity adjustment means *no adjustment at all!* This occurs because, similar to what is shown in the output from Program 12.2, the permutation distributions for `test1vs3` and `test2vs3` cannot generate as small a p-value as produced by the `test1vs2` test. Further, in the step-down hierarchy, the `test2vs3` distribution does not have any p-values as small as 0.0020, so the `test1vs3` p-value also remains unadjusted. At the last step, the algorithm calculates $P(P_{23} \leq 0.4587) = 0.4587$, since only the data from groups 2 and 3 are considered at this point. Finally, we see that we no longer have the anomalous (and invalid) situation where the adjusted p-value is less than the unadjusted p-value.

While not a problem in the example above, the DB method suffers by not incorporating correlations. It *does* account for discreteness, and profitably so, as shown in the previous example where no adjustment at all was required because of discreteness. However, in general, you would prefer to account for dependencies to improve power further. In the next section we show how you can do this using the closure principle described in Chapter 8, using multiple calls to PROC MULTTEST.

12.3.3   Closed Binary Comparisons against a Control Using PROC MULTTEST

Recall from Chapter 8 the closure method, which tells you that, in order to reject a particular hypothesis, you must reject it and all intersection hypotheses that imply (or contain) it. In the case of pairwise comparisons with a control, you can easily specify and test all these intersection hypotheses using PROC MULTTEST.

The following data set is taken from a toxicity study in which the number of animals exhibiting a particular adverse event are measured. The study consists of data from historical controls, concurrent controls, and two dose groups, low and high. We want to compare the active doses and the historical control against the concurrent control, all with one-sided tests. Data and an incorrect PROC MULTTEST analysis (as described in the preceding section), are given in Program 12.7.

PROGRAM 12.7   Toxicity Data and Incorrect Comparisons against Control

```
data Toxicity;
   do Group='Hist','Curr','Low','High';
      do Outcome=0 to 1;
         input Freq @@;
         output;
         end;
      end;
datalines;
326 4
 49 1
 42 7
 44 4
;
proc multtest data=Toxicity order=data stepperm seed=121211;
   class Group;
   freq Freq;
   test fisher(Outcome/lower);
   contrast ''Hist vs Curr'' -1  1  0  0 ;
   contrast ''Low  vs Curr''  0  1 -1  0 ;
   contrast ''High vs Curr''  0  1  0 -1 ;
run;
```

Output from Program 12.7

Discrete Variable Tabulations

Variable	Group	Count	NumObs	Percent
Outcome	Hist	4	330	1.21
Outcome	Curr	1	50	2.00
Outcome	Low	7	49	14.29
Outcome	High	4	48	8.33

p-Values

Variable	Contrast	Raw	Stepdown Permutation
Outcome	Hist vs Curr	0.8692	0.7687
Outcome	Low vs Curr	0.0277	0.0093
Outcome	High vs Curr	0.1685	0.1437

Output from Program 12.7 shows the incorrect situation where the adjusted p-value is smaller than the raw. To fix this problem we apply the full closure method described in Chapter 8, testing all of the following intersection families:

1. The global intersection hypothesis: Hist = Curr = Low = High

2. The three-group intersection hypotheses which contain control: (1) Hist = Curr = Low, (2) Hist = Curr = High, (3) Curr = Low = High, and

3. the two-group pairwise hypotheses: (1) Hist = Curr, (2) Curr = Low, (3) Curr = High.

The results for the global and pairwise hypotheses already are given above in the output from Program 12.7. $p = 0.0093$ is the p-value for a test of the global null, and the raw p-values are the two-group comparison p-values. So all that remains is to test the three-group intersection hypotheses. You can perform these tests as follows in Program 12.8.

PROGRAM 12.8   Adjunct Program Used for Closed Pairwise Testing

```
proc multtest data=Toxicity(where=(Group ^= ''High''))
              order=data seed=121211 permutation;
    title ''Hist=Curr=Low'';
    class Group;
    freq Freq;
    test fisher(Outcome/lower);
    contrast ''Hist vs Curr'' -1  1  0;
    contrast ''Low  vs Curr''  0  1 -1;
    ods select pValues;
run;
proc multtest data=Toxicity(where=(Group ^= ''Low''))
              order=data seed=121211 permutation;
    title ''Hist=Curr=High'';
    class Group;
    freq Freq;
    test fisher(Outcome/lower);
    contrast ''Hist vs Curr'' -1  1  0;
    contrast ''High vs Curr''  0  1 -1;
    ods select pValues;
run;
proc multtest data=Toxicity(where=(Group ^= ''Hist''))
              order=data seed=121211 permutation;
    title ''Curr=Low=High'';
    class Group;
    freq Freq;
    test fisher(outcome/lower);
    contrast ''Low  vs Curr''  1 -1  0;
    contrast ''High vs Curr''  1  0 -1;
    ods select pValues;
run;
```

Output from Program 12.8

Hist=Curr=Low

p-Values

Variable	Contrast	Raw	Permutation
Outcome	Hist vs Curr	0.8692	0.8840
Outcome	Low vs Curr	0.0277	0.0025

Hist=Curr=High

p-Values

Variable	Contrast	Raw	Permutation
Outcome	Hist vs Curr	0.8692	0.7746
Outcome	High vs Curr	0.1685	0.0364

```
                              Curr=Low=High

                                 p-Values

        Variable     Contrast              Raw    Permutation

        Outcome      Low  vs Curr        0.0277      0.0256
        Outcome      High vs Curr        0.1685      0.1581
```

The *p*-values for the joint tests HistCurrLow, HistCurrHigh, and CurrLowHigh are the smaller of the two *p*-values in each table, which are 0.0025, 0.0364, and 0.0256, respectively. The following points summarize our conclusions:

- For the History vs. Current comparison, the raw *p*-value is 0.8692, and the *p*-values for containing hypotheses are 0.0025, 0.0364, and 0.0093. Since we must reject the individual hypotheses and all containing hypotheses, we will reject the null only for α-levels of 0.8692 or more. Thus the adjusted *p*-value is 0.8692.

- For the Low vs. Current comparison, the raw *p*-value is 0.0277, and the *p*-values for containing tests are 0.0025, 0.0256, and 0.0093. Thus the adjusted *p*-value is .0277.

- For the High vs. Current comparison, the raw *p*-value is 0.1685, and the *p*-values for containing tests are 0.0364, 0.0256 and 0.0093. Thus the adjusted *p*-value is 0.1685.

Thus, the Low vs. Current comparison is statistically significant, and the other comparisons are not. Note that, in following the closure principle, no adjusted *p*-values can be smaller than the raw *p*-value. Also note that no *p*-values require adjustment at all in this example.

The previous analysis is computationally intensive. You can get results much more quickly using the DB approximation, discussed in Section 12.3.2 at the expense of a slightly more conservative procedure. Again, you need to use the missing value trick shown in Program 12.6. This is shown in Program 12.9, which is a re-analysis of the pairwise tests in the toxicity data.

PROGRAM 12.9   Closed Testing of Pairwise versus Control with Binary Data Using Discrete Bonferroni

```
data HistVsCurr; set Toxicity(where=(Group in ('Hist','Curr')));
   HistVsCurr = Outcome;  DummyGroup = (Group='Hist');
data Low_VsCurr; set Toxicity(where=(Group in ('Low', 'Curr')));
   Low_VsCurr = Outcome;  DummyGroup = (Group='Low');
data HighVsCurr; set Toxicity(where=(Group in ('High','Curr')));
   HighVsCurr = Outcome;  DummyGroup = (Group='High');
data TrickToxicity; set HistVsCurr Low_VsCurr HighVsCurr;
   run;
proc multtest data=TrickToxicity stepbon;
   title ''Complete Null'';
   class DummyGroup;
   freq Freq;
   test ca(HistVsCurr Low_VsCurr HighVsCurr/lower permutation=20);
   contrast ''PairTest'' 1 -1;
   ods select pValues;
run;
```

```
proc multtest data=TrickToxicity stepbon;
    title ''HistVsCurrLow'';
    class DummyGroup;
    freq Freq;
    test ca(HistVsCurr Low_VsCurr/lower permutation=20);
    contrast ''PairTest'' 1 -1;
    ods select pValues;
run;

proc multtest data=TrickToxicity stepbon;
    title ''HistVsCurrHigh'';
    class DummyGroup;
    freq Freq;
    test ca(HistVsCurr HighVsCurr/lower permutation=20);
    contrast ''PairTest'' 1 -1;
    ods select pValues;
run;

proc multtest data=TrickToxicity stepbon;
    title ''CurrLowHigh '';
    class DummyGroup;
    freq Freq;
    test ca(Low_VsCurr HighVsCurr/lower permutation=20);
    contrast ''PairTest'' 1 -1;
    ods select pValues;
run;
```

Output from Program 12.9

Complete Null

p-Values

Variable	Contrast	Raw	Stepdown Bonferroni
HistVsCurr	PairTest	0.8692	0.8692
Low_VsCurr	PairTest	0.0277	0.0529
HighVsCurr	PairTest	0.1685	0.1685

HistVsCurrLow

p-Values

Variable	Contrast	Raw	Stepdown Bonferroni
HistVsCurr	PairTest	0.8692	0.8692
Low_VsCurr	PairTest	0.0277	0.0277

HistVsCurrHigh

p-Values

Variable	Contrast	Raw	Stepdown Bonferroni
HistVsCurr	PairTest	0.8692	0.8692
HighVsCurr	PairTest	0.1685	0.1685

```
                                 CurrLowHigh

                                  p-Values

                                                       Stepdown
               Variable       Contrast        Raw     Bonferroni

             Low_VsCurr       PairTest      0.0277      0.0529
             HighVsCurr       PairTest      0.1685      0.1685
```

The conservative DB p-values for the joint tests HistvsCurrLow, HistvsCurrHigh, and CurrLowHigh are 0.0277, 0.1685, and 0.0529, respectively. The following points summarize our conclusions:

- For the History vs. Current comparison, the raw p-value is 0.8692, and the p-values for containing hypotheses are 0.0277, 0.1685, and 0.0529. Since we must reject the individual hypotheses and all containing hypotheses, we will reject the null only for α-levels of 0.8692 or more. Thus the adjusted p-value is 0.8692.
- For the Low vs. Current comparison, the raw p-value is 0.0277, and the p-values for containing tests are 0.0277, 0.0529, and 0.0529. Thus the adjusted p-value is .0529.
- For the High vs. Current comparison, the raw p-value is 0.1685, and the p-values for containing tests are 0.1685, 0.0529 and 0.0529. Thus the adjusted p-value is 0.1685.

In this more conservative approach, the Low vs. Current comparison is statistically insignificant, with adjusted p-value 0.0529, whereas before, using the distributions fully, the adjusted p-value for this comparison was 0.0277. The other comparisons remain unadjusted, as before.

Despite the loss of power, you might prefer the DB approach because it is quicker and free of Monte Carlo error. Resampling-based adjusted p-values can take a while to compute and will vary slightly with different random seeds.

You can use the conservative DB approach for closed testing with all pairwise comparisons as well. To identify the intersection hypotheses that you need to specify in this case, see Chapter 8, specifically Figure 8.1 in Section 8.2. However, you cannot get full closure-based tests for all pairwise comparison using PROC MULTTEST, such as those shown in Program 12.8. The reason is that PROC MULTTEST only permutes complete null distributions, and not partial nulls of the form $(\mu_1 = \mu_2)$, $(\mu_3 = \mu_4)$. It is possible to use the DB approximation with PROC MULTTEST to evaluate such hypotheses, and use the complete null distributions for other cases, to arrive at a reasonably powerful closed procedure, but we do not pursue this further.

12.4   Improving the Power of Multiple Binary Tests

Rom (1992) proposed another procedure for exploiting the discreteness of the distribution of statistics arising from binary variables. Recall that the adjusted p-value for the smallest p-value is calculated as $\tilde{p}_j = P[P_{(1)} \leq p_{(1)}]$. We can define an alternative global p-value for testing the global null hypothesis H_0 as:

$$
P_{H_0} = P \left[\begin{array}{l}
\{P_{(1)} < p_{(1)}\} \\
\cup \quad \left(\{P_{(1)} = p_{(1)}\} \cap \{P_{(2)} < p_{(2)}\}\right) \\
\cup \quad \left(\{P_{(1)} = p_{(1)}\} \cap \{P_{(2)} = p_{(2)}\} \cap \{P_{(3)} < p_{(3)}\}\right) \\
\vdots \\
\cup \quad \left(\{P_{(1)} = p_{(1)}\} \cap \ldots \cap \{P_{(n-1)} = p_{(n-1)}\} \cap \{P_{(n)} \leq p_{(n)}\}\right)
\end{array} \right].
$$

The P_{H_0} is never larger, and quite often, much smaller than $\tilde{p}$. Thus, the test which rejects H_0 based on P_{H_0} is more powerful than the test based on $\tilde{p}$. This procedure is quite powerful for testing H_0 when there is evidence against the null hypothesis in few of the individual tests, that is, when few of the p-values are small. However, the cost of a more powerful test for testing H_0 is that we have lost the simplicity of the procedure based on $\tilde{p}$. In particular, we can no longer designate P_{H_0} as an adjusted p-value for $H_{(1)}$; rather, it should be viewed as a p-value for testing the global null hypothesis only. We can, however, make assessment on individual hypotheses, and even calculate adjusted p-values by using the closure principle.

The calculation of P_{H_0} is done using a complete enumeration when feasible (as with Fisher's Exact test), and otherwise using resampling-based Monte Carlo.

We will now illustrate this procedure with an example. A pharmaceutical company has conducted a study to compare a new antifungal treatment with a competitor, on the following three endpoints:

- the patient is judged to be cured based on the physician's rating.
- the patient is judged to be cured based on the patient's self-assessment.
- the patient is judged to be cured based on fungal cultures as assessed in the lab.

Program 12.10 uses the %romex macro, provided in the appendix, to analyze the fungal data.

PROGRAM 12.10   Improving the Power of Binary Tests

```
data fungal;
   input ep1 ep2 ep3 treat1 treat2;
datalines;
   1       0       0       1       2
   0       1       0       1       2
   0       0       1       0       2
   1       1       0       0       0
   1       0       1       1       2
   0       1       1       0       1
   1       1       1       57      61
   0       0       0       10      0
   ;

data par;
   nep=3;
   nt=2;
run;
%romex(2, fungal, par);
```

The input data set contains 0-1 indicators for the three different endpoints, with $2^3 = 8$ possible different collections of assessments of cured or not cured by the three methods. There is an observation in the data set for each different collection of assessments, with the number of subjects exhibiting that collection for the competitor (Treat1) and for the new drug (Treat2). For example, the first dataline, 1 0 0 1 2, means that among the subjects who were cured successfully according to the physician's assessment but not according to either self-assessment or the fungal culture (ep1=1, ep2=0, ep3=0), one used the existing (competitive) drug, and two used the new drug. Similarly, the dataline 1 1 1 57 61 means that there were 57 and 61 subjects who used the competitor and the new drug, respectively, who were assessed as cured by all three methods. The %romex macro requires an initial parameter specifying the alternative hypotheses; "1" specifies lower-tailed tests, "2" specifies upper-tailed tests, and "3" specifies two-tailed tests. In this case, we use an upper-tailed since the purpose of the study is to show superiority of the new treatment.

**Output from
Program 12.10**

```
                   ROM DISCRETE MULTIPLE ENDPOINTS ANALYSIS


       I           ENDPOINT                       P-VALUE*
       ----------------------------------------------------------
       1              3                            0.0301
       2              1                            0.0914
       3              2                            0.1030
       ----------------------------------------------------------
            EXACT GLOBAL P-VALUE:                  0.0339
```

The output consists of p-values corresponding to the individual endpoints, a p-value for testing the global null hypothesis H_0, and an indication for sidedness. Note that the endpoints are sorted by the corresponding p-values. Another important point to note is that, for this data set, the global p-value is not much larger than the smallest of the individual p-values. This is due to the fact that all three p-values are quite small, strengthening the evidence against the global null hypothesis. Based on the global p-value, we can state that the evidence shows that the new drug (TREAT 2) has better efficacy overall. However, for the reasons stated at the beginning of the section, we cannot claim that the new drug is better on any particular endpoint, even the one with the smallest p-value.

You can make individual claims by using the closure method as described in Section 12.3.3. To illustrate this consider testing $H_1 \cap H_3$. All you need to do is run the %romex macro on the data collapsed over these two endpoints.

PROGRAM 12.11   Joint Test of Endpoint 1 and Endpoint 3

```
proc sort data=fungal out=fungal;
   by ep1 ep3;
proc summary data=fungal;
   by ep1 ep3;
   var treat1 treat2;
   output out=fungal13 sum=treat1 treat2;
run;

data par; nep=2; nt=2; run;
%romex(2, fungal13, par);
```

The p-value for this test is 0.0338, leading to the rejection of $H_1 \cap H_3$. Similarly, you can conduct a test for $H_2 \cap H_3$ by collapsing the data for these two endpoints and running %romex again. This gives you the p-value 0.0274, leading to the rejection of $H_2 \cap H_3$.

Since all tests containing H_3 as a component are rejected, we can conclude that H_3 can be rejected. Note that the maximum p-value for testing all hypotheses containing H_3 is $\max\left(P_{H_0}, P_{H_1 \cap H_3}, P_{H_2 \cap H_3}, P_{H_3}\right) = 0.0339$. This can serve as the adjusted p-value for p_3 because it is the smallest FWE for which H_3 can be rejected. For this example, only H_3 can be rejected (with an adjusted p-value of 0.0339), because none of the other p-values is less than 0.05. The final conclusion is that the new drug is superior to its competitor on endpoint 3 (the fungal cultures), but has not been shown to be superior on the other endpoints.

When the data sets are too large, the exact calculation of P_{H_0} becomes infeasible. However, you can use the %rommc macro to compute the p-values via permutation resampling. The statistic used for each endpoint is the asymptotic z-score approximation instead of Fisher's Exact statistic. You will need an additional data set containing the desired number of samples, and the seed, as shown in Program 12.12.

PROGRAM 12.12   **Monte Carlo Calculation of P_{H_0}**

```
data par; nep=3; nt=2;
data mcn; n_sample=1000; seed=1235;
run;
%rommc(2, fungal, par, mcn);
```

Output from
Program 12.12

```
                 ROM DISCRETE MULTIPLE ENDPOINTS ANALYSIS


         I            ENDPOINT                    P-VALUE*
      -------------------------------------------------------
         1               3                         0.0171
         2               1                         0.0561
         3               2                         0.0656
      -------------------------------------------------------
         MONTE CARLO GLOBAL P-VALUE                 0.0370
         95% CONFIDENCE INTERVAL           (  0.0253  0.0487 )
         NUMBER OF SAMPLES                 1000



            *: ASYMPTOTIC P-VALUE FOR UPPER-TAILED TREND
```

The Monte Carlo analysis gives an estimated global *p*-value of 0.0370, not far from the exact global p-value of 0.0339. The confidence interval can be used to assess the precision of the calculations. Increasing the number of samples from 1000 will lead to a decrease in the width of the confidence interval. This test can be used to test all subset intersection hypotheses in a closure manner.

12.4.1   Comparison with PROC MULTTEST

Finally, we close with a comparison of Rom's P_{H_0} method with that of PROC MULTTEST. Program 12.13 shows the corresponding data (in PROC MULTTEST format) and calculations using PROC MULTTEST.

PROGRAM 12.13   **Analysis of Fungal Data Using PROC MULTTEST**

```
data fungal_mult; set fungal;
   Freq = treat1; Treatment = 1; if (Freq) then output;
   Freq = treat2; Treatment = 2; if (Freq) then output;
run;

proc multtest data=fungal_mult stepperm n=100000 seed=121211;
   class Treatment;
   freq Freq;
   test fisher(ep1-ep3/upper);
   contrast ''New-Old'' -1 1;
   ods select pValues;
run;
```

Output from
Program 12.13

		p-Values	
Variable	Contrast	Raw	Stepdown Permutation
ep1	New-Old	0.0914	0.1084
ep2	New-Old	0.1030	0.1084
ep3	New-Old	0.0301	0.0515

The smallest adjusted *p*-value 0.0515 is larger than the value $P_{H_0} = 0.0339$, showing the improvement in the power of Rom's discrete method.

12.5 Multiple Linear Contrast Tests

Up to this point in the chapter we have considered only tests that involve pairwise differences between groups. PROC MULTTEST can also analyze more general contrasts, such as those involving a linear trend or a comparison of one level with the average of others. The ca test with permutation resampling is a useful technique for multiplicity-adjusting such tests, much as we have done in continuous applications with the %Sim* macros. Again, the methods cannot be considered exact because of the lack of subset pivotality, but if the results seem sensible, it is probably safe to use them. (If there are no instances of adjusted *p*-values being smaller than the unadjusted *p*-values, or other anomalies, then the results are sensible). We also note that when you perform such analyses where subset pivotality is known to fail, you should identify the results as approximate, rather than exact, much in the same way that you would identify MCPs using PROC MIXED as approximate, rather than exact.

In many cases of practical interest, the multiple inferences using PROC MULTTEST are perfectly adequate, despite failure of the subset pivotality assumption. Simulations performed by Westfall (1998) suggest that problems are likely to arise when there is great imbalance, where the group with the largest sample size has a very small occurrence rate. However, in many cases involving imbalance and differing rates, the excess Type I errors in these simulations were minor or nonexistent, even in cases where the data sets frequently showed an adjusted *p*-value that was smaller than its corresponding raw *p*-value.

EXAMPLE: **Comparing Patient Mortality and Morbidity Rates for Different Surgeons**

Pearce and Westfall (1997) give a practical application of PROC MULTTEST for a problem in healthcare quality. Six different surgeons are to be compared on the basis of the following adverse surgical outcomes:

- Hospital death (HDeath)
- Perioperative myocardial infarction (MI_EKG)
- Reoperation for bleeding (RFB)
- Surgical wound infection (Infect)
- Cerebrovascular accident (Neuro)
- Pulmonary complications (Pulm)
- Renal failure (RenFail).

The comparisons of interest are each surgeon's proportion against the average proportions from all other surgeons. Thus, for each adverse outcome, there are six comparisons. With seven adverse outcomes, there are $k = 6 \times 7 = 42$ tests in all. It is extremely important to multiplicity-adjust surgeon comparisons because, as pointed out by Pearce and Westfall, false significances reflect negatively on specific surgeons, leading to fear and mistrust in the quality improvement process. On the other hand, the tests should be as powerful as possible in order to identify real quality improvement opportunities, therefore, it is important to utilize the discrete character of the data.

Program 12.14 gives the data and analysis of Pearce and Westfall.

PROGRAM 12.14   Comparing Multiple Contrasts for Multiple Binary Variables

```
data Doctors;
   keep Doctor HDeath MI_EKG RFB Infect Neuro Pulm RenFail;
   array AE{7} HDeath MI_EKG RFB Infect Neuro Pulm RenFail;
   input Doctor nTotal nNone @@;
   do i = 1 to dim(AE); AE{i} = 0; end;
   do iobs = 1 to nNone; output; end;
   do iobs = 1 to nTotal-nNone;
      input nAE @@;
      do i = 1 to dim(AE); AE{i} = 0; end;
      do i = 1 to nAE; input iAE @@; AE{iAE} = 1; end;
      output;
      end;
   datalines;
1 38 32   1 7   1 2   2 2 6   1 1     1 1        3 1 5 6
2 26 20   1 6   1 6   1 6     2 3 6   3 2 5 6    2 2 3
3 36 32   1 3   1 3   1 3     1 2
4 52 45   1 7   1 5   1 2     2 2 5   2 1 3      2 1 2
         5 1 2 3 4 7
5 43 36   1 7   1 5   1 5     1 5     1 2        1 2
         1 2
6 30 26   1 6   1 6   1 4     1 1
;

proc multtest data=Doctors stepbon stepperm seed=121211 n=50000;
   class Doctor;
   test ca(HDeath MI_EKG RFB Infect Neuro Pulm RenFail/lower permutation=50);
   contrast ''1 vs rest'' -5  1  1  1  1  1 ;
   contrast ''2 vs rest''  1 -5  1  1  1  1 ;
   contrast ''3 vs rest''  1  1 -5  1  1  1 ;
   contrast ''4 vs rest''  1  1  1 -5  1  1 ;
   contrast ''5 vs rest''  1  1  1  1 -5  1 ;
   contrast ''6 vs rest''  1  1  1  1  1 -5 ;
   ods output pValues=pValues;
proc sort data=pValues out=pValsort;
   by raw;
data top5;
   set pValsort;
   if _n_ <= 5;
proc print noobs data=top5;
run;
```

Output from Program 12.14

Variable	Contrast	Raw	Stepdown Bonferroni	Stepdown Permutation
Pulm	2 vs rest	0.0013	0.0164	0.0168
RFB	3 vs rest	0.0835	1.0000	0.8332
HDeath	1 vs rest	0.0957	1.0000	0.8767
Neuro	5 vs rest	0.1299	1.0000	0.9580
RFB	2 vs rest	0.1876	1.0000	0.9923

The conclusion is that Surgeon 2 is significantly worse than the rest with respect to the pulmonary complications, and that the difference between this surgeon and the rest for this outcome is not attributable to chance differences between surgeon 2's patients and the remaining patients. Of course, this latter comment presumes that the patients are randomly assigned to the surgeons, and that surgeon 2 does not get a significantly worse patient pool. You can control for such effects using a discrete "risk stratification score" (see, for example, Edwards et al., 1997) as a STRATA variable in PROC MULTTEST.

12.6 Multiple Animal Carcinogenicity Tests

PROC MULTTEST is especially convenient for performing unadjusted and multiplicity-adjusted analyses for multiple animal carcinogenicity tests; in fact, that was the original intended application of the software. Data from such studies are essentially multivariate binary, with multivariate vectors of 1s and 0s that indicate presence or absence of any of dozens of tumor types that are found in the animals at necropsy.

Often, animals in the higher dose groups die early because of drug toxicity, unrelated to any particular tumor type. Therefore, you must control for age at death, either by logistic regression or discrete stratification. PROC MULTTEST allows you to perform discrete stratification with the STRATA variable. A typical stratification for a two-year rodent carcinogenicity study looks like the following:

- stratum 1: early death between 1 and 52 weeks
- stratum 2: early death between 53 and 65 weeks
- stratum 3: early death between 66 and 78 weeks
- stratum 4: early death between 79 and 91 weeks
- stratum 5: early death between 92 and 104 weeks
- stratum 6: terminal sacrifice.

Besides time of death strata, you must also account for status of tumor, whether incidental (or prevalent), lethal, or palpable. If lethal or palpable, then the test should use survival analysis methods as described in Peto et al. (1980). Such methods require actual survival (or palpation) time for the analysis, not just the death time stratification. PROC MULTTEST computes the Peto mortality-prevalence test with both asymptotic and permutation-based approximations. You must code tumor occurrences that are incidental to survival as a "1," and tumor occurrences that are lethal or palpable as a "2" in the input data set.

The following data and Program 12.15 illustrate the use of PROC MULTTEST to calculate the permutation approximation and discrete Bonferroni multiplicity adjustments for multiple tumor data.

PROGRAM 12.15   Multiple Peto Mortality-Prevalence Carcinogenicity Tests Using Discrete Distributions and Discrete Bonferroni Multiplicity Adjustments

```
data Carcinogenicity;
   keep TGroup Day Tumor1-Tumor44;
   array Tumor{44};
   input TGroup nTotal @@;
   do iobs = 1 to nTotal;
      input Day nTumor @@;
      do i = 1 to dim(Tumor); Tumor{i} = 0; end;
      do i = 1 to nTumor;
         input iTumor Tumori @@;
         Tumor{iTumor} = Tumori;
         end;
      output;
      end;
   datalines;
1 60
729 0                      729 1 7 1                  564 0
675 1 10 1                 598 1 22 2                 613 2 5 1    10 1
729 1 21 1                 729 2 1 1    36 1          505 1 5 2
689 1 44 2                 704 0                      682 1 5 2
697 2 10 1    34 1         729 1 10 1                 556 0
729 2 10 1    14 1         617 0                      661 1 5 1
112 1 42 2                 729 2 10 1    27 1         729 1 10 1
729 3 10 1    20 1    25 1 465 0                      729 1 25 1
729 0                      588 0                      729 1 5 1
595 0                      532 2 10 1    38 1         620 1 5 2
680 1 5 2                  561 0                      578 2 6 1    10 1
682 2 5 1    8 2           729 0                      713 1 10 1
729 1 5 1                  541 1 5 1                  689 1 32 1
729 1 6 1                  729 1 10 1                 638 0
693 1 9 1                  729 1 26 1                 729 2 15 1    21 1
729 1 42 1                 729 1 33 1                 729 0
602 3 10 1    14 1    42 2 556 3 5 1    10 1    11 2  576 0
729 0                      623 0                      729 1 1 1
639 1 10 1                 638 0                      729 2 10 1    34 1
729 0                      729 1 6 1                  575 0
2 60
732 1 10 1                 415 0                      732 1 10 1
732 0                      576 0                      581 1 5 2
634 2 5 1    10 1          595 0                      667 1 5 1
618 3 1 1    10 1    42 2  732 1 10 1                 586 0
640 1 9 1                  493 0                      426 1 5 2
419 1 10 1                 658 1 10 1                 661 1 10 1
689 1 19 2                 643 0                      697 0
648 1 10 1                 706 0                      566 0
732 1 6 1                  451 1 27 1                 568 1 42 2
686 3 5 1    18 2    31 1  508 1 10 1                 732 0
508 0                      662 0                      732 0
217 1 12 2                 732 2 5 1    10 1          485 0
644 1 10 1                 732 2 5 1    10 1          683 1 6 1
678 1 10 1                 732 4 1 1    5 1    9 1    10 1  556 2 5 2    10 1
732 1 13 1                 732 1 6 1                  581 0
536 0                      732 1 10 1                 732 1 6 1
544 0                      591 1 5 2                  615 0
290 1 42 2                 732 1 10 1                 732 1 9 1
732 1 1 1                  446 2 1 1    10 1          473 0
667 1 10 1                 531 0                      683 3 5 1    10 1    27 1
```

```
3 60
562 2 5 1   10 1        590 0                514 1 5 2
543 0                   543 1 10 1           731 0
641 2 10 1   28 1       731 2 5 1   29 1     588 0
580 0                   645 2 10 1   40 2    633 1 10 1
674 0                   718 2 2 1   5 1      578 2 4 2   25 1
644 3 5 2   10 1   31 1 679 0                596 1 5 2
702 1 5 1               731 2 10 1   25 1    651 0
402 0                   569 1 10 1           600 1 10 1
711 0                   702 1 10 1           731 0
731 2 3 1   10 1        599 0                576 1 10 1
470 0                   729 1 10 1           548 1 9 1
729 1 10 1              710 2 5 1   42 2     613 1 43 2
731 1 10 1              616 0                731 2 10 1   25 1
724 1 10 1              570 1 39 1           731 1 5 1
731 2 1 1   41 1        708 2 5 1   10 1     534 1 10 1
497 0                   718 0                652 2 10 1   30 1
727 1 5 2               573 0                663 0
731 0                   510 1 10 1           579 1 10 1
686 1 5 1               693 1 10 1           731 2 10 1   24 1
731 0                   731 0                573 0
4 60
700 3 1 1   10 1   11 2 475 0                566 1 10 1
617 2 10 1   37 1       476 0                542 1 10 1
581 0                   655 0                446 2 10 1   35 1
547 2 5 1   10 1        719 2 10 1   36 1    678 1 10 1
603 2 5 1   10 1        683 1 8 1            543 1 10 1
730 2 1 1   10 1        624 1 10 1           449 1 10 1
639 0                   475 0                609 1 10 1
511 0                   696 1 10 1           556 1 10 1
620 1 5 2               392 1 10 1           661 1 32 1
676 1 10 1              556 1 16 1           605 0
496 0                   532 1 5 2            505 0
482 0                   591 0                556 1 10 1
730 1 10 1              635 0                669 0
730 2 10 1   42 1       568 1 10 1           702 1 17 2
618 0                   630 3 10 1   14 1   23 1   730 2 6 1   10 1
730 0                   519 0                382 0
633 1 10 1             451 0                576 0
549 1 10 1             610 1 23 2           654 1 10 1
524 2 10 1   42 2      669 2 5 1   10 1     593 1 10 1
730 0                 659 2 1 1   10 1       24 0
;

data Carcinogenicity; set Carcinogenicity;
   select;
      when (Day <= 365) Stratum = 1;
      when (Day <= 455) Stratum = 2;
      when (Day <= 546) Stratum = 3;
      when (Day <= 637) Stratum = 4;
      when (Day <= 730) Stratum = 5;
      otherwise         Stratum = 6;
      end;
   run;
```

```
ods listing close;
proc multtest data=Carcinogenicity stepbon;
   class TGroup;
   strata Stratum;
   test peto(Tumor1-Tumor44/upper time=day permutation=10 continuity=.5);
   contrast ''Dose trend'' 0 1 2 3;
   ods output pValues = pValues;
run;
ods listing;

proc sort data=pValues out=pvalsort; by raw;
data top5; set pvalsort; if _n_ <= 5;
proc print data=top5 noobs;
   run;
```

Output from Program 12.15

Variable	Contrast	Raw	Stepdown Bonferroni
Tumor10	Dose trend	0.0010	0.0040
Tumor23	Dose trend	0.0614	0.6645
Tumor17	Dose trend	0.1026	0.9782
Tumor16	Dose trend	0.3284	1.0000
Tumor37	Dose trend	0.3284	1.0000

Thus, Tumor10 has an increasing trend in carcinogenicity; all other trends might be spurious.

Note that, even though there are $k = 44$ tests, the multiplicity adjustment is minimal because the method incorporates discreteness. The effective Bonferroni multiplier for Tumor10 is about 4, much less than the ordinary multiplier $k = 44$; likewise, the effective Bonferroni multiplier for the Tumor23 trend test is 10.8, still much smaller than the step-down Bonferroni multiplier of $44 - 1 = 43$.

This analysis is essentially equivalent to that of Heyse and Rom (1988), who proposed using the independence-based discrete adjustments. Westfall and Wolfinger (1997) noted that the independence-based adjustments can be liberal for discrete one-sided tests, but that in most cases the independence-based adjustments also are conservative. You can get the independence-based adjustments of Heyse and Rom exactly using PROC MULTTEST, simply by specifying "stepsid" instead of "stepbon."

Usually, there is relatively little effect of incorporating correlations in typical animal carcinogenicity studies—the stepbon and stepsid methods incorporate discreteness, and that is the major effect. An important point regarding the use of PROC MULTTEST for this application:

- You **must** specify permutation= in the ca or peto tests in order for the stepbon and stepsid options to incorporate discreteness. Otherwise, those options will treat the data as continuous, and you lose the great advantage of incorporating discreteness.

If you really want to assess the effect of correlation in your tumor study, and you have fatal or palpable tumors, here is a strategy that can help you understand the effect of correlation on your analysis.

1. Create a new tumor data set, with all fatal and palpable "2" codes replaced by incidental "1" values. In other words, recode the 2s as 1s.

2. Specify all of stepbon, stepsid and stepperm, and analyze the data using ca, not peto, with the given strata and no time= variable. Compare the results of the three

multiplicity adjustments. This should give you a rough idea of how well the `stepbon` and `stepsid` adjustments approximate the more correct `stepperm` adjustments, when all data are classified as incidental. Note that the `stepperm` method incorporates correlations, while the other two do not.

3. Perform either the `stepsid` or `stepbon` adjustments with the original data set, using `peto`, `strata`, and the `time=` variable. Using your analysis of (2.), you should have a good idea of how well the `peto` analysis would compare to a method that incorporates correlation structure.

When performing multiple animal carcinogenicity tests using the `peto` test of PROC MULTTEST, resampling options are unavailable for various technical reasons. See Soper and Westfall (1990) for more details.

As a final note concerning carcinogenicity, if you have palpable tumors, the ordinary PROC MULTTEST syntax may not be appropriate, since palpation time usually differs from death time. However, you can restructure the input data using the missing value trick shown earlier in this chapter, and calculate the exact `peto` *p*-values and associated discrete `stepbon` or `stepsid` multiplicity adjustments. You have to change the `time=` variable from the death time to palpation time, but you should leave the strata variable fixed, related to death time and not palpation time, for all tumor types.

12.7 Miscellaneous PROC MULTTEST Applications

12.7.1 Freeman-Tukey (FT) Test

As we have seen, the subset pivotality problem is most pronounced in cases of heteroscedasticity. One way to alleviate the problem is to use a variance-stabilizing transformation. The Freeman-Tukey double-arcsine transformation makes the distribution of the sample proportion approximately free of the underlying rate, and can therefore alleviate some of the problems that are associated with performing component tests under global resampling. If a proportion π is estimated using the fraction of occurrences y/n, then the double arcsine transformation is defined as

$$f(y, n) = \arcsin\{[y/(n+1)]^{1/2}\} + \arcsin\{[(y+1)/(n+1)]^{1/2}\}.$$

Freeman and Tukey (1950) show that if Y has the binomial distribution with parameters π and n, then the variance of $f(Y, n)$ is approximately

$$\mathrm{Var}\big(f(Y, n)\big) \approx \frac{1}{n+.5}$$

which does not depend on π.

Westfall (1998) showed in a set of simulations that the FT test has dramatically fewer excess Type I Errors than Fisher exact test under global resampling, and that the occurrences of adjusted *p*-values less than corresponding unadjusted *p*-values also are dramatically reduced.

For further technical details concerning the FT test, see Westfall and Young (1993, pp. 153–155, and p. 162).

Program 12.16 reanalyzes the toxicity data from Program 12.7, using the Freeman-Tukey double-arcsine transformation of the proportions.

PROGRAM 12.16   Multiple Binary Comparisons Using Freeman-Tukey Tests

```
proc multtest data=Toxicity order=data stepboot seed=121211;
   class Group;
   freq Freq;
   test ft(Outcome/lower);
   contrast ''Hist vs Curr'' -1  1  0  0 ;
   contrast ''Low  vs Curr''  0  1 -1  0 ;
   contrast ''High vs Curr''  0  1  0 -1 ;
run;
```

Output from Program 12.16

		p-Values	
			Stepdown
Variable	Contrast	Raw	Bootstrap
Outcome	Hist vs Curr	0.7595	0.7252
Outcome	Low vs Curr	0.0114	0.0320
Outcome	High vs Curr	0.0856	0.1782

The following notes concern this analysis and compare it to the analysis using the Fisher test shown in the output from Program 12.7:

- The conclusion is that Low differs from Current, with adjusted *p*-value 0.0320. This conclusion is similar to that obtained using the Fisher test in Program 12.7, which we noted was an incorrect analysis, but also obtained using the more valid closure-based testing method that followed.

- Note that, with the FT tests, you no longer have the adjusted *p*-value smaller than the unadjusted. The results look reasonable, consistent with common sense and expectations. In particular, the adjusted *p*-value for Low vs Current is larger by a factor of approximately 3, the Bonferroni multiplier. In addition, in Program 12.7 there is an uncomfortably large difference between the Hist vs Curr raw and adjusted *p*-values 0.8692 and 0.7687. Since this is the last step in the step-down tests, you want the raw and adjusted to coincide here. They do not because the global null distribution is used to obtain the adjusted, rather than the pairwise null distribution. However, there is a much closer agreement between these two *p*-values with the FT tests, 0.7595 and 0.7252, despite the fact that the adjustment is calculated under the global null. This similarity shows the benefit of stabilizing the variances using the Freeman-Tukey transformation.

- The unadjusted *p*-values are smaller using the FT test than the Fisher test. This difference reflects the fact that the Fisher exact test is not at all exact from the population sampling model standpoint; it is in fact conservative (true Type I error level always below α). The FT test has a true Type I error that is much closer to (but can occasionally exceed) α.

- We use bootstrap sampling here to be consistent with the base test. Because the Fisher exact test is a permutation test, it is philosophically consistent to use permutation resampling for its multiplicity adjustment. The same comment can be made when you use the ca test along with the permutation= specification. On the other hand, the ft test is not a permutation test, and is justified using the population sampling model. Therefore, we recommend bootstrap sampling in this case, since bootstrapping also has the population sampling model as its rationale. This distinction is more philosophical than substantive; if you replace stepboot with stepperm in Program 12.16, the resulting adjusted *p*-values change very little.

12.7.2   Mixing Binary and Continuous Variables

With PROC MULTTEST, you can mix binary and continuous variables in your analysis. Multiplicity adjustments are computed by resampling the mixed binary/continuous vectors, centering the continuous measures by default with bootstrap sampling, and not centering them with permutation sampling. In this way, correlations between binary and continuous variables are incorporated into the multiplicity adjustments. To illustrate this feature, we return to the adverse events data analyzed in Program 12.1, and create a new variable, total adverse events, which we analyze as a continuous variable. Of course, the variable is discrete and not continuous, but nonnormality will be accommodated via resampling.

PROGRAM 12.17   Mixing Continuous and Discrete Variables

```
data Adverse; set Adverse;
   TotalAdverse = sum(of AE1-AE27);
proc multtest data=Adverse stepperm seed=121211;
   class Group;
   test mean  (TotalAdverse/upper)
        fisher(ae1-ae28    /upper);
   contrast ''Treatment-Control'' -1 1;
   ods output pValues=pValues;
run;

proc sort data=pValues out=pValues; by raw;
data Top5; set pValues; if _n_ <= 5;
proc print noobs data=Top5;
run;
```

Output from Program 12.17

Variable	Contrast	Raw	Stepdown Permutation
AE1	Treatment-Control	0.0008	0.0023
AE8	Treatment-Control	0.0293	0.1480
AE6	Treatment-Control	0.0601	0.2784
TotalAdverse	Treatment-Control	0.1027	0.3416
AE5	Treatment-Control	0.2213	0.6268

Note that the adjusted *p*-values for the three most significant tests are slightly larger here than in the output from Program 12.1, reflecting the slightly larger family of tests. Note also that the included `total` variable does not achieve significance, even without multiplicity adjustment, reinforcing our earlier observation that unadjusted combined tests are not necessarily more sensitive than adjusted component tests.

12.7.3   Multiple Comparisons of Survival Functions

You can use PROC MULTTEST to perform the log-rank test for comparing survival functions (identical to that of PROC LIFETEST) simply by coding fatal occurrences as "2" and censored occurrences as "0."

Program 12.18 analyzes data from a study of the survival rates of laboratory animals exposed to a certain agent. Both the LIFETEST and MULTTEST procedures are used, and you can see the correspondence between data input formats.

PROGRAM 12.18   Corresponding PROC MULTTEST and PROC LIFETEST

```
title1 'Lifetimes of Rats';

data DMBA_LIFETEST;
   input Group Days @@;
   Censored = (Days < 0);
   Days = abs(Days);
datalines;
1 143  1 164  1 188  1 188  1 190  1 192  1 206
1 209  1 213  1 216  1 220  1 227  1 230  1 234
1 246  1 265  1 304  1 -216  1 -244
2 142  2 156  2 163  2 198  2 205  2 232  2 232
2 233  2 233  2 233  2 233  2 239  2 240  2 261
2 280  2 280  2 296  2 296  2 323  2 -204  2 -344
;

proc lifetest data=DMBA_LIFETEST;
   title2 ''Comparisons of Survival Curves via the LIFETEST Procedure'';
   time Days*Censored(1);
   strata Group;
   ods select HomTests;
run;


title2 'Logrank Test via the MULTTEST Procedure';
data DMBA_MULTTEST; set DMBA_LIFETEST;
   t = 2*(1-Censored);
run;

proc multtest data=DMBA_MULTTEST;
   title3 ''Asymptotic Analysis'';
   class Group;
   test peto(t/time=Days);
   ods select pValues;
run;
proc multtest data=DMBA_MULTTEST;
   title3 ''Permutation Analysis'';
   class Group;
   test peto(t/time=Days permutation=10);
   ods select pValues;
run;
```

Output from Program 12.18

```
        Comparisons of Survival Curves via the LIFETEST Procedure

                       The LIFETEST Procedure

                      Test of Equality over Strata

                                                   Pr >
            Test        Chi-Square      DF      Chi-Square

            Log-Rank      3.1227        1         0.0772
            Wilcoxon      2.6510        1         0.1035
            -2Log(LR)     0.0775        1         0.7807
```

```
          Logrank Test via the MULTTEST Procedure
                    Asymptotic Analysis

                         p-Values

          Variable      Contrast            Raw

             t            Trend           0.0772

                   Permutation Analysis

                         p-Values

          Variable      Contrast            Raw

             t            Trend           0.0943
```

You can see that the log-rank *p*-value from PROC LIFETEST is identical to the asymptotic *p*-value from PROC MULTTEST. So why bother with PROC MULTTEST? Because you can exploit the discrete character of the log-rank survival test to get improved multiplicity adjustments!

The final table shows the log-rank *p*-value obtained using PROC MULTTEST's permutation test. If you have multiple groups, you can use those permutation distributions to improve upon the usual Bonferroni adjustments. To do so, use the missing value trick, creating a distinct variable for each pairwise comparison, as shown for example, in Program 12.9; use the `peto` test along with the `permutation=` specification, and use the `stepbon` or `stepsid` multiplicity adjustment options.

12.8 Concluding Remarks

In this chapter we have shown numerous capabilities of PROC MULTTEST for handling discrete data, and have highlighted some problems as well. To summarize,

- PROC MULTTEST is ideally suited for multiple permutation tests with multivariate binary data where there is only one test per variable. That test can be the Fisher exact or the Cochran-Armitage trend.
- With multiple tests per variable, the subset pivotality condition fails, and you risk excess Type I errors. An indication that you have a problem is when an adjusted *p*-value is smaller than a corresponding unadjusted *p*-value. To overcome the problem, you have several options:

  1. Use the missing value coding trick, and perform discrete Bonferroni or discrete Šidák adjustments. This method is valid, does not have excess Type I errors, and the adjusted *p*-values do not require Monte Carlo.
  2. Use the closure-based method with the discrete Bonferroni adjustments. This method is more powerful than 1., does not have excess Type I errors, and the adjusted *p*-values do not require Monte Carlo. However, the method requires extensive DATA step manipulations.

3. Use the closure-based method with resampling-based multiplicity adjustments. This method is the most powerful among these three, does not have excess Type I errors, but the adjusted *p*-values do require Monte Carlo, and the method requires extensive DATA step manipulations.

4. Use the FT tests with step-down bootstrap resampling adjustments instead of permutation tests and permutation adjustments. This method is quite simple to code, and can greatly lessen the excess Type I error problem. However, the method is only a large-sample approximation, and excess Type I errors can occur.

- You can further improve the power of global null hypothesis tests involving discrete data by using Rom's method, with the provided %romex macro (or the corresponding %rommc macro for larger problems).

- PROC MULTTEST is particularly convenient for performing multiple animal carcinogenicity tests.

- You can perform multiple comparisons of survival distributions using PROC MULTTEST.

A parenthetical note: Several applications in this chapter formulate safety and toxicity studies using tests of null hypotheses. As in all hypothesis testing procedures, you should be aware that the conclusion "accept H_0" does not necessarily imply safety, as the sample size might not have been large enough to detect an important difference.

Chapter 13

Bayesian Multiple Comparisons and Multiple Tests

13.1 Introduction

The Bayesian paradigm offers a perspective on multiple comparisons that is completely different from the frequentist point of view we have considered so far. For Bayesians, frequentist constructs like p-values and confidence intervals, which have been fundamental to our development up to this point, are not generally viable; in fact, they violate basic principles of Bayesian inference. In this chapter we discuss some of the fundamental differences between the two philosophies and then present Bayesian analyses of a few of the examples considered in earlier chapters.

The dispute between the two camps has actually been going on for decades, but frequentist techniques have generally been favored because of their ease of use. However, with the availability of modern computing power and Monte Carlo algorithms, Bayesian methods are currently enjoying a surge of new interest. This revival is bringing many of the foundational issues into the forefront as researchers realize that both alternatives are viable.

Table 13.1 describes some of the primary distinctions between the two viewpoints. In many respects the Bayesian approach is more appealing because of its coherent nature and understandability. For example, frequentists typically test a sharp null hypothesis by constructing a p-value, the probability of observing data at least as extreme as the given data given that the hypothesis is true. If this probability is small, frequentists conclude that the hypothesis is unlikely to be true. Bayesians argue that this appeal to *reductio ad absurdum* as evidence against the hypothesis is unreasonable because it is based on data that never occurred. Instead, they directly compute the probability of a hypothesis given the data using Bayes rule. The conclusions between the two methods can be dramatically different; refer to Jeffreys (1961), Lindley (1971), Berger and Sellke (1987), Berger and Berry (1988), and Schervish (1996).

TABLE 13.1   Distinctions between Frequentists and Bayesians

Frequentists	Bayesians
Interpret probability in terms of long-run frequencies	Interpret probability as a subjective degree of belief
Require a probabilistic model and a repeated sampling space	Require a probabilistic model and prior distribution
Employ a loose collection of techniques containing some inconsistencies	Enjoy a coherent, self-contained system
Condition on the parameters and contemplate the data varying	Condition on the data and contemplate the parameters varying
Envision hypothetical repetitions of the experiment	Condition on the knowns and average over unknowns
Subjectively select the model and the sampling space	Subjectively select the model and the prior distribution
Simulate via bootstrap or permutation resampling	Simulate via Markov chain Monte Carlo

The basic components of a typical Bayesian analysis are

- the data, $\mathbf{Y}$
- a probabilistic model for the data in terms of unknown parameters, $\boldsymbol{\theta}$
- a prior distribution for $\boldsymbol{\theta}$.

Unlike the frequentist approach, the unknown parameter vector $\boldsymbol{\theta}$ is assumed to be random. Uncertainty about it is described using probability theory, and we let $P(\boldsymbol{\theta})$ denote its prior density.

Let $L(\mathbf{Y}|\boldsymbol{\theta})$ denote the probabilistic model for the data given $\boldsymbol{\theta}$, which is also known as the likelihood function. Bayes Theorem states that

$$P(\boldsymbol{\theta}|\mathbf{Y}) \propto L(\mathbf{Y}|\boldsymbol{\theta})P(\boldsymbol{\theta}),$$

where $P(\boldsymbol{\theta}|\mathbf{Y})$ is known as the posterior density for $\boldsymbol{\theta}$. In words, the posterior density of the parameters is proportional to the likelihood times the prior. All Bayesian inferences are based on the posterior density $P(\boldsymbol{\theta}|\mathbf{Y})$, and Bayes Theorem provides a way of computing it.

At first, we focus on Bayesian methods that incorporate little or no prior information, although the methods presented easily extend to informative priors. Using noninformative or reference priors is useful when there is little prior information about the parameters in a model relative to the information about them contained in the data. In this case the data will overwhelm any prior distribution and so you might as well choose convenient ones. Noninformative priors are also useful when you want to let the data "speak for themselves" or when you want to report results to other investigators in a form that is convenient for them to incorporate their own prior beliefs. In addition, noninformative priors offer you the chance to compare results with the frequentist methods we have already employed. Kass and Wasserman (1996) provide an extensive review and discussion of reference priors.

The Bayesian analysis strategy we present is based on simulation. Using Markov chain Monte Carlo, we generate a large pseudorandom sample from the joint posterior density $P(\boldsymbol{\theta}|\mathbf{Y})$. Details of how the simulation is carried out are in Wolfinger and Kass (1998).

This sample is then used to make all subsequent inferences. Simple statistics like means, medians, standard deviations, and percentiles are the basic tools for making inferences about quantities of interest such as least-squares means or their differences. Appropriate adjustments can be made when necessary to account for multiple inferences. Working with the sample is usually much easier than trying to derive the analytical form of various posterior summaries, especially when they involve multiple variables. The resulting solutions do involve Monte Carlo error, but this can be reduced to a negligible level by increasing the simulation sample size.

13.2   The Variance Component Model

As with the general model considered in Chapter 10, the model for the data is assumed to be

$$\mathbf{Y} = \mathbf{X}\boldsymbol{\beta} + \mathbf{Z}\boldsymbol{\gamma} + \boldsymbol{\epsilon},$$

where $\mathbf{Y}$ is an observation vector, $\mathbf{X}$ and $\mathbf{Z}$ are known design matrices, and $\boldsymbol{\beta}$, $\boldsymbol{\gamma}$, and $\boldsymbol{\epsilon}$ are unknown vectors.

The vector $\boldsymbol{\beta}$ contains fixed-effect parameters and models the mean of the data. We assume the prior for $\boldsymbol{\beta}$ is completely flat; that is $p(\boldsymbol{\beta}) = 1$. The vector $\boldsymbol{\gamma}$ contains random-effect parameters and models covariance in the data. It is assumed to have a normally distributed prior, with mean 0 and diagonal variance matrix $\boldsymbol{\Gamma}$. The vector $\boldsymbol{\epsilon}$ models residual errors in the usual way, as a random sample from a $N(0, \sigma^2)$ density. The elements of $\boldsymbol{\Gamma}$ along with σ^2 form the variance components of the model.

The joint prior density for $\boldsymbol{\beta}$, $\boldsymbol{\Gamma}$, and σ^2 is assumed to be the noninformative prior of Jeffreys (1961), which is routinely employed in Bayesian analysis of linear models such as those presented in Box and Tiao (1973) and Broemeling (1985). This prior does not contain $\boldsymbol{\beta}$ and consists of products of reciprocals of various linear combinations of the variance components, depending upon the model. This prior is invariant to reparameterizations of the model and incorporates very little information about any of the parameters.

We limit ourselves to this variance component model because it is fairly flexible and contains the general linear model and randomized block model as special cases. Also, we can easily generate a sample from it using PROC MIXED. Other models have been used in this book, such as the repeated measures model using an unstructured covariance matrix, but sampling methods for these are not yet available in PROC MIXED. General methods such as Gibbs sampling can be used in this case (refer to Gelfand et al., 1990), although we do not cover them in this chapter.

13.3   Analysis of an Incomplete Block Design

13.3.1   The Model

To illustrate a Bayesian analysis of a variance component model, we use the detergent data from Program 9.8 in Section 9.2.7 and Program 10.5 in Section 10.3.2. The data are from an incomplete block design and follow the mixed model

$$y_{ij} = \mu + \alpha_i + \beta_j + \epsilon_{ij}$$

with i denoting detergent and j block. Using notation from the previous section, the fixed effects vector $\boldsymbol{\beta}$ consists of μ and the α_i, the random effects vector $\boldsymbol{\gamma}$ contains the β_j, and the residuals $\boldsymbol{\epsilon}$ the ϵ_{ij}. The variance components are $\sigma_b^2 = \text{Var}(\beta_j)$ and $\sigma_e^2 = \text{Var}(\epsilon_{ij})$.

Because of the imbalance in the design, there is not a simple expression for Jeffreys prior here, although it is close to being proportional to $\sigma_e^{-2}(\sigma_e^2 + 2.8\sigma_b^2)^{-1}$.

13.3.2 Generating the Sample

Program 13.1 generates a Bayesian sample.

PROGRAM 13.1   **Bayesian Sample for an Incomplete Block Design**

```
data detergent;
   do detergent=1 to 5;
      do block =1 to 10;
         input plates @@;
         output;
      end;
   end;
   datalines;
27 28 30 31 29 30  .  .  .  .
26 26 29  .  .  .  30 21 26  .
30  .  . 34 32  . 34 31  . 33
 . 29  . 33  . 34 31  . 33 31
 .  . 26  . 24 25  . 23 24 26
run;

proc mixed data=detergent;
   class block detergent;
   model plates = detergent;
   random block;
   lsmeans detergent / cl adjust=simulate(seed=121211);
   prior / out=sample seed=1283470 nsample=10000;
run;
```

The prior statement requests PROC MIXED to generate a Bayesian sample and output it to the data set sample. The seed= option specifies the random number seed, and the nsample= option specifies the number of samples, here 10,000. Besides the sample data set, the prior statement generates the following tables at the end of the PROC MIXED output:

Output from Program 13.1

Posterior Sampling Information

Prior	Jeffreys
Algorithm	Independence Chain
Sample Size	10000
Seed	1283470

Base Densities

Type	Parm1	Parm2
ig	4.4974	33.777
ig	8.0335	15.097

Acceptance Rates

Boundary Constraints	Sampling
0.99	1.00

The Posterior Sampling Information Table presents basic information about the sampling. The Base Densities table describes the so-called "proposal" distribution used in generating the sample, a product of independent inverted gamma densities with the indicated parameters. A proposal is a candidate simulated sample point, which may or may not be selected for the final sample based on various criteria which aim to ensure that it comes from the intended posterior distribution. The Acceptance Rates table indicates how often a proposal is selected for the final sample. A proposal can be rejected because it violates boundary constraints (here, negative variance components) or because of a Markov chain Monte Carlo rejection due to differences between the proposal density and the true posterior density. A perfect proposal density matching the posterior density exactly would always produce an acceptance rate of $1.0 = 100$ percent, and we have achieved that level of acceptance here to within two decimal places.

Keep in mind that for other problems the sampling acceptance rates may not be nearly as large. For these more difficult cases the PROC MIXED proposal density is not as close to the true posterior. Lower acceptance rates mean that there will be a larger number of duplicate observations in the sample and thus a larger degree of dependence in the sampled observations. Nevertheless, you can still obtain valid inferences in these case.

13.3.3   Simultaneous Intervals

Proceeding now to inference using the posterior sample from the detergent data set, our interest focuses on the LS-means of the five detergent levels and their differences. Because an LSMEANS statement was specified in the PROC MIXED code, the `sample` data set will contain separate variables for each LS-mean, denoted `lsm1`, `lsm2`, ..., `lsm5`. Also, because the `adjust=` option was specified, the variables `dif1`, `dif2`, ..., `dif10` are also included, corresponding to the pairwise differences of the five LS-means. An informative first step in conducting a Bayesian analysis of these variables is to look at various univariate statistics for each of them. For example, the following statements use PROC UNIVARI-ATE to compute the 2.5th and 97.5th percentiles of `dif1`, which represent an interval that contains the difference of the first two LS-Means with subjective probability 0.95.

Computing the 95 Percent Central Range of dif1

```
proc univariate data=sample noprint;
   var dif1;
   output out=dif1Range95 pctlpts =2.5    97.5
                          pctlname=Lower Upper
                          pctlpre =dif1;
proc print data=dif1Range95 noobs;
   run;
```

The results are shown as follows.

dif1Lower	dif1Upper
0.56025	4.13866

To account for multiplicity in this setting, we construct a set of intervals that has probability 0.95 of *simultaneously* containing the parameters of interest. Different approaches can be used to accomplish this; we adopt one that is fairly simple to understand and compute. The method is to begin with the collection of unadjusted 95 percent intervals and then inflate all the individual percentage levels by the same factor until the simultaneous coverage over the Bayesian sample equals 95 percent. This approach has been implemented in the %BayesIntervals macro. Its invocation and output are as follows:

Using the %BayesIntervals Macro

```
%BayesIntervals(data=sample,vars=dif1-dif10)
```

with output

Iteration	Alpha	Coverage
1	0.05	0.7402
2	0.025	0.853
3	0.0125	0.9178
4	0.00625	0.9548
5	0.009375	0.9359
6	0.0078125	0.9446
7	0.00703125	0.9498

OBS	_NAME_	Lower	Upper
1	dif1	-0.17985	5.0957
2	dif2	-5.96572	-0.8408
3	dif3	-4.93210	0.1421
4	dif4	1.66916	7.0323
5	dif5	-8.46664	-3.2912
6	dif6	-7.51397	-2.1952
7	dif7	-0.65683	4.5272
8	dif8	-1.56578	3.5971
9	dif9	5.17189	10.3302
10	dif10	4.22270	9.2344

The macro begins by computing the simultaneous coverage of the unadjusted intervals (the 2.5th and 97.5th percentiles of each variable); for this example it is 0.7402. It then conducts a bisection search until the simultaneous coverage is sufficiently close to 0.95. New percentiles are computed at each step until an effective α value of 0.00703125 produces the desired coverage.

The output contains the intervals adjusted for multiplicity. They are fairly similar to the frequentist adjusted intervals obtained in the Output from Program 10.5 and lead to similar conclusions about the LS-Means differences.

13.3.4   Multiple Hypothesis Testing: A Loss Function Approach

Hypothesis testing can take on quite a different flavor in a Bayesian context than it has in a frequentist one. In the Bayesian context, inferences stem from the actual (posterior) probabilities of hypotheses, and these are generally only superficially related to p-values and their adjustments (refer to Berger and Sellke, 1987, and Berger and Berry, 1988).

One common approach to multiple hypothesis testing in a Bayesian framework is to define a loss function on one-sided null and alternative hypotheses. Among the most well-known methods of this kind is the one proposed by Waller and Duncan (1969), who define the loss associated with deciding that the null hypothesis $H_0^{ij}: \mu_i \leq \mu_j$ is true to be

$$L(H_0^{ij}) = \begin{cases} 0, & \text{if } \delta_{ij} \leq 0, \\ \delta_{ij}, & \text{if } \delta_{ij} > 0, \end{cases}$$

and the loss associated with deciding conversely that the alternative hypothesis H_A^{ij} : $\mu_i >$ μ_j is true to be

$$L(H_A^{ij}) = \begin{cases} -k\delta_{ij}, & \text{if } \delta_{ij} \leq 0, \\ 0, & \text{if } \delta_{ij} > 0, \end{cases}$$

where $\delta_{ij} = \mu_i - \mu_j$ (the difference of the ith and jth LS-Means), and k is a constant defining the ratio of severity of Type 1 to Type 2 errors. You can obtain results for this method in the general linear model by using the WALLER option in the MEANS statement of PROC GLM, with the default value of $k = 100$.

For a variance component model, you can set up differences of the Waller-Duncan loss functions for each observation in the Bayesian sample and then average them across all observations. Program 13.2 performs this analysis with the Bayesian sample from the detergent data.

PROGRAM 13.2   Calculating Average Differences in Losses

```
%let k = 100;
data s;
   set sample;
   array lsm[5] lsm1-lsm5;
   array Loss[5,5] Loss1-Loss25;
   do i = 1 to 5;
      do j = 1 to 5;
         delta = lsm[i] - lsm[j];
         if (delta > 0) then Loss[i,j] =    delta;
         else                Loss[i,j] = &k*delta;
      end;
   end;
run;

proc means data=s mean noprint;
   var Loss1-Loss25;
   output out=o mean=mean1-mean25;
run;

data o1;
   set o;
   array mean[5,5] mean1-mean25;
   do i = 1 to 5;
      do j = 1 to 5;
         if (i ne j) then do;
            LossDiff = mean[i,j];
            output;
         end;
      end;
   end;
   keep i j LossDiff;
proc print noobs;
run;
```

	i	j	LossDiff
Output from	1	2	2.176
Program 13.2	1	3	-346.880
	1	4	-234.206
	1	5	4.374
	2	1	-234.718
	2	3	-581.418
	2	4	-468.565
	2	5	1.247
	3	1	3.458
	3	2	5.814
	3	4	-3.657
	3	5	7.848
	4	1	2.150
	4	2	4.686
	4	3	-117.638
	4	5	6.720
	5	1	-437.952
	5	2	-204.185
	5	3	-784.816
	5	4	-671.964

The lossdiff entries refer to the average difference in losses: $L(H_0^{ij}) - L(H_A^{ij})$ for $i = 1, \ldots, 5; j = 1, \ldots, 5; i \neq j$. The negative entries refer to cases where the null hypothesis is favored and positive entries refer to cases where the alternative is favored. This table leads to the ordering 3 4 1 2 5 (largest to smallest), with all means significantly different except for 3 and 4. Different loss functions such as those suggested by Shaffer (1998) can be easily programmed in a similar fashion.

Another approach to hypothesis testing in a Bayesian context is to define an *a priori* value determining meaningful difference, and base your inference on the posterior probability of that difference. For example, in the detergent data, suppose you determine that means different by 2 or more units should be considered meaningful. Program 13.3 constructs new 0-1 indicator variables in the sample corresponding to whether or not the null hypothesis $|\mu_i - \mu_j| > 2$ is satisfied, and then employ PROC SUMMARY to estimate the associated probabilities by counting up how often these meaningful differences occur in the sample data set.

PROGRAM 13.3   Probabilities of Meaningful Differences

```
data s1; set sample;
   array lsm[5];
   array M[5,5];
   do i=1 to 4; do j=i+1 to 5;
      M[i,j] = (abs(lsm[i] - lsm[j]) > 2);
      end; end;
proc summary data=s1;
   var M:;
   output out=s2(where=(_STAT_='MEAN'));
proc iml;
   use s2; read all var ("M1":"M25") into M;
   title "Probabilities of Meaningful Differences";
   print (shape(M,5,5)) [rowname=("1":"5") colname=("1":"5")];
```

Output from
Program 13.3

```
                   Probabilities of Meaningful Differences

                  1         2         3         4         5

         1        .       0.6578    0.9493    0.6448    0.9946
         2        .         .       0.9998    0.9977    0.5227
         3        .         .         .       0.1626    1
         4        .         .         .         .       0.9999
         5        .         .         .         .         .
```

Probabilities of joint hypotheses can be computed in the same way.

As this example shows, the sample from the joint posterior density is a powerful and flexible tool for carrying out a wide variety of useful Bayesian inferences.

13.4   Multiple Bayesian Tests of Point Nulls

In the preceding section we showed how you can use Bayesian methods to test hypotheses H_i directly by calculating $P(H_i$ is true$| \mathbf{Y})$. In this section we consider the case where the H_i are point nulls like $H_i : \theta_i = 0$, rather than interval nulls. While you might not think that such an hypothesis could really be true (to the last decimal), the use of point nulls provides a good approximation for the perhaps more realistic hypothesis $H_i : -\epsilon < \theta_i < \epsilon$, where ϵ is very small. (See Berger and Delampady, 1987.)

To perform such an analysis, you must specify your priors carefully. Not only do you have to specify your prior probability $P(H_i$ is true$)$, but you must also specify a proper prior for the effect size, given that H_i is false. Use of improper priors, as in the previous section, provides answers that are nonsensical in that the posterior probabilities on the point nulls become 1.0. (See Berger and Sellke, 1987.)

As a Bayesian, you must calibrate your prior distributions to be consistent with your prior beliefs. If you think that H_i has a moderate probability of truth, then you might set $P(H_i$ is true$)$ to be 0.5. This implies that the joint probability $P(H_i$ is true, for all $i)$ must be much smaller than 0.5, perhaps near zero in the case of many independent hypotheses.

Often, such joint prior probabilities should be much larger than zero, for example, when there is doubt whether the treatment affects *any* of the outcomes. In such a case, you must revise the probability $P(H_i$ is true, for all $i)$ upward, perhaps to 0.5, to suggest a moderate prior belief in the joint null hypothesis. Westfall, Johnson and Utts (1997) prove that, for independent variables and priors, the posterior probability $\tilde{p}_j = \tilde{P}(H_j|\mathbf{Y})$ obtained using the prior $P(H_i$ is true, for all $i) = 0.5$ is $\tilde{p}_j \approx k\sqrt{2}p_j$, where $p_j = P(H_j|\mathbf{Y})$ is the posterior evidence obtained using the prior $P(H_i$ is true$) = 0.5$. (The approximation becomes precise for larger k and smaller p_j.) Thus, there is a rough correspondence between a Bayesian posterior probability and a frequentist Bonferroni-adjusted p-value, since the multiplier k appears in both.

Still, you might like to calculate these Bayesian probabilities, and see for yourself how they depend on the priors. Gönen and Westfall (1998) developed a method for calculating these Bayesian posterior probabilities, extending the Westfall et al. (1997) method to allow both prior correlations and data correlations. Specifically, they define $\mathbf{z} = (z_1, \ldots, z_k)$, the k-dimensional vector of two-sample t-statistics, with asymptotic (conditional on $\boldsymbol{\theta}$ and $\boldsymbol{\Sigma}$) distribution $N_k(\boldsymbol{\theta}, \boldsymbol{\Sigma})$. The vector $\boldsymbol{\theta}$ contains noncentrality parameters of the tests. The matrix $\boldsymbol{\Sigma}$ is assumed to be estimated with adequate precision from the data (you can use the partial correlation matrix in the case of multivariate two-sample tests), and the estimate $\hat{\boldsymbol{\Sigma}}$ will be substituted for it. The asymptotic approach of estimating the variance-covariance matrix from the given data, and treating it as fixed and known, is a common practice in Bayesian statistics where sample sizes are reasonably large (for example, Berger and Deely, 1988).

The null hypotheses of interest are $H_j : \theta_j = 0$, $j = 1, \ldots, k$, which you can test by computing the posterior probabilities $p_j = P(H_j$ is true $\mid \mathbf{z})$, as an alternative to the usual frequentist p-values.

To calculate these posterior probabilities, you need priors. The following prior has the properties (1) it allows positive probability on each H_j, (2) it allows correlation among the binary outcomes (H_j either true or false), and (3) it allows correlation among the nonzero θ_j realizations. We will model the prior distribution of $\boldsymbol{\theta}$ using two independent multivariate normal random vectors, $\mathbf{u}$ and $\mathbf{v}$. The elements of $\mathbf{u}$ will model the prior probabilities of the individual point nulls as $\pi_j = P(u_j < c_j)$, and the elements of $\mathbf{v}$ will model the distributions of the θ_i when the point nulls are false, as equicorrelated normal random variables.

To be specific, let $\mathbf{u}$ and $\mathbf{v}$ be independent k-dimensional multivariate normal random vectors with

$$E(\mathbf{u}) = 0, \;\; \text{Var}(\mathbf{u}) = \boldsymbol{\rho}, \;\; E(\mathbf{v}) = \boldsymbol{\lambda}, \;\; \text{Var}(\mathbf{u}) = \sigma^2 \boldsymbol{\rho}.$$

where $\boldsymbol{\rho}$ be a $k \times k$ compound symmetric correlation matrix, with 1 on the diagonals and ρ on the off-diagonals, with $-1/(k-1) < \rho < 1$. Then we will model $\boldsymbol{\theta}$ as

$$\theta_j = \begin{cases} 0 & \text{if } u_j < c_j \\ v_j & \text{else.} \end{cases}$$

The parameters of this prior are $\boldsymbol{\lambda}$ and σ^2, which reflect the expected size and uncertainty surrounding the noncentrality parameter, respectively; and ρ, which is the common prior correlation among the binary outcomes and among the nonzero θ_j realizations. The value of c_j is another prior input; for example, if set $c_j \equiv 0$, then the prior probability for the jth hypothesis is 0.5. For simplicity, assume $c_j \equiv c$, so that $\pi_j \equiv \pi_0$. The value of c is determined from your specification of π_0 using the inverse normal cdf.

Details of the posterior probability calculation are given by Gönen and Westfall (1998). Their method is coded in the %BayesTests macro of the appendix. You need to set up an %Estimates macro similar to those used in the %SimIntervals and %SimTests macros discussed in Chapters 5 and 8, except that %BayesTests requires the *standardized* estimates $\hat{\theta}_i$ (divided by their standard errors) and their *correlation* matrix, rather than the raw estimates and their covariance matrix. Also, the %BayesTests analysis is asymptotic, so the error degrees of freedom and MSE are not required. Once such an %Estimates macro has been defined, you invoke the macro as follows

```
%BayesTests(meanmuz  = <values> ,
            sigmamuz = <value>  ,
            rho      = <value>  ,
            Piall    = <value>  ,
            Pi0      = <value>  );
```

where

meanmuz   is the prior mean of the effect size, given that the effect is nonzero. This term is called "λ" in the development above. The default is 2.5 2.5 ..... Why? Because typical studies are designed to have power .80, translating to an expected noncentrality parameter of 2.5.

sigmamuz   is the prior variance (called σ^2 above) of the nonzero effect sizes. This number is assumed to be a constant value 2.0 by default; which, in conjunction with the mean effect size of 2.5, admits a small probability (0.039) that the effects are in opposite of expected directions.

rho　is the prior correlation of the effect sizes (ρ above), given that they are nonzero. It is also used to define the simultaneous null outcomes (specifically, it is the tetrachoric correlation of binary null outcomes). There is no default, but if you specify both `Piall` and `Pi0`, then you cannot specify rho; it will be computed for you.

Piall　is your prior value for $P(H_i$ is true, for all $i)$. There is no default, but if you specify both rho and `Pi0`, then you cannot specify `Piall`; it will be computed for you.

Pi0　is your prior value for $P(H_i$ is true) $= \pi_0$. There is no default, but if you specify both rho and `Piall`, then you cannot specify `Pi0`; it will be computed for you.

Program 13.4 shows how to use `%BayesTests` to reanalyze the multiple endpoint data, in multivariate form, as analyzed in Program 11.5.

PROGRAM 13.4   Multiple Bayes Tests of Point Null Hypotheses

```
data MultipleEndpoints;
   Treatment = 'Placebo';
   do Subject = 1 to 54;
      input Endpoint1-Endpoint4 @@;
      output;
   end;
   Treatment = 'Drug';
   do Subject = 54+1 to 54+57;
      input Endpoint1-Endpoint4 @@;
      output;
   end;
datalines;
4 3 3 5   5 0 1 7   1 0 1 9   4 0 3 5   3 0 2 9   4 1 2 6   2 0 4 6
2 2 5 5   3 0 1 7   2 0 1 9   4 6 5 5   2 0 2 8   2 7 1 7   1 2 2 9
4 0 3 7   3 0 1 6   3 0 1 6   4 1 4 6   6 0 4 7   3 0 1 8   3 0 1 9
2 1 2 7   6 2 3 5   3 0 4 7   3 0 1 9   2 0 1 9   6 9 6 3   4 9 2 6
2 0 1 7   1 0 1 9   4 0 4 7   3 1 4 6   3 0 3 7   1 0 1 8   6 7 5 4
4 6 2 5   6 19 7 5 6 3 6 6   3 0 5 6   2 4 2 8   1 0 1 8   4 21 5 5
2 0 2 9   4 7 3 5   3 1 2 8   3 3 3 8   4 3 4 6   1 0 1 10 1 0 2 9
3 0 4 5   3 1 1 6   3 4 4 6   5 8 5 5   5 1 5 4   1 0 4 8   1 0 1 10
1 0 1 9   2 1 2 7   4 1 2 5   5 0 5 6   1 4 5 6   5 6 4 6   2 0 2 9
2 2 2 5   1 0 1 10 3 2 3 6   5 4 6 6   2 1 2 8   2 1 2 6   2 1 1 8
3 0 3 9   3 1 2 6   1 0 2 9   1 0 1 9   3 0 3 9   1 0 1 10 1 0 1 9
1 0 1 10 2 0 4 7   5 1 2 6   4 0 5 7   4 0 4 6   2 1 3 6   2 1 1 6
4 0 4 6   1 0 1 8   1 0 2 9   4 1 3 6   4 3 4 5   4 2 5 5   1 0 1 10
3 0 2 8   4 2 2 8   3 0 2 9   1 0 1 10 1 0 1 9   2 0 2 9   2 1 2 8
3 0 3 8   2 4 2 6   2 1 1 9   2 2 2 9   4 0 1 4   3 3 1 8   4 4 3 6
2 0 1 10 4 2 3 6   1 0 1 8   2 0 2 8   5 1 5 5   4 0 4 6
;

data multend1;
   set MultipleEndpoints;
   Endpoint4 = -Endpoint4;
run;
```

```
ods listing close;
proc glm data=multend1;
   class Treatment;
   model Endpoint1-Endpoint4 = Treatment;
   estimate "Treatment vs Control" Treatment -1 1;
   manova h=Treatment / printe;
   ods output Estimates  =Estimates
              PartialCorr=PartialCorr;
run;
ods listing;

%macro Estimates;
   use Estimates;
   read all var {tValue}                  into EstPar;
   use PartialCorr;
   read all var ("Endpoint1":"Endpoint4") into cov;
%mend;


%BayesTests(rho=.5,Pi0  =.5);
```

The reason for the Endpoint4 = -Endpoint4 line in the DATA step that creates the multend1 data set is that, *a priori*, the drug was expected to lower all responses but y4 (if the drug indeed is efficacious). It is **not** based on the estimated sign of the difference between means. The output from Program 13.4 is as follows:

Output from Program 13.4

```
                    Prior Probability on Individual Nulls is .5
                    Prior Probability on Joint Null is 0.2000000001
                       Prior Correlation Between Nulls is .5
```

		Prior					
	Prior Mean	StdDev					
Z	Effect	Effect	Posterior				
Statistic	Size	Size	Probability	Cov1	Cov2	Cov3	Cov4
2.55256	2.5	1.41421	0.09780	1.00000	0.38262	0.63745	0.69522
2.49145	2.5	1.41421	0.08925	0.38262	1.00000	0.44755	0.42592
1.29349	2.5	1.41421	0.26810	0.63745	0.44755	1.00000	0.63235
2.37971	2.5	1.41421	0.11358	0.69522	0.42592	0.63235	1.00000

You can make decisions concerning whether the nulls are true by using the posterior probabilities. Noting that Bayesian posterior probabilities tend to be much larger than ordinary frequentists *p*-values (for example, Berger and Sellke, 1987), it is reasonable to consider a probability of 0.10 or less as reasonable evidence against the null hypothesis.

The preceding analysis used rho=.5 and implied a joint prior probability of 0.2 for all null hypotheses. In this study, there was doubt as to whether any of the endpoints were affected by the drug, but there was no doubt that the hypotheses are correlated *a priori*. A second analysis uses Piall = .50 to reflect more doubt about the composite null.

PROGRAM 13.5   **Evaluating Sensitivity to Priors—Recalibrating the Joint Prior**

```
%BayesTests(rho=.5,PiAll=.5);
```

Output from Program 13.5

```
            Prior Probability on Individual Nulls is 0.7644590384
                  Prior Probability on Joint Null is .5
                  Prior Correlation Between Nulls is .5
```

		Prior					
	Prior Mean	StdDev					
Z	Effect	Effect	Posterior				
Statistic	Size	Size	Probability	Cov1	Cov2	Cov3	Cov4
2.55256	2.5	1.41421	0.41174	1.00000	0.38262	0.63745	0.69522
2.49145	2.5	1.41421	0.37826	0.38262	1.00000	0.44755	0.42592
1.29349	2.5	1.41421	0.60591	0.63745	0.44755	1.00000	0.63235
2.37971	2.5	1.41421	0.44095	0.69522	0.42592	0.63235	1.00000

Now you see that the posterior probabilities are substantially higher. Much as in the case of frequentist multiplicity adjustment, the Bayesian posterior probabilities are quite sensitive to the choice of family, when you compare the results from using $Pi0 = .5$ and $Piall = .5$.

As a footnote, the analysis with $Piall=0.5$ turned out to be correct for this particular pharmaceutical product. The clinical trial was replicated several times, with none of the four endpoints ever approaching statistical significance, and product development was halted.

Finally, we note that the %BayesTests macro is designed for use with logically unconstrained (free combination) tests, as is the case with multiple endpoints. You cannot perform constrained tests, such as pairwise comparisons using this macro, but see Gopalan and Berry (1998) and Westfall et al. (1997) for related approaches to the pairwise comparisons problem.

13.5 Concluding Remarks

Bayesian methods are becoming increasingly popular as a coherent means of interpreting data. Multiple testing and multiple comparisons issues are as important in Bayesian statistics as they are in the frequentist framework although the analytic tools differ greatly. In this chapter we have introduced three types of Bayesian methods for multiple inferences, two for testing hypotheses and one for simultaneous Bayesian intervals (the %BayesIntervals macro). The resulting inferential quantities are posterior probabilities and posterior intervals instead of p-values and confidence limits.

The following Bayesian methods are described and illustrated with examples:

- Markov chain Monte Carlo simulation for a variance components model using PROC MIXED
- Computation of the Waller-Duncan loss function and the probability of meaningful differences
- Testing multiple point null hypotheses using the %BayesTest macro
- Evaluation of sensitivity to prior probabilities and prior correlations

Validity of a Bayesian procedure depends upon the reasonableness of its prior assumptions. If the priors used by the %BayesIntervals macro, as described in Section 13.3.1, are reasonable for your situation, and if you are comfortable with the model assumptions, then you may use the %BayesIntervals macro.

We have provided two hypothesis testing methods, with different assumptions on the priors. If you believe there is some probability that the point null hypotheses are true, and want to test these hypotheses, then you may use the %BayesTests macro. If you feel that the null point has no probability of being true, and if you want to calculate probabilities of meaningful differences, then you may prefer the Loss Function method described in Section 13.3.4.

Additional Topics

14.1   Introduction

No book is complete. Our focus in this book admittedly reflects preferences of the authors (although, with so many authors, a fairly wide collection of views is present!) In this chapter, we attempt to fill in the gaps somewhat, presenting material that is useful, but doesn't quite fit in any previous chapter. Of course, there still will be methods left untouched. If you have a great interest in one of these other methods, send any of us an e-mail, or e-mail sasbbu@sas.com. Who knows, maybe it will wind up in the second edition!

In any event, the topics addressed in this chapter are necessarily disjoint, without much in the way of a common theme (other than MCPs, of course!) In this chapter we discuss large-sample comparisons, multiple comparisons with "the best," infinite family sizes with multivariate tests, and repeated significance tests (interim analysis) in clinical trials.

14.2   Large-Sample Multiple Comparisons Using PROC LOGISTIC, PROC LIFEREG, PROC PHREG, PROC CATMOD, PROC GENMOD

We developed the %Sim* macros with the intention that you would be able to use them with any SAS procedure that provides estimates and their covariance matrix, thus enabling you to perform multiple comparisons in a broad range of applications. Many procedures use large-sample asymptotic normal approximations for their significance levels and critical values. In order to be consistent with such methods, the %Sim* macros allow asymptotic normal approximations as well. When you specify $df = 0$ in the %Estimates macro, the %Sim* macros will sample from the appropriate multivariate normal distribution, rather than the multivariate t distribution.

The following example of this capability, taken from Stokes, Davis, and Koch (1995), uses PROC LOGISTIC to analyze a study designed to compare the cure rates from urinary infection using three treatments (A, B and C). A second factor in the study is the diagnosis of the infection, either "complicated" or "uncomplicated." In our analysis, we perform multiple comparisons of the differences among the A, B and C levels, and we include the comparison of the cure rates for complicated and uncomplicated diagnoses, for a total of $k = 4$ elements of the family. Our inference will concern log odds ratios initially, which we will convert to odds ratios.

PROGRAM 14.1   Multiple Comparisons in Logistic Regression

```
data uti;
    format diagnosis $13.;
    do Diagnosis = "complicated", "uncomplicated";
        do treatment = "A", "B", "C";
            input cured total @@;
            AminusC = (treatment="A");
            BminusC = (treatment="B");
            CompminusUnComp = (Diagnosis="complicated");
            output;
            end;
        end;
datalines;
78 106   101 112   68 114    40 45   54 59   34 40
;
proc logistic data=uti outest=stats covout;
    model cured/total = AminusC BminusC CompminusUnComp;
run;

%macro Contrasts;
    C = { 0   1   0   0 ,
          0   0   1   0 ,
          0   1  -1   0 ,
          0   0   0   1 };
    C = C';
    Clab = {"trt(A-C)" ,
            "trt(B-C)" ,
            "trt(A-B)" ,
            "Diag(Comp-UnComp)" };
%mend;
```

```
%macro estimates;
    use stats(where=(_TYPE_='PARMS'));
    read all var {INTERCEPT  AminusC BminusC CompminusUnComp} into EstPar;
    EstPar = EstPar';
    use stats (where=(_TYPE_='COV'));
    read all var {INTERCEPT AminusC BminusC CompminusUnComp} into Cov;
    df = 0;
%mend;

%SimIntervals(seed=121211, nsamp=100000);
```

Output from Program 14.1

```
                      Estimated 95% Quantile = 2.447601
                        Asymptotic Normal Approximations
```

Contrast	Estimate	Standard Error	t Value	Pr > |t| Raw	Adjusted	95% Confidence Interval	
trt(A-C)	0.5847	0.2641	2.21	0.0268	0.0912	-0.0617	1.2312
trt(B-C)	1.5608	0.3160	4.94	<.0001	<.0001	0.7874	2.3341
trt(A-B)	-0.9760	0.3311	-2.95	0.0032	0.0119	-1.7863	-0.1657
Diag(Comp-UnComp)	-0.9616	0.2998	-3.21	0.0013	0.0048	-1.6954	-0.2278

In this case, all comparisons but the A-C treatment comparisons are statistically significant. Note also,

- We specified df = 0 in the %Estimates macro to get the asymptotic analysis.
- The t Value and Pr > |t| really refer to z, not t, but the heading Asymptotic Normal Approximations clues you in to this fact.
- The Raw p-values are the Wald test p-values, and could be obtained identically using the TEST statement in PROC LOGISTIC.
- Our method uses the correlation information, thus the inferences are more precise than the Bonferroni inferences. In particular, the trt(A-C) comparison would not be significant at the FWE= 0.10 level using Bonferroni's method with $k = 4$, but is significant using our method.
- As with the unadjusted analysis, the adjusted p-values and confidence intervals are asymptotic, and thus FWE control is only assured for large sample sizes.
- The confidence intervals are for log odds ratios. You can convert them to simultaneous intervals for odds ratios simply by exponentiating them. For example, the odds of cure with treatment B are between $e^{0.7874} = 2.20$ and $e^{2.3341} = 10.32$ times higher than they are for treatment C.
- Our analysis assumes a no interaction model, as suggested by Stokes et al. You can assess interaction effects using multiple comparisons using this method by constructing the appropriate cross-products of the indicator variables, and expressing the six interaction tetrad differences as linear combinations of the resulting model parameters.

You can also perform this analysis using %SimTests, if you are willing to give up the confidence intervals for risk ratios. Simply substitute %SimTests (with type=LOGICAL) for %SimIntervals in Program 14.1, and you get

Output from Program 14.1 Using %SimTests instead of %SimIntervals

```
    Logically Constrained (Restricted Combinations) Step-Down Tests
                   Asymptotic Normal Approximations


                                Standard     ----- Pr > |t| -----
      Contrast         Estimate   Error     Raw     Bon     Adj     SE(AdjP)

      trt(A-C)          0.5847   0.2641    0.0268  0.0268  0.0268      0
      trt(B-C)          1.5608   0.3160    <.0001  <.0001  <.0001      0
      trt(A-B)         -0.9760   0.3311    0.0032  0.0032  0.0032      0
      Diag(Comp-UnComp) -0.9616  0.2998    0.0013  0.0027  0.0027      0
```

In this case, all comparisons are statistically significant at the FWE= 0.050 level. Again, this is an asymptotic analysis.

14.3   Multiple Comparisons with the Best

Material in this section is largely reproduced from the corresponding sample program in the SAS/STAT sample library, which is available on the Web at www.sas.com/techsup/download/sample/samp_lib/statsampMultiple_Comparisons_with_the_Be.html.

Suppose you are conducting an experiment on the effects of several alternative drugs for treating a certain disease. The goal is to determine which drugs are most effective. However, in this case not all pairwise differences are of interest: you only want to compare each drug with the true best drug.

This situation is called multiple comparisons with the best, or MCB (Hsu, 1996). It is related to several other multiple inference techniques, such as bioequivalence testing and ranking and selection. MCB is designed to allow you to make two different kinds of assertions with statistical confidence:

- certain treatments are inferior to the true best
- other treatments are close enough to the true best that you may consider them to be practically equivalent to it.

By giving up the ability to say precisely *how inferior* the not-the-best treatments are, MCB provides sharper inference than can be achieved by evaluating all pairwise comparisons. On the other hand, if you need to know how inferior the not-the-best treatments are, unconstrained multiple comparisons with the best (UMCB) provides this sort of analysis. MCB is executed by multiply performing a one-sided Dunnett's test for comparisons with a control, in turn treating each of the alternative drugs as the control which is potentially the best; UMCB deduces from two-sided Dunnett's tests (or alternatively from Tukey's all-pairwise test).

You can use the %MCB macro to perform MCB analysis, and the %UMCB macro to perform UMCB analysis, where in both cases the best population mean is defined as the maximum one; use %MCW and %UMCW, respectively (for multiple comparisons with the *worst* and its associated unconstrained version), if you want to compare to the minimum population mean. These macros use the MIXED procedure and the output manager to perform Dunnett's and Tukey's tests and write the results to SAS data sets, which are then processed to compute the standard form of MCB and UMCB analysis, respectively.

The following arguments are required by each of the macros. They must be the first three arguments and they must be in this order. Do not use keywords for these arguments.

1. the SAS data set containing the data to be analyzed
2. the response variable
3. the grouping variable

The following additional arguments may be listed in any order, separated by commas:

MODEL=   is a linear model for the response, specified using the effects syntax of PROC GLM. The default is a one-way model in the required grouping variable.

CLASS=   are classification variables involved in the linear model. The default is the required grouping variable.

ALPHA=   is the level of significance for comparisons among the means. The default is 0.05.

OUT=   is the name of the output data set containing the MCB analysis. The default is _LEV.

OPTIONS=   is a string containing either of the following options:

- NOPRINT: suppresses printed output of results
- NOCLEAN: suppresses deletion of temporary datasets

EXAMPLE: Comparing Water Filters

Hsu (1984) reports the results of a study undertaken to compare seven different brands of water filter. For each brand, samples of water were run through three filters and then the filters were incubated; the response is the number of bacterial colonies grown on filter. A better filter is one that captures more bacteria and thus has a higher colony count. Thus, the %MCB macro is appropriate. Program 14.2 creates the FILTER data set and analyzes it with %MCB.

PROGRAM 14.2   MCB Analysis of Water Filters

```
data Filter;
   do Brand = 1 to 7;
      do i = 1 to 3;
         input NColony @@;
         output;
         end;
      end;
   cards;
 69 122  95
118 154 102
171 132 182
122 119   .
204 225 190
140 130 127
170 165   .
;

%MCB(Filter,NColony,Brand);
```

Note that some of the data are missing. The %MCB results are as follows:

Output from Program 14.2

Effect	Brand	Estimate	StdErr	cllo	clhi	rval	sval
Brand	1	95.3333	11.7075	-153.941	0.0000	0.00006	.
Brand	2	124.67	11.7075	-124.608	0.0000	0.00087	.
Brand	3	161.67	11.7075	-87.608	0.0000	0.04184	.
Brand	4	120.50	14.3387	-133.843	0.0000	0.00130	.
Brand	5	206.33	11.7075	-7.950	86.8429	.	0.10065
Brand	6	132.33	11.7075	-116.941	0.0000	0.00189	.
Brand	7	167.50	14.3387	-86.843	7.9499	0.10065	.

The filter brand with the highest colony count was number 5, but because the lower endpoint of the 95 percent confidence interval for the difference between it and the best is negative, we cannot assert that this particular brand is the best. However, we can say that either brand 5 or 7 is the best, since these are the only two brands for which the confidence interval properly contains 0. These conclusions are corroborated by the two *p*-values associated with MCB analysis, labeled `rval` and `sval` in the output. `rval` is the *p*-value for whether the associated mean is equal to the best, and `sval` is the *p*-value for whether the sample best mean is equal to the second best. In this case, the `rval` for brand 7 and the `sval` for the sample best mean associated with brand 5 are not significant, indicating that either of them might be the true best.

14.4   Infinitely Many Comparisons with Multivariate Data

In Chapter 2, Section 2.4.3, we introduced the spouse study, where each partner in a married couple was asked to rate their passionate and companiate love felt for their partners, as well as perceived reciprocations. We tested the multivariate hypothesis $H_0: \mu_H = \mu_W$ that average response on each of the four questions was the same for the husbands and wives, where μ_i is the four-dimensional response for husbands and wives, respectively; and we found a significant difference (derived $F(4, 26) = 2.9424$, unadjusted $p = 0.0394$). We also performed various comparisons of the form $H_\mathbf{d}$: : $\mathbf{d}'\boldsymbol{\mu}_H = \mathbf{d}'\boldsymbol{\mu}_W$, with the $\mathbf{d}$ identifying linear combinations of interest. (For example, to compare the average of the husbands' four responses with the average of the wives' four responses, we set $\mathbf{d}' = (1\ 1\ 1\ 1)$.)

Noting that the global null hypothesis H_0 is true if and only if all components $H_\mathbf{d}$ are true, Roy (1953) devised a *union-intersection* (UI) test procedure, which rejects H_0 if at least one of the components $H_\mathbf{d}$ is rejected. This is the union part of UI; the rejection region for the test of H_0 is $\cup_\mathbf{d}\{$Reject $H_\mathbf{d}\}$. The intersection part of UI refers to the acceptance region, which is the complement $\cap_\mathbf{d}\{$Accept $H_\mathbf{d}\}$.

The useful thing about the UI principle is that it gives a test for all members of the infinite family (indexed by $\mathbf{d}$), such that the FWE is controlled. The trick is to identify the rejection regions so that $\cup_\mathbf{d}\{$Reject $H_\mathbf{d}\}$ will occur with probability α for FWE protection.

In the output from Program 2.7, each hypothesis $H_\mathbf{d}$ can be tested using a paired-difference t-test, with rejection rule, Reject if $|t_\mathbf{d}| \geq c_\alpha$, or equivalently, Reject if $t_\mathbf{d}^2 \geq c_\alpha^2$, and $\cup_\mathbf{d}\{$Reject $H_\mathbf{d}\}$ therefore refers to the rule $\max_\mathbf{d} t_\mathbf{d}^2 \geq c_\alpha^2$. We can set the critical value of the UI test to be the $1 - \alpha$ quantile of the null distribution of $\max_\mathbf{d} t_\mathbf{d}^2$.

The Scheffé procedure discussed in Chapter 6, Section 6.3.1, provides an example where the null distribution of $\max_\mathbf{d} t_\mathbf{d}^2$ is found, and is simply related to the F-distribution. In that case, however, the responses are univariate, and in this example the responses are multivariate. With multivariate data, the appropriate distribution is related to Roy's greatest root distribution; which, in many cases, is still related to the F.

Applying Result 5.3 of Johnson and Wichern (1998, p. 241) to the Husband-Wife paired differences, the $1 - \alpha$ quantile of $\max_\mathbf{d} t_\mathbf{d}^2$ is exactly (assuming multivariate normal data) $c_\alpha^2 = 4(30 - 1)F_{4,30-4}(1 - \alpha)/(30 - 4)$. Thus, simultaneous 95 percent confidence tests for all individual $H_\mathbf{d}$ are obtained by comparing $|t_\mathbf{d}|$ to $c_\alpha = 3.498$. You can also get simultaneous 95 percent confidence intervals by using this critical value in the usual way. This allows you to test all linear combinations, even the most significant ones that are suggested by the data, and to conclude significant differences when the critical value is exceeded.

For the husband and wife data, you can get the most significant linear combination by using the `canonical` option in the REPEATED statement as follows:

PROGRAM 14.3 **Finding the Most Significant Linear Combination with Multivariate Data**

```
ods select Spouse_Question.Canonical.CanCoefficients;
proc glm data=husbwive;
   model HusbQ1-HusbQ4 WifeQ1-WifeQ4 = / nouni;
   repeated Spouse 2, Question 4 identity/canonical;
run;
```

Output from Program 14.3

Canonical Coefficients

	Standardized Can1	Raw Can1
Spouse_1*Question_1	-0.24229896	-0.26708818
Spouse_1*Question_2	0.56932610	0.63289897
Spouse_1*Question_3	1.98961840	2.65384153
Spouse_1*Question_4	-1.37852307	-1.77626607

The Raw canonical coefficients identify the most significant test with $\mathbf{d} = (-0.267$ $0.632\ 2.654\ -1.776)$. You can construct a valid test and confidence interval for this linear combination using Program 14.4:

PROGRAM 14.4   **Confidence Interval and Test for Most Significant Linear Combination**

```
data _null_;
   tcrit = sqrt(4*(30-1)*finv(1-0.05,4,30-4)/(30-4));
   alpha = 2*(1-probt(tcrit,29));
   call symput('alpha',alpha); run;
data one;
   set HusbWive;
   maxdiff =  -0.26708818*DiffQ1 + 0.63289897*DiffQ2
              +2.65384153*DiffQ3 - 1.77626607*DiffQ4;
proc means alpha=&alpha n mean lclm uclm prt;
   title "Interval and Test for max Diff, Alpha=&alpha";
   var maxdiff;
run;
```

Output from Program 14.4

```
         Interval and Test for max Diff, Alpha=0.0015324805

                      The MEANS Procedure

                   Analysis Variable : maxdiff

                    Lower 99.8%      Upper 99.8%
     N       Mean    CL for Mean     CL for Mean     Pr > |t|
   --------------------------------------------------------------
     30   -0.6615094   -1.3001539     -0.0228649      0.0011
   --------------------------------------------------------------
```

Thus, the husbands and wives differ along this dimension determined by $\mathbf{d}$. This can be seen because the confidence interval excludes zero, and because the *p*-value 0.0011 is smaller than 0.0015324805.

Since $\mathbf{d}$ weighs the companionate love responses most heavily, and in opposite directions, you might conclude that the husbands and wives differ significantly with respect to a dimension related to "perceived reciprocation of companionate love."

For more general multivariate models, the critical values of the UI test are not simply related to the F distribution, but are given in tables of the distribution of Roy's greatest root. See, for example, Morrison (1990), who provides a good general discussion with examples and tables.

A Parenthetical Note about Union-Intersection Tests

Since most of the tests considered in this book use such a max t^2 statistic (or closely related variation), most of the methods we have discussed are in fact UI procedures. In some cases intersection-union methods, or IU methods, are justified; see Hochberg and Westfall, 1999, for an overview.

14.5 Interim Analysis and Repeated Significance Tests in Clinical Trials

The conduct of a clinical study sometimes requires a continuous monitoring for a variety of reasons. In comparative clinical trials, we are sometimes compelled to look at the data before the study has been completed to get an idea about the relative efficacy (or safety) of two or more competing drugs. If based on an early look at the data, one treatment can be identified as superior, and based either on its efficacy or safety profiles, the study can be terminated early. There is a common statistical problem in analyzing a clinical study at several time points when partial data have been accumulated. If the goal is to prove the superiority of one treatment over another, and we allow ourselves to compare the two treatments at two or more time points, we are more likely to make a Type I error if we use the nominal α level test at each time. This problem is identical to the multiple testing problem. To control the FWE, we have to lower the α level at each analysis time so that the overall Type I error remains intact. Numerous methods have been developed to allow a comparison of two treatments at several times, with Type I error control. The most widely known are the O'Brien-Fleming and Pocock methods. We will highlight here only a few issues related to such methods.

Considering again the problem of comparing two treatments (one of which may be a placebo) on the basis of either an efficacy or a safety endpoints. Our goal in conducting several treatment comparisons while the study is ongoing may be one or more of the following:

- Stop the trial when sufficient evidence indicates that the new drug is superior, to allow patients to switch to it (the ethical objective).

- Stop the trial when sufficient evidence indicates that the new therapy is no better (or inferior), thereby saving resources (the administrative or financial objective).

We must be aware that the above goals may be conflicting at times, and special care must be taken so as to balance these goals. This point is of special importance considering that for both ethical and financial reasons, clinical trials are conducted with an appropriate power to meet the objective. To illustrate this point, suppose you design a study to find a clinically relevant difference with 80 percent power, requiring say 200 patients on each treatment arm. Your usual α will be 0.05 if your design calls for one analysis at the end of the trial when all data are considered. If you now decide to conduct an interim analysis at, say, a point where roughly half of the patients have completed the study, you will have to change your α in order to control the overall Type I error. To simplify things, let's assume that you decide to test the difference between the two treatments at 0.01 level at the interim analysis (and stop the trail if you find a significant difference) and at 0.04 level if you had to continue to the end of the trial. (The choice of 0.01 and 0.04 levels conservatively ensures the Type I error and is used here only for illustration. Obviously, more optimal allocations can be calculated.) You should be aware of the consequence of your interim analysis. On one hand, you allow to stop the trial early if the new drug is proven early to be safer or more efficacious, but on the other hand, you reduced the chance to show that difference at the end of your trial based on your original target of 80 percent power. This is because of the requirement to lower the α level at the end of the trial from 0.05 to 0.04. So to preserve power, you must increase the number of patients from your original target of 200. You can balance your desire to stop early, and your desire to meet your power criterion by allocating your overall α of 0.05 in a way that meets your goal: reducing α at your interim analysis will minimize your ability to stop early, but maximize your power at the end of the trial. The ultimate choice may take into consideration some other relevant issues, like your expectation and experience with the new drug, how critical the treatment is to fight the disease, regulatory and financial considerations, and so on. In choosing an appropriate procedure to meet your objectives, you have to take into consideration other administrative and statistical constraints. For example,

- how fast can you enroll patients
- do you need to unblind the data when you conduct an interim analysis
- how many times would you like to look at the data

- does your interim analysis require a certain number of subjects, or should it be based on the amount of time elapsed
- is the parameter on which you base your comparison discrete or continuous?

In closing, we emphasize again that this important area is mentioned here as some of the issues are related to concepts of multiple testing. While we do not provide examples in this edition, you can find SAS/IML code for certain interim analyses in *SAS/IML Software: Changes and Enhancements through Release 6.11* (SAS Institute, 1995, p. 63).

14.6 Concluding Remarks

In this last chapter, we have attempted to tie up some loose ends regarding multiple testing methods. If a favorite method of yours has somehow been excluded, we apologize! It is impossible to cover everything in a book. Feel free to contact one of us if you want to discuss particular methods further; it is possible that there will be another edition of this book.

Despite possible shortcomings, we feel that the methods and macros described in this book substantially increase the scope of applications to which MCPs may be applied. In particular, as shown in Section 14.1, the %SimIntervals and %SimTests macros can interface quite easily with most parameter estimation procedures in SAS. Thus, multiple comparisons and multiple testing inferences are now easy in cases where they were previously very difficult. In addition, since these macros incorporate correlations and closure (in the case of %SimTests), the methods are among the most powerful of those that are currently available.

Appendix: Macro Code

Many of the methods discussed in this book have been implemented as SAS macro programs, and this appendix contains all of these. Each macro includes header comments listing the author and any relevant references, and briefly explains the input and output for the program. Note that the macros have different primary authors and thus exhibit different styles, both externally (e.g., how the macros are invoked) and internally (programming style). Note also that while some of the macros work in Release 6.12 and earlier, others use features such as ODS and long variable names that require more recent releases of the SAS System. If you have questions or problems with a macro, please feel free to contact its primary author.

A.1   The %Rom Macro

This macro computes multiplicity adjustments usings Rom's (1990) method.

```
/*------------------------------------------------------------------*/
/* Name:      Rom                                                   */
/* Title:     Rom Step-Up procedure                                 */
/* Author:    Dror Rom, rom@prosof.com                              */
/* Reference: Rom, D.M. (1990). A sequentially rejective test       */
/*               procedure based on a modified Bonferroni           */
/*               inequality. Biometrika, 77, 663--665.              */
/* Release:   Version 6.11                                          */
/*------------------------------------------------------------------*/
/* Input:                                                           */
/*                                                                  */
/*   DATASET=   the SAS data set containing the data to be          */
/*              analyzed (required)                                 */
/*                                                                  */
/*   PV=        the p-values (required)                             */
/*                                                                  */
/*   FWE=       the level of significance for comparisons           */
/*              among the means.  The default is 0.05.              */
/*                                                                  */
/* Output:                                                          */
/*                                                                  */
/*   The output dataset contains one observation for each           */
/*   P-value in the dataset.  The output dataset contains the       */
/*   following variables:                                           */
/*                                                                  */
/*      i    - The index of the ordered P-value                     */
/*                                                                  */
/*    CRIT   - The critical value                                   */
/*                                                                  */
/*  PVALUE   - The P-value                                          */
/*                                                                  */
/*    ADJP   - The adjusted P-value                                 */
/*                                                                  */
/*     DEC   - The decision on the corresponding hypothesis         */
/*------------------------------------------------------------------*/

%MACRO ROM(dataset=,pv=,FWE=0.05);
data a;
set &dataset;
p=&pv;
keep p;
proc sort;
by descending p;
proc means noprint data=a;
var p;
output out=b n=N;
proc transpose data=a prefix=pv out=a;
data adjp;merge b a;
array critv{200};
array pv{200};
minim=1;
do z=1 to n;
w=0;
converge='false';
```

```
do while ((converge='false')or(w<=6));
  w=w+1;
  if (w=1) then do;
   if (z=1) then alpha=pv(z);
    else if (z=2) then alpha=2*pv(2);
    else alpha=(-1+(1+4*z*pv(z))**0.5)/2;
   end;
   else do;
   if abs(alpha-adjp)<=0.0001 then converge='true';
     alpha=adjp;
    end;
critv(2)=alpha;
critv(1)=alpha/2;
critv(n)=alpha;
critv(n-1)=alpha/2;
do i=3 to n;
 m=n-i+1;
 do j=1 to i-1;
  critv(i+1-j)=critv(i-j);
 end;
 critv(1)=0;
 do j=1 to i-2;
*** calculates n choose m *****;
 c=1;
 k=j;
 jj=i-j;
 do ii=1 to k;
  jj=jj+1;
  c=c*jj/ii;
 end;
 comb=c;
  critv(1)=critv(1)+critv(i)**j-comb*critv(i-j)**(i-j);
 end;
 critv(1)=(critv(1)+critv(i)**(i-1))/i;
end;
adjp=alpha*pv[z]/critv[n-z+1];
end;
minim=min(adjp,minim);
adjp=minim;
output;
end;
data adjp;set adjp;i=_N_;keep adjp i;
data critp;merge b a;
array critv{200};
alpha=&fwe;
critv(2)=alpha;
critv(1)=alpha/2;
critv(n)=alpha;
critv(n-1)=alpha/2;
do i=3 to n;
 m=n-i+1;
 do j=1 to i-1;
  critv(i+1-j)=critv(i-j);
 end;
 critv(1)=0;
 do j=1 to i-2;
*** calculates n choose m *****;
 c=1;
 k=j;
 jj=i-j;
```

```
  do ii=1 to k;
   jj=jj+1;
   c=c*jj/ii;
  end;
  comb=c;
   critv(1)=critv(1)+critv(i)**j-comb*critv(i-j)**(i-j);
  end;
 critv(1)=(critv(1)+critv(i)**(i-1))/i;
end;

data c;
merge a b critp;
array pv{200};
array critv{200};
alpha=&fwe;
dec='retain';
do i=1 to n;
crit=critv(n+1-i);
pvalue=pv(i);
if(pv(i)<=crit)then dec='reject';

output;
end;
run;
data c;set c;i=_N_;
title1 ' ';
TITLE2 'ROM STEP-UP PROCEDURE';
title3 ' ';
DATA _NULL_;
FILE PRINT;
merge c adjp END=EOF;by i;
IF _N_=1 THEN DO;
PUT @8 'I' @12 'CRITICAL VALUE' @30 'P-VALUE' @45 'ADJUSTED P'
@60 'DECISION';
PUT @5 65*'-';
END;
put @8 i @12 crit f7.6 @30 pvalue @45 adjp f7.6 @60 dec;
if EOF=1 then do;
PUT @5 65*'-';
put @8 'ALPHA=' @16 alpha;
end;
RUN;
%MEND ROM;
```

A.2 The %HochBen Macro

This macro performs multiplicity adjustments using Hochberg and Benjamini's (1990) graphical method.

```
/*--------------------------------------------------------------*/
/* Name:      HochBen                                           */
/* Title:     Hochberg and Benjamini graphical analysis of      */
/*            multiple P-values                                 */
/* Author:    Dror Rom, rom@prosof.com                         */
```

```
/* Reference: Hochberg, Y., and Benjamini, Y. (1990). More     */
/*            Powerful Procedures for Multiple Significance     */
/*            Testing. Statistics in Medicine, 9, 811-818.      */
/* Release:   Version 6.11                                      */
/*-------------------------------------------------------------*/
/* Input:                                                       */
/*                                                              */
/*   DATASET=   the SAS data set containing the data to be      */
/*              analyzed (required)                             */
/*                                                              */
/*   PV=        the p-values (required)                         */
/*                                                              */
/*   FWE=       the level of significance for comparisons       */
/*              among the means.  The default is 0.05.          */
/*                                                              */
/* Output:                                                      */
/*                                                              */
/*   The output dataset contains one observation for each       */
/*   P-value in the dataset.  The output dataset contains the   */
/*   following variables:                                       */
/*                                                              */
/*       i    - The index of the ordered P-value               */
/*                                                              */
/*    CRIT    - The critical value                             */
/*                                                              */
/*  PVALUE    - The P-value                                    */
/*                                                              */
/*    ADJP    - The adjusted P-value                           */
/*                                                              */
/*     DEC    - The decision on the corresponding hypothesis   */
/*                                                              */
/*    NHAT    - The estimated number of true hypotheses        */
/*-------------------------------------------------------------*/

%MACRO HOCHBEN(dataset=,pv=,FWE=0.05);
data a;
set &dataset;
p=&pv;
q=1-p;
proc sort;
by q;
data b;
set a;
i=_N_;
slope=q/i;
nhat=1/slope-1;
title1 ' ';
title2 'HOCHBERG & BENJAMINI GRAPHICAL ANALYSIS OF MULTIPLE P-VALUES';
proc sort;
by p;
data c;
set b;
lags=lag1(slope);
data c;
set c;
diff=slope-lags;
if (diff='.') or(diff>=0) then diff='.';
else diff=0;
data d;
set c;
```

```
if (diff=0);
ii=1;
data d;
set d;
by diff;
if first.diff;
keep nhat q i ii;

data c1;set c;if(diff='.');
data c1;set c1;by diff;if last.diff;ii=1;
keep nhat q i ii;
run;
data d;set c1 d;by ii;if last.ii;
keep nhat q i;
data d1;
set d;
i=nhat+1;
q=1;
keep i q;
data d3;
set d;
i=nhat;
drop q;
do j=0,10;
qqq=j/10;
output;
end;
data d2;
q=0;
i=0;
data d1;
set d1 d2 d;
qq=q;
keep qq i;
data c;
set c;
drop nhat;
proc sort;
by i;
data e;
merge c d;
by i;
data f;
set e d1 d3;
symbol1 v=PLUS i=none;
symbol2 v=none i=join;
symbol3 v=none i=join;
title1 ' ';
title2 'HOCHBERG & BENJAMINI GRAPHICAL ANALYSIS OF MULTIPLE P-VALUES';
title3 'PLOT of 1-PVALUES VS. THEIR ORDER';
goptions colors=(black) cback=white;
label q='q';
proc gplot data=f;
plot q*i=1 qq*i=2 qqq*i=3/overlay frame;
run;
data a;set a;keep p;
proc sort;
by p;
proc means noprint;
var p;
```

```
output out=b n=N;
data b;set b;
data c1;set f;
nhat=round(nhat);
if not(nhat='.');
data c2;merge b c1;if not(n='.');
alpha=&fwe;
keep n alpha nhat;
proc transpose data=a prefix=pv out=a;
run;
data c;
merge a c2;
data c;set c;
array pv{200};
dec='reject';

do i=1 to n;
crit1=alpha/(n+1-i);
if (nhat=0)then crit2=alpha;
                else crit2=alpha/nhat;
crit=max(crit1,crit2);
if(nhat<1)then adjp=pv(i);
 else adjp=max(min((n+1-i)*pv(i),nhat*pv(i),1),adjp);
pvalue=pv(i);
if((pv(i)<=crit)
    and(dec='reject'))then dec='reject';
else dec='retain';
output;
end;
run;
title1 ' ';
title2 'HOCHBERG & BENJAMINI GRAPHICAL ANALYSIS OF MULTIPLE P-VALUES';
title3 ' ';
title4 'CRITICAL VALUES ADJUSTED BY ESTIMATED NUMBER OF TRUE HYPOTHESES';
title5 ' ';
DATA _NULL_;
FILE PRINT;
SET c END=EOF;
I=_N_;
IF _N_=1 THEN DO;
PUT @8 'I' @12 'CRITICAL VALUE' @30 'P-VALUE' @45 'ADJUSTED P'
@60 'DECISION';
PUT @5 65*'-';
END;
put @8 i @12 crit f7.6 @30 pvalue @45 adjp f7.6 @60 dec;
if EOF=1 then do;
PUT @5 65*'-';
put @8 'ALPHA=' @16 alpha;
put @8 'ESTIMATED NUMBER OF TRUE HYPOTHESES:' @56 nhat;
end;
RUN;
%MEND HOCHBEN;
```

A.3 The %SimIntervals Macro

This macro computes simultaneous confidence intervals for a general collection of linear functions of parameters, using Edwards and Berry (1987).

```
/*---------------------------------------------------------------*/
/* Name:      SimIntervals                                       */
/* Title:     Simultaneous Confidence Intervals for General      */
/*            Linear Functions                                   */
/* Author:    Randy Tobias, sasrdt@sas.com,                     */
/* Reference: Edwards and Berry (1987). The efficiency of        */
/*            simulation-based multiple comparisons.             */
/*            Biometrics 43, 913-928.                            */
/* Release:   Version 7.01                                       */
/*---------------------------------------------------------------*/
/* Inputs:                                                       */
/*                                                               */
/*     NSAMP =  simulation size, with 20000 as default          */
/*                                                               */
/*     SEED  =  random number seed, with 0 (clock time)         */
/*              as default                                       */
/*                                                               */
/*     CONF  =  desired confidence level, with 0.95 as default   */
/*                                                               */
/*     SIDE  = U, L or B, for upper-tailed, lower-tailed         */
/*              or two-tailed, respectively. SIDE=B is default.  */
/*                                                               */
/* Additionally, %SimIntervals requires two further macros to    */
/* be defined that use SAS/IML to construct the estimates and    */
/* the contrasts of interest.  In particular, make sure the      */
/* following two macros are defined before invoking              */
/* %SimIntervals:                                                */
/*                                                               */
/*    %Estimate: Uses SAS/IML code to define                     */
/*        EstPar - (column) vector of estimated parameters       */
/*        Cov    - covariance matrix for the for the estimates   */
/*        df     - error degrees of freedom; set to 0 for        */
/*                 asymptotic analysis                           */
/*                                                               */
/*    %Contrasts: Uses SAS/IML code to define                    */
/*        C      - matrix whose columns define the contrasts of  */
/*                 interest between the parameters               */
/*        CLab   - (column) character vector whose elements      */
/*                 label the respective contrasts in C           */
/*                                                               */
/*  You can either define these macros directly, or use the      */
/*  %MakeGLMStats macro to define them.                          */
/*                                                               */
/*---------------------------------------------------------------*/
/* Output:                                                       */
/*   The output is a dataset with one observation for each       */
/*   contrast and the following variables:                       */
/*                                                               */
/*     Contrast - contrast label                                 */
/*     Estimate - contrast estimated value                       */
/*     StdErr   - standard error of estimate                     */
/*     tValue   - normalized estimate, Estimate/StdErr           */
/*     RawP     - non-multiplicity-adjusted p-value              */
```

```
/*      OneP    - one-step multiplicity-adjusted p-value       */
/*      LowerCL - multiplicity-adjusted lower confidence limit */
/*      UpperCL - multiplicity-adjusted upper confidence limit */
/*                                                             */
/*   This dataset is also displayed as a formatted table, using */
/*   the ODS system.                                           */
/*-------------------------------------------------------------*/

%macro SimIntervals(nsamp   = 20000,
                    seed    =     0,
                    conf    =  0.95,
                    side    =     B,
                    options =      );
%global ANORM quant;

options nonotes;

proc iml;
   %Estimates;
   if (df <= 0) then call symput('ANORM','1');
   else              call symput('ANORM','0');
   %Contrasts;

   Cov = C'*Cov*C;
   D   = diag(1/sqrt(vecdiag(Cov)));
   R   = D*Cov*D;

   evec = eigvec(R);
   eval = eigval(R) <> 0;
   U = (diag(sqrt(eval))*evec')';
   dimU = sum(eval > 1e-8);

   U    = U[,1:dimU];

   ests = C'*EstPar;
   ses  = sqrt(vecdiag(Cov));
   tvals = ests/ses;
   %if      (&side = B) %then %do;
      if df>0 then rawp = 2*(1-probt(abs(tvals),df));
         else rawp = 2*(1-probnorm(abs(tvals)));
      %end;
   %else %if (&side = L) %then %do;
      if df>0 then rawp =       probt(   tvals ,df) ;
      else rawp = probnorm( tvals);
      %end;
   %else                      %do;
      if df>0 then rawp =     1-probt(   tvals ,df) ;
      else rawp = 1-probnorm(tvals);
      %end;

   adjp = j(ncol(C),1,0);
   maxt=j(&nsamp,1,0);
   do isim = 1 to &nsamp;
      Z = U*rannor(j(dimU,1,&seed));
      if df>0 then do;
         V = cinv(ranuni(&seed),df);
         tvalstar = Z / sqrt(V/df);
         end;
```

```
            else do; tvalstar = Z; end;
            %if (&side = B) %then %do; mx = max(abs(tvalstar)); %end;
            %else              %do; mx = max(    tvalstar ); %end;
            maxt[isim] = mx;

            %if        (&side = B) %then %do; adjp = adjp + (mx>abs(tvals)); %end;
            %else %if (&side = L) %then %do; adjp = adjp + (mx>   -tvals ); %end;
            %else                          %do; adjp = adjp + (mx>    tvals ); %end;
            end;
         adjp = adjp/&nsamp;

         confindx = round(&nsamp*&conf,1);
         sorttemp = maxt;
         maxt[rank(maxt),] = sorttemp;
         c_alpha = maxt[confindx];

         start tlc(n,d); return(trim(left(char(n,d)))); finish;

         %if (&side = B) %then %do;
            LowerCL = ests - c_alpha*ses;
            UpperCL = ests + c_alpha*ses;
            %end;
         %else %if (&side = L) %then %do;
            LowerCL = j(ncol(C),1,.M);
            UpperCL = ests + c_alpha*ses;
            %end;
         %else %do;
            LowerCL = ests - c_alpha*ses;
            UpperCL = j(ncol(C),1,.I);
            %end;

         create SimIntOut
            var {"Estimate" "StdErr" "tValue" "RawP"
                "OneP" "LowerCL" "UpperCL"};
         data = ests || ses || tvals || rawp || adjp || LowerCL || UpperCL;
         append from data;
         call symput('confpct',tlc(100*&conf,4));
         call symput('quant'  ,tlc(c_alpha  ,8));

         create labels from clab; append from clab;

      data SimIntOut; merge labels(rename=(COL1=Contrast)) SimIntOut; run;

      %if (^%index(%upcase(&options),NOPRINT)) %then %do;

      proc template;
      delete MCBook.SimIntervals;
      define table MCBook.SimIntervals;
         column Contrast Estimate StdErr tValue RawP OneP LowerCL UpperCL;

         define header h1;
            text "Estimated &confpct% Quantile = &quant";
            spill_margin;
      %if (^&ANORM) %then %do;
            space=1;
      %end;
            end;
```

```
%if (&ANORM) %then %do;
   define header h2;
      text "Asymptotic Normal Approximations";
      space=1;
      end;
%end;

   define column Contrast;
      header="Contrast";
      end;
   define column Estimate;
      header="Estimate"        format=D8. space=1;
      translate _val_ = ._ into '';
      end;
   define column StdErr;
      header="Standard Error" format=D8. space=1;
      translate _val_ = ._ into '';
      end;
   define column tValue;
      header="#t Value"        format=7.2;
      translate _val_ = .I into '  Infty',
         _val_ = .M into ' -Infty',
         _val_ = ._ into '';
      end;

   %if (&side = B) %then %do;
      define header ProbtHead;
         text " Pr > |t| ";
         start=RawP end=OneP just=c expand='-';
         end;
      %end;
   %else %if (&side = L) %then %do;
      define header ProbtHead;
         text " Pr < t ";
         start=RawP end=OneP just=c expand='-';
         end;
      %end;
   %else %do;
      define header ProbtHead;
         text " Pr > t ";
         start=RawP end=OneP just=c expand='-';
         end;
      %end;

   define column RawP;
      space=1 glue=10
      parent=Common.PValue header="Raw";
      translate _val_ = ._ into '';
      end;
   define column OneP;
      parent=Common.PValue header="Adjusted";
      translate _val_ = ._ into '';
      end;

   define header CLHead;
      text "&confpct% Confidence Interval";
      start=LowerCL end=UpperCL just=c;
      end;
```

```
      define LowerCL;
         translate _val_ = .M into ' -Infty';
         space=1 glue=10 format=D8. print_headers=off;
         end;
      define UpperCL;
         format=D8. print_headers=off;
         translate _val_ = .I into '  Infty';
         end;

      end;
   run;

   data _null_; set SimIntOut;
      file print ods=(template='MCBook.SimIntervals');
      put _ods_;
      run;

   %end;

   options notes;

   %mend;
```

A.4 The %MakeGLMStats Macro

This macro creates the %Estimates and the %Contrasts macros that are needed for %SimIntervals and %SimTests.

```
/*-------------------------------------------------------------------*/
/* Name:      MakeGLMStats                                        */
/* Title:     Macro to create %Estimates and %Contrasts macros   */
/*            needed for %SimIntervals and %SimTests             */
/* Author:    Randy Tobias, sasrdt@sas.com                       */
/* Release:   Version 7.01                                       */
/*-------------------------------------------------------------------*/
/* Inputs:                                                        */
/*                                                                */
/*    DATASET = Data set to be analyzed (required)               */
/*                                                                */
/*    CLASSVAR = Listing of classification variables. If absent, */
/*               no classification variables are assumed         */
/*                                                                */
/*       YVAR = response variable (required)                     */
/*                                                                */
/*       MODEL = GLM model specification (required)              */
/*                                                                */
/*    CONTRASTS = CONTROL(effect), ALL(effect), or USER. This    */
/*               creates the %Contrasts macro unless you specify */
/*               USER (the default), in which case you create    */
/*               the %Contrasts macro yourself                   */
/*                                                                */
/*-------------------------------------------------------------------*/
/* Output:  This macro creates the %Estimates macro needed for   */
/* the %SimIntervals and %SimTests macros.  Additionally, if     */
/* you specify CONTRASTS = ALL or CONTROL, it also creates the   */
/* %Contrasts macro.  There is no other output.                  */
/*-------------------------------------------------------------------*/
```

```
%macro MakeGLMStats(dataset= , classvar= , yvar= , model= , contrasts=USER);
   %global nx yvar1 nlev icntl;

   options nonotes;

   %let yvar1 = &yvar;
   proc glmmod data=&dataset noprint outparm=parm outdesign=design;
      %if (%length(&classvar)) %then %do;
      class &classvar;
      %end;
      model &yvar = &model;
   data _null_; set parm; call symput('nx',_n_);
      run;

   %macro Estimates;
      use design;
      read all var ("col1":"col&nx") into X;
      read all var ("&yvar1")        into Y;
      XpXi   = ginv(X`*X);
      rankX  = trace(XpXi*(X`*X));
      n      = nrow(X);
      df     = n-rankX;
      EstPar = XpXi*X`*Y;
      mse    = ssq(Y-X*EstPar)/df;
      Cov    = mse*XpXi;
   %mend;

   %let ctype = %upcase(%scan(&contrasts,1));
   %if (&ctype ^= USER) %then %do;
      %let effect = %scan(&contrasts,2);
      %if (&ctype = CONTROL) %then %do;
         %let icntl = %scan(&contrasts,3);
         %end;
      %end;

   %if (&ctype ^= USER) %then %do;
      ods listing close;
      ods output LSMeanCoef=LSMeanCoef;
      proc glm data=&dataset;
         %if (%length(&classvar)) %then %do;
         class &classvar;
         %end;
         model &yvar = &model;
         lsmeans &effect / e;
      quit;
      ods listing;
      proc transpose data=LSMeanCoef out=temp;
         var Row:;
      data _null_; set temp;
         call symput('nlev',_n_);
      run;
      %end;
```

```
%if (&ctype = ALL) %then %do;
    %macro Contrasts; %global nlev;
        use LSMeanCoef; read all var ("Row1":"Row&nlev") into L;
        free C clab;
        do i = 1 to ncol(L)-1;
            do j = i+1 to ncol(L);
                C    = C    // L[,i]` - L[,j]`;
                clab = clab // (     trim(left(char(i,5)))
                                 +'-'+trim(left(char(j,5))));
                end;
            end;
        C = C`;
        %mend;
    %end;
%if (&ctype = CONTROL) %then %do;
    %macro Contrasts; %global icntl;
        use LSMeanCoef; read all var ("Row1":"Row&nlev") into L;
        free C clab;
        j = &icntl;
        do i = 1 to ncol(L);
            if (i ^= j) then do;
                C    = C    // L[,i]` - L[,j]`;
                clab = clab // (     trim(left(char(i,5)))
                                 +'-'+trim(left(char(j,5))));
                end;
            end;
        C = C`;
        %mend;
    %end;
    options notes;
%mend;
```

A.5 The %IndividualPower Macro

This macro computes power for various multiple comparisons tests using the Individual Power definition.

```
/*-------------------------------------------------------------*/
/* Name:      IndividualPower                                  */
/* Title:     Macro to evaluate individual power of multiple   */
/*            comparisons                                       */
/* Author:    Randy Tobias, sasrdt@sas.com                     */
/* Release:   Version 7.01                                     */
/*-------------------------------------------------------------*/
/* Inputs:                                                     */
/*                                                             */
/*       MCP = RANGE, DUNNETT2, DUNNETT1, or MAXMOD (required) */
/*                                                             */
/*         G = Number of groups (excluding control for         */
/*             DUNNETT2 and DUNNETT1; required)                */
/*                                                             */
/*         D = Meaningful mean difference (required)           */
/*                                                             */
/*         S = Standard deviation (required)                   */
/*                                                             */
```

```
/*          FWE = Desired Familywise Error (0.05 default)          */
/*                                                                 */
/*       TARGET = Target power level (0.80 default)                */
/*                                                                 */
/*-----------------------------------------------------------------*/
/* Output:  This macro plots individual power for a variety of     */
/* Multiple comparisons methods, and plots it as a function of     */
/* n, the within-group sample size                                 */
/*-----------------------------------------------------------------*/

%macro IndividualPower(mcp=,g=,d=,s=,FWE=0.05,target=0.80);
%let mcp = %upcase(&mcp);
options nonotes;
data power;
   keep C_a N NCP DF Power;
   label N="Group size, N";

   ntarget = 1;
   nactual = .;
   dtarget = 1000;

   do N=2 to 1000 until (Power>.99);
      %if (&mcp = MAXMOD) %then %do; ncp = sqrt(N  )*(&d/&s); %end;
      %else                      %do; ncp = sqrt(N/2)*(&d/&s); %end;

      %if (    (&mcp = DUNNETT1)
            or (&mcp = DUNNETT2)) %then %do; df = (&g+1)*(N-1); %end;
      %else                          %do; df = (&g  )*(N-1); %end;

      conf = 1-&fwe;

      %if (&mcp = RANGE) %then %do;
         c_a = probmc("&mcp",.,conf,df,&g)/sqrt(2);
         %end;
      %else %do;
         c_a = probmc("&mcp",.,conf,df,&g);
         %end;

      %if (&mcp = DUNNETT1) %then %do;
         Power = 1-probt(c_a      ,df,ncp   );
         %end;
      %else %do;
         Power = 1-probf(c_a**2,1,df,ncp**2);
         %end;

      if (abs(Power - &target) < dtarget) then do;
         ntarget = N;
         nactual = Power;
         dtarget = abs(Power - &target);
         end;
      output;
   end;
   call symput('ntarget',trim(left(ntarget)));
   call symput('nactual',trim(left(nactual)));
run;
```

```
data target;
   length xsys ysys position $ 1;
   retain xsys ysys hsys color;
   xsys = '2'; ysys = '2'; color = 'black';
   x = 0        ; y = &nactual; function = 'MOVE ';                    output;
   x = &ntarget; y = &nactual; function = 'DRAW '; line=1; size=1; output;
   x = &ntarget; y = 0;        function = 'DRAW '; line=1; size=1; output;
   x = &ntarget+2; y = &nactual/2; function = 'LABEL';
   style = 'swissb';
   text  = "Power(N=&ntarget)";
   position = '0';
   output;
   x = &ntarget+2; y = &nactual/2-0.12; function = 'LABEL';
   style = 'swissb';
   text  = "  = "||put(&nactual,pvalue6.);
   position = '0';
   output;

goptions ftext=swissb vsize=6 in hsize=6 in;
axis1 style=1 width=2 minor=none order=0 to 1 by 0.2;
axis2 style=1 width=2 minor=none;
symbol1 i=join;
proc gplot data=power annotate=target;
   title2 "Power for detecting an individual difference of &d";
   title3 "Using the &mcp method with FWE=&FWE";
   title4 "With &g groups and standard deviation = &s";
   plot power*n=1 / vaxis=axis1 haxis=axis2 frame;
run;
quit;
title2;
title3;
title4;
options notes;
%mend;
```

A.6   The %SimPower Macro

This macro computes several versions of power for multiple comparisons procedures, in
addition to FWE and directional FWE.

```
/*------------------------------------------------------------------*/
/* Name:      SimPower                                              */
/* Title:     Macro to simulate power of multiple comparisons       */
/*            using various definitions                             */
/* Author:    Randy Tobias, sasrdt@sas.com                          */
/* Release:   Version 7.01                                          */
/*------------------------------------------------------------------*/
/* Inputs:                                                          */
/*                                                                  */
/*     METHOD = TUKEY, DUNNETT, DUNNETTL, DUNNETTU, or REGWQ        */
/*              (TUKEY is the default)                              */
/*                                                                  */
/*       NREP = number of Monte Carlo samples (1000 default)        */
/*                                                                  */
/*          N = Within-group sample size (if equal)                 */
/*              or listing of group sample sizes (if unequal)       */
```

```
/*                                                             */
/*          S = Standard deviation (required)                  */
/*                                                             */
/*        FWE = Desired Familywise Error (0.05 default)        */
/*                                                             */
/*  TRUEMEANS = A listing of the true group means (no default) */
/*                                                             */
/*       SEED = Seed value for random numbers (0 default)      */
/*                                                             */
/*-------------------------------------------------------------*/
/* Output:  This macro simulates multiple power, using the     */
/* complete, minimal, and proportional definitions.  It also   */
/* simulates FWE (ordinary and directional), for a variety     */
/* of MCPs. The results are presented in a formatted table.    */
/*-------------------------------------------------------------*/


options ls=76 nodate generic;


/*
/  Use the binomial estimation options in PROC FREQ to compute
/  confidence limits for the Complete and Minimal power, which are
/  proportions; and use PROC MEANS to compute confidence limits for
/  the proportional power.
/-----------------------------------------------------------------*/

%macro EstBin(Input,Var,Output,Label);
proc freq  data=&Input noprint;
    table &Var / measures bin out=Freq;
    output out=&Output bin;
data _null_; set Freq;
    if (_N_ = 1) then call symput('First',&Var);
data &Output; set &Output;
    keep Quantity Estimate LowerCL UpperCL;
    Quantity = &Label;
    Estimate = _BIN_;
    LowerCL  = L_BIN; label LowerCL = "Lower 95% CL";
    UpperCL  = U_BIN; label UpperCL = "Upper 95% CL";
    if (&First = 0) then do;
        Estimate = 1 - Estimate;
        temp = LowerCL; LowerCL = UpperCL; UpperCL = temp;
        LowerCL = 1 - LowerCL;
        UpperCL = 1 - UpperCL;
        end;
run;
%mend;



%macro SimPower(method=TUKEY,nrep=1000,n=,s=,FWE=0.05,TrueMeans=
=,seed=0);


%let method = %upcase(&method);


/*
/  Determine the number of groups from the true means.
/-----------------------------------------------------------------*/
```

```
%let g = 1;
%do %while(%length(%bquote(%scan(%bquote(&TrueMeans),&g,%bquote(','))))));
   %let g = %eval(&g+1);
   %end;
%let g=%eval(&g-1);

options nonotes;

/*
/   Create &nrep random normal data sets using the true means.
/-----------------------------------------------------------------------*/

%if ("%substr(&n,1,1)" = "(") %then %do;
   data a;
      array mu{&g} &TrueMeans;
      array _n{&g} &n;
      do rep = 1 to &nrep;
         do a = 1 to dim(mu);
            do i = 1 to _n{a};
               y = mu{a} + &s*rannor(&seed);
               output;
               end;
            end;
         end;
   run;
   %end;
%else %do;
   data a;
      array mu{&g} &TrueMeans;
      do rep = 1 to &nrep;
         do a = 1 to dim(mu);
            do i = 1 to &n;
               y = mu{a} + &s*rannor(&seed);
               output;
               end;
            end;
         end;
   run;
   %end;

/*
/   Analyze the random data sets.  For the methods that return pairwise
/   results, we put the confidence limits in the CLDiffs dataset; for
/   REGWQ we assemble all the LINES results in the MCLines dataset.
/-----------------------------------------------------------------------*/

ods listing close;
%if (&method = REGWQ) %then %do;
   ods output MCLines(match_all=mv)=MCLines;
   %end;
%else %do;
   ods output CLDiffs=CLDiffs;
   %end;
proc glm data=a;
   by rep;
   class a;
   model y = a / nouni;
   means a / alpha=&fwe &method
```

```
      %if (&method ^= REGWQ) %then cldiff;
      ;
      quit;
ods listing;


%if (&method = REGWQ) %then %do;


/*
/ Combine the MCLines# datasets, putting all the Lines info into a
/ single L variable.
/------------------------------------------------------------------*/

data temp; set &mv;
data MCLines; set temp(drop=Effect Dependent Method N);
   length _Name_ $ 8;
   array Line{26};
   where (Mean ^= ._);
   L = '                          ';
   do i = 1 to 26; substr(L,i,1) = Line{i}; end;
   _Name_ = trim(left('Level' || trim(left(Level))));
run;


/*
/ Turn the results from REGWQ into a data set that has a variable
/ "Correct" with the number of correctly rejected hypotheses
/ for each random data set.  Each of the three combined definitions
/ of power can be computed from this number.
/------------------------------------------------------------------*/

proc sort data=MCLines out=MCLines;
   by rep Level;
proc transpose data=MCLines out=Lines;
   by rep;
   var L;
proc transpose data=MCLines out=Means prefix=Mn;
   by rep;
   var Mean;
data True; merge Lines Means;
   array Level{&g};
   array eq{&g,&g};
   array mu{&g} &TrueMeans;
   array Mn{&g};

   if (_n_ = 1) then do;
      ndiff = 0;
      nsame = 0;
      do a1=1 to &g-1; do a2 = a1+1 to &g;
         if (mu{a1} ^= mu{a2}) then ndiff = ndiff + 1;
         if (mu{a1}  = mu{a2}) then nsame = nsame + 1;
         end; end;
      retain ndiff nsame;
      end;
```

```
            do i = 1 to &g;
               do j = i+1 to &g;
                  eq{i,j} = 0;
                  do k = 1 to 26;
                     lik = substr(Level{i},k,1);
                     ljk = substr(Level{j},k,1);
                     if ((lik ^= ' ') & (ljk ^= ' ') & (lik = ljk)) then eq{i,j} = 1;
                     end;
                  end;
               end;


            CorrectA = 0;
            Correct0 = 0;
            DirectionalError = 0;
            do i = 1 to &g-1;
               do j = i+1 to &g;
                  if    ((mu{i} ^= mu{j}) & (^eq{i,j})) then CorrectA = CorrectA + 1;
                  if    ((mu{i}  = mu{j}) &   eq{i,j} ) then Correct0 = Correct0 + 1;
                  if (  ((mu{i}  = mu{j}) &  ^eq{i,j} )
                      | ((mu{i}  < mu{j}) & (^eq{i,j}) & (Mn{i} > Mn{j}))
                      | ((mu{i}  > mu{j}) & (^eq{i,j}) & (Mn{i} < Mn{j}))) then
                     DirectionalError = 1;
                  end;
               end;
            %end;
      %else %do;
      /*
      / Turn the results from the tests into a data set that has a
      / variable "Correct" with the number of correctly rejected hypotheses
      / for each random data set.  Each of the three combined definitions
      / of power can be computed from this number.
      /-------------------------------------------------------------------*/

      proc transpose data=CLDiffs out=Sig  prefix=Reject;
         var Significance;
         by rep;
      proc transpose data=CLDiffs out=Comp prefix=Comp;
         var Comparison;
         by rep;
      proc transpose data=CLDiffs out=Diff prefix=Diff;
         var Difference;
         by rep;
         run;


      %if       (&method = TUKEY)    %then %let npair = %eval(&g*(&g-1));
      %else %if (&method = DUNNETT)  %then %let npair = %eval(   &g-1 );
      %else %if (&method = DUNNETTU) %then %let npair = %eval(   &g-1 );
      %else %if (&method = DUNNETTL) %then %let npair = %eval(   &g-1 );

      data True; merge Sig(keep=Reject:) Comp(keep=Comp:) Diff(keep=Diff:);
         array mu{&g} &TrueMeans;
         array Comp{&npair};
         array Reject{&npair};
         array Diff{&npair};
```

```
    if (_n_ = 1) then do;
       ndiff = 0;
       nsame = 0;
       %if (&method = TUKEY) %then %do;
          do a1=1 to &g; do a2 = 1 to &g; if (a1 ^= a2) then do;
             if (mu{a1} ^= mu{a2}) then ndiff = ndiff + 1;
             if (mu{a1}  = mu{a2}) then nsame = nsame + 1;
             end; end; end;
          %end;
       %else %if (&method = DUNNETT) %then %do;
          do a2 = 2 to &g;
             if (mu{1} ^= mu{a2}) then ndiff = ndiff + 1;
             if (mu{1}  = mu{a2}) then nsame = nsame + 1;
             end;
          %end;
       %else %if (&method = DUNNETTL) %then %do;
          do a2 = 2 to &g;
             if (mu{a2} - mu{1} <  0) then ndiff = ndiff + 1;
             if (mu{a2} - mu{1} >= 0) then nsame = nsame + 1;
             end;
          %end;
       %else %if (&method = DUNNETTU) %then %do;
          do a2 = 2 to &g;
             if (mu{a2} - mu{1} >  0) then ndiff = ndiff + 1;
             if (mu{a2} - mu{1} <= 0) then nsame = nsame + 1;
             end;
          %end;
       retain ndiff nsame;
/*
       put "For G=&g and TrueMeans=&TrueMeans, NDiff=" ndiff;
*/
       end;

    CorrectA = 0;
    Correct0 = 0;
    DirectionalError = 0;
    do i = 1 to dim(Reject);
       a1 = 1*scan(Comp{i},1,' ');
       a2 = 1*scan(Comp{i},3,' ');

       if ((mu{a1} ^= mu{a2}) & Reject{i}) then CorrectA = CorrectA + 1;

       %if (&method = DUNNETTL) %then %do;
          if ((mu{a1} - mu{a2} >= 0) & ^Reject{i}) then Correct0 = Correct0 +
1;
          if ((mu{a1} - mu{a2} >= 0) &  Reject{i}) then DirectionalError = 1;
          %end;
       %else %if (&method = DUNNETTU) %then %do;
          if ((mu{a1} - mu{a2} <= 0) & ^Reject{i}) then Correct0 = Correct0 +
1;
          if ((mu{a1} - mu{a2} <= 0) &  Reject{i}) then DirectionalError = 1;
          %end;
```

```
          %else %do;
             if (    (mu{a1} = mu{a2}) & ^Reject{i}                    ) then
                Correct0 = Correct0 + 1;
             if (   ((mu{a1} = mu{a2}) &  Reject{i}                )
                  | ((mu{a1} < mu{a2}) &  Reject{i} & (Diff{i} > 0))
                  | ((mu{a1} > mu{a2}) &  Reject{i} & (Diff{i} < 0))) then
                DirectionalError = 1;
             %end;
          end;

       %end;

       call symput('ndiff',trim(left(put(ndiff,20.))));
       call symput('nsame',trim(left(put(nsame,20.))));
       if (ndiff) then do;
          CompletePower     = CorrectA=ndiff;
          MinimalPower      = CorrectA>0    ;
          ProportionalPower = CorrectA/ndiff;
          end;

       if (nsame) then do;
          TrueFWE = 1 - (Correct0=nsame);
          end;

    run;


    data Sim; if (0); run;

    %if (&ndiff) %then %do;
       %EstBin(True,CompletePower,CompletePower,'Complete Power    ');
       data Sim; set Sim CompletePower;
       run;

       %EstBin(True,MinimalPower,MinimalPower,'Minimal Power     ');
       data Sim; set Sim MinimalPower;
       run;

       proc means data=True noprint;
          var ProportionalPower;
          output out=ProportionalPower(keep=Estimate LowerCL UpperCL)
                 mean=Estimate lclm=LowerCL uclm=UpperCL;
       data ProportionalPower; set ProportionalPower;
          keep Quantity Estimate LowerCL UpperCL;
          Quantity = 'Proportional Power';
       data Sim; set Sim ProportionalPower;
       run;
       %end;

    %if (&nsame) %then %do;
       %EstBin(True,TrueFWE,TrueFWE,'True FWE          ');
       data Sim; set Sim TrueFWE;
       run;
       %end;

    %EstBin(True,DirectionalError,DirectionalError,'Directional FWE   ');
    data Sim; set Sim DirectionalError;
       run;
```

```
data Sim; set Sim;
   CI = "(" || put(LowerCL,5.3) || ',' || put(UpperCL,5.3) || ")";
   label CI = "---95% CI----";
run;
options ls=76 nodate generic;
proc print data=Sim noobs label;
   var Quantity Estimate CI;
   title1 "Method=&method, Nominal FWE=&FWE, nrep=&nrep, Seed=&seed";
   title2 "True means = &TrueMeans, n=&n, s=&s";
   run;
title1;
title2;

options notes;
%mend;
```

A.7 The %PlotSimPower Macro

This macro computes power using various definitions, for various sample sizes, and plots the results.

```
/*-------------------------------------------------------------*/
/* Name:      PlotSimPower                                     */
/* Title:     Macro to plot the simulated power of multiple    */
/*            comparisons procedures                           */
/* Author:    Randy Tobias, sasrdt@sas.com                     */
/* Release:   Version 7.01                                     */
/*-------------------------------------------------------------*/
/* Inputs:                                                     */
/*                                                             */
/*      METHOD = TUKEY, DUNNETT, DUNNETTL, DUNNETTU, or REGWQ  */
/*               (TUKEY is the default)                        */
/*                                                             */
/*        NREP = number of Monte Carlo samples (100 default)   */
/*                                                             */
/*           S = Standard deviation (required)                 */
/*                                                             */
/*         FWE = Desired Familywise Error (0.05 default)       */
/*                                                             */
/*   TRUEMEANS = A listing of the true group means (no default)*/
/*                                                             */
/*        SEED = Seed for random numbers (0 default)           */
/*                                                             */
/*        STOP = type/maxpower, specifies the type of power    */
/*               whether COMPLETE, MINIMAL, or PROPORTIONAL,   */
/*               and the maximum power to stop simulation.     */
/*               The default is COMPLETE/0.9                   */
/*                                                             */
/*      TARGET = desired power level (default 0.8)             */
/*                                                             */
/*-------------------------------------------------------------*/
/* Output: A graph of the power function, indicating the n for */
/* which the target power is acheived.                         */
/*                                                             */
/*-------------------------------------------------------------*/
```

```
%macro PlotSimPower(method    =          TUKEY,
                    nrep      =          100,
                    s         =             ,
                    FWE       =          0.05,
                    TrueMeans =             ,
                    seed      =             0,
                    stop      = Complete/0.9,
                    target    =           0.8);


    %let StopType  = %scan(&stop,1,'/');
    %let StopValue = %scan(&stop,2,'/');

    data plot; if (0); run;
    %do n = 2 %to 100;
        %SimPower(TrueMeans = &TrueMeans,
                  s         =        &s,
                  n         =        &n,
                  nrep      =     &nrep,
                  method    =   &method,
                  seed      =     &seed);
        data Sim; set Sim(where=(scan(Quantity,1)="%scan(&stop,1,'/')"));
            n = &n;
            put "For N=&n, &StopType power = " Estimate;
            if (LowerCL >= &StopValue) then call symput('n','1001');
        data plot; set plot Sim;
        %end;

data probit;
    set plot;
    Estimate = round(100*Estimate);
    c=100;
    sqrtn = sqrt(n);
    call symput('MaxN',trim(left(put(n,best20.))));
proc probit data=probit outest=ests noprint;
    model Estimate/c=sqrtn;
data _null_; set ests;
    call symput('IParm',trim(left(put(Intercept,best20.))));
    call symput('NParm',trim(left(put(sqrtn     ,best20.))));
    run;
%put IParm=&IParm;
%put NParm=&NParm;
data plot; set plot;
    EPower = probnorm(&IParm + sqrt(n)*&NParm);
    label EPower="Power";
    run;

data target;
    length xsys ysys position $ 1;
    retain hsys color;

    sqrtn   = (probit(&target) - &IParm)/&NParm;
    ntarget = int(sqrtn*sqrtn + 1);
    actual  = probnorm(&IParm + sqrt(ntarget)*&NParm);
```

```
        color = 'black';
        xsys = '1'      ; ysys = '2'    ;
        x    = 0       ; y    = actual; function = 'MOVE ';                output;
        xsys = '2'     ; ysys = '2'    ;
        x    = ntarget; y    = actual; function = 'DRAW '; line=1; size=1; output;
        xsys = '2'     ; ysys = '1'    ;
        x    = ntarget; y    = 0      ; function = 'DRAW '; line=1; size=1; output;

        xsys = '2';                 ysys = '2';
        x    = (&MaxN+ntarget)/2; y    = actual/2; function = 'LABEL';
        style = 'swissb';
        text  = "Power(N="||trim(left(put(ntarget,best6.)))||")";
        position = '0';
        output;

        xsys = '2';                 ysys = '2';
        x    = (&MaxN+ntarget)/2; y = actual/2-0.1; function = 'LABEL';
        style = 'swissb';
        text  = "  = "||put(actual,5.3);
        position = '0';
        output;

    goptions ftext=swissb vsize=6 in hsize=6 in;
    axis1 style=1 width=2 minor=none;
    axis2 style=1 width=2 minor=none;
    symbol1 color=BLACK i=join;
    symbol2 color=BLACK i=none v=dot height=0.5;
    proc gplot data=plot(where=(scan(Quantity,1)="&StopType")) annotate=target;
       title2 "&StopType power using the &method method with FWE=&FWE";
       title4 "With true means &TrueMeans and standard deviation = &s";
       plot EPower*n=1 Estimate*n=2 / vaxis=axis1 haxis=axis2 frame overlay;
    run;
    quit;
    title2;
    title3;
    title4;

    %mend;
```

A.8 The %BegGab Macro

This macro performs multiple comparisons using the Begun and Gabriel (1981) method.

```
/*------------------------------------------------------------*/
/* Name:      BegGab                                          */
/* Title:     Begun and Gabriel Closed Testing Procedure      */
/* Author:    Dror Rom, rom@prosof.com                        */
/* Reference: Begun, J., and Gabriel, K. R. (1981). Closure of */
/*            the Newman-Keuls multiple comparisons procedure.*/
/*            Journal of the American Statistical Association,*/
/*            76, 241-245.                                     */
/* Release:   Version 6.11                                     */
/*------------------------------------------------------------*/
/* Input:                                                     */
/*                                                            */
/*   DATASET=   the SAS data set containing the data to be    */
/*              analyzed (required)                           */
```

```
/*                                                              */
/*    GROUPS=    the grouping variable (required)               */
/*                                                              */
/*    RESPONSE=  the response variable (required)               */
/*                                                              */
/*    FWE=       the level of significance for comparisons      */
/*               among the means.  The default is 0.05.         */
/*                                                              */
/* Output:                                                      */
/*                                                              */
/*    The output dataset contains one observation for each      */
/*    pairwise comparison in the dataset.  The output dataset   */
/*    contains the following variables:                         */
/*                                                              */
/*       GRi    - The index of a (smaller) mean being compared  */
/*                                                              */
/*       Grj    - The index of a (larger) mean being compared   */
/*                                                              */
/*       PVALUE - The P-value for the comparison                */
/*                                                              */
/*       DECISION - Reject or Retain the corresponding hypothesis */
/*--------------------------------------------------------------*/

%macro BegGab(dataset=,groups=,response=,FWE=0.05);
options nonotes;
proc sort data=&dataset;
by &groups;
proc means data=&dataset noprint;
   var &response;
   by &groups;
   output out=bg mean=mean std=sd n=n;
proc print;
var trt mean sd n;
data bg;set bg;
samps=n;drop n;
proc sort;
by mean;
proc means noprint;
var samps;
output out=b n=m;
data a;set b;
call symput('m',m);
run;

%let mm=%eval(&m*&m);
%let m=%eval(&m);

data a;set bg;
i=_N_;
grp=trt;
trt=i;
m=&m;
array t(&m);
array gr(&m) $;
t(i)=trt;
gr(i)=grp;
array meanss(&m);
meanss(i)=mean;
array stds(&m);
```

```
stds(i)=sd;
array samp(&m);
samp(i)=samps;
array p(&m,&m);
retain meanss1-meanss&m;
retain stds1-stds&m;
retain samp1-samp&m;
retain p1-p&mm;
retain t1-t&m;
retain gr1-gr&m;
df=0;
mse=0;
do i=1 to m;
  mse=mse+stds(i)**2*(samp(i)-1);
  df=df+samp(i)-1;
end;
mse=mse/df;
do i= 1 to (m-1);
  do j= (i+1) to m;
    msamp=0;
    do k=i to j;
    msamp=msamp+samp(k);
    end;
    msamp=msamp/(j-i+1);
    tr=j-i+1;
    if (tr>2) then do;
      tval=abs((meanss(j)-meanss(i)))/
           ((mse/2)*((1/samp(i))+(1/samp(j))))**0.5;
      if not(tval='.')then
      p(i,j)=1-probmc('RANGE',tval,.,df,tr);
    end;
    else do;
      tval=abs((meanss(j)-meanss(i)))/
           (mse*((1/(samp(i)))+(1/(samp(j)))))**0.5;
      if not(tval='.')then
      p(i,j)=2*(1-probt(tval,df));
    end;
  end;
end;
run;

data a;set a;by j;if last.j;
data a;set a;
  j=m;
  array p{&m,&m};
  array g{&m};
  array dec{&m,&m} $;
  do i= 1 to m;
   g(i)=0;
  end;
  do i=1 to (m-1);
    do j=(i+1) to m;
      dec(i,j)='.';
    end;
  end;
```

```
      do i=1 to (m-1);
      do j=(i+1) to m;
       if(not(dec(i,j)='Retain'))then
        do;
        if p(i,j)>&FWE then
                              do;
                               dec(i,j)='Retain';
                                do k=i to (j-1);
                                 do l=(k+1) to j;
                                   dec(k,l)='Retain';
                                 end;
                                end;

                              end;
        else
        if (p(i,j)<=(&FWE*(j-i+1)/m))then dec(i,j)='Reject';

        else
        if (0.05>=p(i,j)>(&FWE*(j-i+1))/m)then
            do;
                if
                  (((i>2)and(p(1,(i-1))<=(&FWE*(i-1))/m))
                        and
                  ((j<(m-1))and(p((j+1),m)<=(&FWE*(m-j))/m)))
                            then do;
                                  dec(i,j)='Reject';
                                  do k=1 to (i-2);
                                   do l=(k+1) to (i-1);
                                     if(p(k,l)>(&FWE*(l-k+1)/m)) then
                                         dec(i,j)='Retain';
                                   end;
                                  end;
                                  do k=(j+1) to (m-1);
                                   do l=(k+1) to m;
                                     if(p(k,l)>(&FWE*(l-k+1)/m)) then
                                         dec(i,j)='Retain';
                                   end;
                                  end;

                                 end;

                  if
                    (((i>2)and(p(1,(i-1))<=(&FWE*(i-1))/m))
                          and
                       ((j>=(m-1))))
                            then do;
                                  dec(i,j)='Reject';
                                  do k=1 to (i-2);
                                      do l=(k+1) to (i-1);
                                        if(p(k,l)>(&FWE*(l-k+1)/m)) then
                                            dec(i,j)='Retain';
                                      end;
                                  end;
                                 end;
```

```
                      if
                           (((i<=2))
                               and
                ((j<(m-1))and(p((j+1),m)<=(&FWE*(m-j))/m)))
                           then do;
                                   dec(i,j)='Reject';
                                   do k=(j+1) to (m-1);
                                       do l=(k+1) to m;
                                         if(p(k,l)>(&FWE*(l-k+1)/m)) then
                                             dec(i,j)='Retain';
                                       end;
                                     end;
                                   end;

                 if((i<=2)and(j>=(m-1)))then dec(i,j)='Reject';

              if(not(dec(i,j)='Reject'))then
                             do k=i to (j-1);
                              do l=(k+1) to j;
                                dec(k,l)='Retain';
                              end;
                            end;

              end;
           end;
         end;
      end;
run;
data a1;set a;
  array t{&m};
  array p{&m,&m};
  array dec{&m,&m} $;
  array gr(&m) $;

 do i=1 to m;
  do j=1 to m;
   ti=t(i);
   tj=t(j);
   gri=gr(i);
   grj=gr(j);
   decision=dec(i,j);
   pvalue=p(i,j);
   if not(pvalue='.')then output;
  end;
 end;

title1 ' ';
title2 'Begun-Gabriel Closed Testing Procedure';
title3 "Based on the Range Statistic, FWE=&FWE";
TITLE4 ' ';
DATA _NULL_;
FILE PRINT;
set a1 end=eof;
IF _N_=1 THEN DO;
PUT @20 't_i' @26 '-' @30 't_j' @37 'P-VALUE' @48 'DECISION';
PUT @20 36*'-';
END;
if pvalue>=0.0001 then put @20 gri @26 '-' @30 grj @37 pvalue 6.4 @48
   decision;
```

```
else put  @20 gri @26 '-' @30 grj @37 '<.0001' @48 decision;
if EOF=1 then do;
PUT @20 36*'-';
end;
RUN;

data b;set a;
 array dec(&m,&m) $;
 array g(&m);
 array gr(&m) $;
 do i=1 to (m-1);
  do j=(i+1) to m;
   if((dec(i,j)='Reject'))then g(j)=g(j)+1;
  end;
 end;
data b1;set b;
array g(&m);
array gr(&m) $;
 do j=1 to m;

   if(j=1)then hfb=0;
   else
     hfb=g(j);
   output;
 end;
data c;set b;
 array dec(&m,&m) $;
 array g(&m);
 do i=1 to (m-1);
  do j=(i+1) to m;
        if((dec(i,j)='Retain'))then do l=i to j;
                               g(l)=g(j);
                            end;
        end;
        end;
data c1;set c;
array g(&m);
array gr(&m) $;
 do j=1 to m;
   tj=gr(j);
   if(j=1)then hfa=0;
   else
     hfa=g(j);
   output;
 end;

data d;merge b1 c1;by j;
keep hfa hfb j tj;
goptions colors=(black) cback=white;
proc gplot;
label tj='Treatment';
title1 ' ';
title2 'Begun-Gabriel Closed Testing Procedure';
title3 "Based on the Range Statistic, FWE=&FWE";
title4 'Schematic Plot of Significant Differences';
title5 ' ';
symbol1 i=join value=dot;
symbol2 i=join value=dot;
axis1 label=(angle=90 rotate=0 'Response') value=none major=none
```

```
minor=none;
axis2 minor=none;
plot (hfa hfb)*tj/vaxis=axis1 haxis=axis2 overlay frame;
run;

options notes;
%MEND BEGGAB;
```

A.9 The %RCC Macro

This macro performs closed dose-response tests using the Rom, Costello, and Connell (1994) method.

```
/*----------------------------------------------------------------*/
/* Name:      RCC                                              */
/* Title:     Rom, Costello, and Connell Closed Testing       */
/*            Procedure for Dose Response analysis             */
/* Author:    Dror Rom, rom@prosof.com                        */
/* Reference: Rom, D. M., Costello, R. and Connell, L. (1994). */
/*            On closed test procedures for dose response     */
/*            analysis. Statistics in Medicine, 13, 1583-1596. */
/* Release:   Version 6.11                                    */
/*----------------------------------------------------------------*/
/* Input:                                                     */
/*                                                            */
/*   DATASET=   the SAS data set containing the data to be    */
/*              analyzed (required)                           */
/*                                                            */
/*   GROUPS=    the grouping variable (required)              */
/*                                                            */
/*   RESPONSE=  the response variable (required)              */
/*                                                            */
/*   FWE=       the level of significance for comparisons     */
/*              among the means.  The default is 0.05.        */
/*                                                            */
/* Output:                                                    */
/*                                                            */
/*   The output dataset contains one observation for each     */
/*   trend test among successive means.  The output dataset   */
/*   contains the following variables:                        */
/*                                                            */
/*     Di    - The index of a (smaller) dose being compared   */
/*                                                            */
/*     Dj    - The index of a (larger) dose being compared    */
/*                                                            */
/*     PVALUE - The P-value for the comparison                */
/*                                                            */
/*     DECISION - Reject or Retain the corresponding hypothesis */
/*----------------------------------------------------------------*/
%MACRO rcc(dataset=,groups=,response=,FWE=0.05);
proc means data=&dataset noprint;
var &response;
by &groups;
output out=rcc n=samps std=sd mean=mean;
data meanss;set rcc;
proc sort;
```

```
        by &groups;
        proc means noprint;
        var samps;
        output out=b n=m;
        data a;set b;
        call symput('m',m);
        run;

        %let mm=%eval(&m*&m);
        %let m=%eval(&m);

        data a;set meanss;
        i=_N_;
        m=&m;
        array d(&m);
        d(i)=&groups;
        array meanss(&m);
        meanss(i)=mean;
        array stds(&m);
        stds(i)=sd;
        array samp(&m);
        samp(i)=samps;
        array p(&m,&m);
        retain meanss1-meanss&m;
        retain stds1-stds&m;
        retain samp1-samp&m;
        retain p1-p&mm;
        retain d1-d&m;
        df=0;
        mse=0;
        do i=1 to m;
          mse=mse+stds(i)**2*(samp(i)-1);
          df=df+samp(i)-1;
        end;
        mse=mse/df;
        do i= 1 to (m-1);
            do j= (i+1) to m;
              expec=0;
              do k=i to j;
                expec=expec+k;
              end;
              expec=expec/(j-i+1);
              num=0;
              den=0;
              do k=i to j;
                  num=num+(k-expec)*meanss(k);
                  den=den+(k-expec)**2/samp(k);
              end;
              t=num/(mse*den)**0.5;
              p(i,j)=1-probt(t,df);
            end;
          end;
        run;
```

```
data a;set a;by j;if last.j;
data a;set a;
alpha=0.05;
  j=m;
  array p{&m,&m};
  array g{&m};
  array dec{&m,&m} $;
  do i= 1 to m;
   g(i)=0;
  end;
  do i=1 to (m-1);
     do j=(i+1) to m;
      dec(i,j)='.';
     end;
  end;


do i=1 to (m-1);
 do j=(i+1) to m;
  if(not(dec(i,j)='Retain'))then
    do;
    if p(i,j)>alpha then
                       do;
                        dec(i,j)='Retain';
                         do k=i to (j-1);
                          do l=(k+1) to j;
                             dec(k,l)='Retain';
                           end;
                         end;

                       end;
    else
    if (p(i,j)<=(alpha*(j-i+1)/m))then dec(i,j)='Reject';

    else
    if (0.05>=p(i,j)>(alpha*(j-i+1))/m)then
        do;
             if
               (((i>2)and(p(1,(i-1))<=(alpha*(i-1))/m))
                        and
              ((j<(m-1))and(p((j+1),m)<=(alpha*(m-j))/m)))
                        then do;
                              dec(i,j)='Reject';
                              do k=1 to (i-2);
                               do l=(k+1) to (i-1);
                                  if(p(k,l)>(alpha*(l-k+1)/m)) then
                                      dec(i,j)='Retain';
                                end;
                              end;
                              do k=(j+1) to (m-1);
                               do l=(k+1) to m;
                                  if(p(k,l)>(alpha*(l-k+1)/m)) then
                                      dec(i,j)='Retain';
                                end;
                              end;

                          end;
```

```
                          if
               (((i>2)and(p(1,(i-1))<=(alpha*(i-1))/m))
                         and
                    ((j>=(m-1))))
                     then do;
                             dec(i,j)='Reject';
                             do k=1 to (i-2);
                                 do l=(k+1) to (i-1);
                                     if(p(k,l)>(alpha*(l-k+1)/m)) then
                                         dec(i,j)='Retain';
                                   end;
                                 end;
                             end;
                  if
                      (((i<=2))
                         and
             ((j<(m-1))and(p((j+1),m)<=(alpha*(m-j))/m)))
                     then do;
                             dec(i,j)='Reject';
                             do k=(j+1) to (m-1);
                                 do l=(k+1) to m;
                                     if(p(k,l)>(alpha*(l-k+1)/m)) then
                                         dec(i,j)='Retain';
                                   end;
                                 end;
                             end;

              if((i<=2)and(j>=(m-1)))then dec(i,j)='Reject';

              if(not(dec(i,j)='Reject'))then
                             do k=i to (j-1);
                               do l=(k+1) to j;
                                 dec(k,l)='Retain';
                               end;
                             end;
                 end;
               end;
             end;
           end;
         data a1;set a;
           array d{&m};
           array p{&m,&m};
           array dec{&m,&m} $;
          do i=1 to m;
           do j=1 to m;
            di=d(i);
            dj=d(j);
            decision=dec(i,j);
            pvalue=p(i,j);
            if not(pvalue='.')then output;
           end;
          end;

         title1 ' ';
         title2 'ROM-COSTELLO-CONNELL CLOSED TESTING PROCEDURE';
         title3 'FOR UPPER-TAILED';
         TITLE4 'DOSE RESPONSE ANALYSIS';
         title5 ' ';
         DATA _NULL_;
```

```
FILE PRINT;
set a1 end=eof;
IF _N_=1 THEN DO;
PUT @15 'd_i' @21 '-' @25 'd_j' @32 'P-VALUE' @43 'DECISION';
PUT @15 36*'-';
END;
if pvalue>=0.0001 then put @15 di @21 '-' @25 dj @32 pvalue 6.4 @43 decision;
else put @15 di @21 '-' @25 dj @32 '<.0001' @43 decision;
if EOF=1 then do;
PUT @15 36*'-';
put @15 'ALPHA=' @23 alpha;
end;
RUN;

data b;set a;
 array dec(&m,&m) $;
 array g(&m);
 do i=1 to (m-1);
  do j=(i+1) to m;
   if((dec(i,j)='Reject'))then g(j)=g(j)+1;
  end;
 end;
data b1;set b;
array g(&m);
 do j=1 to m;

   if(j=1)then hfb=0;
   else
     hfb=g(j);
   output;
 end;
data c;set b;
 array dec(&m,&m) $;
 array g(&m);
 do i=1 to (m-1);
  do j=(i+1) to m;
        if((dec(i,j)='Retain'))then do l=i to j;
                               g(l)=g(j);
                               end;
       end;
      end;
data c1;set c;
array g(&m);
array d(&m);
 do j=1 to m;
   dj=d(j);
   if(j=1)then hfa=0;
   else
     hfa=g(j);
   output;
 end;

data d;merge b1 c1;by j;
keep hfa hfb j dj;
goptions colors=(black) cback=white;
proc gplot;
label dj='TREATMENT';
title1 ' ';
title2 'ROM-COSTELLO-CONNELL CLOSED TESTING PROCEDURE';
```

```
title3 ' ';
title4 'SCHEMATIC PLOT OF THE DOSE RESPONSE';
title5 ' ';
symbol1 i=join value=dot;
symbol2 i=join value=dot;
axis1 label=(angle=90 rotate=0 'Response') value=none major=none minor=none;
axis2 minor=none;
plot (hfa hfb)*dj/vaxis=axis1 haxis=axis2 overlay frame;
run;
%MEND rcc;
```

A.10   The %Williams Macro

This macro performs a step-down test for the Minimal Effective Dose using Williams
(1971, 1972) method.

```
/*-----------------------------------------------------------------*/
/* Name:      Williams                                             */
/* Title:     Williams step-down test for minimal effective dose  */
/* Author:    Dror Rom, rom@prosof.com                            */
/* Reference: Williams, D. A. (1971). A test for difference       */
/*            between treatment means when several dose levels     */
/*            are compared with a zero dose level.                 */
/*            Biometrics, 27, 103-117.                            */
/*            Williams, D. A. (1972). The comparison of several    */
/*            dose levels with a zero dose control.                */
/*            Biometrics, 28, 519-531                             */
/* Release:   Version 6.12                                        */
/*-----------------------------------------------------------------*/
/* Input:                                                          */
/*                                                                 */
/*    DATASET=   the SAS data set containing the data to be        */
/*               analyzed (required)                               */
/*                                                                 */
/*    TRT=       the grouping variable (required)                  */
/*                                                                 */
/*    RESPONSE=  the response variable (required)                  */
/*                                                                 */
/*                                                                 */
/* Output:                                                         */
/*                                                                 */
/*    The output dataset contains one observation for each        */
/*    pairwise comparison in the dataset.  The output dataset      */
/*    contains the following variables:                            */
/*                                                                 */
/*       i    - The index of a dose being compared with the       */
/*              control (zero dose)                                */
/*                                                                 */
/*       M1   - The mean of the control                           */
/*                                                                 */
/*       M    - The mean of the dose being compared with the      */
/*              control                                            */
/*                                                                 */
/*       W    - The Williams statistics for the dose being        */
/*              compared with the control                          */
/*                                                                 */
```

```
/*      PV     - P-value for the comparison                    */
/*------------------------------------------------------------*/

%macro Williams(dataset=,trt=,response=);

options nonotes;

*********************** Get Stats *****************;
proc glm data=&dataset noprint outstat=stat;
class trt;
model &response=&trt;
run;
data stat;set stat;
keep _source_ mse ss df;
if _source_='ERROR';
mse=ss/df;

proc means data=&dataset noprint;
var &response;
by &trt;
output out=means mean=mean n=samp;

data means;set means;
proc means noprint;
var samp;
output out=a n=m;
data a;set a;
keep m;

data b;merge a stat;
d=df;
e=mse;
call symput('m',m);
run;
data b;set b;
%let m=%eval(&m);

proc sort;
by m;
data c;set means;
m=&m;

array means(&m);
array samps(&m);

means(trt)=mean;
samps(trt)=samp;
retain means1-means&m;
retain samps1-samps&m;
data c;set c;if &trt=m;
data d;merge c b;
array means(&m);
array samps(&m);
array will(&m);
                   ************** Pool adjacent violators *********=
*;
control=means(1);
do j=1 to m-1;
if (means(j)>means(j+1)) then
```

```
       do;
        emean=means(j+1);
        l=0;
        do k=j to 1 by -1;
         l=l+1;
         if emean<means(k) then do;
                                emean=emean*l/(l+1)+means(k)/(l+1);
                                  do r=k to j+1;
                                    means(r)=emean;
                                  end;
                            end;
        end;
       end;
      do k=2 to m;
      will(k)=(means(k)-control)/(mse*((1/(samps(1))+(1/(samps(k))))))**0.5;
      end;
      end;
                        *************** Get P-values **********;
      data williams;
      set d;
      array means(&m);
      array will(&m);
      array p(&m);
      do i=2 to m;
      p(i)=1-probmc("williams",will(i),.,df,i-1);
      *** P-values are based on number of doses ***;
      end;

      data williams;set williams;
      format means1-means&m f4.3 will2-will&m f4.3 p2-p&m f5.4;
      proc print;
      var means1-means&m will2-will&m p2-p&m;
      run;
      options notes;
      %MEND Williams;
```

A.11 The %SimTests Macro

This macro performs closed multiple tests for general functions parameters, incorporating logical constraints and correlations using Westfall's (1997) method.

```
/*-------------------------------------------------------------*/
/* Name:      SimTests                                         */
/* Title:     Simultaneous Hypothesis Tests for General Linear */
/*            Functions, using Correlations and Constraints    */
/* Author:    Peter Westfall, westfall@ttu.edu                 */
/* Reference: Westfall, P.H. (1997). Multiple testing of       */
/*            general contrasts using logical constraints and  */
/*            correlations.  JASA 92, 299-306                  */
/* Release:   Version 7.01                                     */
/*-------------------------------------------------------------*/
/* Inputs:                                                     */
/*                                                             */
/*      NSAMP =  simulation size, with 20000 as default        */
/*                                                             */
/*      SEED  =  random number seed, with 0 (clock time)       */
/*               as default                                    */
/*                                                             */
/*      SIDE  = U, L or B, for upper-tailed, lower-tailed      */
/*               or two-tailed, respectively. SIDE=B is default. */
/*                                                             */
/*      TYPE  = LOGICAL or FREE, for logically constrained or  */
/*               unconstrained tests, respectively. TYPE=FREE  */
/*               is the default.                               */
/*                                                             */
/* Additionally, %SimTests requires two further macros to be   */
/* defined that use SAS/IML to construct the estimates and     */
/* the contrasts of interest.  In particular, make sure the    */
/* following two macros are defined before invoking            */
/* %SimTests:                                                  */
/*                                                             */
/*    %Estimate: Uses SAS/IML code to define                   */
/*      EstPar - (column) vector of estimated parameters       */
/*      Cov    - covariance matrix for the for the estimates   */
/*      df     - error degrees of freedom; set to 0 for        */
/*               asymptotic analysis                           */
/*                                                             */
/*    %Contrasts: Uses SAS/IML code to define                  */
/*      C      - matrix whose columns define the contrasts of  */
/*               interest between the parameters               */
/*      CLab   - (column) character vector whose elements      */
/*               label the respective contrasts in C           */
/*                                                             */
/* You can either define these macros directly, or use the     */
/* %MakeGLMStats macro to define them.                         */
/*                                                             */
/*-------------------------------------------------------------*/
/* Output:                                                     */
/*   The primary output is a dataset with one observation for  */
/*   each contrast and the following variables:                */
/*                                                             */
```

```
/*      Contrast - contrast label                              */
/*      Estimate - contrast estimated value                    */
/*      StdErr   - standard error of estimate                  */
/*      tValue   - normalized estimate, Estimate/StdErr         */
/*      RawP     - non-multiplicity-adjusted p-value           */
/*      BonP     - Bonferroni multiplicity-adjusted p-value    */
/*      BonMult  - corresponding Bonferroni multiplier         */
/*      AdjP     - stepwise multiplicity-adjusted p-value      */
/*      SEAdjP   - standard error for AdjP                     */
/*                                                             */
/*   This dataset is also displayed as a formatted table, using */
/*   the ODS system.                                           */
/*                                                             */
/* This macro also produces a data set called SUBSETS that has */
/* has a variable STEPJ indicating the particular (ordered)    */
/* hypothesis being considered; as well as variables          */
/* (TEST1--TESTk) identifying the particular subset hypotheses */
/* that contain the hypothesis indicated by the STEPJ variable,*/
/* that do not contradict falsehood of the previous hypotheses.*/
/* The order of the TEST1--TESTk variables is from most to     */
/* least significant.                                          */
/*-------------------------------------------------------------*/

%macro SimTests(nsamp   = 20000  ,
                seed    = 0      ,
                side    = B      ,
                type    = FREE   ,
                options =        );
%global ANORM;

options nonotes;

proc iml;
%Estimates;
if (df <= 0) then call symput('ANORM','1');
else              call symput('ANORM','0');
%Contrasts;
C = C`;
side="&side";
type="&type";
if side = "U" then C=-C;

EstCont = C*EstPar;
CovCont = C*Cov*C`;
SECont = sqrt(vecdiag(CovCont));
tvals = EstCont/SECont;
if side = "B" then do;
   tvals = -abs(tvals);
   if df=0 then pvals = 2*probnorm(tvals);
      else pvals = 2*probt(tvals,df);
   end;
else do;
   if df=0 then pvals=probnorm(tvals);
      else pvals = probt(tvals,df);
   end;
```

```
k = nrow(c);
nests = nrow(EstPar);
call symput('k',char(k));
call symput('g',char(nests));
r  = rank(Pvals`);
ir = r;
ir[,r] = 1:nrow(PVals);
origord  = ir`              ;
cord      = c       [ir,];
clabord  = clab    [ir,];
tvalsord = tvals   [ir,];
pvalsord = pvals   [ir,];
ccord     = CovCont[ir,ir];
crrccord = inv(sqrt(diag(ccord)))*ccord*inv(sqrt(diag(ccord)));
ct = t(cord);

start ztrail;
   ii=1;
   zz=kk;
   do while(mod(zz,2)=0);
      ii=ii+1;
      zz=zz/2;
      end;
finish;

if type = "LOGICAL" then do;
do iout  = 1 to k-2;
   limit = 2**(k-iout-1);
   in=J(k-iout-1,1,0);
   zero =J(k,1,0);
   in1 =zero;
   y = ct[,1:iout];

   do kk=1 to limit;
      if kk=limit then in=j(k-iout-1,1,0);
      else do;
         run ztrail;
         in[ii,]=^in[ii,];
         end;

      locbin  = j(iout, 1, 0) // {1} // in;
      loc1 = loc(locbin);
      x = ct[,loc1];

      res = y - x*ginv(x`*x)*x`*y;
      ssemat = vecdiag(res`*res);

      if ssemat > .00000001 then do;
         if in1=0 then in1 = locbin;
         else do;
            check = in1 - repeat(locbin, 1, ncol(in1));
            diff = check[<>,] - check[><,];
            if min(diff) = 2 then  in1 = in1||locbin;
            else do;
               mindx = diff[,>:<];
               if check[+,mindx]=-1 then in1[,mindx] = locbin;
               end;
            end;
```

```
         end;
       end;
   in1  = in1';
   ncont = nrow(in1);
   in1 = j(ncont,1,iout+1)||in1;
   if iout = 1 then inbig = in1;
   else inbig = inbig//in1;
   end;
end;

big = j(1,k+1,1)//inbig;
lastset = j(1,1,k)||j(1,k-1,0)||{1};
big = big//lastset;
stepj = big[,1];
if type="FREE" then do;
   stepj = 1:k;
   stepj = stepj';
end;
SubsetK = big[,2:ncol(big)];
if type="FREE" then do;
   m = j(1,k,1);
   do i = 2 to k;
      r = j(1,i-1,0)||j(1,k-i+1,1);
      m= m//r;
   end;
SubsetK = m;
end;

subsets = subsetk||stepj;
create subsets var (("t1":"t&k")||"StepJ");
append from subsets;
nbig = nrow(big);
if type="LOGICAL" then des = design(big[,1]);
   else des=design(stepj);
if type="LOGICAL" then contonly = big[,2:k+1];
   else contonly = subsetk;
tcmpr = des*tvalsord;
h = root(crrccord);
if type="FREE" then nbig=k;
count = j(nbig,1,0);
countc = count;
countc2 = count;
if type="LOGICAL" then totals =  contonly[,+];
   else do; totals=k:1; totals=totals'; end;
if side = "B" then do;
   if df = 0 then bon = 2*(probnorm(tcmpr))#totals;
      else bon = 2*(probt(tcmpr,df))#totals;
      end;
   else do;
      if df = 0 then bon = (probnorm(tcmpr))#totals;
      else bon = (probt(tcmpr,df))#totals;
      end;
```

```
if &nsamp>0 then do;
file log;
do isim = 1 to &nsamp;
   if mod(isim,5000) = 0 then put isim;
   z = h'*rannor(j(k,1,&seed));
   if df=0 then s=1; else do;
      chi = 2*rangam(&seed,df/2);
      s = sqrt(chi/df);
      end;
   t = z/s;
   if side = "B" then t = -abs(t);
   try = (contonly#(j(nbig,1,1)*t'));
   try1 = (10000*(try=0)) + try;
   maxind =     (try1[,><] <= tcmpr);

   sumind = (try1 < ((tcmpr)*j(1,ncol(try),1)))[,+];
   countc = countc + sumind;
   countc2 = countc2 + sumind##2;
   count = count +  maxind;
end;

smpl = count/&nsamp;
cv = bon + smpl - countc/&nsamp;
avec = countc/&nsamp;
avec2 = countc2/&nsamp;
varx = smpl#(j(nrow(smpl),1,1)-smpl);
varz = avec2 - avec##2 + smpl - smpl##2 -2*avec#(j(nrow(smpl),1,1)-smpl);
covzx = (avec-smpl)#(j(nrow(smpl),1,1)-smpl);
a1 = varz+covzx;
a2 = varx+covzx;
atot = a1+a2;
atot = (atot=0) + atot;
a1 = a1/atot;
a2 = a2/atot;
atot = a1+a2;
a2 = a2+(atot=0);
gls = a1#smpl + a2#cv;

stdgls = sqrt(abs((a1##2#varx + a2##2#varz -2*a1#a2#covzx)/&nsamp));
stdsmpl = sqrt(varx/&nsamp);
stdcv = sqrt(abs(varz/&nsamp));
glsbig = des#(gls*j(1,k,1));
glsp = glsbig[<>,];
glsin = glsbig[<:>,];

stdgls = stdgls[glsin,];
glsptry = glsp';
smplbig = des#(smpl*j(1,k,1));
smplp = smplbig[<>,];
smplin = smplbig[<:>,];
stdsmpl = stdsmpl[smplin,];
cvbig = des#(cv*j(1,k,1));
cvp = cvbig[<>,];
cvin = cvbig[<:>,];
stdcv = stdcv[cvin,];
```

```
            do i = 2 to k;
                if smplp[1,i] < smplp[1,i-1] then do;
                    smplp[1,i] = smplp[1,i-1];
                    stdsmpl[i,1] = stdsmpl[i-1,1];
                    end;
                if cvp[1,i] < cvp[1,i-1] then do;
                    cvp[1,i] = cvp[1,i-1];
                    stdcv[i,1] = stdcv[i-1,1];
                    end;
                if glsp[1,i] < glsp[1,i-1] then do;
                    glsp[1,i] = glsp[1,i-1];
                    stdgls[i,1] = stdgls[i-1,1];
                    end;
            end;

            adjpsmpl = smplp`;
            adjpcv = cvp`;
            adjpgls = glsp`;
            adjp=adjpgls;
            SEAdjp = stdgls;
            end;

        bonbig = des#(bon*j(1,k,1));
        bonp = bonbig[<>,];
        bonmult = bonp`/pvalsord;

        do i = 2 to k;
            if bonp[1,i] < bonp[1,i-1] then bonp[1,i] = bonp[1,i-1];
            end;

        rawp = pvalsord;
        estimate = EstCont[ir,];
        if side ="U" then estimate=-estimate;
        stderr = SECont[ir,];
        contrast = cord;
        if side = "U" then contrast=-contrast;
        adjpbon = bonp`;
        adjpbon = (adjpbon<1)#adjpbon +(adjpbon>=1);

        if &nsamp>0 then do;
            outres =    origord
                     ||contrast
                     ||estimate
                     ||stderr
                     ||rawp
                     ||bonmult
                     ||adjpbon
                     ||adjp
                     ||SEAdjp;
            create SimTestOut var (     "OrigOrd"
                                    ||("Est1":"Est&g")
                                    ||"Estimate"
                                    ||"StdErr"
                                    ||"RawP"
                                    ||"BonMult"
                                    ||"BonP"
                                    ||"AdjP"
                                    ||"SEAdjP");
            append from outres;
            end;
```

```
        else do;
            outres =    origord
                     ||contrast
                     ||estimate
                     ||stderr
                     ||rawp
                     ||bonmult
                     ||adjpbon;
            create SimTestOut var (    "OrigOrd"
                                    ||("Est1":"Est&g")
                                    ||"Estimate"
                                    ||"StdErr"
                                    ||"RawP"
                                    ||"BonMult"
                                    ||"BonP");
            append from outres;
            end;

    create labels from clabord; append from clabord;

    data SimTestOut; merge SimTestOut labels;
        rename col1=Contrast;
    proc sort data=SimTestOut out=SimTestOut; by origord;
    data SimTestOut; set SimTestOut; drop origord;
        run;

    %if (^%index(%upcase(&options),NOPRINT)) %then %do;

    proc template;
    delete MCBook.SimTests;
    define table MCBook.SimTests;
        column Contrast Estimate StdErr RawP BonP AdjP SEAdjP;

        define header h1;
            spill_margin;
    %if (%upcase(&type) = LOGICAL) %then %do;
            text "Logically Constrained (Restricted Combinations) Step-Down Tests";
        %end;
    %else %do;
            text "Unconstrained (Free Combinations) Step-Down Tests";
        %end;
    %if (^&ANORM) %then %do;
            space=1;
    %end;
            end;
    %if (&ANORM) %then %do;
        define header h2;
            text "Asymptotic Normal Approximations";
            space=1;
            end;
    %end;

        define column Contrast;
            header="Contrast";
            end;
        define column Estimate;
            header="Estimate"        format=D8. space=1;
            translate _val_ = ._ into '';
            end;
```

```
         define column StdErr;
            header="Standard Error" format=D8.;
            translate _val_ = ._ into '';
            end;

      %if (&nsamp) %then %let LastPValCol = AdjP;
      %else               %let LastPValCol = BonP;

      %if (&side = B) %then %do;
         define header ProbtHead;
            text " Pr > |t| ";
            start=Rawp end=&LastPValCol just=c expand='-';
            end;
         %end;
      %else %if (&side = L) %then %do;
         define header ProbtHead;
            text " Pr < t ";
            start=Rawp end=&LastPValCol just=c expand='-';
            end;
         %end;
      %else %do;
         define header ProbtHead;
            text " Pr > t ";
            start=Rawp end=&LastPValCol just=c expand='-';
            end;
         %end;

      define column RawP;
         space=1 glue=10
         parent=Common.PValue header="Raw";
         translate _val_ = ._ into '';
         end;
      define column BonP;
         space=1 glue=10
         parent=Common.PValue header="Bon";
         translate _val_ = ._ into '';
         end;
      define column AdjP;
         parent=Common.PValue header="Adj";
         translate _val_ = ._ into '';
         end;

      define column SEAdjP;
         header="SE(AdjP)" format=d8.;
         translate _val_ = ._ into '';
         end;

      end;
   run;

data _null_; set SimTestOut;
   file print ods=(template='MCBook.SimTests');
   put _ods_;
   run;

%end;

options notes;

%mend;
```

A.12 The %RomEx Macro

This macro computes exact discrete tests using Rom's (1992) method.

```
/*------------------------------------------------------------*/
/* Name:     RomEx                                            */
/* Title:    Rom exact discrete multiple comparison procedure */
/* Author:   Chung-Kuei Chang, prosof@prosof.com             */
/* Reference: Rom, D. M. (1992). Strengthening some common    */
/*               multiple test procedures for discrete data.  */
/*               Statistics in Medicine, 11, 511-514.         */
/* Release:  Version 6.11                                     */
/*------------------------------------------------------------*/
/* Input:                                                     */
/*                                                            */
/*   The following arguments are required and must be in this */
/*   order.                                                   */
/*                                                            */
/*    - the tail of the test 1-lower, 2-upper, 3-two-sided    */
/*    - the SAS data set containing the data to be analyzed   */
/*    - the SAS data set containing the number of endpoints and */
/*       number of treatments.                                */
/*                                                            */
/* Output:                                                    */
/*                                                            */
/*   The output dataset contains one observation for each     */
/*   P-value in the dataset.  The output dataset contains the */
/*   following variables:                                     */
/*                                                            */
/*        i    - The index of the ordered P-value             */
/*                                                            */
/*  ENDPOINT   - The index of the corresponding endpoint      */
/*                                                            */
/*  P_VALUE    - The Fisher Exact P-value for the endpoint    */
/*                                                            */
/*     ADJP    - The P-value for the global null hypothesis   */
/*------------------------------------------------------------*/

%MACRO ROMEX(TAIL, dsdat, dspar);
%let con=1e-10;
%GLOBAL ADJP;
DATA PAR;
 SET &DSPAR;
 DIGNEP=INT(LOG10(NEP))+1;
 DIGNT=INT(LOG10(NT))+1;
 CALL SYMPUT('DIGNEP',DIGNEP);
 CALL SYMPUT('DIGNT',DIGNT);
proc print;
run;
RUN;

DATA PAR;
 KEEP NEP NT;
 SET PAR;
 LENGTH TT $&DIGNEP. TG $&DIGNT.;
 TT=NEP;
 TG=NT;
 CALL SYMPUT('TT',TT);
```

```
                      CALL SYMPUT('TG',TG);
                  TITLE 'DATA = MULTCOMP.PAR';
                  RUN;
                  DATA DISMULEP;
                   N=_N_;
                   SET &DSDAT END=EOF;
                   IF EOF=1 THEN DO;
                      CALL SYMPUT('NC', N);
                                   END;
                  proc print;
                  RUN;
                  title1 'MULTIPLE ENDPOINTS DATA';
                  title2 ' ';
                  proc print data=dismulep;
                  id ep1;
                  VAR EP2-EP&TT TREAT1-TREAT&TG;
                  run;

                  PROC TRANSPOSE DATA=DISMULEP OUT=TEMP1;
                   BY N;
                   VAR EP1-EP&TT TREAT1-TREAT&TG;
                  *PROC PRINT;
                  TITLE 'TEMP1';
                  RUN;

                  DATA TEMP1;
                   SET TEMP1;
                   DROP _NAME_ N;
                  RUN;

                  PROC TRANSPOSE DATA=TEMP1 OUT=TEMP2 PREFIX=TAO;
                   VAR COL1;
                  *PROC PRINT DATA=TEMP2;
                  TITLE 'TEMP2';
                  RUN;

                   %LET NCOLO=%EVAL(&TT+&TG);
                   %LET NROW=&NC;
                   %LET NCOL=&TG;
                   %LET TOT=%EVAL(&NC*&NCOLO);
                  DATA ZPZ(KEEP=P_VALUE  ENDPOINT);
                  SET TEMP2;
                  ARRAY P(&TT);
                  ARRAY POBS(&TT);
                   ARRAY TAO(&NROW,&NCOLO);
                   ARRAY Q(&NROW, &NCOL);
                   ARRAY MINM(&NROW, &NCOL);
                   ARRAY C(&NCOL);
                   ARRAY R(&NROW);
                   ARRAY NN(&TT,2,&TG);
                  ARRAY    BR{&NCOL};
                  ARRAY    BC{&NROW};
                  ARRAY CY{&NROW,&NCOL    };
                  ARRAY RY{&NROW,&NCOL    };
                  ARRAY SR(2);
                  ARRAY SRY(2,&TG);
                  ARRAY SMINM(&TG);
                  %MACRO SMTABLE(B);
```

```
    DO SJ=&B TO &K;
     IF SJ>1 THEN DO;
      DO SJI=1 TO 2;
        SRY(SJI,SJ)=SRY(SJI,SJ-1)+NN(I,SJI,SJ-1);
      END;
                    END;
     MMR=SR(1)-SRY(1,SJ);
     NN(I,1,SJ)=MIN(MMR,C(SJ));
     NN(I,2,SJ)=C(SJ)-NN(I,1,SJ);
     MMR2=SR(2)-SRY(2,SJ);
     MMC=C(SJ)-MMR2;
     SMINM(SJ)=MAX(0,MMC);
    END;
%MEND SMTABLE;

%MACRO SPROB;
 SPP=SFIX;
 DO SI=1 TO 2;
 DO SJ=1 TO &K;
  DO SS=2 TO NN(I,SI,SJ);
    SPP=SPP-LOG(SS);
  END;
 END;
 END;
 SPP=EXP(SPP);
%MEND SPROB;

%MACRO TWOXK(K);
 SR(1)=0;
 SR(2)=0;
 STOTAL=TOTAL;
 DO II=1 TO 2;
  DO J=1 TO &K;
   SR(II)=SR(II)+NN(I,II,J);
  END;
 END;

STOBS=0;
EXPMAR=0;
DO K=2 TO &K;
 STOBS=STOBS+(K-1)*NN(I,1,K);
 EXPMAR=EXPMAR+(K-1)*SR(1)*C(K);
END;
EXPMAR=EXPMAR/TOTAL;
DISOBS=ABS(STOBS-EXPMAR);
SFIX=0;
DO J=1 TO 2;
 DO S=2 TO SR(J);
  SFIX=SFIX+LOG(S);
 END;
END;
DO K=1 TO &K;
 DO S=2 TO C(K);
  SFIX=SFIX+LOG(S);
 END;
END;
DO S=2 TO STOTAL;
 SFIX=SFIX-LOG(S);
END;
```

```
SRY(1,1)=0;
SRY(2,1)=0;
P_VALUE=0;
%SMTABLE(1)
* N_TABLE=0;
DO UNTIL (NN(I,1,1)<SMINM(1));
DO UNTIL (NN(I,1,&K-1)<SMINM(&K-1));
STPRO=0;
DO SI=2 TO &K;
 STPRO=STPRO+(SI-1)*NN(I,1,SI);
END;
DISPRO=ABS(STPRO-EXPMAR);
%IF &TAIL=1 %THEN %DO;
    IF STPRO-STOBS<&con THEN DO;   %END;
%ELSE %IF &TAIL=2 %THEN %DO;
    IF STPRO-STOBS>-&con THEN DO;   %END;
%ELSE %IF &TAIL=3 %THEN %DO;
    IF DISPRO-DISOBS>-&con THEN DO;   %END;
 %SPROB
 P_VALUE=P_VALUE+SPP;
                                                      END;
 NN(I,1,&K-1)=NN(I,1,&K-1)-1;
 NN(I,2,&K-1)=NN(I,2,&K-1)+1;
 NN(I,1,&K)=NN(I,1,&K)+1;
 NN(I,2,&K)=NN(I,2,&K)-1;
END;***************FOR DO UNTIL;
IF &K>2 THEN DO;
U=(&K-1);
DO UNTIL (NN(I,1,1)<SMINM(1) OR NN(I,1,U)>=SMINM(U));
 U=U-1;
 NN(I,1,U)=NN(I,1,U)-1;
 IF NN(I,1,U)>=SMINM(U) THEN DO;
  NN(I,2,U)=NN(I,2,U)+1;
  U=U+1;
  %SMTABLE(U)
                                END;
END;
END;
END;****************** FOR THE DO UNTIL REPLACING SSTART;
%MEND TWOXK;

  DO I=1 TO &NROW; R(I)=0;END;
  DO J=1 TO &NCOL; C(J)=0;END;
TOTAL=0;
    DO I=1 TO &NROW;
    DO J=1 TO &NCOLO;
    IF J>&TT THEN DO;
    Q(I,J-&TT)=TAO(I,J);
     R(I)=R(I)+TAO(I,J);
     C(J-&TT)=C(J-&TT)+TAO(I,J);
     TOTAL=TOTAL+TAO(I,J);
                    END;
    END;
    END;
```

```
 BR(&NCOL)=0;
 BC(&NROW)=0;
   DO I=(&NCOL-1) TO 1 BY -1;
     BR(I)=BR(I+1)+C(I+1);
   END;
   DO I=(&NROW-1) TO 1 BY -1;
     BC(I)=BC(I+1)+R(I+1);
   END;

 DO I=1 TO &TT;
  DO J=1 TO &TG;
   NN(I,1,J)=0;
    DO K=1 TO &NC;
     IF TAO(K,I)=1 THEN NN(I,1,J)=NN(I,1,J)+Q(K,J);
    END;
    NN(I,2,J)=C(J)-NN(I,1,J);
  END;
  %TWOXK(&TG)
  ENDPOINT=I;
  OUTPUT ZPZ;
 IF I=1 THEN POBS(I)=P_VALUE;
 ELSE DO;
   LE=0;
   DO B=1 TO (I-1);
      IF P_VALUE-POBS(B)<&con THEN DO;
         DO CC=(I-1) TO B BY -1;
            POBS(CC+1)=POBS(CC);
         END;
      POBS(B)=P_VALUE;
      LE=1;
      GOTO ORDER;
                                                        END;
   END;
ORDER: ;
   IF LE=0 THEN POBS(I)=P_VALUE;
       END;
 END;

 FIX=0;
 DO I=1 TO &NROW;
DO S=2 TO R(I);  FIX=FIX+LOG(S);  END;
 END;
 DO J=1 TO &NCOL;
DO S=2 TO C(J);  FIX=FIX+LOG(S);  END;
 END;
DO S=1 TO TOTAL;
 FIX=FIX-LOG(S);
END;
DO S=1 TO &NROW; RY(S,1)=0;END;
DO S=1 TO &NCOL; CY(1,S)=0;END;

%MACRO MTABLE(A,B);
   DO II=&A TO &NROW;
   DO JJ=1 TO &NCOL;
    IF (II>&A OR JJ>=&B) THEN DO;
    IF (JJ=&NCOL AND II<&NROW) THEN DO;
       Q(II,JJ)=R(II)-RY(II,&NCOL-1)-Q(II,&NCOL-1);
        IF II>1 THEN CY(II,JJ)=CY(II-1,JJ)+Q(II-1,JJ);
                                       END;
```

```
        IF II=&NROW THEN DO;
          IF JJ<&NCOL THEN Q(II,JJ)=C(JJ)-CY(II-1,JJ)-Q(II-1,JJ); ELSE DO;
           LAST=R(&NROW);
           DO S=1 TO (&NCOL-1);
             LAST=LAST-Q(&NROW,S);
           END;
             Q(&NROW,&NCOL)=LAST;                                      END;
                         END;
        IF (II<&NROW AND JJ<&NCOL) THEN DO;
         IF II>1 THEN CY(II,JJ)=CY(II-1,JJ)+Q(II-1,JJ);
         IF JJ>1 THEN RY(II,JJ)=RY(II,JJ-1)+Q(II,JJ-1);
                   MMR=R(II)-RY(II,JJ);
                   MMC=C(JJ)-CY(II,JJ);
                 Q(II,JJ)=MIN(MMR,MMC);
           MXR=MMR-BR(JJ);
          IF II>1 THEN DO;
          DO L=(JJ+1) TO &NCOL;
            MXR=MXR+CY(II-1,L)+Q(II-1,L);
          END;         END;
          MXC=MMC-BC(II);
          MINM(II,JJ)=MAX(0,MXR,MXC);
                                           END;
                                        END;
      END;
      END;
  %MEND MTABLE;
  %MACRO PROB;
   PP=FIX;
    DO II=1 TO &NROW;
    DO J=1 TO &NCOL;
  DO S=2 TO Q(II,J);  PP=PP-LOG(S);  END;
    END;
    END;
        PP=EXP(PP);
  %MEND PROB;


  %MTABLE(1,1)
  P_ONESID=0; N_TABLE=0;
  N_TABLE=N_TABLE+1;
  START: ;
  DO UNTIL (Q(&NROW-1,&NCOL-1)<MINM(&NROW-1,&NCOL-1));
   DO I=1 TO &TT;
    DO J=1 TO &TG;
     NN(I,1,J)=0;
     DO K=1 TO &NC;
      IF TAO(K,I)=1 THEN NN(I,1,J)=NN(I,1,J)+Q(K,J);
     END;
     NN(I,2,J)=C(J)-NN(I,1,J);
    END;
    %TWOXK(&TG)
   IF P_VALUE-POBS(1)<-&con THEN DO;
     P(1)=P_VALUE;
     GOTO CALP;
                                                   END;
```

```
ELSE DO;
 IF I=1 THEN P(I)=P_VALUE;
 ELSE DO;
   LE=0;
   DO B=1 TO (I-1);
     IF P_VALUE-P(B)<&con THEN DO;
        DO CC=(I-1) TO B BY -1;
           P(CC+1)=P(CC);
         END;
       P(B)=P_VALUE;
       LE=1;
       GOTO ORDER2;
                                                            END;

   END;
    IF LE=0 THEN P(I)=P_VALUE;
ORDER2: ;
     END;


 IF P(1)-POBS(1)<-&con THEN GOTO CALP;
ELSE IF I<&TT THEN DO;
 IF P(1)-POBS(1)>&con THEN GOTO NEXTI;
 ELSE IF ABS(P(1)-POBS(1))<&con THEN DO;
         DO B=2 TO I;
       IF P(B)-POBS(B)>&con THEN GOTO NEXTI;
       ELSE IF P(B)-POBS(B)<-&con THEN GOTO CALP;
       ELSE IF (ABS(P(B)-POBS(B))<&con AND I<&TT)
            THEN GOTO NEXTI;
       ELSE IF (ABS(P(B)-POBS(B))<&con AND I=&TT)
             THEN GOTO CALP;
           END;
                                                            END;

             END;
ELSE IF I=&TT THEN DO;
 IF P(1)-POBS(1)>&con THEN GOTO SKIP;
 ELSE IF ABS(P(1)-POBS(1))<&con THEN DO;
         DO B=2 TO I;
       IF P(B)-POBS(B)>&con THEN GOTO SKIP;
       ELSE IF P(B)-POBS(B)<-&con THEN GOTO CALP;
       ELSE IF (ABS(P(B)-POBS(B))<&con AND B<&TT)
            THEN GOTO NEXTB;
       ELSE IF (ABS(P(B)-POBS(B))<&con AND B=&TT)
            THEN GOTO CALP;
           NEXTB: ;
           END;
                                                            END;

                 END;
     END;
NEXTI: ;
END;
 GOTO SKIP;
 CALP: ;
   %PROB
 P_ONESID=P_ONESID+PP;
SKIP:;
Q(&NROW-1,&NCOL-1)=Q(&NROW-1,&NCOL-1)-1;
Q(&NROW-1,&NCOL)=Q(&NROW-1,&NCOL)+1;
Q(&NROW,&NCOL-1)=Q(&NROW,&NCOL-1)+1;
Q(&NROW,&NCOL)=Q(&NROW,&NCOL)-1;
END;
```

```
        DO I=&NROW-1 TO 1 BY -1;
        DO J=&NCOL-1 TO 1 BY -1;
          IF (I<&NROW-1 OR J<&NCOL-1) THEN DO;
         Q(I,J)=Q(I,J)-1;
          IF Q(1,1)<MINM(1,1) THEN GOTO FINISH;
          IF Q(I,J)>=MINM(I,J) THEN DO;
            J=J+1;
            %MTABLE(I,J)
            GOTO START;
                                    END;
                                            END;
          END;
          END;
        FINISH: ;
        CALL SYMPUT('ADJP', P_ONESID);
        RUN;

        PROC SORT DATA=ZPZ OUT=ZPZ;
         BY P_VALUE;
        RUN;

        TITLE1 ' ';
        title2 'ROM DISCRETE MULTIPLE ENDPOINTS ANALYSIS';
        title3 ' ';
        title4 ' ';
        title5 ' ';
        DATA _NULL_;
         FILE PRINT;
         SET ZPZ END=EOF;
         ADJP=&ADJP;
         I=_N_;
         IF _N_=1 THEN DO;
          PUT @18 'I'  @28 'ENDPOINT'          @57 'P-VALUE*';
          PUT @15 51*'-';
                    END;
          PUT @18 I    @24 ENDPOINT 8.              @55 P_VALUE 8.4;
         IF EOF=1 THEN DO;
          PUT @15 51*'-';
          PUT @18  'EXACT ADJUSTED P-VALUE' @55 ADJP 8.4;
          PUT ///;
        %IF &TAIL=1 %THEN %DO;
          PUT @18 '*: P-VALUE FOR LOWER-TAILED TREND';   %END;
        %ELSE %IF &TAIL=2 %THEN %DO;
          PUT @18 '*: P-VALUE FOR UPPER-TAILED TREND';   %END;
        %IF &TAIL=3 %THEN %DO;
          PUT @18 '*: P-VALUE FOR TWO-TAILED TREND';   %END;

                    END;
         RUN;
        %MEND ROMEX;
```

A.13 The %RomMC Macro

This macro simulates discrete tests using Rom's (1992) method.

```
/*--------------------------------------------------------------*/
/* Name:      RomMc                                             */
/* Title:     Rom Monte-Carlo discrete multiple comparison      */
/*            procedure                                         */
/* Author:    Chung-Kuei Chang, prosof@prosof.com              */
/* Reference: Rom, D. M. (1992). Strengthening some common     */
/*            multiple test procedures for discrete data.      */
/*            Statistics in Medicine, 11, 511-514.             */
/* Release:   Version 6.11                                     */
/*--------------------------------------------------------------*/
/* Input:                                                       */
/*                                                              */
/*   The following arguments are must be in this order.         */
/*                                                              */
/*      - the tail of the test 1-lower, 2-upper, 3-two-sided   */
/*      - the SAS data set containing the data to be analyzed  */
/*      - the SAS data set containing the number of endpoints and */
/*        number of treatments.                                */
/*      - the SAS data set containing the number of Monte-Carlo */
/*        samples.                                             */
/*                                                              */
/* Output:                                                      */
/*                                                              */
/*   The output dataset contains one observation for each       */
/*   P-value in the dataset.  The output dataset contains the   */
/*   following variables:                                       */
/*                                                              */
/*        i      - The index of the ordered P-value            */
/*                                                              */
/*   ENDPOINT    - The index of the corresponding endpoint     */
/*                                                              */
/*   P_VALUE     - The Fisher Exact P-value for the endpoint    */
/*                                                              */
/*        ADJP   - The P-value for the global null hypothesis  */
/*                                                              */
/*        L95    - The lower limit of the confidence interval for */
/*                 the P-value                                 */
/*                                                              */
/*        U95    - The upper limit of the confidence interval for */
/*                 the P-value                                 */
/*--------------------------------------------------------------*/

%MACRO ROMMC(TAIL, dsdat, dspar, dsnmc);
%let con=1e-10;
%GLOBAL ADJP MM L95 U95;
%MACRO ZSCORE(K);
 SR(1)=0; ****************** SUM OF THE ELEMENTS IN THE FIRST ROW;
 SR(2)=0; ****************** SUM OF THE ELEMENTS IN THE SECOND ROW;
          ****************** C(J) IS THE JTH COLUMN SUM;
```

```
         STOTAL=TOTAL;
      DO II=1 TO 2;
       DO J=1 TO &K;
         SR(II)=SR(II)+NN(I,II,J);
        END;
       END;
      TOBS=0;
      EXPMAR=0;
      UR2=SR(1);
      U2=(SR(1)**2)/TOTAL;
      VC2=0;
      V2=0;
      DO K=2 TO &K;
       TOBS=TOBS+(K-1)*NN(I,1,K);
       EXPMAR=EXPMAR + SR(1)*C(K-1)*(K-1);
       VC2=VC2+(K-1)**2*C(K);
       V2=V2+(K-1)*C(K);
      END;
      EXPMAR=EXPMAR/TOTAL;
      V2=V2**2/TOTAL;
      VAR=(UR2-U2)*(VC2-V2)/(TOTAL-1);
      IF VAR>0 THEN DO;
      Z=(TOBS-EXPMAR)/VAR**0.5;
      PVAL=PROBNORM(Z);
      %IF &TAIL=1 %THEN %DO; PZ=PVAL;   %END;
      %ELSE %IF &TAIL=2 %THEN %DO; PZ=1-PVAL; %END;
      %ELSE %IF &TAIL=3 %THEN %DO; PZ=2*MIN(PVAL,1-PVAL); %END;
      P_VALUE=PZ;
                      END;
      ELSE PZ=1;
      %MEND ZSCORE;

      DATA N_SAMPLE;
       SET &DSNMC;
       IF SEED=. THEN SEED=0;
      CALL SYMPUT('MM',N_SAMPLE);
      CALL SYMPUT('SEED',SEED);
      RUN;

      DATA PAR;
       SET &DSPAR;
       DIGNEP=INT(LOG10(NEP))+1;
       DIGNT=INT(LOG10(NT))+1;
       CALL SYMPUT('DIGNEP',DIGNEP);
       CALL SYMPUT('DIGNT',DIGNT);
      RUN;

      DATA PAR;
       KEEP NEP NT;
       SET PAR;
       LENGTH TT $&DIGNEP. TG $&DIGNT.;
       TT=NEP;
       TG=NT;
       CALL SYMPUT('TT',TT);
       CALL SYMPUT('TG',TG);
      TITLE 'DATA = MULTCOMP.PAR';
      RUN;
```

```
DATA DISMULEP;
 SET &DSDAT END=EOF;
 N=_N_;
 IF EOF=1 THEN DO;
    CALL SYMPUT('NC', N);
               END;
RUN;

PROC TRANSPOSE DATA=DISMULEP OUT=TEMP1;
 BY N;
 VAR EP1-EP&TT TREAT1-TREAT&TG;
TITLE 'TEMP1';
RUN;

DATA TEMP1;
 SET TEMP1;
 DROP _NAME_ N;
RUN;
title1 'MULTIPLE ENDPOINTS DATA';
title2 ' ';
proc print data=dismulep;
id ep1;
 VAR EP2-EP&TT TREAT1-TREAT&TG;
 run;
PROC TRANSPOSE DATA=DISMULEP OUT=TEMP1;
 BY N;
 VAR EP1-EP&TT TREAT1-TREAT&TG;
RUN;

PROC TRANSPOSE DATA=TEMP1 OUT=TEMP2 PREFIX=TAO;
 VAR COL1;
RUN;

 %LET NCOLO=%EVAL(&TT+&TG);
 %LET NROW=&NC;
 %LET NCOL=&TG;
 %LET TOT=%EVAL(&NC*&NCOLO);

DATA TEMP2;
 SET TEMP2;
 ARRAY TAO(&NROW,&NCOLO);
 ARRAY Q(&NROW, &NCOL);
 ARRAY C(&NCOL);
 ARRAY R(&NROW);
  DO I=1 TO &NROW; R(I)=0;END;
  DO J=1 TO &NCOL; C(J)=0;END;
TOTAL=0;
    DO I=1 TO &NROW;
    DO J=1 TO &NCOLO;
    IF J>&TT THEN DO;
     Q(I,J-&TT)=TAO(I,J);
     R(I)=R(I)+TAO(I,J);
     C(J-&TT)=C(J-&TT)+TAO(I,J);
     TOTAL=TOTAL+TAO(I,J);
                    END;
    END;
    END;
CALL SYMPUT('N',TOTAL);
RUN;
```

```
DATA ZPZ(KEEP= P_VALUE ENDPOINT);
SET TEMP2;
TRIAL=&MM;

%MACRO SMTABLE(B);
 DO SJ=&B TO &K;
  IF SJ>1 THEN DO;
   DO SJI=1 TO 2;
     SRY(SJI,SJ)=SRY(SJI,SJ-1)+NN(I,SJI,SJ-1);
   END;
              END;
  MMR=SR(1)-SRY(1,SJ);
  NN(I,1,SJ)=MIN(MMR,C(SJ));
  NN(I,2,SJ)=C(SJ)-NN(I,1,SJ);
  MMR2=SR(2)-SRY(2,SJ);
  MMC=C(SJ)-MMR2;
  SMINM(SJ)=MAX(0,MMC);
 END;
%MEND SMTABLE;

%MACRO SPROB;
 SPP=SFIX;
 DO SI=1 TO 2;
 DO SJ=1 TO &K;
  DO SS=2 TO NN(I,SI,SJ);
    SPP=SPP-LOG(SS);
  END;
 END;
 END;
 SPP=EXP(SPP);
%MEND SPROB;


 ARRAY TAO(&NROW,&NCOLO);
 ARRAY Q(&NROW, &NCOL);
 ARRAY MINM(&NROW, &NCOL);
 ARRAY C(&NCOL);
 ARRAY R(&NROW);
 ARRAY NN(&TT,2,&TG);
 ARRAY    BR{&NCOL};
 ARRAY    BC{&NROW};
 ARRAY SR(2);
 ARRAY SRY(2,&TG);
 ARRAY SMINM(&TG);

 ARRAY P(&TT);
 ARRAY POBS(&TT);
 ARRAY CY{&NROW,&NCOL   };
***CY(I,J)=Q(1,J)+Q(2,J)+...+Q(I-1,J);
 ARRAY RY{&NROW,&NCOL   };
***RY(I,J)=Q(I,1)+Q(I,2)+...+Q(I,J-1);

 ARRAY acumr(&NROW);
 ARRAY acumc(&NCOL);
      acumr(1)=R(1);
      acumc(1)=C(1);
DO I=2 TO &NROW;
  acumr(I)=acumr(I-1)+R(I);
END;
```

```
    DO I=2 TO &NCOL;
      acumc(I)=acumc(I-1)+C(I);
    END;


      BR(&NCOL)=0;
      BC(&NROW)=0;
        DO I=(&NCOL-1) TO 1 BY -1;
          BR(I)=BR(I+1)+C(I+1);
        END;
        DO I=(&NROW-1) TO 1 BY -1;
          BC(I)=BC(I+1)+R(I+1);
        END;
    DO I=1 TO &TT;
      DO J=1 TO &TG;
        NN(I,1,J)=0;
        DO K=1 TO &NC;
          IF TAO(K,I)=1 THEN NN(I,1,J)=NN(I,1,J)+Q(K,J);
        END;
        NN(I,2,J)=C(J)-NN(I,1,J);
      END;
/* %TWOXK(&TG)  */
%ZSCORE(&TG)
ENDPOINT=I;
OUTPUT ZPZ;
  IF I=1 THEN POBS(I)=P_VALUE;
  ELSE DO;
    LE=0;
    DO B=1 TO (I-1);
      IF P_VALUE-POBS(B)<&con THEN DO;
        DO CC=(I-1) TO B BY -1;
            POBS(CC+1)=POBS(CC);
        END;
      POBS(B)=P_VALUE;
      LE=1;
      GOTO ORDER;
                                                        END;
    END;
ORDER: ;
    IF LE=0 THEN POBS(I)=P_VALUE;
      END;
  END;

ADJP=0;
N_TABLE=0;
ARRAY XX(&N);
ARRAY YY(&N);
DO KL=1 TO &MM;
DO I=1 TO &N;
  XX(I)=I;
END;
DO I=1 TO &N;
 RR=0;
  YY(I)=XX(INT((&N+1-I)*RANUNI(&SEED)+1));
 J=0;
DO UNTIL (RR>0);
 J=J+1;
 IF XX(J)=YY(I) THEN RR=J;
  END;
```

```
        DO J=RR TO (&N-I);
         XX(J)=XX(J+1);
        END;
    END;
DO I=1 TO &NROW;
 IF I=1 THEN RMIN=0;ELSE RMIN=acumr(I-1);
 RMAX=acumr(I)+1;
 DO J=1 TO &NCOL;
  Q(I,J)=0;
  IF J=1 THEN CMIN=1;ELSE CMIN=acumc(J-1)+1;
  CMAX=acumc(J);
  DO KK=CMIN TO CMAX;
   IF RMIN<YY(KK)<RMAX THEN Q(I,J)=Q(I,J)+1;
  END;
 END;
END;

EQUAL='NO ';
   DO I=1 TO &TT;
     DO J=1 TO &TG;
        NN(I,1,J)=0;
        DO K=1 TO &NC;
           IF TAO(K,I)=1 THEN NN(I,1,J)=NN(I,1,J)+Q(K,J);
        END;
        NN(I,2,J)=C(J)-NN(I,1,J);
     END;
/*      %TWOXK(&TG)     */
%ZSCORE(&TG)
  IF I=1 THEN P(1)=P_VALUE;
 IF P_VALUE-POBS(1)<-&con THEN DO;
    P(1)=P_VALUE;
    ADJP=ADJP+1;
    GOTO NEXTKL;                          END;
  ELSE IF ABS(P_VALUE-POBS(1))<&con THEN DO;
EQUAL='YES';
      IF &TT=1 THEN DO; ADJP=ADJP+1; GOTO NEXTKL; END;
      ELSE IF &TT>1 AND I>1 THEN DO;
            DO CC=(I-1) TO 1 BY -1;
              P(CC+1)=P(CC);
            END;
            P(1)=P_VALUE;
            DO CC=2 TO I;
             IF P(CC)-POBS(CC)<-&con
               OR (ABS(P(CC)-POBS(CC))<&con AND CC=&TT)
                   THEN DO; ADJP=ADJP+1; GOTO NEXTKL; END;
             ELSE IF P(CC)-POBS(CC)>&con THEN GOTO NEXTI;
            END;
                                          END;
                                                            END;
  ELSE IF P_VALUE-POBS(1)>&con THEN DO;
      IF &TT=1 THEN GOTO NEXTI;
      ELSE IF &TT>1 AND I>1 THEN DO;
 LE=0;
 DO B=1 TO (I-1);
   IF P_VALUE-P(B)<&con THEN DO;
     DO CC=(I-1) TO B BY -1;
        P(CC+1)=P(CC);
     END;
```

```
              P(B)=P_VALUE;
              LE=1; ********THE P_VALUE IS LESS THAN ONE OF THE PREVIOUS ONES.;
              GOTO ORDER2;
                                                          END;
                                     END;
        END;
      IF LE=0 THEN P(I)=P_VALUE;
ORDER2: ;
        IF EQUAL='YES' THEN DO;
            DO CC=1 TO I;
              IF P(CC)-POBS(CC)<-&con
                OR (ABS(P(CC)-POBS(CC))<&con AND CC=&TT)
                    THEN DO; ADJP=ADJP+1; GOTO NEXTKL; END;
              ELSE IF P(CC)-POBS(CC)>&con THEN GOTO NEXTI;
            END;
                             END;
                                                       END;
NEXTI: ;
END;  ********************** END FOR I;
NEXTKL: ;
END;  ********************** END FOR KL;
ADJP=ADJP/&MM;
L95=MAX(0,ADJP-PROBIT(.975)*(ADJP*(1-ADJP)/&MM)**.5);
U95=MIN(1,ADJP+PROBIT(.975)*(ADJP*(1-ADJP)/&MM)**.5);
CALL SYMPUT('ADJP', ADJP);
CALL SYMPUT('L95', L95);
CALL SYMPUT('U95', U95);
RUN;

PROC SORT DATA=ZPZ OUT=ZPZ;
 BY P_VALUE;
*PROC PRINT;
RUN;

title1 ' ' ;
TITLE2 'ROM DISCRETE MULTIPLE ENDPOINTS ANALYSIS';
title3 ' ';
TITLE4 ' ';
title5 ' ';
DATA _NULL_;
 FILE PRINT;
 SET ZPZ END=EOF;
 ADJP=&ADJP;
 L95=&L95;
 U95=&U95;
 I=_N_;
 MM=&MM;
 IF _N_=1 THEN DO;
  PUT @18 'I'  @28 'ENDPOINT'          @57 'P-VALUE*';
  PUT @15 51*'-';
              END;
  PUT @18  I   @24 ENDPOINT 8.              @55 P_VALUE 8.4;
 IF EOF=1 THEN DO;
  PUT @15 51*'-';
  PUT @18  'MONTE CARLO GLOBAL P-VALUE' @55 ADJP 8.4;
  PUT @18  '95% CONFIDENCE INTERVAL'
          @54 '(' @55 L95 8.4  @63 ',' @63 U95 8.4 @72 ')';
  PUT @18  'NUMBER OF SAMPLES' @50 MM 8.;
  PUT //;
```

```
%IF &TAIL=1 %THEN %DO;
   PUT @18 '*: ASYMPTOTIC P-VALUE FOR LOWER-TAILED TREND'; %END;
%ELSE %IF &TAIL=2 %THEN %DO;
   PUT @18 '*: ASYMPTOTIC P-VALUE FOR UPPER-TAILED TREND'; %END;
%ELSE %IF &TAIL=3 %THEN %DO;
   PUT @18 '*: ASYMPTOTIC P-VALUE FOR TWO-TAILED TREND';   %END;
             END;
RUN;
%MEND ROMMC;
```

A.14 The %BayesIntervals Macro

This macro computes Bayesian simultaneous confidence intervals.

```
/*------------------------------------------------------------*/
/* Name:      BayesIntervals                                  */
/* Title:     Bayesian simultaneous intervals based on        */
/*            percentiles                                      */
/* Author:    Russell D. Wolfinger, sasrdw@sas.com            */
/* Release:   Version 6 or later                              */
/*------------------------------------------------------------*/
/* Inputs:                                                    */
/*                                                            */
/*    data=   data set representing a sample from the         */
/*            posterior distribution (required)               */
/*                                                            */
/*    vars=   the variables in the data set for which to compute */
/*            simultaneous intervals (required)               */
/*                                                            */
/*    alpha=  the joint significance level, default=0.05      */
/*                                                            */
/*    tail=   the tail type of the intervals, must be L, U, or */
/*            2, default=2                                     */
/*                                                            */
/*    maxit=  maximum number of iterations in the search,      */
/*            default=50                                      */
/*                                                            */
/*    tol=    convergence tolerance, default=0.001            */
/*                                                            */
/* Output:                                                    */
/*                                                            */
/*    The macro begins by computing the joint coverage of the */
/*    naive unadjusted alpha-level intervals, computed as      */
/*    percentiles across the sample.  It then decreases alpha  */
/*    using a bisection search until the joint coverage comes  */
/*    within the tol= value of alpha.  A history of this search */
/*    is printed and then the simultaneous intervals.          */
/*                                                            */
/*------------------------------------------------------------*/

%macro BayesIntervals(data=,vars=,alpha=.05,tail=2,maxit=50,tol=0.001);

   options nonotes;
   %if %bquote(&data)= %then %let data=&syslast;
```

```
/*---do bisection search to find adjusted alpha---*/
%let lowera = 0;
data _null_;
   uppera = &alpha * 2;
   call symput('uppera',uppera);
run;
%let iter = 0;

%put %str(         )The BayesIntervals Macro;
%put;
%put Iteration    Alpha         Coverage;

%do %while(&iter < &maxit);

    /*---compute quantiles---*/
    data _null_;
       alf = (&lowera + &uppera)/2;
       %if (&tail = 2) %then %do;
          lowerp = 100 * alf/2;
          upperp = 100*(1 - alf/2);
       %end;
       %else %if (&tail = L) %then %do;
          lowerp = 100 * alf;
          upperp = 100;
       %end;
       %else %do;
          lowerp = 0;
          upperp = 100*(1 - alf);
       %end;
       call symput('alf',left(alf));
       call symput('lowerp',left(lowerp));
       call symput('upperp',left(upperp));
    run;

    proc univariate data=&data pctldef=1 noprint;
       var &vars;
       output pctlpts=&lowerp,&upperp pctlpre=&vars pctlname=l u out=p;
    run;

    proc transpose data=p out=pt;
    run;

    /*---load limits and variable names into macro variables---*/
    data _null_;
       set pt nobs=count end=last;
       retain i 0;
       if (mod(_n_,2)=1) then do;
          i = i + 1;
          mname = "v" || left(put(i,8.));
          len = length(_NAME_);
          vname = substr(_NAME_,1,len-1);
          call symput(mname,left(vname));
          mname = "lv" || left(put(i,8.));
          call symput(mname,left(put(COL1,best8.)));
       end;
       else do;
          mname = "uv" || left(put(i,8.));
          call symput(mname,left(put(COL1,best8.)));
       end;
```

```
                    if last then do;
                        call symput('nvar',left(put(count/2,8.)));
                    end;
                run;

                /*---pass through data and determine simultaneous coverage---*/
                data _null_;
                    set &data nobs=no end=last;
                    retain count 0;
                    bad = 0;
                    %do i = 1 %to &nvar;
                        if (&&v&i < &&lv&i) or (&&v&i > &&uv&i) then bad = 1;
                    %end;
                    if (bad = 0) then count = count + 1;
                    if last then do;
                        coverage = count / no;
                        target = 1 - &alpha;
                        if (abs(coverage - target) < &tol) then conv = 1;
                        else do;
                            conv = 0;
                            alf = &alf;
                            if (coverage < target) then do;
                                call symput('uppera',left(alf));
                            end;
                            else do;
                                call symput('lowera',left(alf));
                            end;
                        end;
                        call symput('conv',left(conv));
                        call symput('coverage',left(coverage));
                    end;
                run;

                %let iter = %eval(&iter+1);
                %put %str(  ) &iter %str(      ) &alf %str( ) &coverage;
                %if (&conv=1) %then %let iter=&maxit;

            %end;

            options notes;
            %if (&conv=1) %then %do;
                data BayesIntervals;
                    %do i = 1 %to &nvar;
                        _NAME_ = "&&v&i";
                        Lower = &&lv&i;
                        Upper = &&uv&i;
                        output;
                    %end;
                run;
                proc print data=BayesIntervals;
                run;
            %end;
            %else %do;
                %put Did not converge;
            %end;

        %mend BayesIntervals;
```

A.15 The %BayesTests Macro

This macro computes Bayesian posterior probabilities for a set of free-combination tests using Gönen and Westfall's (1998) method.

```
/*-----------------------------------------------------------------*/
/* Name:      BayesTests                                           */
/* Title:     Multiple tests of hypotheses using Bayesian          */
/*            posterior probabilities                              */
/* Author:    Peter H. Westfall, westfall@ttu.edu,                 */
/* Reference: Gonen, M. and Westfall, P.H. (1998).  Bayesian       */
/* multiple testing for multiple endpoints in clinical trials.     */
/* Proceedings of the American Statistical Association,            */
/* Biopharmaceutical Subsection.                                   */
/* Release:   Version 7.01                                         */
/*-----------------------------------------------------------------*/
/* Inputs:                                                         */
/*                                                                 */
/*   MEANMUZ = The mean vector of the prior distribution for the   */
/*             noncentrality parameters of the test statistics,    */
/*             given that they are nonzero. Default is 2.5 2.5.    */
/*                                                                 */
/*   SIGMAMUZ = The variance of the prior distribution of the      */
/*             noncentrality parameters (assumed constant),        */
/*             given that the noncentrality parameters are         */
/*             nonzero.  The default is 2.0.                       */
/*                                                                 */
/*   You must specify two out of three of the following            */
/*   parameters.  The third will be calculated from the            */
/*   two that you specify.                                         */
/*                                                                 */
/*     RHO = The prior correlation (assumed constant) of the       */
/*           prior distribution of the noncentrality               */
/*           parameters (assumed constant), given that the         */
/*           noncentrality parameters are nonzero;  AND ALSO        */
/*           the tetrachoric correlation of the binary             */
/*           outcomes (Hi true, Hj true).                          */
/*                                                                 */
/*     Piall = The prior probability that all null hypotheses      */
/*             are true.                                           */
/*                                                                 */
/*     Pi0 = The probability that an individual hypothesis         */
/*           is true (assumed identical for all hypotheses)        */
/*                                                                 */
/* Additionally, %BayesTests requires a further macro to be        */
/* defined that uses SAS/IML to construct the estimates and        */
/* their covariance, as follows:                                   */
/*                                                                 */
/*   %Estimate: Uses SAS/IML code to define                        */
/*       EstPar - (column) vector of estimated parameters          */
/*       Cov    - covariance matrix for the for the estimates      */
/*                                                                 */
/* You can either define this macro directly, or use the          */
/* %MakeGLMStats macro to define it.                               */
/*                                                                 */
```

```
/* Output:                                                         */
/*                                                                 */
/*   The output shows the values of Pi0, PiAll, and Rho (two of    */
/*   which were input and the third calculated.)                   */
/*   The formatted output contains the following variables:        */
/*                                                                 */
/* Z Statistic  - The values of the test statistics defined in     */
/*                the %Estimates macro                             */
/*                                                                 */
/*   Prior Mean                                                    */
/*   Effect Size - The prior mean of the noncentrality parameter   */
/*                 (meanmuz)                                       */
/*                                                                 */
/*   Prior Std Dev                                                 */
/*   Effect Size - The prior std dev of the noncentrality          */
/*                 parameter (sqrt(sigmamuz))                      */
/*                                                                 */
/*   Posterior                                                     */
/*   Probability - The probability that the null hypothesis is     */
/*                 true, given the data (and the prior inputs)     */
/*                                                                 */
/*     Cov1-Covk - The correlation matrix of the test statistics,  */
/*                 from the %Estimates macro                       */
/*                                                                 */
/*---------------------------------------------------------------*/


%macro BayesTests(
                meanmuz = j(1,k,2.5) ,
                sigmamuz = 2.0        ,
                rho     =            ,
                Piall   =            ,
                Pi0     =            );

proc iml;

%Estimates;
zsample = EstPar';
sigma   = cov;

%if &rho    ^= %then %let flag1 = 1; %else %let flag1 = 0;
%if &piall  ^= %then %let flag2 = 1; %else %let flag2 = 0;
%if &pi0    ^= %then %let flag3 = 1; %else %let flag3 = 0;

%if %eval(&flag1+&flag2+&flag3) ^= 2 %then %do;
    print "Please specify exactly two of the three inputs: rho, PIall, pi0";
    print "The other will be implied by the two you specify";
%end;

k = ncol(zsample);
mu = &meanmuz;
sig2 = &sigmamuz;
pstd = j(k,1,sqrt(sig2));
if ssq(sigma-sigma')>.0000001 then print "Warning: Asymmetric Cov Matrix";
in = j(1,k,0);

START FUN(Z) GLOBAL(K1,K2,Z0,RHO);
    V1 = SQRT(RHO);
    V2 = SQRT(1-RHO);
    V3 = Z0-V1*Z;
```

```
    V4 = PROBNORM(V3/V2);
    V5 = 1 - V4;
    V6 = (1/SQRT(2*3.14159265))*EXP(-(Z**2)/2);
    IF K1 = 0 THEN V = (V4**K2)*V6;
        ELSE IF K2 = 0 THEN V = (V5**K1)*V6;
            ELSE V = (V4**K2)*(V5**K1)*V6;
RETURN(V);
FINISH FUN;

START JPROB(PROB,IN,CRIT,CORR) GLOBAL(K1,K2,Z0,RHO) ;
    Z0 = CRIT;
    RHO = CORR;
    K1 = SUM(IN);
    K2 = NCOL(IN) - K1;
    A  = {.M .P};
    CALL QUAD(PROB,"FUN",A);
FINISH JPROB;

start mnorm(x, mu, sig);
    p = nrow(sig);
    log1 = -(p/2)*log(2*3.14159265);
    log2 = -.5*log(det(sig));
    log3 = -.5*(x-mu)'*inv(sig)*(x-mu);
    log = log1 +log2 + log3;
    f = exp(log);
    return (f);
finish mnorm;

%if &Pi0  = %then %do;
    Piall = &Piall;
    corr  = &rho;
clower = probit(Piall);
cupper = probit(Piall**(1/K));
    CALL JPROB(PROB1,IN,Clower,CORR);
    CALL JPROB(PROBu,IN,Cupper,CORR);
do t = 1 to 50;
    cchk = (clower+cupper)/2;
    call  JPROB(PROBchk,IN,Cchk,CORR);
    if cupper-clower <.0000001 then do;
        Pi0 = probnorm(cchk);
        t=51;
        end;
    if probchk < PIall then clower = cchk;
        else cupper=cchk;
    end;
    crit=cchk;
    call symput('Pi0',char(Pi0));
%end;

%if &rho = %then %do;
    Piall = &Piall;
    Pi0   = &Pi0;
    crit=probit(Pi0);
pilower = pi0**k;
piupper = pi0;

*print "critical value is " crit;
if Piall <= pilower then print "error: PIAll is too low
        or Pi is too high";
```

```
      if Piall >= piupper then print "error: PIAll is too high
            or Pi is too low";
   Corrl = 0;
   Corru = .999;
   if (Piall > pilower) & (Piall < piupper) then
      do t = 1 to 50;
      corrchk = (corrl+corru)/2;
      call  JPROB(PROBchk,IN,crit,CORRchk);
      if corru-corrl <.0000001 then do;
      corr = corrchk;
            t=51;
              end;
      if probchk < PIAll then corrl = corrchk;
            else corru=corrchk;
       end;
      call symput('Rho',char(corr));
%end;


%if &Piall = %then %do;
   corr =  &rho;
   Pi0  = &Pi0;
   crit=probit(Pi0);
   CALL JPROB(Piall,IN,CRIT,CORR);
   call symput('Piall',char(Piall));
%end;

priprob = j(k,1,Pi0);
call symput('k',char(k));


sumnum = j(k,1,0);
rho1=corr;
sumdenom = 0;
%do ii = 1 %to &k;
   do i&ii = 0 to 1; %end;
   in = i1
%do ii = 2 %to &k;
   ||i&ii %end;  ;
      call jprob(prob,in,crit,rho1);
      mean = in#mu;
      cov = sig2*(rho1*in`*in + (1-rho1)*diag(in)) + sigma  ;
      f = mnorm(zsample`, mean` , cov);
%do ii = 1 %to &k;
      if i&ii = 0 then sumnum[&ii] = sumnum[&ii] + prob*f; %end;
  sumdenom = sumdenom + prob*f;
%do ii = 1 %to &k;
   end; %end;
postprob =sumnum/sumdenom;

bf = (postprob/(1-postprob))#((1-priprob)/priprob);



 todata = zsample`||mu`||pstd||postprob||sigma;

 create imlout from todata;
 append from todata;

 quit;
```

```
       proc print data=imlout noobs label;
           title  "Prior Probability on Individual Nulls is &Pi0";
           title2 "Prior Probability on Joint Null is &Piall";
           title3 "Prior Correlation Between Nulls is &Rho";
              label col1 = 'Z Statistic'
                    col2 = 'Prior Mean Effect Size'
                    col3 = 'Prior StdDev Effect Size'
                    col4 = 'Posterior Probability'
                    %do ii = 1 %to &k; %let ii1 = %eval(&ii+4); col&ii1 = Cov&ii %end; ;
   run ;
   quit;


   %mend;
```

A.16 The %MCB Macro

This macro computes confidence intervals for Hsu's (1984, 1996) multiple comparisons with the best.

```
/*------------------------------------------------------------------*/
/* Name:     MCB                                                    */
/* Title:    Multiple Comparisons with the Best                     */
/* Author:   Randy Tobias, sasrdt@sas.com                           */
/* Reference: Hsu, Jason C. (1996).  _Multiple_Comparisons:_        */
/*                 _Theory_and_methods_, Chapman & Hall, NY.         */
/* Release:   Version 7.01                                          */
/*------------------------------------------------------------------*/
/* Input:                                                           */
/*                                                                  */
/*   The following arguments are required.  They must be the        */
/*   first three arguments and they must be in this order.  Do      */
/*   not use keywords for these arguments.                          */
/*                                                                  */
/*     - the SAS data set containing the data to be analyzed        */
/*     - the response variable                                      */
/*     - the grouping variable                                      */
/*                                                                  */
/*   The following additional arguments may be listed in any        */
/*   order, separated by commas:                                    */
/*                                                                  */
/*     MODEL=   a linear model for the response, specified          */
/*              using the effects syntax of GLM.  The default       */
/*              is a one-way model in the required grouping         */
/*              variable.                                           */
/*                                                                  */
/*     CLASS=   classification variables involved in the            */
/*              linear model.  The default is the required          */
/*              grouping variable.                                  */
/*                                                                  */
/*     ALPHA=   the level of significance for comparisons           */
/*              among the means.  The default is 0.05.              */
/*                                                                  */
/*     OUT=     the name of the output dataset containing the       */
/*              MCB analysis.  The default is MCBOUT.               */
/*                                                                  */
```

```
/*        OPTIONS= a string containing either of the following    */
/*                 options                                        */
/*                                                                */
/*                    NOPRINT - suppresses printed output of      */
/*                              results                           */
/*                    NOCLEAN - suppresses deletion of temporary  */
/*                              datasets                          */
/*                                                                */
/* Output:                                                        */
/*                                                                */
/*   The output dataset contains one observation for each         */
/*   group in the dataset.  The output data set contains the      */
/*   following variables:                                         */
/*                                                                */
/*     LEVEL  - formatted value of this group                     */
/*                                                                */
/*     LSMEAN - sample mean response within this group            */
/*                                                                */
/*     SE     - standard error of the sample mean for this        */
/*              group                                             */
/*                                                                */
/*     CLLO   - lower confidence limit for the difference         */
/*              between the population mean of this group and     */
/*              the best population mean                          */
/*                                                                */
/*     CLHI   - upper confidence limit for the difference         */
/*              between the population mean of this group and     */
/*              the best population mean                          */
/*                                                                */
/*     RVAL   - the smallest alpha level at which the             */
/*              population mean of this group can be rejected     */
/*              as the best, for all groups but the one with      */
/*              the best sample mean                              */
/*                                                                */
/*     SVAL   - the smallest alpha level at which the             */
/*              population mean of this group can be selected     */
/*              as the best treatment, for the group with the     */
/*              best sample mean                                  */
/*--------------------------------------------------------------*/

%macro mcb(data,
           resp ,
           mean,
           model   = &mean,
           class   = &mean,
           alpha   = 0.05 ,
           out     = mcbout ,
           options =       );

  /*
  / Retrieve options.
  /--------------------------------------------------------------*/
     %let print = 1;
     %let clean = 1;
     %let iopt = 1;
     %do %while(%length(%scan(&options,&iopt)));
         %if     (%upcase(%scan(&options,&iopt)) = NOPRINT) %then
             %let print = 0;
```

```
        %else %if (%upcase(%scan(&options,&iopt)) = NOCLEAN) %then
            %let clean = 0;
        %else
            %put Warning: Unrecognized option %scan(&options,&iopt).;
        %let iopt = %eval(&iopt + 1);
        %end;


/*
/  Count number of variables in grouping effect.
/-------------------------------------------------------------------*/
    %let ivar = 1;
    %do %while(%length(%scan(&mean,&ivar,*)));
        %let var&ivar = %upcase(%scan(&mean,&ivar,*));
        %let ivar = %eval(&ivar + 1);
        %end;
    %let nvar = %eval(&ivar - 1);


/*
/  Compute ANOVA and LSMEANS
/-------------------------------------------------------------------*/
    ods listing close;
    proc mixed data=&data;
        class &class;
        model &resp = &model;
        lsmeans &mean;
        make 'LSMeans' out=&out;
    run;
    ods listing;
    data &out; set &out; orig_n = _n_;
    proc sort data=&out out=&out; by &mean;
    run;


/*
/  Retrieve the levels of the classification variable.
/-------------------------------------------------------------------*/
    data &out; set &out;
        drop tvalue probt;
        length level $ 20;

        level = '';
        %do ivar = 1 %to &nvar;
            level = trim(left(level)) || ' ' || trim(left(&&var&ivar));
            %end;
        call symput('nlev',trim(left(_n_)));
        call symput('lev'||trim(left(_n_)),level);
        run;


/*
/  Now, perform Dunnett's comparison-with-control test with each
/  level as the control.
/-------------------------------------------------------------------*/
    ods listing close;
    proc mixed data=&data;
        class &class;
        model &resp = &model / dfm=sat;
```

```
        %do ilev = 1 %to &nlev;
          %let control =;
          %do ivar = 1 %to &nvar;
              %let control = &control "%scan(&&lev&ilev,&ivar)";
              %end;
          lsmeans &mean / diff=controlu(&control) cl alpha=&alpha
                                  adjust=dunnett;
          %end;
       make 'Diffs' out=_mcb;
     run;
     ods listing;
     data _mcb; set _mcb;
        length level1 $ 20 level2 $ 20;

        level1 = '';
        level2 = '';
        %do ivar = 1 %to &nvar;
           %let v1 = &&var&ivar;
           %let v2 = _&&var&ivar;
           %if (%length(&v2) > 8) %then
              %let var2 = %substr(&v2,1,8);
           level1 = trim(left(level1)) || ' ' || trim(left(&v1));
           level2 = trim(left(level2)) || ' ' || trim(left(&v2));
           %end;
     run;


  /*
  / Sort results by first and second level, respectively.
  /----------------------------------------------------------------------*/
     proc sort data=_mcb out=_tmcb1; by level1 level2;
     proc transpose data=_tmcb1 out=_tmcb1 prefix=lo; by level1; var adjlow;
     data _tmcb1; set _tmcb1; ilev = _n_;
     proc sort data=_mcb out=_tmcb2; by level2 level1;
     proc transpose data=_tmcb2 out=_tmcb2 prefix=lo; by level2; var adjlow;
     data _tmcb2; set _tmcb2; ilev = _n_;
     run;


  /*
  / From Hsu (1996), p. 94:
  /     Di+ = +( min_{j!=i} m_i - m_j + d^i*s*sqrt(1/n_i + 1/n_j))^+
  /         = +(-max_{j!=i} m_j - m_i - d^i*s*sqrt(1/n_i + 1/n_j))^+
  /     G = {i : min_{j!=i} m_i - m_j + d^i*s*sqrt(1/n_i + 1/n_j) > 0}
  /     Di- = 0                                          if G = {i}
  /         = min_{j!=i} m_i - m_j + d^j*s*sqrt(1/n_i + 1/n_j) otherwise
  /----------------------------------------------------------------------*/
     data clhi; set _tmcb2; keep level2 clhi ilev;
        rename level2=level;
        clhi = -max(of lo1-lo%eval(&nlev-1));
        if (clhi < 0) then clhi = 0;
     data _g; set clhi; if (clhi > 0);
     run;

     %let ng = 0;
     %let g  = 0;
     data _null_; set _g
        call symput('ng',_n_ );
        call symput('g' ,ilev);
     run;
```

```
    data cllo; set _tmcb1; keep level1 cllo ilev;
        rename level1=level;
        if ((&ng = 1) & (&g = ilev)) then cllo = 0;
        else                            cllo = min(of lo1-lo%eval(&nlev-1));
    run;

    data cl; merge cllo clhi;
        by level;
    data &out; merge &out cl;
        drop df ilev;
    run;

  /*
  / Compute RVAL and SVAL.  RVAL is just the p-value for Dunnett's
  / test for all means except the best, and SVAL is the maximum RVAL.
  /------------------------------------------------------------------*/
    data _slev; set &out; _i_ = _n_;
    proc sort data=_slev out=_slev; by descending estimate;
    %let ibest = 0;
    data _null_; set _slev;
        if (_n_ = 1) then call symput('ibest',_i_);
    proc sort data=_mcb out=_pval; by level2 adjp;
    proc transpose data=_pval out=_pval prefix=p; by level2; var adjp;
    data _pval; set _pval; keep level2 rval;
        rename level2=level;
        if (_n_ = &ibest) then rval = .;
        else                    rval = p1;
    proc sort data=_pval out=_spval; by descending rval;
    data _null_; set _spval; if (_n_ = 1) then call symput('sval',rval);
    data _pval; set _pval;
        if (_n_ = &ibest) then sval = &sval;
    data &out; merge &out _pval; by level; drop level;
    proc sort data=&out out=&out; by orig_n;
    data &out; set &out; drop orig_n;
    run;

  /*
  / Print and clean up.
  /------------------------------------------------------------------*/
    %if (&print) %then %do;
        proc print uniform data=&out noobs;
        run;
        %end;

    %if (&clean) %then %do;
        proc datasets library=work nolist;
            delete cllo clhi cl _slev _spval _pval _mcb _tmcb1 _tmcb2 _g;
        run;
        %end;

%mend;
```

A.17 The %MCW Macro

```
/*----------------------------------------------------------------*/
/* Name:     MCW                                                  */
/* Title:    Multiple Comparisons with the Worst                 */
/* Author:   Randy Tobias, sasrdt@sas.com                        */
/* Reference: Hsu, Jason C. (1996).  _Multiple_Comparisons:_     */
/*                  _Theory_and_methods_, Chapman & Hall, NY.    */
/* Release:   Version 7.01                                        */
/*----------------------------------------------------------------*/
/* Input:                                                         */
/*                                                                */
/*   The following arguments are required.  They must be the     */
/*   first three arguments and they must be in this order.  Do   */
/*   not use keywords for these arguments.                       */
/*                                                                */
/*     - the SAS data set containing the data to be analyzed     */
/*     - the response variable                                   */
/*     - the grouping variable                                   */
/*                                                                */
/*   The following additional arguments may be listed in any     */
/*   order, separated by commas:                                 */
/*                                                                */
/*     MODEL=    a linear model for the response, specified      */
/*               using the effects syntax of GLM.  The default   */
/*               is a one-way model in the required grouping     */
/*               variable.                                       */
/*                                                                */
/*     CLASS=    classification variables involved in the        */
/*               linear model.  The default is the required      */
/*               grouping variable.                              */
/*                                                                */
/*     ALPHA=    the level of significance for comparisons       */
/*               among the means.  The default is 0.05.          */
/*                                                                */
/*     OUT=      the name of the output dataset containing the   */
/*               MCB analysis.  The default is MCBOUT.           */
/*                                                                */
/*     OPTIONS= a string containing either of the following      */
/*               options                                         */
/*                                                                */
/*                   NOPRINT - suppresses printed output of       */
/*                             results                           */
/*                   NOCLEAN - suppresses deletion of temporary   */
/*                             datasets                          */
/*                                                                */
/* Output:                                                        */
/*                                                                */
/*   The output dataset contains one observation for each        */
/*   group in the dataset.  The output data set contains the     */
/*   following variables:                                        */
/*                                                                */
/*     LEVEL  - formatted value of this group                    */
/*                                                                */
/*     LSMEAN - sample mean response within this group           */
/*                                                                */
/*     SE     - standard error of the sample mean for this       */
/*              group                                            */
```

```
/*                                                                 */
/*      CLLO   - lower confidence limit for the difference         */
/*               between the population mean of this group and     */
/*               the worst population mean                         */
/*                                                                 */
/*      CLHI   - upper confidence limit for the difference         */
/*               between the population mean of this group and     */
/*               the worst population mean                         */
/*                                                                 */
/*      RVAL   - the smallest alpha level at which the             */
/*               population mean of this group can be rejected     */
/*               as the worst, for all groups but the one with     */
/*               the worst sample mean                             */
/*                                                                 */
/*      SVAL   - the smallest alpha level at which the             */
/*               population mean of this group can be selected     */
/*               as the worst treatment, for the group with the    */
/*               worst sample mean                                 */
/*-----------------------------------------------------------------*/

%macro mcw(data,
           resp ,
           mean,
           model   = &mean,
           class   = &mean,
           alpha   = 0.05 ,
           out     = mcbout ,
           options =        );

 /*
 / Retrieve options.
 /--------------------------------------------------------------------*/
   %let print = 1;
   %let clean = 1;
   %let iopt = 1;
   %do %while(%length(%scan(&options,&iopt)));
       %if       (%upcase(%scan(&options,&iopt)) = NOPRINT) %then
          %let print = 0;
       %else %if (%upcase(%scan(&options,&iopt)) = NOCLEAN) %then
             %let clean = 0;
       %else
          %put Warning: Unrecognized option %scan(&options,&iopt).;
       %let iopt = %eval(&iopt + 1);
       %end;

 /*
 / Copy the dataset but reverse the sign of the response, so that
 / the worst is the maximum response.
 /--------------------------------------------------------------------*/
   data _tmpds; set &data; &resp = -&resp; run;

   %mcb(_tmpds,
        &resp ,
        &mean ,
        model   = &model  ,
        class   = &class  ,
        alpha   = &alpha  ,
        out     = &out    ,
        options = &options);
```

```
   /*
   / Reverse the sign of the results, so that the worst is again the
   / minimum response.
   /-------------------------------------------------------------------*/
      data &out; set &out;
         rename cllo=cllo;
         rename clhi=clhi;
         estimate = -estimate;
         tvalue = -tvalue;
         _temp = -cllo; cllo = -clhi; clhi = _temp; drop _temp;
      run;


    /*
    / Print and clean up.
    /-------------------------------------------------------------------*/
      %if (&print) %then %do;
         proc print uniform data=&out noobs;
         run;
         %end;

      %if (&clean) %then %do;
         proc datasets library=work nolist;
            delete _tmpds;
         run;
         %end;

   %mend;
```

A.18   The %UMCB Macro

```
   /*-------------------------------------------------------------------*/
   /* Name:      UMCB                                                   */
   /* Title:     Unconstrained Multiple Comparisons with the Best       */
   /* Author:    Randy Tobias, sasrdt@sas.com                           */
   /* Reference: Hsu, Jason C. (1996).  _Multiple_Comparisons:_         */
   /*                 _Theory_and_methods_, Chapman & Hall, NY.          */
   /* Release:   Version 7.01                                           */
   /*-------------------------------------------------------------------*/
   /* Input:                                                            */
   /*                                                                   */
   /*   The following arguments are required.  They must be the         */
   /*   first three arguments and they must be in this order.  Do       */
   /*   not use keywords for these arguments.                           */
   /*                                                                   */
   /*      - the SAS data set containing the data to be analyzed        */
   /*      - the response variable                                      */
   /*      - the grouping variable                                      */
   /*                                                                   */
   /*   The following additional arguments may be listed in any         */
   /*   order, separated by commas:                                     */
   /*                                                                   */
   /*     MODEL=   a linear model for the response, specified           */
   /*              using the effects syntax of GLM.  The default        */
   /*              is a one-way model in the required grouping          */
   /*              variable.                                            */
```

```
/*                                                               */
/*     CLASS=   classification variables involved in the         */
/*              linear model.  The default is the required       */
/*              grouping variable.                               */
/*                                                               */
/*     ALPHA=   the level of significance for comparisons        */
/*              among the means.  The default is 0.05.           */
/*                                                               */
/*     OUT=     the name of the output dataset containing the    */
/*              MCB analysis.  The default is MCBOUT.            */
/*                                                               */
/*     OPTIONS= a string containing either of the following      */
/*              options                                          */
/*                                                               */
/*                      NOPRINT - suppresses printed output of   */
/*                                results                        */
/*                      NOCLEAN - suppresses deletion of temporary */
/*                                datasets                       */
/*                                                               */
/* Output:                                                       */
/*                                                               */
/*   The output dataset contains one observation for each        */
/*   group in the dataset.  The output data set contains the     */
/*   following variables:                                        */
/*                                                               */
/*     LEVEL  - formatted value of this group                    */
/*                                                               */
/*     LSMEAN - sample mean response within this group           */
/*                                                               */
/*     SE     - standard error of the sample mean for this       */
/*              group                                            */
/*                                                               */
/*     CLLO   - lower confidence limit for the difference        */
/*              between the population mean of this group and    */
/*              the best population mean                         */
/*                                                               */
/*     CLHI   - upper confidence limit for the difference        */
/*              between the population mean of this group and    */
/*              the best population mean                         */
/*-------------------------------------------------------------*/
%macro umcb(data,
          resp ,
          mean,
          model   = &mean,
          class   = &mean,
          alpha   = 0.05 ,
          out     = mcbout ,
          method  = EH   ,
          options =      );

 /*
 / Retrieve options.
 /-------------------------------------------------------------------*/
   %let print = 1;
   %let clean = 1;
   %let iopt = 1;
   %do %while(%length(%scan(&options,&iopt)));
       %if     (%upcase(%scan(&options,&iopt)) = NOPRINT) %then
          %let print = 0;
```

```
            %else %if (%upcase(%scan(&options,&iopt)) = NOCLEAN) %then
                %let clean = 0;
            %else
                %put Warning: Unrecognized option %scan(&options,&iopt).;
            %let iopt = %eval(&iopt + 1);
            %end;

    /*
    /  Count number of variables in grouping effect.
    /-----------------------------------------------------------------------*/
        %let ivar = 1;
        %do %while(%length(%scan(&mean,&ivar,*)));
            %let var&ivar = %upcase(%scan(&mean,&ivar,*));
            %let ivar = %eval(&ivar + 1);
            %end;
        %let nvar = %eval(&ivar - 1);

    /*
    /  Compute ANOVA and LSMEANS
    /-----------------------------------------------------------------------*/
        ods listing close;
        proc mixed data=&data;
            class &class;
            model &resp = &model;
            lsmeans &mean;
            make 'LSMeans' out=&out;
        run;
        ods listing;
        data &out; set &out; orig_n = _n_;
        proc sort data=&out out=&out; by &mean;
        run;

    /*
    /  Retrieve the levels of the classification variable.
    /-----------------------------------------------------------------------*/
        data &out; set &out;
            drop tvalue probt;
            length level $ 20;

            level = '';
            %do ivar = 1 %to &nvar;
                level = trim(left(level)) || ' ' || trim(left(&&var&ivar));
                %end;
            call symput('nlev',trim(left(_n_)));
            call symput('lev'||trim(left(_n_)),level);
            run;

        %if (%upcase(&method) = TK) %then %do;
            ods listing close;
            proc mixed data=&data;
                class &class;
                model &resp = &model;
                lsmeans &mean / diff=all cl alpha=&alpha adjust=tukey;
                make 'Diffs'   out=_mcb;
            run;
            ods listing;
            proc sort data=_mcb out=_mcb;
                by &mean _&mean;
            run;
```

```
     /*
     /  Add reverse differences.
     /-------------------------------------------------------------------*/
          data _mcb; set _mcb; keep level1 level2 adjlow adjupp adjp;
             length level1 $ 20 level2 $ 20;

             level1 = '';
             level2 = '';
             %do ivar = 1 %to &nvar;
                 %let v1 = &&var&ivar;
                 %let v2 = _&&var&ivar;
                 %if (%length(&v2) > 8) %then
                     %let var2 = %substr(&v2,1,8);
                 level1 = trim(left(level1)) || ' ' || trim(left(&v1));
                 level2 = trim(left(level2)) || ' ' || trim(left(&v2));
                 %end;
             output;
             _tmplev = level1; level1 = level2; level2 = _tmplev;
             _tmpcl  = -adjlow; adjlow = -adjupp; adjupp = _tmpcl;
             output;
          run;


     /*
     /  Confidence limits are the minimum lower and upper CL's for each
     /  level.
     /-------------------------------------------------------------------*/
          proc sort data=_mcb out=_mcb; by level1 level2;
          proc transpose data=_mcb out=cllo prefix=lo; by level1; var adjlow;
          proc transpose data=_mcb out=clhi prefix=hi; by level1; var adjupp;
          data cllo; set cllo;
             rename level1=level;
             cllo = min(of lo1-lo%eval(&nlev-1));
          data clhi; set clhi;
             rename level1=level;
             clhi = min(of hi1-hi%eval(&nlev-1));
          data cl; merge cllo(keep=level cllo) clhi(keep=level clhi);
          run;

          data &out; merge &out cl; drop level;
          run;

          %if (&clean) %then %do;
             proc datasets library=work nolist;
                delete _mcb cllo clhi cl;
                run;
             %end;
          %end;
      %else %do;


     /*
     /  Now, perform Dunnett's comparison-with-control test with each
     /  level as the control.
     /-------------------------------------------------------------------*/
          ods listing close;
          proc mixed data=&data;
             class &class;
             model &resp = &model / dfm=sat;
```

```
              %do ilev = 1 %to &nlev;
                 %let control =;
                 %do ivar = 1 %to &nvar;
                    %let control = &control "%scan(&&lev&ilev,&ivar)";
                    %end;
                 lsmeans &mean / diff=control(&control) cl alpha=&alpha
                                              adjust=dunnett;
                 %end;
              make 'Diffs' out=_mcb;
           run;
           ods listing;
           data _mcb; set _mcb;
              length level1 $ 20 level2 $ 20;

              level1 = '';
              level2 = '';
              %do ivar = 1 %to &nvar;
                 %let v1 = &&var&ivar;
                 %let v2 = _&&var&ivar;
                 %if (%length(&v2) > 8) %then
                    %let var2 = %substr(&v2,1,8);
                 level1 = trim(left(level1)) || ' ' || trim(left(&v1));
                 level2 = trim(left(level2)) || ' ' || trim(left(&v2));
                 %end;
           proc sort data=_mcb out=_mcb; by level2 level1;
           data cl; keep cllo clhi;
              array m{&nlev,&nlev}; /* m[i1]-m[i2] - |d|^i2*s[i1,i2] */
              array p{&nlev,&nlev}; /* m[i1]-m[i2] + |d|^i2*s[i1,i2] */
              array s{&nlev};
              array l{&nlev};
              array u{&nlev};

              do i = 1 to &nlev; do j = 1 to &nlev;
                 m[i,j] = .; p[i,j] = .;
                 end; end;
              do obs = 1 to %eval(&nlev*(&nlev-1));
                 set _mcb point=obs;

                 j  = mod((obs-1),%eval(&nlev-1)) + 1;
                 i2 = int((obs-1)/%eval(&nlev-1)) + 1;
                 if (j < i2) then i1 = j;
                 else             i1 = j + 1;

                 m[i1,i2] = adjlow;
                 p[i1,i2] = adjupp;
                 end;


        /*
        / From Hsu (1996), p. 120:
        /     S = {i : min_{j!=i}   m_i - m_j + |d|^i*s[i,j] > 0}
        /       = {i : min_{j!=i} -(m_j - m_i - |d|^i*s[i,j]) > 0}
        /       = {i : min_{j!=i} -m[j,i] > 0}
        /---------------------------------------------------------------------*/
              ns = 0;
              do i = 1 to &nlev;
                 minmmji = 1e12;
                 do j = 1 to &nlev; if (j ^= i) then do;
                    if (-m[j,i] < minmmji) then minmmji = -m[j,i];
                    end; end;
```

```
                s[i] = (minmmji > 0);
                ns = ns + s[i];
                end;


 /*
/  From Hsu (1996), p. 115:
/     Lij = (i ^= j) * (m_i - m_j + |d|^j*s[i,j])
/         = (i ^= j) * p[i,j]
/     Li  = min_{j in S} Lij
/
/     Uij = (i ^= j) * -(m_i - m_j + |d|^j*s[i,j])^-
/         = (i ^= j) * min(0,p[i,j])
/     Ui  = max_{j in S} Uij
            put "Edwards-Hsu intervals";
            do i = 1 to &nlev;

                li = 1e12;
                do j = 1 to &nlev; if (s[j]) then do;
                   if (i = j) then lij = 0;
                   else          lij = m[i,j];
                   if (lij < li) then li = lij;
                   end; end;

                ui = -1e12;
                do j = 1 to &nlev; if (s[j]) then do;
                   if (i = j) then uij = 0;
                   else          uij = min(0,p[i,j]);
                   if (uij > ui) then ui = uij;
                   end; end;

                put li 7.3 " < mu" i 1. " - max_j muj < " ui 7.3;
                end;
/----------------------------------------------------------------------*/


 /*
/  From Hsu (1996), p. 120:
/     If S = {i} then
/        Li* = (min_{j!=i}   m_i - m_j - |d|^i*s[i,j] )^+
/            = (min_{j!=i} -(m_j - m_i + |d|^i*s[i,j]))^+
/            = (min_{j!=i} -p[j,i])^+
/     Otherwise
/        Li* = min_{j in S,j!=i} m_i - m_j - |d|^j*s[i,j]
/            = min_{j in S,j!=i} m[i,j]
/----------------------------------------------------------------------*/
            do i = 1 to &nlev;
                if ((ns = 1) & s[i]) then do;
                   minmpji = 1e12;
                   do j = 1 to &nlev; if (j ^= i) then do;
                      if (-p[j,i] < minmpji) then minmpji = -p[j,i];
                      end; end;
                   l[i] = max(0,minmpji);
                   end;
                else do;
                   minpmij = 1e12;
                   do j = 1 to &nlev; if (s[j] & (j ^= i)) then do;
                      if (m[i,j] < minpmij) then minpmij = m[i,j];
                      end; end;
                   l[i] = minpmij;
                   end;
                end;
```

```
          /*
         /  From Hsu (1996), p. 120:
         /      If i in S then
         /          Ui* = min_{j!=i}   m_i - m_j + |d|^i*s[i,j]
         /              = min_{j!=i} -(m_j - m_i - |d|^i*s[i,j])
         /              = min_{j!=i} -m[j,i]
         /      Otherwise
         /          Ui* = -(max_{j in S,} m_i - m_j + |d|^j*s[i,j])^-
         /              = -(max_{j in S,} p[i,j])^-
         /-------------------------------------------------------------------*/
                  do i = 1 to &nlev;
                      if (s[i]) then do;
                        minmmji = 1e12;
                        do j = 1 to &nlev; if (j ^= i) then do;
                            if (-m[j,i] < minmmji) then minmmji = -m[j,i];
                            end; end;
                        u[i] = minmmji;
                        end;
                      else do;
                        minppij = -1e12;
                        do j = 1 to &nlev; if (s[j]) then do;
                            if (p[i,j] > minppij) then minppij = p[i,j];
                            end; end;
                        u[i] = minppij;
                        end;
                      end;

                  do i = 1 to &nlev;
                      cllo = l{i}; clhi = u{i};
                      output;
                      end;

                  stop;
              data &out; merge &out cl; drop level;
              run;

              %if (&clean) %then %do;
                  proc datasets library=work nolist;
                      delete _mcb cl;
                      run;
                  %end;

              %end;

          proc sort data=&out out=&out; by orig_n;
          data &out; set &out; drop orig_n;
          run;

          /*
         / Print and clean up.
         /-------------------------------------------------------------------*/
          %if (&print) %then %do;
              proc print uniform data=&out noobs;
              run;
              %end;

      %mend;
```

A.19 The %UMCW Macro

```
/*----------------------------------------------------------------*/
/* Name:      UMCW                                               */
/* Title:     Unconstrained Multiple Comparisons with the Worst */
/* Author:    Randy Tobias, sasrdt@sas.com                      */
/* Reference: Hsu, Jason C. (1996).  _Multiple_Comparisons:_    */
/*                _Theory_and_methods_, Chapman & Hall, NY.      */
/* Release:   Version 7.01                                      */
/*----------------------------------------------------------------*/
/* Input:                                                       */
/*                                                              */
/*   The following arguments are required.  They must be the    */
/*   first three arguments and they must be in this order.  Do  */
/*   not use keywords for these arguments.                      */
/*                                                              */
/*      - the SAS data set containing the data to be analyzed   */
/*      - the response variable                                 */
/*      - the grouping variable                                 */
/*                                                              */
/*   The following additional arguments may be listed in any    */
/*   order, separated by commas:                                */
/*                                                              */
/*     MODEL=   a linear model for the response, specified      */
/*              using the effects syntax of GLM.  The default    */
/*              is a one-way model in the required grouping      */
/*              variable.                                       */
/*                                                              */
/*     CLASS=   classification variables involved in the        */
/*              linear model.  The default is the required      */
/*              grouping variable.                              */
/*                                                              */
/*     ALPHA=   the level of significance for comparisons       */
/*              among the means.  The default is 0.05.          */
/*                                                              */
/*     OUT=     the name of the output dataset containing the   */
/*              MCB analysis.  The default is MCBOUT.           */
/*                                                              */
/*     OPTIONS= a string containing either of the following     */
/*              options                                         */
/*                                                              */
/*                    NOPRINT - suppresses printed output of    */
/*                              results                         */
/*                    NOCLEAN - suppresses deletion of temporary */
/*                              datasets                        */
/*                                                              */
/* Output:                                                      */
/*                                                              */
/*   The output dataset contains one observation for each       */
/*   group in the dataset.  The output data set contains the    */
/*   following variables:                                       */
/*                                                              */
/*     LEVEL  - formatted value of this group                   */
/*                                                              */
/*     LSMEAN - sample mean response within this group          */
/*                                                              */
/*     SE     - standard error of the sample mean for this      */
/*              group                                           */
```

```
/*                                                          */
/*      CLLO   - lower confidence limit for the difference    */
/*              between the population mean of this group and  */
/*              the worst population mean                      */
/*                                                          */
/*      CLHI   - upper confidence limit for the difference    */
/*              between the population mean of this group and  */
/*              the worst population mean                      */
/*----------------------------------------------------------*/
%macro umcw(data,
           resp ,
           mean,
           model   = &mean ,
           class   = &mean ,
           alpha   = 0.05  ,
           out     = mcbout,
           method  = EH    ,
           options =       );

  /*
  / Retrieve options.
  /-----------------------------------------------------------------------*/
    %let print = 1;
    %let clean = 1;
    %let iopt = 1;
    %do %while(%length(%scan(&options,&iopt)));
       %if      (%upcase(%scan(&options,&iopt)) = NOPRINT) %then
           %let print = 0;
       %else %if (%upcase(%scan(&options,&iopt)) = NOCLEAN) %then
           %let clean = 0;
       %else
           %put Warning: Unrecognized option %scan(&options,&iopt).;
       %let iopt = %eval(&iopt + 1);
       %end;

  /*
  / Copy the dataset but reverse the sign of the response, so that
  / the worst is the maximum response.
  /-----------------------------------------------------------------------*/
     data _tmpds; set &data; &resp = -&resp; run;

     %umcb(_tmpds,
           &resp ,
           &mean ,
           model   = &model  ,
           class   = &class  ,
           alpha   = &alpha  ,
           out     = &out    ,
           method  = &method ,
           options = &options);

  /*
  / Reverse the sign of the results, so that the worst is again the
  / minimum response.
  /-----------------------------------------------------------------------*/
    data &out; set &out;
       rename cllo=cllo;
       rename clhi=clhi;
```

```
        estimate = -estimate;
        tvalue = -tvalue;
        _temp = -cllo; cllo = -clhi; clhi = _temp; drop _temp;
    run;


 /*
/  Print and clean up.
/----------------------------------------------------------------*/
    %if (&print) %then %do;
        proc print uniform data=&out noobs;
        run;
        %end;

    %if (&clean) %then %do;
        proc datasets library=work nolist;
            delete _tmpds;
        run;
        %end;

%mend;
```

References

Bailar, J.C. III (1991). Scientific inferences and environmental health problems. *Chance* 4 (2), 27–38.

Bartholomew, R.E. (1959). A test of homogeneity for ordered alternatives. *Biometrika* 46, 36–48.

Bauer, P. (1997). A note on multiple testing procedures in dose finding. *Biometrics* 53, 1125–1128.

Begun, J. and Gabriel, K.R. (1981). Closure of the Newman-Keuls multiple comparisons procedure. *Journal of the American Statistical Association* 76, 241–245.

Benjamini, Y. and Hochberg, Y. (1995). Controlling the false discovery rate: A new and powerful approach to multiple testing. *Journal of the Royal Statistical Society, Series B* 57, 1289–1300.

Berger, J.O., and Berry, D.A. (1988). Statistical analysis and the illusion of objectivity. *The American Scientist* 76, 159–165.

Berger, J.O., and Deely, J.J. (1988). A Bayesian approach to ranking and selection of related means with alternatives to ANOVA methodology, *Journal of the American Statistical Association* 83, 364–373.

Berger, J.O., and Sellke, T. (1987). Testing a point null hypothesis: the irreconcilability of *p*-values and evidence. *Journal of the American Statistical Association* 82, 112–122.

Berry, D.A. (1988). Multiple comparisons, multiple tests, and data dredging: A Bayesian perspective," in *Bayesian Statistics* 3, eds. J.M. Bernardo, M.H. DeGroot, D.V. Lindley, and A.F.M. Smith, New York: Oxford University Press, 79–94.

Berry, D.A., and Hochberg, Y. (1998). On Bayesian and Quasi-Bayesian approaches to multiple comparison problems. manuscript.

Blazer, D., George, L.K., Landerman, R., Pennybacker, M., Melville, M.L., Woodbury, M., Manton, K.G., Jordan, K., Locke, B. (1985). Psychiatric disorders: A rural/urban comparison. *Archives of General Psychiatry* 42, 651–656.

Box, G.E.P. (1950). Problems in the analysis of growth and wear curves. *Biometrics* 6, 262–289.

Box, G.E.P. and Meyer, R.D. (1986). An analysis of unreplicated fractional factorials. *Technometrics*, 28, 11–18.

Box, G.E.P., and Tiao, G.C. (1973). *Bayesian Inference in Statistical Analysis,* Reading, MA: Addison-Wesley.

Broemeling, L.D. (1985). *Bayesian Analysis of Linear Models,* New York: Marcel Dekker, New York.

Casella, G. and Berger, R.L. (1987). Reconciling Bayesian and frequentist evidence in the one-sided testing problem. *Journal of the American Statistical Association* 82, 106–111.

Conforti, M. and Hochberg, Y. (1987). Sequentially rejective pairwise testing procedures. *Journal of Statistical Planning and Inference* 17, 193–208.

Conover, W.J. and Iman, R.L. (1981). Rank transformation as a bridge between parametric and nonparametric statistics. *The American Statistician* 35, 124–129.

Cook, R.J. and Farewell, V.T.(1996). Multiplicity considerations in the design and analysis of clinical trials. *Journal of the Royal Statistical Society, Series A.* 159, 93–110.

Duncan, D.B. (1965). A Bayesian approach to multiple comparisons. *Technometrics* 7, 171–222.

Dunnett, C.W. (1955). A multiple comparison procedure for comparing several treatments with a control. *Journal of the American Statistical Association* 50, 1096–1121.

Edwards, D. and Berry, J.J. (1987). The efficiency of simulation-based multiple comparisons. *Biometrics* 43, 913–928.

Edwards F.H., Grover F.L., Shroyer L.W., Schwartz M., and Bero J. (1997). The Society of Thoracic Surgeons National Cardiac Surgery Database: Current Risk Assessment. *The Annals of Thoracic Surgery* 63, 903–908.

Edwards, S., Koch, G.G., Sollecito, W.A., and Peace, K.E. (1990). Summarization, analysis, and monitoring of adverse experiences. Chapter 2 in *Statistical Issues in Drug Research and Development*, Karl Peace ed., New York: Marcel Dekker Inc.

Ernhart, C.B. Landa, B. and Schnell, N.B. (1981). Subclinical levels of lead and development deficit—A multivariate follow-up reassessment. *Pediatrics* 67, 911–919.

Finner, H. and Roters, M. (1998). Asymptotic comparison of step-down and step-up multiple test procedures based on exchangeable test statistics. *Annals of Statistics* 26, 505–524.

Fisher, R.A. (1936). The coefficient of racial likeness and the future of craniometry. *Journal of the Royal Anthropological Society* 66, 57–63.

Fleming, T.R. (1992). Current issues in clinical trials. *Statistical Science* 7, 428–456.

Freeman, M.F. and Tukey, J.W. (1950). Transformations related to the angular and square root. *Annals of Mathematical Statistics* 21, 607–611.

Gelfand, A.E., Hills, S.E., Racine-Poon, A., and Smith, A.F.M. (1990). Illustration of Bayesian inference in normal data models using Gibbs sampling. *Journal of the American Statistical Association* 85, 972–985.

Giesbrecht, F.G. (1986). Analysis of data from incomplete block designs. *Biometrics* 42, 437–448.

Gönen, M. and Westfall, P.H. (1998). Bayesian Multiple Testing Using a SAS macro. *Proceedings of the American Statistical Association, Biopharmaceutical Subsection*, 108–113.

Gopalan, R. and Berry, D.A. (1998). Bayesian multiple comparisons using Dirichlet process priors. *Journal of the American Statistical Association* 93, 1130–1139.

Grechanovsky, E. and Hochberg, Y. (1998). Closed procedures are better and often admit a shortcut. *Journal of Statistical Planning and Inference*, 76, 79–91.

Green, J., and Wintfeld, N. (1995). Sounding board: Report cards on cardiac surgeons—Assessing New York state's approach. *The New England Journal of Medicine* 332 (18), 1229–1232.

Hayter, A.J. (1984). A proof of the conjecture that the Tukey-Kramer multiple comparisons procedure is conservative. *Annals of Statistics* 12, 61–75.

Heyse, J.F. and Rom, D. (1988). Adjusting for multiplicity of statistical tests in the analysis of carcinogenicity studies. *Biometrical Journal* 30, 883–896.

Hochberg, Y. (1988). A sharper Bonferroni procedure for multiple tests of significance. *Biometrika* 75, 800–802.

Hochberg, Y., and Benjamini, Y. (1990). More powerful procedures for multiple significance testing. *Statistics in Medicine* 9, 811–818.

Hochberg, Y. and Rom, D.M. (1995). Extensions of Simes' test for logically related hypotheses. *Journal of Statistical Planning and Inference* 48, 141–152.

Hochberg, Y. and Tamhane, A.C. (1987). *Multiple Comparison Procedures*. New York: John Wiley & Sons.

Hochberg, Y., Weiss, G., and Hart, S. (1982). On graphical procedures for multiple comparisons. *Journal of the American Statistical Association* 77, 767–772.

Hochberg, Y. and Westfall, P.H. (1999). On some multiplicity problems and multiple comparisons procedures in biostatistics. *Handbook of Statistics*, P.K. Sen, ed.

Holland, B.S. and Copenhaver, M.D. (1987). An improved sequentially rejective Bonferroni test procedure. *Biometrics* 43, 417–424.

Holm, S. (1979). A simple sequentially rejective multiple test procedure. *Scandinavian Journal of Statistics* 6, 65–70.

Hommel, G. (1988). A comparison of two modified Bonferroni procedures. *Biometrika* 75, 383–386.

Hommel, G. and Krummenauer, F. (1998). Improvements and modifications of Tarone's multiple test procedure for discrete data. *Biometrics* 54, 673–681.

Hsu J.C. (1984). Ranking and selection and multiple comparisons with the best. in *Design of Experiments: Ranking and Selection (Essays in Honor of Robert E. Bechhofer)*, T.J. Santner and A.C. Tamhane, eds, New York: Marcel Dekker, 23–33.

Hsu J.C. (1992). The factor analytic approach to simultaneous inference in the general linear model. *Journal of Computational and Graphical Statistics* 1, 151–168.

Hsu, J.C. (1996). *Multiple Comparisons: Theory and Methods*, London: Chapman and Hall.

ICH (1998). *International Conference on Harmonisation; Statistical Principles for Clinical Trials*, U.S. Food and Drug Administration, 5600 Fishers Lane, Rockville, MD 20857; www.fda.gov:80/cder/guidance/

Jeffreys, H. (1961). *Theory of Probability*, Oxford: Clarendon Press.

Johnson, R.A. and Wichern, D.W. (1998). *Applied Multivariate Statistical Analysis*, 4th ed, New Jersey: Prentice-Hall. Source: E. Hatfield.

Kass, R.E. and Wasserman, L. (1996). The selection of prior distributions by formal rules. *Journal of the American Statistical Association* 91, 1343–1370.

King, R.T. (1995). The tale of a dream, a drug, and data dredging. *The Wall Street Journal* Feb. 7, 1995.

Koch, G.G., Carr, G.J., Amara, I.A., Stokes, M.E. and Uryniak,T.J. (1990). Categorical data analysis. Ch. 13 in *Statistical Methodology in the Pharmaceutical Sciences*, Donald A. Berry, ed, New York: Marcel Dekker.

Kramer, C.Y. (1956). Extension of the multiple range test to group means with unequal numbers of replications. *Biometrics* 12, 307–310.

Lenth, R.V. (1989). Quick and easy analysis of unreplicated factorials. *Technometrics* 31, 469–473.

Lin, D.K.J. (1995). Generating systematic supersaturated designs. *Technometrics* 37, 213–225.

Lindley, D.V. (1972). *Bayesian Statistics: A Review,* Society for Industrial and Applied Mathematics.

Lindley, D.V. (1990). The 1988 Wald Memorial Lectures: The present position in Bayesian statistics. *Statistical Science* 5, 44–65.

Littell, R.C., Milliken, G.A., Stroup, W.W. and Wolfinger, R.D. (1996). *SAS System for Mixed Models*, Cary, NC: SAS Institute Inc.

Ludbrook, J. and Dudley, H. (1998). Why permutation tests are superior to t and F tests in Biomedical research. *The American Statistician* 52, 127–132.

Mantel, N. (1963). Chi-Square tests with one degree of freedom: extensions of the Mantel-Haenszel procedure. *Journal of the American Statistical Association* 58, 690–700.

Marcus, R., Peritz, E. and Gabriel, K.R. (1976). On closed testing procedures with special reference to ordered analysis of variance. *Biometrika* 63, 655–660.

Milliken, G.A. and Johnson, D.E. (1992). *Analysis of Messy Data, Volume I: Designed Experiments*. New York: Chapman and Hall. Reprinted with permission. Copyright CRC Press, Boca Raton, Florida.

Morrison, D.F. (1990). *Multivariate Statistical Methods*, 3rd ed, New York: McGraw-Hill.

Needleman, H.L., Gunnoe, C., Leviton, A., Reed, R., Peresie, H., Maher, C. and Barrett, P. (1979). Deficits in psychologic and classroom performance of children with elevated dentine lead levels. *The New England Journal of Medicine* 300, 689–695.

Neter, J., Kutner, M.H., Nachtsheim, C.J. and Wasserman, W. (1996). *Applied Linear Regression Models*, 3rd ed, Chicago: Irwin.

O'Brien, P. and Fleming, T. (1979). A multiple testing procedure for clinical trials. *Biometrics* 35, 549–556.

Ott, L. (1988). *An Introduction to Statistical Methods and Data Analysis*, 3rd Edition, Boston: PWS-Kent.

Palca, J. (1991). Get-the-lead-out guru challenged. *Science* 253, 842–844.

Patterson and Thompson (1971). Recovery of inter-block information when block sizes are unequal. *Biometrika* 58, 545-554.

Pearce, G.L. and Westfall, P.H.(1997). Identifying clinical practice improvement opportunities using resampling techniques in PROC MULTTEST. *Proceedings of the Fifth Annual Conference of the SouthEast SAS User's Group*, 394–99.

Peritz, E. (1970). A note on multiple comparisons. Unpublished manuscript, Hebrew University, Israel.

Peto, R., Pike, M., Day, N., Gray, R., Lee, P., Parish, S., Peto, J., Richards, S. and Wahrendorf, J. (1980). Guidelines for simple, sensitive significance tests for carcinogenic effects in long-term animal experiments. *Long-Term and Short-Term Screening Assays for Carcinogens: A Critical Appraisal* IARC Monographs, Annex to Supplement 2, 311–426. Lyon: International Agency for Research on Cancer.

Petrondas, D.A. and Gabriel, K.R. (1983). Multiple comparisons by randomization tests. *Journal of the American Statistical Association* 78, 949–957.

Pocock, S.J. (1982). Interim analyses for randomized clinical trials: the group sequential approach. *Biometrics* 38, 153–162.

Rom, D.M. (1990). A sequentially rejective test procedure based on a modified Bonferroni inequality. *Biometrika* 77, 663–665.

Rom, D.M. (1992). Strengthening some common multiple test procedures for discrete data. *Statistics in Medicine* 11, 511–514.

Rom, D.M., Costello, R. and Connell, L. (1994). On closed test procedures for dose response analysis. *Statistics in Medicine* 13, 1583–1596.

Rom, D.M. and Holland, B. (1995). A new closed multiple testing procedure for hierarchical family of hypotheses. *Journal of Statistical Planning and Inference* 46, 265–275.

Rothman, K.J. (1990). No adjustments are needed for multiple comparisons. *Epidemiology* 1, 43–46.

Roy, S.N. (1953). On a heuristic method of test construction and its use in multivariate analysis. *Annals of Mathematical Statistics* 24, 220–238.

Sarkar, S., and Chang, C.K. (1997). Simes method for multiple hypothesis testing with positively dependent test statistics. *Journal of the American Statistical Association* 92, 1601–1608.

SAS Institute Inc. (1989), *SAS/STAT User's Guide, Version 6, Fourth Edition, Volumes 1 and 2*, Cary, NC: SAS Institute Inc.

SAS Institute Inc. (1995), *SAS/IML Software: Changes and Enhancements through Release 6.11*, Cary, NC: SAS Institute Inc.

SAS Institute Inc. (1999). *SAS/STAT User's Guide*, Version 7-1, Cary, NC: SAS Institute Inc.

Saville, D.J. (1990). Multiple comparison procedures: The practical solution. *The American Statistician* 44, 174–180.

Scheffé, H. (1953). A method for judging all contrasts in the analysis of variance. *Biometrika* 40, 87–104.

Scheffé, H. (1959). *The Analysis of Variance*, New York: John Wiley & Sons.

Schervish, M.J. (1996). *P* values: what they are and what they are not. *The American Statistician* 50, 203–206.

Schweder, T. and Spjøtvoll, E. (1982). Plots of *p*-values to evaluate many tests simultaneously. *Biometrika* 69, 493–502.

Searle, S.R. (1971). *Linear Models*, New York: John Wiley & Sons.

Searle, S.R., Speed, F.M., and Milliken, G.A. (1990). Population marginal means in the linear model: an alternative to least squares means. *The American Statistician* 34, 216–221.

Shaffer, J.P. (1986). Modified sequentially rejective multiple test procedures. *Journal of the American Statistical Association* 81, 826–831.

Shaffer, J.P. (1998). A semi-Bayesian study of Duncan's Bayesian multiple comparison procedure. manuscript.

Šidák, Z. (1967). Rectangular confidence regions for the means of multivariate normal distributions. *Journal of the American Statistical Association* 62, 626–633.

Siddiqui, M.M. (1967). A bivariate *t* distribution. *Annals of Mathematical Statistics* 38, 162–166.

Simes, R.J. (1986). An improved Bonferroni procedure for multiple tests of significance. *Biometrika* 73, 751–754.

Soper, K.A. and Westfall, P.H. (1990). Monte Carlo estimation of significance levels for carcinogenicity tests using univariate and multivariate models. *Journal of Statistical Computation and Simulation* 37, 189–209.

Stokes, M.E., Davis, C.S., and Koch, G.G. (1995). *Categorical Data Analysis Using the SAS System*, Cary, NC: SAS Institute Inc.

Tarone, R.E.(1990). A modified Bonferroni method for discrete data. *Biometrics* 46, 515–522.

Tukey, J.W. (1953). The problem of multiple comparisons. *Mimeographed Notes*, Princeton University.

Tukey, J.W., Ciminera, J.L. and Heyse, J.F. (1985). Testing the statistical certainty of a response to increasing doses of a drug. *Biometrics* 41, 295–301.

Utts, J. (1991). Replication and meta-analysis in Parapsychology. *Statistical Science* 6, 363–378.

Utts, J. (1995). An assessment of the evidence for psychic functioning. In *An Evaluation of Remote Viewing: Research and Applications* eds. M.D. Mumford, A.M. Rose and D.A. Goslin, Washington: The American Institutes for Research. Reprinted in *The Journal of Scientific Exploration*, 1996, 10 (1), 3–30.

Waller, R.A., and Duncan, D.B. (1969). A Bayes rule for the symmetric multiple comparisons problem. *Journal of the American Statistical Association* 64, 1484–1503.

Westfall, P.H. (1997). Multiple testing of general contrasts using logical constraints and correlations. *Journal of the American Statistical Association* 92, 299–306.

Westfall, P.H. (1998). Applications of resampling methods in the pharmaceutical industry. Plenary session of the Midwest Biopharmaceutical Statistics Workshop. (unpublished; slides available).

Westfall, P.H., Johnson,W.O., and Utts, J.M. (1997). A Bayesian perspective on the Bonferroni adjustment. *Biometrika* 84, 419–427.

Westfall, P.H., Lin,Y. and Young, S.S. (1990). Resampling-based multiple testing. *Proceedings of the Fifteenth Annual SAS Users Group International*, 1359–1364.

Westfall, P.H. and Wolfinger, R.D. (1997). Multiple tests with discrete distributions. *The American Statistician* 51, 3–8.

Westfall, P.H. and Young, S.S. (1993). *Resampling-Based Multiple Testing: Examples and Methods for P-Value Adjustment*, New York: John Wiley & Sons.

Williams, D.A. (1971). A test for difference between treatment means when several dose levels are compared with a zero dose level. *Biometrics* 27, 103–117.

Williams, D.A. (1972). The comparison of several dose levels with a zero dose control. *Biometrics* 28, 519–531.

Winer B.J. (1971) *Statistical Principles in Experimental Design*, 2nd ed, New York: McGraw-Hill.

Wolfinger, R.D. and Kass, R.E. (1999). Non-conjugate bayesian analysis of variance component models. Carnegie Mellon Department of Statistics Technical Report #693.

Index

B O O K S
by
USERS

SAS Institute's
Author Service

Call your local SAS® office to order these other books and tapes available through the Books by Users℠ program:

An Array of Challenges — Test Your SAS® Skills
by **Robert Virgile**..Order No. A55625

Applied Multivariate Statistics with SAS® Software, Second Edition
by **Ravindra Khattree**
and **Dayanand N. Naik**..............................Order No. A56903

Applied Statistics and the SAS® Programming Language, Fourth Edition
by **Ronald P. Cody**
and **Jeffrey K. Smith**................................Order No. A55984

Beyond the Obvious with SAS® Screen Control Language
by **Don Stanley** ....Order No. A55073

Carpenter's Complete Guide to the SAS® Macro Language
by **Art Carpenter** ....Order No. A56100

The Cartoon Guide to Statistics
by **Larry Gonick**
and **Woollcott Smith**................................Order No. A55153

Categorical Data Analysis Using the SAS® System
by **Maura E. Stokes, Charles S. Davis,**
and **Gary G. Koch** ....Order No. A55320

Common Statistical Methods for Clinical Research with SAS® Examples
by **Glenn A. Walker**...................................Order No. A55991

Concepts and Case Studies in Data Management
by **William S. Calvert**
and **J. Meimei Ma**......................................Order No. A55220

Efficiency: Improving the Performance of Your SAS® Applications
by **Robert Virgile**.......................................Order No. A55960

Essential Client/Server Survival Guide, Second Edition
by **Robert Orfali, Dan Harkey,**
and **Jeri Edwards**......................................Order No. A56285

Extending SAS® Survival Analysis Techniques for Medical Research
by **Alan Cantor**...Order No. A55504

A Handbook of Statistical Analyses Using SAS®
by **B.S. Everitt**
and **G. Der** ....Order No. A56378

The How-To Book for SAS/GRAPH® Software
by **Thomas Miron** ....Order No. A55203

In the Know ... SAS® Tips and Techniques From Around the Globe
by **Phil Mason** ....Order No. A55513

Integrating Results through Meta-Analytic Review Using SAS® Software
by **Morgan C. Wang** and
Brad J. Bushman ....Order No. A55810

Learning SAS® in the Computer Lab
by **Rebecca J. Elliott** ....Order No. A55273

The Little SAS® Book: A Primer
by **Lora D. Delwiche** and
Susan J. Slaughter ....Order No. A55200

The Little SAS® Book: A Primer, Second Edition
by **Lora D. Delwiche** and
Susan J. Slaughter ....Order No. A56649
(updated to include Version 7 features)

Logistic Regression Using the SAS System: Theory and Application
by **Paul D. Allison** ....Order No. A55770

Mastering the SAS® System, Second Edition
by **Jay A. Jaffe** ....Order No. A55123

Multiple Comparisons and Multiple Tests Using the SAS® System
by **Peter H. Westfall, Randall D. Tobias,**
Dror Rom, Russell D. Wolfinger,
and **Yosef Hochberg** ....Order No. A56648

The Next Step: Integrating the Software Life Cycle with SAS® Programming
by **Paul Gill** ....Order No. A55697

Painless Windows 3.1: A Beginner's Handbook for SAS® Users
by **Jodie Gilmore** ....Order No. A55505

Painless Windows: A Handbook for SAS® Users
by **Jodie Gilmore** ....Order No. A55769
(for Windows NT and Windows 95)

Painless Windows: A Handbook for SAS® Users, Second Edition
by **Jodie Gilmore** ....Order No. A56647
(updated to include Version 7 features)

PROC TABULATE by Example
by **Lauren E. Haworth** ....Order No. A56514

Professional SAS® Programmers Pocket Reference, Second Edition
by **Rick Aster** ....Order No. A56646

Professional SAS® Programming Secrets, Second Edition
by **Rick Aster**
and **Rhena Seidman** ....Order No. A56279

Professional SAS® User Interfaces
by **Rick Aster** ....Order No. A56197

Audio Tapes

JMP® Books

*Welcome * Bienvenue * Willkommen * Yohkoso * Bienvenido*

SAS® Publications Is Easy to Reach

Visit our SAS Publications Web page located at www.sas.com/pubs

You will find product and service details, including

- **sample chapters**
- **tables of contents**
- **author biographies**
- **book reviews**

Learn about

- **regional user groups conferences**
- **trade show sites and dates**
- **authoring opportunities**
- **custom textbooks**

Order books with ease at our secured Web page!

Explore all the services that Publications has to offer!

Your Listserv Subscription Brings the News to You Automatically

Do you want to be among the first to learn about the latest books and services available from SAS Publications?
Subscribe to our listserv **newdocnews-l** and automatically receive the following once each month: a description
of the new titles, the applicable environments or operating systems, and the applicable SAS release(s). To subscribe:

1. Send an e-mail message to **listserv@vm.sas.com**

2. Leave the "Subject" line blank

3. Use the following text for your message:

      subscribe newdocnews-l *your-first-name your-last-name*

    For example: subscribe newdocnews-l John Doe

    Please note: newdocnews-l ◄——— that's the letter "l" not the number "1".

For customers outside the U.S., contact your local SAS office for listserv information.

Create Customized Textbooks Quickly, Easily, and Affordably

SelecText® offers instructors at U.S. colleges and universities a way to create custom textbooks for courses that teach students how to use SAS software.

For more information, see our Web page at **www.sas.com/selectext**, or contact our SelecText coordinators by sending e-mail to **selectext@sas.com**.

You're Invited to Publish with SAS Institute's User Publishing Program

If you enjoy writing about SAS software and how to use it, the User Publishing Program at SAS Institute Inc. offers a variety of publishing options. We are actively recruiting authors to publish books, articles, and sample code. Do you find the idea of writing a book or an article by yourself a little intimidating? Consider writing with a co-author. Keep in mind that you will receive complete editorial and publishing support, access to our users, technical advice and assistance, and competitive royalties. Please contact us for an author packet. E-mail us at **sasbbu@sas.com** or call 919-677-8000, then press 1-6479. See the SAS Publications Web page at **www.sas.com/pubs** for complete information.

Read All about It in *Authorline*®!

Our User Publishing newsletter, *Authorline*, features author interviews, conference news, and informational updates and highlights from our User Publishing Program. Published quarterly, *Authorline* is available free of charge. To subscribe, send e-mail to **sasbbu@sas.com** or call 919-677-8000, then press 1-6479.

See *Observations*®, Our Online Technical Journal

Feature articles from *Observations*®: *The Technical Journal for SAS*® *Software Users* are now available online at **www.sas.com/obs**. Take a look at what your fellow SAS software users and SAS Institute experts have to tell you. You may decide that you, too, have information to share. If you are interested in writing for *Observations*, send e-mail to **sasbbu@sas.com** or call 919-677-8000, then press 1-6479.

Book Discount Offered at SAS Public Training Courses!

When you attend one of our SAS Public Training Courses at any of our regional Training Centers in the U.S., you will receive a 15% discount on any book orders placed during the course. Each course has a list of recommended books to choose from, and the books are displayed for you to see. Take advantage of this offer at the next course you attend!

SAS Institute Inc.
SAS Campus Drive
Cary, NC 27513-2414
Fax 919-677-4444

E-mail: sasbook@sas.com
Web page: www.sas.com/pubs
To order books, call Fulfillment Services at 800-727-3228*
For other SAS Institute business, call 919-677-8000*

* Note: Customers outside the U.S. should contact their local SAS office.

SAS®